ROUTLEDGE HANDBOOK ON ELECTIONS IN THE MIDDLE EAST AND NORTH AFRICA

This *Handbook* analyzes elections in the Middle East and North Africa and seeks to overcome normative assumptions about the linkage between democracy and elections.

Structured around five main themes, contributors provide chapters detailing how their case studies illustrate specific themes within individual country settings. Authors disentangle the various aspects informing elections as a process in the Middle East by taking into account the different contexts where the electoral contest occurs and placing these into a broader comparative context. The findings from this *Handbook* connect with global electoral developments, empirically demonstrating that there is very little that is "exceptional" about the Middle East and North Africa when it comes to electoral contests.

Routledge Handbook on Elections in the Middle East and North Africa is the first book to examine all aspects related to elections in the Middle East and North Africa. Through such comprehensive coverage and systematic analysis, it will be a key resource for students and scholars interested in politics, elections, and democracy in the Middle East and North Africa.

Francesco Cavatorta is Professor in the Department of Political Science, Université Laval, Québec, Canada. He is currently working on a collaborative project examining political parties and coalition governments in the Middle East and North Africa.

Valeria Resta is Guest Lecturer in the Department of Social and Political Sciences, Bocconi University, Milan, Italy. She is currently working on a collaborative project examining political parties and coalition governments in the Middle East and North Africa.

ROUTLEDGE HANDBOOK ON ELECTIONS IN THE MIDDLE EAST AND NORTH AFRICA

Edited by Francesco Cavatorta and Valeria Resta

LONDON AND NEW YORK

Designed cover image: Majid

First published 2023
by Routledge
4 Park Square, Milton Park, Abingdon, Oxon OX14 4RN

and by Routledge
605 Third Avenue, New York, NY 10158

Routledge is an imprint of the Taylor & Francis Group, an informa business

© 2023 selection and editorial matter, Francesco Cavatorta & Valeria Resta; individual chapters, the contributors

The right of Francesco Cavatorta & Valeria Resta to be identified as the authors of the editorial material, and of the authors for their individual chapters, has been asserted in accordance with sections 77 and 78 of the Copyright, Designs and Patents Act 1988.

All rights reserved. No part of this book may be reprinted or reproduced or utilised in any form or by any electronic, mechanical, or other means, now known or hereafter invented, including photocopying and recording, or in any information storage or retrieval system, without permission in writing from the publishers.

Trademark notice: Product or corporate names may be trademarks or registered trademarks, and are used only for identification and explanation without intent to infringe.

British Library Cataloguing-in-Publication Data
A catalogue record for this book is available from the British Library

Library of Congress Cataloging-in-Publication Data
A catalog record has been requested for this book

ISBN: 978-1-032-02874-3 (hbk)
ISBN: 978-1-032-02884-2 (pbk)
ISBN: 978-1-003-18562-8 (ebk)

DOI: 10.4324/9781003185628

Typeset in Bembo
by Deanta Global Publishing Services, Chennai, India

CONTENTS

List of Figures ix
List of Tables xi
Acknowledgements xiii
Notes on Contributors xiv

1 Elections in the Middle East and North Africa 1
  Francesco Cavatorta and Valeria Resta

PART 1
Elections in authoritarian settings 11

2 The functions of authoritarian elections: Symbolism, safety valves, and clientelism 13
  Matt Buehler and Calista Boyd

3 Elections and the bureaucratic management of plurality in Algeria 26
  Thomas Serres

4 Parliamentary elections under Mohammed VI's reign (2002–2021) 39
  Inmaculada Szmolka

5 Electoral districts in Jordan: An analytical study 54
  Mohammed Torki Bani Salameh

6 Elections in Mauritania: The role of the military 66
  Raquel Ojeda-Garcia and Samara López-Ruiz

7 "Only me": Repression, legal engineering, and
   state-managed elections in Sisi's Egypt   78
   Hesham Sallam

PART 2
Elections in democratic and quasi-democratic settings   95

8 Israel's electoral system and political instability: Electoral fragmentation,
   party unity, and the prime minister's political leadership   97
   Maoz Rosenthal

9 When free and fair elections are not enough: Party fragmentation and
   unaccountability in Tunisia   109
   Ester Sigillò

10 Pre-electoral coalitions in Iraq: The case of the Communist–Sadrist alliance   121
   Paride Turlione

11 Elections and democratic backsliding in Turkey   134
   Sebnem Gumuscu

12 From one-sect one-vote to one-man one-vote? Demands for reforming
   the electoral system in Lebanon   147
   Rosita Di Peri

13 Competition under systemic religious constraints: Presidential elections
   in Iran   160
   Pejman Abdolmohammadi

PART 3
Rules, institutions, and the infrastructure of elections   173

14 The management of elections in Tunisia: The Independent High
   Authority for Elections   175
   Mohamed Chafik Sarsar and Nidhal Mekki

15 Partial and non-partisan: The municipal council elections in Saudi Arabia   187
   Hendrik Kraetzschmar

16 Elections in the Arab World: International monitoring and assistance   201
   Pietro Marzo

17	The independence referendum in Kurdistan *Sara Dilzar Mustafa*	214
18	Gender quotas, constituency service, and women's empowerment: Lessons from Algeria *Meriem Aissa*	222

PART 4
Elections and campaigning   235

19	A minority goes to the polls: Arab voters in Israel *Arik Rudnitzky*	237
20	Elections in Occupied Palestine: Control, resistance and contention *Francesco Saverio Leopardi*	251
21	Electoral campaigns in post–Ben Ali's Tunisia: Electoral expertise and renewed clientelism *Déborah Perez-Galan*	263
22	Digital strategies of Tunisian political parties: The case of the 2018 municipal elections *Bader Ben Mansour*	277
23	The role of media in electoral campaigns in the pandemic era: the case of Kuwait *Geoffrey Martin*	292
24	Opposition coordination under a competitive authoritarian regime: the case of the 2019 local elections in Turkey *Berk Esen and Hakan Yavuzyılmaz*	310
25	Polarisation and elections under competitive authoritarianism: The case of Turkey after 2013 *Şebnem Yardımcı Geyikçi*	329
26	From ballots to bullets: Libyan 2012 elections as the origin of the unachieved transition *Chiara Loschi*	342

PART 5
Voting behaviour — 353

27 The rationality of Arab voters: why and how people vote in non-democratic regimes across the MENA region — 355
Valeria Resta

28 Clientelism in MENA elections — 366
Miquel Pellicer and Eva Wegner

29 The consequences of Arab parties' divide and quest for power in Israeli politics on Arab voters — 378
Sawsan Khalife

30 Class and religious cleavages: the case of Lebanon — 387
Joseph Daher

31 Ideology and Electoral Choices in Arab Elections — 401
Enea Fiore

32 The Arab Generation Z: From Disillusionment to Pragmatism — 412
Dina Shehata and Abdalmajeed Abualela

Index — *429*

FIGURES

1.1	V-Dem Electoral Component Index, 2021	3
4.1	Perception of Electoral Integrity (PEI) in Middle East and North African countries	44
4.2	Electoral and parliamentary parties/coalitions in Morocco	45
4.3	Electoral participation in the election of the Moroccan House of Representatives (2002–2021)	46
4.4	Parliamentary representation of the main Moroccan political parties (percentage of seats)	47
8.1	Effective number of parliamentary parties, 1948–2021	102
11.1	Electoral and liberal democracy in Turkey, 2000–2021	139
11.2	Electoral fairness in Turkey, 2000–2021	142
19.1	Breakdown of the Arab vote in Knesset elections, 1949–1973	241
19.2	Breakdown of the Arab vote in Knesset elections, 1977–1999	245
19.3	Breakdown of the Arab vote in Knesset elections, 2003–2021	248
22.1	Strategic objectives assigned to digital campaigns (inspired by Giasson et al., 2018, 2019)	281
22.2	Distribution of strategic objectives by political parties	282
23.1	Media sample topics	298
23.2	What is the role of government media in elections?	298
23.3	What is the most important medium for campaigning?	299
23.4	Was the quality of media content by candidates better than in previous elections?	300
23.5	Overall, how would you rate the quality of media content in 2020?	301
23.6	How would you rate the quality of candidates?	301
23.7	What were the most important topics in the election?	302
23.8	What are the most important topics concerning corruption?	303
23.9	Does media influence your voting preferences?	304
23.10	What does influence your voting preferences?	304

23.11	What were the main challenges for women candidates winning in the 2020 elections?	305
23.12	Were you surprised by the election results?	305
24.1	The 2014 local election results in Turkey by province	316
24.2	The 2019 local election results in Turkey by province	317
24.3	The local organizational strength (AKP and CHP). Four indicates that the party has local offices in all municipalities, zero indicates that the party has negligible presence locally	321
24.4	Clientelistic electoral mobilization in Turkey (AKP and CHP). Four indicates that the party uses clientelist voter mobilization as its main mobilizational strategy	322
25.1	Social and political polarisation in Turkey	331
28.1	Clientelistic linkages and vote-buying in the MENA	368
28.2	Polyarchy and clientelism in the MENA	369
32.1	The generations defined	413
32.2	Generational difference	415
32.3	Trust in government	416
32.4	Arab youth keep away from politics.	418
32.5	Youth's self-reported turnout in referendums and elections from 2011 to 2012, and gender and wealth quintile, 2014 (%)	423

TABLES

4.1	Moroccan electoral system for the House of Representatives	41
4.2	Perception of Electoral Integrity (PEI) of Moroccan elections—general indicators (scale–100)	44
4.3	Concentration and competitiveness in Moroccan parliamentary elections	49
4.4	Electoral and Parliamentary Party Fragmentation in Moroccan parliamentary elections	50
5.1	The number of seats in the Jordanian House of Representatives and the number of electoral districts for the period of years from 1989 to 2016	60
5.2	Justice or misdistribution of electoral districts in Jordan	62
5.3	The rate of variance in the division of electoral districts in Jordan	62
8.1	Leadership patterns of prime ministers in parliamentary democracies	101
8.2	Historical periods, prime ministers, and leadership patterns	105
9.1	Results of 2011 elections for the National Constituent Assembly (turnout 52.0%)	111
9.2	The 2014 parliamentary elections	113
9.3	Results of the 2019 elections	116
11.1	Electoral integrity in Turkey, 2014–2018	141
15.1	Electoral regulations factsheet	189
15.2	Voter registration and turnout	191
15.3	Municipal councils, elective seats and candidacies	192
15.4	Registered female voters and turnout, 2015	194
15.5	Female candidacies and winners, 2015	195
19.1	Knesset elections turnout (%), 1949–1973	240
19.2	Knesset elections turnout (%), 1977–1999	244
19.3	Knesset elections turnout (%), 2003–2022	247
22.1	Number of mentions of communication objectives	288
22.2	Number of mentions of political objectives	288
22.3	Number of mentions of marketing objectives	288

23.1	Media analysis	294
23.2	Survey	295
24.1	Membership density and membership strength figures of AKP 2006–2018	322
25.1	Results of 2014 presidential elections in Turkey	334
25.2	Results of June and November 2015 general elections in Turkey	335
25.3	Results of November 2015 and June 2018 parliamentary elections in Turkey	337
25.4	Results of 2018 presidential elections in Turkey	339
26.1	Composition of General National Congress' seats (party lists and independents). Personal elaboration based on Lacher 2013 and Smith 2012	347
28.1	Data on clientelism in the MENA	367
28.2	Dominant linkage types in the MENA according to V-Dem	370
28.3	Targeting of different types of voters according to DALP	371
28.4	Demand for different types of clientelism in Tunisia	372
28.5	Support for democracy, trust, and demand for clientelism	373

ACKNOWLEDGEMENTS

This work is supported by a grant (number 435-2020-0539) from the Social Sciences and Humanities Research Council of Canada (SSHRC). We would like to acknowledge the phenomenal work completed by our contributors. All were exceptionally patient with us throughout the two years needed to complete this project. We are truly grateful for their commitment and their excellent research.

NOTES ON CONTRIBUTORS

Pejman Abdolmohammadi is Senior Assistant Professor of Middle Eastern Studies at the University of Trento's School of International Studies. He was formerly a Resident Visiting Research Fellow at the London School of Economics – Middle East Centre (2015–2018) and a Lecturer in Political Science and Middle Eastern Studies at the American University "John Cabot" in Rome (2013–2015). Since November 2019, he has been the Coordinator of the Jean Monnet European Project entitled "North Africa and Middle East Politics and EU Security" (NAMEPES), and he is Associate Research Fellow at the Italian Institute for International Political Studies in Milan (ISPI). His latest book (with Gianpiero Cama) is titled *The Domestic and Foreign Policy of Modern Iran*, which was published in 2020.

Abdelmajeed Abualela is Research Assistant at Ahram Center for Political and Strategic Studies (ACPSS) in Cairo. He earned his BA in political science from Beni Suef University Faculty of Economics and Political Science, where he is currently completing his Master's degree. He has published many articles on youth and on extremism in Egypt and the Arab world.

Meriem Aissa is Post-Doctoral Research Associate at Texas Woman's University. Her research interests lie in gender and politics and comparative politics, with a particular focus on gender quotas and women's representation in Arab legislatures.

Bader Ben Mansour holds a doctorate in public communication from Laval University and is Associate Researcher with the Groupe de recherche en communication politique and Centre interdisciplinaire de recherche sur l'Afrique et le Moyen-Orient at Laval University in Québec. His research focuses on political communication and more specifically on the strategies and uses of social media by public and political organizations in emerging and established democracies. He is interested in the role of the internet and social media in the development of democracy as well as new forms of political participation. He is also a communication strategist and advisor to several public and political organizations in Canada and internationally.

Calista Boyd is a PhD student in political science at the University of Tennessee Knoxville. She is studying the comparative politics of the Middle East and North Africa. She also serves as the managing editor for the *Review of Middle East Studies (RoMES)*.

Notes on Contributors

Matt Buehler is Associate Professor of Political Science and Global Security Fellow at the University of Tennessee's Howard H. Baker Center for Public Policy, where he researches contemporary politics of the Middle East and North Africa. He has held research fellowships at Harvard University's Middle East Initiative at the John F. Kennedy School of Government and Georgetown University's Center for International and Regional Studies in Qatar. He has served as an editor of *Mediterranean Politics* since 2019 and serves as co-editor of the *Edinburgh Series on the Maghreb*. He is the author of *Why Alliances Fail: Opposition Coalitions between Islamists and Leftists in North Africa* (2018). His book received the 2019 best book award from the Southeast Regional Middle East and Islamic Studies Society (SERMEISS). He was a recipient of a 2018 Early Career Excellence in Research and Creative Achievement Award from the University of Tennessee's College of Arts and Sciences. His articles have appeared in *International Studies Quarterly*, *Political Research Quarterly*, the *Journal of Immigrant and Refugee Studies*, the *Nonproliferation Review*, the *British Journal of Middle Eastern Studies*, *Mediterranean Politics*, and others.

Joseph Daher teaches at the University of Lausanne, Switzerland, and is Affiliate Professor at the European University Institute in Florence, Italy, where he participates in the Wartime and Post-Conflict in Syria Project. He is the author of *Syria after the Uprisings, The Political Economy of State Resilience* (2019) and *Hezbollah, The Political Economy of Lebanon's Party of God* (2016).

Rosita Di Peri is Associate Professor of Political Science and International Relations at the Department of Culture, Politics and Society at the University of Turin. Her research interests focus on the transformation of political institutions in the Middle East with specific attention to Lebanon. She is the scientific coordinator of the Summer School "Understanding the Middle East" (https://www.tomideast.com/) and a member of the board of SeSaMO (Italian Association for Middle Eastern Studies). She has published several articles in Italian and international journals, including *Rivista Italiana di Politiche Pubbliche*, *Rivista Italiana di Scienza Politica*, the *British Journal of Middle Eastern Studies*, *Politics Religion and Ideology*, and *Mediterranean Politics*. She has authored two books (in Italian), one about Lebanese politics (*Il Libano contemporaneo*, 2017) and the other about Middle East Politics (with Francesco Mazzucotelli, *Guida alla Politica Medio Orientale*, 2021), and co-edited several books and special issues. Her last co-edited book *Mediterranean in Dis/Order: Space, Power and Identity* is about to be published.

Berk Esen is Assistant Professor of Political Science at the Faculty of Arts and Sciences, Sabancı University, Turkey, and IPC-Stiftung Mercator fellow at the Centre for Applied Turkey Studies in the German Institute for International and Security Affairs (SWP). He received his PhD in Government from Cornell University in 2015. Before joining Sabancı University, he served as Assistant Professor at the Department of International Relations at Bilkent University. His research interests include the political economy of development, party politics, and authoritarian regimes with a focus on Latin America and the Middle East. His research has been funded by the Science and Technology Institute of Turkey (TUBITAK) and published in political science journals such as *Party Politics*, *Journal of Democracy*, *Third World Quarterly*, *Armed Forces & Society*, *PS: Political Science & Politics*, *South East European Society and Politics*, the *Journal of Near East and Balkan Studies*, *Mediterranean Politics*, the *Middle East Journal*, *Turkish Studies*, *Review of Middle East Studies*, and the *Middle East Review of International Affairs*. Berk has received numerous prestigious awards, including the Sakıp Sabancı International Research Award and the Turkish Science Academy Young Scientist Award (BAGEP).

Enea Fiore is a PhD candidate in Political Science in co-supervision at Laval University and the University of Geneva. He is also affiliated with the Centre Interdisciplinaire de Recherche sur l'Afrique et le Moyen-Orient (CIRAM) at Laval University in Québec, Canada. His academic field is comparative politics and political sociology. His research focus is on the interactions between political parties and social movements in the MENA region. His current research focuses on the Lebanese parties' membership and how militancy intersects with membership in social movements, and how this shapes parties' organization, policies, and ideological positions.

Sebnem Gumuscu is Associate Professor of Political Science at Middlebury College and the author of *Democracy or Authoritarianism: Islamist Governments in Turkey, Egypt, and Tunisia* (forthcoming). She is also the co-author (with E. Fuat Keyman) of *Democracy, Identity, and Foreign Policy in Turkey: Hegemony Through Transformation* (2014) and the author of numerous journal articles on political Islam, democratic backsliding, and dominant parties.

Sawsan Khalife publishes political analyses on regional dynamics. She studied Political Science at the University of Haifa in Israel and International Relations at the University of Glasgow in Scotland, UK. Her Master's thesis investigated the regional dynamics in the Persian Gulf during the Yemen war.

Hendrik Kraetzschmar is Associate Professor in the Comparative Politics of the MENA at the University of Leeds, United Kingdom. He has published on electoral, associational, and party politics in the Middle East and North Africa in peer-reviewed journals and is the co-editor of *Islamists and the Politics of the Arab Uprisings: Governance, Pluralisation and Contention* (2018) and *Democracy and Violence: Global Debates and Local Challenges* (2010) as well as the editor *of Opposition Cooperation in the Arab World: Contentious Politics in Times of Change* (2012).

Francesco Saverio Leopardi is Research Fellow at the Marco Polo Centre for Global Europe-Asia Connections, Ca' Foscari University of Venice. He also teaches Global Asian Studies at Ca' Foscari International College and International History at the University of Bologna. He is currently working on a project focusing on the history of Arab Countries' economic cooperation with China and Chinese economic presence in the region. During his time as a research fellow at the University of Bologna, Dr Leopardi worked on the history of the 1980s and 1990s debt crisis in Algeria, particularly in its international dimension. Over the last five years, Dr Leopardi also continued to pursue his longstanding interest in the history of the Palestinian national movement and its leftist factions. In 2020 he published his first monograph, *The Palestinian Left and Its Decline. Loyal Opposition*. Research for this book was conducted during his doctoral studies at the University of Edinburgh, where he earned his PhD in 2017.

Samara López-Ruiz is a PhD candidate in Social Science at the University of Granada and teacher assistant in the Department of Political Science and Administration. She holds a MBA and a Master's in High international and European studies, along with a Bachelor's in Political Science and Administration. Her research interests are human rights, water security, sustainable development, and natural resources in conflict areas. She has written several scientific articles and has participated in more than ten international conferences on these topics.

Chiara Loschi is Post-Doctoral Researcher at the University of Bologna for the ERC-funded project Processing Citizenship led by Professor Pelizza. From 2018 to 2020, she was a postdoctoral researcher at the Centre for European Integration Research at the University of Vienna for a project led by Dr Peter Slominski titled *The EU-Border Protection Regime: The Cooperation between EU Agencies and Its Consequences for Fundamental Rights*. From 2017 to 2018, she was based in Tunis as CNRS Post-Doctoral Researcher for an EU HORIZON2020 project led by the Norwegian Institute for Foreign Affairs titled EUNPACK. Good Intention Mixed Results, focusing on EU crisis response in Libya.

Geoffrey Martin is a PhD candidate in Political Science at the University of Toronto, as well as an entrepreneur and economic analyst based in Kuwait. His focus is on political economy, food logistics, and labour law in Kuwait and the wider GCC. He tweets @bartybartin.

Pietro Marzo is Assistant Professor at TELUQ University (Québec, Canada). His research focuses on the international relations of the Middle East. His latest academic articles have appeared in *Middle East Law and Governance*, *Third World Quarterly*, *Cambridge Review of International Affairs*, and *Middle Eastern Studies*. He is currently working on his book *International Influence in the Tunisian Democratization*.

Nidhal Mekki is a PhD candidate and Lecturer in the School of Law at Laval University, Québec, Canada. He is a member of CIRAM (Interdisciplinary Centre for Research on Africa and the Middle East) and of the Research Chair in International Law and International Courts, Faculty of Legal, Political and Social sciences at the University of Tunis. He is interested in the relationship between international human rights law and the new Arab constitutions, with a focus on Egypt, Morocco, and Tunisia). He has published several articles on human rights in the Arab world and on the democratic transition in Tunisia.

Sara Mustafa is a PhD candidate in Political Science at the Universidad Nacional de Educación a Distancia (UNED) in Madrid and is also a Lecturer at the University of Kurdistan-Hewler in the Department of Politics and International Relations.

Raquel Ojeda-García is Senior Lecturer in Political Science and Administration at the University of Granada (Spain). She has been a visiting scholar at Canadian, European (United Kingdom, Ireland, Sweden, and France) and Moroccan universities. Thanks to two Teaching Mobility Erasmus+ grants, she taught at the University of Sapienza (Italy) and Lille 2 (France). She is a member of the Forum of Researchers on the Arab and Muslim World (FIMAM) and the research group on Political Science at the University of Granada. Her articles have appeared in the following academic journals: the *British Journal of Middle Eastern Studies*, the *Journal of Modern African Studies*, the *Nationalities Papers*, *Transmodernity*, *Revista de Estudios Políticos*, *CIDOB d'Afers Internacionals*, *Afkar/Ideas*, *Revista de Investigaciones Políticas y Sociológicas*, *Revista de Estudios Internacionales Mediterráneos*, and *Gestión y Análisis de Políticas Públicas*.

Miquel Pellicer is Professor of Inequality and Poverty at the Centre for Conflict Studies, Philipps-University Marburg. He holds a PhD in Economics from the European University Institute. Previously, he was Senior Lecturer at the University of Cape Town and Senior Researcher at the GIGA German Institute for Global and Area Studies. His core research interest is in the interactions between inequality and politics. He studies support for redistribution, voting behaviour, and protests in Sub-Saharan Africa as well as the Middle East and North Africa. Together with Eva Wegner, he is PI of The Demand Side of Clientelism, a project investigating demand for different forms of clientelism in South Africa and Tunisia. His articles have appeared in journals such as *Perspectives on Politics*, the *Quarterly Journal of Political Science*, *Governance*, the *Journal of Development Economics*, and *Party Politics*.

Déborah Perez-Galan is Assistant Professor in Political Science at the FGSES, University Mohamed VI Polytechnic. An Ecole Normale Superieure and SciencePo alumni, she defended in 2021 her PhD dissertation on the Tunisian national constituent assembly at the IEP of Aix-en-Provence. Her research focuses on parliaments, regime changes, elections, and good governance policies in the Maghreb. She recently published with Quentin Deforge "La fabrique transnationale de l'accountability," *Revue internationale des études du développement*, 248, 2022; "Les dynamiques de l'ancrage politique dans la Tunisie d'après Ben Ali" (Political anchorage dynamics in post-Ben Ali Tunisia), in Vincent Geisser, Amin Allal (ed.) *Tunisie An V*, Paris, CNRS Éditions, 2018; "Becoming a decision maker in the Parliament of post-revolutionary Tunisia" *Middle East Law and Governance*, 8, 2016.

Valeria Resta is Adjunct Professor at the Catholic University of the Sacred Heart in Milan, Italy. Her research deals with the functioning of political parties in authoritarian and transitional settings of the Arab World. She is the author of *Tunisia and Egypt after the Arab Spring: Party Politics in Transitions from Authoritarian Rule* (forthcoming), and she co-authored the *Routledge Handbook of Political Parties in the Middle East and North Africa*. Her latest works have appeared in the *British Journal of Middle Eastern Studies*, *Politics and Religion*, and in the *Italian Political Science Review*.

Maoz Rosenthal holds a PhD in Political Science from Tel Aviv University. He is Senior Lecturer at Reichman University's Lauder School of Government, Diplomacy, and Strategy. Dr Rosenthal held visiting positions at Binghamton University and Yale University. He is a project leader at the programme for Democratic Resilience and Development at Reichman University and a Principal Investigator at the Israeli Policy Agendas project. Dr Rosenthal's fields of study include executive politics, judicial politics, and ethnic voting, with a focus on Israeli politics. His book from 2017 examined Israel's governability crisis. He has published papers in outlets such as *Political Studies*, the *Journal of Law and Courts*, *Ethnic and Racial Studies*, and many others. His main research projects currently are presidential prime ministers, judges' ideological preferences, and the effect of education on ethnic voting.

Arik Rudnitzky is Researcher on Arab society affairs in Israel at the Moshe Dayan Center for Middle Eastern and African Studies, Tel Aviv University, and at the Israel Democracy Institute, Jerusalem. His fields of expertise cover political, national, and social developments in Israel's Arab society, government policies on Arab citizens and Jewish–Arab relations in Israel. Dr Rudnitzky serves as a regular commentator on Israeli Arab issues in the local and international media. Some of his notable publications include: *Arab Voter Turnout in Knesset Elections: The Real, the Ideal, and Hope for Change* (2020, Hebrew); *The Arab Minority in Israel and the Discourse on the "Jewish State"* (2015, Hebrew); and "Do the Jews have a right to self-determination in Palestine? Islamic discourse in Israel," in: Meir Hatina and Mohammad al-Atawnah (editors), *Muslims in the Jewish State: Religion, Politics, Society* (2018, in Hebrew).

Mohammed T. Bani Salameh is Professor of Political Science in the Political Science Department at Yarmouk University, Jordan. He holds a PhD in Comparative Politics from Clark Atlanta University, USA. His research focuses on identity, political reforms, human rights, Political Islam, social network analysis, elections, immigration, terrorism, and contemporary politics of the Middle East. He has also published his work in numerous peer-reviewed journals. His publications appear in *Digest of Middle East Studies*, the *Journal of Middle Eastern and Islamic Studies (in Asia)*, *Nationalities Papers: The Journal of Nationalism and Ethnicity*, the *Journal of Research in Political Sociology*, the *International Journal of Human Rights and Constitutional Studies*, the *World Affairs Journal*, *Middle East Quarterly*, the *Journal of Politics and Law*, the *Asian Journal of Comparative Politics*, and *Middle East Policy*. Bani Salameh is a member of the Board of Trustees of Hashemite University and a member of the Global V-Dem team 2016–2022. He was a Fulbright Scholar at Clark Atlanta University from 1995 to 1997.

Notes on Contributors

Hesham Sallam is Research Scholar at Stanford University's Center on Democracy, Development, and the Rule of Law, where he also serves as the Associate-Director of the programme on Arab Reform and Democracy. He is also a co-editor of the *Jadaliyya* ezine and a former programme specialist at the US Institute of Peace. His research focuses on Islamist movements and the politics of economic reform in the Arab World. Sallam's research has previously received the support of the Social Science Research Council and the US Institute of Peace. Sallam is the author of *Classless Politics: Islamist Movements, the Left, and Authoritarian Legacies in Egypt* (forthcoming 2022) and editor of *Struggles for Political Change in the Arab World* (with Lisa Blaydes and Amr Hamzawy) (forthcoming 2022) and *Egypt's Parliamentary Elections 2011–2012: A Critical Guide to a Changing Political Arena* (2013). Sallam received a PhD in Government (2015), an MA in Arab Studies (2006) from Georgetown University, and a BA in Political Science from the University of Pittsburgh (2003).

Mohamed Chafik Sarsar is Professor of Public Law at the Naief Arab University for Security Sciences (NAUSS) in Riyadh, Saudi Arabia. He is the former President of the Independent High Authority for Elections and was previously Law Professor at the Faculty of Law and Political Sciences, University of Tunis. He has held several public positions, including the member of the Committee of Experts within the High Authority for the Achievement of the Objectives of the Revolution and Secretary General of the Tunisian Association for Democratic Transition (ARTD). He is a founding member of the Arab Organization of Constitutional Law. His writings focus on constitutional theory, political parties, and democratic transitions.

Thomas Serres is Assistant Professor in the Politics Department at the University of California Santa Cruz. He is a specialist in North African and Mediterranean politics, and his scholarship focuses on questions of crisis, economic restructuring, and authoritarian upgrading. His first book studies the politics of catastrophization in post-civil war Algeria. His new monograph is titled *Managing the Crisis, Blaming the People: The Suspended Disaster in Bouteflika's Algeria* (*Gérer la Crise, Blâmer le Peuple: De la Catastrophe Suspendue dans l'Algérie de Bouteflika*). He has also co-edited the volume *North Africa and the Making of Europe: Governance, Institutions, Culture*, which was published in 2018.

Dina Shehata is Senior Researcher and Head of Egyptian Studies Unit at Al Ahram Center for Political and Strategic Studies (ACPSS) in Cairo. She is also the editor-in-chief of *Almalaf Almasry*, a monthly policy journal published by ACPSS. Her areas of expertise include political parties, social movements, civil society, and authoritarian politics in the Arab world. She has a PhD in Comparative Politics from Georgetown University, an MSc in political theory from the London School of Economics, and a BA in Middle East Politics from the American University in Cairo.

Ester Sigillò is Post-Doctoral Researcher at the University of Bologna, at the Department of Political and Social Sciences, and Adjunct Professor of Comparative Politics in the Mediterranean region at Georgetown University (Florence campus). She is responsible for research in the MENA area under the framework of the ERC-funded project BIT-ACT. Ester holds a PhD in Political Science from Scuola Normale Superiore. Her dissertation, under the supervision of Donatella della Porta, focused on the politicization of civil society in post-authoritarian Tunisia vis-à-vis the intervention of international donors. During her doctorate, she served as Visiting Fellow at the Institut de recherche sur le Maghreb Contemporain (IRMC) in Tunis and as Research Fellow in the ERC project TARICA focused on the political and institutional changes in North Africa after the Arab Uprisings. After her PhD, Ester served as Max Weber Fellow at the

European University Institute in Florence, at the Robert Schuman Center for Advanced Studies, under the supervision of Olivier Roy. Her current research interests include international relations in the MENA, democratization, social movements, and Islamic activism in the Maghreb.

Inmaculada Szmolka is Professor at the Department of Political Science and Administration at the University of Granada (Spain). Her main research interests focus on political regimes, political change processes, party systems, elections, and government formation, mainly in relation to Middle East and North African countries. She has published in journals such as *Mediterranean Politics*, the *British Journal of North African Studies*, the *Journal of North African Studies*, *Arab Studies Quarterly*, *Revista de Estudios Políticos*, *Revista de Estudios e Investigaciones Sociológicas*, and *Revista Española de Ciencia Política*. She coordinated two research projects on Authoritarianism Persistence and Political Change Processes in North Africa and Middle East: Consequences on Political Regimes and International Scene" from 2012 to 2018, supported by the Spanish government and the Andalusian government. She has been Visiting Researcher at the Middle East Centre at the University of Oxford (19 May 2022–1 October 2022), the Institute of Arabic and Islamic Studies at Exeter University (8 June 2019–30 September 2019), the École de Gouvernance et d'Economie in Rabat (18 June 2014–15 September 2014), the Centro de Investigaciones Sociológicas in Madrid (31 May 2006–31 August 2006), and the Center d'Analyse et d'Interventions Sociologiques at the École des Hautes Études en Sciences Sociales in Paris (1 April 2004–30 June 2004). She has been co-editor of the *Spanish Journal of Political Science* (RECP) from May 2012 to August 2020, and she is currently a member of its editorial board. For further information, see: www.inmaculadaszmolka.wordpress.com

Paride Turlione is a PhD candidate at the Laval University (Québec City) and Research Assistant in the Centre Interdisciplinaire de Recherche sur l'Afrique et le Moyen-Orient (CIRAM). He has an MA in International Relations from the University of Turin. His current research focuses on comparative politics and party politics in the Middle East and North Africa, mainly in Iraq and Lebanon.

Eva Wegner is Professor of Comparative Politics at Philipps-University Marburg. Her research focuses on political behaviour and accountability in the Middle East and Sub-Saharan Africa. Her previous work includes work on Islamist parties and voters in the Middle East and North Africa and work on protest and voting in South Africa. Together with Miquel Pellicer, she is PI of The Demand Side of Clientelism, a project investigating demand for different forms of clientelism in South Africa and Tunisia. Her work has appeared in *Perspectives on Politics*, the *Journal of Conflict Resolution*, *International Political Science Review*, *Governance*, and *Party Politics*, among others.

Şebnem Yardımcı-Geyikçi is Associate Professor of Politics at Hacettepe University, Ankara. She completed her PhD in Government at the University of Essex in 2013. She has a second PhD degree in Political Science from Bilkent University, received in 2015. Her primary area of research is comparative politics, with a special focus on parties, party systems, regime change, and contentious politics. Previously, her works on aspects of party politics, contentious politics, and democratization in Turkey and beyond have appeared in *Party Politics*, *Democratization*, *Government and Opposition*, *PS: Politics and Political Science*, *Mediterranean Politics*, and *The Political Quarterly*. She was Fellow at the Netherlands Institute for Advanced Studies (NIAS) and a Visiting Fulbright Scholar at the University of Michigan. She received the Young Scientists Award in the field of Political Science given by the Science Academy in 2022. Currently, she serves as a board member of the Turkish Political Science Association.

Notes on Contributors

Hakan Yavuzyılmaz received his PhD from Hacettepe University and conducted research on the dynamics of party (de)institutionalization under electoral authoritarian regimes as Post-Doctoral Researcher at the University of Nottingham, School of Politics and International Relations. He is currently working as Research and Policy Development Coordinator at the Checks and Balances Network, Istanbul Policy Center, Sabancı University and teaching at Başkent University, Department of Political Science and International Relations. His research mainly focuses on political parties, party systems, and political regimes. His research appeared in journals such as *Party Politics* and the *Journal of Balkan and Near Eastern Studies*.

1
ELECTIONS IN THE MIDDLE EAST AND NORTH AFRICA

Francesco Cavatorta and Valeria Resta

Introduction

Research on elections and campaigning in the Middle East and North Africa has attracted scant attention for many years because the vast majority of the countries in the region, with very few and contested exceptions, were authoritarian regimes. Formal institutions such as elections, when they were held at all, did not actually matter very much because informal networks of privilege and power were more central to explaining political developments (Heydemann 2004; Anceschi et al. 2014). However, building on authoritarian elections elsewhere in the world (Schedler 2002), Middle East scholars began in the early 2000s to question the assumption that studying elections in authoritarian contexts was meaningless (Posusney 2002; Lust-Okar 2006). While there was a consensus on the fact that elections in authoritarian states were held to 'upgrade authoritarianism' through the self-serving adoption of liberal institutions (Heydemann 2007; Schlumberger 2007), these elections were nevertheless important for both the regime and the opposition. Through them, the regime could, for instance, come to 'know' social trends better and prevent resistance through the co-optation of key actors and their demands (Blaydes 2010; Lust-Okar 2005; Brownlee 2011), while for the opposition parties and candidates elections were a means to test their popularity and 'practice' for the day when electoral competition would actually matter (Brown 2012; Masoud 2008). Authoritarian elections were also a safety valve for regimes as well as an instrument they could employ to secure financial and diplomatic support from the international community (Heydemann 2007). For voters more broadly, authoritarian elections represented a means through which they could acquire material benefits, as elected representatives had access to state resources, no matter how limited they might have been (de Miguel et al. 2015; Ellen Lust 2009; Corstange 2012). It should be noted though that not all elections in the Middle East and North Africa during this time were held in authoritarian regimes. Elections in Israel have always been free and fair and hotly contested since the establishment of the state, and such electoral contests see the active participation of the Arab Palestinian minority. Free and fair elections have characterised Turkish political life for decades, allowing scholars to note, for instance, the emergence and electoral strength of Islamist parties before they were actually allowed to run in several Arab countries later on. Despite military occupation, a disastrous security situation and a severe economic crisis, Iraq has held a number of free elections since 2005. Lebanon, after the civil war, also experienced several free and fair elections,

DOI: 10.4324/9781003185628-1

although the country was under some sort of Syrian protectorate for three decades. Iraqi and Lebanese contests provided the literature with insights about the appeal of sectarianism, as well as its rejection later on, for instance. Finally, after the 2011 Arab uprisings, Tunisia, Egypt and Libya experienced genuinely free and fair elections, although they were held during unstable transitioning times. Such elections illustrated trends that scholars suspected existed in society and that now found confirmation at the polls, such as the appeal of Islamism, the weakness of the left and endurance of electoral clientelism. In all of these cases, meaningful tools for the selection of the political elite brought about government alternation. In the midst of all of this, it should also be noted that Palestine and Iraqi Kurdistan – two non-state entities – also experienced what can be defined as democratic elections. Yet, in line with the global trend of autocratisation (Maerz et al. 2020), the democratic potential of electoral contests has been defused in the wake of democratic erosion in settings such as Palestine, Lebanon and Turkey. Exceptions to this rule are Israel, Iraq and Tunisia, although the 2021 constitutional coup places the Tunisian consolidation of democracy in danger.

MENA elections

Elections are today part of the ordinary course of political life in authoritarian, democratic and quasi-democratic settings across the region (Brumberg 2002; Schedler 2013; Ellen Lust 2009). Since the 1980s, compliance with the Structural Adjustments Programmes (SAPs) formulated by the International Monetary Fund (IMF) and the World Bank forced regional autocrats to introduce measures of political liberalisation in exchange for enormous loans with the hope these would trigger a genuine democratisation process (Achcar 2013; Carothers 2002). At the same time, the end of the Cold War empowered the Western international community further, instigating calls to ditch alliances with authoritarian regimes, admittedly useful during the struggle against the Soviet Union, and live instead up to the liberal-democratic ideals that allowed it to 'win' the Cold War. In this context of considerable external pressure (Durac and Cavatorta 2009; Pace et al. 2009) and combined with increasing domestic demands for political openings after decades of underperforming authoritarianism (Pratt 2006), MENA regimes implemented a set of liberalising institutional reforms. The first of such measures were the holding of multi-party elections, which soon turned to be one of the pillars for the maintenance of authoritarianism in the region (Albrecht and Schlumberger 2004; Heydemann 2007). Through several constraints placed in electoral laws, in the design of districts and in access to the media, authoritarian regimes emptied elections of their significance, and very few countries consistently held democratic elections.

The aftermath of the 2011 Arab Uprisings further illustrated the relevance of elections, with a number of countries holding free and fair electoral contests for the first time in their history. Scholars therefore began to focus more on elections and all that they entailed, from candidate selection to campaigning and from the study of parties' manifestos to the way in which electoral systems operated (Aydogan 2021; Geisser and Perez 2016; Resta 2019, 2022). In addition, a number of studies examined voters, their preferences and attitudes (Masoud 2014; Wegner and Cavatorta 2019; Spierings 2019). Thus, even though the region is not known for its good governance and strong democratic institutions, elections across the Middle East and North Africa are now part of the political routine. As Figure 1.1 shows, according to V-dem, in 2021 almost all the countries of the region could be classified as electoral regimes, confirming that elections are one of the hallmarks of regional politics. The exception to this rule is, as it appears, Saudi Arabia, even though elections rarely occur in the other Gulf Monarchies of Qatar and the United Arab Emirates and in Yemen, which has recently worsened its track record following the 2014 civil war.

Elections in the Middle East and North Africa

Figure 1.1 V-Dem Electoral Component Index, 2021. *Source*: Author

In the wake of this empirical reality, several studies have seen the light and aim to explain the reasons why regular elections are not accompanied by democratic empowerment. Scholars focused on incumbents' manipulations of electoral rules and results, or their use (or threat) of violence at the ballot box to obtain their preferred outcome (Kraetzschmar and Cavatorta 2010). In a slightly different vein, others have looked instead to the manipulation of the structures of competition to defuse the democratic potential of elections from the start (Brownlee 2011; Buehler 2013). Another strand of studies insisted on the importance of corruption, clientelism and networks of kinship in hampering the emergence of issue-based politics that is meant to come with (democratic) elections (Corstange 2018; Çarkoğlu and Aytaç 2015; Hibou 2006). Coming from a different perspective, a recent study has unveiled how the perceived quality of elections among citizens bolsters regimes' legitimation, thus shedding new light on the foundations of electoral authoritarianism and it's survival (Williamson 2021). While these works have been incredibly important to explain how elections can sustain 'upgraded autocracies', elections *per se* – and all that comes with them – have been overlooked and there are therefore very few studies about, among many others, rules and procedures, about the institutions supervising elections, about candidate selection, about the coverage of elections, and about the way in which preferences and attitudes of voters shape electoral debates and outcomes. The reason for this is twofold. First, elections are still inherently associated with democracy (Hamad and al-Anani 2014). Despite the growth of the literature on elections under authoritarian constraints, many aspects of elections and electioneering are still under-examined. Given the relative paucity of genuine democracies in the region, elections have generally been regarded as just one of the tools in the hand of autocrats to sustain authoritarianism or, at best, competitive authoritarianism (Levitsky and Way 2002). Second, the poor institutionalisation of parties and party systems in the region (Storm 2014) has strengthened the belief that elections are playfields without players (Eyadat 2015; Völkel 2019). Even though institutionalisation alone cannot capture the complexities of partisan engagement in the region (Bermeo and Yashar 2016; Storm 2014), this has bolstered the narrative of regime survival, inducing scholars to approach elections largely for their contribution to authoritarianism (Albrecht 2005; Maghraoui 2019). This is not necessarily erroneous, but it is not the only story that can be told about elections in the MENA.

Re-connecting with the literature on elections in the Middle East and North Africa and focusing on their relevance in their own right, the contention of this project is that elections do matter and are worth investigating as autonomous processes. This claim does not mean understating the fact that elections have been a powerful tool in the hand of autocrats in the region to consolidate their rule. Nor it is here argued that elections are to be regarded as gateways to democracy in the region. Rather, this project upholds the idea that the mere institutionalisation and routinisation of elections in the region is in itself a valid rationale to study them as a stand-alone political fact, regardless of its implications for broader structures of power. First, elections are *procedures*; hence, it might be worth investigating how the entire electoral process takes place across the Middle East and North Africa. Second, the variety of regime types in the region might shed light on the complexity of elections and, as a consequence, on the partiality of the extant literature on regime survival (Martinez-Fuentes 2017). Lastly, even in authoritarian settings, the mere recurrence of elections might have changed the political landscape in ways that go beyond the survival of authoritarianism (Croissant and Hellmann 2017; Schedler 2013), as unintended consequences of institutional changes might appear when one least expects it (Pierret and Selvik 2009). This holds particularly true in light of the vitality of Arab, Turkish and Iranian civil society and the venues of politicisation and participation in the Arab Spring, among other powerful movements of social mobilisation, contributed to the expansion. It should also be noted that despite the retrenchment of authoritarian rule and the presence of civil strife in some countries, such spaces of mobilisation are still present (Cavatorta and Clark 2022).

Main themes

There are five themes that emerge from this study of elections as processes in the Middle East and North Africa, and they are teased out in individual country settings. These in-depth case studies illustrate specific national dynamics and issues, but, at the same time, speak to broader themes. The first theme has to do with how elections take place in authoritarian settings. However, rather than insisting on how competitive authoritarian elections strengthen authoritarianism, the chapters dealing with the first theme offer an analysis of the specific instruments and discourses that affect electoral contests. What emerges is a complex picture of regimes resorting to very detailed instruments – military oversight, district design, media access – to conduct elections, ensuring the survival of the regime while providing the appearance of competition. One overarching and innovative element that characterises elections in MENA authoritarian settings is the degree of legal engineering implemented to ensure that a competitive façade is kept. This is rather surprising insofar as both the international community and, crucially, voters are aware that electoral contests are a charade. Plummeting turnout is a clear indication of voters' dissatisfaction and disengagement, confirming what Brumberg (2002) had already hinted at over two decades ago when he suggested that electoral competitions in authoritarian settings held in the name of democracy or democratisation do nothing but cheapen the concept and practice of democracy itself.

While all this is well-known and unproblematic for both scholars and policy-makers, several traits and elements of competitive authoritarian elections have found their way into elections in MENA democratic or quasi-democratic settings. Israel, Turkey, Tunisia, Iraq and Lebanon have all experienced what Bermeo (2016) labelled 'democratic backsliding', albeit to different degrees and starting from different points on the 'democracy' spectrum. The second theme of the book has therefore to do with the way in which elections, while remaining central features of these countries and enjoying the label of 'free, fair and competitive', are still subject to considerable constraints. Such constraints in turn weigh quite heavily on how voters and citizens more broadly feel disenfranchised. Since the revolution, Tunisia has held regular legislative and presidential elections in addition to the 2018 local elections, but these contests are increasingly perceived as rather meaningless by citizens because they are unable to produce strong governments capable of facing the country's challenges. In fact, elections are held responsible for fostering party fragmentation and unaccountability. Since 2005, elections in Iraq have been genuinely competitive, but have been held in a precarious security environment and have reinforced sectarian cleavages. More recently, Iraqi consociationalism has been challenged and alternative political visions have been put forth, but without fundamentally undermining the way in which political power is distributed in the state's institutions. These two examples suggest that elections are both central to democratic politics and increasingly perceived as incapable of functioning as mechanisms to allocate policy-making power. In the Turkish case, democratic backsliding through elections is even clearer with the ruling party and its leader employing electoral mechanisms to reinforce authoritarian tendencies, while in the Iranian case the religious constraints on elections significantly limit their actual competitiveness. Exploring the laws and statutes that govern elections in democratic and quasi-democratic settings paints a rather disappointing picture of democratic elections in the Middle East and North Africa.

A further examination of the rules, institutions and infrastructure of elections is the third theme of the book. It deals specifically with a range of different elections – presidential, parliamentary, local – and the broader infrastructure of electoral competition. As mentioned above, elections have become central mechanisms of legitimacy across different and opposing political systems. Their centrality has led to the establishment, development and implementation of rules governing them. In fact, a complex architecture has been created to manage and carry out elections ranging from independent authorities charged with overseeing them to the imposition of gender quotas to ensure greater female representation in elected institutions. Although this architecture is established to either serve the needs and goals of ruling elites in authoritarian countries or to support pluralism and fairness in democratic ones, the consequences of creating it go well beyond the initial intention. Unintended dynamics have flowed from the electoral architecture put in place. In the Tunisian case, for instance, the independent high authority for elections has become a terrain of confrontation between political parties and state institutions rather than being simply allowed to carry out its functions autonomously as specified in the 2014 constitution. The introduction of gender quotas in Algeria, implemented to signal to the international community the country's liberalising agenda and to appease the more secular sectors of the population, has led female MPs to acquire considerable prominence through their work for individual citizens once elected and performing better on this measure than their male counterparts. Greater familiarity with competition and 'democratic' mechanisms has flowed from the setting up of elected local councils in Saudi Arabia, a country where political parties do not exist, and national elections are for the moment unthinkable. Designed to appease demands for reform and to provide the regime with accurate information about political and social trends in broader society, these local elections have achieved these objectives, but they have also socialised some Saudis to competitive politics with potential future repercussions on the regime. The fact that such an architecture exists and is taken seriously in some quarters of society partly explains why many political actors spend time and resources on campaigning for elected office.

The fourth theme in the book is how campaigns are carried out on the ground, what is the role of mass media and what is the role of social media. This theme is preoccupied with the way in which the public scene is invested at election time and how it influences voters and political parties. These issues are relevant to all institutional contexts. Elections in the MENA display both traditional and more modern elements of campaigning. On the one hand, several elections, whether in democracies or authoritarian systems, still witness the central role of brokers and intermediaries between parties and voters. Their role is to connect political leaders and candidates with reservoirs of voters in exchange for material goods or rewards. This is not necessarily outright corruption or vote-buying, which is increasingly negatively perceived, but it is part of an exchange that both politicians and voters have come to expect. The patronage networks that emerge during campaigns may seem like a throwback to a different era, but they still are relevant to explain how parties attempt to engage voters and secure their support. On the other, MENA elections have also become more 'modern' and the increasingly significant role of social media, notably Facebook and Twitter, is the most evident manifestation of this. This does not mean that social media campaigning has replaced traditional methods of engagement; rather, it complements off-line campaigning, which still evolves around physical social networks. Campaigning though is not only about the instruments being used to campaign. During campaigns, several political strategies can be seen at work, including innovative alliances between former rivals deciding to pool their resources together to defeat a particularly powerful incumbent, as the case of Turkey clearly demonstrates. In this case, campaigns might see the withdrawal of candidates in certain districts to favour an ally, who in turn will withdraw elsewhere. Thus, campaigns are also moments when other processes occur and influence the way in which the political system works.

In all of this, voters and voting behaviour should not be forgotten. The fifth and final theme is preoccupied with the way in which voters approach elections and participate – or not – in them. Of particular relevance are issues related to turnout, what are the issues that drive voters, how social structures and demographic traits (sectarianism, tribalism, class, age or education) influence the way in which voters approach elections and what are the material rewards that voters expect, if any. While there is a degree of truth, as we have seen, in that elections in the MENA are largely about clientelism and patronage – for parties and voters alike – it is equally true that ideological commitment plays a substantial role in some elections and for significant numbers of voters. Class divisions or sectarian allegiances can be powerful motivators for turning out, although turnout overall is quite low across regimes and across countries. In part, this is due to the low trust that parties, politicians, and institutions more broadly enjoy, particularly among the youth, which prefers alternative modes of political mobilisation and participation.

Conclusion: MENA elections in a global context

Although the region is often analysed in isolation due to its supposedly 'exceptional' politics, the reality is that the political and social phenomena occurring there are often part of trends that can be seen elsewhere across the world, and elections are no different. While the systematic examination of elections presented here highlights some region-specific trends about the way in which they function and are carried out, notably the authoritarian constraints affecting the majority of the electoral contests, it is important to underline several connections with findings of the comparative politics literature has presented (Lynch 2021).

First of all, elections have on average poor or very poor turnouts. Although this might be understandable in authoritarian settings, whereby dissent with the regime can be demonstrated through abstention from voting, this should not occur in democracies, particularly new ones, as enthusiasm for newly found freedoms and the chance to finally have a saying in policy-making should be high. However, and in line with decreasing rates in established democracies, turnout has been disappointing in Tunisia and Iraq, as well as Lebanon. This points to a 'convergence' among large sectors of the electorate whereby elections are no longer capable of delivering radical political change, particularly when it comes to economic policy-making (Hopkin 2020).

As research on Arab voters demonstrates (Teti et al. 2019), democracy for Arabs is equated with procedures and mechanisms such as elections as well as socio-economic rights and redistributive outcomes. This means that when the latter do not follow from the adoption of democracy, the whole concept of democracy is questioned. This, in turn, has significant implications for democracy-promotion, which Western countries and international organisations still equate with the holding of free and fair elections.

Second, the rules and laws governing elections are manipulated across the region as they are elsewhere, including in established democracies. The design of the electoral system and gerrymandering are but two of the ways in which political parties and ruling elites attempt to tilt the playing field in their favour. In this context, the issue of gerrymandering does not only concern Jordanian or Lebanese elections, but American (Engstrom 2020) ones too, for instance. Rather complex and obscure rules, at least to the majority of the electorate, have become a battlefield for political actors in both authoritarian and democratic settings across the MENA and elsewhere.

Third, campaigns increasingly resemble each other too, in particular, when it comes to social media. Much like across the rest of the globe, social media have become increasingly crucial in running campaigns to promote parties and candidates. Whether it is for Tunisian local elections or Kuwaiti legislative ones, candidates and parties have placed social media at the centre of their campaigns, often employing professionals to run them. However, and in line with the literature's findings, the role of social media in driving people to the polls or changing the course of elections is rather limited, as off-line social networks seem to be more relevant.

This is in part due to the fact that 'identity' issues have become more important for voters and when this occurs, they tend to operate in a sort of echo chamber. The expectation that voters in the Middle East and North Africa are keener on voting on identity issues is in many cases validated, whether it is because such issues are clearly reflecting divides in society – sectarian, ethnic or linguistic – or because of the legal framework and political system – the rule of consociationalism. Such identity issues and the subsequent voting behaviour are increasingly seen in established democracies and other settings too.

These and other trends confirm therefore that *elections as processes* in the Middle East and North Africa deserve to be studied in their own right, as they can tell us something about elections more broadly and connect with a comparative politics literature that rarely engages with them.

References

Achcar, Gilbert. 2013. *The People Want: A Radical Exploration of the Arab Uprising*. Oakland, CA: University of California Press.
Albrecht, Holger. 2005. 'How Can Opposition Support Authoritarianism? Lessons from Egypt'. *Democratization* 12(3): 378–397.
Albrecht, Holger, and Oliver Schlumberger. 2004. '"Waiting for Godot": Regime Change without Democratization in the Middle East'. *International Political Science Review* 25(4): 371–392.
Anceschi, Luca, Andrea Teti, and Gennaro Gervasio. 2014. *Informal Power in the Greater Middle East*. Abingdon, Oxon: Routledge.
Aydogan, Abdullah. 2021. 'Party Systems and Ideological Cleavages in the Middle East and North Africa'. *Party Politics* 27(4): 814–826.
Bermeo, Nancy, and Deborah J. Yashar. 2016. *Parties, Movements and Democracy in the Developing World*. New York: Cambridge University Press.
Blaydes, Lisa. 2010. *Elections and Distributive Politics in Mubarak's Egypt*. Cambridge: Cambridge University Press.
Brown, Nathan J. 2012. *When Victory Is Not an Option: Islamist Movements in Arab Politics*. Ithaca, NY: Cornell University Press.
Brownlee, Jason. 2011. 'Executive Elections in the Arab World: When and How Do They Matter?' *Comparative Political Studies* 44(7): 807–828.

Brumberg, Daniel. 2002. 'The Trap of Liberalized Autocracy'. *Journal of Democracy* 13(4): 56–68.
Buehler, Matt. 2013. 'Safety-Valve Elections and the Arab Spring: The Weakening (and Resurgence) of Morocco's Islamist Opposition Party'. *Terrorism and Political Violence* 25(1): 137–156.
Çarkoğlu, All, and S. Erdem Aytaç. 2015. 'Who Gets Targeted for Vote-Buying? Evidence from an Augmented List Experiment in Turkey'. *European Political Science Review* 7(4): 547–566.
Carothers, Thomas. 2002. 'The End of the Transition Paradigm'. *Journal of Democracy* 13(1): 5–21.
Cavatorta, Francesco, and Janine A. Clark. 2022 forthcoming. 'Political and Social Mobilization in the Middle East and North Africa after the 2011 Uprisings'. *Globalizations*.
Corstange, Daniel. 2012. 'Vote Trafficking in Lebanon'. *International Journal of Middle East Studies* 44(3): 483–505.
Corstange, Daniel. 2018. 'Kinship, Partisanship, and Patronage in Arab Elections'. *Electoral Studies* 52(April): 58–72.
Croissant, Aurel, and Olli Hellmann. 2017. 'Introduction: State Capacity and Elections in the Study of Authoritarian Regimes'. *International Political Science Review* 39(1): 3–16.
Durac, Vincent, and Francesco Cavatorta. 2009. 'Strengthening Authoritarian Rule through Democracy Promotion? Examining the Paradox of the US and EU Security Strategies: The Case of Bin Ali's Tunisia'. *British Journal of Middle Eastern Studies* 36(1): 3–19.
Engstrom, Richard L. 2020. 'Partisan Gerrymandering: Weeds in the Political Thicket'. *Social Science Quarterly* 101(1): 23–36.
Eyadat, Zaid. 2015. 'A Transition without Players: The Role of Political Parties in the Arab Revolutions'. *Democracy and Security* 11(2): 160–175.
Geisser, Vincent, and Déborah Perez. 2016. 'De La Difficulté à 'Faire Parti' Dans La Tunisie PostBen Ali'. *Confluences Méditerranée* 98(3): 21.
Hamad, Mahmoud, and Khalil al-Anani. 2014. 'Elections and Beyond: Democratization, Democratic Consolidation, or What?'. In: Mahmoud Hamad and Khalial Al-Anani (eds.), *Elections and Democratization in the Middle East*, 203–221. London: Palgrave Macmillan.
Heydemann, Steven. 2004. *Networks of Privilege in the Middle East: The Politics of Economic Reform Revisited*. New York: Palgrave.
Heydemann, Steven. 2007. 'Upgrading Authoritarianism in the Arab World'. *The Saban Center for Middle East Policy at the Brooking Institution* 13.
Hibou, Béatrice. 2006. *La Force de l'obéissance: Économie Politique de la Répression en Tunisie*. Paris: La Découverte.
Hopkin, Jonathan. 2020. *Anti-system Politics: The Crisis of Market Liberalism in Rich Democracies*. New York: Oxford University Press.
Kraetzschmar, Hendrik, and Francesco Cavatorta. 2010. 'Bullets over Ballots: Islamist Groups, the State and Electoral Violence in Egypt and Morocco'. *Democratization* 17(2): 326–349.
Levitsky, Steven, and Lucan Way. 2002. 'The Rise of Competitive Authoritarianism'. *Journal of Democracy* 13(2): 51–65.
Lust, Ellen. 2009. 'Competitive Clientelism in the Middle East'. *Journal of Democracy* 20(3): 122–135.
Lust-Okar, Ellen. 2005. *Structuring Conflict in the Arab World: Incumbents, Opponents, and Institutions*. Cambridge: Cambridge University Press.
Lust-Okar, Ellen. 2006. 'Elections under Authoritarianism: Preliminary Lessons from Jordan'. *Democratization* 13(3): 456–471.
Lynch, Marc. 2021. 'Taking Stock of MENA Political Science after the Uprisings'. *Mediterranean Politics* 26(5): 682–695.
Maerz, Seraphine F., Anna Lührmann, Sebastian Hellmeier, Sandra Grahn, and Staffan I. Lindberg. 2020. 'State of the World 2019: Autocratization Surges – Resistance Grows'. *Democratization* 27(6): 909–927.
Maghraoui, Driss. 2019. 'On the Relevance or Irrelevance of Political Parties in Morocco'. *The Journal of North African Studies* 25(6): 939–959.
Martinez-Fuentes, Guadalupe. 2017. 'Elections and Electoral Integrity'. In: Inmaculada Szmolka (ed.), *Political Change in the Middle East and North Africa*, 89–114. Edinburgh: Edinburgh University Press.
Masoud, Tarek. 2008. 'Islamist Parties and Democracy: Are They Democrats? Does It Matter?' *Journal of Democracy* 19(3): 19–24.
Masoud, Tarek. 2014. *Counting Islam: Religion, Class and Elections in Egypt*. New York: Cambridge University Press.
Miguel, Carolina de, Amaney A. Jamal, and Mark Tessler. 2015. 'Elections in the Arab World'. *Comparative Political Studies* 48(11): 1355–1388.

Pace, Michelle, Peter Seeberg, and Francesco Cavatorta. 2009. 'The EU's Democratization Agenda in the Mediterranean: A Critical inside-out Approach'. *Democratization* 16(1): 3–19.

Pierret, Thomas, and Kjetil Selvik. 2009. 'Limits of "Authoritarian Upgrading" in Syria: Private Welfare, Islamic Charities, and the Rise of the Zayd Movement'. *International Journal of Middle East Studies* 41(4): 595–614.

Posusney, Marsha Pripstein. 2002. 'Multi-party Elections in the Arab World: Institutional Engineering and Oppositional Strategies'. *Studies in Comparative International Development* 36(4): 34–62.

Pratt, Nicola. 2006. *Democracy and Authoritarianism in the Arab World*. Boulder, CO: Lynne Rienner.

Resta, Valeria. 2019. 'The Effect of Electoral Autocracy in Egypt's Failed Transition: A Party Politics Perspective'. *Italian Political Science Review/Rivista Italiana di Scienza Politica* 49(2): 157–173.

Resta, Valeria. 2022 forthcoming. 'The "Myth of Moderation" Following the Arab Uprisings: Polarization in Tunisia and Egypt's Founding Elections'. *British Journal of Middle Eastern Studies*.

Schedler, Andreas. 2002. 'The Menu of Manipulation'. *Journal of Democracy* 13(2): 36–50.

Schedler, Andreas. 2013. *The Politics of Uncertainty: Sustaining and Subverting Electoral Authoritarianism*. Oxford: Oxford University Press.

Schlumberger, Oliver. 2007. *Debating Arab Authoritarianism: Dynamics and Durability in Nondemocratic Regimes*. Stanford: Stanford University Press.

Spierings, Niels. 2019. 'Democratic Disillusionment? Desire for Democracy after the Arab Uprisings'. *International Political Science Review* 41(4): 522–537.

Storm, Lise. 2014. *Party Politics and the Prospects for Democracy in North Africa*. Boulder, CO: Lynne Rienner.

Teti, Andrea, Pamela Abbott, and Francesco Cavatorta. 2019. 'Beyond Elections: Perceptions of Democracy in Four Arab Countries'. *Democratization* 26(4): 645–665.

Völkel, Jan Claudius. 2019. 'The "Chicken and Egg" Problem of Relevance: Political Parties and Parliaments in North Africa'. *Journal of North African Studies* 25(6): 865–880.

Wegner, Eva, and Francesco Cavatorta. 2019. 'Revisiting the Islamist–Secular Divide: Parties and Voters in the Arab World". *International Political Science Review* 40(5): 558–575.

Williamson, Scott. 2021. 'Elections, Legitimacy, and Compliance in Authoritarian Regimes: Evidence from the Arab World'. *Democratization* 28(8): 1483–1504.

PART 1

Elections in authoritarian settings

2
THE FUNCTIONS OF AUTHORITARIAN ELECTIONS
Symbolism, safety valves, and clientelism

Matt Buehler and Calista Boyd

Introduction

Elections in advanced industrialized democracies – like the United States, Canada, and Western Europe – serve to aggregate citizens' interests, helping the elites who run for office better understand the preferences of their constituencies. In democratic contexts, elections determine which political parties and elites control institutions that wield influence over society and how that political power can be reordered over time. Elections, as Schedler (2006: 6) and Levitsky and Way (2010 observe, also occur in many authoritarian systems, though irregularities and fraud often mar them. Further, in authoritarian regimes, elections do not necessarily reorder or redistribute power – indeed, autocrats' right-hand men may retain ironclad control over key institutions (e.g., military, police) regardless of electoral results. Thus, this chapter asks what the purposes of elections are in authoritarian regimes if they do not help to genuinely signal citizens' preferences or redistribute power. We address this topic, focusing on the different functions of elections within the authoritarian regimes of the Middle East and North Africa (MENA). The MENA region differs from other world regions insomuch as, except for Israel (for Israeli citizens, at least), it features only solidly authoritarian regimes or transitional democracies trending toward authoritarianism, like Turkey and Sudan. In recent history, it also includes a handful of Arab states – specifically Iraq, Lebanon, and Tunisia – that typically have held free and fair elections from a procedural perspective, yet issues of sectarian control, political instability, authoritarian tendencies, and military interference often constrain how much political power gets genuinely redistributed through voting.

Elections in the MENA's authoritarian regimes serve different functions that reinforce non-democratic rule. Drawing on existing literature, this chapter examines these different functions, focusing on elections occurring at the executive (i.e., presidential or prime ministerial levels), legislative (i.e., parliamentary level), and local (i.e., municipal) levels. In a landmark article focused on the Arab world's executive elections, Brownlee (2011b) surveyed the existing literature finding that scholars theorize three main functions or purposes for elections under authoritarianism. These include, as Brownlee avers (2011b: 807), acting as "safety valves, patronage networks, and performance rituals." That is, Brownlee theorizes that autocrats – here, we mean mostly presidential dictators or monarchs in the MENA – utilize elections for three major functions:

to help release or assuage political pressure, to distribute clientelist resources, and to cultivate political symbolism. In the remainder of this chapter, we apply Brownlee's theoretical framework to examine three different types of elections in the MENA – those at the executive, legislative, and local levels. We also explore, conversely, the relatively rare circumstances when opponents of autocrats, most notably opposition parties (like Islamists and leftists), may also use elections under authoritarianism as safety valves, patronage networks, or political symbolism to advance their own interests and contest regimes. Some of these functions may be more or less prevalent according to election type, yet they all manifest – to a lesser or greater degree – across all three different levels of elections.

Elections in the "gray" regimes of the MENA

Most regimes in the MENA are considered "gray" regimes, with institutions exhibiting features resembling both consolidated, open democracies (e.g., Canada) and also full, closed autocracies (e.g., North Korea). Their internal institutions, including elections, seem to straddle these two ideal regime types, falling somewhere in between. Some scholars have considered the MENA's regimes "liberalized autocracies" or "electoral authoritarian" regimes (Carothers 2002; Brumberg 2002; Diamond 2006). Moving beyond terminology, the MENA's regimes are similar insofar as they exhibit characteristics of democracies, such as the existence of opposition parties, reoccurring elections, and written constitutions. However, these institutions are limited in power due to their lack of meaningful popular representation, limits on political participation, and widespread corruption (Carothers 2002: 9). Scholars who compare these MENA states with those in other geographic regions view them as non-democracies with an overarching dictator, king, or autocrat possessing absolute (penultimate) ruling powers, while pseudo-democratic institutions' habits and practices exist at a subordinate, lower level. In short, gray regimes feature parallel institutions: popular elections that are often manipulated and unfair, electing politicians in institutions at lower and subordinate levels of governance, while non-democratic institutions lay above these elected ones, controlled solely by the autocrat and his allies. What this means is that, compared to other authoritarian regimes like North Korea, Eritrea, or Turkmenistan, which are labeled "closed autocracies" without elections at all (Brumberg 2002: 59), scholars see the MENA's gray regimes as featuring at least limited elections containing constrained forms of multiparty or other political competition (Schedler 2006: 6). Yet, because authoritarian rulers and their allies can exercise power outside of gray regimes' elections, they fail to serve as a method of accountability that could be used to take elites to task for engaging in practices or implementing policies contrary to the citizenry's preferences (Schedler 2006: 6).

Morocco provides an ideal example in which such parallel pseudo-democratic institutions operate at a lower level, below more powerful non-democratic ones. Morocco's political system features regular elections across multiple levels of governance, a plethora of political parties, and alternations of power in which different elites control the elected government. Like other Arab regimes, Morocco also has a written constitution that (formally speaking, at least) guarantees citizens' basic rights. Yet, simultaneously, the country's monarch – Mohammed VI – rules over the regime and holds penultimate decision-making power. He appoints the ministers of what are known as "sovereign ministries," like the defense, interior, and finance ministries, that possess power over the most important policy areas (Daadaoui 2011: 56–57). Mohammed VI also turns to an unelected royal cabinet of experts – including elites like Fouad Ali al-Himma, senior advisor for domestic political affairs – for advice before promulgating new policies or decrees. And although citizens have the right to elect local representatives for municipal and regional councils, the monarch simultaneously appoints provincial intelligence officials – what are called Wālis (or préfets) and Caids – who act as his representatives locally and are powerful decision-makers (Hoffman 2011: 8; Daadaoui 2011: 152). These different unelected institutions controlled by Morocco's monarch work in parallel with (but, in reality, above) the elected ones. In many liberalized autocracies of the Arab world, like Morocco, citizens often become confused about this complex web of elected and unelected institutions that simultaneously governs politics and often have difficulty figuring out which ones they can and cannot control via elections at the ballot box. In reality, elected institutions that do exist often have limited authority or perhaps only narrow authority in specific (and typically less important) policy areas.

Elections in the MENA's autocracies: symbolism, safety valves, and clientelism

Executive elections: presidents and prime ministers

Different types of executive elections exist in the MENA. These include direct executive elections for the presidency, as in the cases of Egypt, Syria, Algeria, Mauritania, and Iran. Algeria's, Egypt's, Mauritania's, and Syria's presidents, per their constitutions, need to compete every five, six, or seven years, respectively, for their posts. Iran, similarly, has an elected president. Yet, in the cases of Algeria, Egypt, Syria, and Mauritania, several formal and informal conditions limit who can become president. In all these Arab regimes, for example, the president must be a Muslim and likely must have the tacit backing of the military establishment, which holds true power. Other candidates compete in the Egyptian and Syrian presidential elections, yet their presence is largely symbolic without any real likelihood of success. The fact that, in both Egypt and Syria, incumbent rulers received around 97 and 95 percent of votes, respectively, in the recent 2018 and 2021 presidential elections illustrates the lopsided nature of these elections. In Iran, elections for the presidency are generally more competitive than in Egypt or Syria, though the country's Council of Guardians restricts which candidates are eligible to compete. Although politicians need to prove they meet a variety of criteria to become eligible to run for Iran's presidency, one of the most important is that a candidate must have true revolutionary bona fides, meaning that they actively participated in the 1979 Islamic Revolution. Additionally, regimes often use state-owned media to unequally promote their preferred candidates in presidential campaigns, which disproportionately affects poorer people with less access to satellite television (Blaydes 2011: 112). In sum, citizens of the MENA can often cast ballots for their chief executives, yet unfair electoral conditions produce predetermine winners.

However, if such executive elections are not free and fair, why do regimes hold them and why do citizens participate? The first reason is due to their capacity to exert symbolic (or performative) power over citizens, which helps to reinforce perceived regime authority and legitimacy. By forcing citizens to participate in elections, even when those elections are patently unfair and of limited importance, regimes demonstrate their capacity to manipulate citizens and force their compliance into engaging in activities that rationally they should decline to do.

Lesch's account of Syria's executive elections exemplifies how regimes can create an environment in which symbolic support is elicited from citizens. Examining the 2007 presidential elections, Lesch shows how Syria's regime forced performative support from citizens through voter manipulation and subtle intimidation with the aim of building legitimacy for Bashar al-Assad's re-election campaign. Lesch documents seemingly widespread support for al-Assad in the streets, with pro-Bashar images everywhere (Lesch 2010: 76). And during the actual electoral process inside polling stations, voters were surveilled (Lesch 2010: 77), which means they were less likely to display any kind of opposition. The 2007 election in Syria is a clear example of results being a product of symbolic voter participation. In her earlier research on Syria in the 1990s, Wedeen (1999, 1998) found a similar symbolic power of elections in support of the previous dictator, Hafez al-Assad (r. 1971–2000). She emphasizes that Syrians often have ambiguous – if not outright oppositional – feelings toward their dictators and are not expected to believe their "flagrantly fictions statements" (Wedeen 1998: 506). Yet, the regime ensures that Syrians outwardly behave "as if" they do by compelling their participation in political rituals (like faux elections and campaign rallies) to help legitimize its rule by cultivating the impression of mass support (Wedeen 1998: 506).

Wedeen also utilizes Yemen to illustrate how executive elections can be used to exert symbolic power over citizens. During the 1999 presidential elections, which were the first following North and South Yemen's unification, Wedeen describes how they were largely performative in nature, with the opposition candidates running against dictator 'Ali 'Abdullah Saleh having virtually zero chance of victory. Because the parliament rejected the opposition's original choice of candidate, Salafi Sheikh Muqbil al-Wadi'i, the regime installed its own hand-picked opposition candidate to run against Saleh. The regime's change in candidates made the election appear even more performative, because no legitimate competition existed from a genuinely oppositional candidate (Wedeen 2008: 71). In addition, Saleh's regime drove voter turnout numbers up through intimidation tactics, like checking voters' thumbs to ensure they had participated (Wedeen 2008: 72).

Both Syria's 2007 election and Yemen's 1999 election represent how elections project regime dominance over the population through lack of competition on the executive level and voter intimidation tactics to force citizens' symbolic compliance (Wedeen 1999: 84). Like other regimes in the MENA, Syria's and Yemen's regimes drive citizens to vote in elections, yet their participation is hollow because they either fear declining to participate or genuine opposition is nonexistent. Therefore, the number of participants in elections is unrepresentative and largely symbolic, but the symbolic power of their support nonetheless reinforces the regime's overall authority and perceived legitimacy.

These symbolic practices have continued despite recent civil wars and ongoing instability. Commenting on his country's 2021 presidential election, a Syrian journalist described the election as a "celebratory kind of pro-Assad great spectacle that has been played and replayed in every part of the country" (Sherlock 2021). Although three candidates were permitted to compete, they were given only ten days to campaign, meaning Bashar al-Assad had a clear and easy path to victory. On election day, furthermore, al-Assad and his wife specifically chose to cast their ballots at a polling station in the Damascene suburb of Douma, a historic seat of resistance to Syria's regime during the civil war. In doing so, they sought to symbolically assert their control and rule over this traditional hotbed of resistance (Sherlock 2021).

The second way by which executive elections enhance regime power includes their capacity to distribute clientelist resources. Examining the case of Egypt in the 2000s, Blaydes (2011) finds that Egyptians' caloric intake increases substantially during election years. She emphasizes that presidential candidates – and especially the frontrunner from Egypt's former ruling party – distributed food (particularly meat) to convince citizens to vote in elections and carry their support at the ballot box. Such practices proliferated during Hosni Mubarak's 2005 presidential re-election, which was Egypt's first multi-candidate contest. The distribution of food to encourage pro-regime voting did not occur equally across socio-economic classes but rather took place disproportionately among voters with lower levels of educational attainment (Blaydes 2011: 115). Indeed, Blaydes' book looks at literacy and turnout rates to find a relationship showing a higher turnout rate among illiterate citizens. Blaydes also mentions how local government officials have threatened citizens with fines or unemployment if they do not vote

(Blaydes 2011: 111). Blaydes' findings are not without critique, however. Brownlee (2011a: 959) points out that clientelism is not very telling of the connection between elections and their ability to enhance regime power if the overall voter turnout is low, as occurred in Egypt's 2005 presidential election. Brownlee continues, moreover, that the possible link between illiteracy and turnout may be overstated because of the unreliability of voter turnout data, which the regime doctors to convey higher numbers (Brownlee 2011a: 959). Given new constraints on social scientific research in Egypt under the new reign of coupist-cum-president General Abdel Fattah al-Sisi, it is difficult to discern how much this clientelist system continues to exist in more recent Egyptian presidential elections. However, preliminary media accounts from the 2014 and 2018 elections reported citizens receiving a variety of goodies for casting their votes on behalf of the regime: subsidy boxes (of cooking oil, rice, and sugar), cash payments (between $3 and $9 per person), and free pilgrimage trips to Mecca (Walsh and Youssef 2018).

The third way by which executive elections help reinforce regime power entails their utility as safety valves to relieve citizens' discontent. This occurs most often not with direct presidential elections but with indirect executive elections for a prime minister. Morocco and Jordan, for example, are monarchies with kings as the ultimate rulers and arbiters. But they do allow for legislative and parliamentary elections, which result in the election of prime ministers. The prime minister – in the cases of Morocco and Jordan – acts as Head of Government, while the king is the Head of State. If the elected government causes a scandal or makes mistakes, which generate popular anger, the Jordanian and Moroccan kings will often dismiss the Head of Government or his ministers to pacify discontent (Ryan 2002; Buehler 2018: 177). By swapping one prime minister out for a new one, Jordan's regime projects an impression of political change to the population, which is, in reality, of a limited nature. Similarly, in the case of Morocco, the king retains the authority to dismiss the prime minister and often does so, if the country is experiencing a major crisis (often an unexpected economic downturn). This move helps to assuage citizen anger, and redirects it toward the elected government and elected political parties rather than the unelected king and his elite allies.

Some scholars (Brites et al. 2021: 1–4) have documented a similar strategy to assuage citizen anger in Mauritania's presidential autocracy, wherein unelected military overlords backed rotating in a new presidential dictator, Mohamed Ould Ghazouani, for the sitting one, Mohamed Ould Abdel Aziz, in 2019 to project an image (of largely superficial) change. Arguably, a similar dynamic occurred the same year after popular protests in Algeria when the military establishment endorsed removing President Abdelaziz Bouteflika and swapping in President Abdelmadjid Tebboune.

Legislative elections: parliaments and legislatures

Like most kingdoms of the Persian Gulf, most authoritarian regimes of the MENA include elected assemblies in their political systems that act as law-making bodies. Across the region, these legislative bodies have different names: in some states, like Morocco, Algeria, and Jordan, they are called parliaments, whereas in other states like Syria and Egypt they are termed people's assemblies (*majlis al-sha'ab*). Kuwait, the one Persian Gulf monarchy with a robust elected legislature, calls it the National Assembly (or *majlis al-ummah*). Despite these different labels, these legislative bodies are similarly staffed by deputies who obtain their positions via elections. Like the example of executive elections, elections at this lower level of political power can also serve the three aforementioned purposes: symbolism, safety valves, and clientelist distribution.

While executive elections act symbolically as performance rituals of political loyalty, legislative elections can be symbolic insomuch as autocrats use them to cultivate a sense of faux pluralism. Before their collapse during the 2011 Arab uprisings, Tunisia's and Egypt's presidential autocracies in the 1990s and 2000s used legislative elections to symbolically project fake pluralism to their citizens. Although in both Tunisia and Egypt the regimes' ruling parties – the *Rassemblement constitutionnel démocratique* (RCD) and National Democratic Party (NDP) – possessed overwhelming majorities in their parliaments, they still permitted a number of small, weak opposition parties. These parties, though limited in their capacity to authentically resist ruling parties or implement true policy, did help to generate a veneer of debate, contestation, and pluralism within parliaments.

For example, in 2005, Egypt's regime permitted the Muslim Brothers to gain about 20 percent of seats, running as independent candidates. These opposition parties did not have sufficient power within the parliaments to pass laws or enact real change. Yet, as Shehata and Stacher show (2006), they could act as gadflies, criticizing the regime's actions, highlighting its misguided policies, and advocating for investigations. This was particularly true in the case of Egypt's Muslim Brothers. The Brothers called for parliamentary inquiries into the Mubarak regime's mishandling of the 2006 avian flu and its economic fallout, investigating a loss of $217 million and 1 million jobs (Shehata and Stacher 2006). But without a large presence, opposition parties who gained some representation through legislative elections could not meaningfully alter or resist their regimes' policies. However, this veneer of pluralism created by allowing weak opposition parties not only helped regimes partially assuage citizen pressure for reform but also appeased international donors – like the United States, European Union, and World Bank – who periodically threatened to make economic aid contingent on gradual liberalization.

Tunisia and Syria provide examples of how regimes can use legislative elections to cultivate a sense of pluralism. In 1994, Tunisia's regime legalized several opposition parties, allowing them to compete in legislative elections (Angrist 1999: 90). This move built upon the prior legalization of a handful of socialist-inspired parties, such as *Parti démocrate progressiste* (PDP) and *Ettajdid* (formerly the Tunisian communist party), who gained permits to operate in the late 1980s and early 1990s. These socialist parties, however, were unable to compromise their ideologies or coordinate their opposition, and thus gained little electoral or political influence (Haugbølle and Cavatorta 2011: 330–331). Some opposition parties during the Ben Ali era, like the *Parti de l'unité populaire* (PUP), did little to oppose the regime's ruling party and often considered cooperation with it as more beneficial (Haugbølle and Cavatorta 2011: 332). These parties' operations were hampered by harassment from the ruling party and financing laws that forced them to reveal their private fundraising (Angrist 1999: 93–95). Despite these restrictions, Tunisia's regime allowed an increase in the percentage of opposition-held seats during this period from 7 percent following the 1994 elections to nearly 19 percent after the 1999 elections, hoping to cultivate a sense of pluralism within the chamber (Sadiki 2002: 64). "Tunisia," as Sadiki (2002: 63) concludes, "gives the impression of having moved a long way from single party rule and exclusivity." Yet, legislative elections "have done very little in terms of tilting the balance of power towards society or away from the ruling party."

One ruling party dominates Syrian politics, much like in Tunisia and Egypt in the 1990s and 2000s. This is the Syrian Ba'ath Party. Yet, the regime has permitted legislative elections – though highly rigged and unfair – to allow the formation and limited electoral representation of nine small, alternative parties to generate a sense of pluralism within Syria's parliament. Compared with the cases of Tunisia and Egypt, however, Syria's opposition parties have even less power and are generally considered "cardboard" opposition. These opposition parties constitute what is known as the National Progressive Front and possess ideological views that differ little from the Ba'ath Party (US State Department 2007). They regularly recognize and defer to the rule of the al-Assad family and even publicly endorsed Bashar al-Assad's candidacy in the

2007 presidential elections. In short, these political parties could barely be called "oppositional," possessing very little interest in genuinely criticizing the regime's hegemony over politics. One exception to this trend appeared in the area of economic policy in the 2000s: some debate occurred among leaders from the Ba'ath Party and various National Progressive Front parties over macro-economic planning, though these discussions were limited to financial and other highly technocratic topics considered uncontroversial (US State Department 2007). Prior to the 2011 Arab uprisings, nearly all serious criticism of Syria's regime occurred among the banned Islamist opposition or secular writers and intellectuals, mostly living in exile (Leiken and Brooke 2007: 115).

In other Arab authoritarian regimes, notably in the Arab monarchies, elections have a role as a safety valve. In these states, unlike in the presidential autocracies, opposition parties have relatively more strength and have greater power to potentially shape policy. Legislative elections and elected bodies, like parliaments, can be used as safety valves in these contexts. Especially prevalent in the Arab monarchies, regimes manipulate and alter electoral rules, laws, and legal permits to practice divide-and-rule against the opposition. Lust, in her landmark book *Structuring Conflict in the Arab World*, describes how this process works. She introduces her concepts of *unified* or *divided* "structures of contestation" (2006: 36–40). In unified structures of contestation, nearly all opposition groups are banned, as is the case in the most politically closed Persian Gulf monarchies, such as Saudi Arabia or the United Arab Emirates. Yet, in partially liberalized monarchies like Jordan and Morocco, the regimes ban some opposition groups while allowing others to become legal political parties. This is what Lust terms "divided structures of contestation" (2006: 36–40). Fearing that they may lose their legally permitted status, the legal opposition parties often tone down their rhetoric, moderate their tactics, and decline to cooperate with illegal opposition groups. This means that cross-ideological coalitions become less likely, and fragmentation increases among social groups that may – in theory, at least – have a common cause in resisting authoritarian regimes. Because these regimes allow some opposition groups to become legalized (while keeping others banned), the legalized opposition acts as a safety valve in legislative elections, helping to release society's discontent and demands for liberalization. But the regimes are ultimately able to keep the opposition weak by simultaneously creating incentives for the legal and illegal opposition parties to remain divided and in competition with each other.

Morocco and Jordan provide examples of how legislative elections serve as safety valves. After the 1971 and 1972 coup attempts, Morocco's erstwhile ruler, King Hassan II, allowed different opposition groups to enter the political system in Morocco and compete in elections as a safety valve. These groups were oppositional insomuch as they pressured for greater reform and democracy, yet many were not anti-systemic in that they did not vocalize (publicly, at least) a desire to overthrow Morocco's regime or oust its sitting monarch. In effect, they were opposition parties participating in legislative elections to voice the concerns of the public toward the regime but exhibited a degree of loyalty insofar as they did not question its underlying legitimacy (Lust 2004: 162). By allowing such quasi-loyalist opposition groups to compete in legislative elections, Morocco's regime developed a low-cost method to relieve some social pressure and dissent from the citizenry (Lust 2004: 161). As Brumberg (2002: 64) notes, a regime's inclusion of quasi-opposition parties in legislative elections discourages or minimizes the use of violence by the opposition, because they have alternative methods to voice dissent and advocate for change.

In its most extreme manifestation, this safety valve approach was exemplified in Morocco's 1997 and 2011 legislative elections when the regime permitted the legal opposition parties – in this case, the socialist and Islamist parties – to gain control of the elected government and appoint a Head of Government (prime ministers) from their parties. In both cases, however, the regime limited the Head of Government's powers to bring about only incremental reforms, without undermining the overall authoritarian system. Another example occurred in 1993 with civil society in which Hassan II granted concessions through legislative changes to appease Morocco's women's rights movement, *L'union de l'action féministe*. This process intensified under the rule of his successor, who sought to further enhance women's rights through the reform process of personal status and family laws. Although Islamists and other traditionalists resisted these legislative reforms, Mohammed VI intervened to ensure they were successful. This helped convince women's rights and other progressive activists to support Morocco's regime or, at least, divide them from the more radical anti-systemic leftist opposition, the Democratic Way (*al-nahj al-diyymuqraṭi*) (Cavatorta and Dalmasso 2009: 496–497).

Like Morocco's regime, Jordan's has also used legislative elections as a safety valve to deflate social pressure for reform. Although Jordan's regime permits legislative elections and has legalized dozens of political parties, it has simultaneously manipulated the electoral code to limit the legalized opposition's capacity to drive meaningful reform. This strategy ultimately limited the influence of Jordan's Islamist party, which garnered considerable success in the 1989 legislative election by winning 34 out of 80 seats (Ryan 2011: 375). Following this success of Islamists in 1989, Jordan's regime altered the electoral system from a proportional system into a one-man, one-vote system. This change in the electoral code led to a smaller percentage of Islamists winning seats in parliament, which not only constrained their political power domestically but also facilitated easier passage of an internally important diplomatic treaty. This treaty was Jordan's 1993 peace pact with Israel, which motivated the regime to change the composition of parliament to dilute the power of Islamists (who opposed the diplomatic rapprochement) (Lust and Jamal 2002). After the 1993 peace treaty, Jordan's regime further reformed the electoral code to make it more restrictive, leading to a dwindling of Islamist electoral presence during that decade. Indeed, by 2007, Islamists held only 6 of 110 seats in Jordan's parliament, even though Islamists were experiencing electoral success in legislative elections in Egypt, Morocco, and elsewhere in the mid-2000s (Ryan 2011). In sum, by using its legislative elections as a safety valve, Jordan's regime successfully projected an appearance of reform without giving up real political power.

Like executive elections, legislative elections can also aid regimes in distributing clientelist benefits to win over citizens' political loyalty. In a pioneering article in the *Journal of Democracy*, Lust describes how parliamentary deputies consider themselves "service deputies" (*nāʾib khidma*) and use their "position and influence to pressure ministers and bureaucrats" within the regimes' federal ministries into "dispensing jobs, licenses, and other state resources to their constituents" (Lust 2006: 124). Lust (2006: 124) describes that they accomplish this, in part, by threatening to use legislative speeches or media outreach to "cast doubt" on these federal ministries' "performance should their requests go unmet." In his book, Corstange (2016) discovers that citizens see elected deputies as carrying out such services in Yemen's and Lebanon's parliaments, while Benstead and Lust (2018), furthermore, find that citizens view female parliamentary deputies as less corrupt in delivering such services in Tunisia and Jordan.

Local elections: cities, towns, and villages

Like the examples of executive and legislative elections, those at the local level can similarly act as vehicles of symbolism, safety values, and clientelism in the authoritarian political systems of the MENA. They, in effect, reflect trends locally that analogously manifest at the national level, in executive and parliamentary elections.

Before proceeding, however, we should note that the political stakes at hand in local elections vary considerably in different countries of the MENA. For countries like Egypt, elections for local municipalities (what are known as *maḥaliyāt* in Arabic) do not matter much for politics, yet in other countries they matter much more, sometimes even surpassing the importance of elections in national-level elections. In Morocco, for instance, elections for local municipalities and communes (what are called there *baladiyyah* or *muqāṭa'a* in Arabic) carry great importance and have had consistently higher voter turnout rates since the 1990s than those for elections in the legislative realm (Buehler 2018). What seems clear in the case of Morocco, at least, is that citizens perceive more importance in electing their local mayor and city councilors, who control building their community's roads, distributing its public contracts and jobs, and implementing other local projects, compared to electing their parliamentary deputies (who are posted in the nation's capital, and debate more abstract policy topics with less pertinence to their daily lives).

Symbolism manifests in several different ways in local elections in the MENA. Symbolism in local elections, however, is often more important for the opposition parties than for the regimes. In Turkey and Algeria, for example, local elections were harbingers of change in opposition politics that would presage future developments in national-level politics. In effect, symbolic changes can occur at the local level, during local elections, which seem to trickle up as changes in national-level political trends. For example, prior to becoming Turkey's deeply entrenched Islamist president, with autocratic leanings, Recep Tayyip Erdoğan burst onto his country's political scene by winning the Istanbul mayoral race in the local elections of 1994 as president of the Islamist Refah Party (the Welfare Party), which was the precursor to today's Justice and Development Party (AKP). During the 1994 local elections, the Welfare Party experienced huge success, winning a total of 327 municipalities (Akinci 1999). Modeling Erdoğan's leadership as mayor of Istanbul, Islamist mayors and city officials focused on increasing the effectiveness of service provision and Islamist influence on those processes. The Islamists also sought to shift clientelist benefits toward their supporters, like middle-class entrepreneurs. For example, after the 1994 local elections, the city of Istanbul's electricity, telephone, and transportation agency awarded a newly formed company – the Magic company – a $1.45 million advertising contract to reward its pro-Islamist owner who was a prominent businessman (Akinci 1999). Fearing Erdoğan's victory endangered Turkey's Atatürk-style secularism, military generals (supported by Kemalist political elites) intervened in 1998 to oust him from the mayor's office and ban the Refah party altogether. The Refah party's widespread success in Turkey's local elections posed a threat to the status quo, showing how their pledges to uproot corruption, develop the economy, improve social service provision, and restore public morality could be a persuasive message to ordinary Turkish voters (Kamrava 1998).

Similarly, few recall that, before their controversial landslide election in the legislative elections of December 1991, Algeria's Islamist party – the Islamic Salvation Front (*Front Islamique du Salut* or FIS) – also achieved unexpected success in the previous year's local elections. Indeed, this Islamist party won 53 percent of all votes in Algeria's 1990 local elections, which presaged their victory the following year in national-level elections. The success of the FIS in local elections showed the decline in support of Algeria's ruling party with the middle class. This trend continued during the parliamentary elections, resulting in 24.5 percent of votes for the FIS and only 12.2 percent for the ruling party (Chhibber 1996). Frustrations with Algeria's ruling party began when it downsized the public sector and opened internal markets in response to the fiscal crisis of the 1980s. The former policy negatively affected low-level government workers, whereas the latter increased transaction costs for small business owners. Thereafter, both voting constituencies switched their support from the ruling party to the Islamist party, initially in the local elections and, later, in the parliamentary elections (Chhibber 1996). Thus, local elections in both Turkey and Algeria demonstrate how they symbolize oncoming, future changes occurring in the national-level politics of the MENA.

Local elections can similarly serve as safety valves. Compared with legislative elections for parliaments, which clearly have stakes at the national level, regime leaders often view local elections as carrying less import, with only local-level implications. Because local elections seem to ostensibly have lower stakes, regimes will allow the opposition to mobilize within them, thereby allowing them to "let off steam" without truly empowering them. The case of Morocco illustrates this point. As Lust (2006), Clark (2010), and Browers (2007) argue, one of the most threatening oppositional activities for regimes is the formation of cross-ideological alliances in which political parties or movements of diverse backgrounds form stable coalitions to contest regimes. Following Morocco's local elections of 2009, such cross-ideological alliances emerged in over a dozen different cities between two important opposition parties, the Islamists (The Justice and Development Part or "PJD") and the socialists (Socialist Union of Popular Forces or the "USFP"). Although Morocco's regime disliked these alliances and sought to break them, it – ultimately – chose to permit them given that they only affected local politics in their respective cities and did not catalyze cooperation between the opposition parties in national politics, like in parliament. Thus, the regime utilized local elections to help contain opposition coordination, confining it to local-level forms of contestation that did not challenge broader regime control or stability.

Wegner and Pellicer (2014) detail these local-level alliances between Islamists and socialists in Morocco. In their account, the PJD had seen the most amount of repression in the 1990s and 2000s, so it had greater incentives to seek opposition coordination with leftist groups. At the very least, tight coordination between Islamists and leftists could provide greater physical protection for both opposition parties. Yet, ideological differences made the USFP reluctant to build coalitions with the PJD, as it did not want to give its voters the impression it had stopped supporting gender equality or abandoned secularism (Wegner and Pellicer 2014). At the local level, however, the PJD and USFP found commonalities in city governance, given their similar social bases and their desire to implement reforms aimed at benefiting urban members of the middle class and reducing corruption in city governance (Buehler 2018). Both the PJD's leader, Abdelilah Benkirane, and the USFP's leader, Driss Lachgar, recognized their parties as having common interests in anti-corruption and city efficiency reforms (Buehler 2018). One of the clearest examples of collaboration at the local level between Islamists and leftists came in the city of Agadir following the 2009 local elections. The leftist mayor, Tariq Kabbage, sought out the support of the Islamists, led by local leader Ismael Shukri, to oust city councilors seeking to benefit materially from a local real estate project. With the Islamists' support, Kabbage was able to continue his leadership in Agadir, and the city saw improvements in service provisions to the middle class and better city planning (Buehler 2018). In Agadir, Morocco's regime allowed local elections to act as a safety valve wherein the opposition parties could coordinate and win limited reforms to improve governance. These small victories, however, were unlikely to trickle up to drive larger reform or democratization in Morocco's authoritarian system, so the regime found them unthreatening.

Finally, local elections can also act as channels to disperse clientelist benefits and services. Local institutions staffed through local elections – municipalities and local councils – serve as the frontline of the state, delivering services to citizens directly. That is, while legislative and executive institutions are more distant and aloof from ordinary citizens, local institutions based in their neighborhoods or villages have close proximity to them. This close proximity to the citizens makes them exceptionally more accessible than other institutions to traditional clientelist systems that pervade the MENA region (Buehler 2018). Clientelist systems become intertwined in local elections because traditional elites – notables from influential local families or tribal groups – often serve as candidates in such contests. In his book *Why Alliances Fail*, for example, Matt Buehler details how local elections in Morocco's rural countryside are often predetermined by tribal congresses that nominate and decide on a candidate before the elections are held (Buehler 2018: 109–110). These extended kinship networks serve to nominate a tribe's most competitive leader for electoral office, regardless of his or her specific political party list or ideological affiliation. These tribal congresses focus mainly on an individual candidate's capacity to deliver goods and services to their region, rather than their specific party or ideological orientation (Buehler 2018: 109–110).

Lindsay Benstead has also examined service delivery and clientelism in the context of local elections of the MENA. In particular, she looks at how women's quotas enhance female representation within a system with a legacy of clientelism in local elections. In Tunisia, locally elected politicians typically depend on their relationship with regional or central governments for strength and resources. Traditional clientelist networks tend to be built by and for men and are constructed through interactions and socialization under patriarchal norms, minimizing women's participation in network-building and excluding their representation (Benstead 2019). Looking at local elections, Benstead (2019) finds that having a quota system increases the amount of female representation and can increase the provision of services to women from women representatives in Algeria and Morocco. In this way, clientelism within the context of local elections can take on different dynamics, depending on whether or not the elected representative is male or female (and whether they seek to intercede on behalf of either male or female voters).

Similarly, examining Algeria, Benstead finds that trends in clientelism in local elections can manifest differently, given the type of political party and, more specifically, whether the party was pro or anti-regime. She discovers that Algeria's legal Islamist party – the Movement for Society and Peace (MSP), known formally as HAMAS – works to reach out and deliver services to citizens historically marginalized from traditional patron-client networks, notably women (Benstead 2020). Benstead (2020) finds that the MSP in coalition with the government was able to reach citizens better than the Islamist Islah Party due to its good standing with the government, giving MSP members better access to bureaucratic resources. By contrast, Islah was not trusted to work with the government and so had less access to such clientelist resources. Benstead (2020) argues that Islamist parties are supported by their own members' ideological commitment, which increases the parties' desire to have a direct impact on local communities and transcend patron-client networks by distributing services and resources to the wider population of potential voters (Benstead 2020). They have more access to local communities through local religious organizations; the proliferation of poorly developed institutions that rely on patron-client networks is what creates the large numbers of marginalized communities to which Islamists can cater (Benstead 2020).

Conclusion

Following the 2011 Arab uprisings, optimism soared that elections in the Middle East and North Africa (MENA) might evolve, becoming more democratic. And indeed, several Arab states implemented largely free and fair elections, which helped signal citizens' preferences, adjudicate between competing elites, and redistribute political power. For instance, Egypt, a country long known for unfair elections under previous authoritarian rulers, held the 2012 presidential elections and several legislative elections in 2011–2012, which facilitated the rise of democratically elected President Mohammed Morsi and an opposition-controlled parliament.

Tunisia, similarly, organized the 2011 Constituent Assembly elections to form a congress, which ultimately produced the democratically elected government of President Moncef Marzouki. Thereafter, several elections in Tunisia, like the 2014 and 2019 legislative and 2018 local contests, were free and fair. Today, this momentum behind elections evolving into a method of genuine democratic accountability has largely collapsed. In both Egypt and Tunisia, democratically elected governments have been ousted by new authoritarian rulers, often subtly backed by military forces. Reminiscent of Hosni Mubarak's era, Egypt's most recent 2018 presidential elections produced about a 97 percent victory for General Abdel Fattah al-Sisi. A party pledging loyalty to him won over 55 percent of seats in Egypt's lower chamber and 75 percent in its upper chamber, reinforcing his hegemony over the legislature.

Given that elections in the MENA have again turned away from democratic meaningfulness, this essay has sought to explore their different functions and purposes within authoritarian regimes. It has centered on explaining how elections – at the executive, legislative, and local levels – can project political symbolism, act as safety valves, and facilitate clientelism. These three functions of elections, no doubt, operate to reinforce authoritarian regimes and redouble autocrats' authority in the face of opposition from political parties, civil society, and ordinary citizens.

References

Angrist, Michele Penner. 1999. 'Parties, Parliament and Political Dissent in Tunisia.' *Journal of North African Studies* 4(4): 89–104.

Akinci, Ugur. 1999. 'The Welfare Party's Municipal Track Record: Evaluating Islamist Municipal Activism in Turkey.' *The Middle East Journal* 53(1): 75–94.

Benstead, Lindsay J. 2019. 'Do Female Local Councilors Improve Women's Representation?' *Journal of the Middle East and Africa* 10(2): 95–119.

Benstead, Lindsay. 2020. 'Do Islamist Parties Reach Marginalized Citizens?' Presented at the annual meeting of the Association for the Study of Middle East and North Africa (ASMEA), November 18–20, 2020.

Benstead, Lindsay J., and Ellen Lust. 2018. 'Why Do Some Voters Prefer Female Candidates? The Role of Perceived Incorruptibility in Arab Elections.' In: Helena Stensöta and Lena Wängnerud (eds.), *Gender and Corruption: Historical Roots and New Avenues for Research*. London: Palgrave: 83–104.

Blaydes, Lisa. 2011. *Elections and Distributive Politics in Mubarak's Egypt*. New York: Cambridge University Press.

Brites, Jorge, Camille Evrard, Paul Melly, and Erin Pettigrew. 2021. 'La Mauritanie de Ghazouani: L'illusion de l'alternance.' *L'Année du Maghreb* 26: 1–25.

Browers, Michaelle. 2007. 'Origins and Architects of Yemen's Joint Meeting Parties.' *International Journal of Middle East Studies* 39(4): 565–586.

Brownlee, Jason. 2011a. Review of Lisa Blaydes' *Elections and Distributive Politics in Mubarak's Egypt*. New York: Cambridge University Press, 2010. Perspectives on Politics 9 (4): 958–960.

Brownlee, Jason. 2011b. 'Executive Elections in the Arab World: When and How Do They Matter?' *Comparative Political Studies* 44(7): 807–828.

Brumberg, Daniel. 2002. 'The Trap of Liberalized Autocracy.' *Journal of Democracy* 13(4): 56–68.

Buehler, Matt. 2018. *Why Alliances Fail: Islamist and Leftist Coalitions in North Africa*. Syracuse, NY: Syracuse University Press.

Carothers, Thomas. 2002. 'The End of the Transition Paradigm.' *Journal of Democracy* 13(1): 5–21.

Cavatorta, Francesco, and Emanuela Dalmasso. 2009. 'Liberal Outcomes through Undemocratic Means: The Reform of the *Code de Statut Personnel* in Morocco.' *Journal of Modern African Studies* 47(4): 487–506.

Chhibber, Pradeep K. 1996. 'State Policy, Rent Seeking, and the Electoral Success of a Religious Party in Algeria.' *The Journal of Politics* 58(1): 126–148.

Clark, Janine A. 2010. 'Threats, Structures, and Resources: Cross-Ideological Coalition Building in Jordan.' *Comparative Politics* 43(1): 101–120.

Corstange, Daniel. 2016. *The Price of a Vote in the Middle East: Clientelism and Communal Politics in Lebanon and Yemen*. Cambridge: Cambridge University Press.

Daadaoui, Mohamed. 2011. *Moroccan Monarchy and the Islamist Challenge: Maintaining Makhzen Power*. New York: Palgrave Macmillan.
Diamond, Larry. 2006. 'Authoritarian Learning: Lessons from the Colored Revolutions.' *Brown Journal of World Affairs* 12(2): 215–222.
Haugbølle, Rikke, and Francesco Cavatorta. 2011. 'Will the Real Tunisian Opposition Please Stand Up? Opposition Coordination Failures Under Authoritarian Constraints.' *British Journal of Middle Eastern Studies* 38(3): 323–341.
Hoffmann, Anja. 2011. 'Decentralization and Re-centralization in Morocco: A View from the Middle Atlas.' *CERAM Working Paper*.
Kamrava, Mehran. 1998. 'Pseudo-Democratic Politics and Populist Possibilities: The Rise and Demise of Turkey's Refah Party.' *British Journal of Middle Eastern Studies* 25(2): 275–301.
Leiken, Robert S., and Steven Brook. 2007. 'The Moderate Muslim Brotherhood.' *Foreign Affairs* 86(2): 107–121.
Lesch, David W. 2010. 'The Evolution of Bashar Al-Asad.' *Middle East Policy* 17(2): 70–81.
Levitsky, Steven, and Lucan Way. 2010. *Competitive Authoritarianism: Hybrid Regimes after the Cold War*. Cambridge: Cambridge University Press.
Lust-Okar, Ellen, and Amaney Ahmad Jamal. 2002. 'Rulers and Rules: Reassessing the Influence of Regime Type on Electoral Law Formation.' *Comparative Political Studies* 35(3): 337–366.
Lust-Okar, Ellen. 2004. 'Divided They Rule: The Management and Manipulation of Political Opposition.' *Comparative Politics* 36(2): 159–179.
Lust-Okar, Ellen. 2006. *Structuring Conflict in the Arab World*. Cambridge: Cambridge University Press.
Ryan, Curtis R. 2002. *Jordan in Transition: From Hussein to Abdullah*. Boulder, CO: Lynne-Rienner Publishers.
Ryan, Curtis R. 2011. 'Political Opposition and Reform Coalitions in Jordan.' *British Journal of Middle Eastern Studies* 38(3): 367–390.
Sadiki, Larbi. 2002. 'Ben Ali's Tunisia: Democracy by Non-democratic Means.' *British Journal of Middle Eastern Studies* 29(1): 57–78.
Schedler, Andreas. 2006. *Electoral Authoritarianism: The Dynamics of Unfree Competition*. Boulder, CO: Lynne Rienner Publishers.
Shehata, Samer, and Josh Stacher. 2006. 'The Brotherhood Goes to Parliament.' *Middle East Report*: 1–4.
Sherlock, Ruth. 2021. 'Syrian Election Shows the Extend of Assad's Power.' *NPR News*, May 27.
U.S. State Department, Bureau of Near Eastern Affairs. 2007. 'Background Note: Syria.' Available at: https://2001-2009.state.gov/r/pa/ei/bgn/3580.htm.
Walsh, Declan, and Nour Youssef. 2018. 'For as Little as $3 a Vote, Egyptian Trudge to Election Stations.' *New York Times*, March 27.
Wedeen, Lisa. 1998. 'Acting "As-If": Symbolic Politics and Social Control in Syria.' *Comparative Studies in Society and History* 40(3): 503–523.
Wedeen, Lisa. 1999. *Ambiguities of Domination: Politics, Rhetoric, and Symbols in Contemporary Syria*. Chicago, IL: University of Chicago Press.
Wedeen, Lisa. 2008. *Peripheral Visions Publics, Power, and Performance in Yemen*. Chicago, IL: University of Chicago Press.
Wegner, Eva, and Miquel Pellicer. 2014. 'Socio-economic Voter Profile and Motives for Islamist Support in Morocco.' *Party Politics* 20(1): 116–133.

3
ELECTIONS AND THE BUREAUCRATIC MANAGEMENT OF PLURALITY IN ALGERIA

Thomas Serres

Introduction

In June 1990, Algeria held local elections, the first multiparty electoral process since its independence. In less than 18 months, the country had experienced a rapid transition from a single party toward a pluralist system. An opposition party, the Islamic Salvation Front (FIS), prevailed at the polls and seized control of most local and regional assemblies. The former ruling party, the National Liberation Front (FLN), secured roughly 30% of the votes and one-third of the assemblies. Behind these two main contenders, a handful of mostly leftist organizations attracted the remaining 15% of the votes. Overall, these elections were perceived as a turning point in Algeria and in the region, as they suggested a progressive liberalization of Arab polities. Yet, almost 30 years later, in December 2019, the election of Abdelmajid Tebboune as president contradicted the teleological expectations of the early 1990s. The candidate selected by the military and administrative elites prevailed in an electoral process with a historically low voter turnout (less than 40%). While state-run newspapers lauded the "democratic transparency"[1] of the polls, this umpteenth turning point engineered by the state apparatus merely confirmed the systematic instrumentalization of electoral processes to maintain the *status quo*.

After the waning of the third wave of democratization and the failure of US military adventurism in the Middle East, the belief in the universal appeal of liberal democracy has gradually dissipated worldwide (Carothers and Brechenmacher 2014). Scholars interested in transitology have noted that many authoritarian regimes did not transform into proper "democratic" ones but, rather, instrumentalized the institutional processes and liberal frameworks Western states and NGOs had promoted for a long time (Ruzza et al. 2019; Vollmann et al. 2022). Some observed the emergence of a "grey zone" between democracy and authoritarianism, which combines formally democratic institutions with informal practices to perpetuate authoritarian domination (Diamond 2005; Reich 2002). Among the processes these ambiguous regimes appropriated, elections became a crucial tool for engineering façade pluralism while maintaining a form of centralized state power (Wilson 2009). Noticing that these elections led to actual struggles between political parties (or interest groups posing as such), scholars of democracy and authoritarianism crafted different terms to describe a seemingly contradictory situation. Some argued that the post-Cold War era witnessed the rise of "competitive authoritarianism," a type of hybrid regime clearly distinct from democracy (Levitsky and Way 2002). Others used the notion of "electoral authoritarianism" to describe a pattern of "unfree competition" widespread in the developing world and resulting from the constant violation of minimal democratic standards (Schedler 2006).

Specialists of Algeria have occasionally appropriated the latter term to capture the evolution of the political system under Abdelaziz Bouteflika (1999–2019), as the ruling coalition weaponized electoral processes to trump the political uncertainty that followed the 2011 uprisings (Hachemaoui 2012; Tlemçani 2012). Nevertheless, because they rely on a normative spectrum defined by two poles (democracy vs authoritarianism), such accounts overlook the complex nature of the social and political arrangements shaping changing political systems in the global south. Speaking of hybrid regimes or electoral authoritarianism notably ignores the existence of competing understandings of democracy and non-liberal modes of grassroots claim-making (Volpi 2004). As such, elections in Algeria illustrate some of the tensions and limits inherent in reducing democracy to formal processes and normative expectations. Yet, they should not be perceived as merely cosmetic tools that allow for the perpetuation of autocratic rule. Undoubtedly, elections can serve multiple functions, including permitting the management of a genuinely pluralistic polity and shaping a non-threatening form of popular sovereignty.

This chapter examines elections in Algeria as a democratic technology of power aiming to discipline and integrate a threatening population in the structures of power under the control of bureaucratic-military apparatuses. It presents the problem inherent to popular consultations, as they are seen as both a potential moment of upheaval threatening to jeopardize the country's economic and political development and a necessity to produce legitimacy at the local and international levels. Moreover, elections also allow for the management of political parties and the making of the modern Algerian subject. Through clientelism or the promotion of female participation, the state apparatus can thus integrate various political actors and shape their behaviour. Yet this bureaucratic management of plurality results in forms of coercion and resistance that illustrate the tensions arising from any disciplinary project. As elections are met with calls for boycott and low turnout, state apparatuses struggle to shape "credible" electoral results and "responsible" forms of participation.

The problem of popular consultations

Popular consultations have represented a challenge for the Algerian regime since independence. The potential disorder associated with voting has thus long legitimized bureaucratic control and military oversight. At the same time, relatively free and pluralist elections have increasingly become necessary in light of domestic and international pressure.

Electoral disorders

In Algeria, the notion of popular sovereignty lies at the heart of a political culture shaped by anti-colonial populism, as a vestige of the War of Independence allegedly waged "for the people and by the people." Yet, it remained disconnected from competitive electoral processes until the late 1980s. After independence, elections were not a priority for the new regime. During the constituent elections of 1962, there was only one FLN list per district, with the clear objective of demonstrating the union and support of the population for one single political project. Under Houari Boumediene (1965–1978), local consultations served to reinforce the alliance between local elites, single-party executives and the nationalist middle classes. Yet, these plebiscites failed to generate enthusiasm (Ammour et al. 1974: 152–153). Indeed, the ruling coalition was above all preoccupied with the implementation of a top-down revolutionary agenda and prioritized collegial leadership to manage its internal plurality without public debates (McDougall 2017: 250). In official discourses, popular sovereignty was conceptualized in a pyramidal fashion, through an amalgamating discourse that brought together the people, the army and the party, with Boumediene at the top of the edifice. The negation of the cultural, political and social diversity of the country was aimed at preserving order and fostering the development of the state and the nation.

The political unrest of the 1980s, which culminated in the October 1988 uprising, put an end to the single-party system. A new pluralist constitution was adopted in 1989, and a relatively independent and critical private press emerged rapidly. Despite constant tensions and the government's attempts to mitigate its losses through gerrymandering, the 1990 local elections and the 1991 legislative elections were truly competitive, "free and fair by most standards" and gave the Islamic Salvation Front "a clear popular mandate to govern" (Cavatorta 2009). Profound uncertainty and rapid institutional change characterized the period between 1989 and 1992. While some among the bureaucratic-military elites and Islamist activists viewed seemingly democratic rules with suspicion or as purely formal and non-binding, the FIS's leadership eventually decided to follow the legalist and political path (Cook 2007: 135; McDougall 2017: 285). Under Abdelkader Hashani's stewardship, the Islamist party ran an effective blitz campaign and secured the majority of the seats before the second round of the 1991 legislatives.

Nevertheless, the triumph of the FIS also generated profound hostility within the state and beyond, notably in secularist circles. The discourses of some of its representatives, which vilified francophone elites and pushed for a puritan re-ordering of the polity, legitimated calls for military intervention. As then-President Chadli Bendjedid had started to negotiate a power-sharing agreement with Hashani, a coalition bringing together trade unions, feminist and secularist groups, as well as army generals, emerged to prevent the FIS from exercising power. Spokespersons of the ruling elites portrayed the rise of the FIS as a greater threat to democracy and human rights than the interruption of the elections. This discourse was received favourably abroad, notably in France.[2] The Islamist triumph during the 1991 legislatives thus came to illustrate the dangers resulting from electoral processes held without sufficient control and "maturity" – in the Arab world and beyond (Cavatorta 2009: 191). Eventually, the reaction against the first free pluralist legislative elections in the history of Algeria culminated in the military coup of January 1992 and a purge of all "non-loyal" Islamist activists, which led to a decade-long civil war.

The possibility of a military takeover

The coup of 1992 was not an exception but rather a return to an underlying paradigm in Algerian politics, according to which the National People's Army (ANP) is above formal politics and entitled to intervene directly to protect the nation and the people. Since 1989, successive constitutions have consistently left open the possibility of a "heroic" intervention of the military, which allegedly generates "pride" and "gratitude" among the people.[3] This *de facto* delegation of popular sovereignty has inscribed the military *coup-de-force* in the political tradition of the country and allowed for the perpetuation of a form of praetorianism that also helps settle internal disputes within the ruling coalition (Tlemçani 2014).

Consequently, the *coup d'état* became an alternative mode of designation of the country's leadership. As such, it is a possibility associated with each popular consultation, should the military consider that the choice of the masses is at risk of being ignored by unscrupulous politicians or that the masses themselves are voting against the nation's interest. This means that elections are reversible if needs be, as is the case in other countries in the region (Cook 2007: 48). Accordingly, the 1992 coup has been repeatedly portrayed by state officials as a successful effort to correct the outcome of a derailed political process. One longstanding figure of the nationalist movement and member of the High Committee of State that replaced Chadli after the coup, Ali Haroun, explained in 2002 that interrupting the elections was necessary to prevent a fundamentalist takeover that would have been almost impossible to overturn (Chagnollaud and Haroun 2002: 235). The following year, the chief of staff of the ANP, Mohamed Lamari (1993–2004), argued that the army had to intervene to "save republican institutions" after "a fringe of the population fell into [a trap] when it was offered the establishment of a theocratic regime."[4] In 2004, just before the presidential elections that saw Bouteflika re-elected for the first time, Lamari explained that the military would no longer intervene in politics. Yet, he immediately added that he might consider civilian requests in case of irregularities and promised that any attempt "to change the republican order" would "find the army on its way."[5] In short, the possibility of a military takeover was – and remains – a response to the danger posed by elections, an *ultima ratio* that impacts the strategies of civilian actors.

Nevertheless, while military *coups-de-force* respond to the danger of popular consultations, their possibility also fuels the anguish in each electoral process. Thus, elections have become synonymous with a potential descent into chaos. The period of 1989–1992 represents the model of a political crisis aggravated by uncontrolled electoral processes, which culminated in the fateful 1991 legislatives. Despite the recurring attempts to depoliticize the civil war, the link between the cancellation of these elections and the horrific violence of the "Dark Decade" of the 1990s is obvious (Cavatorta 2009: 145). Consequently, during the twenty years of Bouteflika's rule, electoral processes and especially presidential elections also evoked the risk of a military takeover.

An unescapable necessity

Since the end of the Dark Decade, specialists in Algerian politics have described political elites as secondary in decision-making processes, while military elites truly occupy the centre stage (Roberts 2003; Benchikh 2003; Werenfels 2007; Arezki 2020). Some even portray a system where civilian actors are completely manipulated by a Machiavellian deep state centred on the security services and the ANP's leadership (Hachemaoui 2016). Despite the relative weakness of elected officials and the risk of destabilization associated with elections, the latter nonetheless remained a key feature punctuating the political life of the country. Even during the second half of the Dark Decade, at the height of terrorist violence, elections appeared essential to preserve the status quo and institutionalize power relations within the ruling coalition (Tlemçani 2012: 165). The presidential race of 1995 and the legislatives of 1997 served to demonstrate the strength of the ruling coalition and its ability to shape a sanitized form of popular sovereignty after the purge of the radical Islamist alternative.

Electoral processes are also necessary for domestic and international legitimacy. The collapse of the single-party system occurred after a decade of intense crisis in the 1980s, with the rise of Islamist and Berberist movements that expressed contentious political and cultural claims. Despite their differences and inner contradictions, these oppositions forced the ruling coalition to reckon with the fact that social plurality could not be represented in the sole framework of the FLN. At the same time, these internal pressures also came with a "democratic" turn at the international level after the end of the Cold War. In this context, the transition to political pluralism also became a matter of international recognition. Crucially, international recognition proved to be compatible with the repression of Islamist movements, as they have been repeatedly framed as a greater threat to international security than the interruption of an electoral process. Moreover, foreign support could also boost the legitimacy of popular consultations held under the close supervision of the bureaucracy (Cavatorta 2009: 124, 154). It would nevertheless be simplistic to see electoral processes as a mere attempt to attract external support. The anti-colonialist ethos shaping Algerian political culture implies that the slightest scepticism coming from abroad is rapidly dismissed as an insult to the country's independence. In any case, the routinization of electoral processes since the end of the 1990s is also symptomatic of a quest for normalcy amid longstanding economic and political upheavals. As former prime minister and figure of the nationalist movement Rheda Malek once explained, conforming to universal democratic norms was necessary to follow the zeitgeist of the 1990s (2001: 196). Thus, from the Dark Decade to the 2019 Hirak, the obsession of Algerian state apparatuses for the organization of pluralist elections illustrates their centrality in demonstrating the polity's normalcy, its return to the routine of national development, economic growth and political modernization.

Elections as a technology of power

As popular sovereignty remains essential in Algerian political culture, it is also associated with the dangers inherent to past uprisings and uncontrolled popular consultations. In this context, pluralist elections function as a technology of power; they are not only a way to rule in the name of the people but also normalize and euphemize a system of domination. In other words, they contribute to making a polity more manageable and its unequal power distribution more acceptable, notably by shaping and regulating the behaviour of political actors. Understanding elections as a technology of power invites us to study them as part of a broader disciplinary process through which "subjects are gradually, progressively, really and materially constituted through a multiplicity of organisms, forces, energies, materials, desires, thoughts etc." (Foucault 1980: 97). As such, popular consultations participate in the construction and disciplining of a multitude of subjects and aim to neutralize their threatening features. They are not merely cosmetic, as they echo widespread demands for a greater inclusion of the governed in a more transparent system of government, demands that have been expressed under various forms since the early 1980s. As a technology of power, pluralist elections create a limited and regulated space of free expression of these aspirations "for the shaping of conduct in the hope of producing certain desired effects and averting certain undesired ones" (Rose 1999: 52).

Regulating the political field

Since February 1989 and the transition to multipartyism, the Algerian political field has become remarkably diverse and includes various tendencies (nationalist, Islamo-conservative, liberal, Berberist and Trotskyist, among others). Some of these movements have been associated historically with radical projects directly challenging the political order inherited from the War of Independence. This was notably the case of the FIS, but also of the Socialist Forces Front (FFS) or the Party of Socialist Workers (PST). From this perspective, elections have served to foster the integration and institutionalization of opposition movements. For a Trotskyist movement like the PST, partaking in elections represented an alternative way to make their radical criticism heard in a legal framework created and managed by the state.[6] Even more than that of fringe leftist movements, the institutionalization of Islamist parties was of utmost importance after the 1992 coup. For instance, Abdallah Djaballah, an Islamist who has been a longstanding adversary of the regime, has created multiple political movements that participated in elections over the years. Since the 1990s, foreign observers have portrayed Djaballah as an example of the "virtues of legality, competitive multipartyism, popular political sovereignty and non-violence," who abandoned his more radical claims to remain in the sphere of acceptable politics (Willis

1998: 66). Thus, even without becoming part of the ruling coalition, the participation of Islamist movements in elections demonstrated their bowing to the rules of the system of domination and a relative opening of the said system to a fraction of its population (Benzenine 2020a).

Elections also serve as mechanisms of co-option, integrating individuals in the party structure and political parties in the ruling coalition. From the perspective of the bureaucratic and military elites in the regime, the co-option of small movements representing diverse tendencies allowed for the government to include former opponents, such as Amara Benyounes and Khalida Toumi (both former Rally for Culture and Democracy (RCD) executives). Members of the Movement for the Society of Peace (MSP – islamo-conservative), which participated in the government from 1997 to 2012, explained that this co-option also came with a change in their political behaviour. As they adopted a doctrine of "critical support," they also developed a sense of political compromise and greater ideological flexibility.[7] Meanwhile, the entire party system changed throughout the 2000s and 2010s, with the growing inclusion of businessmen seeking to turn their economic capital into political influence. As financially insecure political parties monetized eligible positions, successive elections also contributed to the commodification of the entire field.

During Bouteflika's tenure, the practice of *shkara* (selling an eligible position to the highest bidder) became more common and illustrated the broader reconfiguration of the political field under the effect of clientelist networks. Thus, electoral processes contributed to the routinization of the exchanges of services between candidates and voters, as local big men demonstrated their influence by organizing feasts, sending gifts or hiring an army of young supporters (Hachemaoui 2012). They shaped a vertical power structure where local patrons served as intermediaries between the governed and the state and could influence the distribution of public resources (subsidies, public housing, procurements) from the centre to the peripheries.[8] The ensuing clientalization of society served to contain popular discontent and create a model of representation centred on the distribution of material resources under state control.

Lastly, popular consultations also fuelled the fragmentation of the political field. Since the end of the Dark Decade, political parties have been subjected to moments of intense stress following their decision to take part in or boycott national elections. This has especially been the case for the Berberist tendency embodied by movements such as the Socialist Forces Front or the Rally for Culture and Democracy. While Berberism is the oldest opposition force in Algeria, it has been consistently weakened since the transition to multipartyism. After the violent repression of the 2001 popular uprising in Kabylia, both parties have faced an electoral conundrum: whether to participate in elections and face the denunciation coming from more radical members or boycott the elections and risk the defection of party officials. Meanwhile, elections have also accentuated competition between the two movements and the centrifugal dynamics within each party, for instance, with the defection of Amara Benyounes from the RCD and the exclusion of Karim Tabbou from the FFS.[9] Overall, clientelization and fragmentation shape an extremely fluid political field, where politicians can move from one party to another without clear ideological convictions. This fluidity, exacerbated during electoral processes, serves the status quo as it increases the vulnerability of political organizations (Dris 2018).

Shaping the modern Algerian subject

Holding pluralist elections is also a way for the government to shape subjectivities. Since independence, Algerian public authorities have tried to develop civic-mindedness and political consciousness, that is to say to promote acceptable and non-threatening forms of political participation. In the 1970s, Boumediene explained that involving the masses in decision-making processes was a matter of method. He prioritized an approach based on the election of local officials (at the level of the city and the region) and considered that the people were not sufficiently mature for national elections, which he feared would reveal the divisions among the population (Balta 2012: 210–211). After the 1988 uprising and the shift to multipartyism, the first local elections of 1990 represented a new kind of challenge. Both the administration and political parties invested a considerable amount of energy in explaining the electoral process, its goals and steps, to the population (Aït-Aoudia 2013, 2015: 187–242). Among the ruling elites, the support received by the FIS and the violence of the 1990s reinforced the idea that a lot of work needed yet to be done to develop a non-threatening political subjectivity (Chagnollaud and Haroun 2002: 214).

Since 1995 and the election of Liamine Zeroual as president, successive Algerian governments have made voting a keystone in the process of normalization and modernization of the country's political life. Parties instrumentalizing cultural and religious references and allegedly susceptible to dividing the nation were banned from participating in politics.[10] Successive presidents and prime ministers have announced reforms and demanded that the people demonstrate their commitment to supporting democratization and peace. One of the most iconic illustrations of this top-down state reformism was the passing of a law introducing suppress quotas of women for the People's National Assembly (APN). The 2011 organic law designed to "augment women chances to become representatives in elected assemblies" was indeed successful in increasing the participation of women in the electoral process and their chance to be elected at the national level (from less than 8% of the MPs at the national level in 2007 to more than 30% in 2012). At the same time, it illustrated a state-organized, vertical and legalistic approach to the modernization of the polity, an effort to fit within the broader global discussion on "gender equality" that was devoid of any grassroots and feminist input (Benzenine 2013).

Elections are a form of "governmental power" that produce behaviours and shape subjectivities. While the Algerian state has been historically involved in many attempts to modernize and reform its population, such disciplinary endeavour is not necessarily limited to the nation-state (Baez 2014). Several non-state actors have also contributed to this effort (these include foreign NGOs, international organizations such as the European Union, as well as local journalists), notably by promoting various forms of "active citizenship" or monitoring elections.[11] For example, in 2017, Minister of the Interior Noureddine Bedoui announced the creation of an award for the "female representative of the year" in partnership with the UN Women programme.[12] The following year, Bedoui received the praise of the head of the UN Development Programme in the region, who lauded the work of the ministry in promoting the role of women in society, notably through the implementation of political training programmes organized by the UN agency.[13] Together, state and international organizations have worked to turn electoral processes into a reform mechanism shaping a politically active and non-subversive female subject.

Other actors have played a more peripheral role in this process of subject formation through the organization of elections. From 1989 to 1992, the emergence of pluralist political competition in Algeria was concomitant with the rise of a diverse private printed press. During the Dark Decade, some journalists critical of the regime and fearful of fundamentalist violence viewed elections with suspicion and welcomed military oversight as a way to "impose a democratic apprenticeship," with the support of the "conscious fraction of the population" (Borgmann 2008: 111–113). Yet, in the aftermath of the Arab uprisings of 2010–2011, the mistrust of non-institutional ways to express discontent has led liberal elites to insist on the need for the population to vote. Prior to the legislative elections of 2021, figures such as journalist Kamel Daoud or the liberal political opponent Soufiane Djilali advocated for participation as a constructive approach that would help build a system based on the rule of law. Partaking in elections, from their perspectives, would lead to the development of "reasonable" behaviours and a "culture of citizenship" that could trump "demagogy and populism."[14] Nevertheless, these attempts to shape the modern Algerian subject were also intertwined with a bureaucratic effort to control and manage political plurality.

The bureaucratic management of plurality

As elections are perceived as both necessary and potentially dangerous, state apparatuses have developed different strategies to shape their outcome. This bureaucratic effort to manage the representation of the population has allowed for the continuous domination of pro-regime parties since the 1992 coup. But it has also progressively eroded the belief in the legitimacy of representative institutions.

Bureaucratic control

State apparatuses have developed various strategies to limit the reach of opposition parties competing in local and national elections. First among them are the legal barriers created over the years. The Ministry of the Interior has withheld the accreditation of newly founded political parties, especially during the period from 1999 to 2012. As for organizations that have received the green light to take part in electoral processes, they face various obstacles resulting from the interference of security apparatuses, such as the last-minute cancellation of their rallies or the impossibility of booking venues in large cities.[15] Combined with lesser access to national media and the strength of clientelistic networks, these legal barriers undermine the ability of opposition parties to be truly competitive.

Legal obstacles are coupled with the use of electoral fraud. Since the triumph of the National Democratic Rally in the legislative and local elections of 1997, the widespread use of fraud to boost friendly parties with limited popular support is a well-known fact of Algerian politics. In 1997, some observers viewed such bureaucratic arrangements as a minor obstacle on the path to democratization. In their eyes, they allowed for the management of tensions among ruling elites and did not prevent opposition figures from maintaining pressure on the ruling coalition (Bouandel and Zoubir 1998). Since then, electoral fraud has nonetheless remained a key practice for the management of the country's plurality. In a confidential cable revealed by Wikileaks, the US embassy thus described the re-election of Bouteflika in 2009 as "heavily managed."[16] Among the various tactics frequently mentioned by opponents and independent observers are the registration of dead people on electoral lists and the mobilization of soldiers and policemen to vote twice (as civilians and in their barracks, where they are under the supervision of their hierarchy).

It is worth noting that electoral fraud does not aim at providing one party with an overwhelming majority but at distributing political legitimacy and positions among the various components of the political field. Consequently, fraud serves to maintain the dependence of parties, whose co-option and political relevance is ultimately decided by the security services (Cavatorta 2009: 173). As it purports to the distribution of seats in elected assemblies and power positions in the government, fraud also serves as a system of political regulation within the ruling coalition, notably among factional power brokers in the security services, the army and the administration (Tlemçani 2012: 166; McDougall 2017: 298).

Lastly, the bureaucratic management of plurality also relies on a formalist approach, which emphasizes the procedural dimension of each electoral process and glosses over its flaws. *De facto*, during the 2021 legislative elections, the combination of the first-past-the-post system, political fragmentation and low voter turnout ensured a seemingly legal victory for the FLN and the RND (National Democratic Rally), despite the fact that they had in fact received together the support of less than 2% of the total electorate.[17] In addition, public authorities routinely insist on the number of seats secured by each party and the percentage of votes cast for each presidential candidate. They emphasize that the election unfolded without major upheaval and that it was validated by the constitutional council. The press, both private and state-owned, has echoed this narrative, focusing on technical details and the congratulations other governments sent in an effort to normalize the entire process.

Indiscipline

Efforts to control and normalize the electoral process have nonetheless faced growing hostility at the grassroots level. On social media, Algerians have long criticized the politicians who accept to partake in a rigged political competition and labelled them as "hares" (*lièvres* or *a'rānib*). They have also turned various food products into symbols of the shameless effort to buy the support of the miserable masses. After people participating in pro-Bouteflika rallies in 2014 were rewarded with sandwiches made of *cashir*, an Algerian beef charcuterie, the term "cashirism" became synonymous with selling out to the regime. Overall, elections have been increasingly perceived as a way for clientelized elites to secure a seat (*koursi*) without any regard for popular sovereignty. Since the beginning of the Hirak in 2019, this trend has only accelerated.

The boycott of elections has long provoked debates among political opponents due to rampant popular distrust in the process. From 1989 to 1992, leading members of the FIS disagreed on the possibility of bringing about a genuinely Islamic regime by competing in elections organized by an impious state. Under Bouteflika, Berberist movements such as the FFS and the RCD oscillated between boycott and participation. For parties, boycotts proved costly politically and financially. The strategy was nonetheless supported by grassroots activists who resisted what they saw as a mockery of the popular will by heckling touring candidates or ransacking polling stations. In 2021, two years after the beginning of the Hirak, most parties on the left, including the RCD and the FFS, decided to snub the polls.

Organized boycott has been instrumentalized to discredit opposition movements, which are portrayed as irresponsible or anti-national, and ensure the dominance of governmental parties. Meanwhile, popular abstention has proved to be a sharper thorn in the side of the ruling coalition. In 2009, the US embassy noted that voter turnout was the government's main concern.[18] Despite the bombastic claims of state officials presenting each election as "historical" or a matter of "safeguarding the nation," plummeting turnout rates demonstrate growing disaffection. The inflated official voter turnout for the presidential election went from 74% in 2009, to 51% in 2014 and to less than 40% in 2019. As for the legislative elections, it decreased from 43% in 2012 to 35% in 2017 to reach an all-time low of 23% in 2021. While some observers speak about "voter apathy" in Algeria (Sardar 2018), this diagnosis overlooks the fact that despite their refusal to take part in rigged electoral processes, Algerians are far from being politically passive. Rather, they take interest in the political, social and economic issues their country deals with and are particularly vocal on social media (Benzenine 2020b). Indeed, abstention progressively turned into a mode of contestation and posed a systematic challenge to the legitimacy of the country's ruling elites (Dris-Aït Hamadouche 2009).

Consequently, elections appear meaningless in the eyes of the public, which puts the entire institutional framework in jeopardy (Volpi 2020: 164). As a democratic technology of power, electoral processes aim to integrate, normalize and organize the threatening plurality of the masses. Yet, more than 30 years after pluralist political competition was introduced, it fails to appear as anything else but a travesty. The population thus remains politically unmanageable and unrepresentable. In 2007, the Ministry of the Interior sent a letter to more than 4 million abstentionists to identify the reasons for their lack of engagement with the process. This moral pressure was soon complemented by a more coercive approach: in the 2010s, activists calling for an electoral boycott were frequently harassed by the police and even jailed under phony pretexts (such as deteriorating state property after tagging electoral posters). After the beginning of the 2019 Hirak, as elections were more critical than ever in the effort of re-legitimation, repression intensified. Dozens of activists opposing the polls were jailed, and reluctant parties were suspended by the government. More importantly, a new law introduced severe sanctions for "arming the right to vote" and "hindering the polling process."[19] Yet, after the massive boycott of the June 2021 elections, even a staunch advocate for political participation such as Soufiane Djilali had to acknowledge the complete lack of legitimacy of the institutions and the impossibility of taking part in any government coalition.[20]

Conclusion

Algerian opponents and disgruntled citizens often portray the ruling coalition as the offspring of French colonialism that usurped the state after independence. They notably point to its autocratic ways, lack of transparency and violence. The organization of flawed popular consultations is yet another technique the colonial state once used. The discriminatory and rigged elections organized under colonialism once fuelled independentist claims among Algerians. From the early 20th-century exclusion of Muslims to the massive fraud and corruption of the late colonial period, the systematic travesty of popular will discredited reformist discourses and legitimized the militarization of the struggle (Peyroulou 2009: 329–338; McDougall 2017: 185–189, Savarese 2016). In the early 1990s, the debates within the Islamic movement regarding the legitimacy of political participation were settled by the cancellation of the legislative elections and a military coup, leading again to the militarization of politics (Ainine 2016). During the decades of Bouteflika's rule, the progressive erosion of the legitimacy of the entire institutional edifice, including local and national elected offices, reinforced the disaffection of the generation born after 1988 (Tlemçani 2012: 169–170). Once again, the rejection of flawed electoral processes, which were viewed as ignoring popular will, was a key motive for the 2019 uprising. This time, nonetheless, the effort to challenge the system of power avoided the pitfalls of factionalism and militarization.

The Hirak has taken the form of a grassroots yet populist, radical yet peaceful mobilization, whose leaderless and informal structure consciously evades institutional politics to trump the strategies of bureaucratic control of the ruling coalition. In response to the organization of weekly marches, the latter has resorted to elections as a default strategy: the state apparatus aims to create legitimacy, co-opt new political elites, organize a convenient representation of social plurality, and promote an acceptable and non-subversive form of citizenship. The resulting stalemate points to both the impossibility of a peaceful alternative to emerge completely outside the sphere of organized politics and the complete discrediting of electoral processes that aim to control and shape the population rather than giving the people genuine influence over their political destiny. Together, the Hirak and the legislative elections of June 2021 illustrate the difficulty to effectively de-bureaucratize democracy without resorting to violence or falling into the trap of advocating for "responsible" participation that in fact serves the status quo. Between these two ills, the possibility of inclusive and non-violent political competition remains uncharted territory.

Notes

1. Feriel Bouchouia, "Al-ri'āsiyāt sābiqa naw'aiya fī tajsīd al-dīmuqrāṭiya wa-l-shafāfiya," *El-Chaâb*, 16 December 2019.
2. Interview with a French member of the European Parliament during the Dark Decade, Lyon, 2016.
3. Preamble of the revised constitution adopted in December 2020.
4. Jean Guisnel, "Interview: Le general de corps d'armée Mohamed Lamari," *Le Point*, 15 January 2003.
5. Nasir Benseba, "Mohamed Lamari réagit," *Le Matin*, 15 January 2004.
6. Interview with a member of the PST, Algiers, Spring 2012.
7. Interviews with members of the national council of the MSP, Algiers 2008.
8. Interview with a local official of Jabhat al-Mustaqbal, Chlef, 2014.
9. Interviews with members of the RCD (Tizi Ouzou & Paris, 2011) and of the FFS (Algiers, 2014). See also Aït-Aoudia (2003: 14) and Baamara (2016).
10. According to article 5 of the ordonnance n° 97-09 of 6 March 1997, political parties cannot be based on religion, language, gender, race, or regionalism.
11. Tellingly, "active citizenship" was the theme of the Euro-Algerian forum co-organized by the European delegation and the Algerian government during Algiers book fair in November 2019, a month before the controversial presidential elections.
12. www.interieur.gov.dz/index.php/fr/actualit%C3%A9s/1934-%C2%AB-l%E2%80%99institution-d%E2%80%99un-prix-annuel-de-l%E2%80%99%C3%A9lue-de-l%E2%80%99ann%C3%A9e-%C2%BB.html
13. "Bedoui: la présence de la femme dans les Assemblées élues constitue une fierté pour notre société algérienne" *APS*, 18 March 2021.
14. See Kamel Daoud, "L'appel au boycott et l'appel à la raison," *Liberté*, 1 April 2021; "Jīl Jadīd: Tawaqqi'a nisbat mushārika "ma'aqūla jiddan," *El-Chaâb*, 31 May 2021.
15. Interview with a local official of the RCD, Tizi Ouzou, 2011.
16. Cable 09ALGIERS370_a, available here: https://wikileaks.org/plusd/cables/09ALGIERS370_a.html (3 July 2021)
17. Out of 24.4 million potential voters, 5.6 million actually cast a ballot. Among these, more than 1 million ballots were invalidated and 3.3 were cast for candidates who were not elected. In other words, the legislative assembly elected in June 2021 represents less than 1.3 million voters, that is to say 5.3% of the electorate.
18. Cable 09ALGIERS370_a
19. Articles 295 and 299 of the order n°21-01 published on 10 March 2021.
20. "Al-muqāṭa'a samaḥat bi'awdat a'ḥzāb al-niẓām al-sābiq," *El-Khabar*, 19 June 2021.

References

Ainine, Bilel. 2016. *Islam politique et entrée en radicalité violente. Le cas des salafistes radicaux violents algériens*. Université Paris-Saclay. Available at: https://tel.archives-ouvertes.fr/tel-01633855.

Aït-Aoudia, Myriam (as Emma Tilleli). 2003. 'Les transformations de la société au regard des élections législatives et municipales de 2002'. *CERI*. Available at: https://www.sciencespo.fr/ceri/sites/sciencespo.fr.ceri/files/artet.pdf.

Aït-Aoudia, Myriam. 2013. 'Les dilemmes des nouveaux partis face à la participation à la première élection pluraliste post-autoritaire. Retour sur un impensé à partir du cas algérien'. *Revue Internationale de Politique Comparée* 20(2): 15–32.

Aït-Aoudia, Myriam. 2015. *L'expérience démocratique en Algérie (1988–1992)*. Paris: Presses de Sciences Po.

Ammour, Kader, Christan Leucate and Jean-Jacques Moulin. 1974. *La voie algérienne. Les contradictions d'un développement national*. Paris: François Maspéro.

Arezki, Saphia. 2020. 'Quand l'armée algérienne occupe le devant de la scène politique. Retour sur des phases de transition depuis 1962'. *Mouvements* 102(2): 147–156.

Baamara, Layla. 2016. 'Une campagne à part, mais pour le parti. Le cas d'un candidat FFS aux élections législatives de 2012 à Alger'. In: Layla Baamara, Camille Floderer and Marine Poirier (eds.), *Faire campagne, ici et ailleurs*. Aix-en-Provence: Karthala, 149–170.

Baez, Benjamin. 2014. *Technologies of Government: Politics and Power in the "Information Age."* Charlotte: Information Age Publishing.

Balta, Paul. 2012. 'Mes rencontres avec Boumediène'. *Confluences Méditerranée* 81(2): 207–212.

Benchikh, Madjid. 2003. *Algérie: Un système politique militarisé*. Paris: L'Harmattan.
Benzenine, Belkacem. 2013. 'Les femmes algériennes au Parlement: La question des quotas à l'épreuve des réformes politiques'. *Égypte/Monde Arabe* 10(3). Available at: https://journals.openedition.org/ema/3196.
Benzenine, Belkacem. 2020a. 'Les députés islamistes algériens (2012–2017): Ce que le passage à l'opposition fait à la modération'. *L'Année du Maghreb* 22(22): 25–40.
Benzenine, Belkacem. 2020b. 'La démocratie de l'abstention en situation autoritaire : Retour sur les élections législatives et locales de 2017 en Algérie'. *Maghreb – Machrek* 243(1): 77–96.
Borgmann, Monika. 2008. *Saïd Mekbel, une mort à la lettre*. Paris: Téraèdre.
Bouandel, Youcef and Yahia H. Zoubir. 1998. 'Algeria's elections: The prelude to democratisation'. *Third World Quarterly* 19(2): 177–190.
Carothers, Thomas and Saskia Brechenmacher. 2014. 'Closing space: Democracy and human rights support under fire'. *Carnegie Endowment for International Peace*. Available at: https://carnegieendowment.org/files/closing_space.pdf.
Cavatorta, Francesco. 2009. *The International Dimension of the Failed Algerian Transition: Democracy Betrayed?* Manchester: Manchester University Press.
Chagnollaud, Jean-Paul and Ali Haroun. 2002. 'Il fallait arrêter le processus electoral'. *Confluences Méditerranée* 1(1): 213–238.
Cook, Steven A. 2007. *Ruling but Not Governing: The Military and Political Development in Egypt, Algeria, and Turkey*. Baltimore, MD: Johns Hopkins University Press.
Diamond, Larry. 2005. 'The State of Democratization at the Beginning of the 21st Century'. *The Whitehead Journal of Diplomacy and International Relations* 11(1): 13–18.
Dris, Chérif. 2018. 'Algérie 2017: De quoi les élections législatives et locales sont-elles le nom?' *L'Année du Maghreb* 19(19): 169–183.
Dris-Aït Hamadouche, Louisa. 2009. 'L'abstention en Algérie: un autre mode de contestation politique'. *L'Année du Maghreb* 5(V): 263–273.
Foucault, Michel. 1980. 'Two lectures'. In: Colin Gordon (ed.), *Power/Knowledge: Selected Interviews and Other Writings, 1972-1977*. New York: Pantheon Books, 78–108.
Hachemaoui, Mohammed. 2012. 'Y a-t-il des tribus dans l'urne?' *Cahiers d'études africaines* 205(205): 103–163.
Hachemaoui, Mohammed. 2016. 'Qui gouverne (réellement) l'Algérie?' *Politique africaine* 142(2): 169–190.
Levitsky, Steven and Lucan Ahmad Way. 2002. 'Elections Without democracy: The rise of competitive authoritarianism'. *Journal of Democracy* 13(2): 51–65.
Malek, Redha. 2001 [1991]. *Tradition et révolution, Le véritable enjeu*. Alger: ANEP.
McDougall, James. 2017. *A History of Algeria*. Cambridge: Cambridge University Press.
Peyroulou, Jean-Pierre. 2009. *Guelma, 1945. Une subversion française dans l'Algérie coloniale*. Paris: La Découverte.
Reich, Gary. 2002. 'Categorizing political regimes: New data for old problems'. *Democratization* 9(4): 1–24.
Ruzza, Stefano, Gabusi Giuseppe and Davide Pellegrino. 2019. 'Authoritarian resilience through top-down transformation: Making sense of Myanmar's incomplete transition'. *Italian Political Science Review* 49(2): 193–209.
Roberts, Hugh. 2003. *The Battlefield Algeria, 1988–2002*. London: Verso.
Rose, Nikolas. 1999. *Powers of Freedom: Reframing Political Thought*. Cambridge: Cambridge University Press.
Sardar, Minakshi. 2018. 'Parliamentary elections in Algeria, 2017'. *Contemporary Review of the Middle East* 5(1): 74–86.
Savarese, Éric. 2016. 'L'acte électoral revisité en situation coloniale. Voter à Oran dans la première partie du XXe siècle'. *Pôle Sud* 44(1): 97–109.
Schedler, Andreas. 2006. *Electoral Authoritarianism: The Dynamics of Unfree Competition*. Boulder, CO: Lynne Rienner Publishers.
Tlemçani, Rachid. 2012. 'Algérie: un autoritarisme électoral'. *Tumultes* 38–39(1–2): 149–171.
Tlemçani, Rachid. 2014. 'Le coup de force permanent en Algérie. Armée, élections et islamisme'. *Maghreb, - Machrek* 221(3): 91–107.
Vollman, Erik, Miriam Bohn, Sturm Roland and Thomas Demmelhuber. 2022. 'Decentralisation as authoritarian upgrading? Evidence from Jordan and Morocco'. *The Journal of North African Studies* 27(2): 362–393.
Volpi, Frédéric. 2004. 'Pseudo-democracy in the Muslim world'. *Third World Quarterly* 25(6): 1061–1078.
Volpi, Frédéric. 2020. 'Algeria: When elections hurt democracy'. *Journal of Democracy* 31(2): 152–165.

Werenfels, Isabelle. 2007. *Managing Instability: Elites and Political Change in Algeria*. London: Routledge.
Willis, Michael. 1998. 'Algeria's other Islamists: Abdallah Djaballah and the Ennahda movement'. *Journal of North African Studies* 3(3): 46–70.
Wilson, Kenneth. 2009. 'Party-system reform in democracy's grey zone: A response to Moraski'. *Government and Opposition* 44(2): 188–207.

4
PARLIAMENTARY ELECTIONS UNDER MOHAMMED VI'S REIGN (2002–2021)

Inmaculada Szmolka

Introduction

Morocco has the longest record of contested elections in the Arab world, as its first local elections took place in 1960. While other Arab countries established one-party systems, Morocco opted for a multi-party system after the country's independence in 1956. Moroccan pluralism has its origins in the various factions that comprised the national liberation movement and in the political strategy adopted by the monarchy to prevent any group from challenging royal power (Rézette 1954). Thus, the royal palace has historically encouraged the creation of new parties favourable to the regime and promoted rifts and splits between political parties born from the national movement (Zartman 1967; Waterbury 1970; Moore 1970; López-García 1979; Entelis 1980). Multi-party politics was also inherent to the monarchy's conception of its position, wherein the king stands at the centre of the political system and acts as an arbitrator as well as an element of cohesion binding the different social and political groups (López-García 2000).

In short, Morocco can be characterised as an "electoral autocracy." While authoritarian electoral regimes do not practise democracy, they do not regularly resort to open repression. Periodically, they organise elections and, in so doing, they attempt to create a semblance of democratic legitimacy for international and domestic consumption. At the same time, these regimes impose authoritarian controls on the elections, with the aim of buttressing their own hold on power. Their objective is to harvest the fruits of electoral legitimacy without running the risks of democratic uncertainty. They seek a balance between control and electoral credibility, placing themselves in a hazy, ambivalent zone (Schedler 2002).

As in other electoral autocracies, Moroccan elections have sought to legitimise the political system, offering an image of pluralism and political competition (Storm 2017: 67). Additionally, elections have served to co-opt opposition parties by ensuring their participation in institutional politics instead of resorting to coercion; such parties are offered positions of responsibility, consequently producing a "loyal opposition" that does not threaten the system (Willis 2006; Cavatorta 2007; Wegner and Pellicer 2009; Boukhars 2010; Haugbølle and Cavatorta 2011; Storm 2014; Daadaoui 2017; Hinnebusch 2017). Moroccan elections have been one of the ruling power's strategies for survival or adaptation to new external or internal demands for change, thereby contributing to the resilience of the authoritarian regime (Heydemann 2007; Maghraoui 2020; Desrues 2020).

Nevertheless, elections not only serve the goals of the political regime but also matter for political parties. Elections determine access to state institutions, public resources and office, enabling political parties to create and sustain their own clientelistic networks among their members and supporters. In addition, elections are the institutional way to reorganise the party landscape and to configure the balance of power among political parties, placing some of them in government roles and some in opposition.

Moroccan elections have become more significant in recent decades, even though they remain under the monarchy's control. Elections have periodically been held during the reign of Mohammed VI (1999–), with a broad spectrum of political parties taking part. They provide a degree of genuine choice to voters and have not been subject to serious accusations of fraud. The majority of the parties accept the electoral rules and the final outcome. Electoral integrity has improved with respect to the voting process, although some political parties benefit from their proximity to the monarchy, and certain irregular practices, such as vote buying, persist. As a result of this emphasis on pluralistic elections, government formation now depends more on electoral results than in the past. The constitution requires the king to appoint the head of government from the winning party in the parliamentary elections. Due to the traditional fragmentation of the House of Representatives (HR), the largest party has to form a coalition government to secure a parliamentary majority. However, the king continues to intervene in the composition of the government, appointing key ministers (including the interior, foreign affairs, religious affairs and defence ministers) and influencing the partners in the government coalition. In addition, the king sets the political agenda and controls the decision-making and policy-making processes. Therefore, although political parties now have more opportunities to reach parliament and government, their real legislative and executive powers are limited.

The aim of this chapter is to analyse the five parliamentary elections that have taken place under the reign of Mohammed VI: September 27, 2002; September 7, 2007; November 25, 2011; October 7, 2016; and September 8, 2021. These elections are examined through the electoral system, the integrity of the electoral processes, the number of parties running for election and gaining representation, the electoral turnout and the Voting Age Population (VAP) turnout, the electoral performance by the main Moroccan parties, and electoral behaviour and its consequences for the party system (concentration, competitiveness and fragmentation).

Electoral system

The first parliamentary elections held during the reign of Mohammed VI took place on September 27, 2002. For these elections, a proportional party list system replaced the plurality system in single-member constituencies, which had been used since the 1963 elections. In the five elections under Mohammed VI's rule, Moroccans have elected the HR for a five-year term through a direct vote. Parliamentary seats have been assigned proportionally using the largest remainder method applied to closed and blocked lists of candidates. Other elements of the electoral system have been changed from one election to another: (a) the size of the chamber; (b) the type, number and distribution of the electoral constituencies; (c) the electoral threshold; and (d) the calculation of the electoral quota to allocate seats among parties (see Table 4.1).

In relation to the size of the chamber, the composition of the HR was set at 325 seats for the elections of 2002 and 2007. This number was increased to 395 seats for the snap election of 2011, which took place during the Arab uprisings. The aim was to boost the representation of women and to promote the participation of younger people in parliament. Thus, the number of

Parliamentary elections under Mohammed VI's reign (2002–2021)

Table 4.1 Moroccan electoral system for the House of Representatives

	Parliamentary elections				
	2002	2007	2011	2016	2021
Size of legislature	325	325	395	395	395
Legislative term	5 years	5 years	5 years	5 years	5 years
Type and number of constituencies	91 local constituencies for 295 seats	95 local constituencies for 295 seats	92 local constituencies for 305 seats	92 local constituencies for 305 seats	92 local constituencies for 305 seats
	1 national constituency for 30 seats	1 national constituency for 30 seats	1 national constituency for 90 seats (60 seats for women + 30 seats for male young people under 40)	1 national constituency for 90 seats (60 seats for women + 30 seats for young people under 40)	12 regional constituencies for 90 seats for women
Voting system	Largest Remainder method, Hare quota (for 2002, 2007, 2011 and 2016 elections)				Largest Remainder method, quota based on registered voters
Electoral threshold	3% for local and national constituencies	6% for local and national constituencies (for all elections)	6% for local constituencies 3% for national constituency	3% for local and national constituencies	None
Ballot structure	Closed and blocked lists				
Mode of suffrage	Universal (over 20 years) and direct vote	Universal (over 18 years) and direct vote (for 2007, 2011, 2016, 2021 elections)			

Source: Produced by the author based on Moroccan electoral laws

seats reserved for women was raised from 30 to 60, and a new quota of 30 seats was established for people under the age of 40, both groups elected from a single nationwide constituency.[1] For the 2021 elections, only one quota for women was set, allocating 90 seats through regional constituencies.

Regarding the electoral constituencies, in the 2002, 2007, 2011 and 2016 elections, seats were allocated through valid votes obtained by political parties in a large number of local multi-member districts and a national constituency. In the 2021 elections, the local districts were maintained, but the national constituency was replaced by 12 regional districts to reflect the constitutional role of the region in the territorial organisation of the country. With respect to local districts, the number of districts and the boundaries has been modified from one election to the other by a ministerial decree issued before elections, according to the criteria of population and representativeness. Local constituencies correspond to the administrative division of provinces and prefectures (currently 62 and 13, respectively), although certain provinces or prefectures are divided into more than one electoral district, grouping several municipalities (*communes*). Less populated rural provinces have traditionally been over-represented at the expense of the populated urban prefectures. This constitutes a form of gerrymandering benefitting pro-regime parties, which are better able to mobilise voters through the local notables and *moqqadems* and *chioukhs* (representatives of the local authority).[2]

Since 2002, seats in the HR have been assigned proportionally using the largest remainder method applied to closed and blocked lists of candidates in each electoral district. According to the largest remainder method, political parties need to obtain a certain number of votes to be assigned a seat in each electoral district, the so-called quota. Each party is first awarded as many seats as it has full quotas, and, second, the unfilled seats are distributed to the parties that present the largest remainders. From the 2002 to the 2016 elections, Morocco has used the Hare quota, the simplest one, which is obtained by dividing the total valid vote by the number of seats to be filled in each electoral district. Nevertheless, for the 2021 elections, an amendment to the electoral law was implemented consisting of calculating the electoral quota based on the number of registered voters instead of valid votes, which is without precedent in comparative electoral politics. The effect of the new way of calculating the electoral quota is a higher quota, and so an increase in the number of votes required to secure a seat. In practice, the chance of any party winning a second seat diminished, and as many parties as seats at stake get representation, regardless of the number of votes received. Analysts expected that the new voting rule would benefit small and medium-sized parties to the detriment of the largest parties, mainly the Islamist Justice and Development Party (PJD).[3] Thus, the electoral reform is consistent with the monarchy's strategy of favouring party system fragmentation. Although the PJD suffered a disastrous result at the polls in September 2021, the severity of the collapse cannot be attributed to the change in the electoral quota. On the contrary, the new electoral quotient allowed the Islamists to take the few seats they won in these elections.

As far as the electoral threshold is concerned, it was set at 6% of the valid votes in the local and national constituencies for the 2002 and 2007 elections. In 2011, the electoral threshold was reduced to 3% for the national constituency but maintained at 6% in local districts. In the 2016 elections, seats were allocated using a 3% threshold in both constituencies. The effect of a lower electoral threshold was a higher quota that made it more difficult for the largest parties to obtain additional seats, hence the PJD's reluctance towards the diminution of the electoral threshold. On the contrary, the electoral barrier had no effect on the entry of small parties to parliament as elected parties considerably surpassed the legal threshold in Morocco elections (Szmolka 2010: 25; Szmolka 2019: 562). Lastly, the electoral threshold was removed in the 2021 elections as the new way to allocate seats makes it meaningless.

Electoral integrity in Morocco

Morocco follows a governmental model of electoral management. The Ministry of the Interior oversees the organisations of the entire election process, from registration on the electoral lists to the result of the voting. In the run-up to the 2021 elections, a Central Monitoring Committee and regional committees were established to check the integrity of Morocco's elections.

In the absence of an independent electoral commission, Morocco allows electoral observation. Electoral observation was regulated for the first time in 2011 (Dahir 1-11-62 of September 29, promulgation of Law No. 30-11 establishing the modalities of independent and neutral observation of elections). In compliance with these new regulations, the National Council of Human Rights, which had already overseen previous elections, was tasked with following the elections and accrediting national and international observers. The function of electoral observers is limited to gathering information and making an informed assessment of how the process unfolded. For the 2021 elections, the National Council of Human Rights accredited 4,600 national observers representing 44 national NGOs and around 100 international observers from 19 international organisations. International observers reported that the electoral process was generally clean, although they highlighted several minor incidents regarding procedural inconsistencies during the closing of polling stations and vote counting, access to the polling stations, and the fact that most polling stations were presided over by men.[4]

According to the Perceptions of Electoral Integrity Index (PEI), the electoral integrity of Moroccan elections can be considered "moderate" (Norris and Grömping 2019).[5] This index only assesses the parliamentary elections of 2016 in the case of Morocco. As Figure 4.1 shows, Morocco ranks fourth among Middle East and North African (MENA) countries, with 57 points (out of 100) behind Israel (74 points), Tunisia (68 points) and Oman (61 points), where a consultative assembly is directly elected.

When it comes to the elements of the electoral process, the lowest scores of the PEI index for the 2016 Moroccan elections correspond to the voting process, voter registration and campaign finance. Conversely, the 2016 elections were assessed as having "high electoral integrity" in the categories of electoral laws, vote counting, results, electoral procedures, district boundaries and media coverage (see Table 4.2).

Party competition: electoral and parliamentary parties

As Figure 4.2 shows, Moroccan voters can choose from a wide range of political parties in parliamentary elections. Depending on the election, there have been more than 20 or 30 parties running for office. In the last elections of 2021, 29 political parties and one coalition of two parties (Alliance of the Democratic Left) competed. Nevertheless, the large number of electoral districts (92 local and 12 regional) makes it difficult for small parties to run candidates in all of them. As a result, only four political parties ran in all constituencies and 14 covered more than half of the local districts.[6] In addition, due to the small size of several local districts, minor parties opt to concentrate their resources in targeted constituencies where they have the best chance of winning a seat.

Nevertheless, many of the political parties that run for election do not secure parliamentary representation, and only a few of them win more than 3% of the seats. The number of parliamentary parties has decreased since the 2011 elections, when 18 political parties won seats, whereas 22 and 23 political parties were represented in the previous legislatures of 2002 and

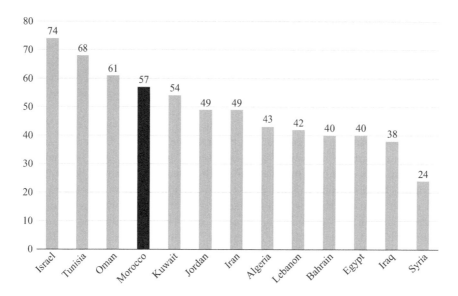

Figure 4.1 Perception of Electoral Integrity (PEI) in Middle East and North African countries. *Source*: Norris and Grömping, "Electoral Integrity Worldwide," PEI 7.0 (May 2019)

Table 4.2 Perception of Electoral Integrity (PEI) of Moroccan elections—general indicators (scale–100)

	Morocco's 2016 parliamentary elections	
	Score	PEI category of electoral integrity
PEI index	57	57
Rank	158	158
Electoral laws	74	High
Electoral procedures	69	High
District boundaries	63	High
Voter registration	42	Low
Party and candidate	50	Moderate
Media coverage	60	High
Campaign finance	42	Low
Voting process	41	Low
Vote count	73	High
Results	72	High
Electoral authorities	56	High

Source: Norris and Grömping, "Electoral Integrity Worldwide," PEI 7.0 (May 2019)

2007, respectively. The number dropped to 12 in 2016 and remained the same after the 2021 elections, despite analysts forecasting that the change in the electoral quota would increase parliamentary fragmentation.

On the other hand, several political parties prefer not to take part in the electoral processes. A point in case is the Marxist party *Annahj Democrati* (the Democratic Way), which has

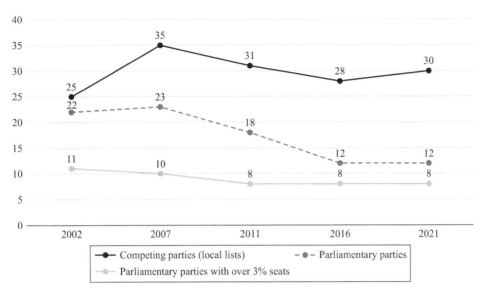

Figure 4.2 Electoral and parliamentary parties/coalitions in Morocco. *Source*: Produced by the author

boycotted all the elections held since the party's creation in 1995. This far-left party claims that the process is used by authorities to "promote fake democracy and false promises, and convince people to participate in voting to endorse a pre-determined political map."[7] Other leftist parties have swung between participating in and boycotting the elections. The Socialist Democratic Vanguard Party (PADS), the Unified Socialist Party (PSU) and the Democratic Socialist Party (PSD) called for the boycott of the elections of November 2011, the first electoral process after Morocco adopted a new constitution in July. However, they decided to participate in the 2016 and 2021 elections, arguing that a permanent boycott leaves leftist seats vacant to be filled by co-opted parties. Regarding the Islamist opposition, the popular movement al-Adlwa al-Ihsan has refused to become a political party and has maintained its position in favour of boycotting the elections. The Islamist movement considers the electoral process "absurd," claiming that the "competition is only in service of the ruler," and "governments in Morocco do not rule."[8]

Electoral participation

Parliamentary elections under Mohammed VI's reign have been characterised by high levels of electoral abstention. The average turnout of the five elections is 45.3%. Turnout reached 51.6% in the 2002 elections but fell to 37% in the following elections in 2007, the lowest in Morocco's history. Even the snap election of 2011, called in response to the social protests, only managed to mobilise 45% of voters. Participation declined to 42.3% in the election of 2016, which took place in a political context of normality and continuity. In an attempt to increase turnout, the 2021 parliamentary elections were held on the same day as municipal and regional elections, which usually have higher participation. This can partly explain the rise in electoral participation, which reached 50.86%.

It is worth noting the difference between voter turnout according to the voter register and the Voting Age Population turnout, that is, relative to the overall population of legal voting

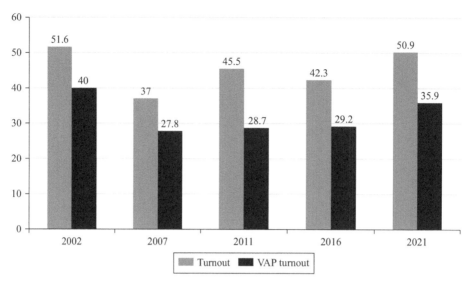

Figure 4.3 Electoral participation in the election of the Moroccan House of Representatives (2002–2021). *Source*: Produced by the author based on electoral data of the Moroccan Ministry of the Interior for turnout and the Institute for Democracy and Electoral Assistance (IDEA) for VAP turnout (https://www.idea.int/data-tools/country-view/200/40)

age. In Morocco, the voter register does not contain all potential voters. Before each election, the voter register is updated, and new voters have to apply for inclusion in the electoral census. Aware of the importance of citizens' votes in legitimising the political regime, the Ministry of the Interior as well as its local authority officials encourage Moroccans to register on electoral lists and to go to the polls. Nevertheless, the fact is that the Moroccan electoral register is not accurate, and some citizens are not listed. Its accuracy is more important than ever since the distribution of seats in the Moroccan parliament is now based on the voter census and not on the votes cast. A total of 17,509,127 million people were eligible to vote in the 2021 elections, of whom 1,806,535 were new voters. This represents an increase of 11.5% over the previous elections. However, the VAP is estimated at 24,445,917, so Moroccans' electoral participation is significantly lower in terms of VAP turnout, at around 36%, as Figure 4.3 shows. In the absence of studies on electoral abstention in Morocco, we can speculate that the low turnout at least partially reflects mistrust in the legitimacy of the elections and the political system.

Electoral evolution of Moroccan political parties (2002–2021)

In this section, we examine the electoral results of the eight Moroccan political parties that exceeded 3% of seats in all the elections in which they ran for office during the study period. They are the Islamist PJD; the so-called parties of the national movement, namely, the Party of Independence (PI), the Socialist Union of Popular Forces (USFP), the Party of Progress and Socialism (PPS); and, those that are usually known as administrative parties such as the National Rally of Independents (RNI), the Popular Movement (MP) and the Constitutional Union (UC), parties promoted by the royal inner-circle with the purpose of supporting monarchy's policies and countering the opposition parties (see Figure 4.4).

Parliamentary elections under Mohammed VI's reign (2002–2021)

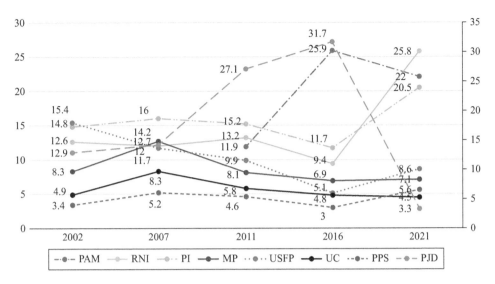

Figure 4.4 Parliamentary representation of the main Moroccan political parties (percentage of seats).
Source: Produced by the author based on electoral data of the Moroccan Interior Ministry

Regarding the PJD, the Islamists were heavily defeated in the 2021 elections, gaining only 13 seats and coming eighth in the electoral race after a decade of being the largest party in parliament. Until then, the PJD had made steady electoral progress since the first elections it contested in 1997, by building up a strong party organisation, maintaining the full support of the broader Islamist movement in civil society, and positioning itself as the only credible opposition party (Wegner 2011). In 1997, the Islamists won eight seats in the HR and formed their own parliamentary group after winning more seats in partial elections, reaching a total of 14 seats at the end of the legislature. In 2002, the PJD became the third-largest party in the HR with 42 seats. Its success would probably have been greater if the party had run in all constituencies.[9] During the 2007 elections, the PJD became the first party in terms of the number of votes received but the second in terms of the number of seats, behind the nationalist and conservative PI (46 and 52 seats, respectively, out of 325). Thus, the PJD became the main opposition party and a real alternative to the government. Finally, the Islamist party came first in the post-Arab Spring elections of November 2011 with 22.8% of the vote and 107 out of the 395 seats in the HR. Consequently, Mohammed VI appointed the general secretary of the PJD, Abdelilah Benkirane, as head of government. The PJD won the elections again in 2016. Nevertheless, the RNI succeeded in blocking for months the negotiations to form a government undertaken by the re-elected head of government Abdelilah Benkirane, which led to his resignation and the subsequent appointment of Saadeddine el-Othmani, president of the national council of the PJD, who formed a government under the conditions set by the RNI.

The undisputed winner of the 2021 elections was the liberal party RNI, led by the billionaire agriculture minister, Aziz Akhannouch, which took 102 seats in the 395-seat parliament. Following the RNI's victory, Mohammed VI appointed Aziz Akhannouch as head of government. The results achieved by the RNI represent a significant electoral change since they had only taken 37 seats in the 2016 elections. In the legislatures of 2002, 2007 and 2011, the RNI had an even more modest presence in parliament, with just over 10% of the seats. The RNI's political influence in Moroccan politics increased as a result of its success in blocking Benkirane's negotiations to form a government in 2016 and its position within the subsequent El Othmani government coalition, taking on relevant portfolios linked to the economy. In preparation for the 2021 elections, the RNI built an effective organisation and wove an optimal territorial network thanks to the influence of local notables and entrepreneurs who campaigned for the party. The RNI also carried out an active and expensive campaign on social media, which became essential due to the restrictions on meetings imposed by the COVID-19 pandemic. Lastly, the proximity of the RNI to the monarchy made it the winning bet.

Thanks to this victory, the RNI has displaced the PAM as the main pro-palace party. Despite being called to become the lead government party when it was established in 2008, the PAM did not meet the expectations placed on it.[10] The PAM suffered the consequences of the Arab uprisings, being the target of criticism on the part of the February 20 protest movement. The PAM only came fourth in the elections of November 2011, although it became the main opposition party during the 2011–2016 legislature due to the participation of the three biggest parties in the coalition government and its strong opposition to the PJD. In the 2016 elections, the PAM came close to the Islamists, taking second place with 102 seats. The pro-regime party was also the runner-up in the 2021 elections, although its number of seats dropped to 87.

The progression of the PJD as an opposition party reduced the electoral weight of the national movement parties, which also suffered a crisis due to their participation and co-optation in the government of *alternance* formed in 1998 by the socialist Abderrahmane el-Youssefi. The percentage of seats gained in 2011 by the PJD alone (27.1%) almost equalled that of all the national movement parties combined (29.7%). Nevertheless, the national movement parties regained electoral strength and political influence in the 2021 elections. As for the PI, the conservative party took about 15% of the parliamentary seats in the 2002, 2007 and 2011 elections. With only 52 out of 325 seats, the PI became the largest parliamentary party in the 2007 elections, which allowed it to lead a coalition government under Abbas el-Fassi from 2007 to 2011. After the 2011 elections, the PI took part in Benkirane's coalition government until the withdrawal of the *Istiqlal* ministers in 2013. The number of seats won by the PI fell to 11.7% in 2016 elections, although it remained the third-largest party. The new secretary-general, Nizar Baraka, elected in 2017, managed to restore the electoral weight of the PI in the 2021 elections, raising the number of seats from 46 to 81. After a poor performance in the elections held between 2002 and 2016, both the USFP and the PPS have increased their parliamentary representation in the 2021 election, securing 34 and 22 seats, respectively.

Finally, the MP and the UC have followed a similar electoral path as secondary parties close to the monarchy. Both parties have been part of the two coalition governments headed by El Othmani. In the 2021 elections, the MP and the UC achieved almost the same electoral results as they did in 2016, winning 28 and 18 seats, respectively.

Dimensions of electoral behaviour and party system

Concentration and competitiveness

Despite the fact that the electoral system favours fragmentation, this effect has been offset by a greater concentration in support for the two largest parties since 2007, and especially in the 2016 elections. As Table 4.3 shows, the highest concentration of votes and seats of the two largest parties was a consequence of the substantial rise in votes and seats achieved by the PJD in 2016. In that year, the PJD and the PAM together won 47.96% of the votes in local constituencies and 57.47%

Table 4.3 Concentration and competitiveness in Moroccan parliamentary elections

	2021	2016	2011	2007	2002
Percentage of the vote of the largest party in the local constituencies	27.66 RNI	27.14 PJD	22.80 PJD	10.9 PJD	11.82 USFP
Percentage of seats of the largest party in the local constituencies	28.20 RNI	32.13 PJD	27.21 PJD	15.59 PI	15.25 USFP
Total percentage of seats of the largest party	25.82 RNI	31.65 PJD	27.10 PJD	20.00 PI	15.38 USFP
Ratio of seats between the first and second parties	1.17 RNI:PAM	1.2 PJD:PAM	1.8 PJD:PI	1.1 PI:PJD	1.0 USFP:PI
Ratio of seats between the second and third parties	1.07 PAM:PI	2.2 PAM:PI	1.1 PI:RNI	1.1 PJD:MP	1.1 PI:PJD
Electoral concentration in the local constituencies	46.11 RNI+PAM	47.96 PJD+PAM	34.63 PJD+PI	21.1 PJD+PI	21.70 USFP+PI
Parliamentary concentration in the local constituencies	52.79 RNI+PAM	58.69 PJD+PAM	42.28 PJD+PI	29.15 PI+PJD	30.16 USFP+PI
Parliamentary concentration in all constituencies	47.84 RNI+PAM	57.47 PJD+PAM	42.30 PJD+PI	40.00 PI+PJD	30.15 USFP+PI
Local electoral competitiveness in the local constituencies	9.21 RNI–PAM	6.32 PJD–PAM	10.91 PJD–PI	0.2 PJD–PI	1.94 USFP–PI
Local parliamentary competitiveness in the local constituencies	3.61 RNI–PAM	5.57 PJD–PAM	11.81 PJD–PI	2.03 PI–PJD	0.34 USFP–PI
Parliamentary competitiveness in all constituencies	3.8 RNI–PAM	5.83 PJD–PAM	11.90 PJD–PI	1.85 PI–PJD	0.61 USFP–PI

Note: At the time of writing, the Moroccan Ministry of the Interior has only provided provisional and aggregated data on the seats won by each party in the September 8, 2021, elections
Source: Produced by the author based on electoral data of the Moroccan Interior Ministry

of the seats: 13.3 and 15 points more, respectively, than the percentage of votes and seats won by the PJD and PI in 2011. In addition, the ratio between the numbers of seats taken by the second (PAM) and third party (PI) in 2016—at 2.2, double that of the previous legislature—also reveals the distance in the parliamentary representation of the PJD and PAM with respect to other parties. Nevertheless, the 2021 elections have entailed a ten-point decrease in parliamentary concentration, since the RNI has fewer seats than the PJD in the last legislature, and the PAM has lost seats. In addition, there is a smaller distance between the second and third parties, so parliament currently has three largest parties (RNI, PAM, PI) instead of two as in 2016 (PJD, PAM).

With the exception of the 2011 elections, the aggregate electoral results also show a high level of party competitiveness; that is, a low percentage difference in votes and seats between the winning party and the runner-up. However, in multi-member proportional constituencies, such as those in Morocco, there is not one single electoral race, but multiple races, one in each local district and, currently, in the regional constituencies. Parties need to receive a certain number of votes (quota) to be allocated seats in each district. This sometimes means that one party can get the same number of seats as another but with far fewer votes. Therefore, parliamentary competitiveness can be high even when there is a large difference in the number of votes won by the leading parties. In particular, the analysis of competitiveness at the local constituency level in the 2016 elections shows that the degree of local competitiveness between the PJD and the PAM was generally very low, and in most districts the Islamists held a big advantage over the PAM. Other third parties also played a significant role and became the voters' first or second choice in some districts, with the effect of increasing parliamentary fragmentation and reducing competitiveness between the PJD and the PAM (Szmolka 2019).

Fragmentation

Party system fragmentation has traditionally been high, particularly during the period 2002–2016 (Szmolka 2010, 2021; Szmolka and Moral 2019). The element of the electoral system that explains parliamentary fragmentation is the large number of small local constituencies in which the proportional quota formula is applied.[11] The combination of both elements of the electoral system makes it difficult for the larger parties to win more than one seat in these districts and allows smaller parties to obtain representatives in the districts where they are electorally strong. The higher quota that Moroccan parties have to reach since the electoral amendment of 2021 also fosters parliamentary fragmentation. To sum up, the Moroccan electoral system makes it practically impossible for any party to win an absolute majority in the HR and therefore prevents the existence of a predominant party.

In this section, we address party fragmentation in the elections held between 2002 and 2016 because, at the time of writing, the Moroccan Ministry of the Interior has only provided provisional data on the total seats won by each party. Electoral and parliamentary fragmentation diminished considerably in the 2016 elections, having reached a peak in the 2002–2007 legislature (see Table 4.4). The HR went from 22 parties in 2002 to 12 in 2016, with parliamentary fragmentation declining from 0.904 to 0.800 in this 15-year period. In addition, the Effective Number of Parliamentary Parties (ENPP) shows the fragmentation of the HR. In the 2016 elections, the ENPP was five, indicating an extreme multi-party system. This figure has declined since 2011 (ENPP 6.6), and especially in relation to the scenario of fragmentation in 2007, when the ENPP was 10.4, and in 2002 with 10.1. The reduction in fragmentation is primarily explained by the rise in electoral support for the largest parties (PJD and PAM) and the smaller number of parties that enter parliament (Szmolka 2021: 15). Data from the 2021 elections show that parliamentary fragmentation has increased, both in terms of Rae's index and the ENPP, although not as much as expected.

Table 4.4 Electoral and Parliamentary Party Fragmentation in Moroccan parliamentary elections

	2021	2016	2011	2007	2002
Rae's electoral fragmentation index (using local votes)	0.842	0.846	0.886	0.933	0.936
Rae's parliamentary fragmentation index	0.824	0.800	0.849	0.901	0.904
Effective number of electoral parties (using local votes)	6.3	6.5	8.8	15.0	15.6
Effective number of parliamentary parties	5.7	5.0	6.6	10.1	10.4

Note: Electoral data for the calculation of Rae's electoral index and ENEP are not available
Source: Produced by the author based on electoral data of the Moroccan Interior Ministry

Conclusion

Pluralist elections do not necessarily mean democracy, as the case of Morocco shows. Despite a degree of genuine choice for Moroccan voters and moderate electoral integrity, the electoral processes are controlled and orchestrated by the monarchy. The electoral system favours parliament fragmentation to prevent the emergence of a dominant party that could challenge royal power. Moreover, state neutrality is called into question by the advantages that parties close to the monarchy have in terms of funding and voter mobilisation. In addition, elections only partially fulfil their function of producing a government. Political parties in the governmental coalitions do not have genuine power to determine government policies. The king, with the help of his cabinet, sets the political agenda and controls the decision-making and policy-making processes. Therefore, although political parties now have more opportunities to reach parliament and government, their real legislative and executive powers are limited.

The vast majority of Moroccan political parties have accepted the rules of the game, even the traditional opposition parties such as the PJD, the USFP, the PI and the PPS. Elections are essential for political parties as they determine access to state institutions, public resources and positions in office, enabling political parties to create their own clientelistic networks among their members and supporters. Moroccan parties are aware that the electoral system will reward them with a minimal representation at least, so they are prone to accept the electoral rules designed by the palace and take part in elections. Through this co-optation strategy, the political regime achieves broad parliamentary representation, rotation of government under control and legitimisation. In this way, electoral processes are contributing to the resilience of authoritarianism in Morocco.

Finally, elections have traditionally been a factor in political change in Morocco (Parejo and Veguilla 2008). The recycling of party coalitions in government after the legislative elections has allowed the Moroccan monarchy to respond to democratic demands and adapt the political regime to adverse circumstances. This occurred with the so-called government of *alternance* in 1998, when the socialist Abderrahmane el-Youssefi was appointed prime minister and the parties of the Democratic Bloc (*Kutla al-Democratiya*) took part in the coalition government. Likewise, the victory of the PJD in 2011 brought about another alternation in power but also failed to meet democratic aspirations and the socioeconomic demands of the public. The elections of 2021 have marked the end of Islamist influence in Moroccan politics and the opening of a new political cycle. The winning party, the RNI, has formed a coalition government with the PAM—also a party close to the monarchy—and the historic PI. The new government is aimed to implement the "New Development Model," promoted by the royal palace and designed to last until 2035. It is expected that the monarchy will continue to dominate Moroccan politics through his control of the party system, institutions and political processes.

Notes

1 The national district was created in 2002 in order to ensure the representation of women in parliament, and following women's rights activists' disappointment over the failed reform of the Moroccan Islamic family code (*Moudawana*) (Sater, 2003: 136).
2 The local constituencies for the 2021 elections comprised 6 six-member districts, 5 five-member, 22 four-member, 38 three-member and 21 two-member.
3 The electoral reform passed with the support of the majority of the parliamentary parties, which argued that the new seat allocation guaranteed equal opportunities and pluralism in parliament. On

the contrary, the PJD voted against the electoral amendment considering that it intentionally sought to prevent their victory in the elections. In addition, the minority party Federation of Democratic Left (FGD), which had two seats in the HR, rejected the electoral quota based on the voter census, but abstained in the parliamentary vote so as not to take a position on the side of the Islamists.
4 See for example Council of Europe News: https://www.coe.int/en/web/congress/-/congress-concludes-electoral-observation-mission-in-morocco.
5 The PEI is produced by Harvard University and the University of Sydney. This index offers complete coverage of 166 countries holding elections and includes all stages of the electoral cycle for national elections held between 2012 and 2018. The PEI categorises the level of electoral integrity as one of the following: very high, 70–100 points; high, 69–60; moderate, 59–50; low, 49–40; and very low, less than 40.
6 See the number of electoral lists submitted by each party in local and regional constituencies in Medias24, August 27, 2021: https://www.medias24.com/2021/08/27/legislatives-2021-31-partis-1704-listes-et-6-815-candidats-y-participent/
7 See *Annahj Democrati* statement in favour of a boycott, August 21, 2021: https://annahjaddimocrati.org/ar/6793.
8 See declarations of the Islamist movement's leaders on a video on its website, August 21, 2021: https://tinyurl.com/bdnnz2zn.
9 The PJD and the inner circle of the monarchy negotiated a deal in which the PJD agreed to step aside in a number of constituencies in exchange for the right to participate in the elections. Thus, the Islamists competed in only 57 local constituencies out of 91 (Willis 2004).
10 The PAM emerged as an attempt to bring together loyalist parties and create a strong anti-Islamist contender as a bulwark against the electoral rise of the PJD. The PJD was founded by the merger of five small parties (the National Democratic Party, the Citizens Initiative for Development, the *Al Ahd* Party, the Alliance of Liberties and the Environment and Development Party) (Boussaid, 2009; Eibl, 2011).
11 The average size of the local districts was 3.31 seats in both the 2016 and 2021 elections.

References

Boukhars, Anouar. 2010. *Politics in Morocco: Executive Monarchy and Enlightened Authoritarianism*. London: Routledge.
Boussaid, Farid. 2009. 'The rise of the PAM in Morocco: Trampling the political scene or stumbling into it?' *Mediterranean Politics* 14(3): 413–419.
Cavatorta, Francesco. 2007. 'More than repression: The significance of divide et impera in the Middle East and North Africa –The case of Morocco.' *Journal of Contemporary African Studies* 25(2): 187–203.
Daadaoui, Mohamed. 2017. 'Of Monarchs and Islamists: The "Refo-lutionary" promise of the PJD Islamists and regime control in Morocco.' *Middle East Critique* 26(4): 355–371.
Desrues, Thierry. 2020. 'Authoritarian resilience and democratic representation in Morocco: Royal interference and political parties' leaderships since the 2016 elections.' *Mediterranean Politics* 25(2): 254–262.
Eibl, Ferdinand. 2011. 'The party of authenticity and modernity (PAM): Trajectory of a political deus ex machina.' *The Journal of North African Studies* 17(1): 45–56.
Entelis, John P. 1980. *Comparative Politics of North Africa: Algeria, Morocco and Tunisia*. Syracuse, NY: Syracuse University Press.
Haugbølle, Rikke H. and Francesco Cavatorta. 2011. 'Will the real Tunisian opposition please stand up? Opposition coordination failures under authoritarian constraints.' *British Journal of Middle Eastern Studies* 38(3): 323–341.
Heydemann, Steven. 2007. 'Upgrading authoritarianism in the Arab World.' The Brookings Institution, Analysis Paper, 13. Available at: http://www.brookings.edu/,/media/Files/rc/papers/2007/10arab-world/10arabworld.pdf.
Hinnebusch, Raymmond. 2017. 'Political parties in MENA: Their functions and development.' *British Journal of Middle Eastern Studies* 44(2): 159–175.

López-García, Bernabé. 1979. *Procesos electorales en Marruecos (1960–1977)*. Madrid: CIS.

López-García, Bernabé. 2000. *Marruecos político. Cuarenta años de procesos electorales (1960–2000)*. Madrid: CIS.

Maghraoui, Driss. 2020. 'On the relevance or irrelevance of political parties in Morocco.' *The Journal of North African Studies* 25(6): 939–959.

Moore, Clement H. 1970. *Politics in North Africa: Algeria, Morocco and Tunisia*. Boston, MA: Brown.

Norris, Pippa and Max Grömping. 2019. 'Electoral integrity worldwide, PEI 7.0.' May 2019 https://static1.squarespace.com/static/58533f31bebafbe99c85dc9b/t/5ce60bd6b208fcd93be49430/1558580197717/Electoral+Integrity+Worldwide.pdf.

Parejo, Maria Angustias and Victoria Veguilla. 2008. 'Elecciones y cambio político. Análisis diacrónico de los procesos electorales en Marruecos.' *Awraq: Estudios Sobre el Mundo Árabe e Islámico Contemporáneo* 25: 11–41.

Rézette, Robert. 1954. *Les Partis Politiques Marocains*. Paris: Presses de la Fondation National des Sciences Politiques.

Sater, James N. 2003. 'Morocco after the parliamentary elections of 2002.' *Mediterranean Politics* 8(1): 135–142.

Schedler, Andreas. 2002. 'The menu of manipulation.' *Journal of Democracy* 13(2): 51–65.

Storm, Lise. 2014. *Party Politics and the Prospects for Democracy in North Africa*. Boulder, CO: Lynne Rienner.

Storm, Lise. 2017. 'Parties and party system change.' In: Inmaculada Szmolka (ed.), *Political Change in the Middle East and North Africa: After the Arab Spring*. Edinburgh: Edinburgh University Press: 63–88.

Szmolka, Inmaculada. 2010. 'Party system fragmentation in Morocco.' *The Journal of North African Studies* 15(1): 13–37.

Szmolka, Inmaculada. 2019. 'A real electoral duel between the PJD and the PAM? Analysing constituency-level competitiveness in the 2016 Moroccan elections.' *British Journal of Middle Eastern Studies* 46(4): 535–563.

Szmolka, Inmaculada. 2021. 'Bipolarisation of the Moroccan political party arena? Refuting this idea through an analysis of the party system.' *The Journal of North African Studies* 26(1): 73–102.

Szmolka, Inmaculada and Lucía G. del Moral. 2019. 'A proposal of party systems typology for democratic and pluralist authoritarian regimes: Its application to the Maghreb countries.' *Revista de Estudios e Investigaciones Sociológicas* 168: 93–110.

Waterbury, John. 1970. *The Commander of the Faithful: The Moroccan Political Elite - A Study of Segmented Politics*. New York: Columbia University Press.

Wegner, Eva. 2011. *Islamist Opposition in Authoritarian Regimes: The Party of Justice and Development in Morocco*. Syracuse, NY: Syracuse University Press.

Wegner, Eva and Miquel Pellicer. 2009. 'Islamist moderation without democratization: The coming of age of the Moroccan party of justice and development?' *Democratization* 16(1): 157–175.

Willis, Michael. 2004. 'Morocco's Islamists and the legislative elections of 2002: The strange case of the party that did not want to win.' *Mediterranean Politics* 9(1): 53–81.

Willis, Michael. 2006. 'Containing radicalism through the political process in North Africa.' *Mediterranean Politics* 11(2): 137–150.

Zartman, William I. 1967. 'Political pluralism in Morocco.' *Government and Opposition* 2(4): 568–583.

# 5

ELECTORAL DISTRICTS IN JORDAN

An analytical study

Mohammed Torki Bani Salameh

Introduction

The role of electoral systems in improving the quality of representation, and with it the quality of democracy, has long attracted the attention of intellectuals, researchers and legislators in the West (Berelsons and Lazarsfeld 1944; Duverger 1972; Nagler 1991; Lijphart 1994), particularly because of declining turnout (Blais 2000; Gray and Caul 2000). With it, the importance of electoral geography and electoral districts has quickly emerged, as these are directly related to the equality of representation.

When it comes to the Arab world, interest in electoral engineering is rather new – first and foremost because of the late appearance of elections in the region – and the issue of the division of electoral districts for a long time has not received much attention. The reason for this gap owes in large part to the fact that electoral policy-making, including the division of electoral districts, is the charge of the sole executive authority. This demonstrates the fragility of democratic practices, the difficulty of clarifying the spatial dimension of elections, the lack of sufficient information about the results and the fear of approaching this issue for political reasons related to the political systems themselves.

This state of affairs seemed to change following the Arab uprisings, when issues concerning electoral laws and the division of electoral districts began to be considered an essential topic in the process of democratic transition, as several researchers, as well as political actors, began to realize that changing the social reality and strengthening the process of democratic transformation required a review of the divisions of electoral districts as part of the electoral reform process. Yet, in Jordan, the regime continues to manipulate the division of electoral districts based on a strict legal framework, while neglecting geography and demography in such division.

Jordan has been experiencing intense political debates since King Abdullah II formed, in 2021, a committee consisting of 92 political figures headed by Samir Al-Rifai to modernize the country's political system. According to the committee's roadmap, this is to be done through the development of two draft laws for elections and political parties; potential constitutional amendments related to the two laws and parliamentary work mechanisms; the expansion of participation in decision-making, and the creation of a legislative and political environment that guarantees the role of youth and women in public life. All these measures are meant to bring about a qualitative shift in political and parliamentary life through the establishment of an effective political party system, and to ensure an equitable representation of citizens – the latter being highly dependent on the division of electoral districts in Jordan.

This study analyzes the division of electoral districts in Jordan, where the executive authority has full control over the determination of electoral districts as part of its hegemony on the general policy governing elections. Electoral districts have remained divided in a way that does not consider changes in demography, thus undermining the representativeness of the House of Representatives. This un-representativeness has led to increasing protests about the performance of the House of Representatives, electoral laws and the distribution of seats. These protests crystallized interest in electoral districting and the number of parliamentary seats allocated to each, as several political actors began to realize that changing social reality requires not only a review of the electoral law but also the division of electoral districts. In this environment, it is expected that a new election law will be approved, one that includes amendments to the representation system or the division of electoral districts on the one hand, and an emphasis on genuinely free, fair and regular elections on the other.

The theoretical framework for the analysis of electoral districts

The size, or magnitude, of electoral districts – i.e., the number of seats therein allocated – is one of three constitutive elements of any given electoral system, along with the electoral formula and the structure of the vote (Kelly et al. 2005). In dividing the national territory into small constituencies, electoral districts are crucial in guaranteeing the representativeness of the whole electoral system. In fact, even though electoral systems are usually defined according to their electoral formula (the way in which votes are converted into seats), which either favors governability over representativeness (as the majoritarian systems) or the other way round (as the proportional ones), it has been noted that under the same electoral formula an electoral system might be more or less proportional depending on how electoral districts are designed. Thus, there is significant interest in developing an integrated legal framework that works to ensure justice in the distribution of electoral districts and to promote the principles of equality among citizens. In general, electoral districts are defined within the electoral law. The full legal framework for elections can be based on a variety of sources, including, among others, *international documents*, such as the International Covenant on Civil and Political Rights, *regional documents*, such as the African Charter on Democracy, Elections and Governance, the *national constitution*, *national laws* providing for the electoral process, *provincial or state laws*, which in federal countries may govern the processes for provincial or state and local electoral events (as in Australia) or for national electoral events (as in the United States), *ordinances and regulations* made by national or lower-level authorities or *codes of conduct* (voluntary or otherwise) that may have a direct or indirect impact on the electoral process (Cat et al. 2014).

Patterns of electoral district division

Electoral districts are a form of spatial organization of society, an administrative division intended to set boundaries for each geographical or administrative region within the territory of the state so that all sectors of the population are represented in parliament by several representatives commensurate with the size of the voting power of each region (Jacob 1964: 266). The choice of an electoral system affects how district boundaries are drawn, how voters are registered, how ballot papers are designed, how votes are counted and many other aspects of the electoral process (Kelly et al. 2005: 18).

Most electoral systems require the division of electoral districts and the determination of the number of seats and voters in each district. The boundaries of the districts may follow the administrative division in place or may be carried out on other bases. Since the process of dividing districts has important political consequences, it must be regulated in the electoral law. In some cases, districts are partially redrawn within a singular law issued by the Cabinet, as is the case in Jordan, or within the same law as is the case with the Egyptian electoral law.

The process of defining district boundaries is regulated by the international obligation of an equal ballot. In accordance with Article 25 of the International Covenant on Civil and Political Rights, "every citizen, without any form of discrimination, has the right to vote and be elected, in just objective elections conducted periodically by general and equal ballot guarantee the electors by secret ballot, and ensures the free expression of the will of the electors". Accordingly, the process of defining district boundaries should not affect the votes of the electors belonging to a particular group or residing in a particular part of the country (Kamel 2015: 1). An example of this is the adoption by the Jordanian government of an electoral system to enter parliament that makes the Bedouin regions in the north, center and south closed regions, as this feature has ensured the representation of Bedouins in the Jordanian parliament since the return of parliamentary elections in 1989.

The distribution and division of electoral districts depend on the distributive justice and the reasons behind the decisions on how to draw district boundaries (Al-Deeb 2008: 743, Karam 1988: 76–77). First is the proportion or disproportion between the number of residents in the district and the number of seats allocated to it. When disproportion wins out, this misallocation takes two forms. On the one hand, the proportion of allocated seats is greater than the proportion of the population; that is, the number of people in a district is less than the number in other districts to which the same number of seats have been allocated, which is known as the high level of representation. On the other, the proportion of the allocated seats is less than the proportion of the population; that is, the number of people in a district is greater than the number of people in another district with the same number of seats, which is known as a low level of representation. The second pattern has to do with how boundaries are drawn. In fact, drawing the boundaries of electoral districts is based on partisan political or geographic considerations, such as interest in the district's population because of their racial, religious, linguistic and ethnic characteristics and their geographical distribution (Abdul Salam 2019: 47). Drawing the boundaries of electoral districts thus relies on different calculations, (Al-Deeb 2008: 765). For instance, linking the scope of the pro-state groupings to certain electoral districts to avoid introducing areas that are not in favor of them, which is what is called the term "stacked". There is also drawing the boundaries of electoral districts in a way that leads to the concentration of voters supporting the state's political system in one or two areas at most, where the candidate of the state obtains an overwhelming majority of the votes there, provided that the candidates of opposition parties receive only a limited number of seats in parliament. Finally, there is the division of the area opposed to the state into several parts, provided that each part is attached to one of the neighboring electoral districts, and thus the individuals or party's opposition do not win a large majority in this area.

Geographical division of electoral districts

The geographical division of electoral districts is mainly related to the principle of proportional balance in the electoral vote. This principle assumes that the number of electors that make up an electoral district is equal to the number of electors in another electoral district.

Electoral boundaries draw geographical divisions to enable the people to elect their representatives. These electorates are made up of subgroups of all eligible voters in the country, defining the people who can vote to elect those who represent their geographic area and their social and political interests. Electoral districts are usually based on the principles of equivalent and proportional voting, which means that if two districts elect one seat each in parliament, they must have an equal number of electors so that all voters have an equal chance of determining their representative. In this context, demographic data, based on voter registration, are essential for the delimitation of electoral district boundaries.

Access to district delimitation data provides an opportunity to assess "equality of voting" by comparing the proportion of voters to representatives across districts. Moreover, with access to data on electoral boundaries, groups can identify distinctions in delimitation or evidence of "qualitative division of districts" (Brown and Krieger-Benson 2015); states usually establish a set of formal rules or criteria for defining the boundaries of electoral districts. These rules are usually included in the electoral law and may sometimes be found in the country's constitution. Electoral districts are not only geographical boundaries; they represent political and social components that will ultimately determine the nature of the electoral count and its final results. The controversy and the struggle over districts, then, are fundamentally political struggles.

There are many basic criteria that countries of the world take when dividing electoral districts, the most important of which are: equality of population in different districts (52.8% of the countries in the world); conformity with the administrative borders in the country (41.8%); respect for natural borders and geographical characteristics (24.2%); geographical area of the electoral district (18%); and communities with shared interests (16.7%).

The Jordanian regime has deliberately tampered with the distribution of electoral districts, as it established large and multi-seat districts in the stronghold of opposition parties to further disperse the votes opposition candidates could gain. More seats were allocated to pro-regime areas and fewer seats to districts in which Islamists and Jordanians of Palestinian origin reside. In the district with the greatest underrepresentation in the parliament, there were over 46,000 electors for each representative, while the figure was less than 8,000 in the pro-regime overrepresented districts (Kao 2012). There are several indicators through which it is possible to reveal the manifestations of the poor geographical division of the electoral districts – malapportionment (Al-Deeb 2008: 785). One could measure *the degree of extremism*. This is done by monitoring the relationship between the number of voters in the largest and smallest constituencies. If the largest district includes 60,000 voters and the smallest district includes 20,000 voters, this indicates that each vote in the second circle is equivalent to three times its counterpart in the first district. One can also measure *the rate of deviation*. This is done by comparing the size of each district with the general average of electoral districts, which can be obtained by dividing the number of voters at the national level by the total number of seats. Thus, if the total number of voters is 2,272.182 million and the number of electoral districts is 117, the average number of voters in each district is 19,420, and if there is no deviation from this average (equal to zero), then there is no geographical distribution of voters among the electoral districts, but if the deviations from the average are large, this means a poor geographical distribution of voters between constituencies. This measure is valid if it is applied to any of the two electoral systems (list and individual). The global deviation rates range from the minimum applied in the United States, which does not exceed 1%, while the average deviation is 3% to 10%, as is the case in Australia, Macedonia and Albania, and the deviation rate is at its highest, from 15% to 25%, in Armenia and Germany, Canada and the United Kingdom. Finally, one could measure *the deviation ratio*. This is done by calculating the ratio of the population of each governorate to the total number of the population and the ratio of seats in each governorate to the total number of seats, and the difference between the two ratios gives the deviation percentage negatively or positively from the optimal allocation.

Election laws and the division of electoral districts in Jordan

Since 1989, when the regime introduced a degree of political liberalization, Jordan has conducted several parliamentary elections with different electoral laws and, accordingly, different divisions of electoral districts. In particular, four electoral laws and regulations have been adopted since 1989, namely Election Law No. 23 (1989), i.e., the open list system; Election Law No. 15 (1993), a single vote system; Election Law No. 28 (2012), the mixed system; and the Election Law No. 6 (2016), which introduced an open proportional list system.

The evolution of electoral laws in Jordan

The legal framework for elections in Jordan consists of the 1952 Constitution and the electoral laws that were issued since the holding of the first parliamentary elections in the country. The legal framework clarifies the conditions under which elections are held, the electoral system that is applied, as well as the approved division of the country into electoral districts. The first election law came into effect after the return of parliamentary life to Jordan in 1989. The law provided for the open list election system, whereby voters had the right to choose as many candidates equal to the number of seats allocated in each district. This was the only and the last time that parliament was elected according to this system (Freihat 2011: 307).

In 1993, the election law changed to the single non-transferable vote and remained in use until 2007. This law restricted voters to choose only one candidate, regardless of the number of parliamentary seats allocated to his district. The elections for the 12th parliament (on November 8, 1993) and then the elections for the 13th parliament (on November 4, 1997) were held according to this system. In 1997, the House of Representatives promulgated the temporary Election Law No. 24. This law maintained the one-vote system for voters, but it included an amendment related to the number of electoral districts, which increased from 20 to 21.

In 2001, Election Law No. 34 saw the light. The law increased the number of seats in the House of Representatives from 80 to 120, six of which were reserved for women even though they maintained the right to vote and compete over all the seats of the House of Representatives. In 2003, other amendments to the election law were issued, the most significant of which was the reduction of the number of parliament seats to 110 while the female quota was kept at six seats.

In 2010, the House of Representatives issued the temporary Election Law No. 9. Known as the "virtual electorate law". The law divided electoral districts into several sub-electorates equal to the number of seats allocated to the original electorate (the main electorate). A candidate could register in only one sub-electorate, while a voter could vote in any sub-electorate. The virtual districts were not based on official divisions, whether demographic or geographic, but were based on political considerations with the aim of dispersing the voices of the partisan opposition in their area of presence. While maintaining the basics of one-man one-vote, the new law changed how elections worked in multi-member districts. It divided them into multiple contiguous subdistricts, determined not by geography but by voter choice. Candidates chose which virtual subdistrict they would run in, and voters voted in the subdistrict of their choice. The 2012 election law eliminated this fictitious system and increased the number of seats in the House of Representatives from 120 to 150. The number of national seats out of the 150 was increased from 17 to 27 to be elected in a nationwide single district under a largest-remainder, closed-list proportional representation system. The number of seats allocated to the women's quota was increased to 15, and each voter was given two votes: one vote for the closed list and one vote for the electorate candidate. The primary concern relates to the fact that the legal framework for the parliamentary elections did not sufficiently address the need for a genuinely representative electoral system. The primary issues of contention – malapportionment and the single non-transferable vote (SNTV) – all remained in place for the 2013 parliamentary elections. This system favored tribal candidates over party-based ones and resulted in significant variance in the equality of suffrage for voters, especially in multi-member electoral districts. As a result, many who participated in the elections saw the electoral system as flawed, while many opposition forces refused to participate (Carter Center Report 2013).

The political movements, tribal youth, retired military officers and a wide range of opposition political parties led by the Islamists considered that the allocation of only 27 seats to national lists out of 150 seats was not in line with the reform process, calling for an increase in the seat numbers, while the process of calculating the winners of the district electorate lists faced widespread criticism, as candidates winning 40,000 votes gained one seat just like those that instead received 13,000 preferences.

In 2016, Election Law No. 6 was issued, and the proportional open list system was adopted; the number of parliament seats was reduced to 130 seats, and 15 seats were reserved for the women's quota. Parliamentary seats are allocated to the electoral district using the open proportional list method, the number of list members must not be less than three members and must not exceed the number of parliamentary seats allocated to the electoral district, and votes are equal to the number of seats allocated to the electoral district, provided that the votes for only one list of candidate lists (Aburumman 2017: 36–37).

The division of electoral districts in the Jordanian electoral laws

Although the Jordanian constitution does not address the issue of distributing or dividing electoral districts, it emphasizes equality and non-discrimination among Jordanians. Nevertheless, data show the government's manipulation of the division of electoral districts based on demographic, political and social reality (Bani Salameh and Edwan 2016). Re-designing districts in Jordan is not new, as the custom since the beginning of the kingdom's establishment has been to modify the number of parliamentary seats and to redistribute electoral districts in accordance with what the regime wants. Broadly speaking, the name of the game in Jordan has been to reduce the number of party representatives and independents opposing the government to the lowest level in return for increasing the number of pro-government loyalists, as the Jordanian identity and duality play (Jordanian–Palestinian) an important role in this, in addition to allocating fixed seats to the Jordanian clans (Bedouins of the north, center and south) and considering them independent electoral districts closed to Bedouins only.

Before parliamentary elections, the government usually divides the country into electoral districts and determines the number of seats for each of them according to a system. The core of the political forces' disagreements is on how to "adopt" districts; for instance, should the governorate constitutes one district, or should the governorate be divided into several electoral districts? The following table shows the number of seats in the Jordanian House of Representatives and the number of electoral districts for the period from 1989 to 2016.

Table 5.1 shows that the number of electoral districts in Election Law No. 23 from 1989 amounted to 20 electoral districts. In 1997, as mentioned previously, it was increased to 21 electoral districts, then it was increased according to the electoral laws issued since 1997–2001, or the so-called one-vote law, to 45. The one-vote law was supposed to be based on dividing the kingdom into electoral districts by the number of seats in the House of Representatives so

Table 5.1 The number of seats in the Jordanian House of Representatives and the number of electoral districts for the period of years from 1989 to 2016

Number	Governorate	1989 Law Number of constituencies	1989 Law Number of seats	2001 Law Number of constituencies	2001 Law Number of seats	Number Dropping of seats	2010 Law Number of constituencies	2010 Law Number of seats	2012 Law Number of constituencies	2012 Law Number of seats	2016 Law Number of constituencies	2016 Law Number of seats
1	Amman	5	18	7	23	5	7	25	7	22	5	29
2	Middle Bedouin	1	2	1	3	1	1	3	1	3	1	4
3	Al-Zarqa	1	6	4	10	4	4	11	4	11	2	13
4	Al-Balqa	1	8	4	10	2	4	10	4	9	1	11
5	Madba	1	3	2	4	1	4	4	2	4	1	5
6	Al-Mafraq	1	3	1	4	1	4	4	1	4	1	5
7	Northern Bedouin	1	2	1	3	1	3	3	1	3	1	4
8	Irbid	3	14	9	16	2	9	17	9	16	9	4
9	Ajloun	1	3	2	4	1	4	4	2	4	1	5
10	Jerash	1	2	1	4	2	4	4	1	4	1	5
11	Al-Karak	1	9	6	10	1	6	9	6	10	1	11
12	Al-Tafila	1	3	2	4	1	4	4	2	4	1	5
13	Ma'an	1	3	3	4	1	3	4	3	4	1	5
14	Southern Bedouin	1	2	1	3	1	3	3	1	3	1	4
15	Al-Aqba	1	2	1	2	0	2	2	1	2	1	4
Total		21	80	45	104		93	108	45	108	23	105
Women Seats		0	0		6			12		15 Women quota (27) National Electoral list		15
Total summation		21	45		110			120		150		130

Note: There are quotas for Circassians, Chechens and Christians within the quotas of the provinces that each electoral district had one representative, as is the case in Britain, to achieve justice and equality among citizens, and to encourage political parties.

In the 2010 law, which is the law of virtual constituencies, the number of sub-constituencies was increased to 93. Virtual constituencies do not depend on demographic or geographic divisions but rather divide the candidates into imaginary groups according to their choices, and the competition between them is carried out according to these groups, and a seat is created in each constituency for "fake" circles because they do not exist on the ground. The system did not give equal weight to the voters in many electoral districts, as in some districts you find a seat and in others two, three, four and five seats, the voter can select one candidate while other candidates win from his district and represent him without having a hand in deciding who represents him for these seats. In the general election law of 2012, the electoral districts went back down to 45 and then down again to 23 in 2016.

The rationale for the geographical division of electoral districts in Jordan

The Minister of Political Development stated in a press conference held on August 30, 2016, that three factors govern the process of dividing the electoral districts in the governorates: "demography, geography and development". How can this be verified?

Equitable distribution of electoral districts in Jordan

When it comes to the distribution of districts, the analysis of Table 5.2 shows three main points. First, the low level of representation in the three main governorates in Jordan – Amman, Zarqa and Irbid – emerges strongly. These are the governorates in which Jordanians of Palestinian origin are concentrated, and they are also the governorates in which elections are based on partisan bases away from sub-identities. It follows that such low representation limits the opposition. Second, the high level of representation in the governorates of Karak, Tafileh, Ma'an and Aqaba, where Jordanians are concentrated, boosts the numbers of pro-regime deputies. Finally, the high level of representation in the Bedouin areas, which are characterized by historical loyalty to the Jordanian political system, also boosts the regime, as elections are often held on tribal and sub-tribal identities.

The rate of variance in the division of electoral districts in Jordan

The most widely accepted rule for electoral districting is that districts must be relatively equal in population (Shawqi 2012), whereby representation by population is a fundamental principle of democracy, and constituencies of equal population are necessary for voters to have equal weight in the election process. Table 5.3 shows the rate of variance (deviation) in the distribution of electoral districts:

Two points emerge from looking at the deviation rate in the different governorates. First, the highest deviation rates were in the governorates of Ma'an and Tafileh, reaching about 10,000 voters in both governorates, with a very high deviation rate of 52% in the Ma'an governorate and 51% in Tafileh governorate. This is followed by the average percentage in the seats for the Bedouins in the north, south and middle (7,738 voters), with a deviation rate of 39%, then the Karak governorate (7,120 voters), with a deviation percentage of 36%, then the Capital governorate with a deviation rate of 30% and Mafraq with a deviation rate of 24%, and finally Zarqa with a deviation rate of 18%, which is a high percentage of deviation and indicates a poor distribution of electoral districts in provinces with large populations. Second, the lowest devia-

Table 5.2 Justice or misdistribution of electoral districts in Jordan

Governorates		Districts in Jordan	Number of voters	Polling percentage	Percentage of voters per seat per thousand	Distributive justice
Amman		28	707,977	43.5	25.280	Low level of representation
Al-Balqa		10	190,106	61.9	19.0	Balanced
AL-Zarqa		12	276,445	47.9	23.04	Low level of representation
Madba		4	71,731	69.8	17.925	Balanced
Irbid		19	451,360	59.4	23.752	Low level of representation
Al-Mafraq		4	58,817	73.6	14.700	High level of representation
Jerash		4	72,265	71.8	18.066	Balanced
Ajloun		4	71,048	70.9	17.750	Balanced
Al-Karak		10	122,907	71.1	12.300	Low level of representation
Al-Tafila		4	38,115	70.3	9.500	High level of representation
Ma'an		4	36,590	67.7	9.147	High level of representation
Al-Aqapa		3	41,630	62.4	13.870	High level of representation
Bedouins	Northern	3	58,867	75.4	19.620	Balanced
	Middle	3	41,790	74.7	13.930	High level of representation
	Southern	3	42,520	73.3	14.173	High level of representation
	Total	12	140,186	74.6	11.682	High level of representation
Total summation		117	2,272,182	56.7		

Source: Prepared by the author based on the data of the Independent Election Commission for 2013

Table 5.3 The rate of variance in the division of electoral districts in Jordan

Governorates		Districts in Jordan	Number of voters	Polling percentage	Percentage of voters per seat per thousand	deviation rate	Deviation %	The ratio of seats in each governorate to the total number of seats
Amman		28	707,977	43.5	25.280	5860	0.30	23.9
Al-Balqa		10	190,106	61.9	19.0	−420	−0.02	0.08
AL-Zarqa		12	276,445	47.9	23.04	3580	0.184	0.102
Madba		4	71,731	69.8	17925	−1495	−0.07	0.034
Irbid		19	451,360	59.4	23.752	−4332	−0.22	0.16
Al-Mafraq		4	58,817	73.6	14.700	4700	0.24	0.034
Jerash		4	72,265	71.8	18.066	1354	0.06	0.034
Ajloun		4	71,048	70.9	17.750	1670	0.08	0.034
Al-karak		10	122,907	71.1	12.300	7120	0.36	0.08
Al-Tafila		4	38,115	70.3	9.500	9920	0.51	0.034
Ma'an		4	36,590	67.7	9.147	10273	0.52	0.034
Al-Aqapa		3	41,630	62.4	13.870	5550	0.28	0.025
Bedouins	Northern	3	58,867	75.4	19.620	−200	−0.01	0.025
	Middle	3	41,790	74.7	13.930	5490	0.28	0.025
	Southern	3	42,520	73.3	14.173	5247	0.27	0.025
	Total	12	140,186	74.6	11.682	7738	0.39	0.102
Total summation		117	2,272,182	56.7		19420.3		100

Source: Prepared by the author based on the data of the Independent Election Commission for 2013

tion rates were in the governorates of Irbid, where it reached about 4,300 voters with a negative deviation of minus 22%, followed by the Madaba governorate (1,495 voters), with a negative deviation percentage of minus 7%, then the Al-Balqa governorate, with a negative deviation (420 voters) percentage of minus 2%.

The effect of the distribution of electoral districts on the outcomes of the electoral process

The delimitation of electoral districts is a strong geographic link between voters and their representatives, allowing the former to hold the latter accountable for their actions. In so doing, it shows the extent of equality in voting by comparing the proportion of voters to representatives across the various districts. The distribution of electoral districts in Jordan played an important role in limiting the success of parties or independents opposing governments. In the 1989 elections, there were 20 electoral districts and an open electoral system, which allowed the Jordanian Islamic Front and leftist parties to win 37 seats, and the strength of its composition and its political personalities characterized the 1989 parliament of (Al-Awamleh 2020: 780)

Because of local and regional circumstances and modifications, and the circumstances of the peace process that led to the Jordanian–Israeli peace agreement in 1993, which required a weak opposition, the government modified the electoral system and manipulated the distribution of electoral districts, giving the Jordanian regions and governorates dominated by the East Jordanian clans (Karak, Ma'an, Tafileh, Aqaba) a greater weight in the degree of representation. At the same time, the regime re-divided some districts in the densely populated Jordanian governorates like Amman, Zarqa and Irbid, where dual or sub-identities and political parties opposed to the regime are traditionally stronger. The outcomes of those elections led to a decline in the presence of Islamic, national and leftist parties and personalities in the Jordanian parliament at the expense of the emergence of non-partisan personalities and the growth of tribal, clan and regional identities, which in turn led to the formation of parliaments based on tribal and local representation and service-oriented representatives (Bani Salameh 2017).

In 2010, the government invented a fictitious district distribution system, where the original 23 districts were divided into 93 sub-electoral districts, the aim of which was to destroy the ability of any party to obtain a high percentage of parliamentary seats, in addition to making room for elite personalities figures of tribal and military career backgrounds (most of whom are loyal to the political system) can enter parliament and facilitate the work of Jordanian governments away from any real opposition.

In the 2012 elections, in which the fictitious sub-constituencies were abolished, the parties in the national list gained only 10 seats out of 27 because of the large number of lists. In addition, these lists and nominations were not limited to political parties. It was open in terms of candidacy on a national basis and not on a party basis (Abu Rumman 2014). Despite the amendment of the 2016 election law, which adopted the proportional representation system (the open proportional list), the results obtained by the parties were the opposite of what was expected, as the parties obtained 24 seats out of 130 seats, with a lower representation to the representation of parties in the 18th election (Al-Majali and Jawad 2016).

Conclusion

The choice of an electoral system is one of the most important institutional decisions for any democracy. It has a profound effect on the future political life of the country concerned. Since the beginning of the Arab Spring, Jordan has witnessed increasing demands for political and economic reforms from a widening set of opposition. Jordanians view electoral reforms as one of the most influential of all political issues and of crucial importance to meaningful political reform, but the regime does not respond positively to these demands, using the electoral system instead for manipulation. Throughout the history of the country, designing electoral districts (combined with other factors) has contributed to the survival of authoritarianism. The delimitation of the constituencies, as well as the number of seats per district, is determined by decree from the Cabinet of Ministers upon recommendation of the Ministry of the Interior. Neither the previous nor the current electoral law provides any criteria for the allocation of seats or the process of boundary delimitation. In sum, the electoral process in Jordan is characterized by fragility and immaturity. Continuing to change the electoral laws and electoral systems and the unfair distribution of electoral seats, on the one hand, and the continued tampering with the elections, on the other, has led to the loss of credibility of elections. Establishing the Independent Election Commission did not provide legitimacy to the electoral process. The commission was supposed to be responsible for the integrity of the electoral process, but it was not up to the level of ambition or responsibility, so it lost credibility and failed to build good relations with the main partners, especially political parties, civil society institutions and Jordanian society in general.

While it is argued that the electoral system will have a greater chance of being accepted as fair and legitimate if it is considered to work in an inclusive manner, all the electoral systems implemented in Jordan are perceived by voters to be unfair, and that the mechanisms of the electoral system, especially gerrymandering, overtly discriminate against specific groups in the society. Therefore, the ultimate success of the electoral reform in Jordan requires the passage of a new consensus-based election law to create a more representative electoral system that can serve as a genuine mechanism of democratic accountability and a venue for further reform. An electoral system that is more representative of the Jordanian population, while also suited to the political realities of the country. In accordance with good international practice, the drawing of electoral districts should be done at regular intervals in an impartial and transparent manner with the inclusion of different stakeholders, and should ensure equal representation. Despite some procedural improvements, the legal framework for the parliamentary elections does not sufficiently address the need for a genuinely representative electoral system. The primary issue of contention is malapportionment, a system favoring tribal candidates over party-based ones, which results in a significant variance in the equality of suffrage for voters, especially in multi-member electoral districts. As a result, many who participated in the elections see the electoral system as flawed, while many opposition forces refuse to participate. Significant reforms in the electoral process and the broader institutional structure are to move political reform forward in Jordan. International obligations do not stipulate the type of electoral system that should be used, but the electoral system and the delimitation of boundaries must uphold fundamental rights and freedoms, including universal and equal suffrage. Consequently, the desired electoral reforms are a test for both the legitimacy of the electoral process as well as for the broader democratic transition

During a quarter of a century after the adoption of the one-vote law and the accompanying manipulation of the divisions of electoral districts, parliamentary elections have not produced parliaments that are respected and accepted by Jordanian society. All government committees, seminars and dialogues failed to agree on a modern electoral law, a fair distribution of electoral districts and a full legal framework that works to ensure fair representation of citizens, the independence and integrity of the electoral process.

References

Abu Rumman, Hussein. 2014. *The Impact of the 2012 Election Law and the Distribution of Electoral Seats on the Representation of Political Parties in the House of Representatives.* Amman: Al-Quds Center for Political Studies.

Aburumman, Hussein. 2017. *The Impact of the 2016 Elections Law on the Structure and Performance of the Eighteenth Parliament.* Amman: Al-Quds Center for Political Studies, pp. 36–37.

Al-Awamleh, Raad Abdel Karim. 2020. 'The Role of Election Laws in Representing Political Parties in Parliamentary Assemblies in Jordan after the Democratic Transition (1989–2016)'. *Journal of Human and Social Sciences Studies* 47(1): 772–789.

Al-Deeb, Mohamed Mahmoud Ibrahim. 2008. *Geopolitics from a Contemporary Perspective.* Cairo: Anglo-Egyptian Library.

Al-Majali, Ayman and Al-Hamad Jawad. 2016. *The 2016 Jordanian Parliamentary Elections, a Political Study.* Amman: Center for Middle East Studies

Bani Salameh, Mohammed Torki. 2017. 'Political Reform in Jordan: Reality and Aspirations'. *World Affairs Journal* 180: 139–160. https://doi.org/10.1111/dome.12068

Bani Salameh, Mohammed Torki and Khalid Issa Edwan. 2016. 'The Identity Crisis in Jordan: Historical Pathways and Contemporary Debates'. *Nationalities Papers* 44(6): 985–1002.

Berelsons, Bernard and Paul Lazarsfeld. 1944. *The People's Choice: How the Voter Makes up His Mind in a Presidential Campaign.* New York: Columbia University Press.

Blais, Andre. 2000. *To Vote or Not to Vote? The Merits and Limits of Rational-Choice Theory.* Pittsburgh, PA: University of Pittsburgh Press.

Brown, Michelle and Ilana Krieger-Benson.2015. *Electoral Data Directory Google Inc.* Available at: https://openelectiondata.net/ar/guide/key-categories/electoral-boundaries.

Carter Center Report. 2013. *The Carter Center Releases Study Mission Report on Jordan's 2013 Parliamentary Elections.* Available at: https://www.cartercenter.org/resources/pdfs/news/peace_publications/election_reports/jordan-2013-study-mission-eng.pdf.

Cat, Helena, Andrew Ellis, Michael Maley, Alan Wall and Peter Wolf. 2014. *Electoral Management Design.* International Idea's Resources on Electoral Processes. Available at: https://www.idea.int/sites/default/files/publications/electoral-management-design-2014.pdf.

Duverger, Maurice. 1972. *Party Politics and Pressure Groups.* New York: Thomas Y. Crowell.

Freihat, Iman. 2011. 'The Historical Development of Election Laws in Jordan 1928–2011'. *The Jordanian Journal of History* 5(4): 98–160.

Gray, Mark and Miki Caul. 2000. 'Declining Voter Turnout in Advanced Industrial Democracies, 1950 to 1997'. *Comparative Political Studies* 33(9): 1091–1121.

Jacob, Hebert. 1964. The Consequences of Malapportionment, Note of Caution. *Social Forces* 43(2): 256–261.

Kamel, Osama. 2015. *Delimitation of Electoral Districts between International Standards and the Consequences of the Electoral Division Law in Egypt.* Cairo: The Egyptian Initiative for Personal Rights Center.

Karam, Jassim Muhammad. 1988. 'The Geography of Elections, Its Development and Methodology'. *Journal of Social Sciences, Kuwait University* 23(16): 167–190.

Kelly, Tania, Aqeel Abbas, Muneer Al-Mawri and Muneeza Hussein 2005. Elections and Electoral Systems. (In Arabic). *Journal of Democratic Papers* 4:18. Published by the Iraq Center for Democracy Information. On the following website: https://constitutionnet.org/sites/default/files/volume5web.pdf.

Kao, Christina. 2012. *The Electoral Law Crisis Continues, so what are the Elements of the Dispute and what is their Impact on the electoral Process?* (In Arabic). Beirut, Lebanon: Carnegie Middle East Center.

Lijphart, Arend. 1994. *Electoral Systems and Party Systems: A Study of Twenty-Seven Democracies, 1945–1990.* Oxford: Oxford University Press.

Nagler, Jonathan. 1991. 'The Effect of Registration Laws and Education on US Voter Turnout'. *American Political Science Review* 85(4): 1393–1405.

Salam, Mohamed Abdel. 2019. *The Geography of Elections between Theory and Practice.* Cairo: National Book House.

Shawqi, Tamam. 2012. The Mechanisms of Electoral Districts Division: A Theoritical Study. *Journal of Legal Sciences and Politics*, Volume 3 (June 5): 259–282.

6
ELECTIONS IN MAURITANIA
The role of the military

Raquel Ojeda-Garcia and Samara López-Ruiz

Introduction

The military has become a fixture in Mauritanian politics since the country's independence (N'Diaye 2017). The succession of *coups d'état* and attempts to interfere continued unabated until 2019. This became evident for the first time in 1978, only 18 years after Mauritania gained independence, with the *coup d'état* that deposed the first president, Mokhtar Ould Daddah. Between 1978 and 1984, there was one *coup d'état* and two failed attempts (Hochman 2009: 221). A military officer, the young commander Maaouya Ould Sid'Ahmed Taya (Marty 2002), led the *coup d'état* in 1984 and provided the longest period of presidential stability in the country. In 2005, another military coup put an end to Taya's regime after 21 years in power, and in 2008 a process of openness and liberalization that had begun only two years earlier was terminated with the inauguration of Mohamed Ould Abdel Aziz (2008–2019). This means that, except for 2019, every change in the presidency since 1978 has been brought about by a military intervention.

The opposition feared that Ould Abdel Aziz would run again in the 2019 presidential elections for a third term.[1] This was not the case and his party, the Union for the Republic (UPR), was represented by Mohamed Ould Ghazouani, the eventual winner. However, this simply demonstrates the fact that the military presence in government is not limited to periods of dictatorship or strictly military governments, as Ghazouani also held high positions in the military, serving as a general and defence minister under Ould Abdel Aziz. Nevertheless, he is the first president to fill the post without benefiting from any direct military intervention, although he had joined his former ally and predecessor, Ould Abdel Aziz, in the last two *coups d'état* in the country in 2005 and 2008. Actually, with Ghazouani as president, there was no inkling that his former comrade-in-arms (and government) would end up behind bars;[2] rather, a situation of continuity and control with the military elite at the helm of the country seemed more likely (Ojeda and López-Ruiz 2019).

Mauritania might be most clearly defined as a militarized semi-presidential system in which the institution of military presidents is quite stable, while the institution of the prime minister is unstable and of lesser significance. Given the difficulty in separating the military from Mauritanian politics – described as a 'restrictive and hegemonic pluralist authoritarian system' (Szmolka 2011) – this chapter explores the role of the military in the Mauritanian political system through an analysis of its elections. In line with Jourde (2005), who highlighted the need to study the inner workings of the institutions in authoritarian regimes that appear to be democratic, this chapter provides an analysis of the military as decision-makers in elections (Marty 2002; N'Diaye 2006).

To understand the extent of the power of the military in Mauritania and how it manages elections so as to remain in power (as in the last presidential elections in 2019), it is necessary to examine a number of elements that define the electoral process. The procedural elements of elections improve the legitimacy of the regimes applying them (Ani 2021). This means that the assessment of elections will be more positive if it focuses only on the fulfilment of their formal aspects.[3] From this perspective, Morse (2018: 712) also recognizes the 'democratic socializing' power of elections in terms of greater protection of individuals and civil liberties, an increase in public deliberation and a more equitable distribution of resources for authoritarian regimes.

It is necessary to analyse different dimensions of the political and electoral reality to understand the impact of the army on the system due. We therefore address the role of the military in electoral processes, but we also examine the space that the political parties occupy in the electoral system, and the degree of institutionalization of the party system, to discover whether the elections are free and fair. By the same token, by identifying and studying the electoral system and the presidential and legislative electoral contests, it becomes easier to understand the actions taken by the military to control the elections and how they remain a fixture in Mauritanian politics. This requires, most essentially, having in-depth knowledge of the guarantees that underpin electoral processes and the oversight institutions that review and control the procedures and results, like the Mauritanian National Independent Electoral Commission (CENI) and international election observers.

The political role of the military in the Arab World

In several countries in the Middle East and North Africa (MENA), the army often plays a crucial role in controlling the political system (Arlinghaus 2019), having a clear impact on election results. Indeed, Algeria, Turkey and Egypt are just some examples of other countries where the situation was – and in some cases still is – quite similar (Dekmejian 2021; Blaydes 2008; Lounici 2011). Military intervention to end a term of office or a dictatorship falls into two major categories: *coup d'état* or revolution (Bishara 2018: 12). Unlike revolutions, which involve military interventions for the purpose of overthrowing a political regime that it opposes and undertaking a process of radical socio-political change, *coups d'état* seek instead to overthrow an incumbent, without necessarily changing the regime. In other words, the aim is to change the leadership, although the action often turns into a struggle between factions within the army itself. Neither are coups with revolutionary ambitions free of risk, like the establishment of another authoritarian regime or descent into anarchy (Bishara 2018: 18). Moreover, if a civil ally does not back the military or the necessary links with political or social captors are not forged, the coup cannot be successful because it is impossible to give it continuity with a stable government. This was true in the case of the attempted *coup d'état* in Turkey in 2016, which failed, and the one in Egypt in 2013, which had the support of some of the most important political actors in the country.

While Basedau (2020: 1) has asserted that the democratization of soldiers and the maintenance of an army's loyalty towards a regime stabilize democracies, he also recognizes that in Arab countries, to date, the military has usually been one of the biggest supporters of autocratic regimes. Bishara notes several factors that must be considered when analysing the extent of an army's politicization and direct military intervention in politics: the degree of national cohesion provided by the army; its contribution to the construction and consolidation of the state; its rise or formation after independence; its relationship with or support of the president of the republic and the political parties; as well as any links the army has with neighbouring countries (Bishara 2018).

In some cases, the army serves as a vector for cohesion and the creation of a national identity; it has even contributed to the process of state-building (Bishara 2018). The social background of military personnel is another variable affecting their degree of politicization (Haddad 2012; Gaub 2014). The military does not only play a decisive role in leadership changes but also has veto power within the system, and it is able to design national and foreign policies autonomously (Basedau 2020). In the same respect, Gaub (2014) has observed that, even after 2011, armed forces in Arab countries have continued to be 'political agents'. In addition, the more that the military intervenes, the more it is believed that it should continue to intervene. The image of military personnel as guarantors of stability in the face of threats like ethnic divisions and religious radicalization reinforces its interventionism and direct actions in the political system (Kalu 2004).

Finally, according to Bishara (2018: 22, 23), the military struggle to control power is not based on a single ideological point of view opposed to moderate Islamism but is opposed to the fragility of a model of liberal democracy that is very weak or scarcely institutionalized in Arab countries. In short, there is an incompatibility between establishing a democratic model and the interventionism of the military in politics.

The party system

Elections in formal democracies are structured around political parties that represent and articulate the interests of citizens. The degree of institutionalization of the party system is a sign of a solid democratic political regime because it guarantees the participation and representation of the citizenry in political institutions (Cavatorta and Storm 2018). The Mauritanian party system has the following characteristics: high parliamentary fragmentation, high electoral volatility (Ojeda 2018: 366) and a high degree of politicians changing party affiliation. The most relevant parties are the Union for the Republic (UPR), Tawassoul, Union for Democracy and Progress, Rally of Democratic Forces (RFD), Union of the Forces of Progress (UFD), El Karam, National Democratic Alliance (AND), Action for Change, People's Progressive Alliance, Sawab, El Wiam, National Pact for Democracy and Development, IRA-Mauritania and AJD/MR.

The Union for the Republic (UPR) was created by Ould Abdel Aziz in 2009 to run for president. Since its creation, the party has won every election: the 2009, 2014 and 2019 presidential elections and the 2013 and 2018 legislative and local elections. One explanation for the party's striking electoral success is the fact that it 'absorbed' former leaders and members of dissolving parties like the Democratic and Social Republican Party (PRDS).

During the earlier transition period, Ould Abdallahi won the elections with the National Pact for Development and Democracy (PNDD), despite being a party with few social links and, moreover, one that was divided due to the presence of former members of the PRDS in its ranks; in fact, the PNDD occupied the space left by the PRDS on the political chessboard (Ould Khattat 2011). The PRDS changed its name to the Democratic Party for Democracy and Renewal (PRDR) and, in 2018, joined the majority UPR party to form a coalition that also included Democratic Renewal (RD), the Mauritanian Party for Unity and Change (HATEM-PMUC) and the Union of the Democratic Centre (UCD). Thanks to this coalition, the UPR was able to gain majority control of the National Assembly and executive branch.

Elections in authoritarian contexts show that the parties in government have more resources, in addition to controlling state institutions of coercion used in a patrimonial way (Mozaffar and Scarritt 2005: 415). Since independence, Mauritanian parties in government have always been led by a military man. Another characteristic is the weakness of the opposition and its lack of coordination. The opposition is in fact unable to create a common front with respect to the holding of elections, which are affected by fraud and unequal access to the media, amongst other shortcomings. For example, several Afro-Mauritanian voters are even left off the electoral rolls to stave off social demands that political elites are unable and unwilling to meet. Interestingly, the domination of Arab tribes over Afro-Mauritanians both in the social and the military spheres is reproduced in the political one.

Additionally, the structure of the Mauritanian National Independent Electoral Commission (CENI) before 2019 is useful for understanding the extent to which the military is capable of shaping the party system. The Commission is designed to guarantee clean, transparent elections, but its 11 members are all appointed by authorities with close ties to the UPR party. This means that military officers close to former President Abdel Aziz have a considerable say when appointing those who should guarantee control over the quality of democracy in the country. Specifically, the role and performance of CENI is particularly important in shaping the party system and its democratic health because of its role regarding the mobilization of financial resources. The CENI presents the electoral budget to the higher authorities of the state and prepares round tables with donors to participate in the financing of the election.[4] Therefore, the who, why and how members are selected is of great relevance in shaping electoral contests.

Politicians changing party affiliation and the creation of new parties between elections are two significant traits of the Mauritanian system and contribute to the low level of institutionalization in the party system, excessive personalization and, above all, few social bonds between the party and the electorate. The party in power takes this opportunity to co-opt members of failed parties or simply creates conflicts among leaders. In Mauritania, political nomadism contributes to the weakening of parties that are unable to take root in society. It also affects the stability and legitimacy of the government (Goeke and Hartmann 2011).

The lack of party system institutionalization strengthens the elites, and they are usually military officers who, in line with Gaub (2014), present themselves as guarantors of stability in the face of threats like ethnic divisions and religious radicalization and a shield against vagaries of democratic politics. This reinforces the military's interventionism and direct actions in the political system. Meanwhile, the stability the military seems to bring is reinforced by the weakness and confrontation that define the opposition.

Opposition parties create different coalitions to try to present a common front against the authoritarian drift of the regime. However, because of their lack of rootedness, ideological firmness and strong leadership, they do not pose a real threat to the military's control of public institutions. In short, the cleavages that underpin the party positions are not so much ideological as formed around fighting against an authoritarian leader. Only parties with stronger social bonds or some sense of tradition, like the Rally of Democratic Forces (RFD), Union of the Forces of Progress (UFP), Tawassoul, the Initiative for the Resurgence of the Abolitionist Movement (IRA-Mauritania), the People's Progressive Alliance (APP) and Don't Touch My Nationality (TPMN) have at different times been able to serve as interlocutors or challenge the regime (Ojeda and López-Ruiz 2019). As an Islamist party with strong social support, Tawassoul, along with IRA-Mauritania, which formed in response to the consequences of slavery and the marginalization of the Afro-Mauritanian people, are the leading components of the opposition and have had both a national and international impact. Tawassoul, which is currently led by the historic opposition figure Mohamed Jemil Ould Mansour, came together as a party to support

Biram Dah Abeid when he was imprisoned after running in the most recent legislative elections (August 2018).

The role of opposition parties is key to whether a system allows for real electoral competition and whether there is the possibility of government alternation and parliamentary control over the executive branch. In Mauritania, opposition parties have tried to create coalitions to counteract the power of the president, especially after Abdallahi was overthrown by Abdel Aziz. The Coordination of the Democratic Opposition (COD) was created in 2012 by the following parties: the Rally of Democratic Forces (RFD), the Union of the Forces of Progress, Tawassoul, the National Pact for Development and Democracy (PNDD-ADIL) and Alternative, or Al-Badil. However, just a year later, the first fracture appeared among opposition forces when the Coalition for a Peaceful Alternative decided to present candidates along with the COD. The new coalition included noteworthy parties that had been old travelling companions in opposition to Ould Taya, such as the People's Progressive Alliance (APP) led by Messaoud Ould Boulkheir, who had demanded rights for Afro-Mauritanians and the small parties, El Wiam and Sawab.[5] Boulkheir was not the only one who broke the mould; Tawassoul also ended up running in the 2013 elections, thus violating the boycott proposed by the COD. In addition to confusing the electorate, this produced deep mistrust in the other parties, emphasizing the competition between opposition parties than between the opposition and the party in government.

Not only did the coalitions that formed around the anti-president cleavage break, but also unexpected coalitions emerged, like the aforementioned Tawassoul and IRA-Mauritania alliance. Moreover, in the most recent presidential elections, Tawassoul – once the main opposition party in the era of Abdel Aziz – opted not to present its own candidate, deciding instead to support Ould Boubacar because of his personal prestige. Boubacar, who had filled several ministerial posts and was Mauritania's ambassador to Spain, has a reputation as a good clean technocrat.

Political actors and ethnic diversity

The root of the militarization of power is also due to the traditional tribal rule present in Mauritania (Milošević 2020; N'Diaye 2017). The difficult 'cohabitation' of the country's ethnic-cultural communities is seen as a critical challenge Mauritania has faced throughout its existence as an independent country.

The inability of political parties to represent the demands of citizens is aggravated in the case of Mauritania, as parties must also deal with a considerable degree of social heterogeneity and complexity. The Mauritanian social structure is highly fragmented (Freire 2014), but demands related to questions of identity are met with little or no response from politicians. Some argue that the salience of cultural diversity in most African states poses clear challenges to sustainable democracy (Young 1999). Along these lines, Shoup (2018) argues that in the face of social fragmentation – when ethnic polarization is high with more than two groups involved the political sphere – the chances of democratization are lower, and it does not get any easier when societies are dominated by praetorians (Fayemi 1998). For Shoup (2018), Mauritania is characterized by being less open and more restrictive of the organizational abilities of opposition groups, while simultaneously using coercion and fear to stop opposition activists and followers.

Nevertheless, the military had attempted in the past to generate some sort of cohesive identity. Ould Daddah, overthrown in a coup in 1978 (N'Diaye 2017), tried to forge a Mauritanian national identity, until he decided to introduce Arabic as a compulsory subject matter in the country's school system in 1966. Prior to the coups, the military was a small cohesive institution largely spared of the racial cleavage threatening the country. After the first coup, though, Ould Taya purposely exploited and exacerbated the process of 'de-professionalisation' of the army. Non-Arab military officers were purged in 1987 after their clumsy coup plot, and Ould Taya sought to 'Arabize' all branches of the armed forces, by sending select officers for training in military schools in Arab countries, accentuating their pollicization and the proliferation of Arab nationalist and Islamist groups in the army (Pazzanita 1992).

During the long tenure of Ould Taya's regime, he only exacerbated ethnic divisions. Human rights observers documented the extrajudicial killing of at least 500 black Mauritanians, most of whom were military men. Also, up to 120,000 black Mauritanians were stripped of their citizenship between 1989–1992. Later in his term in power, as Jourde (2001) documents, Ould Taya pursued policies of 'national reconciliation' aimed at co-opting the elites of victimized population, and he attempted to deal with the issue of slavery, although his regime formally denied it still existed. Ultimately, though, social and, importantly, racial fragmentation did not really diminish and according to N'Diaye (2017) Ould Taya ruled through 'divide and rule', as he identified and created frictions among and within tribes and ethnic groups to play one off against others.

Currently, there are movements and parties in Mauritania – IRA-Mauritania and *Touche Pas Ma Nationalité* – moving away from traditional social structures to question their 'exclusionary' effects in politics (Freire 2019). However, Mauritanian politics is shaped by the issue of ethnic heterogeneity. When the military was a small cohesive institution largely spared the racial cleavage, politicians tried to address and resolve ethnic problems, but when the military was de-professionalized and co-opted by mainly Bidan tribes, marginalization policies proliferated, increasing divisions between and within ethnic groups or tribes. This has profound effects on voting patterns and on the way in which political parties respond to cleavages.

Review and control institutions

Successful elections also depend on the officials in charge of setting them up and monitoring the process. Hence, the importance of educating and training individuals to fulfil this task (Maphunye 2017). Despite the efforts made by several NGOs and international foundations that organize training sessions for the administrative staff overseeing elections, this endeavour is not always sufficient, even more so in rural or remote areas of the country. Moreover, international election observers occasionally issue biased reports. The African Union, for example, has been identified by Ani (2021) as producing reports that emphasize the procedural elements of the elections without fully examining whether the guarantees of freedom, fairness and transparency were respected, to legitimize the regime.

The Mauritanian National Independent Electoral Commission (CENI) is one of the few tools that the opposition has access to in order to exercise some level of control over the quality of the democracy in the country, at least during elections. As briefly mentioned earlier though, the Commission used to have only 11 members, all appointed by the authorities with close ties to the party of former President Abdel Aziz, the Union for the Republic (UPR). After exerting pressure and reporting this fact, the opposition candidates managed to increase the number of members in the CENI and include members appointed by opposition parties, thus improving its representativeness and credibility.[6] In this way, the Commission can now serve as a Trojan horse for the opposition.

Voter shuttling by party activists is among the most common complaints made during elections. The fraudulent use of tents (*khaimas*) by candidates for propaganda purposes and to forge a closer personal relationship with voters has also been reported. Some, located next to polling stations, were open on election day in 2019 (Ojeda and López-Ruiz 2019). Additionally, UPR party activists have been reported for handing out ballots to voters with the name and photo of their candidate right before they went in to vote.

Electoral processes and regulation
Presidential elections

Presidential elections use a two-round majority system. In the authoritarian Mauritanian context, there is a clear tendency towards presidentialism; the head of state is completely overlooked, and parliamentary control is token (the Mauritanian National Assembly has had only one chamber since the last constitutional reform in 2017).

In the 2014 presidential elections, Ould Abdel Aziz won with an absolute majority, because no conditions were set for any candidate to compete (Diagana et al. 2016). Clearly, many candidates run in presidential elections in Mauritania,[7] despite the authoritarian context and the fact that campaign financing is private. The 'big man' theory popularized by Diamond explained this situation in which elections allow individuals to access the regime more than to contest it (Morse 2018: 713). Above all, candidates can participate in the partial division of resources through a patronage system, as Van de Walle notes (2003). In a context characterized more by ethno-linguistic differences than ideological ones, the possibility of obtaining benefits for the community the candidate represents helps to explain, as Mozaffar and Scarrit (2005) discuss, the high number of candidates with no possibility of winning. Moreover, the marked presidential nature of the Mauritanian political system favours personalism, as well as populist strategies (Mainwaring and Torcal 2005; Manning 2005).

The elections of 22 June 2019 introduced several changes (Antil 2019), most notably the constitutional limit of two terms for the presidency, which meant that Ould Abdel Aziz had to step down. The election was won by Ghazouani, with 52.01 per cent of the vote, and turnout was high (62.66 per cent). The results for the other candidates were as follows: Biram Dah Abeid, 18.58 per cent; Sidi Mohamed Ould Boubacar, 17.87 per cent; Kane Hamidou Baba, 8.71 per cent; and Mohamed Ould Maouloud, 2.44 per cent. Ghazouani won a majority in all the provinces except for Nouadhibou, where Biram came in first. With regard to the vote itself, there were two major changes: 1) 132,000 new voters were added to the electoral rolls; and 2) all eligible voters voted on the same day as the military for the first time since 1992. To that end, 3,800 polling stations opened their doors for the first round of the elections from 7 am to 7 pm that day.

Legislative elections

Ninety-eight political parties participated in the September 2018 National Assembly elections, including members of the opposition National Front for the Defense of Democracy (FNDU), a coalition that boycotted previous elections.

The 2017 constitutional reform dissolved the Senate, leaving the 157-seat National Assembly as the only legislative body. Members are directly elected for a five-year term in a mixed system of direct and plurality voting (proportional or majoritarian system related to the number of seats by constituency). Four members of the Assembly are directly elected by the diaspora (Freedom House 2021). A zipper system is included in party lists for large constituencies for alternating male and female candidates (UA 2019). In constituencies with three or two seats, women's representation must be guaranteed too.

The 2013 legislative, which should have taken place in 2011, were postponed several times due to the 2008 *coup d'état*. When the elections were finally held, the UPR won a resounding victory, due in part to the opposition's call to boycott the elections (Diagana et al. 2016). Specifically, the UPR won 51.7 per cent of the seats in the National Assembly (Ojeda 2015), with Tawassoul lagging far behind at 10.51 per cent.

The 2018 elections were controversial, but the opposition parties and international observers (Freedom House 2021) finally accepted the results. The governing party once again won the elections (Ojeda 2018), with the UPR coming in with 69.20 per cent of the votes, followed by Tawassoul with 19.47 per cent.[8] Although the opposition parties took part in the elections, the UPR continues to be the dominant party with a strong majority in the legislative elections; only in the local and regional elections was the opposition able to obtain better results (Freedom House 2021).

The year 2018 also saw the adoption of a decree by which the government of Ould Abdel Aziz was required to disband any political party that did not win at least 1 per cent of the vote in two consecutive elections. Consequently, in 2019, 76 parties were dissolved under this regulation (Freedom House 2021).

The political role of the military in Mauritania

From a historical perspective, Mauritania is an example of a country unable to fully break with the occupying colonizer's practices. The early years of the presidency of Mokhtar Ould Daddah were more in continuity with the French colonial structures and policies than in rupture with them, including the role of the army (Nwokedi 1989).

Eventually, Mauritania, like other countries in the MENA, started an Arabization policy of their structures to provide a differentiated identity. The beginning of the policy of Arabization focused on education, with compulsory classes in Arabic, but it also marked the beginning of the domination of the Arab tribes over the other communities, especially the Afro-Mauritanians. Consequently, in the case of Mauritania, the military does not represent unity or the creator of national identity; rather, it reproduces the ethnic conflict between the Bidan tribes and the ethnic Afro-Mauritanian communities (N'Diaye 2009, 2017; Boukhars 2012). The clear control of the army by the Bidan tribes has led to the ranks of the senior officials being purged of Afro-Mauritanians (N'Diaye 2009, 2017; Bouganour 2017) and fuelled the exclusion and marginalization of these sections of the population from positions of responsibility. Therefore, in Mauritania, Arabic is used to exclude Afro-Mauritanian communities from higher-ranking posts in the military. This is aggravated by the fact that the army is often the most organized, disciplined and well-funded institution and even, at times, the symbol of modernity, with tight control over the levers of the state.

On the other hand, the connections established between the members of the military who gain power and neighbouring countries play a role as well when analysing the interventionism of the military in politics. In this respect, the links between Ould Abdel Aziz and Morocco, where the leader spent a significant part of his military training, are well known. The experience with Arabization during training led many military officers to Iraq, Syria, Morocco and Algeria, contributing more to their politicization in Arab nationalism and even Islamism than to the professional aspects of their instruction (N'Diaye 2009: 134). Ould Taya, however, passed through different alliances. One of the most important, from an economic and military point of view, was with Libya under Muammar Gaddafi, whose economic successes had made the country a destination for Mauritanian migrants. However, on more than one occasion, this relationship was disrupted by the personal whims of the leaders. Additionally, this all took place in the context of the Maghreb, characterized by the conflict in Western Sahara between Morocco and the Polisario Front, a movement supported by Algeria.

The relationship between the military and the presidency of the republic is another important determinant of the degree of political interventionism. Mauritania has a semi-presidential system based on the French model, but with a heavy emphasis on the president, given the presidential powers recognized in the Constitution. Article 93 of the Constitution of Mauritania, amended in 2017, lists all the prerogatives and powers that determine the president's central role in the political sphere and his legal immunity.[9]

Given the institutional element of the configuration of the political system itself, the role of the military in the last 40 years has been determined by its effort to fill the position of the presidency of the republic, instead of supporting a particular president. In this way, the military can decide and execute policies and maintain the lofty aims of the presidency and the country's national identity and integrity. In fact, there is only one clear democratic interval in the political life of Mauritania: 2006 to 2008 (Aghrout 2008; Zisenwine 2007; Ojeda and López-Ruiz 2019). The democratic institutions elected between 2006 and 2007 survived only until 2008, when the military decided to act directly in August 2008 to intervene in the political system again. This brief period began with the establishment of a military junta after the 2005 coup, Military Council for Justice and Democracy (CMJD), led by Ely Ould Mohamed Vall. Ould Vall was also a military man, but he honoured the commitment that he made to his fellow citizens and the international organizations that supervised the process (the European Union, African Union and United Nations) to lead the country towards establishing genuine democratic institutions. After meeting the criteria set for the transition, the process resulted in elections qualified as free, fair and transparent (MOE-UE 2007). Moreover, none of the members of the junta ran for office in any of the three elections (local, general and presidential) between 2006 and 2007.

Indeed, Hochman (2009) described the 2005 coup as the 'Good Coup'. The author identified three reasons for the following *coup d'état*, which brought to an end the democratic interval: (1) widespread discontent about the failure of the three successive governments appointed by Abdallahi in only two years; (2) the presence of Islamists in the government; and, above all, (3) the removal of Ould Ghazouani as head of the armed forces and Abdul Aziz as chief of staff in a desperate attempt on the part of Abdallahi to hold on to power (Hochman 2009: 223).

The reaction of the two Mauritanian generals was immediate; Abdallahi and his prime minister, Yahya Ould Ahmed El Waghef, were removed from office in August 2008. Hochman cites political scientist Aqil Shah's observation that in the face of the inexperience of civil leaders, the military believes it has an obligation to intervene to protect the national interest. While the initial coup may be successful, it produces dynamics in which civilians find it difficult to recover their space. As pointed out in the previous analysis, the two main obstacles identified in the relationship between the military and civilians in Mauritania are the complex political system tilted towards strong presidentialism with a highly fragmented parliamentary system, and a divided, multi-ethnic society (Hochman 2009). Additionally, by appointing civilians to the position of prime minister, the semi-presidential system creates the illusion of democratization (Milošević 2020). However, the holders of the said position, usually do not really hold any real power. Moreover, staging a coup has the function of transforming military officers into politicians, and thus into acting civilian officials, blurring the line between the military and the civilians.

The weakness of the governments and prime ministers appointed by President Ould Abdallahi in 2007 and 2008 and, above all, the appearance of the recently legalized Islamist party, Tawassoul, on the scene (Buehler 2020), provided the perfect excuse for Ould Abdel Aziz and Ould Ghazouani to come to the fore in 2008. When the moderate Islamist party Tawassoul – which had a long background in politics and social activism but had been banned until

2007 (Ould Hamed 2008) – appeared on the scene, it highlighted the complicated relationship between the army and political Islam (Gaub 2014). In Mauritania, the fight against terrorism was used as an excuse to keep Tawassoul out of the government.

Concerning political parties, the influence of the military can also be identified. For example, the party created by Abdallahi, the National Pact for Development and Democracy (PNDD-ADIL), was harshly criticized for retaining members of the Democratic and Social Republican Party (PRDS) and incorporating them into the party ranks (N'Diaye 2009: 148). The PRDS, a political movement created by Ould Taya in 1991 (Bouganour 2017), was the dominant authoritarian party from the time of its creation and controlled all the electoral processes until 2005 (Ojeda 2015). The objective of the military in Mauritania, then, is not to support presidents but to overthrow them through direct intervention. Since the aim of military intervention is not a profound change in the political regime but, rather, a change in leadership, what is at play is clearly a *coup d'état* and not a revolution.

Conclusion

The three primary reasons for the continued leading role of the military in elections in Mauritania are: 1) the lack of party system institutionalization; 2) the weakness of a highly fragmented opposition unable to attract voters; and 3) ethnic and tribal conflicts, with their economic impact, social and political exclusion and the high percentage of voters outside the system. Equally important is the authoritarian nature of the political regime and its strong presidentialism, which prioritizes the role of political leaders who are incapable of forming long-lasting coalitions. This is especially true of those who tolerate the presence of the military, not as forces for political change, let alone regime change, but actors seeking to overthrow presidents anchored in power. In effect, then, what is 'institutionalized' in Mauritania is the presence of the military in power, with the consequent increased control over the other political and social actors.

Notes

1 A study published by the African Center for Strategic Studies on 18 African countries showed that regimes without formal limits on presidential terms are more unstable, with one third facing armed conflict (Ani 2021: 2).
2 At the time of writing (August 2021), the former president of the Islamic Republic of Mauritania, Ould Abdel Aziz, had been held in prison since June 2021, after being accused of embezzlement, money laundering and unjust enrichment in 2020. Sahara Médias (2021) 'La cour suprême confirme la décision du juge d'instruction à propos de la détention de l'ex-président'. 24 August 2021. https://cridem.org/C_Info.php?article=748342
3 The formal aspects are (1) deadlines for calling elections are respected; (2) free competition of all candidates and/ or parties in electoral campaigns; (3) organization of polling stations with voter lists; (4) publication of the results in a short period of time; (5) presence of review bodies and national and international electoral observation.
4 https://ceni.mr/fr/node/9
5 www.theodora.com/wfbcurrent/mauritania/mauritania_government.html
6 ceni.mr/fr/node/69 3/, accessed June 2019.
   www.rfi.fr/fr/afrique/20190504-mauritanie-ceni-integration-membres-opposition
7 There were 20 candidates in the 2007 elections, 9 in 2009, 5 in 2014 and 6 in 2019 (www.electionguide.org/elections/id/2393/, www.ndi.org/sites/default/files/MauritaniaElectionsBulletinIssueNo1_0.pdf).
8 www.electionguide.org/elections/id/2646/
9 Khabaz, Mohamed (2021) 'À propos de l'article 93 de la Constitution', 3 September 2021. https://cridem.org/C_Info.php?article=748698

References

Aghrout, Ahmed. 2008. 'Parliamentary and presidential elections in Mauritania 2006 and 2007'. *Electoral Studies* 27(2): 385–390.

Ani, Ndubulsi Christian. 2021. 'Coup or not coup: The African Union and the dilemma of popular uprisings in Africa'. *Democracy and Security* 17(2): 257–277.

Antil, Alain. 2019. 'Les évolutions paradoxales de la démocratie mauritanienne'. *Politique Étrangère* 84(2): 49–59.

Arlinghaus, Bruce E. (Ed.). 2019. *African Armies: Evolution and Capabilities*. London: Routledge.

Basedau, Matthias. 2020. *A Force (Still) to be Reckoned With: The Military in African Politics*. Hamburg: German Institute of Global and Area Studies (GIGA). Available at: https://www.giga-hamburg.de/en/publications/giga-focus/a-force-still-to-be-reckoned-with-the-military-in-african-politics.

Bishara, Azmi. 2018. 'The army and political power in the Arab context: Theoretical Issues'. *AlMuntaqa* 1(1): 11–37.

Blaydes, Lisa. 2008. 'Authoritarian elections and elite management: Theory and evidence from Egypt'. Paper presented at the *Princeton University* Conference on Dictatorships. Available at: https://www.princeton.edu/~piirs/Dictatorships042508/Blaydes.pdf.

Bouganour, Ismail. 2017. 'Civil society and democratic transformation in Mauritania: The paradigm of transition and the antecedents of political change'. *Contemporary Arab Affairs* 10(3): 372–391.

Boukhars, Anouar. 2012. 'The drivers of insecurity in Mauritania'. *Carnegie Endowment for International Peace*. Available at: https://carnegieendowment.org/2012/04/30/drivers-of-insecurity-in-mauritania-pub-47955.

Buehler, Matt. 2020. '"How does legalization alter Islamists" electoral strategies? A comparative study of Mauritania's Tawassoul party in the 2006 and 2013 local elections'. *L'Année du Maghreb* 23(23): 303–323.

Cavatorta, Fracesco and Lise Storm. 2018. *Political Parties in the Arab World: Continuity and Change*. Edinburgh: Edinburgh University Press.

Dekmejian, Richard. 2021. 'Egypt and Turkey: The military in the background'. In: Roman Kolkowicz and Andrzej Korbonski (eds.), *Soldiers, Peasants and Bureaucrats*. London: Routledge, pp. 28–51.

Diagana, Abdoulaye, Alain Antil and Céline Lessourd. 2016. 'Marches et grèves. Les tourments d'une gouvernance face aux tensions sociales et politiques (2014–2015)'. *L'Année du Maghreb* 15(15): 257–277.

Fayemi, J. Kayode. 1998. 'The future of demilitarisation and civil military relations in West Africa: Challenges and prospects for democratic consolidation'. *African Journal of Political Science/Revue Africaine de Science Politique*, 3(1): 82–103.

Freedom House. 2021. 'Mauritania: Country report 2021'. Available at: https://freedomhouse.org/country/mauritania/freedom-world/2021.

Freire, Francisco. 2014. 'Sahara migrant camel herders: Znaga social status and the global age'. *The Journal of Modern African Studies* 52(3): 425–446.

Freire, Francisco. 2019. 'Weapons of the weak, and of the strong: Mauritanian foreign policy and the international dimensions of social activism'. *The Journal of North African Studies* 24(3): 490–505.

Gaub, Florence. 2014. 'Understanding Arab armies: Agents of change? Before and after 2011'. *European Union Institute for Security Studies (EUISS)*. Available at: https://www.files.ethz.ch/isn/182218/Chaillot_Paper_131_Arab_armies.pdf.

Goeke, Martin and Christof Hartmann. 2011. 'The regulation of party switching in Africa'. *Journal of Contemporary African Studies* 29(3): 263–280.

Haddad, Bassam. 2012. 'Syria's state bourgeoisie: An organic backbone for the regime'. *Middle East Critique* 21(3): 231–257.

Hochman, Dafna. 2009. 'Civil-military power struggles: The case of Mauritania'. *Current History* 108(718): 221–226.

Jourde, Cedric. 2001. 'Ethnicity, democratization, and political dramas: Insights into ethnic politics in Mauritania'. *African Issues* 29(1–2): 26–30.

Jourde, Cedric. 2005. '"The president is coming to visit!": Dramas and the Hijack of democratization in the Islamic republic of Mauritania'. *Comparative Politics* 37(4): 421–440.

Kalu, Kalu. 2004. 'Embedding African democracy and development: The imperative of institutional capital'. *International Review of Administrative Sciences* 70(3): 527–545.

Lounici, Rabah. 2011. 'The relation between the military and the political in contemporary Algerian history'. *Contemporary Arab Affairs* 4(3): 288–300.

Mainwaring, Scott and Mariano Torcal. 2005. 'La institucionalización de los sistemas de partidos y la teoría del sistema partidista después de la tercera ola de democratización'. *América Latina Hoy* 41: 141–173.

Manning, Carrie. 2005. 'Assessing African party systems after the third wave'. *Party Politics* 11(6): 707–727.

Maphunye, Kealeboga. 2017. 'Straining without training? Capacity related problems facing African election executives and officials'. *International Journal of African Renaissance Studies - Multi-, Inter- and Transdisciplinarity* 12(1): 55–75.

Marty, Marianne. 2002. 'Mauritania, political parties, neo-patrimonialism and democracy'. *Democratization* 9(3): 92–108.

Milošević, Tanja. 2020. 'Presidential elections as a form of legitimization of power after coups d'état: Mauritania case study'. Available at: http://media1.naukaidrustvo.org/2021/03/broj-13-milosevic.pdf.

MOE-UE. 2007. 'Mission d'observation électorale-Union Éuropéenne: Rapport final. Elections municipales, législatives 2006 et présidentielles 2007'. *Nouackchott*. Available at: http://www.eods.eu/library/FR%20MAURITANIA%202006-2007_fr.pdf.

Morse, Yonatan. 2018. 'Presidential power and democratization by elections in Africa'. *Democratization* 25(4): 709–727.

Mozaffar, Shaheen and James Scarritt. 2005. 'The puzzle of African party systems'. *Party Politics* 11(4): 399–421.

N'Diaye, Boubacar. 2006. 'Mémoire et reconciliation en Mauritanie: Enjeux, intérêts et jeux d'acteurs'. *Cahiers d'Études Africaines* 50(197): 51–67.

N'Diaye, Boubacar. 2009. 'To 'midwife' – And abort – A democracy: Mauritania's transition from military rule 2005–2008'. *The Journal of Modern African Studies* 47(1): 129–152.

N'Diaye, Boubacar. 2017. *Mauritani's Colonels: Political Leadership, Civil-Military Relations and Democratization*. London: Routledge.

Nwokedi, Emeka. 1989. 'France's Africa: A struggle between exclusivity and interdependence'. In: R.I. Ralph Onwuka and Tim Shaw (eds.), *Africa in World Politics*. London: Palgrave Macmillan, pp. 180–197.

Ojeda, Raquel. 2018. 'Transformations in the political party system in Mauritania: The case of the Union for the Republic'. In Francesco Cavatorta and Lise Storm (eds.), *Political Parties in the Arab World: Continuity and Change*. Edinburgh University Press, pp. 252–275.

Ojeda García, Raquel. 2015. '¡Mauritania: Régimen autoritario y reconfiguración del sistema de partidos¡'. In: Inmaculada Szmolka (ed.), *Escenarios post-primavera árabe: Actores y dinámicas de cambio*. Madrid: Revista CIDOB d'Afers Internals, pp. 109–131.

Ojeda, Raquel and Samara López-Ruiz. 2019. 'Mauritania: ¿el fin de la era Abdelaziz?' *Afkar Ideas: Revista Trimestral Para el Diálogo Entre el Magreb, España y Europa* 60: 43–46.

Ould Hamed, Moussa. 2008. 'Menace terroriste en Mauritanie: Un cas d'école'. *L'Année du Maghreb* 4: 337–343.

Ould Khattatt, Mohamed. 2011. 'Pourquoi, à l'UPR, rien ne va plus ou presque?' *Chroniques Politiques Mauritaniennes*. Available at: https://chroniques-politiques-de-mkhattatt.blogspot.com/2011/07/pourquoi-lupr-rien-ne-va-plus-ou.html.

Pazzanita, Anthony. 1992. 'Mauritania's foreign policy: The search for protection'. *The Journal of Modern African Studies* 30(2): 281–304.

Shoup, Brian. 2018. 'Ethnic polarization and the limits of democratic practice'. *Democratization* 25(8): 1419–1440.

Szmolka, Inmaculada. 2011. 'Democracias y autoritarismos con adjetivos. La clasificación de los países árabes dentro de una tipología general de regímenes políticos'. *Revista Española de Ciencia Política* 26: 11–62.

Van de Walle, Nicolas. 2003. 'Presidentialism and clientelism in Africa's emerging party systems'. *Journal of Modern African Studies* 42(2): 297–321.

Young, Crawford. 1999. 'Case-studies in cultural diversity and public policy: Comparative reflections. In: C. Young (Ed.), *The Accommodation of Cultural Diversity*. London: Palgrave Macmillan, pp. 1–18.

Zisenwine, Daniel. 2007. 'Mauritania's democratic transition: A regional model for political reform?' *The Journal of North African Studies* 12(4): 481–499.

7

"ONLY ME"

Repression, legal engineering, and state-managed elections in Sisi's Egypt

Hesham Sallam

"If you really love Egypt … listen to only me", said President Abdel-Fattah Al-Sisi in a memorable televised remark in 2016. Al-Sisi's comment aptly summarizes the hallmarks of his rule: personalism, nationalist rhetoric, and a complete intolerance for opposing political viewpoints. The latter trend is heavily pronounced in the electoral arena, which the Sisi regime has structured to undermine opponents and reward allies. This chapter examines the strategies Sisi employed to shut serious competitors out of electoral contests, namely the 2014 and 2018 presidential elections, and the 2015 and 2020 legislative elections. It also identifies the political challenges and goals that shaped the regime's management of each of the four elections.

Background: Sisi's rise to power

Abdel-Fattah Al-Sisi ascended to power in the wake of a military coup that deposed President Mohamed Morsi on July 3, 2013. The coup ended Egypt's brief experiment with relatively competitive electoral politics and paved the way for a military-backed authoritarian regime with Sisi at its helm.

Sisi initially presented Morsi's ousting as an attempt at resetting the "transition". On the day of the coup, he announced a roadmap that suspended the 2012 constitution and gave presidential powers to the president of the Supreme Constitutional Court, Adly Mansour. Sisi outlined the steps for producing a new constitution and convening presidential and legislative elections. The following week, an interim government was sworn in, featuring individuals widely viewed as sympathetic to the Revolution of January 25. Appointed as vice president was Mohamed ElBaradei, who had come to symbolize demands for political change during the final years of Hosni Mubarak's rule. Senior military officials emphasized that they had no interest in staying in power, and Sisi vowed not to run for president. Some observers took these signals to mean that the army was—to borrow the words of then-US Secretary of State John Kerry—"restoring democracy" (BBC News 2013). The exact opposite was taking place.

As discussions about resetting the so-called transition were underway, the security establishment began repressing the Muslim Brotherhood and allies of the ousted president. The Brotherhood's top leaders, along with several thousands of the movement's members and supporters, were arrested and prosecuted on politically motivated charges. In August 2013, security forces used deadly violence to end pro-Morsi rallies in Rabaa Al-Adawiya and Al-Nahda squares, killing over a thousand people (HRW 2014a). Two months later, the interim president issued a protest law heavily restricting the freedom of assembly and enhancing authorities' power to repress and punish expressions of dissent. A host of prominent activists were detained and prosecuted based on that law (BBC News 2017). These include leaders of the April 6 Youth Movement, a major driver of anti-Mubarak protests in the lead up to the January 25 Uprising.

With this wave of repression in progress, a new constitution was approved by 98 per cent of voters in a popular referendum held in January 2014. The 2014 constitution propped up presidential powers to some degree and enhanced the military's role in selecting ministers of defence (ACRPS 2014). Sisi announced in the spring that he would resign from his military post and run for president (Tawfeeq and Gumuchian 2014), thereby confirming prior suspicions that he had been posturing to retain political power ever since orchestrating the coup. Sisi ended up winning nearly 97 per cent of the votes, defeating his sole challenger Hamdeen Sabbahi, a long-time Nasserist politician.

Upon assuming power, Sisi deployed the security apparatus to curtail political rights, undermine and jail his opponents, and establish control over media outlets. To support these efforts, the president adopted a series of anti-terror laws authorizing state punishment and prosecution of peaceful dissidents (TIMEP 2018). The regime's clampdown against its adversaries widened and intensified in 2017—the same year Sisi enacted a state of emergency—with numerous politicians and activists from across the ideological spectrum routinely prosecuted or imprisoned without charge. A year into Sisi's 2018 presidential re-election, his allies managed to pass a set of constitutional amendments that have afforded him the chance to stay in power until 2030. Legislative elections were convened in late 2020, resulting in even greater dominance by Sisi's allies in parliament.

The following sections examine the strategies Sisi's ruling establishment employed to eliminate political rivals from electoral competition and prevent pockets of opposition from emerging inside the legislature. It situates these strategies in Sisi's broader efforts to consolidate political power and manage various challenges to his rule.

The 2014 presidential election: political intimidation and media bullying

The context for the 2014 presidential election is the violent exclusion of the Muslim Brotherhood and its allies from the political sphere and the marginalization of political actors who had supported anti-military popular mobilization in the past. In the aftermath of the July coup, authorities arrested almost all Muslim Brotherhood senior figures, along with prominent allies of the movement. The state levelled politically motivated charges against them and used deadly violence to disperse pro-Morsi sit-ins and rallies. It also declared the Muslim Brotherhood and its political arm, the Freedom and Justice Party, terrorist organizations, banned them, and froze and confiscated their assets (Zollner 2019).

As Sisi's major rival, the Brotherhood was eliminated from the political scene, and the state was able to do without the ballot-fixing tactics it later adopted in the 2018 election, as described below. Still, compared to the previous one, the 2014 election was rife with barriers that made it harder for qualified opposition candidates to run. For instance, the 2014 presidential election law did away with a provision from the 2012 version allowing each political party to field its own presidential candidate, if it enjoyed representation in the last parliament. Under the new law, an individual could run for president in 2014 only if they gathered 25,000 citizen endorsements from 15 different governorates.[1] Indeed, the minimum number of signatures needed to qualify for candidacy was lower in comparison to that required by the 2012 election law (30,000) (Carter Center 2012). Yet, the new number was still a tall order for candidates who lacked access to large donors.

The extent to which state officials were involved in pressuring certain politicians to stay out of the race is unknown. In any case, Sisi's presidential bid and the political environment in which he announced it was enough to dissuade potential challengers from running. Shortly before Sisi's campaign commenced, the military issued a statement blessing the minister of defence's prospective presidential candidacy (BBC News 2014). The statement made it obvious to all observers that Sisi was the state's chosen candidate. Prior to that development, it had been unclear whether the military was prepared to tolerate some degree of competition in electoral politics—notwithstanding the exclusion of the Muslim Brotherhood. It was in that spirit of uncertainty that a host of prominent politicians expressed interest in running for president. After the military announced its support for Sisi, however, presidential hopefuls began dropping from the race.

Weeks after the said announcement, former Muslim Brotherhood member and Strong Egypt Party leader Abdel-Moneim Aboul-Fotouh revealed he would not run. Aboul-Fotouh, who ran for president in 2012, stated in one interview, "the military establishment's fielding of a candidate, regardless of my own opinion of him, means that there are no elections, and that the matter has already been settled" (Assabeel 2014). Expressing a similar sentiment, Khaled Ali announced his withdrawal from the race while arguing that the vote was nothing more than a theatrical production with a predictable outcome (DW 2014). Presidential hopeful and Mubarak's last prime minister, Ahmed Shafik, who had lost to Morsi by a small margin in 2012, stated that the military's endorsement of Sisi was a sign that it was preparing to rig the contest in favour of its chosen candidate (CNN 2014). Shafik's remarks came in a recorded private conversation that was leaked to the media. He dropped out of the race shortly after the recording surfaced.

Informing the scepticism of qualified contenders were the attacks that military-allied media waged against Sisi's challengers, whose integrity and patriotism was questioned. Among their top targets was former Army Chief of Staff Sami Anan, whom pro-Sisi commentators accused of doing the bidding of the Muslim Brotherhood.[2] Anan eventually dropped his bid, reportedly under pressure from the state (Hassan 2014). These developments were taking place in a political environment in which individuals contradicting the *de facto* official line that Sisi was Egypt's saviour and rightful leader were usually accused of being unpatriotic.

There were additional signs that the presidential election would be nothing more than window dressing for a preordained Sisi presidency. The state's management of the January 2014 constitutional referendum was one of such signs. In the lead up to the vote, authorities arrested activists campaigning on behalf of the "no" vote, whereas state allies were free to promote the draft constitution and slander its critics (HRW 2014b). In one telling incident, one provincial governor blatantly declared, "whoever votes 'no' to the constitution is a traitor" (Khalil 2014). Meanwhile, the state was using anti-terror laws to jail opponents and silence dissidents (El-Sadany 2014). Given this political climate, no serious presidential candidate was to believe that they stood a chance against Sisi, the state's *de facto* candidate. Ultimately, the only politician who agreed to play by the regime's rules and succeeded in getting his name on the ballot alongside Sisi was Hamdeen Sabbahi. Despite his decades-long history as an opposition politician, Sabbahi was by no means a serious challenger to Sisi.

Although a Sisi victory was practically guaranteed, the ruling establishment was clearly seeking more than just a routine victory. After all, the vote was an opportunity to bestow upon the coup a façade of popular legitimacy, and thus, there was real pressure for Sisi to win by an overwhelming margin with a significant turnout. It is perhaps for that reason that Sisi's campaign submitted over 180,000 endorsements in its official petition for candidacy, exceeding the legally mandated threshold (25,000) seven folds. Equally revealingly, both authorities and Sisi supporters stifled Sabbahi's campaign's efforts to gather and notarize endorsements (Lashin 2014; Al-Masry and Aly 2014), presumably to dwarf his perceived popularity relative to that of Sisi. Neither was it surprising that Sisi's allies were unsettled by reports of low turnout when voting was underway. In fact, alarmed pro-Sisi television commentators went as far as scolding viewers for not casting their votes.[3] Eventually, voting was extended for an extra day in the hope that more voters would show up. Finally, when Sisi was declared the winner with 97 per cent of the votes, the state-funded press emphasized that the votes he won were double those received by Morsi in the 2012 election (Ahmed 2014).

To recap, the 2014 presidential election was held in an exclusionary, repressive political environment in which the state signalled very clearly that Sisi was its chosen candidate. That reality dissuaded some competitive presidential contenders from running and intimidated others into dropping out of the race. The legal requirements for candidacy were somewhat restrictive to the extent that political parties with previous parliamentary representation were no longer allowed to field candidates, as was the case in the 2012 presidential election. Although Sisi emerged as the decisive winner, it was apparent that the election turnout did not meet the political leadership's expectations.

The 2015 parliamentary election: the fragmented parliament strategy

Even with the Muslim Brotherhood excluded from the political scene, the first parliamentary elections presented a major predicament for President Sisi. On the one hand, the roadmap announced after the 2013 coup mandated the convening of legislative elections within two months of the ratification of a new constitution.[4] By the time Sisi was sworn in as president, that deadline had already passed, and there was significant pressure to hold a parliamentary election without delay. On the other hand, the new president appeared reluctant to cede legislative power to the prospective parliament. The 2014 constitution gave the House of Representatives the power to withdraw confidence from the president and charge him with high treason, along with sufficient authority to force government resignations. Adding to Sisi's worries, the elected parliament was expected to vote to either approve or repeal the laws he and his predecessor had decreed after the coup. In other words, Sisi had reason to believe that the prospective legislature could have greatly impeded his presidency.

These concerns shaped the state's engineering of the election—or what I refer to as the "fragmented parliament strategy"—which sought to ensure that the legislature would be devoid of a majority bloc capable of challenging the president. Contributing to that strategy was the conspicuous absence of a ruling party akin to Mubarak's National Democratic Party (NDP). That is, a body that can organize regime allies and field candidates who strike the right balance between enjoying public credibility and demonstrating political loyalty to the regime. Although the Nation's Future Party (NFP) would later emerge as the ruling establishment's primary political arm, it had not been decisively tasked with that role prior to the 2015 legislative race. Put simply, lacking a reliable ruling party organization, Sisi was seeking to generate a parliament that was too disorganized to either block his legislative agenda or hold executive bodies to account.

The fragmented parliament strategy was equally apparent in Sisi's proclamations leading up to the election season. He called on all political parties to unite under a single electoral coalition in a veiled attempt to discourage any one political force from contesting a majority of the seats

(Al-Gali 2015). Efforts to devise a unified coalition had already kicked off in 2014 under the leadership of former Prime Minister Kamal Al-Ganzouri. Later, as these efforts proved unwieldy, the political leadership tasked the General Intelligence Services (GIS) with devising a pro-Sisi electoral alliance in collaboration with major political parties. The outcome was the "For Love of Egypt (FLE)" alliance. The FLE included the Al-Wafd Party, the GIS-linked NFP, and the Free Egyptians Party (FEP), which was then associated with business mogul Naguib Sawiris.

The fragmented parliament strategy was also enshrined in the design of the electoral system. Of all the seats up for grabs, about a fifth was designated for party-list races, compared to two-thirds in the 2011–2012 election. The other 80 per cent of the seats were filled through first-past-the-post individual candidacy (IC) races held in relatively small districts. Their reconfiguration in favour of IC races was significant. That arrangement was known to be advantageous to prominent local figures who normally run as non-partisan candidates (El-Shewy 2015). Politicians of such profile have historically sought to court rather than challenge authority, because they usually pursue locally oriented goals that rely on state patronage, as opposed to national agendas that are likely to provoke the ruling establishment. That is to say, the IC races were expected to generate predominantly non-partisan legislators unlikely to antagonize the government. Ultimately, the fragmented parliament strategy worked to the extent that no one party was able to pick up more than 11 per cent of the seats, and half of the parliament was occupied by lawmakers who had run as independents.

The electoral design was also tailored to limit the fortunes of independent political groups that could have run against the state-sponsored coalition. Potential competitors comprised three main communities: Islamist parties like the Salafist Al-Nour, Mubarak regime remnants and business associates who rallied around presidential hopeful Ahmed Shafik, and leftist and liberal parties that housed elements nominally associated with the January 25 Revolution like Al-Dostour, Al-Karama, the Socialist Popular Alliance (SPA), and the Egyptian Social Democratic Party (ESDP).

By replacing the proportional representation (PR) formula used in the 2011–2012 election with a winner-take-all (WTA) one, the 2015 election law made it virtually impossible for any party to enter parliament unless it joined the GIS-sponsored list. The most obvious political casualty of this change was Al-Nour, a Salafist party that generally advocates for a gradual Islamization of society and that has enjoyed a cooperative relationship with the state apparatus since its founding in 2011. Al-Nour's sizeable gains in 2011–2012 were in no small part the result of the PR formula, which enabled it to pick up seats in districts where it failed to secure a majority or plurality of the votes. Because the 2015 election law's WTA formula handed all the seats in each district to the list that secured the majority of the votes and none to second- or third-place winners, Al-Nour was unlikely to repeat the electoral gains it scored in 2011–2012.

The 2015 election law posed additional obstacles to Al-Nour. For instance, the law required each party list to meet certain quotas for the representation of women, Christians, workers and farmers, youth, Egyptians abroad, and persons with disabilities. Naturally, the quota for Christians was expected to disadvantage Islamist contenders, since they were expected to struggle in recruiting Christian candidates.[5]

To the shock of the regime, Al-Nour was able to meet the quota, but it was the target of a smear campaign in the media, accusing it of serving as a proxy for the Muslim Brotherhood (Al-Hanafy and Ghoneim 2015). During this same period, private individuals, likely at the behest of the regime, filed lawsuits petitioning authorities to dissolve Al-Nour on the grounds that it was formed on a religious platform in violation of the constitution (Makhlouf and Al-Qaranshawy 2015). Coinciding with the lawsuits was a broader campaign calling for banning all religious parties, including Al-Nour (Sarhan 2015). Unnerved by this political intimidation, Al-Nour withdrew from two (of the four) party-list races, and in the two it contested it ended up losing to the GIS-sponsored FLE (Bahgat 2016). While it managed to pick up a limited number of seats in the IC contests, its share of the elected seats amounted to a modest 2 per cent.

Another target of regime intimidation was the Ahmed Shafik-tied Egyptian Patriotic Movement Party, founded by supporters of the former prime minister. Seeing that prominent political and business figures were rallying behind the Shafik-supported "Egypt List", the regime began signalling publicly that the former prime minister was *persona non grata*, presumably to dissuade credible candidates from joining his list. In other words, even without formally excluding the Egyptian Patriotic Movement Party, the political leadership tacitly undermined it to drive politicians away from it.

As for smaller parties nominally associated with the goals of the January 25 Uprising, the road to parliament was much more difficult. For these parties, the election law was a major obstacle, as it made electoral districts immensely large. It divided the entire country into only four party-list electoral districts, each spanning several governorates. So even if these nascent, underfunded parties could recruit competitive candidates across such vast regions, they were unlikely to muster enough resources to campaign effectively in large districts. Campaign funding and candidate recruitment aside, the payoffs of contesting the party-list races were largely uncertain because with a WTA formula in place, securing seats required an impossible mission: defeating the state-backed list with a majority of the votes. The IC race may have offered a more viable path to parliament for these parties, since its districts spanned smaller geographical areas. But IC contests still presented an uphill battle because they often featured non-partisan candidates from among local notables who could not be easily defeated without both local support networks and, once again, a level of funding these parties were unlikely to possess. Exacerbating these difficulties was the prevalence of vote-buying in its various forms in IC races, which further undermined the electoral fortunes of these relatively young parties.

Thus, many of the parties that organized under the banner of the "Civil Democratic Movement", including Al-Dostour and Bread and Freedom, ended up boycotting the election in part due to what they viewed as an objectionable election law.[6] They had demanded amending it to allocate more seats for party-list races and reinstituting a PR formula along the lines of the 2011–2012 election, but to no avail (Samir 2016: 12; Al-Quds Al-Araby 2015). These parties' grievances did not stop at the election law. A major concern for them was the increasingly repressive environment in which the contest was scheduled to take place: the 2013 restrictive protest law, the prosecution of political dissidents, and security forces' chronic use of deadly violence against protesters and activists (Arabi21 2015).

The 2018 presidential election: brute force in the face of dissent

As the presidential election was about to kick off in the spring of 2018, the state had already spent years silencing dissidents and closing off political space. In contrast to the immediate aftermath of the 2013 coup when Sisi appeared widely popular, criticism of his policies became more visible in 2015 and 2016, even among social and political forces that once supported him. In February 2016, the Medical Doctors' Syndicate mobilized in protest of police brutality against medical professionals (CNN 2016). Months later, the government was under fire after security forces illegally stormed the Journalists' Syndicate to arrest writers accused of stirring up instability (BBC News 2016a). Protests ensued in large cities in November in response to deteriorating economic conditions (BBC News 2016b). These events were taking place against a backdrop of widespread anger at Sisi's decision to cede sovereignty over the islands of Tiran and Sanafir to Saudi Arabia (France24 2016). That move put the president in a particularly vulnerable position. Sisi had spent his first two years in office convincing the public that his primary mandate as president was protecting Egypt's national security from outside threats. Having relinquished sovereignty over the islands, Sisi was then forced to contend with those questioning his commitment to the patriotic mission he had set out for himself at the outset of his tenure.

With rising opposition, the president grew viscerally intolerant of criticism. Prosecution of political activists and forced disappearances of dissidents became routinized (Amnesty International 2016), and restrictions on the activities of civil society organizations and opposition movements grew markedly (Hamzawy 2017). In parallel, state control of the media tightened. In fact, starting in 2016, security agencies became heavily involved in the media sector not only by ways of regulation and censorship, but also through ownership and management (Reuters 2019b).

In this context, the possibility of allowing a prominent challenger on the 2018 presidential election ballot was out of the question. Facing off with an unfriendly challenger would have forced Sisi to defend his performance and unpopular policies. On a more fundamental level, the very idea of pitting the president against a capable politician risked shattering Sisi's image as a national hero and an unmatched statesman who stands above the fray of conventional politics. Accordingly, in the months leading up to the vote, the political leadership engaged in blatantly aggressive ballot-fixing, robbing the electoral process of the slightest hint of democratic appearance. Every competitive candidate who tried to get on the ballot was eliminated through repression and intimidation. Among them was Ahmed Shafik, who was pressured by officials to drop his presidential bid.

That former military officials like Shafik were seeking to enter the race was a disturbing development for Sisi, because it implied that the military establishment was not unified in its support for the president. During the years preceding the election, Sisi was seemingly preoccupied with pre-empting political challenges from military and intelligence bodies (Gamal 2021). That trend was most visible in the GIS, which the president perceived as a site of subversive potential. He purged the agency's senior leaders and replaced them with a cadre of loyalists, including his own son Mahmoud (Reuters 2019a). Sisi's obsession with competing centres of influence inside military bureaucracies likely deepened his own perception of the threat emanating from the former officers who announced their intent on running for president.

For Sisi, the candidacy of another officer was also threatening because having multiple contenders with a military background raised an uncomfortable question within the ranks of the armed forces. That is, whether their interests would be better served under a military-tied president other than Sisi. Given these stakes, the political leadership was more than alarmed when former Army Chief of Staff Sami Anan revealed his intention to run for president in a widely publicized video statement in January 2018. The statement criticized Sisi's foreign and domestic policies, as well as his overreliance on the military in governing the country. In a show of confidence, Anan called on state institutions to behave impartially toward all candidates, including the current president, while implying that there was a good possibility Sisi would be leaving office at the end of the race.[7] The Sisi regime's response was decisive and unforgiving. Anan was arrested and referred to military prosecution on the grounds that, as a member of the military reserves, he was not authorized to run for public office (Mada Masr 2018). Anan was kept in detention and would not be released until late 2019. Members of his presidential bid team were prosecuted, imprisoned, and, in one case, violently beaten up.

Anan was not alone in suffering the wrath of military prosecution. Joining him was army Colonel Ahmed Konsowa who released a video statement in late November announcing that he would run for president, while criticizing prevailing economic and social policies. Within a few weeks, a military tribunal handed Konsowa a six-year prison sentence for expressing political views in uniform—an act that was deemed a violation of military rules.

To avert a similar fiasco from occurring in the future, Sisi eventually made it even harder for military affiliates and retirees to run against him. In June 2020, he signed a law barring both current and former members of the armed forces from running for public office without prior approval from the military (France24 2020). But as far as the 2018 race was concerned, the intimidation, prosecution, and imprisonment of multiple candidates sent the message loud and clear: the race is closed off to real competition, and the state is not interested in salvaging any pretensions of impartiality.

In mid-January, the leader of the Reform and Development Party, Mohamed Anwar Al-Sadat, dropped his presidential bid. Al-Sadat cited the underlying restrictive political climate, while noting that the authorities made it difficult for him to gather the endorsements necessary to qualify for running (Ghali 2018). Similarly, presidential hopeful Khaled Ali announced his withdrawal from the race, arguing that there was no longer an opportunity to use the election to advance popular aspirations for change (CNN 2018). Accompanying Ali's withdrawal from the race was a wider call for a boycott from the Civil Democratic Movement, which includes the SPA, Al-Karama, Al-Dostour, and the Bread and Freedom parties. The coalition described the election as an "absurd theatrical play", as evidenced by the lack of candidates and the absence of legal guarantees (BBC News 2018).

By the time election season was about the commence, the state had succeeded in preventing every potential contender from running against Sisi, who was therefore poised to run unchallenged. Whereas that reality reinforced the regime's narrative that the president was a legendary leader whom no politician could dare challenge, pressure from the US Government forced Sisi to backtrack on that arrangement and find someone who could run against him. Otherwise, the argument went, it would have been embarrassingly obvious to Sisi's critics in Washington that the entire electoral process was a complete sham (Soliman 2018). And thus, Sisi embarked on a desperate (and dark comedic) search for a "pretend challenger". The first contender for the job was Al-Wafd Party leader Al-Sayyid Al-Badawy, who enjoyed a cooperative relationship with the regime. According to the election law, for an individual to qualify for running, they had to obtain either 25,000 public endorsements, as was the case in 2014, or endorsements from 20 lawmakers. Given that Al-Wafd had over 30 deputies in the House of Representatives, getting Al-Badawy on the ballot seemed quite feasible. Certainly, the Al-Wafd chief was not a perfect choice, because, at that point, the party had already announced that it would not field a presidential candidate and that it would endorse Sisi instead. Yet Al-Badawy seemed receptive to filling the role of pretend challenger and took steps to prepare for running. Al-Wafd's Supreme Council, however, would not play along. It voted down the proposal for Al-Badawy to run, largely out of concern that the move would give the party the stigma of being the president's "political extra". With Al-Badawy out and the official deadline to apply for candidacy only a few days away, Sisi was left in a precarious position.

Ultimately the regime managed to recruit an alternate: Moussa Mostafa Moussa, a politician with a rich history of collaboration with security agencies (Abu-Shanab and Gawish 2008). Getting Moussa on the ballot required asking legislators who had already endorsed Sisi to withdraw their endorsement of the president and redirect it to Moussa so that he can meet the official requirements for candidacy (Soliman 2018). The plan was messy, but it ultimately worked, and Moussa managed to apply for candidacy minutes before the official deadline closed. Moussa still was not able to save the election from embarrassment and mockery. It was crystal clear to all observers that, notwithstanding the regime's pretend challenger, Sisi was, in effect, running unopposed. And when the election results were announced, with Sisi winning 97 per cent of the vote, many commentators baulked at the fact that there were more invalid ballots in the election than there were votes for Moussa (Al-Gamal and Al-Issawi 2018). Others questioned the official turnout figure, 41 per cent, which did not align with reports of largely empty polling sites (Ketchley 2021).

In sum, the 2018 presidential election reflected the Sisi regime's preoccupation with silencing criticism and pre-empting potential challenges from within military and intelligence bodies. Thus, compared to its conduct in the 2014 presidential race, in 2018, the state was much more heavy-handed in eliminating its opponents and fixing the candidate list.

The 2020 parliamentary elections: the party-centred strategy

By the time legislative elections were about to kick off in 2020, the regime had already abandoned the fragmented parliament strategy of the 2015 election. Certainly, the previous strategy had some success in limiting the representation of independent parties, none of which were able to form a legislative bloc large enough to threaten the ruling establishment. Yet as time passed, it became apparent that the GIS-engineered parliament was not as politically pacified as the political leadership had hoped. Even without effective partisan blocs, parliament still had a vocal, albeit small, group of lawmakers who caucused under the banner of the "25–30 Alliance"[8] and tried to challenge the government's positions on a variety of occasions. Although its interventions never stifled Sisi's agenda meaningfully, the Alliance generated a spectacle of opposition the regime was clearly uncomfortable with (Al-Fadali 2018).

The prospect of having a similarly pronounced voice of dissent inside the next parliament was particularly troubling for the political leadership, especially after expressions of popular anger surfaced in 2019. In addition, the president was also showing unease with the incompetence of the regime's parliamentary interlocutors and their inability to manage differences among the ruling establishment's allies (Mada Masr 2019). In other words, the time was ripe for a change in course and with it a new approach to engineering the next parliament.

Replacing the 2015 fragmented parliament plan was a party-driven strategy that sought to achieve a decisive legislative majority through the NFP, which by 2020 became a major vehicle for organizing pro-Sisi elements. The appeal of that approach stemmed in part from the regime's interest in asserting greater control over its own allies and containing the growing visible rivalries among their ranks—tasks that the NFP appeared well-placed to handle. The NFP also seemed a useful instrument for integrating politically valuable stakeholders into Sisi's circle of support, especially prominent political and business families once tied to the Mubarak ruling establishment (Mada Masr 2020a). Thus, as the 2020 legislative election neared, businessmen formerly associated with the defunct NDP were gaining visible roles inside the NFP, including Mohamed Aboul-Enein, who became the party's vice president.[9]

Elevating the NFP's role was not the only element of the party-centred strategy. The regime was also using other political parties to prop up the parliamentary representation of pro-Sisi forces. In addition to the NFP, the regime threw its support behind the security apparatus-linked Republican People's Party (RPP) (Diab 2021), the retired generals-led Homeland Defenders Party (HDP), as well as smaller parties housing disparate elements that hailed from the former ruling NDP.

The party-centred strategy was institutionalized in the 2020 parliamentary election law, which awarded half of the elected seats to party-list races (compared to one-fifth in 2015), with the other half designated to first-past-the-post IC races. The new electoral formula reflected the extent to which the security establishment's grip over party life had tightened since the previous election cycle. And therein lay the key difference between the regime's approaches to the elections in 2015 and 2020, respectively.

In 2015, the political leadership viewed the realm of party politics with a high degree of scepticism, hence its attempts to limit all parties' legislative representation through the fragmented parliament strategy. In 2020, on the other hand, the regime dealt with parties with greater confidence, having successfully neutralized the oppositionist inclinations that permeated many of them. For example, pro-Sisi forces gained complete control over Al-Wafd in 2018 when Sisi's ally and cheerleader, Bahaa Abu-Shoqqah, became party president (Al-Mawqif Al-Misry 2020). Two years earlier, pro-regime leaders in the FEP began antagonizing party affiliates who voiced opposition to government policies (Assaad 2017). By the 2020 election season, the party, which once controlled the largest bloc in parliament, fell into political oblivion due to these internal divisions and the defections they prompted (Ahmed 2020).

The meddling of Sisi's security establishment in the internal affairs of political parties in recent years is not unlike the notorious conduct of the security apparatus during the Mubarak era. The surfacing of these similarities was perhaps the logical outcome of the shifting balance of power inside Sisi's security sector. In 2018, Sisi awarded the National Security Agency (NSA) a greater role in managing domestic political files previously designated to the GIS but that the latter had not handled as effectively as the president would have liked. Legislative elections comprised one such file. Unlike the GIS, the NSA, formerly known as the State Security Investigations Service, had a long experience under Mubarak in directing opposition parties from behind the scenes and striking covert electoral bargains with their leaders. Accordingly, once Sisi developed an interest in controlling independent political parties and pressuring them into executing his own electoral schemes, it was only natural for him to lean on the NSA's help more heavily.

It must be emphasized, however, that asserting Sisi's dominance over party politics took a lot more than just infiltrating parties and co-opting their leaders. It also involved multiple rounds of repression against the president's rivals. For example, after detecting an opposition effort to devise an electoral coalition for the 2020 parliamentary race, authorities arrested over a dozen activists and organizers in the summer of 2019. Defendants were prosecuted on fabricated charges of "terrorism" in what became known as the "Hope Alliance case" (Mohie 2021).

According to the Arabic Network for Human Rights Information, in March 2020, every opposition party had at least several members and/or leaders behind bars for politically motivated reasons. These include Al-Dostour, the SPA, Al-Karama, the ESDP, Bread and Freedom, and Strong Egypt (ANHRI 2020). For some observers, authorities intentionally targeted individuals with known credentials as lead campaigners and coalition-builders for the purpose of stifling the growth of opposition forces and isolating them from their "movers and shakers" (Mada Masr 2020c). Beyond the imprisonment of political activists, pro-regime elements were filing lawsuits seeking the dissolution of opposition parties, including the Strong Egypt and the Bread and Freedom parties (Daaarb 2021). In other words, the context for the 2020 legislative election was one in which licensed independent parties were fighting for their own survival, with no real opportunities to organize and compete effectively in electoral contests.

What was equally significant is that the heightening repression of prominent opposition figures coincided with the political leadership's efforts to build its own cadre of loyal politicians and public servants through state-sponsored youth programmes and associations (Brown and Berlin 2020). Sisi, in other words, was putting his own house in order just as he was working actively on undermining and weakening his opponents' organizational capacities. Put simply, well before the 2020 election, the regime had been structuring the political field to its own advantage. And when the race for parliament came, there was no real political force that could have challenged the state-sponsored coalition.

With all the cards in Sisi's hands in 2020, there was no mystery surrounding the outcome of the election. The lack of uncertainty was the product of not only the repression and co-optation of the opposition but just as equally of a carefully engineered electoral design. Half of the seats up for grabs were due to be elected through four unusually large party-list districts, which, as was the case in 2015, spanned several governorates. Given the inordinate size of the districts, there was virtually no chance for any opposition group to singlehandedly recruit enough candidates from across the vast regions each of these districts covered. And if any of them did, they could not have possibly mustered enough resources to launch a cross-governorate campaign capable of competing with the well-funded state-sponsored coalition.

Indeed, had the seats been distributed according to a PR formula, opposition parties may have stood a chance, since, under such an arrangement, they conceivably could have won seats even if they ended up in second or third place in the vote tally. But the regime had no interest in making the party-list races competitive. Instead, it wanted to make them as arduous as possible for independent parties so that they would have no choice but either to drop out or join the state-sponsored "National List", which, thanks to the WTA formula, was poised to sweep all the seats.

The regime's scheme worked. The sole list that ran in all four party-list races was its own National List. While a few independent lists contested these races on paper, major opposition parties either steered clear of the party-list races or gave into regime pressure and joined the National List—that is, capitulated to the state's own terms and conditions, as described below. Those that did not run for the list races include Al-Nour, which contested the IC seats instead. Al-Dostour boycotted the election altogether (Talab 2020), whereas the SPA, Al-Karama, and Bread and Freedom endorsed a limited number of candidates in the IC races (Salama 2020). The parties that chose to play by the regime's rules and joined the National List, Al-Wafd, the ESDP, Al-Tagammu, and Al-Adl were each allowed 21, 7, 5, and 2 candidates, respectively. The bulk of the 284 candidate slots on the National List went to the NFP (145), the RPP (28), and HDP (19), and the rest was divided among smaller parties linked to the defunct NDP (Rabie 2021).

Within this picture, it becomes embarrassingly clear that as far as any independent party was concerned, getting a parliamentary seat through the party-list races had nothing to do with running a campaign or reaching out to voters. Rather, it entailed negotiating with the security apparatus behind closed doors to get on the regime's National List. Stated differently, despite the façade of competitive, multi-party elections, the ruling establishment was in complete control of who gets to enter parliament and who is left out. For independent parties that agreed to join the National List, the terms of participation were both unfavourable and undignified, as only candidates who were preapproved by security agencies were permitted to run. In some cases, parties were shocked to learn that their proposed list of candidates was basically discarded by the regime, which instead picked outsiders to run on these parties' own behalf. What gave the regime greater latitude in picking and choosing each party's candidates was the fact that it managed to cultivate a network of loyalists at various opposition parties through the political parties' Youth Coordination Committee. The Committee comprised young leaders from a range of political parties and was one of the multiple initiatives the ruling establishment used to recruit dependable political collaborators under the guise of youth empowerment (Al-Ahram 2019). A handful of the Committee's members ran on the National List representing various political parties (Mada Masr 2020b).

The real uncertainty in the 2020 House of Representatives election rested in the IC races, which comprised the other half of the elected seats. In 2020, the number of seats allotted to IC decreased to 284, compared to 448 in 2015. Accordingly, the districts for these races increased in size significantly, which marked a major setback for the opposition. The resizing, as many opposition candidates protested, handed the edge to state-linked wealthy candidates who were more likely to have the financial means to campaign across large regions and set up vote-buying machines (Salama 2020). Adding to the opposition's woes, the regime was pursuing IC seats more aggressively than it did in the 2015 election. Whereas in 2015, the fragmented parliament strategy left the opposition some wiggle room in the IC races, in 2020, the regime was actively working on securing a majority of these seats for the NFP and thus was bound to marginalize opposition and independent candidates.

As anticipated, the results of the IC races spoke to the regime's shifting strategy. The NFP ended up with nearly 60 per cent of these seats, whereas "independent" candidates got only a quarter of them, compared to half in 2015 (Rabie 2021). Meanwhile, the seven lawmakers who comprised the "25–30 Alliance" lost five of their seven IC seats (Gawish 2020). Parties not sponsored by the state apparatus performed rather poorly. In fact, the only parties that won IC seats were the ones that participated in the state-tied National List. The only exception to that trend was Al-Nour, which secured only seven seats. State differently, parties that were not "preapproved" by the security apparatus largely failed to score any victories in the IC contests.

The combined outcome of the IC and party-list races was a parliament controlled by the NFP, which received 55 per cent of the elected seats. The intelligence-tied RPP took 8 per cent, and the HDP and Al-Wafd got 4 per cent each. Each of the remaining parties' share of the elected seats did not exceed 2 per cent. Pro-regime forces comprised a decisive majority in the new legislature and, outside of the NFP, there were no partisan blocs that wielded enough seats to threaten the government's agenda. Accompanying NFP's victory was a reduced representation of independent lawmakers from 325 in 2015 to 93 in 2020. That decline was consistent with the shift in the regime's electoral strategy from a "fragmented parliament" in 2015 to the party-centred approach it adopted in the 2020 contest.

Conclusion

Since the July 3, 2013, coup, Sisi has worked to erect a highly exclusionary political field structured to limit competition against him and his allies. Repression and intimidation tactics have remained central elements in the Sisi regime's management of electoral politics. The regime has also employed a variety of legal engineering tactics to make it impossible for independent political parties to compete effectively in electoral contests without prior negotiations with security officials. The regime's reliance on coercion in managing electoral competition expanded between the two presidential elections of 2014 and 2018 in part due to challenges posed by military figures who sought to enter the race, coupled with growing signs of opposition and popular discontent. Sisi began his presidency with a clear aversion to political parties, as reflected in his management of the 2015 legislative election. Yet the growing dominance of the security apparatus over the realm of party politics through repression and co-optation allowed the regime in the 2020 election to use trusted parties to advance its own electoral schemes. The future of that trend will largely depend on the role the regime will assign the NFP, which remains more of a political arm for the security establishment and less of a ruling party that organizes the country's governing class and political elite.

Notes

1 Each of these governorates must contribute at least 1,000 signatures to the 25,000 required ones (Carter Center 2014).
2 See for example, September 2013 *ONTV* segment, available online at <www.youtube.com/watch?v=e_Wlu9chnIk>

3 See for example, May 2014 *Al-Jazeera* report on Egyptian media's response to the low turnout in the Egyptian presidential election, available online at <www.youtube.com/watch?v=Jt_hnbGAg2o>
4 See unofficial translation of the July 8, 2013 Constitutional Declaration, available online at <www.refworld.org/cgi-bin/texis/vtx/rwmain/opendocpdf.pdf?reldoc=y&docid=5491883b4>
5 The investigative reporting of Hossam Bahgat (2016) indicates that regime insiders were not expecting Al-Nour to be able to meet that requirement.
6 Some like-minded parties including the Socialist Popular Alliance and the Egyptian Social Democratic Parties boycotted the party-list races but contested a limited number of individual candidacy seats.
7 The full video can be accessed online at <www.youtube.com/watch?v=fT8MAs2oE-A>
8 The name references the uprisings of January 25, 2011 and June 30, 2013.
9 Ilhamy Al-Mirghani (2020) discusses the expanding profile of former NDP figures and their families inside the Sisi regime's political machine. In one notable incident, an NDP figure who was campaigning on behalf of NFP candidates in the 2020 election season outrightly said that the NFP was basically the "new NDP" (Mada Masr 2020d).

References

Abu-Shanab, Fatima and Mohamed Gawish. 2008. 'Ihtiraq maqar al-Ghad bi-wasat al-Qahirah baʿd maʿrakah bi-l-mulutuf bayn jabhatay Ayman Nur wa Musa Mustafa'. *Al-Masry Al-Youm*, November 7. Available at: https://www.almasryalyoum.com/news/details/1931574.

ACRPS. 2014. *Dustur bi-l-ghulbah: 'Nazrah muqarinah bayn dustur 2012 wa mashruʿ dustur 2014'*. Doha: Arab Center for Research and Policy Studies. Available at: https://www.dohainstitute.org/ar/lists/ACRPS-PDFDocumentLibrary/document_5E5B2A92.pdf.

Ahmed, Makram Mohamed. 2014. 'Al-Sisy raʾisan li Misr'. *Al-Ahram*, June 3. Available at: https://gate.ahram.org.eg/daily/News/21202/11/291578/الأعمدة/السيسى-رئيسا-لمصر.aspx.

Ahmed, Mohamed. 2020. 'Baʿd tasaduruhu barlaman 2015: Kayf inhar hizb al-Misriyyin al-Ahrar'. *Arabi21*, September 26. Available at: https://arabi21.com/story/1303173/بعد-تصدره-برلمان-2015-كيف-انهار-حزب-المصريين-الأحرار

Al-Ahram. 2019. 'Tansiqyat shabab al-ahzab wa al-siyasiyyin taʿqid salunaha al-siyasy bi-maqar hizb al-tajammuʿ'. *Al-Ahram*, October 12 Available at: https://gate.ahram.org.eg/News/2292302.aspx.

Al-Fadali, Abdel-Aziz. 2018. 'Takatul "25–30"'. *Raseef22*, August 15. Available at: https://raseef22.net/article/159306-تكتل-30-25-قصة-تحالف-المعارضة-الوحيد-في-بر

Al-Gali, Mohamed. 2015. 'Al-Sisy yubdi istiʿdadih daʿm qaʾimah muwahadah li kul al-ahzab fi intikhabat majlis al-nuwab'. *Youm7*, May 27. Available at: https://www.youm7.com/story/2015/5/27/السيسى-يبدى-استعداده-دعم-قائمة-موحدة-لكل-الأحزاب-فى-انتخابات/2200229

Al-Gamal, Ahmed and Ahmed Al-Issawi. 2018. 'Al-Natijah al-kamilah li-intikhabat al-riʾasah 2018'. *Al-Shorouk*, April 2. Available at: https://www.shorouknews.com/news/view.aspx?cdate=02042018&id=d61cd700-f410-46d5-b539-4a2f56e48649.

Al-Hanafy, Heba and Reda Ghoneim. 2015. 'Hizb Al-Nur wa al-Sisy'. *Al-Masry Al-Youm*, October 22. Available at: https://www.almasryalyoum.com/news/details/831483.

Al-Masry, Ayman and Mohamed Aly. 2014. 'Hamlat Sabahy: Tajawuzat ansar al-Sisy mahzalah wa intiqadat Mubarak Wisam'. *Al-Araby Al-Jadid*, April 3. Available at: https://www.alaraby.co.uk/حملة-صباحي-تجاوزات-أنصار-السيسي-22%مهزلة-22%وانتقادات-مبارك22%وسام22%.

Al-Mawqif Al-Misry. 2020. 'Al-Mawqif Al-Misry Facebook Post'. *Facebook*, October 24. Available at: https://www.facebook.com/almawkef.almasry/photos/2942061409227070.

Al-Mirghani, Ilhamy. 2020. 'Khalfiyat walimat Ashmun: Muhawalah li-l-bahth'. *Ahewar*, August 12. Available at: https://www.ahewar.org/debat/s.asp?aid=688168&t=4.

Al-Quds Al-Araby. 2015. 'Misr: Islamiyyun wa libraliyyun yuqarurun muqataʿat al-intikhabat al-barlamaniyya'. *Al-Quds Al-Araby*, February 14. Available at: https://www.alquds.co.uk/%EF%BB%BFمصر-إسلاميون-وليبراليون-يقررون-مقاط/.

Amnesty International. 2016. *Egypt: 'Officially, You Do Not Exist'; Disappeared and Tortured in the Name of Counter-Terrorism*. London: Amnesty International. Available at: https://www.amnesty.org/en/documents/mde12/4368/2016/en/.

ANHRI. 2020. 'Fi-l-sijun waraqat mawqif fi-l-rad ʿala suʾal: Ayn al-ahzab al-madaniyya'. *ANHRI*, March 17. Available at: https://www.anhri.info/?p=15350.

Arabi21. 2015. 'Itisaʿ muqataʿat al-intikhabat bi Misr baʿd indimam hizb sadis'. *Arabi21*, February 8. Available at: https://arabi21.com/story/808859/اتساع-مقاطعة-الانتخابات-بمصر-بعد-انضمام-حزب-سادس.

Assaad, Karim. 2017. 'Hin taʾkul al-ahzab abaʾaha: Qisat itahat al-Misriyyin al-Ahrar bi-Sawiris'. *Ida2at*, January 1. Available at: https://www.ida2at.com/the-story-of-the-sawiris-overthrow-by-almasreyeenalahrrar/.

Assabeel. 2014. 'Abu al-Futuh: Intikhabat al-riʾasah mahsumah'. *Assabeel*, February 20. Available at: https://assabeel.net/news/2014/02/20/أبو-الفتوح-انتخابات-الرئاسة-محسومة.

Bahgat, Hossam. 2016. 'Anatomy of an election'. *Mada Masr*, May 14. Available at: https://www.madamasr.com/en/2016/03/14/feature/politics/anatomy-of-an-election/.

BBC NEWS. 2013. 'Egypt army, "restoring democracy", says John Kerry'. *BBC News*, August 1. Available at: https://www.bbc.com/news/world-middle-east-23543744.

BBC NEWS. 2014. 'Al-Jaysh al-misry yunashid al-Sisy al-tarashuh li-l-riʾasah'. *BBC News*, January 27. Available at: https://www.bbc.com/arabic/middleeast/2014/01/140127_egypt_sisi_army_statement.

BBC NEWS. 2016a. 'Niqabat al-shafiyyin al-misriyya tutalib bi-iqalat wazir al-dakhliyya ithr iqtiham maqaraha'. *BBC News*, May 2. Available at: https://www.bbc.com/arabic/middleeast/2016/05/160501_egypt_press_syndicate_strike.

BBC NEWS. 2016b. 'Misr: Al-miʾat yahtajun ʿala tarady al-awdaʿ al-iqtisadiyya fi ma atlaq ʿalihi nushataʾ thawrat al-ghalabah'. *BBC News*, November 11. Available at: https://www.bbc.com/arabic/middleeast-37951468.

BBC NEWS. 2017. 'Alaa Abdel Fattah: Egypt court upholds activist's sentence'. *BBC News*, November 8. Available at: https://www.bbc.com/news/world-middle-east-41915250.

BBC NEWS. 2018. 'Ahzab misriyya tuqarir muqataʿat intikhabat al-riʾasah al-muqbilah'. *BBC News*, January 30. Available at: https://www.bbc.com/arabic/middleeast-42872494.

Brown, Nathan J. and Mark Berlin. 2020. 'Steering the wide Egyptian state: Ideology or administration?' *Carnegie Endowment for International Peace*, May 28. Available at: https://carnegieendowment.org/2020/05/28/steering-wide-egyptian-state-ideology-or-administration-pub-81924.

Carter Center. 2012. *Presidential Election in Egypt Final Report, May–June 2012*. Atlanta: The Carter Center. Available at: https://www.cartercenter.org/resources/pdfs/news/peace_publications/election_reports/egypt-final-presidential-elections-2012.pdf.

Carter Center. 2014. *Carter Center Statement on the Legal and Political Context of Egypt's Presidential Elections*. The Carter Center. March 16. Available at: https://www.cartercenter.org/resources/pdfs/news/pr/egypt-05162014.pdf.

CNN. 2014. 'Ahmad Shafiq yuqir bi sihhat tasjil hajam fih al-Sisy'. *CNN*, March 12. Available at: https://arabic.cnn.com/middleeast/2014/03/13/shafik-easd-record.

CNN. 2016. 'Alaaf al-atibaʾ yantafidun did iʿtidaʾat al-shurtah al-misriyya'. *CNN*, February 12. Available at: https://arabic.cnn.com/middleeast/2016/02/13/egypt-doctors-police-tensions.

CNN. 2018. 'Khalid ʿAly yatarajaʿ ʿan al-tarashuh li-intikhabat al-riʾasah al-misriyya'. *CNN*, January 24. Available at: https://arabic.cnn.com/middle-east/2018/01/24/egypt-presidential-elections-khalid-ali-out.

Daaarb. 2021. 'Bayan min Al-ʿAysh wa-l-Huriyah hawl qadiyat hazr al-hizb'. *Daaarb*, June 3. Available at: https://daaarb.com/بيان-من-العيش-والحرية-حول-قضية-حظر-الح/.

Diab, Mostafa. 2021. 'Munir al-Shurbagy aminan ʿaman li-hizb Al-Shaʿb Al-Jumhury fi Shamal Saynaʾ'. *Al-Dostor*, April 30. Available at: https://www.dostor.org/3439788.

DW. 2014. 'Al-Nashit al-misry Khalid ʿAly: Lan akhud 'masrahiyat' al-intikhabat al-riʾasiyya'. *DW*, March 26. Available at: https://www.dw.com/ar/الناشط-المصري-خالد-علي-لن-أخوض-مسرحية-الانتخابات-الرئاسية/a-17500004.

El-Sadany, Mai. 2014. 'Legislating terror in Egypt'. *Tahrir Institute for Middle East Policy*, July 19. Available at: https://timep.org/esw/articles-analysis/legislating-terror-in-egypt/.

El-Shewy, Mohamed. 2015. 'Sisi's parliamentary fears'. *Carnegie Endowment for International Peace*, May 6. Available at: https://carnegieendowment.org/sada/59276.

France24. 2016. 'Misr: Iʿtiqal al-ʿasharat min al-mutazahirin did itifaq tarsim al-hudud al-bahariyah maʿa al-Suʿudiyya'. *France24*, April 15. Available at: https://www.france24.com/ar/مصر-مظاهرة-تفريق-شرطة-السعودية-تيران-صنافير-20160415/.

France24. 2020. 'Al-Sisy yusadiq ʿala qanun yashtarit muwafaqat al-jaysh ʿala tarashuh dubatuh li-l-riʾasah'. *France24*, July 29. Available at: https://www.france24.com/ar/السيسي-يصادق-على-قانون-يشترط-موافقة-الجيش-على-ترشح-ضباطه-للرئاسة-20200729/.

Gamal, Mahmoud. 2021. 'Al-Sisy wa siyasat al-haymanah ʿala qiyadat al-jaysh'. *Egyptian Institute for Studies*, June 16. Available at: https://eipss-eg.org/السيسي-وسياسات-الهيمنة-على-قيادات-الجيش/.

Gawish, Mahmoud. 2020. '25–20 yahzur ʿala aʿdaʾuh al-qawaʾim wa yakhud al-nuwab fardiyan'. *Al-Masry Al-Youm*, September 6. Available at: https://www.almasryalyoum.com/news/details/2029447.

Ghali, Mina. 2018. 'Muhamad Anwar al-Sadat yuʿlin tarajuʿhu ʿan khawd al-intikhabat al-riʾasiyya'. *Al-Masry Al-Youm*, January 15. Available at: https://www.almasryalyoum.com/news/details/1245489.

Hamzawy, Amr. 2017. 'Legislating Authoritarianism: Egypt's New Era of Repression'. *Carnegie Endowment for International Peace Report* (March). Available at: https://carnegieendowment.org/files/CP_302_Hamzawy_Authoritarianism_Final_Web.pdf.

Hassan, Aly. 2014. 'Tafasil ijtimaʿ al-saʿat al-6 li iqnaʿ Samy ʿAnan bi-l-tarajuʿ ʿan al-tarashuh li-l-riʾasah'. *Youm7*, March 13. Available at: https://www.youm7.com/story/2014/3/13/تفاصيل-اجتماع-الساعات-الـ6لإقناع-سامي-عنان-بالتراجع-عن-الترشح/1555109.

HRW. 2014a. 'All According to Plan: The Rabʿa Massacre and Mass Killings of Protesters in Egypt'. Human Rights Watch. August 12. Available at: https://www.hrw.org/report/2014/08/12/all-according-plan/raba-massacre-and-mass-killings-protesters-egypt.

HRW. 2014b. 'Misr: Iʿtiqal nushataʾ bi tuhmat al-tarwij li "la"'. Human Rights Watch. January 12. Available at: https://www.hrw.org/ar/news/2014/01/12/252324

Ketchley, Neil. 2021. 'Fraud in the 2018 Egyptian presidential election?' *Mediterranean Politics*, 26(1): 117–129.

Khalil, Mohamed Mahmoud. 2014. 'Muhafiz al-Qaliyubiyya: Man yaqul la li-l-dustur khaʾin wa ʿamil'. *Al-Masry Al-Youm*, January 9. Available at: https://www.almasryalyoum.com/news/details/372989.

Lashin, Sameh. 2014. 'Hamlat Sabahy tuʿlin al-qabd ʿala ʿadad min aʿdaʾaha'. *Al-Ahram*, April 1. Available at: https://gate.ahram.org.eg/News/474225.aspx.

Mada Masr. 2018. 'Former Armed Forces chief of staff arrested, referred to military prosecution after announcing presidential bid'. *Mada Masr*, January 23. Available at: https://www.madamasr.com/en/2018/01/23/news/u/former-armed-forces-chief-of-staff-arrested-referred-to-military-prosecution-after-announcing-presidential-bid/.

Mada Masr. 2019. 'A presidential directive to freeze parliament'. *Mada Masr*, October 1. Available at: https://www.madamasr.com/en/2019/10/01/feature/politics/a-presidential-directive-to-freeze-parliament/.

Mada Masr. 2020a. 'Senate elections: How we moved backward'. *Mada Masr*, August 7. Available at: https://www.madamasr.com/en/2020/08/07/feature/politics/senate-elections-how-we-moved-backward/.

Mada Masr. 2020b. 'The cost of playing monopoly: How the Nation's Future Party has caused rifts among parties in House elections'. *Mada Masr*, October 1. Available at: https://www.madamasr.com/en/2020/10/01/feature/politics/the-cost-of-playing-monopoly-how-the-nations-future-party-has-caused-rifts-among-parties-in-house-elections/.

Mada Masr. 2020c. 'Limadha tusharik ahzab al-muʿaradah fi intikhabat al-nuwab 2020?' *Mada Masr*, October 21. Available at: https://www.madamasr.com/ar/2020/10/21/feature/سياسة/لماذا-تشارك-أحزاب-المعارضة-في-انتخابا/.

Mada Masr. 2020d. 'Intikhabat: Mustaqbal Watan yatabaraʾ min qiyady wasafuh bi-l-Hizb Al-Watany al-jadid'. *Mada Masr*, October 25. Available at: https://www.madamasr.com/ar/2020/10/25/feature/سياسة/انتخابات-مستقبل-وطن-يتبرأ-من-قياد/.

Makhlouf, Mostafa and Shaimaa Al-Qaranshawy. 2015. 'Al-Idariyah al-ʿuliya taqdy bi ʿadam jawaz ihalat daʿwa hal hizb al-Nur'. *Al-Masry Al-Youm*, July 5. Available at: https://www.almasryalyoum.com/news/details/768527.

Mohie, Mostafa. 2021. 'Hossam Moanis: A backstage force in oppositional politics'. *Mada Masr*, January 7. Available at: https://www.madamasr.com/en/2021/01/07/feature/politics/hossam-moanis-a-backstage-force-in-oppositional-politics/.

Rabie, Amr Hashem. 2021. 'Natʾij intikhabat al-barlaman al-misry wa taʾthirataha al-muhtamalah fi ʿadaʾih wa ʿilaqatih al-mustaqbaliyah bi-l-hukumah'. *Emirates Policy Center*, January 20. Available at: https://epc.ae/ar/topic/results-of-egyptian-parliamentary-elections-potential-impact-on-its-performance-and-future-relationship-with-government.

Reuters. 2019a. 'Hakatha shadad Al-Sisy qabdatuh ʿala al-hukm fi misr'. Reuters. August 1. Available at: https://www.reuters.com/article/egypt-governance-ab6-idARAKCN1UR4D9

Reuters. 2019b. 'Al-Sisy yuwasiʿ hamlat al-tadiq li-tashmal khisman jadidan'. Reuters. December 2. Available at: https://www.reuters.com/article/egypt-media-ia6-idARAKBN1YG1C8

Salama, Ahmed. 2020. 'Darb yarsud istiʿdadat al-muʿaradah l-intikhabat al-nuwab'. *Daaarb*, September 30. https://daaarb.com/درب-يرصد-استعدادات-المعارضة-لانتخاب/.
Samir, Mina. 2016. *Muqataʿat al-intikhabat*. Cairo: Arab Forum for Alternatives. Available at: http://www.afalebanon.org/wp-content/uploads/2018/02/YYYYYY_YYYYYYYYYY.pdf.
Sarhan, Hamam. 2015. 'Hizb al-Nur'. *Swissinfo*, September 8. Available at: https://www.swissinfo.ch/ara/مع-ق-رب-انتخابات-مجلس-النواب-في-مصر-حزب-النور-بين-تمثيل-الإسلام-السياسي-و-دعاوى-الحل/41623046.
Soliman, Asmahan. 2018. 'How Sisi has been sidelining his opponents'. *Mada Masr*, February 10. Available at: https://www.madamasr.com/en/2018/02/10/feature/politics/analysis-how-sisi-has-been-sidelining-his-opponents/.
Talab, Ibtisam. 2020. 'Al-Dustur yuʿlin muqataʿat al-intikhabat al-barlamaniyah'. *Al-Masry Al-Youm*, September 22. Available at: https://www.almasryalyoum.com/news/details/2043486.
Tawfeeq, Mohammed and Marie-Louise Gumuchian. 2014. 'Egypt's El-Sisi to resign, paving the way for presidential bid'. *CNN*, March 26. Available at: https://www.cnn.com/2014/03/26/world/meast/egypt-sisi-resignation/index.html.
TIMEP. 2018. *Egypt Security Watch: Five Years of Egypt's War on Terror*. Washington, DC: The Tahrir Institute for Middle East Policy. Available at: https://timep.org/wp-content/uploads/2018/07/TIMEP-ESW-5yrReport-7.27.18.pdf.
Zollner, Barbara. 2019. 'Surviving repression: How Egypt's Muslim Brotherhood has carried on'. *Carnegie Endowment for International Peace*, March 11. Available at: https://carnegie-mec.org/2019/03/11/surviving-repression-how-egypt-s-muslim-brotherhood-has-carried-on-pub-78552.

PART 2

Elections in democratic and quasi-democratic settings

8
ISRAEL'S ELECTORAL SYSTEM AND POLITICAL INSTABILITY

Electoral fragmentation, party unity, and the prime minister's political leadership

Maoz Rosenthal

Introduction

From its establishment in 1948 and until June 2021, Israel went through 24 parliamentary elections and the formation of 36 governments. Thus, on average, Israel holds elections about once every three years, while new governments are sworn in on average about once every two years. Furthermore, in multiparty parliamentary systems a coalition of parties (or cabinets) forms the government. When a party joins or leaves the coalition, its cabinet changes (Müller et al. 2008: 6). By September 2019, Israel saw 76 different government cabinets,[1] reflecting the fact that parties enter and leave Israeli government coalitions at a pace that exceeds any other average per-year rate documented by PARLGOV, a leading data-based observer of parliamentary democracies (Döring and Manow 2020).

Israel has numerous social and political cleavages: doves and hawks, Jews of varying religiosity levels, Arabs and Jews, rich and poor, and different ethnicities within the Jewish population (Arian and Shamir 2008). This diversity is represented in Israel's parliament (Knesset), ensuring that these diverse voices are heard, but also creating a fragmented political system (Shamir and Arian 1999). Israel uses a proportional representation electoral system with a single national electoral district to allocate 120 seats in the Knesset to parties able to overcome the electoral threshold (Shugart 2021). This single electoral district, which is quite a unique feature in parliamentary systems (Carey and Hix 2011), is an outcome of historical reasons rather than a planned attempt to provide a high level of representation (Rosenthal 2017: 29–33).

From 1951 until 1992, Israel's electoral threshold was 1%. At that point, it was increased to 1.5%. It was raised again in 2004 to 2%, and in 2014 it rose to 3.25%. The combination of a diverse society, a high degree of proportional representation and low entry barriers to the parliament results in a high level of what Shugart and Taagepera (2017: 73–77) called the Effective Number of Parties in Parliament (ENPP). While not necessarily increasing the likelihood of regime instability (Diskin et al. 2005), political instability stemming from a multitude of parties in parliament complicates the capacity to govern by creating instability in the cabinet and government (Heller 2001; Huber and Lupia 2001).

In contrast to this institutional instability, during the same 73 years, Israel saw only 13 prime ministers, with two of them serving more than a decade in office. For the most part, Israeli prime ministers served more than the average of 4.4 years, often seen in many parliamentary democracies (Kenig 2020). Thus, unlike Israeli political institutions, the position of the Israeli executive head is quite stable. Hence, the main puzzle this analysis examines is the discrepancy between Israel's political instability and the relative stability of its prime ministers in an environment with a great deal of electoral fragmentation. In short, *how can Israeli election results produce chronic instability in parliament (the Knesset) and the composition of the government but stability in the prime minister's position?*

I maintain that Israel's high degree of electoral fragmentation yields potentially unstable political institutions. These institutions become increasingly more unstable when prime ministers enjoy party unity, little political competition, and high levels of electoral support. Such personal support stems from the public's appreciation of the prime ministers' personal qualities, either real or perceived (Stokes 1966). The public tends to consider these qualities irrespective of the issues that the candidates and parties wish to promote (Schofield 2003; Stokes 1963). In such cases, prime ministers will destabilize the system to maintain their position in office. I maintain that these leadership patterns are an outcome of the leaders' activities in light of various contextual and institutional factors (Elgie 2018). I identify the qualitative differences among four leadership patterns of prime ministers in parliamentary systems as part of a party's leadership collective, party-based, prime ministerialized, or presidentialized. Each of these leadership patterns reflects a different power structure between the prime minister and his/her party with regard to electoral support patterns and institutional rules. I use these concepts to explain the connections between Israel's electoral system and institutional political stability from 1948 until 2021.

Parties in parliamentary regimes, electoral outcomes, and government stability: some general comments

In parliamentary democracies, parliament establishes, removes, and replaces the government (Samuels and Shugart 2010). Furthermore, in parliamentary democracies, party unity is the key to handling the party's decision-making: nominating candidates, creating (or dissolving) coalitions, and handling public policy processes (Samuels and Shugart 2010). Hence, party governance is the key to an effective executive uniting all party factions around the party's policy agenda, leadership, and designated constituency (Andeweg 2020; Hazan 2003). There is a fine line between *party cohesion*, which is a self-enforcing set of joint preferences, and *party discipline*, which is based on institutional incentives for party members to toe the party line (Hazan 2003). Party cohesion is based on an equilibrium of preferences between the different party factions. With party discipline, institutional rules (election rules, the party's financial rules etc.) compel party factions to maintain unity (Hazan 2003).[2] In political systems which are party-focused, parties rule on the basis of collective cohesive leadership that depends on the party's valence: the party's popularity due to its policy positions and the socio-demographic characteristics of its loyal supporters (Schofield and Sened 2006). The result is the party-based leadership model in which the party leadership collectively decides on its positions with little dissent from party activists and supporters (Schofield and Sened 2006).

A key issue for governance as an outcome of election results is a party system's fragmentation: the number of parties and the divergence between these parties' ideologies and values. These two parameters potentially reduce the ability of the reigning political leadership to form coalitions and design and implement public policy (Sartori 1999; Tsebelis 1999). Thus, political fragmentation is a key variable for understanding governance. One indicator of political fragmentation is the Effective Number of Parliamentary Parties. This measure is calculated by summing the inverse of the squared proportions of all seat shares of parties in parliament. A high ENPP denotes the presence of many parties with a smaller number of seat shares in parliament (Shugart and Taagepera 2017).

When the ENPP is large, the formateur party seeking to create a coalition must include a wide variety of different policy preferences in the coalition (Schofield 1995). To create a coalition, parties in parliamentary regimes nominate a leading party member to be the prime minister (Lupia and Strøm 2008). When bargaining to construct cabinets, prime ministers allocate portfolios and budgets to existing or new coalition partners to compensate for any ideological losses the parties entering the coalition need to absorb (Sened 1996). Thus, fragmentation means that parties present diverse policy positions to the electorate. Therefore, prime ministers need to compensate them for convincing them to join the coalition (Sened 1996). Hence, the second leadership pattern is evident when there is a high level of ENPP and a cohesive party. In such cases, the prime minister will preserve the stability of parliament, the government, and the cabinet using policy and portfolio payoffs. Let us refer to this leadership pattern as the premier leadership pattern, as prime ministers might be first in their parties, but they need to consider the party's wishes and preferences.

A qualitatively different situation occurs when prime ministers become more popular than their parties (Schofield and Sened 2005). This situation reflects the personalization of politics (Rahat and Kenig 2018), meaning that the parties' electoral valence is less than the party leader's valence (Schofield and Sened 2005). Such a direct focus on the prime minister as an individual could create the *prime ministerialization* of politics: an increased focus on the prime minister's position as the key figure in the executive (Dowding 2013; Rosenthal 2021). Once the interests of the prime minister and the party diverge, the party is strong enough to remove the prime minister from power. While the prime ministers could destabilize all levels of governance, they still need the support of a united party. In such situations, if the interests of the prime minister and the party diverge, the party will have at least two competing factions: the prime minister's supporters and at least one other group. In such cases, party discipline can be more important than the party's cohesion (Hazan 2003). Hence, in the third leadership pattern, while all party factions accept the prime minister's rule and there is a high ENPP, the prime minister is more popular than the party. In such situations, there will be instability in the parliament, the government, and the cabinet. With intraparty unity decreasing, the party will maintain its discipline but not its cohesion.

Another outcome of the personalization of electoral politics is the presidentialization of executive politics in parliamentary democracies. In such situations, not only do political systems focus on prime ministers and potential candidates for this position during elections (Andeweg 2020), but they also do so throughout all stages of governance (Elgie and Passarelli 2019; Poguntke and Webb 2007; Webb and Poguntke 2013). When a parliamentary system becomes presidentialized, it empowers the executive's leader, potentially creating a differentiation between the leader's incentives and those of the party (Samuels and Shugart 2010). Furthermore, the use of intraparty primaries to select the party leader might promote a leader who is an external candidate and at odds with the party elite s/he just defeated (Samuels and Shugart 2010).

Hence, the presidentialization and prime ministerialization of politics in parliamentary systems mean a focus on the prime minister throughout the policy process. However, in presidentialized parliamentary systems, the prime minister will be the decisive player. Thus, in such systems, when the parties no longer have control over the prime ministers, we would expect that the prime ministers would go against competing party factions even if doing so means splitting the party. Therefore, the final leadership pattern is a presidentialized parliamentary system with a high

ENPP, and instability in the parliament, government, cabinet, *and* the formateur party. Table 8.1 summarizes the results of the various leadership patterns.

Israel's electoral system

Israel's electoral system is based on a single electoral district consisting of 120 representatives drawn from closed party lists, whose seats are allocated using proportional representation. As I showed above, one institutional factor affecting fragmentation in the electoral system is the threshold for entering the Knesset. Israel's first election took place in 1949, with the electoral threshold effectively set at 0.83. From 1951 until 1992, it was 1%. In 1992, it was increased to 1.5%. In 2004, it was raised to 2%, and in 2014 it increased to 3.25% (Hazan et al. 2018). Furthermore, in 1973 the formula used to allocate seats changed from the largest remainder method (Hare) to the highest average method (d'Hondt) (Shugart 2021). The larger parties initiated this move because they benefited from the advantages it offered them (Shugart 1992). Overall, Israel's electoral method simply translates votes into seats proportionally (Shugart and Taagepera 2017). With a relatively inclusive proportional representation system, Israel's social cleavages, which translate into electoral and party politics (Arian and Shamir 2008; Nachmias et al. 2016), result in an Effective Number of Parliamentary Parties generally exceeding theoretical expectations regarding the ENPP that Israel's electoral method is supposed to produce (Shugart and Taagepera 2017). Figure 8.1 shows Israel's ENPP over time and Knessets.

The mean of the ENPP in Israel is 4.23 (Shugart and Taagepera 2017), with only four Knessets, 7–8 and 10–11, having smaller numbers.

Israeli prime ministers' leadership patterns and political stability

Israel's formative years during 1948–1965 were dominated by Mapai (Israel's Labor Party) headed by David Ben-Gurion (Doron 2006). Mapai always formed coalitions because it never won enough seats to govern alone. However, as the winner of the largest number of seats and due to its centrality in the political system, Mapai was the formateur party throughout these years (Schofield 1995). Mapai had several layers of leadership: Ben-Gurion and his close aides, the veteran leadership including people belonging to Ben-Gurion's leadership generation who accepted his leadership from early on, and a variety of political machines spread throughout the country organized around Israel's main labor union, the Histadrut (Shapira 1993). From 1948 to 1963, Ben-Gurion was Mapai's leader (Arian 2005). However, he usually deferred to intraparty power-sharing arrangements in place before the state of Israel was formed (Shapira 1993). Furthermore, when Ben-Gurion breached this arrangement, the party elite practically removed him from power (Arian 2005).

Throughout this period (1948–1965), Israel saw 11 elected governments, 5 Knessets, and 15 Ben-Gurion-led cabinets, alongside three cabinets headed by Moshe Sharett (1954–1955) and two cabinets headed by Levi Eshkol (1963–1965). Ben-Gurion resigned and was replaced by Sharett as prime minister during 1954–1955. Ben-Gurion resigned again in 1963 and was replaced by Eshkol. That last resignation led to his removal from office by the party elite (Arian 2005). Hence, Ben-Gurion's tenure exemplifies the prime-ministerial pattern: a higher than average ENPP with a leader safe in his political position due to his strong valence, who can secure his/her party the formateur's position. As long as s/he coordinates with the party's leadership, this arrangement continues. In such a situation, there is stability in the prime minister's position and that of the formateur party, but complete instability in all structural and systemic parameters. When intraparty conflict erupts, the prime minister's position is also destabilized. In

Table 8.1 Leadership patterns of prime ministers in parliamentary democracies

Parliamentary democracy leadership pattern	Leader's valence	Party unity	Leader's stability	Party's stability	Parliament's stability	Government's stability	Cabinet's stability
Party based	Leader's valence irrelevant	Cohesion	Stable	Stable	Stable	Stable	Stable
Premier	Party's valence greater than leader's valence	Cohesion	Stable	Stable	Stability depends on party's interests	Stability depends on party's interests	Stability depends on party's interests
Prime ministerial	Higher than party's valence	Discipline by party leadership	Stability depends on party's interests	Stable	Stability depends on party's interests	Stability depends on party's interests	Stability depends on party's interests
Presidential	Party's valence irrelevant	Discipline by prime minister	Stable	Stability depends on prime minister's interests	Stability depends on prime minister's interests	Stability depends on prime minister's interests	Stability depends on prime minister's interests

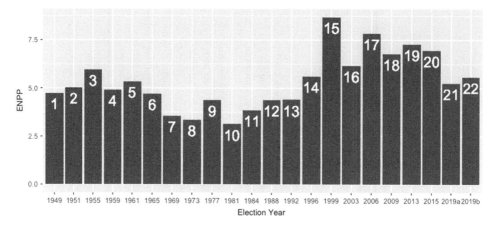

Figure 8.1 Effective number of parliamentary parties, 1948–2021. Note: The data for 71 years in the figure came from PARLGOV. The data for 2020–2021 are my own calculations. Knesset election data are available at: https://main.knesset.gov.il/mk/elections/Pages/default.aspx

our case, Ben-Gurion lost his position. This period ends when Ben-Gurion formed a party and tried to compete against Mapai in the 1965 election. However, the voters remained loyal to the party label (Mapai) rather than to Ben-Gurion (Arian 2005).

The next period goes from 1965 to 1977. During this time, Mapai changed its label to *Maarach* (Alignment). It was led by a series of prime ministers: Levi Eshkol (1965–1969, when he died) and then Golda Meir (1969–1974), who resigned due to the failures of the 1973 Yom Kippur War. Her successor was Yitzhak Rabin, who did not try to get re-elected in 1977 because of a scandal in which he was involved (Arian 2005). During that period, the Alignment leadership was split over various matters. Nevertheless, Golda Meir, the prime minister, remained in a decisive position with little, if any, conflicts with other party leaders (Arian 2005; Weitz 2011). After Meir's resignation, under Rabin, intraparty competition erupted among his generation's leaders who sought to replace him (Shapira 1984).

From 1965 to 1977, there were three Knessets, five governments (including a unity government with the opposition), and nine cabinets. The Knessets completed their full term. The governments were replaced due to elections (Itzhak Rabin), a death (Levi Eshkol), and a resignation (Golda Meir). The ENPP during this period ranged from 4.71 to 3.35. Hence, in the post-Ben-Gurion era, there was a large, cohesive formateur party with a less fragmented Knesset and little instability. Thus, the 1965–1977 period can be viewed as representing the party-based leadership pattern, evident in cohesion, low ENPP, and stability.

In 1977, after the election of the 9th Knesset, Israel witnessed the first replacement of a formateur party. The Likud Party headed by Menachem Begin was a cohesive opposition party that had sought power since its inception during Israel's formative years (Shapira 1991). Begin formed a coalition with the religious parties, which switched from their alliance with the Alignment to cooperate with Likud, alongside a new centrist party called Dash. Begin headed two cabinets during the period of the 9th Knesset. Dramatic changes took place under Begin's first government, most notably, the peace agreement between Israel and Egypt. To make this peace agreement, Begin made territorial compromises that led to the emergence of the Israeli far-right, which opposed them. In 1981, Begin headed the Likud in a tight re-election battle. However, in 1983 after forming two more cabinets, he resigned from office due to health issues and was replaced by another Likud leader, Itzhak Shamir (Arian 2005). Shamir led two further cabinets before seeking re-election in 1984. Hence, we have here a cohesive party under (in Begin's case) a very popular leader's valence. Yet, due to external changes and challenges, Begin and then Shamir saw replacements in their cabinets.

Thus, in this seven-year period there were two Knessets and three governments (due to elections and illness), with transitions in the cabinets. Hence, there was stability on all fronts except the cabinet, which reflects the policy instability of that period: a right-wing party making territorial concessions to Egypt but going to war in Lebanon, while seeking to change Israel's economic structure (Doron and Rosenthal 2008). The Likud years show two prime ministers heading a cohesive party, forming governments from within the existing Knessets, and creating and dissolving cabinets to deal with policy challenges. Thus, this party setting is quite stable and allows for prime ministers' to maintain their position in power, as long as they wish. Due to Begin's personal valence, he can be defined as a prime-ministerial leader. Due to Shamir's lack of personal valence (Rosenthal and Doron 2009), he can be defined as a premier.

In 1984, Likud and Alignment were not able to form a coalition without each other. The same was true after the 1988 elections. Thus, until 1990 both parties shared power, seeking to handle several major challenges on a number of fronts. During the shared power agreement between the sides, Alignment leader Shimon Peres had one cabinet that ruled for two years. In accordance with the agreement between the parties, Shamir replaced Peres for two years. In 1988, the two sides tried to repeat this arrangement. However, this time the Likud had an electoral advantage over the Alignment (40 Knesset seats for the Likud and 39 for the Alignment). That advantage gave the Likud better prospects to form a government without the Alignment than the Alignment had without the Likud. Thus, the coalition agreement determined that Shamir would be the prime minister for all of the government's time in office (Arian 2005).

Nevertheless, 1988–1992 saw two governments and five cabinets due to internal battles between the Likud and Alignment (now called Israel's Labor Party, ILP), which eventually resulted in the ILP's removal from the government in 1990. Furthermore, Shamir faced continuous challenges to his leadership from within the Likud and projected low electoral valence (Rosenthal and Doron 2009; Schofield and Sened 2006). Therefore, the Likud Party was losing its cohesion. In 1992, Shamir lost the election to the ILP, which was headed by Rabin.

The ILP in 1992 was one of the first parties to change the wording on the ballot to "The Labor Party headed by Itzhak Rabin," thereby marking the beginning of an era of personalized campaigns in Israeli mainstream parties (Balmas et al. 2014). An ENPP of 4.39, a party that had more than a ten-seat advantage over the next largest party, and maneuvering in a coalition between parties that had no appetite for new elections allowed the prime minister to implement his policies (Sened 1996). Rabin led a government and three cabinets until his assassination in November 1995. Rabin was replaced by his second in line within the ILP, Shimon Peres, who ruled over one cabinet and decided to hold new elections in May 1996. The fact that Rabin relied on his party and that the party was ready with a replacement after his assassination tells us that despite the personalization of electoral politics associated with Rabin, we can characterize his term as a prime ministerialization period. Rabin was a high-valence leader but had a disciplined party supporting him.

The May 1996 elections took place using a new electoral method: the direct election of the prime minister, which was used between 1996 and 2001. The reform created a hybrid regime that presidentialized the system in that it determined that the voters would vote directly for the head of the executive (Hazan 1996). However, it kept the parliament's power because the Knesset could dismiss the prime minister without new Knesset elections if it could muster 80 votes out of its 120 votes to do so. In addition, the new method allowed the Knesset to dismiss the prime minister's government and call for new elections for all (Doron 2001). Furthermore, the law determined that any candidate for the prime minister's position would have to lead a party competing for the Knesset. Hence, while the method tried to separate the prime minister's position from the Knesset, it actually embedded the former in the Knesset and the party system (Doron 2001).

Moreover, Israeli voters voted strategically for the prime minister's position and sincerely for the Knesset (Doron 2001). With the low electoral threshold of 1.5% to obtain a seat in the Knesset, this voting behavior created a fragmented parliament, with a large number of small parties seeking to attract niche groups within Israel's very divided society (Doron 2001; Sartori 1999; Shamir and Arian 1999). Thus, despite having a direct mandate from the people for the prime minister to head the executive, the executive needed the support of a wide variety of niche parties, each of which sought to attract a set of voters using sincere voting behavior for the Knesset. This method contradicted the needs of a popularly elected prime minister who was seeking the average voter's support. This combination resulted in dysfunctional governments in which there was great instability in the prime minister's position and the composition of the governments that had to deal with very fragmented and unsupportive parliaments (Harris and Doron 1999).

The main parties whose leaders were competing for the prime minister's position found themselves continuously replacing their leaders. Their intense intraparty conflicts affected their ability to act collectively to pursue their goals. This loss of unity was exacerbated by many parties adopting party primaries for the leader and party list (Rahat 2007). Hence, this "era of accelerated reform" (Hazan 1997) dismantled the core of the Israeli party system (Nachmias and Sened 2001), increased the fragmentation within Israel's parliament (Hazan et al. 2018), and the payoffs needed to create coalitions (Nachmias and Sened 2001).

Benjamin Netanyahu was the first to rule using this method. Between 1996 and 1999, the 14th Knesset had a 5.61 ENPP. During that period, Netanyahu created three cabinets. In 1999, Netanyahu lost the election to the ILP's leader Ehud Barak. The 15th Knesset reached a high point of 8.69 ENPP. Barak ruled from July 1999 until December 2000. In this period, the country had two governments and three cabinets. He resigned from his post and called for early elections, but only for the prime minister position. He lost that election to Ariel Sharon, the Likud's leader, who headed the second-largest party in Knesset. With a disciplined party, and other parties unhappy about having new elections, Sharon ruled for two years, during which he switched between five different cabinets. Both Barak and Netanyahu formed joint lists of parties united with their party for the election. However, these lists broke apart during their time in power, prompting them and their parties to seek the next party merger or split (Kenig 2005; Ottolenghi 1999). The direct election method can be associated with a presidentialized leadership pattern in which prime ministers rely on public support rather than their own party's support and survive in office by making and dissolving cabinets and governments.

In the 2003 elections, Sharon kept the prime minister's position. Before this election, Israel re-adopted the single-ballot proportional representation electoral system (Doron 2006) and increased the electoral threshold to 2% (Rahat 2013). Sharon's term between 2003 and 2006 was unique: he was a Likud leader who received an electoral mandate for strict hawkish policy positions. These positions meant negating any withdrawal from the territories Israel occupied in 1967. However, once in power, he advocated the unilateral withdrawal of Israel from the Gaza Strip and evicted all of its Israeli residents, promoting a policy he actually campaigned against (Rosenthal 2014). Paradoxically, while abolishing the direct election method was supposed to reduce the presidentialization of politics in Israel, Sharon acted in a presidentialized manner. He maneuvered against his right-wing coalition, formed four cabinets, and eventually split his own party to create a new party. Hence, Sharon maintained a presidentialized pattern of politics, splitting the Likud, but retaining power due to public support for him and his policies (Akirav et al. 2010; Rosenthal 2014).

Between 2006 and 2009, the party Sharon formed, Kadima (Forward), was the formateur but without Sharon: after suffering a stroke, he fell into a coma during the 2006 election and never returned to politics. Ehud Olmert, Sharon's successor, was less popular than Sharon, had difficulty maintaining his coalition, and resigned due to corruption allegations before the 2009 election. In that election, Netanyahu came back into power to govern for 12 consecutive years, six Knessets, four governments, and ten cabinets.

In 2014, Israel increased the electoral threshold to 3.25% and then introduced a "full" constructive no-confidence rule (Rosenthal 2017: 16–17). Since the 2015 election and until 2021, the ENPP under Netanyahu decreased from 7.28 before the reform to below 7 and toward 5. Between 2009 and September 2019 (which is the end of the PARLGOV data), Netanyahu saw five Knessets, three governments (one would be a caretaker government continuing until March 2020), and nine cabinets. After the March 2020 election, Netanyahu formed a power-sharing government with the Blue-White party. However, this government collapsed. In March 2021, Israel held new elections in which Netanyahu lost his seat as prime minister, and the Likud lost its position as the formateur party (Magen 2021).

During that period, Netanyahu faced a variety of scandals, corruption charges, and criminal proceedings. However, the Likud Party supported him, with Likud leaders and members publicly unsupportive of Netanyahu expelled from the party (Magen 2021). Netanyahu's electoral valence was celebrated by party leaders and activists, who often referred to him as "King Bibi" (Magen 2021). Hence, like Sharon's reign, Netanyahu's reign was also presidentialized, with a leader dominating his party based on his personal public support. Table 8.2 summarizes the main patterns the Israeli case reveals.

Table 8.2 Historical periods, prime ministers, and leadership patterns

Historical periods	Prime ministers	Parliamentary democracy leadership pattern	Knesset#	Avg. ENPP	Parliaments	Governments	Cabinets
1948–1965	Ben-Gurion	Prime ministerial	0–2	4.86	3	5 (including a temporary state council)	7
	Sharett	Party based	2–3	5.96	2	2	3
	Ben-Gurion	Prime ministerial	3–5	5.47	3	4	6
	Eshkol	Party based	5	5.35	1	2	2
1965–1977	Eshkol	Party based	6	4.71	1	1	2
	Meir	Party based	6–8	3.86	3	3	4
	Rabin	Premier	8	3.35	1	1	3
1977–1984	Begin	Prime ministerial	9–10	3.846	2	2	9
	Shamir	Premier	10	3.86	1	1	2
1984–1990	Peres	Premier	11	3.86	1	1	1
	Shamir	Premier	11–12	4.23	2	3	6
1992–1995	Rabin	Prime ministerial	13	4.39	1	1	3
1995–1996	Peres	Premier	13	4.39	1	1	1
1996–2003	Netanyahu	Presidential	14	5.61	1	1	3
	Barak	Presidential	15	8.69	1	1	3
	Sharon	Presidential	15	8.69	1	1	5
2003–2009	Sharon	Presidential	16	6.17	1	1	3
	Olmert	Premier	17	7.84	1	1	4
2009–2021	Netanyahu	Presidential	18–23	6.659	6	3	10

Concluding discussion

My goal was to explore the seeming paradox of the stability of Israel's prime ministers and the instability of its electoral system. I claimed that electoral fragmentation allows popular Israeli prime ministers to keep themselves in power, while destabilizing government, cabinets, and parliaments. I identified four patterns of prime ministers. Those who are more based within their parties and are part of a party compromise, rather than leaders who are popular among voters, I referred to as examples of party-based prime ministers. The second is the premier leadership pattern: a prime minister who is first among equals but needs the party to be in that position. The prime-ministerial pattern involves a prime minister whose personal valence is greater than that of his/her party. Finally, in the presidentialized pattern, the incentives of the prime minister may be different from those of the party. To what extent did these different political leadership patterns affect Israel's political stability?

When an institutional environment, such as Israel's, can be molded with few roadblocks, leaders can re-shape the way institutions function (Riker 1980; Shepsle 2006). Thus, the connection between electoral constraints and political maneuvering allows the different leadership patterns to affect stability. The party-based leadership pattern turns electoral fragmentation into a stable ruling cabinet, government, and parliament. The prime-ministerial leadership pattern relies on electoral valence and party discipline to ensure the prime minister's stability. The presidentialized prime minister can use his/her personal electoral valence to destabilize all political institutions, including all political parties, in order to remain in power. However, one should keep in mind that different cabinets, governments, and parliaments mean different policy agendas and commitments. Hence, the same person could head cabinets that vary in their composition. However, due to the cabinets' varying compositions, they might have to constantly change the government's policy plans. In some cases, that situation meant the lack of a coherent public policy strategy and the emergence of myopic views within Israel's political elite (Rosenthal 2017, chap. 8). Such situations make it difficult for governments to design long-term plans for dealing with issues such as foreign policy, security threats, and environmental hazards (Dror 2001).

Notes

1 PARLGOV data are available online and can be downloaded at: http://www.parlgov.org/explore/ observed June 22, 2021.
2 Hazan and Itzkovitch-Malka (2017) provide a more elaborate conceptual scheme of party unity by adding the concept of party loyalty. For simplicity, I use the two earlier concepts that Hazan suggested influence party unity: party cohesion and party discipline.

References

Akirav, Osnat, Gary W. Cox, and Mathew D. McCubbins. 2010. 'Agenda Control in the Israeli Knesset during Ariel Sharon's Second Government'. *The Journal of Legislative Studies* 16(2): 251–267.
Andeweg, Rudy B. 2020. 'Parties and Executives in Parliamentary Systems'. In Rudy B. Andeweg, Robert Elgie, Ludger Helms, Juliet Kaarbo, and Ferdinand Muller-Rummel (eds.), *The Oxford Handbook of Political Executives*. Oxford: Oxford University Press, 460–478.
Arian, Asher. 2005. *Politics in Israel: The Second Republic*. Washington, DC: CQ Press.
Arian, Asher and Michal Shamir. 2008. 'A Decade Later, the World Had Changed, the Cleavage Structure Remained Israel 1996–2006'. *Party Politics* 14(6): 685–705.
Balmas, Meital, Gideon Rahat, Tamir Sheafer, and Shaul R. Shenhav. 2014. 'Two Routes to Personalized Politics: Centralized and Decentralized Personalization'. *Party Politics* 20(1): 37–51.
Carey, John M. and Simon Hix. 2011. 'The Electoral Sweet Spot: Low-Magnitude Proportional Electoral Systems'. *American Journal of Political Science* 55(2): 383–397.

Diskin, Abraham, Hanna Diskin, and Reuven Y. Hazan. 2005. 'Why Democracies Collapse: The Reasons for Democratic Failure and Success'. *International Political Science Review* 26(3): 291–309.

Döring, Holger and Philip Manow. 2020. 'ParlGov 2020 Release'. Available at: https://doi.org/10.7910/DVN/Q6CVHX, Harvard Dataverse, V1, UNF:6:mUoYp2KfQii0z+5dEZum1w==[fileUNF].

Doron, Gideon. 2001. 'A Recipe for Failure: Public Policy in the Context of Electoral Reform'. In Dan Korn (ed.), *Public Policy in Israel*. London: Lexington Books, 95–108.

Doron, Gideon. 2006. *Presidential Regime for Israel*. Jerusalem: Carmel.

Doron, Gideon and Maoz Rosenthal. 2008. 'Strategic Entrapment of the Extreme Right-Wing Parties in Israel'. *Social Issues in Israel* 6(1): 44–67.

Dowding, Keith. 2013. 'The Prime Ministerialisation of the British Prime Minister'. *Parliamentary Affairs* 66(3): 617–635.

Dror, Yehezkel. 2001. *The Capacity to Govern: A Report to the Club of Rome*. New York: Frank Cass Publishers.

Elgie, Robert. 2018. *Political Leadership: A Pragmatic Institutionalist Approach*. London: Palgrave Macmillan.

Elgie, Robert and Gianluca Passarelli. 2019. 'Presidentialisation: One Term, Two Uses–Between Deductive Exercise and Grand Historical Narrative'. *Political Studies Review* 17(2): 115–123.

Harris, Michael, and Gideon Doron. 1999. 'Assessing the Electoral Reform of 1992 and Its Impact on the Elections of 1996 and 1999'. *Israel Studies* 4(2): 16–39.

Hazan, Reuven. 1996. 'Presidential Parliamentarism: Direct Popular Election of the Prime Minister, Israel's New Electoral and Political System'. *Electoral Studies* 15(1): 21–37.

Hazan, Reuven. 1997. 'Executive-Legislative Relations in an Era of Accelerated Reform: Reshaping Government in Israel'. *Legislative Studies Quarterly* 22(3): 329–350.

Hazan, Reuven. 2003. 'Introduction'. *The Journal of Legislative Studies* 9(4): 1–11.

Hazan, Reuven, Reut Itzkovitch-Malka, and Gideon Rahat. 2018. 'Electoral Systems in Context: Israel'. In Erik S. Herron, Robert J. Pekkanen, and Matthew S. Shugart (eds.), *The Oxford Handbook of Electoral Systems*. Oxford: Oxford University Press, 581–600.

Heller, William B. 2001. 'Making Policy Stick: Why the Government Gets What It Wants in Multiparty Parliaments'. *American Journal of Political Science* 45(4): 780–798.

Huber, John D. and Arthur Lupia. 2001. 'Cabinet Instability and Delegation in Parliamentary Democracies'. *American Journal of Political Science* 45(1): 18–32.

Itzkovitch-Malka, Reut and Reuven Hazan. 2017. 'Unpacking Party Unity: The Combined Effects of Electoral Systems and Candidate Selection Methods on Legislative Attitudes and Behavioural Norms'. *Political Studies* 65(2): 452–474.

Kenig, Ofer. 2005. 'The 2003 Elections in Israel: Has the Return to the "Old" System Reduced Party System Fragmentation?' *Israel Affairs* 11(3): 552–566.

Kenig, Ofer. 2020. 'For the Fourth Time in Two Years: Israel Has the Highest Election Rate'. *Israel Democracy Institute*. Available at: https://www.idi.org.il/articles/33202.

Lupia, Arthur and Kaare Strøm. 2008. 'Bargaining, Transaction Costs, and Coalition Governance'. In Kaare Strøm, Wolfgang Müller, and Torbjorn Bergman (eds.), *Cabinets and Coalition Bargaining: The Democratic Life Cycle in Western Europe*. Oxford: Oxford University Press, 51–84.

Magen, Amichai. 2021. 'The Strange Case of Dr. Netanyahu and Mr. Bibi'. *Israel Journal of Foreign Affairs* 15(2): 195–200.

Müller, Wolfgang, Bergman Torbjörn, and Kaare Strøm. 2008. 'Coalition Theory and Cabinet Governance: An Introduction'. In Kaare Strøm, Wolfgang Müller, and Torbjorn Bergman (eds.), *Cabinets and Coalition Bargaining: The Democratic Life Cycle in Western Europe*. Oxford: Oxford University Press, 1–50.

Nachmias, David, Maoz Rosenthal, and Hani Zubida. 2016. 'National Party Strategies in Local Elections: A Theory and Some Evidence from the Israeli Case'. *Israel Affairs* 22(2): 401–422.

Nachmias, David and Itai Sened. 2001. 'Governance and Public Policy'. *Israel Affairs* 7(4): 3–20.

Ottolenghi, Emanuele. 1999. 'Immobility, Stability and Ineffectiveness: Assessing the Impact of Direct Election of the Israeli Prime Minister'. *The Journal of Legislative Studies* 5(1): 35–53.

Poguntke, Thomas and Paul Webb. 2007. *The Presidentialization of Politics: A Comparative Study of Modern Democracies*. Oxford: Oxford University Press.

Rahat, Gideon. 2007. 'Determinants of Party Cohesion: Evidence from the Case of the Israeli Parliament'. *Parliamentary Affairs* 60(2): 279–296.

Rahat, Gideon. 2013. *Reforming Israel's Government Method*. Jerusalem: Israeli Democracy Institute Press.

Rahat, Gideon and Ofer Kenig. 2018. *From Party Politics to Personalized Politics? Party Change and Political Personalization in Democracies*. Oxford: Oxford University Press.

Riker, William H. 1980. 'Implications from the Disequilibrium of Majority-Rule for the Study of Institutions'. *American Political Science Review* 74(2): 432–446.

Rosenthal, Maoz. 2014. 'Policy Instability in a Comparative Perspective: The Context of Heresthetic'. *Political Studies* 62(1): 172–196.

Rosenthal, Maoz. 2017. *Israel's Governability Crisis: Quandaries, Unstructured Institutions, and Adaptation.* Lanham, MD: Lexington Books.

Rosenthal, Maoz. 2021. 'Strategic Agenda Setting and Prime Ministers' Approval Ratings: The Heresthetic and Rhetoric of Political Survival'. *British Politics, 16(4): 355-374.*.

Rosenthal, Maoz and Gideon Doron. 2009. 'Israel's 1993 Decision to Make Peace with the PLO or How Political Losers (This Time) Became Winners'. *International Negotiation* 14(3): 449–474.

Samuels, David J. and Matthew S. Shugart. 2010. *Presidents, Parties, and Prime Ministers: How the Separation of Powers Affects Party Organization and Behavior.* Cambridge: Cambridge University Press.

Sartori, Giovanni. 1999. 'The Party-Effects of Electoral Systems'. *Israel Affairs* 6(2): 13–28.

Schofield, Norman. 1995. 'Coalition Politics a Formal Model and Empirical Analysis'. *Journal of Theoretical Politics* 7(3): 245–281.

Schofield, Norman. 2003. 'Valence Competition in the Spatial Stochastic Model'. *Journal of Theoretical Politics* 15(4): 371–383.

Schofield, Norman and Itai Sened. 2005. 'Modeling the Interaction of Parties, Activists and Voters: Why Is the Political Center so Empty?' *European Journal of Political Research* 44(3): 355–390.

Schofield, Norman and Itai Sened. 2006. *Multiparty Democracy: Elections and Legislative Politics.* Cambridge: Cambridge University Press.

Sened, Itai. 1996. 'A Model of Coalition Formation: Theory and Evidence'. *The Journal of Politics* 58(2): 350–372.

Shamir, Michal and Asher Arian. 1999. 'Collective Identity and Electoral Competition in Israel'. *American Political Science Review* 93(2): 265–277.

Shapira, Yonatan. 1984. *Elite without Followers: Leadership Generations in Israeli Society.* Tel-Aviv Israel: Sifriat Poalim.

Shapira, Yonatan. 1991. *The Road to Power: Herut Party in Israel.* Albany, NY: SUNY Press.

Shapira, Yonatan. 1993. 'The Historical Origins of Israeli Democracy: Mapai as a Dominant Party'. In Uri Rami (ed.), *Israeli Society: Critical Perspectives.* Tel Aviv: Breirot, 40–53.

Shepsle, Kenneth A. 2006. 'Old Questions and New Answers about Institutions: The Riker Objection Revisited'. In Barry Weingast and Donald Wittman (eds.), *The Oxford Handbook of Political Economy.* Oxford: Oxford University Press, 1031–1050.

Shugart, Matthew S. 1992. 'Electoral Reform in Systems of Proportional Representation'. *European Journal of Political Research* 21(3): 207–224.

Shugart, Matthew S. 2021. 'The Electoral System of Israel'. In Reuven Y. Hazan, Alan Dowty, Menachem Hofnung, and Gideon Rahat (eds.), *The Oxford Handbook of Israeli Politics and Society.* Oxford: Oxford University Press, 331–350.

Shugart, Matthew S. and Rein Taagepera. 2017. *Votes from Seats: Logical Models of Electoral Systems.* Cambridge: Cambridge University Press.

Stokes, Donald. 1963. 'Spatial Models of Party Competition'. *American Political Science Review* 57(2): 368–377.

Stokes, Donald. 1966. 'Some Dynamic Elements of Contests for the Presidency'. *American Political Science Review* 60(1): 19–28.

Tsebelis, George. 1999. 'Veto Players and Law Production in Parliamentary Democracies: An Empirical Analysis'. *American Political Science Review* 93(3): 591–608.

Webb, Paul and Thomas Poguntke. 2013. 'The Presidentialisation of Politics Thesis Defended'. *Parliamentary Affairs* 66(3): 646–654.

Weitz, Yechiam. 2011. 'Golda Meir, Israel's Fourth Prime Minister (1969–74)'. *Middle Eastern Studies* 47(1): 43–61.

9
WHEN FREE AND FAIR ELECTIONS ARE NOT ENOUGH: PARTY FRAGMENTATION AND UNACCOUNTABILITY IN TUNISIA

Ester Sigillò

Introduction

Applauded by scholars and policymakers as the "democratic exception" in the MENA region, Tunisia is the only Arab country that since the fall of Zine El-Abidine Ben Ali's regime in 2011 managed to carry out several rounds of free and fair elections (Teti et al. 2018). Prior to the Revolution, elections were regularly held, but strong restrictions were in place against the participation of political groups with alternative agendas to the regime's party *Rassemblement Constitutionnel Démocratique* (RCD). Contrary to the past, post-revolutionary elections were characterized by a wide political offer, as hundreds of political parties (about 110 were legalized) popped up on the democratized political scene (Ferjani 2012). Thus, Arab nationalists, liberals, conservatives, socialists, Islamists, and communists, for the first time competed in the October 2011 National Constituent Assembly (ANC) elections. After the inaugural elections, which saw the victory of the Islamist party with 37% of the votes, Tunisia carried out two rounds of presidential elections (2014 and 2019), two legislative elections (2014–2019) and one local election (2018), leading many scholars to define the country as the exemplary case of successful democratization in the Arab World.

Despite elections having taken place on a regular basis, some scholars warned about the weakness of the Tunisian party system (Geisser and Perez 2016), recalling the experience of democratic transitions in Eastern and Central Europe (Yardımcı-Geyikçi and Tür 2018; Battera and Ieraci 2019; Kimya 2021). Indeed, the electoral history of this young democracy shows that none of the political parties ever received an absolute majority. Furthermore, the proportional electoral system employed is associated with a fragile party system of unaccountable and unstable governments (Karvonen and Quenter 2002; Grotz and Weber 2012), which can therefore limit the effectiveness of the political system to meet voters' demands.

Thus, ten years after the so-called "Jasmin Revolution", despite the establishment of procedural democracy, the Tunisian political landscape is highly fragmented, and governments are increasingly perceived as unstable and unaccountable. Despite party pluralism on paper, most of the parties seem indistinguishable on crucial issues such as employment or regional inequalities (Grubman and Şaşmaz 2021).

Since the fall of the regime, political competition has been predominantly absorbed by the Islamist/secular divide, thus blurring the ideological boundaries of the different political actors. Moreover, except for *Ennahda*, a lack of experience and resources has prevented most of the new parties from drafting platforms with broad appeal. The lack of political offer in turn has led to widespread discontent among Tunisian voters, who are increasingly alienated from the major political parties and politics more broadly. Over the years, disaffection from politics has led to a growing detachment from the electoral process, visible in the decreasing turnout, endangering the democratic order of the country. This chapter scrutinizes the transformation of the Tunisian political landscape against the backdrop of the legislative and local elections held from the end of the authoritarian rule in 2011 until 2019. In doing so, this contribution sheds light on the political processes leading to parties' fragmentation and governments' unaccountability, two intertwined factors which contributed to the stalemate, and potential reversal, of the democratic process under the presidency of Kaïs Saïed in 2021.

The democratic boom, the 2011 elections, and a rising polarization

Tunisia always held elections during the Ben Ali era, but they were not free and fair because genuine opposition parties were excluded, and the Assembly of the People's Representatives (*Majlis Nuwwāb ash-Shaʿb*) simply played a symbolic function of ratification (Battera and Ieraci 2019) of decisions taken elsewhere. In April 2011, a few months after the collapse of the regime, an electoral commission – the Independent High Authority for the Elections (*Instance supérieure indépendante pour les élections*, better known as ISIE) – was instituted to design a new electoral system, which turned out to be a strong proportional one aiming at favoring post-revolutionary political pluralism. Moreover, a mechanism of "increased proportionalization" was envisaged for those governorates that had suffered from de-population due to the authoritarian regime's unjust public policies. According to this principle, a minimum of four deputies were assigned to the least populated governorates.[1]

Thus, after decades of domination by the Socialist Destourian Party (PSD), renamed the Democratic Constitutional Rally (RCD) under Ben Ali, from 1956 to 2011, the Revolution led to the dissolution of the old party-state and caused a real democratic explosion (Bendana 2012; Ferjani 2012). Hundreds of parties emerged on the political scene, and no less than 11,000 candidates ran in the National Constituent Assembly (ANC) elections in 2011 (Mezghani 2012). Some of these parties existed well before 2011, but they had to either operate in exile and underground or they were reduced to "loyal opposition" roles (Braun 2006).

The most remarkable change in 2011 was the resurgence of Islamist and Salafi parties, which had been harshly repressed by Ben Ali (Cavatorta and Merone 2013). While Salafism was not a new phenomenon in Tunisian history (Torelli et al. 2012; Merone et al. 2021), the presence of Salafi parties such as *Jabhat al-Islah*, *Hizb al-Asala* and the *Rahma Party* was a novelty in Tunisia (Cavatorta and Merone 2019), although they did not manage to be legalized in time to participate in the 2011 elections. The Islamist party *Ennahda*, stemming from the Movement of Islamic Tendency (MTI) – created in 1981 but never legalized – emerged as a new mass party with the backing of a broad pious public not necessarily interested in politics but supporting the party as the representative of its cultural references (Merone et al. 2018).

Ennahda was the only mass party (with already more than 30,000 members at the end of the 1980s) participating in the 2011 elections. Its mode of organization was less of a model inspired by the Egyptian Muslim Brotherhood than by that of large modern parties, with a political bureau, a central leadership, an internal parliament (*majlis al-shura*), and regional and local representations, which allowed it to cover the whole country (Geisser and Perez 2016). The popular support for *Ennahda* after 2011 was linked to the debate over the cultural identity of the country, forged by the previous authoritarian regime in an anti-Islamist perspective. After the Revolution, the conservative milieu challenged the "secular" identity of Tunisia, which had been imposed from above following independence from France, and the secular sector of society feared Islamization. The conflict lies in the supposed divide between the supporters of a Mediterranean vocation for Tunisia, linked to a modernist understanding of society, and those who reaffirmed, in a logic of rupture with the postcolonial era, the belonging of Tunisia to the Arab-Muslim world. Ghorbal (2012) referred to these two groups as "the Bourguiba's orphans and the heirs of the prophet". As emphasized in the literature, this cleavage reflected, at least partially, a divide between social classes, which found expression through a symbolic cultural perspective rather than through socio-economic issues (Merone 2015; Merone and De Facci 2015; Van Hamme et al. 2014; Gana and Van Hamme 2016).

During the electoral campaign for the ANC, the political debate became a controversy over the role of secularism and Islam in public life and their place in the Constitution. While *Ennahda* tried to project the image of a party committed to respecting pluralistic principles such as civil freedoms and equality, most of the secular elites worried about the likelihood that once in power the party would endanger civil rights, and in particular women's rights (Battera and Ieraci 2019). Whereas *Ennahda* emerged as the sole representative of the conservative milieu, the secularist camp's representation was instead quite varied, ranging from the liberal (*Afek Tounès*) to labor-oriented currents (*Parti démocrate progressiste*, PDP; *Ettakatol*, FDTL; *Pôle démocratique moderniste*, PDM), to different movements linked to the former regime. In particular, former RCD partisans were allowed to run for elections, and they gathered around *al-Moubadara* ("The Initiative"). The CPR (*Congrès pour la République*) emerged as standing somewhat between the conservative-secular tendencies, while the PCOT (*Parti communiste des ouvriers de Tunisie*) refused to join the secular camp because it believed it was too strongly linked to liberal and *ancien regime*'s forces (Battera and Ieraci 2019).

Ennahda obtained 37% of the votes and was able to gain 89 seats out of the 217 in the ANC (see Table 9.1). It is noteworthy, however, that the third most voted party was *Al-Aridha*, a per-

Table 9.1 Results of 2011 elections for the National Constituent Assembly (turnout 52.0%)

Party	Votes	%	Seats
Ennahda	1,498,905	37	89
CPR	352,825	8.7	29
FDTL (Ettakattol)	285,530	7	20
Al-Aridha	280,382	6.9	26
PDP	160,692	3.9	16
Al-Moubadara	129,215	3.2	5
PDM	113,094	2.8	5
Afek Tounes	64,498	1.8	4
POCT	57,600	1.5	3

Source: ISIE 2011

sonalistic and populist party founded by businessman Hechmi Hamdi, from the governorate of Sidi Bouzid, the most marginalized region of the country where the uprisings in 2010 first ignited. Unable to form a majority government, *Ennahda* began talks with the other parties to make a coalition arrangement. Common ground with secular forces in the name of national cohesion was eventually found, and *Ennahda* entered into a coalition government (better known as Troika) with CPR and *Ettakatol*. By the end of October 2011, Hamadi Jbeli (*Ennahda*) was elected prime minister. A month later, Mustapha Ben Jaafar, leader of *Ettakatol*, was elected President of the ANC, and on December 12 Moncef Marzouki was elected by the ANC as President of the Republic with 75% of the votes.

The results of the ANC elections and the creation of the Troika triggered widespread discontent in the secular camp. In 2012, in a highly conflictual political scenario and thanks to the initiative of Beji Caïd Essebsi, who had enjoyed for a long-time close relations with the old regime, several political movements gathered under the umbrella of the neo-bourghibist party *Nidaa Tounès* (Call for Tunisia) with the objective of blocking the rising power of the Islamist party. Indeed, the peculiarity of this new party was its unique capacity to hold together a variety of ideological currents, united only by its anti-Islamist positions (Wolf 2018). For instance, the choice of appointing Taïeb Baccouche, a former head of the UGTT and president of the Arab Institute for Human Rights, as *Nidaa Tounès* secretary general, strengthened the party's credentials. The party also includes leftists, represented by figures such as the journalist and activist Lazhar Akremi and the popular activist Mohsen Marzouk, who during Ben Ali's regime was politically active for the outlawed leftist movement *El Amal Ettounsi*,[2] and since 2008 has been secretary general of the non-governmental organization *Arab Democracy Foundation*. In addition, some independents joined the party, including many women.

However, not all secular parties supported Essebsi's call, notably because *Nidaa Tounès* also integrated people who had worked for Ben Ali's Constitutional Democratic Rally (RCD). Among the most powerful members of *Nidaa Tounès* were former members of Ben Ali's party, who had close ties to business – such as Faouzi Loumi, a former member of the RCD party and head of one of Tunisia's top companies, the Elloumi Group, which generated revenue of around $800 million in 2011. In September 2013, Mohamed Ghariani, Ben Ali's ally and last secretary general of the RCD, also joined *Nidaa Tounès*. Significantly, Tunisia's far-left, which had suffered severe repression under the former regime, quickly launched a counter-initiative through the creation of the Popular Front on October 7, 2012. The front brought together 12 political parties, mostly embracing communist and Arab nationalist ideologies, under the leadership of Hamma Hammami (Wolf 2014).

Notwithstanding this heterogeneity, the recomposition of the political scene in 2012 was still largely structured around the Islamist/secular divide. However, this political polarization "met" an electoral system that made it impossible for an absolute majority for one of the two parties to emerge. In addition, the structural fragmentation of the secular camp prevented anti-*Ennahda* parties from fully coalescing.

The politics of consensus and the implosion of the anti-Islamist bloc

The summer of 2013 represented a watershed for Tunisian politics. After the assassination of leftist leaders Chokri Belaid and Mohamed Brahmi, the country plunged into a political and institutional crisis that could have led to a civil war. That outcome was avoided thanks to the efforts of the two major parties' leaders Rached Ghannouchi (*Ennahda*) and Beji Caïd Essebsi (*Nidaa Tounès*), who, after a private meeting in Paris on August 15, paved the way for the initiative of a "National Dialogue" launched by the "National Quartet"[3] in the fall of 2013.

Interestingly, the 2013 crisis opened a phase of "personalistic politics", based on a direct mode of negotiation between the two charismatic figures, far from their respective partisan constraints. Moreover, the technocratic governance put forward by civil society negotiators and the foreign partners tended to limit the say of political parties, which were relegated to a secondary role. The de-sectorization of political relations also favored unofficial transactions between the leaders of the two major parties to the exclusion of all the others, including business circles, foreign states, and international donors. The deal between Ennahda and Nidaa Tounès led to the approval of the Constitution in January 2014 and paved the way for legislative and presidential elections to be held, respectively, in October and December 2014.

Despite having worked together to approve the new constitutional text, the rhetoric surrounding the legislative elections on October 26, 2014, was particularly conflictual, with *Nidaa Tounès* and *Ennahda* each suggesting that the other might jeopardize the democratization process. This confrontational attitude in the public debate has been interpreted by some scholars as a strategy of the two main parties to maintain their electorate in the run-up to the elections (Marzouki 2015; Boubekeur 2016). In this regard, Boubekeur described the "new Tunisian order" created after the 2014 elections as the result of a particular type of post-authoritarian political culture that she labels "bargained competition" consisting of Islamists and old regime elites bargaining on their mutual reintegration and their monopolization of the post-revolutionary political scene while competing over political resources through informal power-sharing arrangements (Boubekeur 2016).

The electoral results sealed the victory of *Nidaa Tounès* with 37.56% of the votes and 86 of the 217 seats in the ARP (*Assemblée Des Représentants du Peuple*), with *Ennahda* coming in the second position with 27.79% of the votes cast and 69 seats (compared to 89 in 2011). Thus, neither of these two parties had an absolute majority of the 109 deputies necessary to obtain the vote of confidence in the Assembly (see Table 9.2). However, rather than forming a government with smaller secular parties of similar ideological persuasion, *Nidaa Tounès* formed a government with its political adversary *Ennahda*, thereby engaging in what scholars defined as a "rotten compromise" (Marzouki 2015). Moreover, instead of appointing a party leader as prime minister, the new government turned the technocrat Habib Essid. The Essid government, without a clear political agenda, was unable to operate effectively. This lack of clear political direction in an increasingly unstable economic and security context paved the way for a series of "national unity" governments, where all parties and independents were invited to take part, sharing the responsibility of ineffectiveness, and thus creating a situation where all are responsible, but nobody is accountable. Against this backdrop, at the end of 2014, Essebsi became the new Tunisian president, after an electoral campaign characterized by the personalization of politics, with huge portraits of the candidate hanging on every street, recalling the cult of personality during the Ben Ali and Bourguiba regimes (Marzouki 2015).

Table 9.2 The 2014 parliamentary elections

Party	Votes	%	Seats
Nidaa Tounès	1,280,000	37.6	86
Ennahda	948,000	27.8	69
Union Patriotique Libre	141,000	4	16
Front Populaire	125,000	3.7	15
Afek Tounes	103,000	3	8
Congrès pour la République	69,894	2.05	4
Tayyar Dimuqrati	66,396	1.95	3

Source: ISIE 2014[4]

The Essid-led government was perceived by some of its members as leading to political stagnation. First, part of the problem within the secular camp was the fear among politicians, businessmen, professionals, and intellectuals of an alleged *Ennahda* hidden agenda of Islamization. Mutual suspicions in a government coalition are not conducive to effective policy-making. In addition, *Nidaa Tounès* had to contend with several internal struggles, especially after Essebsi's election to the presidency, which led to a leadership crisis within the party. Indeed, Essebsi's resignation from the post of party chair created a void, which in turn fueled internal conflicts. A major split occurred between the president's son, Hafedh Caïd Essebsi, designed to lead the party and a supporter of the politics of compromise with *Ennahda*, and the secretary general, Mohsen Marzouk, who criticized the party's nepotism and saw the alliance with the Islamist party as a voters' betrayal. By 2015, dozens of party members had resigned, including Marzouk, who went on to form his own party: *Mashrou' Tounes* (the Tunisia Project), gathering all the anti-Islamist leftist forces originally part of *Nidaa Tounès*. In 2016 Hafedh Caïd Essebsi became the executive director of the party. All this inevitably affected the government's performance.

Against a backdrop of political stagnation and a worsening economic crisis, a new rivalry within *Nidaa Tounès* developed in 2018 between the head of government Youssef Chahed – appointed by president Essebsi in 2016 to form a "government of national unity" that was supposed to stabilize Tunisia according to a largely technocratic program – and Hafedh Essebsi. On August 27, a new parliamentary bloc, called the "National Coalition", was founded to support Chahed and its political agenda. The Coalition quickly attracted several deputies from *Nidaa Tounès*, such as Zohra Driss, Moncef Sellami, Jalel Ghédira, Lamia Dridi, Marwa Bouazzi, Issam Matoussi, Ahmed Saïdi, and Mohamed Rachdi.[5] In light of this, the dismissal of Chahed from the party was discussed. Chahed's membership in *Nidaa Tounès* was eventually suspended in September 2018, and MPs close to him left the party as well, making the party only the third largest bloc in the parliament. This move eventually led to the transformation of the National Coalition into a new party, *Tahya Tounes*, on January 27, 2019.

To be sure, *Ennahda* as well had to cope with emerging internal schisms led by its most conservative figures who did not accept the leadership's pragmatic turn and coalition-making politics (Netterstrøm 2015). Indeed, several party members perceived the compromise with secular forces as a betrayal of the principles of the Revolution, which eventually led them to consider joining other political movements. Discontent notably increased among followers when the party's new policy of specialization was officially launched at its 10th Congress in May 2016. This new policy aimed at separating preaching activities from professional politics. On this occasion, the party leader Rachid Ghannouchi, declared: "there is no longer any justification for political Islam in Tunisia".[6] This statement was followed by the decision of the party's leadership to engage in the process of specialization (*taḥaṣṣuṣ*), aiming at separating the political from the religious dimension. This measure thus entailed a distinction between two intertwined parts of the same political group: the partisan dimension (*hizb*) and the social movement (*haraka*). As Ghannouchi (2016) declared:

> Ennahda has moved beyond its origins as an Islamist party and has fully embraced a new identity as a party of Muslim democrats. The organization is no longer both a political party and a social movement. It has ended all of its cultural and religious activities and now focuses only on politics.

This measure was perceived as unnatural by several currents within the Islamist community, as it envisages a distinction between two dimensions – religion and politics – which are, according to them, inextricably intertwined and inseparable. Thus, the specialization into political affairs created a split between those who refused such a change in the name of the original Islamist ideal and those who thought that the new historical juncture required a separation of politics and preaching. Some activists talked about a "betrayed revolution" and attacked the party accusing it of being a "corrupt establishment disconnected from real society".[7] As a party member stated:

> The party is now playing "professional" politics, negotiating compromises with the old regime. Because of its compromise with the old regime, the party has distanced itself from the Tunisian people and the values of Islam.[8]

Beyond Islamist vs. Secularist cleavage and the rise of new challengers

The apparent two-party system, which seemed to emerge after 2011, providing the electorate with a choice between two parties capable of governing (Hinnebusch 2017), vanished with the electoral results of the 2018 municipal elections and the 2019 legislative elections. Economic and social concerns were a clear priority, particularly in the countryside, where poverty led to the desire to change the existing political personnel, considered unable to put an end to it. The disappointment of voters, compounded by the failures of the "grand coalition" between *Ennahda* and *Nidaa Tounès*, was reflected in opinion polls from November 2018, with the appearance of independent outsiders leading established political figures in the presidential elections organized almost simultaneously.

The implosion of the secular camp, and of *Nidaa Tounès* in particular, was accelerated by the results of the first municipal elections in the country held on May 2018. The results showed a major defeat for *Nidaa Tounès*, which ranked first in just a few municipal councils. The disengagement of its supporters was so high that its executive director – the son of Tunisian president Beji Caïd Essebsi – made a call for the mobilization of his supporters less than four hours before the polls closed. Albeit to a lesser extent, the Islamist party also experienced disappointing results. The "winners" of the municipal elections were independent groups, created by former members of different political parties who had resigned after ideological or personal conflicts with the parties' leaderships. Thus, the municipal elections saw unaffiliated independent lists win the most votes because of the popular disenchantment with both major parties. This occurred though within a context of very low turnout (33.7 percent of the 5.3 million eligible voters), which is in itself an indication of disaffection with the political system.[9] Indeed, approximately two-thirds of the electorate did not vote. More specifically, the poor turnout was mainly due to the considerable frustration of young people in relation to their harsh economic difficulties in a context of political stagnation and social disarray more than seven years after the ousting of Ben Ali.

Overall, a major lesson of these elections was that the traditional narrative of Islamists versus secularists was no longer effective in explaining Tunisian local politics. The results of the 2019 presidential and legislative elections confirmed this and have to be read against a backdrop of disillusionment from politics and rejection of old cleavages. Indeed, the results marked the end of a political system structured primarily around identity questions and the Islamist/secular divide, notwithstanding the obstinacy of political leaders to keep the political debate on these tracks. The presidential campaign was based on populist rhetoric and the personalistic appeal of the two main contenders. In October 2019, Kaïs Saïed was elected president with a turnout of 55,02%. Saïed, a politically independent figure engaged in anti-corruption, who portrays himself as an anti-system law-and-order man and labeled by the national media as "a Robespierre without guillotine" or "Robocop", was a veritable outsider of the Tunisian political system.[10] His main competitor was Nabil Karoui, owner of the popular channel *Nessma TV*, also known as the "Tunisian Berlusconi". He was also the founder of the party *Qalb Tounès* (the "Heart of Tunisia"). The TV magnate used his daily TV show to build popular support, even though he had no experience of ruling, and he was jailed during the electoral campaign on charges of tax evasion and money laundering. In short, both 2018 municipal and the 2019 presidential elections show clearly how Tunisian voters turned away from traditional political parties to embrace independents and savior-like figures with very little to no political experience.

The results of the legislative Tunisian elections further reflected Tunisian voters' increased disillusionment. The parliament elected on October 6, 2019, was even more fragmented than its predecessor elected in 2014 (Table 9.3). Incumbent parties suffered heavy electoral losses, with *Ennahda* losing 17 MPs and *Nidaa Tounès* only keeping three seats following a series of internal splits that led to the setting up of splinter parties *Machrou' Tounès* and *Tahya Tounès*. The two parties that won the most votes, *Ennahda* (52 seats out of 217) and *Qalb Tounes* (38 seats), were eventually unable to form a majority coalition. Thus, the 2019 elections swept away many of the dominant political forces. The resulting political fragmentation was a major challenge, as *Ennahda* tried to form a government. Difficult negotiations between *Ennahda* – having a relative majority – and other parties were carried out over months. The divisions among the political parties became evident when, in January 2020, the Tunisian People's Assembly rejected a confidence vote on the government of independent lawmakers proposed by prime minister-designate Habib Jemli. On February 26, Elyes Fakhfakh, appointed by Kaïs Saïed, won the confidence of parliament with a majority of 129 votes out of 217, with great difficulty in the context of bitter negotiations and at the end of an 18-hour marathon session.

While the 2014 coalition reduced the polarization between Islamists and anti-Islamists, it proved incapable of meeting the socio-economic and institutional challenges of the post-2011 democratic transition. Thus, the two major parties fell victim to the protest vote, while other political forces – drawing on populist rhetoric around the issue of economic sovereignty – benefited from the widespread discontent about the policy deadlock generated by consensual governance, which was ultimately detrimental to Tunisian socio-economic development.

The party *Qalb Tounès*, with 38 seats, called for new sustainable development policies and joined the many critics of the new trade agreement between Tunisia and the EU for the establishment of a Deep and Comprehensive Free Trade Area.[11] *Attayar* (or *Tayyar Dimuqrati*), a party created in 2013 and based on the restoration of a "strong and just state" and an anti-corruption agenda, progressed from being the seventh to the third largest force in parliament with 22 seats. Another force was the People's Movement, which focused on socio-economic issues, and jumped from 3 to 16 seats from 2014 to 2019. The *Parti Destourien Libre* (PDL), led by Abir

Table 9.3 Results of the 2019 elections

Party	Votes	%	Seats
Ennahda	561,132	19.55	52
Qalb Tounes	416,004	14.49	38
Parti Destourien Libre	189,356	6.60	17
Tayyar Dimuqrati	183,473	6.39	22
Itilaf Karama	169,651	5.91	21
Mouvement du peuple	129,604	4.52	15
Tahya Tounes	116,582	4.06	14
Union Populaire Républicaine	59,924	2.09	3

Source: ISIE 2019

Moussi, formerly the assistant secretary general responsible for women within Ben Ali's party, attacked the 2014 politics of consensus during the electoral campaign. Since the new parliament began its work in December 2019, she has been engaged in a political conflict with *Ennahda*, contributing to the renewed polarization of the political scene around the issue of Islamism.

Most importantly, two newcomers, *Itilaf al-Karama* (Coalition of Dignity, 21 seats) and *Hizb al-Rahma* (5 seats), which have been hastily lumped together as "Salafi" parties, have thrived with a program emphasizing *Ennahda*'s inability to implement the popular claims of the Revolution due to its "politics of compromise" with the ancient regime's political forces. Notably, *Itilaf al-Karama* became the fourth political force in the country and gathered a heterogeneous membership bringing together ex-members of the LPR (Leagues for the Protection of the Revolution), both from Islamic or leftist backgrounds, human rights defenders (lawyers, journalists, and bloggers), former *Ennahda* party members who had left the party due to its pragmatism, members of the Salafi party *Jabhat al-Islah*, and some independent Salafi sheikhs (Blanc and Sigillò 2019). Its spokesperson, Seifeddine Makhlouf, one of the most prominent lawyers defending Tunisian Salafi-jihadists, emerged in the spotlight with his repeated attacks on France and its ambassador, accusing them of plundering Tunisia's natural resources and wanting to change the Tunisian way of life (Al-Hebassi 2019).

Although most conservative members of the *Itilaf al-Karama* blame *Ennahda* for "imitating secularist parties",[12] the party did not present itself as religious. Rather, it built a trans-ideological platform giving priority to a *sovereignist* agenda calling on Western powers to stop meddling in Tunisian domestic politics and "bringing dignity back to Tunisian people". Thus, *Itilaf al-Karama* constitutes a group of self-proclaimed "revolutionary" forces whose gathering momentum lies in its refusal to allow the return of former regime officials. The politicization of this new cleavage – compromising actors versus hard-line revolutionaries – which was previously without a partisan basis, represented the main novelty of the 2019 legislative elections (Blanc and Sigillò 2019).

Conclusion

On January 14, 2021, Tunisia celebrated its tenth anniversary since the fall of the authoritarian regime. However, ten years after the so-called "Jasmin Revolution" and despite the establishment of procedural democracy, the country is far from being stable. The political instability resulting from a proportional voting system coupled with fragile parties and voters' disaffection ended up leading to a fragmented party system and governments' unaccountability.

For most of the eight years since the Revolution, Tunisian politics has been organized around two large blocs: one centered on the *Ennahda* party and one on the modernist-secular *Nidaa Tounès*, which Beji Caïd Essebsi founded to counter the Islamists' influence on the country. As such, the post-revolutionary party system was characterized by political actors primarily distinguished through their affiliation to the old regime or their relationship with political Islam. Originally opposed to each other, these blocs reached a compromise after the 2014 elections and formed a coalition government. The 2018 local elections clearly demonstrated the failure of the major political parties. First, they revealed the inability of the secular camp to take root because of its factionalism and lack of a political agenda. Second, they displayed widespread popular distrust vis-à-vis *Ennahda*, a party perceived to be incapable of responding to the pressing socio-economic demands of the country, despite being in power since October 2011. Elections in 2019 reshuffled the political system and brought on the stage new challengers legitimized by the increasing frustration and discontent of Tunisians.

Overall, free and fair elections turned out to be a poor mechanism for choosing accountable representatives. Since the approval of the Constitution in 2014, Tunisia has had four prime ministers, none of whom was a well-known figure in a party chosen by a large number of voters. Three have lasted less than a year. The most important ministries – among them defense, interior, finance, justice and foreign affairs – have been led almost exclusively by technocratic figures unaffiliated with any political party. Moreover, the failure of the two major political parties led to the rise of new political trends drawing on personalism and populism. The newly born political parties stemming from the 2019 legislative elections lack any clear ideological identity, appealing to both the left and the right as well as to different social strata. The government that emerged from the last parliamentary and presidential elections eventually led to a political stalemate which ended with President Saïed appointing Hichem Mechichi as head of government. In the spring of 2021, another institutional conflict occurred between the prime minister and the speaker of the Assembly, Rachid Ghannouchi, a rivalry that has blocked ministerial appointments and diverted resources from tackling Tunisia's many economic and social problems

On July 25, 2021, after a week of protests in several cities across the country in a context of a harsh social and economic crisis worsened by the pandemic, President Kaïs Saïed invoked Article 80, the emergency clause in the Constitution, that allowed him to freeze parliamentary activities for 30 days, remove parliamentary immunity and dismiss Prime Minister Mechichi from office. Interestingly, the presidential initiative was applauded in the streets, with celebrations following the announcement and the positive reception of many media outlets. As a matter of fact, in the eyes of many Tunisians, the institutions targeted by Saïed – the government, the legislature, and the party having the majority within the parliament – had become associated with corruption and incompetence. Following this measure, several politicians, businessmen, and judges, as well as members of parliament who lost their immunity, were banned from traveling abroad or put under arrest. Even if most of these measures had the partial support of a frustrated and disenchanted Tunisian people, the extension of the emergency clause over the delay of 30 days and the dissolution of the Superior Council of the Judiciary in February 2022 casts a long shadow over the MENA's "democratic exception".

Notes

1 In terms of how many seats in the Assembly of the Representatives of the People (ARP) each district is to elect: Each governorate is allocated one seat for every 60,000 inhabitants. If a governorate's population cannot be neatly divided into increments of 60,000 (such as if its population is 109,000), it will receive one more seat should the remainder exceed 30,000 people (in the above example, the remainder would be 49,000 or 109,000 minus 60,000). Governorates with fewer than 270,000 people are granted an extra two seats, while those with a population between 270,000 and 500,000 are granted one extra seat.
2 *Tunisian Perspectives*, also known as *Perspectives* or *The Movement of El Amal Ettounsi* (The Tunisian Worker from the title of its newspaper), was a leftist movement that was considered one of the main Tunisian opposition movements, together with the Islamist movement, in the 1960s and 1970s.
3 The Tunisian General Labour Union (UGTT), The Tunisian Confederation of Industry, Trade and Handicrafts (UTICA), The Tunisian Human Rights League (LTDH), The Tunisian Order of Lawyers.
4 Turnout: 69% of 5,285,136 registered voters; 47,7% of eligible voters. Statistics taken from « Décision de l'Instance supérieure indépendante pour les élections relatives à la proclamation des résultats définitifs » for each election, published on the ISIE website www.isie.tn/.
5 Cf. www.espacemanager.com/huit-deputes-de-nidaa-tounes-demissionnent-du-bloc-de-ce-parti.html
6 Cf. www.lemonde.fr/international/article/2016/05/19/rached-ghannouchi-il-n-y-a-plus-de-justification-a-l-islam-politique-en-tunisie_4921904_3210.html
7 Statements retrieved from activists' Facebook and Twitter profiles.
8 Author's interview, Tunis, July 2, 2019.
9 Organized parties managed to obtain less than 68% of votes, since more than 32% went to independent lists. *Ennahda* obtained 28.6% and *Nidaa Tounès* 20.9% of the votes. *Nidaa Tounès* as expected, lost about 800,000 votes in comparison to the 2014 elections, confirming its crisis (Battera and Ieraci, 2019).

10 www.nytimes.com/2019/10/06/world/africa/tunisia-election-nabil-karoui.html
11 Sigillò, E. and Blanc T., "Tunisia's 2019 Elections: Beyond the Islamists vs. Secularists Cleavage", Middle East Directions Blog, European University Institute, https://blogs.eui.eu/medirections/tunisias-2019-elections-beyond-islamists-vs-secularists-cleavage/
12 Author's interview with a member of Itilaf Karama, Tunis, October 14, 2019.

References

al-Hebassi, Ahmed. 2019. 'Have you heard Seifeddine Makhlouf is one of the giants of the revolution?' *Kapitalis*, February 6. http://bit.ly/2of3nJd.
Battera, Federico and Giuseppe Ieraci. 2019. 'Party system and political struggle in Tunisia. Cleavages and electoral competition after the transition to democracy'. *Poliarchie/Polyarchies* 2(1): 4–44.
Bendana, Kmar. 2012. 'Le parti Ennahdha à l'épreuve du pouvoir en Tunisie'. *Confluences Méditerranée* 82(3): 189–204.
Blanc, Théo and Ester Sigillò. 2019. 'Beyond the "Islamists vs. Secularists" cleavage: The rise of new challengers after the 2019 Tunisian elections' Policy Brief n. 27'. *Middle East Directions*. European University Institute.
Boubekeur, Amel. 2016. 'Islamists, secularists and old regime elites in Tunisia: Bargained competition'. *Mediterranean Politics* 21(1): 107–127.
Braun, Célina. 2006. 'A quoi servent les partis tunisiens? Sens et contre-sens d'une libéralisation politique'. *Revue des Mondes Musulmans et de la Méditerranée* 111–112: 15–62.
Cavatorta, Francesco and Fabio Merone. 2013. 'Moderation through exclusion? The journey of the Tunisian Ennahda from fundamentalist to conservative party'. *Democratization* 20(5): 857–875.
Cavatorta, Francesco and Fabio Merone. 2019. 'Religion and political parties in Tunisia'. In: Jeff Haynes (ed.), *The Routledge Handbook to Religion and Political Parties*. London: Routledge, 358–369.
Ferjani, Mohamed Chérif. 2012. 'Révolution, élections et évolution du champ politique tunisien'. *Confluences Méditerranée* 82(3): 107–116.
Gana, Alia and Gilles Van Hamme. 2016. *Élections et territoires en Tunisie: Enseignement des scrutins post-révolution (2011–2014)*. Paris: IRMC/Karthala.
Geisser, Vincent and Deborah Perez. 2016. 'De la difficulté à «faire parti» dans la Tunisie post-Ben Ali'. *Confluences Méditerranée* 86(3): 21–44.
Ghannouchi, Rachid. 2016. 'From political Islam to Muslim democracy: The Ennahda party and the future of Tunisia'. *Foreign Affairs* 95(5): 58–67.
Ghorbal, Samy. 2012. *Orphelins de Bourguiba et héritiers du prophète*. Tunis: Cérès Editions.
Grubman, Nate and Aytuğ Şaşmaz. 2021. 'The collapse of Tunisia's party system and the rise of kais Saied'. *Middle East Report Online*. Available at: https://merip.org/2021/08/the-collapse-of-tunisias-party-system-and-the-rise-of-kais-saied/.
Grotz, Florian and Till Weber. 2012. 'Party systems and government stability in Central and Eastern Europe'. *World Politics* 64(4): 699–740.
Hinnebusch, Raymond. 2017. 'Political parties in MENA: Their functions and development'. *British Journal of Middle Eastern Studies* 44(2): 159–175.
Hmed, Choukri. 2016. 'Au-delà de l'exception tunisienne: Les failles et les risques du processus révolutionnaire'. *Pouvoirs* 156(1): 137–147.
Karvonen, Lauri and Sven Quenter. 2002. 'Electoral systems, party system fragmentation and government instability'. In: Dork Berg-Schlosser and Jeremy Mitchell (eds.), *Authoritarianism and Democracy in Europe, 1919–39*. London: Palgrave Macmillan, 131–162.
Kimya, Firat. 2021. 'Authoritarian legacies, weakness of political parties, and prospects for Tunisian democracy'. Available at: https://research.sharqforum.org/2021/08/16/authoritarian-legacies-weakness-of-political-parties-and-prospects-for-tunisian-democracy/.
Marzouki, Nadia. 2015. 'Tunisia's rotten compromise'. *Middle East Report*, July 10. Available at: https://merip.org/2015/07/tunisias-rotten-compromise/.
Merone, Fabio. 2015. 'Enduring class struggle in Tunisia: The fight for identity beyond political Islam'. *British Journal of Middle Eastern Studies* 42(1): 74–87.
Merone, Fabio and Damiano De Facci. 2015. 'The new Islamic middle class and the struggle for hegemony in Tunisia'. *Afriche e Orienti* 17(1–2): 56–69.

Merone, Fabio, Ester Sigillò and Damiano De Facci. 2018. 'Nahda and Tunisian Islamic activism'. In: Dara Conduit and Sharham Akbarzadeh (eds.), *New Opposition in the Middle East*. London: Palgrave Macmillan, 177–201.

Merone, Fabio, Théo Blanc and Ester Sigillò. 2021. 'The evolution of Tunisian Salafism after the revolution: From la Maddhabiyya to Salafi-Malikism'. *International Journal of Middle East Studies* 53(3): 455–470.

Mezghani, Ali. 2012. 'Tunisie une révolution, une élection et des malentendus'. *Le Débat* 168(1): 168–177.

Netterstrøm, Kasper Ly. 2015. 'After the Arab Spring: The Islamists' compromise in Tunisia'. *Journal of Democracy* 26(4): 110–124.

Teti, Andrea, Pamela Abbott and Francesco Cavatorta. 2018. *Social, Economic and Political Transformations in the Wake of the Arab Uprisings*. London: Palgrave.

Torelli, Stefano, Fabio Merone and Francesco Cavatorta. 2012. 'Salafism in Tunisia: Challenges and opportunities for democratization'. *Middle East Policy* 19(4): 140–154.

Van Hamme, Gilles, Alia Gana and Maher Ben Rebbah. 2014. 'Social and socio-territorial electoral base of political parties in post-revolutionary Tunisia'. *The Journal of North African Studies* 19(5): 751–769.

Wolf, Anne. 2014. *Can Secular Parties Lead the New Tunisia?* Washington, DC: Carnegie Endowment for International Peace.

Wolf, Anne. 2018. 'What are secular parties in the Arab world? Insights from Tunisia's Nidaa Tounes and Morocco's PAM'. In: Francesco Cavatorta and Lise Storm (eds.), *Political Parties in the Arab World*. Edinburgh: Edinburgh University Press.

Yardımcı-Geyikçi, Şebnem and Ozlem Tür. 2018. 'Rethinking the Tunisian miracle: A party politics view'. *Democratization* 25(5): 787–803.

# 10

PRE-ELECTORAL COALITIONS IN IRAQ

The case of the Communist–Sadrist alliance

Paride Turlione[1]

Introduction

Given the long-running rivalry between the two political camps, the secular–Islamist divide is still considered one of the most prominent frictions in Middle Eastern and North African (MENA) politics (Mahmood 2009; Göle 2010; Blaydes and Linzer 2012). Although Islamists and secular movements might be seen as inherently opposed to each other, there are, however, prominent cases of cross-ideological cooperation present throughout the region (Schwedler and Clark 2006; Browers 2009; Durac 2015). In this respect, the literature has focused mainly on authoritarian contexts, where an anti-regime posture constitutes a powerful driver of cross-ideological cooperation among opposition parties. Little is known though about this issue in other institutional settings, even though some work exists on the Tunisian case (Cavatorta and Merone 2013; Landolt and Kubicek 2014). The Iraqi case represents a quasi-democratic context or a "delegative polyarchy" (O'Donnell 1993) where one can examine such cooperation in the absence of authoritarian structures. In 2015, an alliance between the Iraqi Communist Party and the Islamist Sadrist movement emerged and formed an electoral coalition – the Alliance Toward Reforms or *Sa'irun* – raising questions about the conditions that led to this apparently awkward outcome. Focusing on shifting structural conditions and the role of crucial agents – or "social brokers" – in bridging the two political camps, this chapter sheds light on cross-ideological convergence in a liberalized MENA country. The analysis of the 2018 elections and the following events also highlight the alliance's limits and shortcomings.

Cross-ideological cooperation

The scholarly debate has handled the issue of cross-ideological cooperation through several perspectives. In emphasizing the inclusion-moderation hypothesis and focusing on the consequences of cross-ideological cooperation, some argued that such cooperation does not always lead to the moderation of Islamist parties' ideology (Schwedler 2011; Cavatorta and Merone 2013; Brocker and Künkler 2013). In her study on Jordan, Clark (2006) focuses on the Higher Committee for the Coordination of National Opposition Parties (HCCNOP), an opposition bloc that included the Islamic Action Front and Communist and Ba'thist parties. Clark argues that beyond the struggle for fair democratic procedures and against the normalization of the relationship between the Jordanian regime and Israel, the HCCNOP did not deal with divisive issues. Discussions on how to reach a shared worldview or a national political program were not held. Each party acted independently and could refuse to sign joint declarations. Members usually interpreted the Committee's mission as coordination of opposition parties rather than cooperation. On important sites of recruitment and mobilization, like universities, such cooperation was much more challenging to reach (Clark 2010), highlighting the unwillingness to share power and the limited nature of coordination among these different ideological actors, which is thus more tactical than programmatic. Abdelrahman (2009) and Shehata (2009) present similar findings in Mubarak's Egypt, where the anti-authoritarian alliance between Islamists and the Left had been built around the principles of consensus and independence, limiting their joint activism to specific short-term goals and reducing their alliance as a tactical one.

Other scholars look for the causes and mechanisms of cross-ideological coalition-building and emphasize the role of key political actors within the main parties. In sharp contrast to the inclusion-moderation theory, Browers (2007) claims that, in the Yemeni case, exclusion rather than inclusion in formal politics triggered cooperation among parties with alternative views. Moreover, by analyzing the steps that led to the Joint Meeting Parties formation – an opposition bloc calling for political liberalization that includes ideologically opposed parties among them, such as the Islamist *Islah* and the Yemenite Socialist Party – she asserts that key individuals with excellent negotiation skills represented a necessary condition for cross-ideological cooperation to succeed. In this context, structural changes (the political marginalization of *Islah* by the regime) and the role of critical agents able to bridge ideological differences operated in a dialectical relationship.

However, in other contexts and times, attempts to forge a broad anti-authoritarian alliance among the opposition parties have failed. In their research on Morocco, Wegner and Pellicer (2011) found that differences in ideology seemed to have had a minor impact on the failure of cross-ideological cooperation between the Islamist Party of Justice and Development and the Socialist Union of Popular Forces. Factors such as their asymmetry in electoral strength and the USFP's co-optation by the regime were crucial factors. Similarly, by focusing on "cooperation failures" among opposition parties in Ben Ali's Tunisia, Haugbølle and Cavatorta (2011) observe that ideological differences within and between the Islamist party *al-Nahda* and the secular parties, strategic postures and personal rivalries undermined for quite some time attempts to forge a broad opposition bloc.

Finally, some laudable contributions propose typologies of opposition cooperation by looking at the broader regional picture and trying to highlight some more general trends. Schwedler and Clark (2006) distinguish three levels of cooperation: *tactical* (low-level), characterized by single-issue and short-term forms of coordination, with few political costs and no substantive ideological shifts and compromises; *strategic* (mid-level), where multiple issues of concern are shared and is sustained for longer, but leaves specific issues (especially the role of religion in politics) off the table, thus preventing a common political vision or ideological compromises; finally, *high-level* cooperation sees participants debating core and substantive issues in the attempt to reach a shared worldview. At that time, the authors found that, despite the sharp predominance of small tactical alignments, instances of strategic cooperation were expanding, thus enhancing the chances of the emergence of high-level cooperation. For his part, Kraetzschmar (2011) proposed a slightly different typology that disentangles cooperation's goals and the durability dimensions. The resulting typology is constituted by four categories of cooperation: domestic actors on a single issue; domestic actors on multiple issues (comprising pre- and post-electoral alliances); domestic and foreign actors on a single issue; and domestic and foreign actors on multiple issues.

All these studies show the progress in the understanding of inter-party relations in MENA authoritarian contexts. However, little is known about cross-ideological cooperation in the Arab democracies or quasi-democracies. To fill this gap, the following sections focus on *Sa'irun*, the cross-ideological alliance between the Sadrists and the Communist Party in Iraq, which obtained the relative majority of parliamentary seats in the 2018 national elections.

The Iraqi case is atypical with respect to those mentioned above for multiple reasons. First, the institutional context: Iraq is a transitional democracy in which political power is shared among the three main ethno-sectarian social groups (Sunnis, Shi'is and Kurds), whereas in most Arab countries, autocratic elites strictly control and co-opt opposition groups. The quasi-democratic features of Iraq weaken one of the main drivers of cross-ideological cooperation detected in authoritarian contexts, namely the struggle for more inclusive rules of the game, degrees of power-sharing, or the fall of the regime. Second, *Sa'irun* was a pre-electoral alliance with a shared political program whose core is the product of years of intellectual and social interactions between the Sadrist movement and the Communist Party. Consequently, it goes beyond a purely tactical or strategic move deployed to gain a degree of political power and occupy government seats, as post-electoral agreements in the region and elsewhere are typically set up for. It fits, instead, the more distinctive and high-level form of cooperation. Third, the alliance's political agenda is largely dedicated to substantive internal issues rather than international posturing or struggles for reforming the procedural rules of political participation. As mentioned, these characteristics make this case quite atypical, thus raising questions about the conditions that made this outcome possible, the underlying coalition-building process and the consequences for the Iraqi party system and the country's political landscape.

Sadrists and Communists: an awkward alliance?

Sectarian cleavages and personalism have been the main traits of Iraqi politics, with sectarian identities in particularly being employed to mobilize support and gain power. After the 2003 US-led invasion and the following reconstruction process, ethno-sectarian power-sharing has become the primary organizing principle of Iraqi political institutions under the label of *muhasasa ta'ifyya*, sectarian apportionment (Dodge 2020; Haddad 2020). Similarly to the Lebanese case, political power is shared among ethno-sectarian groups in compliance with their relative demographic weight. However, the marginalization of Sunni communities and the US military occupation provoked widespread discontent and, eventually, sectarian violence (Jacoby and Neggaz 2018). The 2006–2007 civil war between Sunni and Shi'a paramilitary groups, the fall of the region into sectarian violence after the 2011 uprisings and the emergence of the Islamic State are often used as evidence for claiming that sectarianism – considered, in primordialist terms, immutable – is the primary driver of political affiliation and mobilization in the region (Friedman 2013; Wright 2013). However, dealing with Iraq through this lens alone is misleading. First, it assumes a deterministic and static political life in a context that is actually changing rapidly and where the sectarian system itself is cyclically contested from below (Costantini 2021). Second, it reduces the political debate to a struggle among the three main ethno-sectarian identities, overshadowing the more "secular" political issues at stake. Third, it understands sectarian communities as homogeneous and devoid of internal fractures (Makdisi 2017; Sayigh 2017; Majed 2020).

Inter-sectarian tensions dominated Iraqi politics in the earlier stages after the US invasion when the foundational rules of the post-Saddam Iraqi state were designed, and fears of group extinction triggered a "security dilemma" explicitly coded in sectarian terms by sect-centric actors. Nevertheless, the relevance of sectarian identities in shaping political alliances and rivalries has diminished over time, as shown by the rising instances of intra-sectarian contestation and inter-sectarian coalitions from 2015 onwards. This trend finds confirmation in the widespread rejection of the *muhasasa* system itself since the mid-2010s (Haddad 2019).

The emergence of the 2015 protests epitomizes the shift from identity politics to issue politics (Jabar 2018). The 2015 social movement was marked by an intra-sect struggle – mostly Shi'a citizens against their leaders – with protesters arguing for a civil state based on the representation of political preferences and policy positions rather than ethno-sectarian apportionment (Jabar 2018). On the one hand, the social movement's grievances have become a new source of legitimization, opening a window of opportunity for policy issues beyond ethno-confessional affiliations to penetrate political parties' agendas, an essential move for political parties to regain popular consent and legitimacy. On the other hand, the decreasing salience of identity in shaping coalitions aggravated the intra-sect political fragmentation – no longer held together by sect solidarity – and provided an opportunity for the creation of new alliances based on policy issues.

It is in this renewed context that the alliance between Sadrists and Communists emerged, even though, structural conditions constitute only one side of the coin. Actors have a prominent role in bridging groups with a long story of rivalry and different if not opposing ideologies and positions. In this sense, the Sadrist–Communist alliance has been prompted actively by agents of both sides, whose role has been crucial in bringing it about. The fact that individuals not in leadership positions led the brokerage process is in sharp contrast to the top-down or elite-driven bias in Iraqi and MENA party politics.

A window of opportunity: the structural context

Leftist-Sadrist rapprochement would not have been possible without significant developments in the surrounding political and social environment, which changed the political opportunity structure and political actors' preferences (Robin-D'Cruz 2019a; 2019b). More specifically, the rapidly decreasing legitimacy of the governing elite was further exacerbated by the economic crisis, the changing international environment and the cleavages within the leftist and the Islamist socio-political camps interacted and opened a window of opportunity that allowed unlikely readjustments within the Iraqi political system.

The failure of the post-Saddam Islamist-dominated political elite to tackle the country's crucial problems has precipitated a growing legitimacy crisis, making participation in the political field costly in terms of reputation. The emergence of a broad social movement demanding systemic reforms may be considered a causal indicator of the crisis. On the one hand, the demand for changing the identity-based quota system questioned the fundamental principle of power-sharing dominating Iraqi political institutions since the fall of Saddam. On the other hand, the struggle against endemic corruption is directed toward the political elite as a whole, as it benefited from sectarian patronage networks in gaining ever-increasing political power at the expense of marginalized socio-economic groups that suffered (and still suffer) from the lack of investment in welfare measures (Mansour and van der Toorn 2018), infrastructural penury and poor security.

The inability of the Islamist-dominated Iraqi institutions to ensure security, tackle corruption, build infrastructure and fight against sectarian violence – further exacerbated by the fall of Mosul to the Islamic State – unsettled the established symbolic and material legitimacy resources of the democratically elected ruling elites. The economic crisis and the consequent collapse of patronage networks lowered the political field's capacity to repress or co-opt contentious political mobilization, which had previously allowed its reproduction and (precarious) stability. This paved the way for a new agenda to reform the political system according to new values and ideas. Moreover, the strategy of dialogue promoted by the Obama administration toward Iran and the gradual US military disengagement in Iraq weakened one of the most prominent factors of unity among the diverse constellation of Shi'a Islamist forces in the region, leading to the diminution of Iranian interference in Iraq and unveiling a previously concealed heterogeneity within the Shi'a political field (Khalaf 2020). Taken together, the decreasing appeal of traditional symbolic resources of legitimacy, a lower international pressure on Iran and Iraqi Shi'a political actors and the fall of material means for preventing the emergence of inter-sectarian social movements of contestation opened a window of opportunity for a new political agenda. Looking at the mobilization strategies the major political parties deployed during the 2018 electoral campaign, one can clearly detect a shift in their rhetoric from identity to issue politics. In fact, political parties "competed" over the ownership of the social movement's narratives and promised radical reforms under the flag of "civicness", the end of corruption, the development of service provision and greater employment (Mansour 2018).

All this further exacerbated another ongoing process: the deepening of cleavages within the secular and the Islamist ideological camps. These fractures can be seen in the growing conflicts between the Sadrists and the other Shi'a groups (namely the Iranian-backed components of the Shi'a camp) and the mistrust between the Iraqi Communist Party and other secular actors, paving the way for innovative and unprecedented experiments of cross-ideological cooperation (Robin-D'Cruz 2019b). In this regard, the pictures of the 2005 and 2018 electoral alliances are radically different, reflecting ideological, strategical and personal rivalries among the competing Shi'a leaders that, over time, have overcome the power of sectarian solidarity. In 2005, political alliances were strictly organized in compliance with the sectarian principle: the most prominent Shi'a parties, *Da'wa* and the Islamic Supreme Council of Iraq (ISCI) ran together in the United Iraqi Alliance, backed by the Grand Ayatollah Ali al-Sistani and many Sadrist followers (but not Sadr himself). Later, in the 2010 elections, the Sadrists and the ISCI formed the Iraqi National Alliance, whereas Nouri al-Maliki – the outgoing prime minister and leader of the *Da'wa* party who repressed Sadr's Mahdi Army during his mandate – formed his own State of Law coalition in the attempt to gain trans-sectarian support, but ending up splitting the Shi'a vote. The fragmentation process went on in 2014, with the Sadrists forming their own *al-Ahrar* bloc and a split within the ISCI[2] (Edwards 2018; Resta 2021). In 2018, the Shi'a constituency was the object of competition among five different blocs: the *Sa'irun* coalition, the *Fateh* coalition, the Victory Alliance, the National Wisdom Movement and the State of Law coalition, whose leaders – except for the more ambiguous Muqtada al-Sadr – were prominent members or even leaders of the *Da'wa* Party and the ISCI back in 2005 (al-Marashi 2018).

Similar cleavages occurred within the secular and leftist camps. The two most prominent leftist parties, the Iraqi Communist Party (ICP) and the Workers Communist Party of Iraq (WCPI), have a long history of cooperation failure. Both in 2011 and 2015, the ICP did not make any serious attempt to forge a broad secular alliance with the other secular and leftist actors among protesters, even when the WCPI reached out to the ICP[3]. Moreover, the two leftist parties had an antipodal attitude toward the Sadrist mobilization in the 2015 protests. While the ICP agreed to cooperate with Sadrists given their shared demands, the WCPI withdrew from the street rapidly, refusing to mobilize shoulder to shoulder with Islamists. Later, when the alignment between the Sadrists and the ICP began to emerge, the WCPI denounced their leftist counterpart (Majed and Aljabiri 2020). Finally, the opposite attitudes toward Islamists' involvement in the 2015 social movement led to further splits within the secular camp, with the secular and leftist *Mustamerroun* coalition weakened by the departure of anti-Islamist activists, who later formed the *Madaniyoun* coalition (Saad Aldouri 2017, Majed and Aljabiri 2020).

The interactions between the political and economic crisis, the changing international environment favored by the normalization of the US–Iran relationship and the internal cleavages within the secular and the Islamist camps restructured the political space, transforming the previously marginal secularist/leftist actors into a source of political legitimacy and making social and ideological barriers more permeable. For this reason, political actors recognized the necessity of finding a new set of political ideas for restructuring their bases of legitimacy, looking at the civil protest movement as the primary source of renovation. However, the emergence of the social protest movement and intra-camp political fractures alone cannot explain the emergence of the alliance between Sadrists and Leftists. Although structural changes may affect actors' views and strategies, the success of an alliance between two ideologically opposed groups requires a process of rapprochement and reciprocal trust-building that needs active architects. Indeed, even if several political forces tried to build cooperation with secular actors within the 2015 social movement, only the Sadrist–Communist case could be deemed a success. How did therefore this process of cross-ideological convergence occur?

Cross-ideological social brokerage: the relevance of the actors

Despite their crucial role in opening the window of opportunity for cross-ideological convergence, structural reconfigurations constitute only one side of the story. As Browers (2007: 583) pointed out,

> Formulating the question as to how structural arrangements impact ideas neglects the modes of thinking and the character of individuals necessary to bring about the interactions in the first place. […] structures and agents exist within a dialectical relationship, as do material conditions and ideological contexts.

Thus, structural factors and contextual developments might be crucial for cross-ideological alliances to occur, but they should not be considered the only necessary and sufficient condition. Specific actors have a crucial bridging role and focusing on them in prompting cross-ideological rapprochement can shed light on dynamics overshadowed by a purely deterministic analysis. In this sense, McAdam, Tarrow and Tilly (2001: 142) developed the idea of brokerage, defined as "the linking of two or more previously unconnected social sites by a unit that mediates their relations with one another and/or with yet other sites". Key actors with proper skills and social capital to bridge ideological distance have a crucial role in converting a potential convergence – represented by contextual developments – to an active one. Without these "architects" (Browers 2007) of cross-ideological interactions, distrust and previous rivalries are likely to undermine the process long before reaching mutual accommodation. Interestingly, Diani (2003) noted that these individuals are unlikely to be leaders of the collective actors involved, but they enjoy considerable influence due to their role as intermediaries between organizations. As Clarke (2014) showed, potential social brokers in Egypt and Tunisia were present, and when the uprisings occurred, they took advantage of their positioning at the periphery of different social sectors, mediating and coordinating them, thus becoming active social brokers.

In Iraq, "Sadrist actors with a background in leftist political thought and praxis, and civil trend [secular/leftist] actors with a background in Islamist politics" (Robin-D'Cruz 2019a) were confined to the periphery of their respective social groups, marginalized because of their "transgressive" ideas. However, once the barriers between the Sadrist and the autonomous secular camps became more porous due to contextual developments, their hybrid collocation evolved in social capital, making them central to bridging initiatives. They became social brokers inasmuch as they were able to cross social and ideological barriers and actively initiate the process of cross-ideological convergence.

This does not mean that social brokers' position in the 2015–2018 period was achieved by chance and with no resistance. Attempts to bridge the secular/leftist and the Sadrist camps had been made for over a decade, prompting a step-by-step rapprochement and laying the foundations for the alliance's emergence. In 2010, after the harsh confrontation with al-Maliki and several splits within the Sadrist paramilitary group *Jaish al-Mahdi*, Muqtada al-Sadr himself persuaded Sa'ib' Abd al-Hamid – a prominent Iraqi secular intellectual – to take over the Sadrist Foundation, in an attempt to reorient his movement toward the secular intelligentsia that Islamist forces had tried to silence since 2003. After al-Hamid's early refusal, al-Sadr promised to give him complete control over the Foundation's activities and its reform. Al-Hamid's leadership reformed several centers within the institution. In particular, the Iraqi Scientific Centre started welcoming leftist cultural and political publications, among them those of the leftist psychologist Faris Kamal Nadhmi, one of the key brokers and ideologues of the cross-ideological alliance (Robin-D'Cruz 2019a), which he framed in Gramscian terms. Nadhmi's ideas garnered a lot of interest among youth Sadrists, while receiving criticism from the secular left. At the same time, some Sadrists resisted al-Hamid's reform efforts and tried to sabotage his activities, highlighting an intra-Sadrist struggle and the high degree of heterogeneity within the movement. This resistance forced al-Hamid to resign from the Foundation in 2013, but Sadr's closest allies persuaded him to lead the Iraqi Scientific Center after making it completely independent from the Foundation (Robin-D'Cruz 2019b).

These previous interactions constituted the backbone of the cultural and ideological rapprochement between the Sadrist and the secular-leftist groups, building the base for a deeper political common ground wherein the alliance was built. The longstanding process of cultural and political embeddedness contrasts both the purely instrumental interpretation of the cross-ideological alliance and the allegedly elite-driven nature of Iraqi (and Middle Eastern) politics. This claim is reinforced by the resistance grassroots members put up on both sides throughout these previous interactions.

Previous instances of small-scale collaboration between the Sadrists and the leftists facilitated cross-ideological convergence once the contextual factors became favorable in 2015. Later, junior Sadrists actively engaged with secular activists to coordinate their activities within the 2015 movement. In earlier phases, social brokers did not act as representatives of their respective ideological camps but as individuals capable of engaging in dialogue on a shared cultural terrain. The meetings were informal, private and broad, with the primary goal of "testing the waters" before any deeper discussion about formal cooperation could be held. The role of the junior Sadrist 'Ala' al-Baghdadi and other social brokers with a secular background lowered tensions between the two sides and favored the recognition of shared ideas. Later, other junior members acted officially and publicly to mediate the dialogue between the two sides through weekly local meetings and assemblies, building mutual trust. Finally, social brokers drew senior political actors into the dialogue through delegations, eventually prompting the institutionalization of such a cooperation. Out of it, new bodies, like the Muqtada's Committee for the Supervision of the Protests and the Coordinating Sub-Committee, responsible for coordinating leftist-Islamist activities – both formed by leftist/secularist and Sadrist members (Robin-D'Cruz 2019a) – saw the light of day, enhancing the chances for the subsequent electoral alliance to be formed.

In fact, on the eve of the 2018 election campaign, cross-ideological cooperation became a political alliance between secularists (the Iraqi Communist Party in particular) and Sadrists in the *Sa'irun* coalition. In the majority of cases, alliances are formed after parliamentary elections to reach a majority of seats to form a government. The occurrence of such an alliance *before* the election is particularly relevant because it rules out this instrumentalist reading and makes the Iraqi case particularly interesting.

The 2018 and 2021 elections

The national election in May 2018 saw the Shi'a parties and their "supposed" constituency split as never before. On the one hand, parties commonly associated with the establishment that ruled since the first free elections lost large shares of the vote and parliamentary seats. As a glaring example, al-Maliki's State of Law coalition lost 67 seats, finding itself with only 25 deputies. On the other hand, the *Sa'irun* coalition won 54 seats out of 329 seats, 20 more than the *Ahrar* Sadrist Movement had won in 2014 (al Khafaji 2018). This positive outcome represents a reward for the Sadrists and ICP's participation in the protests, their posture against the ruling elites during the electoral campaign and their representation of the socio-economic and political demands coming from the streets. *Sa'irun* was followed by the *Fateh* coalition, which won 47 seats, and the Victory Alliance of outgoing Prime Minister Haider Al-Abadi with 42, both of which capitalized on the popularity of their role in defeating the Islamic State (Mansour and van den Toorn 2018).

During the electoral campaigning, the *Sa'irun* coalition deployed anti-elite rhetoric, put up non-establishment candidates and promoted an issue-based political discourse, acting in compliance with the shift from identity to issue politics demanded by the 2015 movement itself. In both their anti-elite/populist rhetoric and issue-based political platform, the *Sa'irun* coalition proved successful in meeting the demands of the electorate. In fact, recent surveys show that Iraqi citizens have no confidence in the government ("not at all" 52.7%, "not very much" 24.7%), nor in the parliament ("not at all" 65.1%, "not very much" 18.6%) and show high mistrust toward political parties ("not at all" 67.3%, "not very much" 18.2%) (World Value Survey VII 2020). Moreover, the majority of respondents perceive a significant level of systemic corruption (74%), which is considered the most critical challenge facing the country by the relative majority (32%), followed by the economy (Arab Barometer V, 2019). By addressing these issues in its political agenda, and by participating actively in the 2015 social movement, the *Sa'irun* coalition distinguished itself from the political establishment, aligning itself with the general mood of the electorate.

Furthermore, *Sa'irun* campaigning addressed socio-economic issues as well, which constitute one of the most urgent problems to handling Iraqi public opinion. Indeed, in Iraq and elsewhere in the region (Teti et al. 2019), democracy is associated with redistributive economic policies, and poor economic performances are one of the main factors that render public opinion disillusioned toward its democratic system (Arab Barometer V 2019). As a matter of fact, more than 60% of Iraqi citizens claim that providing unemployment aid should be an essential or a very important characteristic of democracy; a similar percentage is favorable to the role of the state in making people's incomes equal (54.8%) and in taxing rich and subsidize the poor (55.7%)[4] (World Value Survey VII 2020). Accordingly, *Sa'irun* addressed socio-economic issues that concern broad social strata, especially in the marginalized south and in poorer neighborhoods in Baghdad. Indeed, these are the typical sites of popular protests – usually led by young Shi'a activists – whose rage is triggered by absent public services and high unemployment. The combination of al-Sadr popularity among disenfranchised, poor Shi'a citizens – mainly from the rural south and in the urban lower-income neighborhood of Sadr City in Baghdad – and the Iraqi Communist Party's traditional posture in favor of the lower classes may be seen as successful class-like solidarity against social inequality and toward the oppressed, at least discursively (Sakai and Suechika 2020). A closer look at the local distribution of seats in each electoral district seems to confirm this claim: the *Sa'irun* coalition gained most of its votes in the South Shi'a provinces, successfully balancing its anti-Iranian positions – which may have alienated pro-Iranian Shi'a citizens – and its "heretical" secular involvement – vigorously attacked by Iranian officials and pro-Iranian Iraqi constituencies. Moreover, it sensationally won in Baghdad, where the 2015 movement was incredibly vibrant, doubling the second-best coalitions, *Fateh* and State of Law (Mansour and van den Toorn 2018). Thus, given the main worry of the average Iraqi citizen – the fear of losing or not finding a job (73.1%) – political disillusionment is not surprising, nor is it the *Sa'irun* electoral success, given the leftist socio-economic values that it tried to represent, explicitly addressing the oppressed and economically marginalized constituencies.

Nevertheless, this electoral success should be nuanced for at least four reasons. First, the coalition did not gain enough seats to form a government alone, thus forcing it to compromise with other coalitions led by the same elites the 2015 social movement opposed. The struggle for forming a post-electoral coalition pushed *Sa'irun* toward Abadi's Victory Alliance and Hakim's National Wisdom Movement, forming the reformist *Islah* bloc against the more conservative *Bina* bloc formed by al-Maliki's State of Law and Ameri's *Fateh*. The fragmentation of the political forces involved prompted an impasse until the end of October 2018, with new protests erupting in Basra against the failures of the political class (Mansour 2019) and the formation of a government led by ISCI leader Abd al-Mahdi. Second, the 44% turnout was the lowest rate in Iraq since 2005, suggesting *Sa'irun* was unable to invert the trend of growing disaffection toward Iraqi politics. Third, in absolute terms, Sadr received a similar number of votes in each province compared to the 2014 elections. This means that the coalition did not gain new portions of the electorate, but it simply "resisted" Iraqi citizens' disillusionment toward their elites better than other political forces, balancing lower support from the Sadrist movement with more support from the secular and leftist constellation led by the Iraqi Communist Party. Finally, Sadr rapidly reapproached his pro-Iranian counterparts and contributed to repressing the 2019 social movement through his "Blue Helmets" paramilitary group.

The latter development reflects a change in the structural conditions that opened the window of opportunity. This speaks to the salience of foreign affairs in Iraq's internal politics. On the one hand, Sadrists joined the October 2019 movement in the early phases of the protests, which presented the same demands of 2015 but in more radical terms. On the other hand, the Trump administration's provocative rhetoric and, later, the assassination of Qasem Soleimani and Abu Mahdi al-Muhandis in Baghdad pushed Sadr into a defensive posture for fear of being next on the US list of enemies. The renewed conflict between the United States and Iran pushed Sadr to withdraw his followers from the protests and realign with Teheran, causing an internal split between the more conservative members and the ones more supportive of the socio-economic demands of the protesters, confirming the shortcomings of an elite-driven understanding of Iraqi politics (Robin-D'Cruz and Mansour 2020).

The 2021 elections are in continuity with the previous ones. None of the contenders won enough seats to form a government on their own, reiterating the political stalemate over reforms that large sections of the public have been clamoring for. Moreover, the turnout further declined, setting a new negative record of 36% eligible voters (Higel 2021), partly due to the boycott protesters called for. However, two changes deserve to be mentioned, which could influence Iraqi political development in the coming years: the overwhelming victory of the Sadrists over the other Shia parties, but this time not in coalition with the Communist Party; and the emergence of independent anti-sectarian parties linked to the 2019 Tishreen (October) protest movement.

The Sadrists, facilitated by the low turnout and solid local roots in strategic regions, won 73 parliamentary seats, outperformed the rivals of *Fateh* and al-Maliki and allied with Barzani's KDP and Halbousi's Sunni Taqadum party (Higel 2021). The *Fateh* party saw its seats plummet from 48 to 16, while al-Maliki's State of Law went from 25 to 35 seats, probably gaining from *Fateh*'s electoral pool. However, the absolute number of votes shows a different picture than the representation in parliament. Sadr's votes were slightly down in 2018 – a likely sign of the loss of some more secular voters following the crackdown on the Tishreen movement – and *Fateh* and State of Law's votes added together slightly exceeded those of the Sadrist party. This shows that, in addition to the low turnout, the Sadrists were able to take advantage of the new electoral law, acting pragmatically and strategically and adapting candidacies and campaigns, and demonstrating a level of pragmatism not usually recognized in Islamist political actors (Mansour and Stewart-Jolley 2021). Moreover, the split between pro-Iranians (*Fateh* and al-Maliki) and anti-Iranians (Sadr) at the electoral level deepened, thus becoming one of the most profound ideological rifts in contemporary Iraq, overtaking identity differences.

The Tishreen movement has influenced Iraqi institutional politics since its emergence in 2019, and its long-term consequences could empower independent and anti-sectarian political forces. First, the protests played a role in the resignation of the al-Mahdi government, which Mustafa al-Kadhimi replaced (Jiyad 2021). Second, a new electoral law, more favorable to small independent parties, has been approved as a concession to the protesters. Eighty-three electoral districts replaced the old 18 provincial districts in the new electoral system. Moreover, the single non-transferable vote was adopted, virtually ensuring a more transparent electoral process and a better connection between voters and elected representatives (Stewart-Jolley 2021; Mansour and Stewart-Jolley 2021).

The issue of participation in the elections divided the protest movement: most protesters do not believe in top-down reform of the political system, fear co-optation by the much more experienced political elites, and have boycotted the elections. However, some protesters set up the Imtidad party, which performed well, winning nine seats with very little investment, coming first in the territories where the social movement was born. Similarly, the Kurdish New Generation Movement, a supporter of the Tishreen movement, won nine seats as well (Higel 2021). The new electoral reform has thus favored the entry of "underdogs", bringing a secular and anti-sectarian opposition into parliament. Although the electoral power of these political formations is not sufficient to reform the system from the ground up, renewed confidence in the electoral process could lead to a reversal of the trend of abstentionism, with a potential impact on the political balance within the institutions (Higel 2021).

Conclusion

In 2011, Ellen Lust (2011) asked how single-issue interactions between different ideological actors affect their mutual perceptions and their chances to cooperate on several more complex issues in the future. These questions are crucial in the contemporary Middle East, especially after a decade of sectarian violence and jihadists' resurgence. The Iraqi case, in this sense, provides a partial and provisional answer.

The intellectual antecedents of the Sadrist–Communist alliance show that the process of ideological convergence needs several steps of reciprocal recognition to build a sufficient level of mutual trust. While tactical and strategic alignments do not require an actual debate on values to forge a genuine alliance based on a joint political agenda, more profound forms of cross-ideological cooperation – such as pre-electoral coalitions – necessitate a long process of cultural and political interactions, the presence of potential social brokers actively working behind the scenes and a window of opportunity for them to emerge from the periphery of their respective groups to propel formal alliances based on shared – in this case, class – grievances. Moreover, the emergence of a social movement, with fluid and informal participation and cooperation attempts, constitutes a facilitating condition for the success of more formal and stable cross-ideological cooperation, involving grassroots members and social brokers drawing their respective party elites into dialogue. Interestingly, the Iraqi case analyzed here is in sharp contrast to a longstanding "conventional wisdom" on MENA politics: the top-down, elite-driven nature of politics and social mobilization. Even if party and movement leaders have a firm grip on their followers, the membership is engaged in a constant dialectical relationship with the leadership, which can be questioned, contested and influenced by grassroots, junior members and their ideas, as shown by the intra-Sadrist movement's splits. Finally, in the MENA region, international pressures from regional powers (Saudi Arabia and Iran) and international actors (United States) have a clear influence on national party politics, changing the contextual conditions. For this reason, it will be essential to observe the consequences of the complete withdrawal of American troops from the country, which could reshape the context and the strategies of all actors (both domestic and external), imposing new rules of the game.

Notes

1 'Work for this article was supported by a grant (number 435-2020-0539) from the Social Sciences and Humanities Research Council of Canada (SSHRC).'
2 The Badr Organization, rooted in the ISCI paramilitary Badr Brigades, joined al-Maliki's State of Law coalition.
3 Between 2011 and 2015, the ICP tried to unify the secular camp within the Civil Democratic Alliance's political platform, but this attempt was strategic failure. In 2017, a second attempt to unify the secular front collapsed when the ICP withdrew (Robin-D'Cruz 2019a).
4 Respondents to these questions had to answer on a scale from 1 ("not an essential characteristic of democracy") to 10 ("an essential characteristic of democracy"). The given percentages are the respondents who answered with 8, 9 and 10 on the World Value Survey's scale.

References

Abdelrahman, Maha. 2009. '"With the Islamists? -Sometimes. With the state? - Never!" Cooperation between the left and Islamists in Egypt'. *British Journal of Middle Eastern Studies* 36(1): 37–54.

Al-Khafaji, Isam. 2018. 'Iraqi 2018 elections: Between sectarianism and the nation'. *Arab Reform Initiative*. Available at: https://www.arab-reform.net/publication/iraq-2018-elections-between-sectarianism-and-the-nation/.

Al-Marashi, Ibrahim. 2018. 'Shia factions in the Iraqi election: Divided and in disarray'. *Italian Institute for International Political Studies (ISPI)*. Available at: https://www.ispionline.it/it/pubblicazione/shia-factions-iraqi-election-divided-and-disarray-20461.

Aldouri, Saad. 2017. 'What to know about Iraq's protest movement'. *Chatham House.* Available at: https://www.chathamhouse.org/2017/06/what-know-about-iraqs-protest-movement.

Arab Barometer. 2019. 'Iraq country report'. *Wave V.* Available at: https://www.arabbarometer.org/wp-content/uploads/ABV_Iraq_Report_Public-Opinion_2019.pdf.

Blaydes, Lisa and Drew A. Linzer. 2012. 'Elite competition, religiosity, and anti-Americanism in the Islamic world'. *American Political Science Review* 106(2): 225–243.

Brocker, Manfred and Mirjam Künkler. 2013. 'Religious parties: Revisiting the inclusion-moderation hypothesis – Introduction'. *Party Politics* 19(2): 171–186.

Browers, Michaelle. 2007. 'Origins and architects of Yemen's joint meeting parties'. *International Journal of Middle East Studies* 39(4): 565–586.

Browers, Michaelle. 2009. *Political Ideology in the Arab World: Accommodation and Transformation.* Cambridge: Cambridge University Press.

Cavatorta, Francesco and Fabio Merone. 2013. 'Moderation through exclusion? The journey of the Tunisian Ennahda from fundamentalist to conservative party'. *Democratization* 20(5): 857–875.

Clark, Janine A. 2006. 'The conditions of Islamist moderation: Unpacking cross-ideological cooperation in Jordan'. *International Journal of Middle East Studies* 38(4): 539–560.

Clark, Janine A. 2010. 'Threats, structures, and resources: Cross-ideological coalition building in Jordan'. *Comparative Politics* 43(1): 101–120.

Clarke, K. 2014. 'Unexpected brokers of mobilization: Contingency and networks in the 2011 Egyptian uprising'. *Comparative Politics* 46(4): 379–397.

Costantini, Irene. 2021. 'The Iraqi protest movement: Social mobilization amidst violence and instability'. *British Journal of Middle Eastern Studies* 48(5): 832–849.

Diani, Mauro. 2003. 'Leaders or brokers? Positions and influence in social movement networks'. In Mauro Diani and Doug McAdam (eds.), *Social Movements and Networks: Relational Approaches to Collective Action* (pp. 105–122). Oxford: Oxford University Press.

Dodge, Toby. 2020. 'Beyond structure and agency: Rethinking political identities in Iraq after 2003'. *Nations and Nationalism* 26(1): 108–122.

Durac, Vincent. 2015. 'Social movements, protest movements and cross-ideological coalitions–the Arab uprisings re-appraised'. *Democratization* 22(2): 239–258.

Edwards, Sophie A. 2018. 'Sectarian friction and the struggle for power: Party politics in Iraq post-2003'. In Francesco Cavatorta and Lisa Storm (eds.), *Political Parties in the Arab World: Continuity and Change* (pp. 164–183). Edinburgh: Edinburgh University Press.

Friedman, Thomas Loren. 2013. 'Same war, different country'. *The New York Times* (7th of September).

Göle, Nilüfer. 2010. 'Manifestations of the religious-secular divide: Self, state, and the public sphere'. In Linell E. Cady and Elizabeth Shakman Hurd (eds.), *Comparative Secularisms in a Global Age* (pp. 41–53). New York: Palgrave Macmillan.

Haddad, Fanar. 2019. 'The Diminishing Relevance of the Sunni-Shi'a divide'. In *POMEPS Studies 35: Religion, Violence, and the State in Iraq* (pp. 47–54). The Project on Middle East Political Science (POMEPS).

Haddad, Fanar. 2020. *Understanding 'Sectarianism'*. Oxford: Oxford University Press.

Haugbølle, Rikke Hostrup and Francesco Cavatorta. 2011. 'Will the real Tunisian opposition please stand up? Opposition coordination failures under authoritarian constraints'. *British Journal of Middle Eastern Studies* 38(3): 323–341.

Higel, Lahib. 2021. 'Iraq's surprise election results'. Brussels: International crisis group (16th of November)'. Available at: https://www.crisisgroup.org/middle-east-north-africa/gulf-and-arabian-peninsula/iraq/iraqs-surprise-election-results.

Jabar, F. A. 2018. *The Iraqi Protest Movement: From Identity Politics to Issue Politics*. LSE Middle East Centre papers series (25). LSE Middle East Centre, London, UK.

Jacoby, Tim and Nassima Neggaz. 2018. 'Sectarianism in Iraq: The role of the coalition provisional authority'. *Critical Studies on Terrorism* 11(3): 478–500.

Jiyad, Sajad. 2021. 'Protest vote: Why Iraq's next elections are unlikely to be game-changers'. LSE Middle East Centre Paper Series (48).

Khalaf, Athbi Zaid. 2020. 'American attitude toward Iran and its reflection on Iran policy towards the Arab region'. *Review of Economics and Political Science*. Available at: https://www-emerald-com.acces.bibl.ulaval.ca/insight/content/doi/10.1108/REPS-09-2019-0119/full/pdf?title=american-attitude-towards-iran-and-its-reflection-on-iran-policy-towards-the-arab-region.

Kraetzschmar, Hendrik. 2011. 'Mapping opposition cooperation in the Arab world: From single-issue coalitions to transnational networks'. *British Journal of Middle Eastern Studies* 38(3): 287–302.

Landolt, Laura K. and Paul Kubicek. 2014. 'Opportunities and constraints: Comparing Tunisia and Egypt to the coloured revolutions'. *Democratization* 21(6): 984–1006.

Lust, Ellen. 2011. 'Opposition cooperation and uprisings in the Arab world'. *British Journal of Middle Eastern Studies* 38(3): 425–434.

Mahmood, Saba. 2009. 'Religious reason and secular affect: An incommensurable divide?' *Critical Inquiry* 35(4): 836–862.

Majed, Rima. 2020. 'The theoretical and methodological traps in studying sectarianism in the Middle East'. In Larbi Sadiki (ed.), *Routledge Handbook of Middle East Politics* (pp. 540–553). London: Routledge.

Majed, Rima and Janan Aljabiri. 2020. *Contemporary Social Movements in Iraq: Mapping the Labor Movement and the 2015 Mobilizations*. Berlin: Rosa Luxemburg Stiftung.

Makdisi, Ussama. 2017. *The Mythology of the Sectarian Middle East*. Houston: Center for the Middle East. Rice University's Baker Institute for Public Policy.

Mansour, Renad. 2018. *Iraq Votes 2018: Election Mobilization Strategies*. LSE Middle East Centre Report, Sleiman-Haidar, Ribale (ed.). Middle East Centre and Institute of Regional and International Studies, London, UK.

Mansour, Renad and Christine van der Toorn. 2018. *The 2018 Iraqi Federal Elections: A Population in Transition?* LSE Middle East Centre Report, Sleiman-Haidar, Ribale (ed.). Middle East Centre and Institute of Regional and International Studies, London, UK.

Mansour, Renad. 2019. *Iraq's 2018 Government Formation: Unpacking the Friction between Reform and the Status Quo*. LSE Middle East Centre report. Middle East Centre, LSE, London, UK.

Mansour, Renad and Victoria Stewart-Jolley. 2021. *Explaining Iraq's Election Results*. London: Chatham House (22nd of October).

McAdam, Doug, Sidney Tarrow and Charles Tilly. 2001. *Dynamics of Contention*. Cambridge: Cambridge University Press.

O'Donnell, Guillermo. 1993. 'On the state, democratization and some conceptual problems: A Latin American view with glances at some post-communist countries'. *World Development* 21(8): 1355–1369.

Resta, Valeria. 2021. '"The terminal": Political parties and identity issue in the Arab world'. In Francesco Cavatorta, Lisa Storm and Valeria Resta (eds.), *Routledge Handbook on Political Parties in the Middle East and North Africa* (pp. 331–343). London: Routledge.

Robin-D'Cruz, Benedict. 2019a. 'Social brokers and leftist-Sadrist cooperation in Iraq's reform protest movement: Beyond instrumental action'. *International Journal of Middle East Studies* 51(2): 257–280.

Robin-D'Cruz, Benedict. 2019b. 'Cultural Antecedents of the Leftist-Sadrist Alliance: A case study of Sadrist institution building'. In *POMEPS Studies 35: Religion, Violence, and the State in Iraq* (pp. 79–84). The Project on Middle East Political Science (POMEPS).

Robin-D'Cruz, Benedict and Renad Mansour. 2020. 'Making sense of the Sadrists: Fragmentation and unstable politics'. In Aaron Stein (ed.), *Iraq in Transition: Competing Actors and Complicated Politics* (pp. 4–38). Philadelphia: Foreign Policy Research Institute.

Sakai, Keiko and Kota Suechika. 2020. 'Sectarian fault lines in the Middle East: Sources of conflicts, or of communal bonds?' In Larbi Sadiki (ed.), *Routledge Handbook of Middle East Politics* (pp. 269–280). London: Routledge.

Sayigh, Yezid. 2017. 'The Arab region at a tipping point: Why sectarianism fails to explain the turmoil'. In Nader Hashemi and Danny Postel (eds.), *Sectarianization: Mapping the New Politics of the Middle East* (pp. 53–60). New York: Oxford University Press.

Schwedler, Jillian. 2011. 'Can Islamists become moderates: Rethinking the inclusion-moderation hypothesis'. *World Politics* 63(2): 347–376.

Schwedler, Jillian and Janine A. Clark. 2006. 'Islamist-leftist cooperation in the Arab world'. *Islam Review* 18(1): 10–11.

Shehata, Dina. 2009. *Islamists and Secularists in Egypt: Opposition, Conflict and Cooperation*. London: Routledge.

Stewart-Jolley, Victoria. 2021. *Iraq's Electoral System: Why Successive Reforms Fail to Bring Change*. London: Chatham House.

Teti, Andrea, Pamela Abbott and Francesco Cavatorta. 2019. 'Beyond elections: Perceptions of democracy in four Arab countries'. *Democratization* 26(4): 645–665.

Wegner, Eva and Miquel Pellicer. 2011. 'Left–Islamist opposition cooperation in Morocco'. *British Journal of Middle Eastern Studies* 38(3): 303–322.

World Value Survey. 2020. 'Wave VII (2017–2020)'. Available at: https://www.worldvaluessurvey.org/WVSDocumentationWV7.jsp.

Wright, Robin. 2013. 'How 5 countries could become 14'. *The New York Times* (28th of September).

11
ELECTIONS AND DEMOCRATIC BACKSLIDING IN TURKEY

Sebnem Gumuscu

Introduction

Unlike many other countries in the Middle East, Turkey has a long history of multiparty politics with free and fair elections dating back to the 1950s. Such qualities allowed the country to meet basic democratic criteria, despite occasional promissory coups, and Turkey consistently featured among exceptional democracies in the region, alongside Israel and Lebanon. Turkey's democratic achievements, however, have begun to slip away in the past decade. Political rights and civil liberties have deteriorated rapidly, while elections have lost their free and fair character. That said, they are still central to Turkish politics.

This chapter explores the changing electoral politics with a specific focus on the ruling party *Adalet ve Kalkınma Partisi* (Justice and Development Party, hereafter AKP). The aim is to explain how and why the AKP instrumentalized elections and altered their free and fair character. Specifically, this chapter argues that elections fulfilled four main purposes for the party, as discussed in greater detail below. First, successive electoral victories, thanks to the party's popular support, largely secured political dominance for the AKP. Second, its electoral hegemony in return allowed the party to govern the country in a largely unilateral and majoritarian fashion, and perhaps more importantly, redesign the entire political system to its liking. In three separate constitutional referenda, the AKP centralized power in Erdoğan's hands and weakened checks and balances in the system. Since such changes happened through referenda, it was easy for the party to conjure popular legitimacy and argue that democracy was therefore at work and in fact it was being strengthened by providing citizens with a clear voice in the design of the new political system for the first time in modern Turkish history. Third, given the significance of electoral outcomes in maintaining dominance, the AKP manipulated the electoral playing field to its advantage, paradoxically, with the support of the people. The party tilted the playing field in its favor by politicizing state institutions, redesigning the entire media landscape, and packing courts as well as independent electoral commissions with party loyalists. Finally, elections lent popular legitimacy to AKP's authoritarian practices, including executive aggrandizement as well as systematic violation of opponents' civil liberties and political rights.

A key aspect of the AKP's electoral hegemony has been its polarizing populist discourse that allowed the party to divide the nation between its supporters (the real people) and opponents (the corrupt elite). These steps, instead of consolidating democratic politics in Turkey, culminated in democratic backsliding. In short, the AKP utilized elections to monopolize power, and elections paradoxically facilitated democratic decline. The rest of the chapter examines each of the four functions in greater detail. First, a brief historical background is in order.

Historical background

The Ottoman Empire collapsed by the end of the First World War and was succeeded by republican Turkey. During the early days of the republic, the country remained under the single-party rule of the *Cumhuriyet Halk Partisi* (Republican People's Party, CHP) with no free or fair elections. The ruling party carried out regular elections for parliament, but did not allow any other party to run, kept the vote count secret, and violated the secrecy of the ballot. The first free and fair elections that complied with the norms of electoral integrity took place in 1950. The *Demokrat Parti* (Democrat Party, DP), the first party to run in a free and fair election in the country's modern history, won in a landslide. Turkey thus completed its peaceful transition to multiparty politics when the ruling CHP conceded.

Elections and multiparty politics have formed the backbone of the Turkish political system since 1950. All governments except those formed in the wake of the rather short-lived military interventions in 1960–1961, 1971, and 1980–1982 came to power through elections.[1] Unlike many other parties in the region, Turkish political parties competed in quite free and fair elections to govern the country by forming majority or coalition governments. That said, the system witnessed transformations over time with changing political dynamics and institutions.

In the 1950s, the electoral system was based on plurality, giving more power to large parties, thus inflating majoritarian tendencies and undermining representativeness in the system. For instance, in the 1954 elections, the Democrat Party won 93 percent of the seats in the parliament, despite receiving only 57 percent of the votes. Again, in the 1957 elections, although the party's vote share dropped to 48 percent (as opposed to CHP's 41 percent), it still captured 70 percent of the seats (whereas the CHP got only 29 percent seat share). The system, in other words, engendered disproportionate majorities for the ruling party until the 1960 coup. The DP relied on its somewhat manufactured electoral and political hegemony to create an uneven playing field and restrict opposition parties' access to the political space. Hence the DP posed a threat to democratic politics immediately after the transition to multiparty politics.

The military 'corrected course' with a promissory coup in 1960. The 1961 constitution introduced several institutional guardrails to keep democracy on track. Most importantly, it replaced the plurality system with proportional representation. In the 1960s and 1970s, elections were free and fair, and remained largely inclusive, as political actors from left and right could join the electoral game with ease, and even the small parties could win seats in the parliament thanks to the new electoral system based on proportional representation with no electoral threshold.[2] Such fragmentation also brought ideological polarization with fringe parties on both the right – Islamists and Turkish nationalists – and the left – socialists – winning seats in the parliament. Smaller parties on the right, in particular, became kingmakers and joined successive coalition governments. Among them were the first iterations of Islamist parties and the predecessor of the AKP, *Milli Selamet Partisi* (MSP). Such smaller parties and their youth organizations contributed to heightened political polarization in parliament and the streets as clashes among politicized youth reached a peak in the late 1970s. Using widespread street violence and political instability as a pretext, the military once again intervened in politics in September 1980. In a much more drastic intervention than in 1960, the armed forces suspended the constitution, banned all political parties and unions, and drafted a new constitution. They also introduced a new electoral system before going back to their barracks. The most important difference to the previous electoral system was the introduction of the 10 percent electoral threshold. This threshold, the highest among democratic countries, was set to produce political stability, by way of excluding smaller parties from parliament. Hence, compared to the 1970s, the electoral system partially lost its inclusivity and representativeness. The new system worked as intended throughout the 1980s and produced majority governments, but it failed to prevent fragmentation in the 1990s, as the center-right and center-left splintered – splits were mostly driven by personal squabbles and rivalries among politicians – and smaller parties with Islamist, Turkish nationalist, and pro-Kurdish ideological persuasions gained traction in Turkish politics. This fragmentation and intra-elite conflict translated into unstable coalitions and ineffective governance with negative repercussions on the economy whose decline saw high inflation, currency devaluation, and high foreign and domestic debt. The economic crisis in 2001 was particularly devastating for millions, with economic contraction, heightened unemployment, and depreciating Turkish lira making the lives of ordinary people much harder.

The AKP came to power in 2002 against this backdrop. The 2002 election was an earthquake in Turkish politics in Özel's words (2003), as parliamentary parties faced a devastating defeat at the polls. They were replaced by two parties, the pro-Islamic AKP and the secular CHP. The AKP, established only a year before the elections (with roots in the Turkish Islamist movement and a successor to the MSP, as mentioned before), captured two-thirds of the seats and formed a majority government. The CHP became the main opposition.

After coming to power, the AKP followed a bewildering course, thanks to its changing position vis-à-vis democracy. The party was established as a conservative democrat party with a platform seeking European Union accession, democratic consolidation, and economic growth. In line with these goals the AKP sought to advance democratic politics in its earlier years in power, enacting several liberalizing reforms. After 2011, however, the party pivoted to an authoritarian path. While the reasons for this turn are explored in another chapter in this edited volume as well as in other works (Gumuscu 2023; Esen and Gumuscu 2021; Akkoyunlu and Öktem 2016; Kubicek 2016), the focus here is the party's securitization of elections, as it pivoted from democracy to authoritarianism. The sections below provide a three-pronged answer: a) elections serve as a means for acquiring political hegemony; b) elections form a space for authoritarian manipulation; and 3) elections serve as a source of popular legitimacy.

Elections as a means for political hegemony and an instrument of autocratization

The 2002 elections were the first of several electoral victories for the AKP. The party built its electoral hegemony in successive elections since then. It increased its vote share in the 2007 and 2011 elections, achieving unrivaled success in Turkish politics. Facing a momentary setback in the June 2015 elections, the party quickly recovered its losses in a snap election in November of the same year (Sayarı 2016). In addition, Tayyip Erdoğan, AKP's charismatic leader, won presidential elections in 2014[3] and again in 2018. The party was also victorious in three constitutional referenda in 2007, 2010, and 2017, each of which introduced major changes to the country's constitutional order.

Such unmatched electoral hegemony entrusted the AKP with significant political power.[4] Landslide victories in general elections delivered parliamentary majorities and single-party governments. Thus, electoral hegemony, as Keyman and Gumuscu (2014) underline, secured political hegemony for the party, and allowed it to dominate foreign, economic, and social policies.

The AKP's strong electoral mandate and growing political hegemony also allowed it to alter the balance of power in Turkish politics. Amassing sufficient power, the party sidelined the armed forces through institutional and legal reforms as well as politicized trials. Some of these institutional reforms had a democratic character as they reduced the power of the military through a set of changes: for instance, thanks to these reforms the secretary general of the National Security Council (MGK) was now appointed among civilians, and the council's prerogatives in several civilian councils related to cultural affairs, education, broadcasting, higher education, among others, were eliminated. Likewise, the military courts' jurisdiction was narrowed, and the protocol that allowed the armed forces to take part in public protests and riots and bypass civilian authorities in responding to terrorist attacks was annulled. Subsequently, the AKP took steps to criminalize military involvement in politics through a set of court cases that began during the party's second term in office (2007–2011). In cases like 'Ergenekon' and 'Sledgehammer',[5] hundreds of retired and on-duty high-ranking military personnel were brought before the courts to answer allegations of conspiring to overthrow the elected AKP government. Ultimately, the military was no longer untouchable, nor were officers above censure by the elected civilian government. The Turkish military hence lost its veto powers and overall influence in Turkish politics and the political balance of power in Turkish politics changed in a dramatic fashion (Kubicek 2016; Satana 2008). Many perceived this process as a step in the right direction and welcomed it as democratic consolidation.

The AKP's subsequent actions were not democratic though. Indeed, the party mobilized its electoral popularity to redesign the entire political system in an undemocratic fashion. In three constitutional referenda, the party altered the political system. In 2007, it introduced direct popular elections for the president – who at the time had limited powers and mostly symbolic authority – and paved the way for much more dramatic changes in the system. In 2010, a larger constitutional reform package helped the party overhaul the judiciary. Finally, in 2017, in a drastic move, the AKP replaced the parliamentary system with a presidential one. In short, thanks to its electoral dominance, as Pempel reminds us (1990), the AKP shaped the country's present as well as its future.

For all these reasons, the AKP has taken elections quite seriously. After all, it is how the party has achieved and consolidated power since 2002. Attesting to this fact, the party machine is one of the best organized and disciplined in Turkey. It has strong grassroots and unrivaled mobilizational capacity to ensure electoral victories. Party members work diligently in election cycles, canvass neighborhoods, mobilize supporters on the day of the election, and remain vigilant at polling stations to make sure no irregularities occur at the party's expense. In more than 177,000 polling stations across the country, the party has several volunteers working hard to sustain and secure its electoral fortunes. These people do not only safeguard the vote and ensure communication across branches, but they also help the elderly, the illiterate, and the disabled to arrive at the polling stations and cast their ballots on election day.[6]

As the leader of the party, Erdoğan has been particularly invested in this process. After all, since the early years of his political career, he has been known for his organizational genius. Cognizant of the instrumental value of elections, Erdoğan kept his focus on the party machine and demanded the rank-and-file work hard. Whenever local branches lost their vibrancy, he repeatedly warned the party organization of growing complacency, and reshuffled local cadres.[7]

With so much political power at its disposal, the AKP instrumentalized its electoral hegemony to build a hegemonic party system with limited electoral uncertainty and semi-permanent government rather than consolidating democracy. The aim has been to maximize the power of the executive at the expense of the legislative and judicial branches. In other words, the party sought what Bermeo (2016, pp. 10–11) calls executive aggrandizement, which 'occurs when elected executives weaken checks on executive power one by one, undertaking a series of institutional changes that hamper the power of opposition forces to challenge executive preferences'.

The AKP paved the way toward executive aggrandizement with legal changes and used both referenda and its parliamentary majorities to redesign the political system. Thus, it joined the trend of autocratic legalism observed in Latin America and Eastern Europe (Kadıoğlu 2021; Corrales 2015; Scheppele 2018) to erode horizontal accountability. A major step in eliminating checks over executive authority was the restructuring of the judiciary. In the 2010 referendum, the party passed more than 20 amendments to the constitution. A major part of the package concerned redesigning the courts, including the Constitutional Court and the body in charge of internal affairs of justices and prosecutors (Özbudun 2015). Following the 2010 referendum, parliament increased the power of the executive over the judiciary by authorizing the justice minister to directly appoint members to the High Council of Judges and to control the inspection board that disciplines judges. Within six months, more than 3000 sitting judges had been removed. Hence, the party started to pack the courts, including hitherto independent electoral commissions.

In the meantime, the party passed a record number of new laws, many of which undercut institutions of accountability (Bermeo 2016). A key method to pass a high number of laws was omnibus bills (*torba kanun*). Originally used to accelerate the EU harmonization process with the support of the opposition parties, the first wave of omnibus bills thus had a coherent agenda and purpose, i.e., to fulfill EU membership criteria (*acquis*). From its second term onwards, however, the AKP appropriated this legislative tool to maximize its agenda-setting power and sideline the opposition in parliament by minimizing the time allotted to legislative deliberations (Hazama and Iba 2017). Several of these changes were unconstitutional, and some of them were eventually annulled by the Constitutional Court. Others remained in effect, among them being defamation and social media and internet regulation laws, which facilitated widespread blocking of websites (Bermeo 2016). These measures severely curtailed freedom of expression and increased self-censorship as government officials used defamation as a weapon to silence critiques among journalists as well as ordinary citizens.[8]

Another critical instrument in executive aggrandizement was the recourse to executive decrees. Although the party promised not to use them before coming to power, the AKP-dominated parliament handed the government the authority to rule by decree in 2011 for a period of six months. Hence Prime Minister Erdoğan restructured several key institutions within the administration without any input from parliament. In the end, several public service institutions lost whatever autonomy they had and came under the direct control of the Prime Minister, giving another boost to executive authority.

Executive aggrandizement hit an unprecedented degree in the wake of the coup attempt of July 2016.[9] Parliament declared emergency rule and bestowed President Erdoğan the authority to rule by decree. As head of the executive, he issued 36 decrees between 2016 and 2018. The decrees purged thousands of civil and military bureaucratic personnel, and shut down hundreds of newspapers, radio and tv stations, as well as civic associations and foundations (Gumuscu 2016). The decrees also replaced several elected mayors from pro-Kurdish parties with centrally appointed figures. Because they were released under emergency rule, the Constitutional Court, partly packed by the AKP, decided that they were not subject to judicial review for the next decade.[10]

As emergency rule continued, the AKP took a major step to institutionalize a heightened level of executive aggrandizement. In 2017 the party proposed to replace the parliamentary system with an executive presidency with weak checks and balances. Because the party lacked a super-majority at the time, it could not change the constitution without a referendum. Thus, for more major changes, the party resorted once again to plebiscitary measures.

Although the referendum passed with a narrow margin, it still instated a presidential system, whereby the executive had very weak checks over his powers, had a right to rule by decree with minimal input from parliament, enjoyed absolute control over the cabinet (including presidential deputies) and bureaucratic appointments with no parliamentary oversight, obtained the authority to define the mission, jurisdiction, and duties of all public institutions tied to the state as well as the right to declare emergency rule (Esen and Gumuscu 2018).

In the 2018 elections, Erdoğan was elected president under the new system and continued to rule by decree. In the first year of the presidential system, he changed more than 1900 law articles, most of which sought to redesign the state structure in line with a highly centralized presidency. In the meantime, the parliament changed or passed only 600 articles marking an 89 percent decline in legislative activity in the parliament,[11] hitting a major marker of executive empowerment at the expense of the legislative branch.

In the end, executive aggrandizement through electoral mechanisms (i.e., parliamentary majorities and referenda) led directly to democratic backsliding instead of consolidation. With massive power at its disposal, the AKP translated its electoral strength to, what Varol (2014) calls, stealth authoritarianism rather than advancing democracy. This trend in democratic backsliding has been obvious in Turkey's freedom scores released by Freedom House and democracy scores published by the Varieties of Democracy Project (V-Dem). When the AKP came to power in 2002, Turkey was classified as an electoral democracy by Freedom House. After a brief improvement in its political rights and civil liberties scores, the country started to decline on both counts. In 2016 Freedom House changed Turkey's standing from partly free to 'not free', claiming that the country was no longer a democracy. V-Dem also showed similar trends. Tracing Turkey's democratic decline back to 2006, both liberal democracy scores and electoral democracy scores deteriorated in the past 14 years (see Figure 11.1).

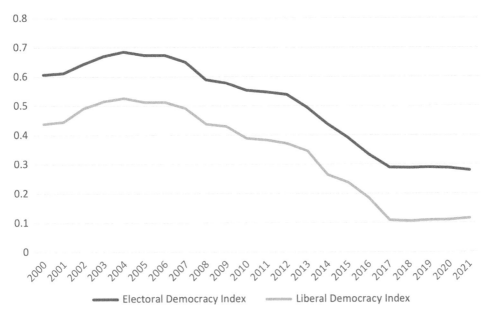

Figure 11.1 Electoral and liberal democracy in Turkey, 2000–2021. *Source*: V-Dem 12.0 (Varieties of democracy project)

Electoral manipulation

Since elections remained central to acquiring and sustaining political power, the AKP has also done its best to secure future electoral victories. To that effect, the party has taken several steps – in addition to building a strong party machine – to ensure sustained electoral dominance. Some of these steps comprised electoral manipulation that tilted the playing field in favor of the AKP and allowed the party to prolong its power, despite its weaknesses and failures in recent years. As Bermeo (2016) claims, in the most recent wave of democratic backsliding, incumbents no longer steal elections, they manipulate them strategically. The AKP, part of this trend, has manipulated elections before the day of the election instead of committing election day fraud. That is, the vote count remained largely clean with no reports of ballot-stuffing. For instance, international observers such as Organization for Security and Co-operation in Europe (OSCE) did not report any major irregularities on the day of elections in 2015 (OSCE 2015). Similarly, a local civil society initiative launched in 2014 has closely monitored elections in several cycles and reported no evidence of election day fraud.

Indeed, as electoral integrity measures released by the Electoral Integrity Project show, Turkish elections have been quite clean, and vote counts have been largely transparent. This does not mean that elections have been fair though. In its first two decades in power, the party did not attempt to redesign the electoral system, but maintained the high electoral threshold, despite its earlier promises to reduce it to a more 'democratic' level. More importantly, the AKP manipulated the campaign cycle by creating an extensive pro-government media and purging critical voices and limiting media access to the opposition (Esen and Gumuscu 2016). The government also enjoyed uneven access to public and private resources, again thanks to its prolonged political dominance. For instance, several AKP campaign events have been funded by the state. Similarly, private actors have made regular donations in cash and in kind to the ruling party, expecting privileged treatment from the government in return (Esen and Gumuscu 2017b, 2021). The party made sure to return these favors in different ways, including public contracts, tax relief, or credit support through public banks. In addition, the party, thanks to its successive electoral victories, politicized state institutions and deployed them against rivals on the campaign trail. As a result, centrally appointed governors imposed greater restrictions on campaign events of the opposition; the police failed to counteract pro-government supporters who attacked and harassed other political parties; public servants on government payroll frequently destroyed opposition's fliers and banners; and the television broadcasting watchdog (RTÜK) fined stations with critical coverage of the government.

The newly designed judiciary also aided the AKP in keeping the opposition in check. The charismatic leader of the pro-Kurdish Peoples' Democracy Party (*Halklarin Demokratik Partisi*, HDP), Selahattin Demirtaş, along with several deputies and local party leaders, has been imprisoned since 2016. Similarly, a CHP deputy and former editor-in-chief of a Turkish daily was arrested on espionage charges because he published a news story on arms transfer to Syria. More recently, the chairwoman of the party's Istanbul branch has been given a prison sentence for terror propaganda and defamation, pending appeal, based on her critical tweets dating back to 2014.

The AKP's hold over the judiciary also allowed it to exercise control over electoral commissions, affecting their decisions pertaining to the electoral process. On the day of the 2017 referendum, for instance, the Turkish electoral board decided to accept unmarked ballots after the polling stations were closed. This was a first in the recent history of Turkish elections and the opposition protested the decision, to no avail. The electoral board made several critical and controversial decisions after the 2019 local elections as well. First, it overturned the results in

Istanbul, the largest city in the country, under intense government pressure. The main opposition candidate had indeed won the elections, but the government demanded a repeat election. In the end, the board decided on a re-run without any proof of wrongdoing in the electoral process (Esen and Gumuscu 2019), while rejecting stronger pleas from the opposition parties elsewhere.

Furthermore, the board annulled results in cities where the pro-Kurdish political movement obtained significant victories. Seven mayors were denied authorization, and their municipalities were overturned by the AKP candidates, who had lost the electoral race. In the year following the elections, the Interior Ministry took over 47 of 65 municipalities the HDP had won (including three metropolitan municipalities), basically canceling 5 million votes cast for the party. In the process, 18 mayors were arrested along with several deputies in local assemblies, while protests were banned in these localities.[12]

All these steps amounted to high levels of electoral manipulation, which led to a rapid decline in electoral integrity in the country over the years. As reported by the Electoral Integrity Project, Turkey's overall integrity scores declined from 51 in 2014 to 35 in 2018. When broken down into its components, it is clear that equal access to media coverage has been quite low all along, while electoral procedures, vote count, voting process, and election results had relatively high integrity in 2014. After only four years, only the voting process maintained its integrity levels, whereas integrity of electoral procedures, vote count, and impartiality of electoral authorities declined drastically (Electoral Integrity Project 2019), as shown in Table 11.1.

The V-Dem project also detected a significant deterioration in fairness in Turkish elections, as Figure 11.2 shows.

In addition to electoral manipulation, the AKP government also took measures to remedy its electoral losses in major metropolitan areas by cutting the municipal budgets and limiting its authority. Istanbul's new mayor, Ekrem Imamoğlu, was a particular target, since the city hosts around one-fifth of the Turkish electorate and is the heart of the Turkish economy. Accordingly, the central government controlled by the AKP largely undermined Istanbul's metropolitan municipality in financial terms and altered bureaucratic structures to curtail the mayor's decision-making power. For instance, the Interior Ministry prohibited fundraising for the municipality and froze its accounts, while the president refused to approve its credit requests and appointed additional bureaucrats to coordination committees to increase the authority of the central government over the mayor.

Elections as source of popular legitimacy

Successive electoral victories, even if they were achieved under unfair conditions, provided the party with popular legitimacy. For the AKP, these victories relayed a strong popular mandate

Table 11.1 Electoral integrity in Turkey, 2014–2018

Election year	Overall electoral integrity scores	Voting procedures	Media access	Voting process	Electoral boards	Vote count	Elections results
2014	51	62	27	53	53	68	68
2015	47	68	28	46	51	70	69
2015	44	60	25	43	45	61	68
2018	35	35	15	48	29	44	60

Source: Norris and Gromping 2019, Electoral Integrity Project

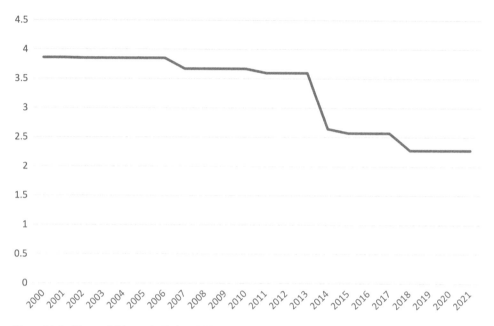

Figure 11.2 Electoral fairness in Turkey, 2000–2021. *Source*: Coppedge et. al., 2022, V-Dem 12.0

and permitted majority rule without any need for deliberation, compromise, or conciliation. In other words, the AKP's perception of democracy has remained procedural and majoritarian (Özbudun 2014; Keyman and Gumuscu 2014; Kubicek 2016).

Underneath AKP's majoritarianism, scholars argue, lies its populist tendencies (Aytaç and Elçi 2019; Selçuk 2016; Baykan 2018; Yabancı 2016). Populism is, as Mudde defines it, 'a thin-centered ideology that considers society to be separated into two antagonistic camps, the pure people and the corrupt elite', within which politics is an expression of the general will of the people (2004: 543). In this Manichean and moralistic outlook, politics is a zero-sum game that unfolds between the people and its enemies (Mudde 2004: 544). Erdoğan constructed this duality in the Turkish context by juxtaposing the conservative masses against 'the secular elite'. One of the early slogans of the party was: 'Enough! It is time for the people to speak up!' As such, the AKP has followed the center-right tradition that sides with the people against the bureaucratic republican establishment. Making frequent references to the early republican elite, which the AKP described as authoritarian and disrespectful of the people's will, the party claimed to be the voice of the silent masses against the powerful state elite (Fisher Onar 2011).

The political implications of AKP's populism are manifold. To begin with, for the party, the only legitimate source of power is the people's will, and it finds its sole expression in elections (including referenda). Accordingly, whoever wins the most votes has the right to rule unilaterally. That is why elections have been so central for the AKP; in Erdoğan's words, the 'ballot box is the indestructible fortress of people's will; it is [the party's] honor'.[13] It is also why the party takes elections seriously and adopts all necessary measures – from canvassing neighborhoods to electoral manipulation – to win. That is also why the AKP leaders often defended and resorted to plebiscitary tools to amplify the voice of the people. Whenever the party failed to find qualified majorities in parliament to change the constitution, it called for a referendum. When other parties opposed such plebiscitary practices, they were accused of having autocratic tendencies by Erdoğan, who often claimed, 'whatever the people wanted, the putschist CHP opposed it'.

These referenda, for AKP leaders, amplified the voice of the people over 'a repressive elite' and allowed the 'real people' to design the political system. Erdoğan expressed this understanding on the night of the 2017 referendum, which replaced the parliamentary system with an executive presidency:

> By the will of the parliament and the will of the people, a very important change has been approved. In the past, our constitutions and political systems were designed in extraordinary times such as the War of Independence or military interventions. For the first time in Turkish history, we are changing our political system through civilian politics. This is very important.[14]

In line with a populist frame, Erdoğan thus claims to facilitate and embody people's empowerment over the repressive elite.

Second, AKP's populism rejects any checks over the power of the people, who is the sole authority and source of sovereignty. Unelected officials, i.e., the judiciary, civilian, and military bureaucracies, often considered to be part of the 'corrupt and repressive elite', should ultimately be subordinate to the will of the people, which is above all other institutions, including the constitution. More specifically, treating democracy solely as vertical accountability through elections leaves no space for horizontal accountability. In this populist frame, checks over the executive power are undemocratic and illegitimate insofar as they limit the power of the 'real people'. This understanding naturally threatens the rule of law as well as the rights of political, religious, and ethnic minorities. The judicial branch and higher courts, Erdoğan often complained, attempted to stop the people's true representatives from coming to power; they exercised 'tutelary powers' over the Turkish people, and their foreign allies, i.e., the EU, and helped them in further curtailing the power of the people. Opposition parties also joined them in their anti-democratic practices and committed treason. Altogether they comprised 'the corrupt, self-interested elite' who acted against the interests of the Turkish people, while the AKP fought for their rights.

This political and intellectual outlook has been a major factor justifying the process of executive aggrandizement. After all, the executive (i.e., Erdoğan), as depicted by the AKP elite, is the embodiment of the people; empowering him meant empowering the people. 'We are the people', Erdoğan has often exclaimed, 'who are you?'

Third, and by extension, since opponents are not just people with different priorities and values holding inalienable rights, but 'evil' (Mudde 2004: 544), their rights and liberties could easily be violated without harming 'democracy'. The opposition parties are illegitimate; not only because they keep losing elections, but also because they represent corrupt minorities (*azgın azınlık*). As such, they do not deserve tolerance, engagement, or equal treatment from the government. Because they have ill intentions, their political rights and civil liberties could be limited, and this would not undermine the democratic system. As a representative of the 'real people', the AKP had an obligation to advance the rights of its supporters and no obligation to tolerate its opponents or commit to institutional forbearance. As he bluntly put in one of his speeches:

> We freed our education system from tutelary policies. Our children are no longer discriminated on the basis of their belief, attire, [or] outlook and [we] established freedom in our country … In the past 16 years *only the terrorists' and their supporters' scope of activity has narrowed* … No one has witnessed any erosion in their liberties or any intervention in their lives … We will continue to develop democracy and expand freedoms and rights.[15] [emphasis added]

The popular legitimacy that came with electoral victories has allowed for the delegitimization of the opposition. The authoritarian steps taken by the party in the name of the 'true' people thus allowed the party to delegitimize its opponents, securitize dissent, and silence critics in the name of 'democracy'. Indeed, the government attacked all civil liberties, including the right to assembly and peaceful protest, since public protests or activism are anti-democratic expressions according to the AKP and the sole legitimate space for political expression is elections. For instance, in 2013 when the Gezi Park protests erupted in Istanbul, and eventually spread to the rest of the country, then Prime Minister Erdoğan claimed that anti-democratic political forces resorted to such autocratic instruments because they had failed to beat his party at the polls. He insisted that the only legitimate democratic venue was elections.[16] As Gümrükçü (2021) aptly puts it, 'the government consider[ed] street protests as a "threat" instead of a normal and ordinary form of political participation'. Meanwhile, he counter-mobilized his supporters in major rallies. Gezi protests marked a critical point in democratic backsliding. Popular mobilization against the government since then, however small-scale, has been met with riot police using disproportionate use of force.

Conclusion

This chapter discussed the centrality of elections in Turkish politics with a particular focus on the AKP era that began in 2002. Since then, the party, under Erdoğan's leadership, has worked hard to establish its electoral hegemony. And it succeeded to a great extent. Successive electoral victories in return allowed the party to build its political dominance in the country and sideline not only the armed forces, which had exercised undue influence in Turkish politics since 1960, but also the democratic opposition. Constitutional reforms through plebiscites also proved essential in the process of redesigning the entire system.

These measures eventually culminated in democratic backsliding since they empowered the executive and weakened the checks on it. Populist discourse legitimized AKP's autocratic actions by providing an ideological frame for executive aggrandizement as well as delegitimization of the opposition. Insofar as the AKP reduced democracy to the ballot box, elections within the broader populist framework have become an invaluable source of legitimacy for the AKP's authoritarian measures taken in the name of the people.

Despite recent trends in democratic backsliding, elections are still central to Turkish politics. AKP's authoritarianism notwithstanding, elections are still real. Their results continue to be uncertain and can deliver victories to the opposition, despite all odds. That is why the end of the AKP era is also likely to come through an election.

Notes

1 These military interventions are, what Bermeo (2016) calls, promissory coups; that is, the armed forces intervened in politics introduced certain institutional changes and then returned to their barracks, handing power back to civilians in free and fair elections.
2 Only in the 1965 elections the country switched to a different system of proportional representation which counted all wasted votes at the national level and allocated seats to all parties proportionately. This system, like the proportional representation system with no threshold in the 1970s, ensured high level of electoral representation.
3 The first direct presidential elections of the parliamentary system took place after 2007 constitutional amendment. 2018 presidential election was the first election after the enactment of the presidential system in 2017.
4 Only recently, the party's electoral fortunes declined slightly when it lost major municipalities in 2019 local elections. These losses, however, did not affect party's hegemony in central government.

5 These were highly politicized trials where the democratic mission of holding armed forces accountable were largely diluted by doctored evidence and frequent violations of defendants' legal rights. For a critical review of the two cases see Rodrik (2011).
6 This section relies on empirical data I collected through participant observation in multiple elections cycles between 2014 and 2019. I monitored seven elections in this time period in an AKP stronghold from 6AM when the election officials meet in the morning till the end of vote counting process is complete at night.
7 www.evrensel.net/haber/321629/şğ-metal-yorgunlugu-var-teskilatlari-yenileyecegiz
8 Between 2014 and 2020 Erdoğan filed more than 38,000 defamation lawsuits, thousands received prison sentences, among them several minors. The five presidents who served before him filed only 1716 lawsuits combined. www.cumhuriyet.com.tr/haber/carpici-rapor-cumhurbaskanlarinin-actigi-dava-sayilari-belirtildi-1863927
9 A group of officers within the Turkish armed forces attempted to overthrow the AKP government on July 15, 2016. It turned out that the putsch included Gulenists – those who were inspired by and followed the leadership of a US-based preacher named Fethullah Gulen – and anti-AKP officers who remained in the minority and were not supported by the top brass. The attempt failed thanks to the weakness of the putschists and extensive mobilization of the people (Esen and Gumuscu 2017a).
10 www.bbc.com/turkce/haberler-turkiye-44799489
11 www.bbc.com/turkce/haberler-turkiye-48788902
12 https://bianet.org/1/17/229222-hdp-den-kayyum-raporu-dort-milyon-oy-gasp-edildi; for further analysis see Tepe and Alemdaroğlu 2021.
13 www.aa.com.tr/tr/politika/cumhurbaskani-erdogan-sandik-milli-iradenin-yikilmaz-kalesidir/1430565
14 www.bbc.com/turkce/live/haberler-turkiye-39613272.
15 Erdoğan, Speech at TUGVA (Turkey's Youth Foundation) Headquarters, 2018.
16 www.yeniasir.com.tr/politika/2013/06/04/millet-gereken-cevabi-sandikta-verecektir

References

Akkoyunlu, Karabekir, and Kerem Öktem. 2016. 'Existential insecurity and the making of a weak authoritarian regime in Turkey'. *Southeast European and Black Sea Studies* 16(4): 505–527.

Aytaç, S. Erdem, and Ezgi Elçi. 2019. 'Populism in Turkey'. In: Daniel Stockemer (ed.), *Populism around the World*. Cham: Springer: 89–108.

Baykan, Toygar Sinan. 2018. *The Justice and Development Party in Turkey: Populism, Personalism, Organization*. Cambridge: Cambridge University Press.

Bermeo, Nancy. 2016. 'On democratic backsliding'. *Journal of Democracy* 27(1): 5–19.

Coppedge, Michael, John Gerring, Carl Henrik Knutsen, Staffan I. Lindberg, Jan Teorell, David Altman, Michael Bernhard, Agnes Cornell, M. Steven Fish, Lisa Gastaldi, Haakon Gjerløw, Adam Glynn, Sandra Grahn, Allen Hicken, Katrin Kinzelbach, Kyle L. Marquardt, Kelly McMann, Valeriya Mechkova, Pamela Paxton, Daniel Pemstein, Johannes von Römer, Brigitte Seim, Rachel Sigman, Svend-Erik Skaaning, Jeffrey Staton, Eitan Tzelgov, Luca Uberti, Yi-ting Wang, Tore Wig, and Daniel Ziblatt. 2022. '"V-Dem Dataset v12"Varieties of Democracy (V-Dem) Project'.

Corrales, Javier. 2015. 'The authoritarian resurgence: Autocratic legalism in Venezuela'. *Journal of Democracy* 26(2): 37–51.

Esen, Berk, and Sebnem Gumuscu. 2016. 'Rising competitive authoritarianism in Turkey'. *Third World Quarterly* 37(9): 1581–1606.

Esen, Berk, and Sebnem Gumuscu. 2017a. 'Turkey: How the coup failed'. *Journal of Democracy* 28(1): 59–73.

Esen, Berk, and Sebnem Gumuscu. 2017b. 'A small yes for presidentialism: The Turkish constitutional referendum of April 2017'. *South European Society and Politics* 22(3): 303–326.

Esen, Berk, and Sebnem Gumuscu. 2018. 'The perils of "Turkish presidentialism"'. *Review of Middle East Studies* 52(1): 43–53.

Esen, Berk, and Sebnem Gumuscu. 2019. 'Killing competitive authoritarianism softly: The 2019 local elections in Turkey'. *South European Society and Politics* 24(3): 317–342.

Esen, Berk, and Sebnem Gumuscu. 2021. 'Why did Turkish democracy collapse? A political economy account of AKP's authoritarianism'. *Party Politics* 27(6): 1075–1091.

Fisher Onar, Nora. 2011. 'Constructing Turkey Inc.: The discursive anatomy of a domestic and foreign policy agenda'. *Journal of Contemporary European Studies* 199(4): 463–473.

Gümrükçü, Selin Bengi. 2021. 'The aftermath of the Gezi Park protests: Rising populism and mobilization for autocracy'. *Jadaliyya*. Available at https://www.jadaliyya.com/Details/42978.

Gumuscu, Sebnem. 2016. 'The Clash of Islamists: The crisis of the Turkish state and democracy'. *Contemporary Turkish Politics, POMEPS Studies* 22, 6–11.

Gumuscu, Sebnem. 2023. *Democracy or Authoritarianism: Islamist Governments in Turkey, Egypt, and Tunisia*, forthcoming. Cambridge: Cambridge University Press.

Hazama, Yasushi, and Şeref Iba. 2017. 'Legislative agenda setting by a delegative democracy: Omnibus bills in the Turkish parliamentary system'. *Turkish Studies* 18(2): 313–333.

Kadıoğlu, Ayşe. 2021. 'Autocratic legalism in new Turkey'. *Social Research: An International Quarterly* 88(2): 445–471.

Keyman, Fuat, and Sebnem Gumuscu. 2014 *Democracy, Identity and Foreign Policy in Turkey: Hegemony through Transformation*. London: Palgrave Macmillan.

Kubicek, Paul. 2016. 'Majoritarian democracy in Turkey: Causes and consequences'. In: Cengiz Erisen and Paul Kubicek (eds.), *Democratic Consolidation in Turkey*. London: Routledge, 135–155.

Mudde, Cas. 2004. 'The populist zeitgeist'. *Government and Opposition* 39(4): 541–563.

Norris, Pippa, and Max Gromping. 'Electoral integrity worldwide 2019'. *Electoral Integrity Project*. Available at: https://www.electoralintegrityproject.com/the-year-in-elections-2019.

OSCE. 2015. 'Election report, 2015'. Available at http://www.osce.org/tr/odihr/86845?download=true.

Özbudun, Ergun. 2014. 'AKP at the crossroads: Erdoğan's majoritarian drift'. *South European Society and Politics* 19(2): 155–167.

Özbudun, Ergun. 2015. 'Turkey's judiciary and the drift toward competitive authoritarianism'. *The International Spectator* 50(2): 42–55.

Özel, Soli. 2003. 'Turkey at the polls: After the tsunami'. *Journal of Democracy* 1 4(2): 80–94.

Pempel, T. John, ed. 1990. *Uncommon Democracies: The One-Party Dominant Regimes*. Ithaca, NY: Cornell University Press.

Rodrik, Dani. 2011. 'Ergenekon and Sledgehammer: Building or undermining the rule of law?' *Turkish Policy Quarterly* 10(1): 99–109.

Satana, Nil S. 2008. 'Transformation of the Turkish military and the path to democracy'. *Armed Forces and Society* 34(3): 357–388.

Sayarı, Sabri. 2016. 'Back to a predominant party system: The November 2015 snap election in Turkey'. *South European Society and Politics* 21(2): 263–280.

Scheppele, Kim L. 2018. 'Autocratic legalism'. *The University of Chicago Law Review* 85(2): 545–584.

Selçuk, Orçun. 2016. 'Strong presidents and weak institutions: Populism in Turkey, Venezuela and Ecuador'. *Southeast European and Black Sea Studies* 16(4): 571–589.

Tepe, Sultan, and Ayça Alemdaroğlu. 2021. 'How authoritarians win when they lose'. *Journal of Democracy* 32(4): 87–101.

Varol, Ozan O. 2014. 'Stealth authoritarianism'. *Iowa Law Review* 100: 1673.

Yabancı, Bilge. 2016. 'Populism as the problem child of democracy: The AKP's enduring appeal and the use of meso-level actors'. *Southeast European and Black Sea Studies* 16(4): 591–617.

12
FROM ONE-SECT ONE-VOTE TO ONE-MAN ONE-VOTE? DEMANDS FOR REFORMING THE ELECTORAL SYSTEM IN LEBANON

Rosita Di Peri

Introduction

Between the end of 2019 and the beginning of 2020, an unprecedented series of crises, worse than anything else the country had experienced since the end of the civil war, hit Lebanon. In October 2019, massive protests began across the country, with demonstrators clamouring for the fall of the sectarian system and the regeneration of the political class. In March 2020, the declaration of bankruptcy by Prime Minister Hassan Diab and the spread of the COVID-19 pandemic intensified the economic and social healthcare crises that had been brewing for years. Finally, in August 2020, the explosion at the port of Beirut, due to the neglect of the authorities, brought death and destruction to the Lebanese capital (Di Peri 2020b). Considered an exception within the Middle East and North Africa (MENA) both for its communitarian composition and for being, at least from a formal point of view, a quasi-democracy (Lijphart 1969; Dekmejian 1978; Fakhoury 2009), Lebanon has nevertheless faced multiple crises since the signing of the Taif Agreement in 1989. These crises have highlighted the contradictions of a system whose legitimacy has gradually been eroded. Although Lebanon respects a series of formal democratic requirements, such as free and fair elections, the presence of accountable institutions, the existence of several political parties and an active and large civil society, from a substantive point of view, the country shows characteristics that significantly distance it from the ones Dahl (1971) identified in his polyarchic model.

A less superficial look reveals how, for example, elections – recognised as crucial indicators of levels of democracy – are anything but free and fair. On the contrary, they are the outcome of sectarian compromises and hostage to more or less secret negotiations. Elections and electoral strategies, as well as voting behaviour, are guided by 'services and money' instead of 'issue and principles' (Corstange 2012). Over the years, this has contributed to the solidification of 'system Lebanon', within which the sectarian communities' pervasive and all-encompassing presence reigns at all levels (political, economic, religious, and social). The system's sole objective is to maintain the status quo for the political and religious elites, as well as for the *zuama* (village leaders), and protect their political and economic interests and privileges (Di Peri 2017, 2018). As a result, the consociational system has become increasingly rigid and devoted almost exclusively to self-preservation. This configuration, which had already been in place before the outbreak of the civil war, was strengthened after the conflict thanks to the ever-deeper intertwining of the political and economic systems, in what has been labelled 'neoliberal sectarianism' (Salloukh 2019; Baumann 2016). Thus, it appears to be far removed from the democratic principles that the consociational model aspires to. In fact, the consociational model has become the basis for all negotiations among political actors, and despite calls to abolish it, its presence remains central to the country's institutional and political life.

Using this analytical lens, I argue here that the Lebanese electoral system is a crucial factor in strengthening 'neoliberal sectarianism', namely how sectarianism intertwines with the economic transformation of the country. Clientelism is the main trait of Lebanese elections (Cammett and Issar 2010; Corstange 2012), and therefore electoral contests are part of power-sharing dynamics that 'imprison' actors and prevent change instead of contributing to a genuine democratisation process. Elections represent a strong source of legitimacy for the sectarian leaders who, through patronage and the allocation of benefits, accumulate political capital to keep the consociational system alive, exploit it and boost their privileges at various levels (Salti and Chaaban 2010). This is in line with the literature on authoritarian resilience, which, along with that of consociationalism, this chapter contributes to.

The processes and dynamics behind elections have contributed to a slow but steady worsening of the economic situation had a negative impact on the living conditions of the Lebanese and called into question the minimal democratic standards in the country. In other words, the configuration, manipulation, and exploitation of elections have helped to fuel 'neoliberal sectarianism', the constitutive characteristic of post-war Lebanon.

The trajectories of consociativism: from 'resilient consociativism' to 'neoliberal sectarianism'

Lebanon has long been studied as an example of consociational democracy – a system that, on paper, protects minorities and their prerogatives. The consociational model focuses on the role of the elites in 'fragmented societies' and emphasises the importance of an agreed-upon division of political power between the different segments – communities in Lebanon – of society. According to the model, the divisions in society tend to balance out when they are cross-cutting, whereas they tend to cause conflict if they are mutually reinforced (Di Peri 2010). The role of the elites is fundamental in this regard, as it is up to them to moderate or exacerbate the conflict (Lijphart 1969). In addition to the elites' convergent and 'preventive' behaviour (i.e. their ability to recognise the inherent dangers in a fragmented political culture, a wish to transcend cultural divisions, at least in terms of group management, and the ability to come up with appropriate institutional solutions to the issues affecting existing sub-cultures), Lijphart (1977) considers four main features: (1) the presence of a grand coalition in power, (2) minorities' mutual veto power, (3) proportional representation, and (4) cultural independence granted to the different segments. Lebanon closely approximated the consociational model between its independence in 1943 and the outbreak of the civil war in 1975, as it was governed by grand coalitions in which the country's main communities had proportional representation in elected institutions. The seats' distribution in parliament followed a ratio of 5:5 between Muslims and Christians, and MPs were elected by adopting the proportional method. The division of constituencies meant a candidate needed to receive not only the vote of those belonging to his confession but also the vote of other communities to be elected. This favoured compromise and the openness of every community to each other. Another aspect distinguishing the consociational system is the relative cultural autonomy granted to the communities. Lebanon's communities enjoyed real independence in all issues concerning their personal status, religion, and, in part, assets.

After the end of the civil war (1975–1990), several of the aspects mentioned above ended, and the system became more rigid and less inclined to compromise, although the communities' autonomy remained unchanged (Fakhoury 2009; Di Peri 2010). This rigidity led to the consolidation of the confessional elites. Lebanese communities, or aggregations of communities, have precise rules for the lives of their members. These rules flow from religious tribunals that are endowed with civil powers, since there is no unified civil code to regulate matters relating to personal status, such as the transmission of citizenship, marriage, inheritance, child protection, adoption, or divorce. According to the rules of the consociational model, this autonomy is 'necessary' for the model to avoid frictions between communities, but the inability to overcome this segmentation, despite the provisions of art. 95 of the Lebanese Constitution, has gradually led to an anachronistic and paradoxical situation in which religious leaders have gained increasing power to regulate the lives of individuals by escaping the control of the state. In addition, and crucially, the strengthening of the prerogatives of religious authorities went hand in hand with an overall deterioration of the conditions that had allowed the consociational model to work, however imperfectly, before the civil war. In the post-war period, Lebanon was under a so-called Syrian protectorate, and Syria had a pervasive presence in the country's political life. Moreover, the sporadic search for a compromise and the fear of new clashes led to a power-sharing agreement between the three main institutions of the state (presidency of the Republic, Council of Ministers, parliament) – the *troika* – which paralysed the decision-making process because of the mutual veto system (Kassir 2000; Assi 2016).

This also resonates in the presence and pervasiveness of large families and community leaders (*zu'ama*), who continue to play a crucial role in Lebanese life both at political and social levels. The large autonomy of confessional communities and *zu'ama* leaders, amidst the difficulties the state encountered to provide basic services like education and healthcare, gave them power and legitimacy within the system (Gates 1998; Kingston 2013; Baumann 2019; Cammett 2014). Therefore, family ties and the pervasiveness of blood bonds are important not only because they allow large families to accumulate political capital – by creating political dynasties, for instance – to fuel clientelistic networks, but also because these ties strengthen the patriarchal system, which is often sustained by state norms.

The profound interweaving between political consociationalism, confessionalism and social patriarchy (Joseph 1999; Geha 2019) made the system resilient and impermeable to change. Despite internal struggles and external interference, it remains a system of power, domination, and control that is able to perpetuate itself (Di Peri 2017, 2020a). This aspect strongly resonates with the literature on authoritarian resilience (Nathan 2003; Posusney 2004; Heydemann 2004; Anderson 2006; Hinnebusch 2014), which, with some exceptions (Fakhoury 2014, 2019; Geha 2019a), has been applied rarely to Lebanese consociationalism. In this literature, the analysis of electoral moments has been considered a crucial part of understanding why and to what extent authoritarian systems become resilient (Lust Okar 2006). Despite the little relevance of the electoral moments *per se*, the authoritarian resilience literature has shown how the study of pre-electoral arrangements, the manipulation of election laws and the design of electoral districts and constituencies provide a clear indication of how these moments are exploited by the political and economic elites to maintain their power and networks of privileges. Although overlooked in the literature on Lebanon, election manipulation has been one of the crucial elements in the hands of the elites to maintain their power and steer the system towards its neoliberal configuration.

This last point introduces the final element, which is decisive in the configuration of 'neoliberal sectarianism': the economic dimension. The unravelling of the consociational model has gone hand in hand with a series of political economy choices that led to a gradual re-orientation of the Lebanese economy towards rentierisation (Tufaro 2019), which benefited only the interests of the elites. The (political, religious or family) elites' exploitation of state resources has allowed them to accumulate not only political capital but, above all, economic capital, which has led to a concentration of wealth in the hands of a few (Baumann 2019). After the civil war, this 'new consortium' – to paraphrase the expression that Traboulsi (2012) uses to describe a small group of families, which often coincided with the political elites and the main business groups of the country – undertook several neoliberal privatisation processes that severely affected the reconstruction of the country (Salloukh et al. 2015; Daher 2016; Halabi and Boswal 2019). The corollaries of these measures were, on the one hand, the withdrawal of the state from its regulatory and distributive role and, on the other hand, the failure to tackle economic and social problems, such as unemployment, rising poverty, increasing corruption, and poor social services (Traboulsi 2014). This has also increased the amount of public debt, which soared from 48% in 1992 to 170% in 2020 (Libnanews 2020). This rise in debt has brought even greater wealth into the hands of the 'new consortium' without producing any improvement for private sector investments or export support, with the result of producing benefits just for a few, while the vast majority of the population remained under the poverty line (Assouad 2017).[1] The destructive interweaving of the state and the economic-financial system led to a consolidation of the neoliberal sectarian system, which, ultimately, became the target of massive protests in October 2019 (Cornish 2020). The deterioration of living conditions and the impossibility of maintaining a system that furthered inequality finally provoked Lebanon's financial default in the spring of 2020 (Di Peri 2020b). In short, the consociational system, in its neoliberal form, showed its limitations in fostering the regime's resilience.

Surfing the Lebanese electoral system

To better understand how and to what extent electoral manipulation has been one of the crucial elements of this transformation, a brief description of the Lebanese electoral system, with a focus on the post-civil war period, is necessary.

Administratively, Lebanon is divided into departments (*muhafaza*), districts (*qada'*) and municipalities. Each *muhafaza*, except for those of Beirut and Akkar, is divided into *qada'* and presents a confessional distribution that depends on the historical context, people's movements during the civil war and other migratory phenomena.[2] Since Lebanon gained independence in 1943, the country's election law has been changed for each electoral round by using either the *muhafaza*, the *qada'* or both as electoral districts (Antoun 1995; El-Khazen 2003). Because of the extremely clientelistic nature of the Lebanese electoral system, the design of electoral districts and, consequently, seat allocation according to confessional lines has been (and is) a powerful tool in the hands of the political elites. Each district takes into account the confession, which is a function of the communitarian distribution for each district. For this reason, there is a strict and effective relationship between voters' electoral communitarian affiliation and that of the deputies who run for each district.[3] This aspect is, of course, connected to the size of the electoral districts: the smaller an electoral district is (*qada'*), the more homogenous it is from a confessional point of view, so it is easier to maintain a correlation between the communitarian affiliation of voters and that of the candidates. Using the *muhafaza* as the electoral district would not change the number of MPs or the parliament's sectarian balance, but many politicians from the minority communities object to this because demographic majorities in larger districts would have the power to 'take over' the minority's seats. They argue that MPs elected by voters belonging to another confession would not be 'real' representatives of their communities but rather 'lackeys' of the majority sect (Milligan 2012). This is one of the reasons why candidates and political parties constantly manipulate the electoral districts to change their size and composition. These practices help to fuel clientelistic networks and facilitate the control of the local electorate by ethno-sectarian parties (Deets and Skulte-Ouaiss 2021). Moreover, as has been demonstrated (Cammett 2014; Cammett and Malesky 2012), practices of vote exchange, vote buying and so forth are commonplace during campaigns and on election day.

From independence, Lebanon has adopted a majoritarian formula that was also maintained for the post-Taif elections. Before the civil war, election laws sought simultaneously to guarantee the best representation of its population, to strengthen national and territorial unity, to favour national cohesion and national integration and to placate the claims of minorities. In short, to be in line with the consociational principles. Once elected, a candidate represents, at least in theory, his/her electoral district as well as his/her community. After the civil war, however, the electoral formula was adapted to the needs of those strong Lebanese families and political elites that emerged victorious after the conflict, and, in particular, their militias (Picard 2000). Pivotal to this new system were the electoral laws related to the design of electoral districts and voters' registration on the electoral lists, a particularly sensitive issue given that the last official census dates back to 1932. The electoral lists do not reflect the real distribution of communities as, paradoxically, many Lebanese appear to be registered in their city of origin where their parents live and not where they actually reside, a practice designed during the French mandate to minimise territorial and administrative mobility and to preserve the historical identity of the regions. This aspect creates a distortion between the distribution of a community in a given district and its actual presence in that place. This is why the design of constituencies, districts and election laws are crucial to grant victory to one or more candidates, but also to strengthen the power of the historic families and *zuama* living in a given district. Because of this system, depending on the election law, it is possible to identify a dominant community for each constituency.[4]

This configuration aligns the system with the consociational desiderata (i.e. protecting minorities and guaranteeing broad autonomy to communities), but also makes it highly pliable to elites' interests. In addition, because of the block voting system in each constituency, the results of the elections are discounted from a sectarian point of view. This aspect, however, does not prevent candidates from using a substantial number of resources during the election campaign, even in those districts that are non-competitive. The collection of votes in these districts serves to accumulate political and bargaining capital to be used when discussions start to form a new government. Likewise, to spend money in non-competitive districts serves to gain accreditation as a communitarian leader at the national and not just at the local level (Corstange 2012). This is why, for example, the value of municipal elections has increased in the post-war era. Even though municipalities are institutions without their own budget and have little decision-making power, municipal elections represent an important moment to give visibility to certain parties and figures who then want to be accredited on the national scene or are used to avoid increasing popular discontent – for example, when there is a political vacuum, like when the legislative elections are postponed (Abu Rish 2016).

Following a similar logic, candidates promote pre-electoral alliances to increase their visibility at the local and national levels, but this does not alter the results of those elected in the various constituencies. For example, in the different electoral rounds, and increasingly since the

2000s, more or less organised movements and electoral coalitions (e.g. the civic lists of Beirut Madinati and Kulluna Watani) were created. These lists called for the abolition of the sectarian system, the introduction of a unified civil code and other modifications to fight the pervasive corruption of the current political classes. Despite not winning seats, these lists often collected hundreds of thousands of votes more than the parties that had won in a particular district (Deets and Skulte-Ouaiss 2021). This was precisely the result of the pre-electoral alliances that impacted some districts, especially those that were non-homogenous from a confessional point of view. This is also connected to the electoral rules. While the right to stand is confessional, the right to vote is non-confessional. Voters can vote for all available confessional seats, regardless of their own confessional group, and in multi-member electoral districts, voters have more than one vote and can cast their choice for as many candidates as there are seats available (block vote system). This, of course, incentivises pre-electoral alliances.

It is evident how the design of constituencies, districts, and election laws is critical to ensure the victory of one or another candidate. The manipulation of this system, according to a client–patron logic is at odds with the principles that guide electoral moments in democratic systems. Furthermore, vote trading, pressure at polling stations, and electoral campaigns monopolised by stronger (richest) candidates are only a few examples of the 'democratic' problems facing Lebanon under neoliberal sectarianism (Corstange 2012).

Behind the elections: debates over election law

Given the system outlined above, the real battle to win the elections plays out not through genuine electoral campaigns but through various arrangements and discussions among the political forces, the economic elites and the *zuama* before the elections, which are also impacted by internal and external factors. Election laws are particularly relevant from this perspective: A comparison of the processes that led to the elaboration of the 2008 and 2017 laws will clarify this point.

The 2008 election law

Discussions about the 2008 election law started in parliament in 2006, shortly after the 2005 elections and the withdrawal of the Syrian army from Lebanon. This was the first time since the end of the civil war that it was possible to design an election law without Syrian influence over Lebanese politics. After the end of the civil war, Syria had strongly interfered in the elaboration of the size of the electoral districts, as Syria worked to create large electoral districts (less homogenous from a confessional point of view) where it would be easier for pro-Syrian candidates to form strategic alliances to be elected (Assi 2016).

An issue that has received significant attention over the years in all the discussions around the election law has been the introduction of the proportional system. Since the first legislatives elections after the end of the civil war in 1992, many groups and experts have called for the introduction of the proportional system or, at least, a mixed system. In fact, when it gained independence, Lebanon adopted a majoritarian system. The use of a proportional system would allow better visibility and representativeness of the minorities in the various districts, as well as a hybridisation of the sectarian composition in the parliamentary blocks (and it would have been more in line with the consociational principles). The most evident result would be a reduction in the weight of confessional presence and their power to make strategic alliances to win parliamentary seats, thereby giving more space to parties and groups emerging from civil society. However, as we will see, political parties and parliament were not very receptive to these demands.

The introduction of the proportional quota was also at the heart of the recommendations made by the 'National Commission on the Parliamentary Election law' established in 2006 (National Commission on the Parliamentary Election law 2006). The idea behind the commission was to foster a productive and synergic process with the representatives of civil society, political forces and independent experts to create a renewed framework for the Lebanese electoral system that could moderate the confessional impact on that system and mitigate the power of the *zuama* and the politicians who had dominated the Lebanese political scene for decades. The most important part of the commission's work was the proposal to introduce a mixed system by using both the *muhafaza* and the *qada'* as electoral districts. A total of 77 seats would be elected from the *qada'* on a majoritarian block vote basis, and 51 seats would be elected from six large *muhafaza* on a proportional representation basis. According to Salem (2006),

> this system would provide a balance between the familiarity of the small districts in which voters and representatives could maintain close links and in which small communities find security; and the promise of large districts with proportional representation which would allow new groups and leaders to enter into parliament, and would end the monopoly of the main *zuama* on representation
>
> (p. 4).

However, the commission's work was severely affected by the evolution of Lebanese politics – first, the 2006 war between Israel and Hezbollah, and second, the violence that erupted in the country in May 2008 after the government's decision to remove the pro-Hezbollah chief of security at the airport of Beirut. This decision sparked armed confrontations in the streets of the capital between the Hezbollah militia and its opponents (mainly the members of the Future Movement) in an escalation of violence. To recompose this confessional fragmentation, another consociational compromise – the Doha Agreement – was reached in May 2008 (Samer 2009). Political consensus on the electoral districts was a core part of the agreement. It proposed the creation of a new government and the preparation of a new election law. It also called for the chief of the army, Michel Suleiman, to be elevated to the presidency, a post that had been vacant since November 2007 (Worth and Bakri 2008).

The 2008 election law, which was finally approved on 28 September 2008, was ultimately based on majoritarian rule and used the *qada'* as electoral district.[5] The new law allocated 128 parliamentary seats among the 26 electoral districts equally distributed between Christians and Muslims. The 26 electoral districts were based on the administrative boundaries of the *qada'* but with some exceptions. It is interesting to note how these districts were homogenous from a confessional point of view. According to a report published in 2011 by the International Foundation for Electoral Systems (IFES 2011), all 26 districts have a clear Sunni, Shi'a, Maronite, Druze or Greek Orthodox majority, except for Metn, Ba'abda, Shuf, and two of Beirut's three districts. As we have seen, the issue of the electoral districts' homogeneity is important, especially concerning the representativeness of the elected officials in relation to the voters. The 2006 election law increased the distortion on this point by disadvantaging Christians. Christians represent about 37% of all registered voters. This means that a total of 38 out of 64 Christian seats were in districts with majority Muslim voters, leading to justifiable complaints from Christian voters that they could not control who represented them. This inflated the Muslim sectarian elite's legislative power at the expense of the Christians and undermined the principle of accountability between voters and many of their deputies because Christian candidates are 'hostages' to Muslim voters and it's then the latter who decide which Christian is elected.

Under the 2008 law, the number of seats allocated to each district ranged from two to ten. There were no formal criteria that outlined the basis for the distribution of seats to different districts or between different confessions in the district. The distribution was similar during the 2000 and 2005 elections. Moreover, the law did not include the recommendations of the 2006 National Commission, in particular those concerning the proportional system method, making them – in the words of Ziyad Baroud, 1 of the 12 members of the National Commission – 'a cup half full' (Khoury 2008).

Thus, it emerges that the design of electoral districts coupled with the high volatility of election laws provides political groups with different tools and opportunities to manipulate votes. In addition to these 'legal' manoeuvres, other instruments are devised during elections to pressure voters through systems that allow identifying those who cast a vote or through different economic incentives (Sarkis 1993). In this regard, a problematic issue that the 2008 election law (as the previous ones) failed to deal with was electoral ballots. Voters are not provided with an official ballot paper listing all the candidates; instead, the 2008 election law, like its predecessors, gave voters two options to cast their ballot. Either voters write the names of their chosen candidates on a blank piece of paper provided at the polling station or the voter brings with them into the polling station a piece of paper (known as a 'prepared ballot') that already contains the names of the candidates they have chosen. This, of course, incentivises clientelistic practices and vote control. It is worth noting that all these possible distortions of the electoral process were seriously considered by the 2006 commission, but the Lebanese parliament did not accept many of its recommendations.[6]

In the case of the 2008 election law, political forces took 18 months to agree on the new law, and only pressure from external actors led to an agreement. In fact, compromise on the 2008 election law was reached thanks to external pressure and following a negotiation process that had put the consociational model, through the Doha Agreement, at the centre once again. The gradual rentierisation of the Lebanese economy and the sectarian leaders' close ties with major external actors like Saudi Arabia and, more broadly, the Gulf countries (Baumann 2017; Abou-Mosleh 2015), as well as the constant influx of petrodollars into the coffers of Lebanese banks, had the effect of pushing for agreement on the new law. Political uncertainty could have damaged national and regional interests in Lebanon with harmful repercussions on the contractor bourgeoisie, which increasingly coincided with the political elites.

The 2017 election law

After 2009, Lebanon went through a long period of time without elections. The inability of the country's political elites to agree on a new electoral law had led to a prorogation of the parliamentary mandate on three occasions, even though security reasons were officially adduced to justify such a delay. As we have seen, one of the most controversial points of the previous electoral laws was the reform of the electoral formula. Already in 2006, along with the National Commission, the Civic Campaign for Electoral Reform was set up and consisted of a national coalition of 66 Lebanese civil society organisations and two coalitions of NGOs to advocate for the reform of the electoral system, through the introduction of the proportional system (Geha 2016). Civil society was not alone in putting pressure on the introduction of the proportional system. Each political party pushed for this as well but with its own idea about what such a proportional system would entail. For example, in 2011, the Progressive Socialist Party (PSP) proposed the Orthodox Gathering Law, according to which MPs could be elected only by members of their own sect, thus creating a sort of apartheid that would distort the proportional aim by deepening the confessional divide (Qifa Nabki 2011). Similarly, in 2012, the 14 March coalition proposed a 50-district law, subsequently modified to 37 districts (Moulahazat 2012), with the clear intent to draw electoral districts for their own interests.

During this period, discussions on the new electoral law were conducted, and proposals were made in a more intricate regional and national scenario. After years of political deadlock and the polarisation of political life between the two main coalitions (8 and 14 March), the 2011 Arab uprisings and the 2015 garbage crisis marked important moments for civil society activism reinvigorating political participation. In this regard, the 2016 municipal elections were crucial. Political leaders understood not only the necessity of having elections to prevent questions about their legitimacy but, particularly, they were seen as key moments to reaffirm the status quo and the neoliberal sectarianism they embody. For the first time in a municipal competition, political elites formed a strategic alliance to oppose emerging actors from civil society (Atallah 2016). The clearest example is the list created for the elections in Beirut, *La'ihat al-Biyarta* (The Beirutis' List), including the Amal Movement, the Future Movement, the Free Patriotic Movement, the Lebanese Forces, the Phalanges Party, and the PSP, to compete against the *La'ihat Bayrut Madinati* (Beirut Is My City List), which included architects, engineers, business persons, and artists, all representatives of civil society. Despite the enormous visibility and sympathy the list attracted, Beirut Is My City failed to secure a single seat on the municipal council even though it garnered nearly 32% of the total votes cast (Abu Rish 2016) due to the block vote system.

The failure to introduce greater proportionality in the 2016 municipal elections led to a renewed reflection on the content and the spirit that the new election law should contain. The spill-over effects of the Syrian war in Lebanon, the gradual deterioration of the socio-economic situation, the increase in inequality, the inability of the political elites to provide basic services to the population and the fear of a new escalation of protests in the country, breathed new life into the push for reforming the election law.

A new round of discussions behind closed doors started in January 2017, and, as in the past, each political party tried to propose a draft law to maximise its own interest. Finally, in June 2017, a proposal from an MP of the Lebanese Forces, Georges Adwan, reached a consensus among political forces and was approved. The law introduced a sort of proportional ratio, but, as we will explain later, it was distorted by technicalities, which, *de facto*, helped political elites to maintain the status quo, namely their power. Despite these limitations, the law was celebrated as the best option for Lebanon (The Daily Star 2017).

The law[7] includes many novelties. First, the number of districts decreased from 26 to 15. Each electoral constituency may have at least one district, and 27 seats are distributed among the sub-districts. The distribution of sets follows the same rules as in the past (64 each for the Christian and Muslim communities), and within each confession, they are further subdivided into 11 confessional branches (4 within Islam and 7 within Christianity). Although the election register does not reflect the demographic reality because voters register according to the place of their family's origin and not according to their actual place of residence, registration rules remained a red line during the discussions over election laws. The most important changes, as we have seen, involve the electoral formula and the type of ballot. According to the new law, the block vote plurality system is replaced with a party-list proportional electoral system that uses an electoral quota and the largest remainder method to allocate seats to lists in the first phase and to individual candidates in the second phase. Seats are allocated proportionally across the lists by considering confessional denomination and the regional allocation of seats (i.e. the distribution of seats among sub-districts). Voters can vote for a list of candidates and for one individual of the same list competing for a seat in their sub-district (or the district, if there are no sub-districts). For the first time, Lebanese citizens living abroad are allowed to vote at embassies, consulates or other locations, provided they are registered in the Lebanese civil registry. However, there were no changes regarding ballot papers. As in 2009, they are provided by the Ministry of the Interior and municipalities for every district and distributed to the polling stations staff along with the elections' material on election day (one instead of four election days as in the past elections). Finally, a permanent Supervisory Commission for Elections was set up to replace the Supervisory Commission for Electoral Campaigns.

Despite the novelty of the proportional quota, the law introduced technical aspects that have altered the aim of the proportionality itself. On the one hand, the electoral quota had to be adjusted according to the Lebanese sectarian system: it was not a fixed threshold but a formula (the number of voters divided by the number of seats in the constituency), and it varies according to the districts. Smaller districts have a higher threshold. This meant that the system generated inequalities in the weight of votes because of the considerable fluctuations from one district to another in the ratio of registered voters per seat and the eligibility quota for seat allocation, with the result that, in some districts, the votes had twice the influence of votes than in other districts. One of the consequences has been that candidates with the highest number of preferential votes lost in many districts because the seat for their sect had already been filled. Also, this determines the result that in the same district, MPs were elected with large gaps between the first and the last vote takers. On the other hand, the law mandates that only lists that reach the quotient are eligible for seat allocation, while 'lists that do not achieve the electoral quotient are excluded from the seat allocation, and the electoral quotient is re-calculated after deduction of the votes obtained by such lists'.[8] Such a provision favours bigger parties while penalising the smaller ones with the consequence of impairing the effects of the proportional formula.

Another aspect of the law that favoured the status quo was a large amount of money candidates had to pay to run. The price has increased four times since 2009, reaching $5,300. This constitutes a serious impediment for independent or poor people or small parties. By contrast, the law increases the financial advantage for established leaders and political parties. During a campaign, a candidate may legally spend up to $100,000 plus $3.33 per registered voter in a relevant district, a 20% increase that allowed established parties and wealthier people to spend millions more in each district than they did in 2009. The amount of money parties can spend during the electoral campaign has an impact on, for example, the number of people they can use to stay at the polls to monitor irregularities or to pressure the voters (Elghossain 2017).

The application of these technicalities is visible in the 2018 electoral results, which did not alter the composition of the Lebanese political spectrum, led to more fragmentation and polarisation, and *de facto* increased the power of neoliberal sectarian elites (Moussa 2018).

Conclusion

Neoliberal sectarianism, an evolution of the resilient sectarianism that became dominant in Lebanon in the post-civil war era, has been supported and fuelled not only by the intertwining of political, economic, social and religious elites in the consociational system but also through skilful manipulation of the electoral system.

It has been widely demonstrated that resilient authoritarianism reproduces itself also through the manipulation of election laws and the design of districts and constituencies. This analysis of the debates behind the most recent electoral laws in Lebanon shows how every attempt to reform the system has been prevented. After the civil war, despite the many attempts to silence it, civil society played an active role in proposing anti-sectarian alternatives and in encouraging movements and civic lists to compete with the traditional elites, but behind-the-scenes manoeuvres, pre-electoral agreements and the impact of actors outside the system (national or international) have led to a stalemate in the reform process and consolidated rather than altered neoliberal sectarianism.

The instrumentalisation of the country's election laws has made the drafting of alternative proposals an exercise dominated by political interests rather than a genuine attempt to reform the consociational model. Thus, it serves as another tool in the hands of the political, religious, and economic elites to self-perpetuate and manipulate the system to ensure that the MPs who will be elected will be able to maintain their political-economic prerogatives.

Notes

1 According to Assouad's estimates, from 2005 to 2014, 48% of personal wealth in Lebanon belonged to 0.3% of the adult population, with two families – Hariri and Mikati – owning 15% of that fortune.
2 About 90,000 Lebanese families were displaced to new territories. According to the Ministry of Refugees, only 70,735 families returned (Feghali 1997).
3 For example, for the 2000 and 2005 elections, Lebanon was divided into 14 electoral districts that did not seem to be based on any formal criteria. The eight *qada'* of North Lebanon formed two districts, the eight *qada'* of South Lebanon formed two districts, and the six *qada'* in Mount Lebanon formed four districts. See IFES (2011).
4 For example, Maronites are the majority in Kesrouan, Jbeil, Metn, Baabda, Jezzine, Zghorta, Bcharre, and Batroun; Shias dominate in Tyre, Nabbatiyeh, Bint Jbeil, Baalbeck, Hermel, Marjeyoun, and north Bekaa; the Sunnis are in the majority in Tripoli, Akkar, Minieh-Dennieh, south Bekaa, and Sidone; and the Druz are dominant in the constituencies of Chouf, and Aley. In Koura, the Greek Orthodox are in the majority, while Beirut, which was previously dominated by Sunnis, now looks equally divided between Christians and Muslims. Those confessions present in constituencies where a dominant community does not prevail appear to be very active, for example, in Zahle and West Bekaa-Rachaya (Verdeil et al. 2007).
5 The law was published by The Daily Star newspaper, which suspended operations while this chapter was in the works www.dailystar.com.lb/elections09/ (accessed 9 March 2010).
6 Not only the introduction of proportional system. The requests include the creation of an Independent Electoral Commission, campaign finance reform, media regulation, the lowering of the voting age from 21 to 18, the lowering of the candidacy age from 25 to 22, out-of-country voting, a 33.33% women's quota on electoral lists, facilitating access for people with special needs, ensuring the secrecy of the vote (pre-printed ballot, vote counting at the polling centre instead of the polling station), the right to vote for the military, ensuring the electoral participation of detainees (Salem 2006).
7 The text of the law in Arabic has been published by An-Nahar (https://bit.ly/3BV46PY) and in English by the Lebanese Ministry of Information (www.ministryinfo.gov.lb/en/22598).
8 As per art. 98/3.

References

Abou-Mosleh, Firas. 2015. 'Lebanon's Economic Dependence on the Gulf: Debunking the Myths'. *Al Akhbar English*, February 23.
Abu Rish, Ziad. 2016. 'Municipal Politics in Lebanon'. *Middle East Report* 280: 4–11.
Anderson, Lisa. 2006. 'Searching Where the Light Shines: Studying Democratization in the Middle East'. *Annual Review of Political Science* 9(1): 189–214.
Antoun, Randa. 1995. 'Municipalities in Lebanon: Past and Present'. *The Lebanon Report* 4: 31–43.
Assi, Abbas. 2016. *Democracy in Lebanon: Political Parties and the Struggle for Power Since Syrian Withdrawal*. London: Bloomsbury Publishing.
Assouad, Lydia. 2017. *Rethinking the Lebanese Economic Miracle: The Extreme Concentration of Income and Wealth in Lebanon 2005–2014*. World Inequality Lab, Working Paper 13. Available at: https://bit.ly/3OstZxR.

Atallah, Sami. 2016. 'Lebanon Needs More than Municipal Elections to Effect Change'. *Center for Lebanese Policy Studies*, April 1. Available at: https://bit.ly/3Exqodm.

Baumann, Hannes. 2016. 'Social Protest and the Political Economy of Sectarianism in Lebanon'. *Global Discourse* 6(4): 634–649.

Baumann, Hannes. 2017. 'Lebanon's Economic Dependence on Saudi Arabia is Dangerous'. *The Washington Post*, December 7. Available at: https://wapo.st/3DhlvUk.

Baumann, Hannes. 2019. 'The Causes, Nature, and Effect of the Current Crisis of Lebanese Capitalism'. *Nationalism and Ethnic Politics* 25(1): 61–77.

Cammett, Melani and Sukriti Issar. 2010. 'Bricks and Mortar Clientelism: Sectarianism and the Logics of Welfare Allocation in Lebanon'. *World Politics* 62(3): 381–421.

Cammett, Melani and Edmund Malesky. 2012. 'Power Sharing in Postconflict Societies: Implications for Peace and Governance'. *Journal of Conflict Resolution* 56(6): 982–1016.

Cammett, Melani. 2014. *Compassionate Communalism*. Ithaca, NY: Cornell University Press.

Cornish, Chloe. 2020. 'Lebanon's Economic Crisis Threatens to Destroy its Middle Class'. *The Financial Time*, June 16.

Corstange, Daniel. 2012. 'Vote Trafficking in Lebanon'. *International Journal of Middle East Studies* 44(3): 483–505.

Daher, Joseph. 2016. *Hezbollah: The Political Economy of Lebanon's Party of God*. London: Pluto Press.

Dahl, Robert. 1971. *Polyarchy: Participation and Opposition*. New Haven, CT: Yale University Press.

Deets, Stephen and Jennifer Skulte-Ouaiss. 2021. 'Breaking into a Consociational System: Civic Parties in Lebanon's 2018 Parliamentary Election'. *Ethnopolitics* 20(2): 157–185.

Dekmejian, Richard Hrair. 1978. 'Consociational Democracy in Crisis: The Case of Lebanon. *Comparative Politics* 10(2): 251–265.

Di Peri, Rosita. 2010. 'Il modello della democrazia consociativa e la sua applicazione al caso libanese'. *Rivista Italiana di Scienza Politica* 2: 1–31.

Di Peri, Rosita. 2017. 'Beyond Sectarianism: Hegemony, Reproduction and Resilience in Lebanon'. *Mediterranean Politics* 22(3): 426–431.

Di Peri, Rosita. 2018. 'Speaking Secular Acting Sectarian: Lebanese Women's Rights beyond the Constitution'. *Oriente Moderno* 98(2): 247–264.

Di Peri, Rosita. 2020a. 'Stretching the margins: Identity, power and new "frontiers" in Lebanon's Maronite community'. *Mediterranean Politics* 25(3): 332–350.

Di Peri, Rosita. 2020b. 'A Sectarianised Pandemic: COVID-19 in Lebanon'. 20/71. Istituto Affari Internazionali. Available at: https://bit.ly/3FLtNEB.

Elghossain, Anthony. 2017. 'One Step Forward for Lebanon's Elections'. *Carnegie Endowment for International Peace*, July 11. Available at: https://bit.ly/3nqcRxw.

El-Khazen, Farid. 2003. 'Political Parties in Postwar Lebanon: Parties in Search of Partisans'. *The Middle East Journal* 57(4): 605–624.

Fakhoury, Tamirace. 2009. *Democracy and Power-Sharing in Stormy Weather: The Case of Lebanon*. Wiesbaden: Vs Verlag.

Fakhoury, Tamirace. 2014. 'Do Power-Sharing Systems Behave Differently amid Regional Uprisings? Lebanon in the Arab Protest Wave'. *The Middle East Journal* 68(4): 505–520.

Fakhoury, Tamirace. 2019. 'Power-Sharing after the Arab Spring? Insights from Lebanon's Political Transition'. *Nationalism and Ethnic Politics* 25(1): 9–26.

Feghali, Kamal. 1997. *Le déplacemnet au Liban la stratégie du retour et du développement* (In Arabic). Beirut: Centre libanais pour la recherché.

Gates, Carolyne. 1998. *The Merchant Republic of Lebanon: Rise of an Open Economy*. London: I.B. Tauris.

Geha, Carmen. 2016. *Civil Society and Political Reform in Lebanon and Libya: Transition and Constraint*. London: Routledge.

Geha, Carmen. 2019. 'The Myth of Women's Political Empowerment within Lebanon's Sectarian Power-Sharing System'. *Journal of Women, Politics and Policy* 40(4): 498–521.

Geha, Carmen. 2019a. 'Resilience through Learning and Adaptation: Lebanon's Power-Sharing System and the Syrian Refugee Crisis'. *Middle East Law and Governance* 11(1): 65–90.

Halabi, Sami and Jacob Boswal. 2019. *Extend and Pretend: Lebanon's Financial House of Cards. How Lebanon's Politicians and Banks Constructed a Regulated Ponzi Scheme That Ran the Country's Economy into the Ground*. Triangle Policy. Available at: https://bit.ly/3kyReJu.

Heydemann, Steven. 2004. *Network of Privileges in the Middle East: The Politics of Economic Reform Revisited*. New York: Palgrave McMillian.

Hinnebusch, Raymond. 2014. 'A Historical Sociology Approach to Authoritarian Resilience in Post-Arab Uprising MENA'. *Project on Middle East Political Science*- POMEPS, December 19. Available at https://bit.ly/3UT3yE3.
IFES – International Foundation for Electoral Systems. 2011. *Electoral Districts in Lebanon*, October 5. Available at: https://bit.ly/3ncYKeI.
Joseph, Suad. 1999. 'Descent of the Nation: Kinship and Citizenship in Lebanon'. *Citizenship Studies* 3(3): 295–318.
Kassir, Samir. 2000. 'Dix ans après, comment ne pas réconcilier une société divisée?' *Monde Arabe Maghreb Machrek* 169: 6–22.
Khoury, Doreen. 2008. 'Lebanon's Election Law: A Cup Half Full'. *Daily Star*, October 11. Available at: https://bit.ly/3Fc3TKg.
Kingston, Paul W. 2013. *Reproducing Sectarianism: Advocacy Networks and the Politics of Civil Society in Postwar Lebanon*. New York: Suny Press.
Libnanews le Média Citoyen du Liban. 2020. *Liban: Nouvelle dégradation de la dette publique qui atteint désormais 91.6 milliards de dollars*. Available at: https://bit.ly/3wA01j7.
Lijphart, Arend. 1969. 'Consociational Democracy'. *World Politics* 21(2): 207–225.
Lijphart, Arend. 1977. *Democracy in Plural Societies: A Comparative Exploration*. New Haven, CT: Yale University Press.
Lust-Okar, Ellen. 2006. 'Elections under Authoritarianism: Preliminary Lessons from Jordan'. *Democratization* 13(3): 456–471.
Milligan, Maren. 2012. 'How to Slice the Pie: Reforming Lebanon's Electoral Law'. *Carnegie Middle East Center*, May 24. Available at: https://bit.ly/3Fp6jVW.
Moulahazat. 2012 (blog). Available at: https://bit.ly/3CoKiEJ.
Moussa, Nayla. 2018. 'The Lebanese Legislative Elections: Fragmentation and Polarization'. *Arab Initiative Reform*, July 12. Available at: https://bit.ly/3c6nxLa.
Nathan, Andrew J. 2003. 'Authoritarian Resilience'. *Journal of Democracy* 14(1): 6–17.
National Commission on the Parliamentary Electoral Law. 2006. Available at: http://www.elections-lebanon.org/elections/docs_2_1_1_e.aspx?lg=en.
Picard, Elizabeth. 2000. 'The Political Economy of Civil War in Lebanon'. In Steven Heydemann (ed.), *War, Institutions, and Social Change in the Middle East*. Berkeley, CA: University of California Press, 292–322.
Posusney, Marsha Pripstein. 2004. 'Enduring Authoritarianism: Middle East Lessons for Comparative Theory'. *Comparative Politics* 36(2): 127–138.
Qifa Nabki. 2011. Available at: https://bit.ly/3DfFjr7.
Salem, Paul. 2006. 'Electoral Law Reform in Lebanon: The Experience and Recommendations of the National Commission'. *Arab Reform Initiative*, July 10. Available at: https://bit.ly/3n4Xz11.
Salloukh, Bassel. 2019. 'Taif and the Lebanese State: The Political Economy of a Very Sectarian Public Sector'. *Nationalism and Ethnic Politics* 25(1): 43–60.
Salloukh, Bassel, Rabie Barakat, Jinan S. Al-Habbal, Lara W. Khattab and Shoghig Mikaelian. 2015. *The Politics of Sectarianism in Postwar Lebanon*. London: Pluto Press.
Salti, Nisreen and Jad Chaaban. 2010. 'The Role of Sectarianism in the Allocation of Public Expenditures in Postwar Lebanon'. *International Journal of Middle East Studies* 42(4): 637–655.
Samer, Abboud. 2009. 'The seige of Nahr Al-Bared and the palestinian refugees in Lebanon'. *Arab Studies Quarterly* 31(1/2): 31–48.
Sarkis, Jean. 1993. *Histoire de la guerre au Liban*. Paris: PUF.
The Daily Star. 2017. 'Lebanese Parliament Approves New Vote Law'. June, 16. Available at: https://bit.ly/3wKa4SJ.
Traboulsi, Fawwaz. 2012. *A History of Modern Lebanon*. London: Pluto Press.
Traboulsi, Fawwaz. 2014. *Social Classes and Political Power in Lebanon*. Berlin: Heinrich Böll Stiftung.
Tufaro, Rossana. 2019. 'Altro che crisi del dollaro: L'economia politica della sollevazione libanese (Pt. 1 and Pt. 2)'. *Global Project*. Available at: https://bit.ly/3krxkjy.
Verdeil, Eric, Ghaleb Faour and Sébastien Velut. 2007. *Atlas du Liban*. Beirut: Institut français du Proche Orient/CNRS Liban.
Worth, Robert F. and Nada Bakri. 2008. 'Deal for Lebanese Factions Leaves Hezbollah Stronger'. *The New York Times*, May 22. Available at: https://nyti.ms/3Hfsq2L.

13
COMPETITION UNDER SYSTEMIC RELIGIOUS CONSTRAINTS

Presidential elections in Iran

Pejman Abdolmohammadi

Introduction

The Iranian political system is very complex, and the historical evolution of its institution-building can be said to be represented in its contemporary history. From 1906, the year of the Iranian Constitutional Revolution, onwards, several political, social, religious, and economic players contributed to institutionalising the political process in the country in a modern way. The intellectuals, the clergy, the merchants (*bazaris*), the courts, the army, and many other players have been the protagonists in the last century and a half in Iranian political history. The Constitutional Revolution of 1906, the rise of the Pahlavi dynasty, declaration of Reza Pahlavi as the Shah of Iran in 1925 and the creation of a proper modern state; the Mosaddeq national government in 1951; Mohammad Reza Shah Pahlavi's reign; and the rise of the Islamic Republic of Iran after the 1979 Revolution represent the main steps that Iranian politics undertook to achieve a more modern political system. In other words, one can state that the forces of tradition, on the one hand, and the forces of modernity, on the other, have challenged each other during different phases in Iranian political history. Sometimes the forces of modernity were successful, and sometimes the forces of tradition were. However, all these forces contributed to the process of modernisation of the country. Some, such as Reza Shah, have been more focused on cultural and economic modernisation and others, such as the constitutional revolutionaries, on political modernisation (Abrahamian 1982; Agiodani 2004; Browne 1966; Kasravi 2002).

The 1979 Islamic Revolution, under the leadership of Ayatollah Ruhollah Khomeini, took Iran into a new phase of its political history. The creation of the Islamic Republic can be seen as a form of compromise between the secular political forces and the religious ones, both protagonists of the 1979 Revolution. In fact, at the institutional level, there are bodies which represent the republican soul and organs that represent the Islamic nature of the regime. However, under the direct influence of Ayatollah Khomeini[1] (Abdolmohammadi 2009; Adib-Moghaddam 2014; Ansari 1994; Djalili 1989; Moin 2000; Taheri 1989) and his collaborators, the Islamic side was able to exercise greater power, both institutionally and politically, than the republican side.

In other words, the republican principles in the Constitution of the Islamic Republic are limited and circumscribed by Islamic principles. Ayatollah Khomeini attributed enormous power to the figure of the *Vali-ye faqih* or the 'jurisconsult', who finds the limits of his authority not in the people but in divine will, and all the articles of the Iranian Constitution guarantee full respect for Islamic principles in the light of *shari'a*. This means that the functioning of republican political institutions must also remain within the limits of shari'a, and the model proposes the establishment of a republican system limited by Islam (Davani 1997).

The 1979 Revolution established a political system based on a fundamental core of values. Frequently, regimes that arise after a revolution are marked by radical core values that configure a 'teleological' path, which is aimed at achieving a final goal that often coincides with utopian designs. In such cases, revolutionary regimes, at least in the initial phase of their existence, set themselves the objective of radical transformation of society to the point, in certain cases, of configuring the creation of a 'new human'. In these circumstances, all the efforts and activities of the political system are directed towards the mobilisation of all social actors in an attempt to involve them in this process. This represents an effort aimed at intervening positively, in a highly dynamic perspective (Edelstein 2004).

The Islamic Republic, especially its clerical component, aims first and foremost to restore a traditional system of values rather than to indicate a new horizon. From the outset, in fact, the application of shari'a concerned the sphere of customs and private behaviour, while it did not precisely define an orthodoxy with regard to economic policies and social structure. The regime of the Iranian Islamic Republic is structured to strictly safeguard the ordering principles of Shari'a in the field of culture and models of civil coexistence, while leaving a certain amount of discretion regarding other public choices.

It can therefore be said that the clerical authorities have secured a sort of 'reserved domain', which is removed from public discussion and political competition. Thus, in many ways, the Islamic Republic is configured as a kind of 'government of the custodian' that combines strict control by the political elite over certain policy areas while granting some space for tolerance and openness in specific policy areas.

By inserting the term 'republic' (*Jomhuri*) in the place of 'government' (*Hokumat*), Ayatollah Khomeini attributed to the state not only the divine legitimacy of the *Vali-ye faqih* but also popular legitimacy. The absolute sovereignty Khomeini theorised for his jurisconsult was shared in part with, popular sovereignty, which could express itself – albeit always under the limits of shari'a – through the vote. Islamic republicanism thus gives rise to an institutional dualism. On the one hand, are constitutional institutions such as parliament and the president of the Republic with his ministers and on the other hand, in order to guarantee the Republic's Islamic nature and the divine sovereignty of the *Vali-ye faqih*, bodies such as the Council of Guardians, the Council of Experts, and the Council for Discernment were established (Schirazi 1997). This political model, unlike 'Islamic government', tries to establish a basis upon which secular principles coexist with religious ones. Therefore, precisely because of the historical-political complexity of Iran, between 1979 and 1980, a unique institutional system was born, which, as will be seen in the following paragraphs, can be defined as a 'hybrid'.

The main Islamic institutions
The Velayat-e faqih (Rahbari)

According to the Imami Shi'a school of thought, the formation of an Islamic government must take place under the guidance of the Prophet or the Imam. The principle of *Velayat-e faqih* becomes the essential root of the state form in the Imami doctrine. This theory was developed during the 1979 Revolution, particularly in the drafting of the Constitution. The form of state that the principle of *Velayat-e faqih* proposes, according to Ayatollah Khomeini, is ensured by a jurist in Islamic law (the jurisconsult), who must be fair and intelligent. He has the task of forming a government and administering it. This ruler will have as much authority over the Islamic state as the Prophet, and the 12 Imams had. The jurisconsult – that is, the *Vali-ye faqih* – is directly nominated by Allah to govern, and no one can deny his authority.

Khomeini's statements provided the legal basis for the establishment in the Iranian Constitution of a central and powerful figure with religious qualifications. This figure is given the name of *Vali-ye faqih*, or Supreme Guide. The principle of *Velayat-e faqih* was introduced in the Iranian legal system, therefore, as a guarantee of the application of shari'a in the Islamic Republic of Iran.

This principle of governance is mentioned once in the first chapter of the Constitution as a cardinal principle of the state, while the eighth chapter, which consists of six articles, is fully dedicated to describing its functions. Article 5 of Chapter 1 of the Constitution states:

> In the absence of the Imam in the Islamic Republic of Iran, the function of protection and guidance of the people is assumed by a faqih of proven virtue and justice, connoisseur of his time, courageous, capable of making the right decisions, recognized and accepted by the majority of the people.
>
> *(Davani and Noruzi 2000)*

What are the requirements of the *Vali-ye faqih* in the Islamic Republic? First, he must be a male; he must be a faqih and have competence in Islamic science and the necessary virtue to pronounce on religious issues. He must be pure and righteous, following Allah's orders. He must have a clear political and social vision, and the strength and leadership skills necessary to be able to lead the people. He must be courageous and able to face the problems of his people. He must be an experienced administrator and must apply wisdom in his functions. He must be recognised and accepted by the majority of the people, through the Council of Experts.

What are the main functions of the *Vali-ye faqih*? The Constitution of 1979 assigns the following tasks and powers to the role: the determination of the general policies of the Islamic Republic of Iran in consultation with the Council for the definition of opportunities; the calling of a referendum; the command of the armed forces and the declaration of a state of war; the appointment of the *faqih* members of the Council of Guardians; the appointment of the highest judicial offices in the country; the command of the IRGC (Islamic Republic Guardians of the Revolution Corps); political mediation in the event of disputes between the three powers of the state (legislative, judicial, and executive); the investiture of the president on the basis of his election by the people; the dismissal of the president of the Republic, in consideration of the interests of the country, following an order of the Court of Cassation for non-fulfilment of duties or following a vote by the Islamic Consultative Assembly relating to the insufficiency of political attitudes; grace and remission of sentences, according to Islamic rules, on the proposal of the head of the judiciary; and appointment of the director general of radio and television (Zanjani 1999).

Some considerations on the role of the Vali-ye faqih in the Islamic Republic of Iran

After examining the role of the *Vali-ye faqih*, it is appropriate to provide a more detailed analysis of the highest office of the Iranian state – the one to which the title of head of state can actually be applied, despite the existence of a president of the Republic, which will be examined later. An

Iranian citizen, to become head of state, encounters three essential obstacles. The first is gender: no woman, in fact, can become head of state of the Islamic Republic. The second obstacle is the religious qualification required. In this case, the citizen must have attended Islamic law school and must have obtained the qualification of *faqih*. Furthermore, it should be emphasised that from the previous requirement, it evidently follows that only a Muslim can access this role, and therefore Iranian religious minorities are automatically excluded. In essence, the *Vali-ye faqih* can only be elected among Muslim men who have the qualification of faqih.

The question becomes more interesting when we study the procedure foreseen by the Constitution for the selection of the head of state. The Iranian Constitution considers the *Vali-ye faqih* as a power fully recognised by the people. In fact, he is elected by the Council of Experts, which in turn acquires its legitimacy through the popular vote. The key issue, however, is the preselection undertaken on the occasion of nominations. Those who want to apply to compete for a place on the Council of Experts are preselected by another body, the Council of Guardians. Therefore, even if in factual terms it is the people who vote for the candidates for the Council of Experts, in reality the Council of Guardians will have already filtered who the people are able to vote for. This is already the first example that highlights an impediment to competitiveness among candidates. But the basic question to be resolved in order to understand whether the *Vali-ye faqih* actually enjoys full popular legitimacy is to question whether the Council of Experts really constitutes a fully representative assembly, by virtue of popular election.

Despite the existence of forms of division of powers in the Iranian Constitution, there is an excessive concentration of key powers in the person of the *Vali-ye faqih*. He is the head of the three legitimate powers of the state and has the necessary means to control them. For example, in the case of legislative power, he exercises indirect control over the laws passed by parliament through the Council of Guardians. In the case of the executive, the Supreme Guide can choose not to sign the presidential mandate, deeming the president unsuitable for the good of the country, even after the popular vote. In addition, bills, even if they originate from the government, are always subject to the control of the Council of Guardians after their approval by parliament and before entering into force. In the case of the judiciary, the influence and control *Vali-ye faqih* exercises are much more direct, since he appoints individuals to high offices. In addition, the *Vali-ye faqih* also enjoys the command of the armed forces, which are under his control. Furthermore, his power is not limited only to the political and legal fields, as he also controls the media. Therefore, the *Vali-ye faqih* also manages to have an important role in the cultural policy of the Iranian state.

The Council of Guardians

The Council of Guardians' major responsibility is to ensure that legislation complies with the Constitution and with shari'a. The Council has a total of 12 members, six of whom are Islamic jurists and the other six of whom are 'regular' jurists. Islamic jurists are shari'a experts, and hence they generally deal with matters relating to the adherence of legislation to Islamic laws. Jurists guarantee that the new laws are in line with the country's Constitution. While the Supreme Leader appoints the Islamic jurists directly, the selection of the six jurists is more complex and includes both the court and parliament. In the Constitution, it is seen as a neutral body that, through its interpretation powers, ensures a continual balance between the executive, legislative, and judicial departments of government (Madani 1997).

The nomination of presidential candidates is also overseen by the Council of Guardians. The Iranian Constitution establishes a number of requirements for people seeking the office of president of the Republic, and the Council of Guardians is the body charged with determining whether a candidate meets these requirements. In other words, the Council conducts candidate preselection procedures before the presidential election.

The approval of the Council of Guardians is required by the Constitution before any Iranian candidate can be recognised as an official candidate to run in the presidential elections. This process of preselection is essential, as it guarantees that the Islamic Republic's ruling elites retain a grip on the republican element (Madani 1997).

The preselection of candidates also depends on the domestic balance of power among the main political factions and on the socioeconomic and international context in which Iran finds itself when presidential elections take place.[2] For this reason, the shortlist also reflects the changing balance of power between the various political forces within the establishment. Such a system determines regular political cycles characterised by alternation between conservative, pragmatic, and reformist groups. It also generates significant shifts in both the internal and foreign policies of the country. Therefore, the electoral contest for the presidency of the Republic is the most distinctive and unique aspect of the Iranian political system (Zanjani 1999), although such contest is preceded by a preselection process of the candidates allowed to run.

The main republican institutions

The president of the Republic

The president of the Republic holds the second-highest office of state and is the head of the government. The presidency is the executive body responsible for the implementation of the Constitution and the maintenance of order in relations between the three branches of the state. Following the reform of the Constitution in 1989 and the removal of the prime minister's office, the president of the Republic now holds the highest executive office, assuming and centralising all of the government's duties formerly shared with the prime minister. The president of the Republic appoints and supervises the cabinet and vice-presidents, who are responsible for overseeing the functioning of the ministries to which they have been appointed. Regarding foreign policy, the president has the authorisation to sign treaties, conventions, and international agreements, subject to approval by parliament. In domestic politics, the president determines public policies in consultation with ministers (Zanjani 1999).

The power of the president of the Republic, when compared with that held by *Vali-ye faqih* and the Council of Guardians, is quite limited. In fact, in Iranian politics, there have been several conflicts and disputes between the presidential body and the office of the Supreme Guide office, since numerous bills proposed by the government, after parliamentary approval, have failed to receive the confirmation vote of the Council of Guardians. In reality, the executive power enjoys quite considerable freedom of action in the field of economic policies, while in domestic politics and foreign affairs, it has its hands tied by the Islamic bodies mentioned above.

The requirements for a passive electorate

According to the Constitution, not all Iranian citizens are eligible to run in the presidential elections. A candidate must in fact possess a certain number of qualifications. First, the candidate must be a man: no woman can become the president of the Republic of Iran. He must be a religious personality, but not necessarily a faqih; it is important that he has a good knowledge of the religious sciences. Possession of political stature is considered the third necessary requirement.

In addition, the candidate must be of Iranian origin and citizenship; must have demonstrated management skills and know how to apply wisdom in the performance of the functions held; must have an irreproachable past and be a pure and honest person; and must believe and adhere to the principles of the Islamic Republic. These are the requirements that an Iranian citizen must meet in order to participate as a candidate in the presidential elections (Zanjani 1999).

The body that has the task of verifying possession of the requisites by candidates and therefore allowing their participation in the elections is, as already discussed, the Council of Guardians. The Council has the task of preselecting all the candidates registered in the presidential elections, on the basis of the criteria outlined above. Therefore, citizens may vote only for those candidates who have managed to pass the preselection process of the Council of Guardians. The president must be elected by an absolute majority of voters. If none of the candidates is likely to win the election outright with an absolute majority, the two candidates who have obtained the greatest number of votes in the first round compete against one another in a second ballot. The elected president must then receive the approval of the Supreme Guide before assuming office. The reason for this latter condition is to be found in the fundamental role of the *Vali-ye faqih*, considered the Imam's representative on earth. On the basis of this, even if the people have given their consent to a candidate, the *Vali-ye faqih* (given his wisdom) may very well not give his consent if he does not deem the winning candidate worthy of assuming the presidency. This has never happened so far in the history of the Islamic Republic of Iran and all candidates elected by a majority of the citizens have received the approval of the *Vali-ye faqih*. However, this element of the Constitution clearly expresses the religious constraint on Iranian electoral competition.

The Islamic government of Ayatollah Khomeini: the basis of systemic religious constraint

Ayatollah Khomeini's original theory, elaborated during a cycle of lectures in Najaf, supported the formation of the *Hokumat-e Eslami* – 'Islamic government' – led by an 'expert in Islamic law'. This Islamic government was to have God as the only legislative source and the expert in the law as the only executor of divine law. The figure of the *Vali-ye faqih*, representative of the Prophet and the 12 Imams on earth, was to be central: he was to enjoy the authority of God on earth and was to be, like the Prophet and the Imams, the point of reference for the people in all issues that concerned their well-being and happiness (Khomeini 1994). His actions and his statements were to constitute orders for Muslims, having to be made effective and unable to be opposed by any legal authority. Khomeini planned the construction of a government where:

> only the expert in the law, and no one else, should hold the responsibility for power. He is the only one who can undertake what the Prophet undertook, without adding anything to it and without deviating from it. He is the only one who can implement the (Islamic) prescriptions as the Prophet implemented them; that he can rule as God has ordained; that he can collect excess wealth from people; who can organize the treasure and receive it in deposit.
>
> *(Khomeini 1994: 55)*

The form of his government, as Khomeini himself explicitly stated, was 'different from constitutional governments, whether monarchical or republican', because in a republican system the representatives of the population govern and in a monarchical system the representatives of the king govern, while the legislative power, in Khomeini's Islamic government, is reserved exclusively for God. In terms of legislative power, Khomeini did not consider the establishment of a national parliament on the model of a 'democratic republic' or a 'parliamentary monarchy', which legislates on the basis of popular legitimacy, to be in conformity with Islamic law. The only and true legislator is God, and therefore the only acceptable law for Islamic government is *shari'a* (Khomeini 1994: 95). Khomeini was convinced that Islamic law contained in itself all the provisions necessary for the realisation of a complete social system:

> In this system, all human needs are met, starting with the relationships between neighbors, parents and children, between members of the same family, between fellow citizens, continuing with all aspects of married life, and concluding with legislation concerning war and peace, international relations, criminal laws, commercial, industrial and agricultural rights. [...] Islam promulgates the law, keeps it alive, makes it effective and intrinsically works for it.
>
> (Khomeini 1994: 29)

These Islamic laws, however, are not enough to reform a society: executive authority is needed. This authority, formerly exercised by the Prophet and the 12 Imams, now belonged to their legitimate successors, 'the experts of the law'. The *Vali-ye faqih*, consequently, is the one who holds executive power in Islamic government: he, enjoying divine legitimacy, on the model of the Prophet and Imam Ali, outlines the political direction of the government, appoints its representatives in the different regions, and administers the Islamic community i. In other words, he exercises the functions of both a head of state and a head of government.

At the judicial level, the *Vali-ye faqih* was to be the supreme judge (*ghazi*) and would designate all judges personally. However, the judges, as in the tradition of the Prophet, were to be independent in the meticulous interpretation and application of Islamic law.

In light of all this, it can be deduced that the form of state Khomeini theorised is an Islamic government based essentially on the principle of *Velayat-e faqih*; this means a government where all power is concentrated in the hands of one person, who by divine sovereignty, holds executive and judicial power, while also having the task of guarding and making effective the legislative power. Khomeini actually theorised an Islamic government (*Hokumat-e Eslami*) that was to follow the model of government of the Prophet Mohammad and the first Shi'ite Imam, Ali, and not an 'Islamic Republic' (*Jomhuri-ye Eslami*).

The choice of the term 'republic' instead of 'government' was a legal constraint to which Khomeini, given the political context in which he found himself, was forced to submit, modifying some parts of his political model. The institutional backbone of the *Velayat-e faqih*-based model was in fact transposed into the Constitution of the Islamic Republic, but it would be wrong to consider the latter the complete realisation of Ayatollah Khomeini's theory of Islamic government for the following reasons. The insertion of the term 'republic' (*Jomhuri*) in place of 'government' (*Hokumat*) gave the state popular legitimacy in addition to divine legitimacy. The absolute sovereignty theorised by Ayatollah Khomeini for his 'expert of the law' was shared in part with popular sovereignty, which could express itself – albeit always within the limits of Shari'a – through the vote and a degree of political competition. Islamic republicanism gave rise to institutional dualism. On the one hand, constitutional institutions such as the parliament and the president of the Republic with his ministers were created. On the other hand, to ensure the Islamic nature of the Republic and the divine sovereignty of the *Vali-ye faqih*, bodies such as the Council of Guardians, the Council of Experts, and Assembly for the Definition of Opportunities were established. Consequently, a political model that sought to allow secular principles to coexist with religious principles was set up, thus also accepting some aspects of Western thought, such as the division of power and the rule of law.

The Islamic Republic: a hybrid and polycentric regime

Hybrid regimes are political systems that combine elements typical of authoritarian regimes and characteristics of democratic systems in different or atypical ways. The spread of hybrid systems has been more common since the end of the Cold War, when several political systems, as a consequence of the fall of their authoritarian regimes, had to face transitional phases. These transitional phases were of different durations, leading to the institution of democratic systems in some cases, the emergence of new authoritarian systems in others, and stalemate and a situation of endemic political instability in others still (Carothers 2002; Diamond 1996).

It could be said that hybrid regimes have taken on different characteristics depending on the historical period. Their common element is the presence of spaces for political competition within a framework which is mostly non-democratic. The nature and scope of these competitive spaces, however, varies among different hybrid regimes. For example, the extent of the limitation of political freedoms granted to the opposition and the powers of the parliament, the executive, and the press and social organisations can vary. Some systems are multi-party (though not all parties compete at the same level); in other systems, elections appear to function merely as a way for the leader or the ruling party to claim plebiscitary legitimacy. Sometimes the limits on public contestation are formally defined through specific constitutional provisions; in other cases, they are the result of the *de facto* power of the rulers (Brumberg 2002; Dahl 1971; Levitsky and Way 2002; Morlino 2009; Ottaway 2003; Schedler 2002). The inclusiveness dimension refers to the extent of political participation allowed in different systems (for instance, the level of inclusiveness is greater when elections are held through universal suffrage and lower where the right to vote is based on census). The variable of public contestation concerns instead the degree of freedom, with regard to the possibility both to challenge the current government and its policies and to eventually replaced said government.

In short, the Iranian system can be considered a hybrid system for two reasons (Abdolmohammadi and Cama 2015; Chehabi 1991; Keshavarzian 2005). The first is linked to the fact that the Islamic Republic is the result of a compromise between the religious and secular forces in the aftermath of the 1979 Islamic Revolution. Since the death of Ayatollah Ruhollah Khomeini in 1989, this compromise has been primarily expressed in the dual nature of the executive, consisting of the Supreme Guide, who represents the religious elite in power, and the president of the Republic. The second reason has to do with the fact that the Islamic Republic, notwithstanding the prevailing authoritarian context, allows some space for genuine political competition. Competition concerns not only parliamentary elections but also the main government office, the presidency of the Republic. This creates competition, among not only mid-level political elites (local notables, provincial or tribal representatives, and supporters of special interests) but also national leaders who control some of the main political factions and institutions.[3]

Presidential elections in the Islamic Republic revolve around major issues of national policy – that is, around macro policies (social justice, the different models of economic development, foreign policy). In this way, the presidential elections become a moment of real confrontation over and resolution of the main political visions that compete within the system.[4]

The genuineness of the competition is shown by at least two factors. The first of these is the endorsement of the various candidates by a diverse set of social and political forces. This demonstrates their anchoring to specific and real interests, ensuring that the candidates are not just the expression of abstract ideological positions, disconnected from social reality. There is, therefore, a link between intra-elite struggles and social conflicts. In this way, a connection between the institutional and the social arena is created, engaging a significant part of society in political competition. Second, the authenticity of the competition is demonstrated by significant developments that have characterised political communication, such as public debates, which have acquired the dynamism and dialectical characteristics typical of consolidated representative democracies – for example, the confrontation between Mir Hossein Mousavi and Mahmoud Ahmadinejad during the election campaign in 2009 and the televised debate of the eight presidential candidates in 2013.

The selection of a shortlist of candidates allows the Islamic Republic to adopt the political offer to different situations and contexts. It enables the inclusion of some innovators who are capable of partially intercepting discontent or a need for change coming from society, while in more stable times the list can be narrowed to include only a more conservative set of candidates. This flexibility of options, guaranteed by presidential elections, is related mainly to ordinary policies, both at the domestic and, particularly in our case studies, at the international level.[5] Therefore, the Islamic Republic represents such a hybrid political laboratory, combining in an original manner elements of pluralism and elements of authoritarianism. Furthermore, this political system, in addition to being hybrid, has a polycentric nature that brings it closer to the cases classified by Samuel Huntington as praetorian regimes (Huntington 1968).[6] In fact, the various institutional actors of the Islamic Republic control their own economic and military resources, which they use to pursue their political strategies. For example, the civilian foreign and defence ministries and the political forces that occupy the government have their own economic and military resources. Similarly, the Revolutionary Guards and their allies control economic and military resources and intelligence apparatuses. Therefore, these factions can develop their own projects, pursue their own interests, and act separately from and sometimes against each other.

In this hybrid and polycentric institutional framework, various and contrasting political factions compete with a level of transparency and uncertainty that is unusual for a non-democratic regime.[7]

Another way in which the Islamic Republic could be defined as a hybrid regime is in terms of symbolic elements. There is a long and illustrious tradition of socio-political and historical research that frames political regimes in terms of their ideological dimensions and the principles of legitimacy upon which they are founded. The varieties of power and political order have been distinguished in connection with the prevalent sources of legitimacy, starting with Weber's (1947) classical research.

The Islamic Republic might be regarded as a hybrid regime within the Weberian framework: it was established on Weber's three legitimation grounds. It may be claimed that one of the roots of the Revolution's legitimation was tied to the clergy, and so constituted a conventional type of legitimation. The involvement of the Islamic Shi'ite clergy in the development of the Islamic Republic should be studied from this viewpoint, notably during and after the 1979 Revolution. In pre-Islamic times, for example, during the Sassanid era, the clergy was one of the three pillars of Persian power, alongside the court and the army, while in the Islamic era, by the time of the foundation of the Safavid Empire in 1501, the clergy had begun to gradually acquire a position of sociocultural and political power.

Instead, the growth of a charismatic power associated with the revolutionary type is highlighted by the figure of Ayatollah Khomeini and his crucial influence in the pre- and post-revolutionary years. Until Khomeini's death in 1989, this form of authority was to provide crucial support to the Islamic Republic. Several incidents demonstrate the attraction and utter loyalty associated with his person, such as the great level of devotion shown to him by many young Iranians during the Iran–Iraq War by fighting against the Iraqi army, or the millions of his admirers who attended his funeral. Khomeini's charisma was institutionalised and largely passed to the Islamic Republic's religious and political authority after his death (particularly the Supreme Guide and the Council of Guardians). Finally, the Islamic Republic's republican component, which is tied to popular will and primarily manifested in constitutional authorities such as the president of the Republic and the parliament, can be linked to a legal/rational power. The legitimacy of these bodies, according to this viewpoint, stems from adherence to established procedures such as elections. Iran is not the only political system in which many sources of legitimacy coexist. However, the challenging balance and high levels of friction among various pillars of legitimacy may be considered unique to Iran. During the 2009 'Green Wave', for example, the invocation of respect for the rules of the game (in the form of a state-issued call for electoral procedures to be followed) and the relatively rational legal legitimacy seemed to take precedence over respect for religious tradition, shaking the regime's foundations.

A future question is whether another type of tradition, such as nationalism (linked to the recovery of ancient Persian identity), can replace religious tradition or whether another type of legal legitimation, not of a democratic nature but linked to the typical practices of an authoritarian system, such as military or plebiscitary, can lead to the adoption of a new secular vision. Finally, these events could be accompanied by the rise of a new charismatic figure, potentially of a populist bent, as has been witnessed in recent times in other parts of the world.

Conclusion

The Islamic Republic had to create several types of power-sharing arrangements to sustain its political dominance, making presidential, parliamentary, and municipal elections a deeply rooted norm in the country, and so implementing a unique hybrid model. This links the Islamic Republic to democratic regimes, albeit with the added filter of pre-election candidate selection by clerical authorities. Political competition and pluralism are built on persons who belong to various ideological factions inside the authoritarian system, rather than on organised and well-structured parties.

It is plausible to argue that allowing for competition has brought stability to the regime. One of the most important factors in the regime's ability to maintain stability is its ability to achieve a balance between competing social, economic, and cultural policies. The willingness to make concessions in these areas, on the other hand, is always matched by an unwavering commitment to protecting the power structures established during the Islamic Revolution. The system's inclusive capacity in regard to new social interests, issues, and groupings is demonstrated by the periods of stability. The cycles of protest, on the other hand, reveal the political arrangement's flaws and vulnerabilities. Yet the lack of actual political parties, and therefore the opposition's organisation and leadership, may make the wave of protests fleeting. Even the limited area for political competition available to reformist forces, however, has succeeded in generating aspirations and expectations.

It can be finally stated that as long as the Islamic Republic is capable of maintaining its hybridity, its political life might be long and stable. On the contrary, if its political system becomes more authoritarian and rigid, losing its flexibilities, its endurance could be undermined and the system could move closer to a sort of implosion and collapse.

Notes

1 On the political biography and thinking of Ayatollah Khomeini, see Baqer Moin (2000), *Khomeini: Life of the Ayatollah*, New York: St Martin's Press; Amir Taheri (1989), *Lo spirito di Allah: Khomeini e la rivoluzione islamica*, Firenze: Ponte Delle Grazie; Hamid Ansari (1373/1994), *The Narrative of Awakening: A Look*

at *Imam Khomeini's Ideal and Political Biography (From Birth to Ascension)*, Tehran: Centro culturale specializzato nelle opere dell'Imam Khomeini; Pejman Abdolmohammadi (2009), *La Repubblica Islamica dell'Iran: il pensiero politico dell'ayatollah Khomeini*, Genoa: De Ferrari Editore; Arshin Adib-Moghaddam (ed.) (2014), *A Critical Introduction to Khomeini*, Cambridge: Cambridge University Press.

2 Normally, those candidates that are considered secular, liberal, or leftists, or Islamist candidates who are critical of the Supreme Guide and the establishment, will not get the approval of the Council of Guardians. Notable examples include former presidents Ali Akbar Hashemi Rafsanjani and Mahmoud Ahmadinejad, both disqualified by the Council of Guardians in the run-up to previous elections. In most cases, the main reason behind disqualification is a candidate's lack of proven loyalty to the Constitution and to Shari'a law.

3 There are three main political factions in the Islamic Republic of Iran: the conservatives, the pragmatists, and the reformists. The conservatives' foreign policy in the region is based on strengthening Iran's leading role in the so-called 'Shi'a Triangle' (Iraq, South Lebanon, Yemen, Syria, and Bahrain), XE " Shi"a triangle:conservative support for " \r "jalambcomWE4t434"while further afield they lean towards a privileged relationship with global powers such as China and Russia. The pragmatists are marked by a technocratic approach that affects all of their policies. Their foreign policy is characterised by a greater propensity to open diplomatic channels to the main Western powers such as the US and the EU. The reformists pursue a foreign policy of openness towards the West that is more cautious than that of the pragmatists. They are also fully anti-Israel and pro-Palestine, like the conservatives. On Iranian political factions, see Darabi (1388/2009); Shadlou (1379/2000).

4 XE " conservatives:term " \r "jalambcomWE1t11"It should be highlighted that these political forces are not organised parties such as those that characterise classic liberal-democratic regimes. Rather, they are political factions that gather around leaders, coalitions of interest, and actors, and are united by common strategic visions. See Abdolmohammadi and Cama (2020: 99).

5 However, it should be noted that this level of flexibility has not been as apparent in relation to changes in the polity or the political structure.

6 A difference from the pure praetorian regime is that there is a power of last resort, represented by the Supreme Guide and the Council of Guardians, who have the last word.

7 There are also hybrid regimes which are not polycentric, such as Russia.

References

Abdolmohammadi, Pejman. 2009. *La Repubblica Islamica dell'Iran: Il pensiero politico dell'ayatollah Khomeini*. Genova: De Ferrari Editore.

Abdolmohammadi, Pejman, and Giampiero Cama. 2015. 'Iran as a Peculiar Hybrid Regime: Structure and Dynamics of the Islamic Republic'. *British Journal of Middle Eastern Studies* 42(4): 558–578.

Abrahamian, Ervand. 1982. *Iran between Two Revolutions*. Princeton, NJ: Princeton University Press.

Adib-Moghaddam, Arshin. 2014. *A Critical Introduction to Khomeini*. Cambridge: Cambridge University Press.

Agiodani, M. 2004. *Mashroute-ye Irani* (Iranian Constitutionalism). Tehran: Akhtaran Edition.

Ansari, H. 1373/1994. *The Narrative of Awakening: A Look at Imam Khomeini's Ideal and Political Biography (From Birth to Ascension)*. Tehran: Cultural Centre on Imam Khomeini's Works.

Browne, Edward. 1966. *The Persian Revolution 1905–1909*. Cambridge: Cambridge University Press.

Brumberg, Daniel. 2002. 'The Trap of Liberalized Autocracy'. *Journal of Democracy* 13(4): 56–68.

Carothers, Thomas. 2002. 'The End of the Transition Paradigm'. *Journal of Democracy* 13(1): 5–21.

Chehabi, Houchang. 1991. 'Religion and Politics in Iran: How Theocratic is the Islamic Republic?' *Dædalus* 120(3): 69–91.

Dahl, Robert A. 1971. *Polyarchy: Participation and Opposition*. New Haven, CT: Yale University Press.

Darabi, A. 1388/2009. *Jaryanshenasi-ye Siasi dar Iran* (The Analysis of Iranian Political Factions). Tehran: Pajouheshgah-e Farhang va Andishe-ye Eslami.

Davani, Qolamhossein. 1376/1997. *Qanun-e Asasi-ye Jomhuri-ye Eslami-ye Iran* (Constitution of the Islamic Republic of Iran). Tehran: Kiumars.

Diamond, Larry. 1996. 'Is the Third Wave Over?' *Journal of Democracy* 7(3): 20–37.

Djalili, Mohammad Reza. 1989. *Diplomatie Islamique: Strategie internationale du khomeynisme*. Paris: Presses Universitaires de France.

Edelstein, Dan. 2004. 'Restoring the Golden Age: Mythology in Revolutionary Ideologies and Culture'. PhD thesis, University of Pennsylvania.

Huntington, Samuel. 1968. *Political Order in Changing Societies*. New Haven, CT: Yale University Press.

Kasravi, Aḥmad. 2002. *Tarikh-e Mashroute-ye Iran* (The History of Iran's Constitutionalism). Tehran: Negah.

Keshavarzian, Arang. 2005. 'Contestation Without Democracy: Elite Fragmentation in Iran'. In Marsha Pripstein Posusney, and Michele Penner Angrist (eds.), *Authoritarianism in the Middle East: Regimes and Resistance*. Boulder, CO: Lynne Rienner.

Khomeini, Ruhollah. 1994. *Velayat-e Faqih* (The Government of the Islamic Jurist). Tehran: Imam Khomeini Editorial Centre.

Levitsky, Steven, and Lucan Way. 2002. 'Elections Without Democracy: The Rise of Competitive Authoritarianism'. *Journal of Democracy* 13(2): 51–65.

Madani, Jalal. 1376/1997. *Hoquq-e Asasi Dar Jomhuri-Ye Eslami-Ye Iran* (Constitutional Law of the Islamic Republic of Iran). Tehran: Sorush.

Moin, Baqer. 2000. *Khomeini: Life of the Ayatollah*. New York: St Martin's Press.

Morlino, Leonardo. 2009. 'Are There Hybrid Regimes? Or Are They Just an Optical Illusion?' *European Political Science Review* 1(2): 273–296.

Noruzi, Mohammad Javad. 1379/2000. *Nezam-e Siasi-ye Eslam* (The Political Institution in Islam). Tehran: Mo'assese-ye Amuzeshi va Pajuheshi Imam Khomeini.

Ottaway, Marina. 2003. *Democracy Challenged: The Rise of Semi-Authoritarianism*. Washington, DC: Carnegie Endowment for International Peace.

Schedler, Andreas. 2002. 'The Menu of Manipulation'. *Journal of Democracy* 13(2): 36–50.

Schirazi, Asghar. 1997. *The Constitution of Iran: Politics and the State in the Islamic Republic*, transl. John O'Kane. London and New York: I.B. Tauris.

Shadlou, A. 1379/2000. *Ettela'ati darbare-ye Ahzab va Jenah-haye Siasi-ye Iran-e Emrouz* (Information about Parties and Factions in Contemporary Iran). Tehran: Edizioni Gostareh.

Taheri, Amir. 1989. *Lo spirito di Allah: Khomeini e la rivoluzione islamica*. Firenze: Ponte alle Grazie.

Weber, Max. 1947. 'The Nature of Charismatic Authority and Its Routinization'. In M. Weber (ed.), *Theory of Social and Economic Organization*, transl. A. R. Anderson, and T. Parsons. New York: Free Press. Originally published 1922 in German as *Wirtschaft und Gesellschaft*.

Zanjani, A.A. 1378/1999. *Nezam-e Siasi va Rahbari dar Eslam* (The Islamic State and the Supreme Leader). Tehran: Islamic Cultural Centre.

PART 3

Rules, institutions, and the infrastructure of elections

14
THE MANAGEMENT OF ELECTIONS IN TUNISIA

The Independent High Authority for Elections

Mohamed Chafik Sarsar and Nidhal Mekki

Introduction

In the aftermath of the fall of the Ben Ali regime, the main concern of the actors of the Tunisian transition was to prevent the return of an undemocratic and authoritarian regime. The creation of the Independent High Authority for Elections (better known under its French acronym ISIE), with a view to organizing the election of a constituent national assembly, was one of the points of rupture with the past in post-revolutionary Tunisia. The ISIE belongs, in fact, to those instances, which, as Rosanvallon (2008) said, 'revolutionize the classic repertoire of the formulation of the democratic question'. It is only with the 2014 Constitution though and at the cost of a tremendous amount of work on the part of this body that it has become a constitutional entity.

The organization of democratic elections has become a key element of democratic transitions (Wall 2010), and it is therefore not surprising that one of the first decisions of those in charge of leading the Tunisian transition was to opt for an Electoral Management Body (EMB) independent of the executive branch to organize the first free and fair elections in the country's history (Sridi 2013). Two simultaneous pieces of legislation – Law No. 2011-27 of April 18, 2011, on the establishment of an Independent High Authority for Elections and Decree Law No. 2011-35 of May 10, 2011, on the election of a National Constituent Assembly – converged toward a common goal: to 'break with the old regime based on arbitrariness and disregard for the will of the people by the seizure of power and the falsification of elections' (Decree 2011-35).

Despite a difficult start, the ISIE has gained the confidence of all stakeholders, although some political parties expressed reservations about the composition of the first ISIE Council, elected in 2011 by the High Instance for the Achievement of Objectives of the Revolution. Ultimately, the ISIE was constitutionalized with the 2014 Constitution (Chapter VI) as one of the five Independent Constitutional Authorities, thereby marking the emergence of a new type of public law person (Sarsar 2018).

Paragraph 1 of Article 126 of the Constitution clearly states that 'the Elections Authority, called the Independent High Authority for Elections, is responsible for the management of elections and referenda, their organization and supervision in their various phases. The Authority guarantees the regularity, integrity and transparency of the electoral process and proclaims the results'. As for its composition, paragraph 3 of the same article adds that 'the body is composed of nine independent, neutral, competent and honest members who carry out their mission for a single term of six years, with the renewal of one-third of its members every two years'. The selection of the nine members was not an easy task. The process began in 2013, but the volatility of the transition interrupted this process

With the resumption of the National Dialogue,[1] one of the key points of the agreement between the political forces was the election of the members of the Council of the ISIE, which was completed on January 8, 2014. The president of the ISIE was elected the next day with 153votes, although the law requires only 109. The ISIE succeeded in organizing the 2014 legislative and presidential elections within the time limit set by the Constitution and in compliance with international norms and standards (The Carter Center 2014).

In ten years, the ISIE has moved from consecration to recognition, to being a target. Thus, initially, it was elevated – consecrated – to constitutional status in the 2014 Constitution to protect it from the vagaries of political life. Then, the recognition of its success in the organization of elections by international and national observers installed it in the institutional and political landscape of the country. However, more recently, the ISIE has faced criticism, with several attempts to interfere in its work, which constitutes a serious challenge to this body. Moreover, the two presidents of the Republic, Béji Caied Essebsi (Jaidi 2017) and Kais Saïed underlined their reservations concerning the organization and the independence of the Independent Bodies.[2] The conception of the ISIE fits into a horizontal rearrangement of powers that affects the executive branch, and it combines certain democratic imperatives with modern administrative management, based on the notions of efficiency, neutrality and transparency in the management of public affairs, but it has experienced, from 2017, a profound crisis of legitimacy (Sarsar and Ben Moualla 2017). Indeed, following the renewal of one-third of the members in February 2017, a conflict within the Council of the ISIE led the president, the vice-president and a third member representing judicial judges to submit their resignations, arguing that they can no longer guarantee the proper functioning of the Authority. These resignations have highlighted the anomalies in the legal framework of the ISIE.

It is important to understand how such a body has come to see its functioning disrupted and its effectiveness limited despite the solid constitutional guarantees it enjoys and the successes it has undoubtedly achieved in fulfilling its primary function. As jurists, we will adopt in the first place an exegetical method to interpret and understand the scope of the texts that established and organized the ISIE. But, as the texts do not evolve in a purely normative universe and they are strongly influenced by the political environment, particular attention is paid to the political considerations and their impact on the functioning of the ISIE. In this respect, our two professional experiences will be of great help since we have been, respectively, president of the ISIE[3] and advisor to the ANC.[4] Thus, we had the opportunity to be at the very head of this constitutional body for one, and privileged witness of the internal workings of the legislative body for the other. It is unfortunate that this subject, despite its extreme importance for the transition and the Tunisian democratic experience, has been poorly studied, and this chapter fills this knowledge gap.

The consecration of the legal guarantees of the ISIE's independence

No one can dispute that the constituent (and later the legislator), as well as the main political forces, were moved, at least in the early stages of the transition and during the first months of application of the new Constitution, by the will to ensure that the ISIE had real independence. This independence allowed the ISIE to break with a long history of elections that were neither free nor fair (ISIE Report 2015) and with state institutions at the service of one party and often one person, namely the Head of State. To this end, the ISIE, like all other constitutional bodies, has benefited from several strong legal guarantees aimed at ensuring its independence. This legal arsenal is consistent with international standards (Sarsar and Ben Moualla 2017). These guarantees relate to the constitutional status, as well as to the appointment of its members and the mode of control.

ISIE's constitutional status

Entrusting the management of elections to an independent body is far from being a general rule today (Sarsar and Ben Moualla 2017). In peaceful and stable democracies, the Ministry of the Interior organizes elections and referenda without affecting their freedom and fairness (IDEA 2002). In contrast, in transitional countries and in emerging democracies, the creation of independent election management bodies (hereafter EMBs) is justified in light of their traditions of bias and election fraud. During its transition from authoritarianism, Tunisia entrusted the management of the first post-Ben Ali elections to an independent body which was further institutionalized as an independent constitutional body with the 2014 Constitution (The Carter Center 2014). This is a first but fundamental guarantee of the independence of this institution, since it places it above the fluctuating parliamentary majorities that could revise its status or even eliminate it through a simple majority if the ISIE had only legislative status. We should not lose sight of the fact that in the early years of the transition, the existence of the ISIE was not guaranteed and, therefore, the temptation among some political actors to get rid of it to entrust the electoral process back to the Ministry of the Interior had to be taken seriously (Sarsar and Ben Moualla 2017). Unfortunately, the fear of seeing independent constitutional bodies abolished is growing stronger, given the ambiguity that has prevailed since the dissolution of the parliament and by President Saïed on July 25, 2021 (Mekki 2021)[5].

A sign of the seriousness of these concerns is that President Kais Saïed did not consult with the ISIE at all before setting the dates for the referendum on constitutional revisions (July 25, 2022) and the parliamentary elections (December 17, 2022). However, the ISIE is the most appropriate body to determine the timing and logistics of any popular consultation.[6]

The very structure of the chapter on constitutional bodies shows the prominent place that the ISIE occupied in the eyes of the drafters of the constitution. After the first article of this chapter (Article 125 of the 2014 Constitution), which deals with the general provisions relating to all the independent constitutional bodies, the constituent deals first with the Elections Body (Article 126 of the Constitution). This is not only due to its historical precedence over other bodies since 2011,[7] but also to the leading role it has played since it organized the first free and fair elections, as attested by national and international observers (The Carter Center 2019). The role and the performance of the ISIE since 2011 have, undoubtedly, contributed to the success of the transitional process, however precarious it might appear since July 25, 2021, and the creation of new electoral traditions in the country.

Article 125 of the Constitution sets out the general philosophy of independent constitutional bodies. It states that they 'work to strengthen democracy'. This is reminiscent of the title of Chapter IX of the South African Constitution– state institutions supporting constitutional democracy[8] – although it should be noted that the South African electoral commission only comes fourth in this chapter. Article 125 of the Tunisian Constitution also enjoins all state institutions to facilitate the work of independent constitutional institutions, which provides them with a special status and aura. Out of this, all other state institutions (and the first to be targeted is certainly the central administration, including, and above all, the Ministry of the Interior) not only have a passive obligation not to interfere with or hinder the work of the independent constitutional bodies, but also a positive obligation to do everything possible to facilitate their work (Sarsar and Ben Moualla 2017). This is a further guarantee, in addition to the one of constitutional status, and is intended to ensure that this body (as well as the other four) has a privileged position. The constituents' awareness of the importance of these bodies led to engraving in the constitutional marble the fact that they are endowed with legal personality and financial and administrative autonomy so as to confirm and guarantee the special status they enjoy within the state (Sarsar 2018).

The method of appointment

The will of the Tunisian constituents to ensure the highest degree of independence for the ISIE went so far as to include the principle of election of its members by the Assembly of People's Representatives (ARP) in the Constitution (Article 125-2). The article specifies that a qualified majority elect the nine members of the Elections Commission. This provision calls for two remarks. The first is that the election guarantees, in itself, a certain degree of independence in view of the pluralistic character of parliamentary assemblies and the public debate that accompanies their work and decisions and which would be reflected in the elections of the members of the constitutional bodies. This is always better than entrusting the designation of the members of constitutional bodies such as the ISIE to the executive, which will act according to a procedure that is less open to the public (or totally opaque), especially in the absence of any debate. In short, the ARP enjoys broad democratic elective legitimacy, which is reflected, albeit indirectly, in the election of the members of the bodies (Sridi 2013).

The second point has to do with the qualified majority required to elect members. The Tunisian Constitution does not specify this majority (it has left it to the Organic Law), but the requirement of a qualified majority constitutes an additional guarantee for an independent body. Indeed, this type of majority prevents a party or coalition with an absolute majority from having a free hand to elect the members of its choice, which would obviously have a negative effect both on the real independence of the EMB and on the public perception of this independence. Organic Law No. 2011-23 set the two-thirds majority for the election of members of the Council of the ISIE. Organic Law No. 47-2018 of August 7, 2018 – on common provisions for independent constitutional bodies – provides this majority for all constitutional bodies and added in its Article 6 that 'the principle of gender parity must be respected in the composition of the Council'. This issue of parity has occupied, since the beginning of the Tunisian transition and throughout the constituent process, an important place in the public and legal debate (Mekki 2021). Article 46-3 of the Constitution requires parity between women and men in elected assemblies. It constitutes a great step forward on the road to equality. Organic Law No. 47-2018 comes, therefore, to consecrate this constitutional requirement for the councils of the authorities (Article 6-2). However, despite this constitutional consecration and this legislative reaffirmation, the composition of the ISIE does not respect this principle, and women remain under-represented.[9]

The two-thirds majority is a qualified majority that aims, as mentioned, to prevent a single party or a single coalition from controlling the election process and 'packing' the ISIE with members loyal to it (Haj Slimane 2021). One should nevertheless not ignore that this majority can pose difficulties in some cases for electing members, especially in a tense and deeply divided political climate where it might be impossible to reach a consensus on the members (Haj Slimane 2021). Article 125-3 also delegates to the Organic Law the determination of the composition of the independent constitutional bodies, the representation within them, modes of election, organization and modalities of their control. However, as an indication of the particular importance of the ISIE in the eyes of the constituents, the latter is the only one, along with the Audiovisual Communication Authority, to have the number of its members fixed by the constitutional text itself (in this case nine members).

Obviously, one can always speculate on the reasons for the choice of this particular number, but it seems that the constituents wanted to set a number that would allow for the inclusion of members representing key sectors and of the utmost importance in electoral matters; a matter that calls for legal and judicial competencies in the narrow sense, as well as in matters of information technology, among others (Sarsar and Ben Moualla 2017). The most important aspect is that the number should neither be too large, which could delay the work and the decision-making process, nor too small, which would prevent certain sectors or expertise from being represented and thus deprive the ISIE of the expertise that they can bring to its work. In any case, the Constitution (Article 126-3) provides that these members must be independent, neutral, competent and honest. The qualities of independence and neutrality are obviously difficult to assess, but to clarify the constitutional provision, the legislator has come up with several guidelines. Thus, Article 7 of Organic Law No. 47-2018 establishes a number of incompatibilities under which the president and members of the Council of the Body may not combine their functions within the body with that of a member of the government, the Constitutional Court, the Supreme Council of the Judiciary or any other elective position. It is also forbidden to hold any other position in the public service or any other professional activity. Article 9 of the same law establishes the obligation for all members to avoid situations of conflict of interest.

The independence of the members is not only ensured through their obligations but also through the protections they enjoy, the most important of which is their immunity to opinions expressed or actions taken during their duties as members of the body. Another guarantee of the independence of the members of the ISIE (Article 126 *in fine*– last paragraph) is that they are elected for a single term of six years. The rather long duration of this term (longer than a legislative or presidential term but not extending to two terms and unlikely therefore to be a coincidence) has a pragmatic aspect to it since it allows members to acquire experience and to pass it on to those who will succeed them.[10] For its part, the fact that members are elected for a single term may also strengthen their independence since they will be less tempted to 'please' a certain party within the ARP, as might have been the case if a second term were possible (Haj Slimane 2021).

The mode of control

Constitutional bodies are independent within the state, but not independent from the state (Sarsar and Ben Moualla 2017). It is therefore normal that they should be subject to control, but this should not limit their independence. The creation of independent constitutional bodies is the embodiment of a new governance of institutions and by extension of a new philosophy of control (Haj Slimane 2021). As far as independent constitutional bodies are concerned, control means 'that bodies are accountable for all of their actions' and they need to provide, 'in a transparent and continuous or regular manner, all data to ensure that their actions obey the legal, ethical, and financial criteria set for them' (Sarsar and Ben Moualla2017: 51). This allows the public to be adequately informed about their policies and the results they pursue as well as the resources they use or intend to use, including public financial resources (Sarsar 2018).

This control has a positive impact on the governance of the bodies insofar as it ensures the transparency of their work and thus strengthens public confidence not only in these institutions, but also in political actors, including those in government. This philosophy is, of course, in total contradiction with the hierarchical or tutelary control the executive power exercises.

Independent constitutional bodies were created precisely to ensure that important and sensitive sectors, notably human rights and public liberties, would not be subject to the control of the executive power (Sarsar and Ben Moualla 2017), which has been and remains the main source of threat to the independence of these bodies and even to their existence, as the past authoritarian experience of Tunisia clearly demonstrates.[11] This explains why the constituents, in Article 125-2, clearly state that these bodies have legal personality and administrative and financial autonomy.

We will limit ourselves, at this level, to examining the only control provided for by the 2014 Constitution over constitutional bodies, namely the control exercised by the ARP. The 2018 law confirms the principle of accountability of constitutional bodies to the ARP in its Article 2-3 in the simplest and clearest terms: 'independent constitutional bodies are accountable to the Assembly of People's Representatives'. Article 125 of the Constitution states that the bodies, including ISIE, are required to submit an annual report to the ARP, which is discussed in a plenary session for this purpose. This logical and necessary obligation does not contradict independence. Due to its democratic elective legitimacy, it is the ARP that elects the members of independent constitutional bodies and reviews their draft budgets. It follows logically that the ARP be entrusted with the responsibility of discussing the activity reports of these bodies.

The control exercised by the ARP is political insofar as the Constitution limits itself to saying that the report is discussed and does not provide for any decision to be taken on it. This discussion in plenary, not sanctioned by a vote, is also taken up and confirmed by Article 32 of Organic Law No. 47-2018, which is titled 'rules relating to the control of independent constitutional bodies'.[12] Taken together, such provisions rule out the possibility of any jurisdictional control[13] of the ARP over the independent constitutional bodies.

The obligation to submit the report to the ARP is necessary because it contributes to the independence of the bodies. For example, if an EMB has noted during the past year attempts to interfere in its work by a public authority or a political party, it may mention this in its report. The public discussion in the ARP of the report might become then an opportunity for members of parliament to point the finger at attempts to interfere and call for an end to them, but also to criticize any other aspect of the management of elections. This gives the ISIE the opportunity to clarify specific points to safeguard public confidence, including political actors', but also to improve certain aspects of its work in view of the remarks and criticism addressed to it. Thus, the annual report is a powerful lever for EMBs to safeguard their independence and improve their governance.

Organic Law No. 23-2012 of December 20, 2012, relating specifically to the ISIE,[14] requires the latter, in addition to the annual report, to prepare a special report on the conduct of any electoral event (Article 3–17), but, just as for the annual report, the ARP is limited to examining and discussing the report without taking any decision on it. However, political control by the ARP over the ISIE, which was supposed to be a key element in the legal system ensuring and strengthening its independence, is the site of a double paradox. Indeed, the practice of submitting annual reports shows that, in the case of the ISIE, problems of tardiness emerge. The first is the delay in the submission of some annual reports to the ARP (for example, that of the year 2014). The second is the delay in the review of reports by the ARP itself. Thus, from 2014 until 2017, the ARP has examined only one ISIE annual report in a plenary session, that of the 2014 elections (Sarsar and Ben Moualla 2017). The suspension (and *de facto* dissolution) of the ARP on July 25, 2021, by the president of the Republic, Kais Saïed, aggravates this problem by further disrupting the control of the ARP on the ISIE and all independent constitutional bodies. This highlights how much the political context in general and transitional more particularly affects the independence of the authorities and of the ISIE more significantly because of the eminently political character of the sector it is responsible for managing and the rights it is supposed to enforce.

A transitional context that puts the ISIE independence into perspective

Although the legal framework of the ISIE seems to be well developed and in line with good practice (The Carter Center 2015), the ISIE, which is the only constitutional body set up seven years after the entry into force of the Constitution, has been in a deep crisis since 2017. To begin with, there are the blockages linked to the political landscape; then its legal framework remains deficient, especially in that its control is exercised in the absence of a control framework and, finally, the poor planning of electoral processes that marked the decade of transition has reduced its room for maneuver.

Blockages linked to the political landscape

Political fragmentation is the most significant trait of the post-revolutionary political landscape (Jendoubi and Giblin 2021) and has become a powerful stumbling block in the institutional progress of the country (Brumberg2019). The municipal elections of May 6, 2018, revealed a massive disavowal of political parties (Mekki 2018), the participation rate did not exceed 35%, and the independent lists obtained almost a third of the votes cast. The presidential election of 2019 confirmed the loss of trust of Tunisians in political parties. Kais Saïd, a populist independent anti-party candidate, was elected as president of the Republic with an overwhelming majority of 72.71% in the second round. This mistrust toward parties can be considered normal for two reasons. First, it is a feature of all democratic transitions, and second recent elections in a number of established democracies show that the loss of trust in parties – with the accompanying decreasing turnout – has become a global phenomenon. Some authors had already evoked the exhaustion or even the death of political parties in the major democracies since the beginning of the 1970s (Burnham 1969). Many in Tunisia believe that it is a pathological state. The reason is that the party landscape in Tunisia is characterized by splintering and fragmentation rarely observed elsewhere. This is reflected first in what can be defined as 'quantitative pluralism', namely the explosion in the number of parties. Thus, the country has moved from having a dozen parties in 2010 to nearly 228 parties in 2021, even though most of them are only parties in name. At least a hundred of them have neither an office, nor structures, nor even members. Moreover, several political parties do not express the diversity of public opinion. They are sometimes simply a springboard to fulfill the personal ambitions of their founders to play a political role and, sometimes, a means to increase their social status by 'posing' as national party leaders.

Finally, most political parties today in Tunisia are not socially anchored. They are neither mass parties, nor cartel parties, nor even parties of effective voters (Jendoubi and Giblin 2021). One of the consequences of this state of affairs is partisan recycling. Over the past ten years, the emergence of dozens of parties is only the result of splits. Transhumance – described as 'partisan tourism' – is often totally devoid of any ideological or political reasons and it has therefore further aggravated the situation. Moreover, most of the leaders of the few effective parties have been present on the political scene since the 1970s, and they continue to lead today's political formations by reproducing the same behavior, the same ways of managing the party and the same ideological struggles of the past.

Tunisian pluralism has produced ephemeral alliances. Between 2011 and 2021, at least ten alliances were formed, but these alliances were unable to structure political life or the party landscape. Some of these alliances lasted only a few weeks, and only one was able to maintain itself for four years – the leftist Popular Front – before shattering just before the 2019 elections. In addition, since 2012, Tunisia has witnessed an exacerbation of divisions between modernists (who rallied around the *NidaaTounes* party for a while) against conservatives (the Islamists of *Ennahda*). The two formations, led by former president Béji Caïd Essebssi (*NidaaTounes*) and

Rachid Gannouchi (*Ennahda*), ended up forming a coalition just after the 2014 elections to govern, which led many within both parties and in the wider public to decry such compromise (Marzouki 2016). In 2019, the same pattern was repeated: *Qalb Tunis*, after a long and virulent campaign against *Ennahda*, allied with the latter to form the government.

The crisis of political parties in Tunisia is structural, and deep and has serious consequences on the democratic transition in general and on the functioning of constitutional institutions in particular. In addition to the very complicated dealings that accompanied the establishment of the ISIE during the national dialogue in 2013, the method of appointing members of the ISIE Council has transformed this most important body from one aimed at ensuring independence to a means of blocking it. The 2016 renewal of one-third of the ISIE Council is an illustration of the impact of the fragmentation of the political scene on the ISIE. This renewal was supposed to take place between September and January 2016, but the ARP took almost a year to choose three new members (Sarsar and Ben Moualla 2017). This renewal did not follow the rules of independence, competence and integrity provided for in Article 126 of the Constitution, and led to the resignation of the president, the vice-president and a third representative of the ISIE. Their replacement also took a year. The election of the new president of the ISIE took four months, but following a motion for his dismissal by the majority of the Council, he preferred to resign from the presidency while retaining his membership. His term as president lasted only 14 months. His successor was elected on February 2, 2019, but his six-year term was due to end on January 8, 2020, and as of November 2021, it had not happened yet. This dysfunction due to the fragmentation of partisan representation within the ARP and the strong tensions running through it can only weaken the position of the ISIE and make it more fragile.

The incomplete legal framework: the absence of a control reference system

Although Organic Law No. 2012-23 multiplied the levels of control of the ISIE, whether in relation to its leaders, its acts or its finances, this control has been poorly exercised and lacks a proper and adequate frame of reference. Thus, the system of control of members provided for by the 2012 Organic Law never worked well over the past ten years.

Article 15 of this law provides that 'in addition to the case provided for in paragraph 5 of Article 13 of this law, the president of the Independent High Authority *for* Elections or one of the members of the council shall be removed from office in the event of gross negligence in the fulfillment of their obligations under this law or in the event of conviction by an irrevocable judgment for an intentional offense or a crime or in cases where they no longer meet any of the conditions required for membership of the council of the Independent High Authority *for* Elections'. The request for dismissal is presented by at least half of the members of the Council of the Body. It is to be submitted to the plenary session of the Legislative Assembly for approval by an absolute majority of its members. In addition, according to Article 3 of the 2012 Organic Law, the ISIE must draw up 'a special report on the conduct of each electoral or referendum operation within a maximum period of three months from the date of the announcement of the final results, which is submitted to the president of the Republic, the President of the Legislative Assembly and the Head of Government and published in the Official Gazette of the Republic of Tunisia and on the body's electronic site', and

> an annual report on the activity of the body during the past year and its action programme for the coming year, which is submitted to the Legislative Assembly in plenary session on the occasion of the vote on the annual budget of the body and published in the Official Gazette of the Tunisian Republic and on the body's electronic site.

The Organic Law of 2012 requires ISIE to create an internal control system on administrative, financial and accounting procedures that is quite sophisticated and complex (Articles 29 and 30 of the Organic Law).

Thus the ISIE 'shall ensure the establishment of an internal control system for administrative, financial and accounting procedures that guarantee the regularity, sincerity and transparency of financial statements and their compliance with the laws in force. To this end, it shall set up an audit and internal control unit chaired by a chartered accountant' (Article 29). In addition, the financial accounts of the Independent High Authority *for* Elections are subject to the control of two auditors registered with the Order of Chartered Accountants, who are appointed by the Council of the Body for a period of three years, renewable only once, in accordance with the legislation in force relating to public establishments and companies (Article 30 of Organic Law No. 2012-23).

The annual financial accounts of the body are approved by the board in the light of the report of the two auditors, which is submitted to the Legislative Assembly for approval and published in the Official Gazette of the Republic of Tunisia and on the body's electronic site within a period not exceeding June 30 of the year following the financial year. In case of non-approval of the financial report by the Legislative Assembly, the latter shall proceed to the creation of a commission of inquiry composed of three chartered accountants registered with the Order of Chartered Accountants that it shall choose. The financial accounts of the Independent High Authority *for* Elections are subject to *a posteriori* control by the Court of Auditors. The Court of Audit draws up a special report on the financial management of the Authority for each electoral or referendum operation. This report shall be published in the Official Gazette of the Tunisian Republic.

In addition to its obvious complexity, the control system is in contradiction, in some of its aspects, with the Constitution. For example, Article 24 of the 2018 Organic Law on common provisions for constitutional bodies not only requires the ISIE to submit a financial report separate from the general report on its activities (whereas the Constitution does not make this distinction), but also submits this financial report to the ARP for approval. This double requirement is contrary to the Constitution and constitutes a limit to the independence of the ISIE and 'an interference of the ARP in its activity through the mechanisms of trusteeship', which is contrary to the philosophy of the Constitution in this matter (Sarsar and Ben Moualla 2017: 42).

Although the ISIE complied with all these requirements, the financial report of the 2014 elections was only approved by the parliamentary committee in 2018, and was not submitted to the vote of the general assembly, so it was not published in the Official Gazette.

It should also be noted that the Organic Law on the budget, promulgated on February 13, 2019, repeals some of the provisions of the Organic Law of 2018, which further complicates the legal framework in this area. It is clear that this cumbersome and complicated control system (Sarsar and Ben Moualla 2017) has failed to develop the new principle of submission 'to the principles of the rule of law, good governance, transparency, efficiency, integrity, good management of public funds and accountability' (Article 6 of the 2018 Organic Law). This is all the truer in the absence of a reference frame for the control of the ISIE, set up either by the Court of Auditors or by the parliament.

Poor planning of electoral processes

The management of electoral cycles should normally respect a circular approach in three stages: the pre-electoral period, the electoral period and finally the post-electoral period. The first period should be used for legal and logistical preparations, the second is the electoral process, which ends with the final proclamation of the results, and finally the third should allow for lessons to be learned and for the reform of texts, institutions and practices.

Over the last decade, this logical approach has not been respected. Indeed, the irregular holding of elections and political blockages have led to a haphazard management of electoral cycles (Sarsar 2018). This is true for the three elections organized in Tunisia between 2011 and 2019.

The 2011 elections were constrained by the transitional timeline. In fact, the decision to hold elections for the National Constituent Assembly on July 24, 2011 (ultimately postponed to October23), was taken on March 23, 2011, even before the adoption of the decree laws establishing the ISIE and the electoral law. The first ISIE was not established until May18, 2011, which made it impossible to hold the elections on the date previously set, and finally the date was pushed back to October 23, 2011.

The post-election period was not properly exploited to learn from this improvisation and to put in place a legal framework to introduce clarity and predictability to the electoral process for the 2014 elections. It was civil society that acted to form a team of national experts who produced a draft electoral law. This draft was endorsed by several members of parliament and integrated into the law-making process to give birth to Organic LawNo.2014-16 of May 26, 2014.

When the ANC members decided that the 2014 elections should be held before the end of the year, the electoral law had not yet been adopted and it was not known whether the parliamentary and presidential elections would be held at the same time or separately. A law dated July 8, 2014, only set the date of the 2014 elections; that is, less than four months before the date of the legislative elections (October 26) and less than five months before the presidential elections (November 21). This improvisation 'has had an impact on the functioning of the ISIE and has necessitated the use of emergency solutions that do not necessarily conform to the principles of good governance' (Sarsar 2018: 24). However, the ISIE, and at the cost of a lot of work, was able to manage the elections within the constitutional timeframe and in compliance with international norms and standards under unfavorable conditions (The Carter Center 2015).

The 2019 elections showed the same improvisation and dysfunction. Indeed, some important legal texts for the organization of the elections were adopted only a few weeks before the elections actually took place. The reason is that during the 2015–2019 legislature, the reform of the electoral system was not among the priorities of the political class. Such improvisation and trial and error limit the capacity of the ISIE to anticipate and prepare quality regulations and to plan the electoral process rationally and efficiently (The Carter Center 2019).

Conclusion

What conclusions and lessons can be drawn from the ten years of existence and experience of the ISIE? The first point to emerge from the analysis of the ISIE is that setting up an entirely new institutional and constitutional structure in a country going through a democratic transition can work. The case of the ISIE shows that rapid institutional improvements, despite the existence of several obstacles, are possible. On the contrary, this new structure can contribute to the success of the transition to democracy and consolidate it. The edifying experience of the Tunisian ISIE in many respects teaches us, however, that for this to be possible, two main conditions must be met: a) a legal framework guaranteeing the independence of the ISIE (as of any other constitutional body) and b) a favorable political context, i.e., well-organized and institutionalized political actors who, above all, sincerely want to make a success of the democratic transition.

The legal framework of the Tunisian ISIE, while not perfect, provides solid guarantees for its independence, but more than its deficiencies, it is the laws (especially the Organic Law No.

2018-47 regarding the report submitted to the ARP and the nature of the control exercised by the latter on the basis of this report),which are contrary to some constitutional requirements, that undermine the independence of this body. Moreover, the Tunisian political context has only deteriorated since 2011, as fragmentation and above all corruption increased further.

To strengthen the independence and effectiveness of the ISIE, it will be necessary to harmonize its legal framework by ensuring the conformity of the law relating to the ISIE and the Organic Law on common provisions for the various constitutional bodies with the Constitution and by developing a harmonious and adequate parliamentary and financial control framework. The process of election of members of the ISIE by the parliament must be streamlined and subject to objective criteria to limit the discretionary choices of members of the ARP and avoid the 'rounds of vote without exits' by a method of preferential voting which can necessarily lead *in fine* to the electing of the members of the bodies. In addition, the planning of electoral processes must be improved to limit improvisation, which can only hinder good electoral management.

At the time of writing, it is not only the implementation of this legislative project that is problematic but the very existence of the ISIE or even of all the independent constitutional institutions. The decree of April 22, 2022, that amends Organic Law No. 2012-23 and allows the president to control the ISIE, is in clear contradiction with the principle of independence of this institution. Even before the new ISIE that will be set up sees the light of day and organizes elections, it is already discredited and its independence and impartiality are open to question. In other words, everything that has been done over a decade – the know-how, the expertise, the credibility – is not far from disappearing.

Notes

1. The national dialogue is a political initiative led by the UGTT and three other Tunisian national organizations (UTICA, LTDH and ONAT) to unblock the political situation and relaunch the constituent process after the serious political crisis in which Tunisia was plunged following in particular the assassination of MP Mohammed Brahmi on July 25, 2013. The success of this initiative of the organizing quartet earned him the 2015 Nobel Peace Prize.
2. In the project 'The new Foundation' of President Kais Saïed there is no mention of constitutional bodies.
3. Mohammed Chafik Sarsar.
4. Nidhal Mekki.
5. Recent developments show that President Saied has realized the strong opposition, both internally and from Tunisia's international partners, to the possibility of abolishing the ISIE altogether. He therefore chose to maintain it but subject it to his control. Thus, he promulgated a decree on April 22, 2022 that modifies Organic Law No. 2012-23 on the ISIE: the number of members will now be reduced to seven (instead of nine), and it is the president who will appoint the members either directly from among the former members of the ISIE (three members) or on the basis of proposals from the councils of judicial, administrative and financial judges and the National Centre for Information Technology (four members). This decree has caused an uproar in the political class and within civil society and is bound to revive opposition to the President and aggravate the political crisis in the country. Available at:www.reuters.com/world/africa/tunisia-pres-appoints-electoral-commission-members-by-decree-latest-power-grab-2022-04-22/
6. Member of the Tunisian Electoral Commission: President Saïd did not consult us about the referendum or the elections – Teller Report
7. The Human Rights Body had a predecessor before 2011, but it had only a legislative rank and very limited competences.
8. See the South African at justice.gov.za.
9. Currently, there are eight members on the ISIE Council (which was supposed to be nine). All of them are men.

10 The principle of rotation for the replacement of members (one third every two years, article 126 in fine) fulfills the same function, since it avoids a complete change in the composition of the Council of the Authority and allows a degree of continuity in the practice and 'jurisprudence' of the body.
11 Calls for the abolition of independent constitutional bodies, which until recently have been muted, are likely to increase and, more importantly, become more explicit in light of President Saied plans for political and constitutional reforms. Even if this project has not materialized to date, it is feared that President Kais Saïed's weakness with regard to the 1959 constitution may lead him to propose the outright abolition of all or some constitutional bodies. On this weakness of President Saied towards the defunct 1959 constitution (Mekki 2021).
12 This is Chapter 6 of the aforementioned law and includes only this one article.
13 However, Article 24 of the 2018 law adds a control not provided for in the Constitution, namely the control of the financial report of the bodies, which is sanctioned by a vote. The establishment by a commission created in this case of administrative or financial mismanagement on the part of the Authority may lead to sanctions.
14 This Organic Law of 2012 relating to the ISIE continues to apply because Article 34 of Organic Law No. 47-2018 on common provisions for independent constitutional bodies provides that 'until the adoption or revision of organic laws specific to each independent constitutional body, the laws and regulations in force relating to the bodies in place continue to apply'.

References

Brumberg, Daniel. 2019. *Tunisia's fragmented and polarized political landscape*. Arab Center Washington DC, March 28. Available at: https://arabcenterdc.org/resource/tunisias-fragmented-and-polarized-political-landscape/.
Burnham, Walter Dean. 1969. 'The end of party politics'. *Trans-Action* 7: 12–23.
Haj Slimane Hanan. 2021. 'The independent authorities: From the will of the foundation to the ambiguity of the concretization'. *Mediterranean Journal of Legal Research*. Available at: الهيئات - حنان ابن الحاج سليمان الدستورية المستقلة من إرادة التأسيس إلى ضبابية التجسيم | MjlrMjlr (mj-lr.com). (In Arabic).
International Institute for Democracy and Electoral Assistance (International IDEA). 2002. *International electoral standards guidelines for reviewing the legal framework of elections*. Stockholm: International IDEA.
Independent High Body for Elections (ISIE). 2015. *Report on the 2014 legislative and presidential elections*. Tunis: ISIE.
Jaidi, Mohammed Afif. 2017. 'Independent authorities: From proliferation to accusation. Reading on a process weakened by the diseases of the past'. Available at: الهيئات المستقلة من الانتشار إلى الاتهام: قراءة في مسار أوهنته أمراض الماضي | Legal Agenda (legal-agenda.com). (In Arabic).
Jendoubi, Kamel and GiblinBéatrice. 2021. 'Tunisie: Un processus démocratique sur le fil du rasoir'. *Hérodote* 180(1): 98–114.
Marzouki, Nadia. 2016. 'La transiton tunisienne : Du compromis démocratique à la réconciliation forcée'. *Pouvoirs* 156(1): 83–94.
Mekki, Nidhal. 2018. 'Local elections in Tunisia: Implementing the constitution and reinforcing the transition'. *Constitutionnet*, 1 June. Available at: https://constitutionnet.org/news/local-elections-tunisia-implementing-constitution-and-reinforcing-transition.
Mekki, Nidhal. 2021. 'On the fragility of new democracies: Tunisia between constitutional order and disorder'. *Constitutionnet*, 30 October. Available at: https://constitutionnet.org/news/fragility-new-democracies-tunisia-between-constitutional-order-and-disorder.
Rosanvallon, Pierre. 2008. 'La légitimité démocratique : Impartialité, réflexivité, proximité' Paris: Seuil.
Sarsar, Mohammed Chafik. 2018. 'Introductory report'. In: *The constitutional independent authorities: What consecration? Symposium on constitutional authorities*. 1st and 2nd March. Faculty of Juridical, Political and Social Sciences (FJPSST). Tunis, 9–26. (In Arabic).
Sarsar, Mohammed Chafik and Mourad BenMoualla Mourad. 2017. *Report on the reality and prospects of independent constitutional authorities*. Tunis: Solidar Tunisia. (In Arabic).
Sridi, Amine. 2013. *L'instance supérieure indépendante pour les élections*. Faculty of Law and Political Sciences of Sousse. Master's thesis.
The Carter Center. 2014. 'Legislative and presidential elections in Tunisia, final report'.
The Carter Center. 2015. 'The Constitution-Making Process in Tunisia: Final Report'.
The Carter Center. 2019. 'Legislative and presidential elections in Tunisia, final report'.
Wall, Alan. 2010. *Concevoir la gestion électorale, le manuel d'IDEA international*. Stockholm: Institute for Democracy and Electoral Assistance (International IDEA).

15
PARTIAL AND NON-PARTISAN
The municipal council elections in Saudi Arabia

Hendrik Kraetzschmar[1]

Introduction

Until about 15 years ago, a chapter on Saudi Arabia would have had no place in a volume on elections in the Arab Middle East and North Africa (MENA). Indeed, prior to 2004–2005 Saudi Arabia belonged to an (albeit diminishing) cluster of Arab states, also including Oman and the United Arab Emirates, where elections and partisan politics were considered divisive and un-Islamic and hence remained banned (Peterson 2012). In the Saudi context, this only changed following the 9/11 terrorist attacks when, driven by growing domestic and foreign pressures for change, then Crown Prince and *de facto* Regent Abdullah bin Abdulaziz al-Saud (1983–2005) pushed through a series of liberalising reforms which included the introduction of plural elections for some of the country's civil associations as well as the nation's municipalities (Kraetzschmar 2015: 184–185).[2] To placate conservative and reform-sceptic elements within the regime, the government at the time decreed that plural elections would be introduced for the lowest tier of government only and that they would be run on a non-partisan basis and under male adult suffrage only. It was further decided that only half of the country's municipal councils were to be elected, with the other half appointed by the Ministry of Municipal and Rural Affairs (MOMRA), most likely as an authoritarian safeguard against the emergence of 'oppositional' councils (Ménoret 2005: 1–2; Kraetzschmar 2010: 515–516).

Back in 2003–2004, the government's decision to open the municipal tier of government to electoral contestation drew mixed responses from local rights activists and pundits of Saudi politics. For some, the turn to electoral politics was nothing short of historic, signifying an important milestone on the path to meaningful citizen participation and potentially broader democratic reforms in the Kingdom (Hamzawy 2006: 12; Al-Sulmani 2008). Others cast a more critical eye on the elections, chastising them as a publicity stunt by the regime to brush up its international image and as little meaningful considering the overarching authoritarian context within which they were to take place. Particularly jarring for these critics was the fact that elected representatives would take up only half of all council seats, that women remained barred from participating and that the councils themselves lacked any substantive authority and decision-making powers (Alghamdy 2011: 128–130, 138–139; Quamar 2016: 434).

This chapter recounts the Saudi experience with municipal elections, covering the founding elections of 2005 as well as the subsequent 2011 and 2015 polls.[3] It suggests that – although run on a non-partisan basis at the lowest tier of government and for institutions holding little substantive decision-making powers – the municipal elections have at times been highly political affairs, engendering elite-level politicking well beyond the day-to-day business of running local government.

The Kingdom's municipalities: organisation and powers

Authoritarianism and administrative centralisation tend to go hand in hand. So too in the Kingdom of Saudi Arabia where, since the formation of the third Saudi state in 1932, power has remained firmly vested within the national executive, with at its apex the ruling House of Saud, and this despite the establishment of distinct sub-national tiers of government (Aazam 2004: 13; Mandeli 2016: 114). As of today, Saudi Arabia is administratively divided into 13 regions, which collectively comprise a total of 118 governorates and 285 municipalities. Each of the 13 regions is headed by an *amir*, who is appointed by the king, usually from within the wider royal family. Carrying the rank of a minister, the *amir* functions as the representative of the central government in the region and is assisted in his duties by a deputy and a regional council. The 118 governorates, in turn, are each headed by a governor, who is appointed by the Minister of the Interior upon the recommendation of the local *amir* and again assisted by a provincial council. The powers of the regional and provincial councils are largely advisory, and although there have been calls for their direct elections, to date they remain fully appointed (Aazam 2004: 19; Fathallah 2018; Law of the Provinces A/92). In this, they differ from the country's lowest tier of government, the municipalities, which – as noted above – feature since 2005 partially elected councils. Unlike any other tier of government, in fact, the municipalities can look back on a rather illustrious history of participatory politics, with local elections having taken place in parts of the country during the 1920s and again between the mid-1950s and early 1960s (Matthiessen 2015).[4]

Whilst the creation of local government institutions dates to the reign of King Abdulaziz bin Abdul Rahman al-Saud (1875–1953), the present-day municipal system is relatively young, resting on the 'Municipalities and Villages Ordinance' M/5 of 1977. Amongst others, this ordinance defines municipalities as legal entities within the Saudi body politic, specifies their responsibilities[5] and places them under the authority of the MOMRA, which itself was only established in 1975 (Aazam 2004: 20–21). Importantly, it stipulates the establishment of local governing institutions, including a municipal administration and council. The latter, however, remained dormant for much of the 1980s and 1990s and was only brought to life by the late King Abdullah bin Abdulaziz al-Saud (2005–2015), who, as part of a broader package of political reforms, announced the formation of partially elected municipal councils in 2003 (Anon 2003; Kapiszewski 2006: 93–94). When, two years later, the municipal councils were eventually established as part of the first nationwide local poll since the 1960s, their total number stood at 178. In 2011, this number was increased to its present total of 285 councils (Quamar 2016: 436).

Throughout the first decade of their existence, the workings of the municipal councils came under intense scrutiny, with local observers and academics alike describing their performance as overall poor and ineffective. At the time, it was widely argued that this poor performance was born out of the limited authority and control powers these councils hold *vis-à-vis* the local executive and the various regional branches and agencies of government, particularly in the fields of public land use, health, education and wastewater management (e.g. Fathallah 2018). To alleviate some of this criticism, and to revive fledging societal interest in the councils, the government in 2013 issued a royal decree that somewhat enhanced the control and supervisory powers of the councils *vis-à-vis* the municipal executive (see Royal Decree No. 61, 2013).

Electoral regulations and management

Elections to the Saudi municipal councils are governed by Ministerial Resolution 38396 and its bylaws. Over time, this body of laws has been subject to several significant amendments, including with regard to suffrage rights and the voting system. Upon the country's return to electoral politics in 2005, the MOMRA devised an electoral regime that was highly suggestive of the authorities' weariness towards genuine democratic reform and unusual by international electoral standards. It stipulated that elections are to be held every four years on a non-partisan basis, with political parties remaining banned, and that only 50 per cent of all council seats are to be filled through competitive elections, whilst the MOMRA would appoint the remaining half (Kraetzschmar 2010: 520).[6] This 50/50 split between elected and appointed councillors was then amended prior to the 2015 poll, raising the proportion of directly elected representatives to currently 75 per cent of all council seats (see Table 15.1).

Suffrage was severely restricted too, with voting and candidacy rights being conferred only to adult Saudi males, and this despite the law being rather ambiguous on the matter. In fact, as devised, the law never explicitly prohibited female electoral participation, and so it was very much the political calculus of the authorities in 2005 and again in 2011 which led to the exclusion of women from the ballot box (Henderson 2005; Kapiszewski 2006: 94). At the time, it was variably argued that the novelty of the electoral experience as well as the challenges of putting in place a gender-segregated electoral infrastructure – yet not matters of principle – prevented

Table 15.1 Electoral regulations factsheet

	2005	2011	2015
No. municipal councils	178	285	285
No. municipal council seats	1,216	2,112	3,159
Mode of designation	– 608 directly elected – 608 appointed by the MOMRA	– 1,056 directly elected – 1,056 appointed by the MOMRA	– 2,106 directly elected – 1,053 appointed by the MOMRA
Voting System	Multiple votes in multiple nomination districts		Single vote in single-member districts
Compulsory voting?	No		
Voter requirements	– age: 21 and over – male only – Saudi nationality – resident in the locality		– age: 18 and over – male and female – Saudi nationality – resident in the locality
Candidate eligibility	– age: 25 and over – male only – Saudi nationality		– age: 25 and over – male and female – Saudi nationality
Incompatibilities	– women – military personnel – resident non-citizens		– military personnel – resident non-citizens

Note: This factsheet lists some of the principal voter requirements and candidate eligibility criteria but does not constitute an exhaustive list thereof.
Sources: Information collated from multiple sources, including Henderson 2005; Abdulaal 2006; Sadek 2011; Alswaid 2015; Sadek 2015; Quamar 2016: 436.

the extension of suffrage rights to women (Kapiszewski 2006: 94; Alswaid 2016; Anon 2011a). In reality, of course, other factors played into this decision too, including the need to tread carefully on the matter due to strong opposition to female political engagement from amongst some of the regime's conservative members and backers.

As stipulated in Table 15.1, alongside women, voting and candidacy rights have also been denied by law to members of the country's armed forces and to resident non-citizens, placing Saudi Arabia alongside those countries globally featuring some of the more severe suffrage restrictions. As of 2005, these restrictions have meant that of a total population of nearly 24 million, only about 3–4 million male citizens were ultimately eligible to vote in, and slightly fewer to stand for, municipal elections. When in 2015, the authorities finally greenlit the participation of women in municipal elections, the total voting population rose concomitantly to about 14 million citizens out of by then nearly 32 million inhabitants.[7]

As concerns the management of the municipal elections themselves and its voting system, the following can be said. Reminiscent of electoral practices elsewhere, the municipal electoral cycle comprises distinct stages, including a voter and candidate registration phase, the actual campaign, the balloting, counting and announcement of results, as well as a period for electoral challenges. Whilst in 2005, balloting took place over three consecutive rounds between February and March, voting in both the 2011 and 2015 municipal elections was conducted on a single day. The MOMRA, in collaboration with the Ministry of the Interior, is in overall charge of managing this electoral cycle and establishes to this effect a range of electoral commissions tasked with organising the municipal poll. These include a General Electoral Commission with overall responsibility for the conduct of the poll, a commission for voter and candidate registration, an Appeals and Grievances Board, as well as local electoral commissions in each of the country's municipalities (Sadek 2015).

Election monitoring too takes place for municipal elections, yet none of it involves internationally-renowned organisations such as the OSCE or UN, and there are question marks over its independence and impartiality, not least because in past elections, the MOMRA licensed quasi-governmental organisations, such as for instance the National Society for Human Rights, to observe the polls. Similar question marks must be raised, in fact, about the key branches of the electoral commission, all of whom are fully appointed by the MOMRA, including the Appeals and Grievances Board which handles electoral challenges (Sadek 2011; Anon 2015e; Sadek 2015).

When it comes to the municipal voting system adopted in 2005, the MOMRA opted for electoral rules that did not chime well with key international electoral standards. Carrying elements of the bloc vote, the voting system created a highly unusual distinction between nomination and voting areas, whereby political hopefuls would register their candidacies in one of several designated nomination districts, whilst voters would be entitled to cast as many votes as there were nomination districts in their municipality.[8] Whichever hopeful received the most votes cast for candidates in his nomination district would then go on to win the seat. As detailed by this author elsewhere, this voting system violated key design principles of plurality-majoritarian systems, not least with regards to 'geographic accountability', which mandates a direct connection between voter and elected representative. In the Saudi voting system, this connection was far from guaranteed, as it offered a realistic prospect for candidates to win a seat without necessarily being the first choice of residents in their (nomination) district (Kraetzschmar 2010: 521–522).

Following two consecutive elections under this voting system, the MOMRA in 2015 replaced these highly contentious provisions with a straightforward simple plurality system in single-member districts. As practised elsewhere, under this new electoral system, voters would cast a single ballot in their electoral district, with the candidate garnering the most votes winning the seat (Anon 2015b). As will be elaborated upon below, it stands to reason that this change in electoral design was driven largely by political considerations, with the regime seeking to put an end to cross-candidate collaboration, which – albeit illegal – had become a prominent vote maximising tactic for many candidates under the previous electoral system (Kraetzschmar 2010).

Prior to each of the past three elections, lastly, the MOMRA issued a set of regulations which spelt out the *dos and don'ts* of electoral campaigning. Being rather prescriptive, they specified where it was permissible to set up headquarters and campaign venues, where to place advertisements and roadside billboards and how to run one's campaign.[9] With regards to the latter, for instance, candidates have been obliged to obtain approval of their campaign materials from the MOMRA, comply with 'good Islamic manners', avoid any recourse to religious, tribal and/or sectarian symbols, and forgo any forms of electoral collaboration with other candidates, either tacitly or in the open. Also featured in these regulations are several violations punishable by imprisonment, a fine or both. These include most notably vote buying and selling, receiving foreign funding, inflicting harm on other candidates and/or their campaigns, as well as any use of public utilities and religious establishments for campaigning purposes (Al-Sulmani 2008: 122; Anon 2015c; Quamar 2016: 437). On the issue of campaign finance, it is worth highlighting that whilst the law has been explicit in banning foreign funding, and mandates candidates to rely on their own resources; it has remained silent on any spending limits for individual campaigns (Alswaid 2016).

Voters, electoral campaigns and results

Despite the fanfare with which they were introduced – and the publicity they received through government advertisements and in the press – over the past 15 years, municipal elections have gained only limited traction among the wider Saudi public. This transpires, first and foremost, from voter registration and turnout data as well as from candidate registration figures. As highlighted in Table 15.2, voter registration has remained incredibly low across the board, with the country's electoral register holding at its peak in 2015 a bare 3.3 per cent of the entire citizen population.[10] After an impressive start, turnout has nosedived too, falling from over 80 per cent of registered voters in the 2005 founding elections to less than 50 per cent by 2015. Candidate registration has remained underwhelming also, with the average number of candidates per elective council seat dropping from a high of 15 to a mere three over the same time period (see Table 15.3).[11] This downward trend in both turnout and candidacy rates was only marginally

Table 15.2 Voter registration and turnout

	2005	2011	2015
Citizen population[1]	17,314,364	~19,837,729	21,531,662
Total number of registered voters	793,432	1,080,000	1,480,096
Percentage registered voters of the citizen population	3.3	~5.4	6.9
Voter turnout	~650,000	~421,000	702,539
Percentage voter turnout of the citizen population	~3.8	~2.1	3.3
Percentage voter turnout of registered voters	~82.0	~39.0	47.0

Note: This figure excludes the resident migrant population of Saudi Arabia, which makes up a sizeable proportion of the total population in the Kingdom.
Sources: Information collated from multiple sources, including World Bank Open Data; Quamar 2016, p. 435, 438.

Table 15.3 Municipal councils, elective seats and candidacies

	2005	2011	2015
Number of elective seats	608	1,056	2,106
Number of candidates	9,330	5,324	6,440
Average number of candidates per seat	~15	~5	~3

Sources: Information collated from multiple sources, including Ménoret 2005; Anon 2011d; Sadek 2015; Quamar 2016: 435, 438; Muhammad 2019.

dented – but hardly reversed – in 2015 with the lowering of the voting age to 18 years and the expansion of full suffrage rights to women.

How then is one to account for such a lack of public engagement with the municipal elections? Observers of Saudi politics seem to concur that this disengagement is being fuelled by a diverse set of motives and that it cuts across all strata of society. For a significant proportion of Saudi citizens, so it is suggested, non-participation has been grounded in either a lack of awareness of, or apathy towards, the workings of the municipalities and their elected councils. Others meanwhile are thought to have stayed clear of the polls because they found the level of electoral choice, particularly under the bloc vote of 2005 and 2011, overwhelming[12] or, more fundamentally, because they were frustrated with the councils' limited statutory powers and their ineffectiveness in pushing for much-needed improvements to local services and in monitoring the performance of the municipal executive (Ménoret 2005: 1–2; Henderson 2005; Kapiszewski 2006: 97; Anon 2015b; Al-Hatlani 2015).[13] Amongst those decrying the democracy deficit of the councils are numerous local writers and activists who in 2011 called for a boycott of the municipal poll, critiquing ongoing restrictions on suffrage rights, the partial election of the councils and the lack of citizen participation at higher tiers of government (Nelson 2011; Wagner 2011). Complementing this pool of non-voters, lastly, are those who, often for religious considerations, object to the idea of an elected government; a view that retains tractions within the country's ulema, parts of the regime and the more conservative/tribal parts segments of society (Kapiszewski 2006: 98; Al-Hatlani 2015; Quamar 2016: 440).

Campaigning in each of the past three elections was a crisp affair – lasting no longer than two weeks – with educated professionals, entrepreneurs and religious as well as tribal candidates making up the bulk of contestants in the race (Ménoret 2005: 3; Al-Rasheed 2009: 591). Reliant on their own sources of funding, candidates would engage in a diverse range of voter outreach and mobilisation activities. These ranged from door-to-door leafleting, the erection of roadside billboards/banners, the placement of adverts in the local print media, the organisation of public talks/lectures, the hosting of cultural events and the provision of hospitality – often in specifically designated campaigning venues – to SMS messaging and telephone marketing (Ménoret 2005: 3; Alghamdy 2011: 116–125).[14] Whilst the wealthier candidates were able to splash out on any of these campaigning activities – and did so at great cost[15] – most ordinary candidates with limited financial means at their disposal tended to limit their outreach activities to the mobilisation of voters through familial and/or tribal connections and networks as well as through social media and telephony. Whatever their wealth, in their campaigns most candidates drew heavily on their professional, religious and/or tribal standing and background – alongside the propagation of their plans for the municipality – as a means of targeting voters, knowing that these personal attributes would chime well with a deeply conservative electorate retaining strong confessional identities and tribal/familial loyalties (Kraetzschmar 2010: 523; Gorney 2015).

Unusual for elections in this part of the world, the Saudi authorities officially refrained from nominating and/or sponsoring its own set of candidates. As such, they are likely to have enhanced the overall competitiveness of a race which, even though political parties remain banned, carried at times a distinct ideological flavour, bringing to the fore marked differences along confessional lines, particularly in the Eastern Province, as well as more widely between Islamist and liberal persuasions (Al-Sulmani 2008: 129; Kraetzschmar 2010: 525–526; Wagner 2011). These persuasions were, in fact, made more visible by an electoral law which – although prohibited – facilitated the formation of informal pacts across nomination districts between like-minded candidates and their supporters. Such took place, for instance, in the 2005 and 2011 campaigns, by means of candidates mutually endorsing their campaigns and through the sponsorship – often by SMS – of specific lists of local candidates particularly by prominent Islamist, Shi'a and tribal leaders (Ménoret 2005: 3–4; Kraetzschmar 2010: 523–525; Alswaid 2016). As this author has demonstrated elsewhere (2010: 526), although highly controversial, for Islamist candidates these informal pacts (also known as 'golden lists') appear to have been key in consolidating electoral support and thus in routing their (liberal) rivals in the 2005 poll.[16]

Female suffrage and electoral participation

As noted earlier, Saudi women only obtained full suffrage rights in 2015. The change in policy was first announced by King Abdullah bin Abdulaziz al-Saud in a speech to the country's Consultative Council (Majlis al-Shura) on the eve of the 2011 campaign, during which he pledged that women would be entitled to fully partake in the following municipal elections scheduled for 2015 (bin Abdulaziz al-Saud 2011).[17] This announcement was then reconfirmed in 2014 by MOMRA in a statement promising that 'women [will] have the right to contest the elections just like men, without facing any discrimination' (Anon 2014).

Throughout the period leading up to the 2015 decision, women's rights activists had campaigned vigorously for their enfranchisement, often against stiff resistance, particularly from within the clerical establishment but also from ordinary citizens who rejected female electoral participation on either doctrinal and/or patriarchal grounds (Alswaid 2015; Batrawy 2015; Gorney 2015; Ottaway 2015). One of the most visible exponents of this campaign was the Baladi ('my country') initiative, a grassroots suffragist movement which was formally launched in 2010–2011 and headed by a group of Saudi businesswomen, academics and activists (Dickinson 2015).[18] Operating without an official licence, the initiative posted its founding statement on Facebook, professing amongst others to 'raising awareness on the individual and institutional levels of the importance of full participation in municipal elections' and to 'working towards securing the right of women to vote and run in the 2011 municipal elections' (Anon 2011b). To this end, Baladi advanced a rights discourse that drew attention to Saudi Arabia's international legal obligations towards gender equality, whilst simultaneously appealing to religious scripture and domestic legislation as a means to underscore the authenticity and legitimacy of its call for the enfranchisement of women (Wagner 2011).[19] In its 2011 campaign, the initiative also actively encouraged Saudi women to register their votes on the electoral register in defiance of the ban and to launch appeals against their exclusion from the poll with the MOMRA's Board of Grievances (Anon 2011b, 2011c; Nelson 2011). Following the enfranchisement of women in 2015 – and in the lead-up to the polls – the Baladi initiative organised an awareness campaign for female citizens, which was to include a series of training workshops for prospective candidates. This campaign was cut short, however, in August 2015 when the authorities ordered the closure of Baladi, officially due to licencing issues and for allegedly using its training programme for commercial purposes (Anon 2015a, 2015b).

With suffrage rights secured, 130,636 Saudi women went on to register their vote for the 2015 elections. Of these, it is estimated that over 100,000 went on to cast their ballots on polling day.[20] Whilst – if accurate – these figures signify a high registration-to-turnout ratio, they also speak to the fact that of a female citizen population of approximately 9.5 million at the time, very few took up their newly-won voting rights in what would have been for most a first-ever experience with electoral democracy. Alongside apathy and/or a lack of awareness (Quamar 2016: 440), local activists have held Saudi Arabia's patriarchal society and its legal underpinning – the guardianship system – largely responsible for the low level of female engagement with the electoral process. This is evident, for instance, with regard to voter registration, which requires proof of identity and residency in the voting district. For many Saudi women, these supporting documents are, however, difficult to obtain largely because their names are not normally listed on housing deeds, rental agreements and/or utility bills – all of which could function as proof of residence – and because they often either do not hold individual ID cards or, if they do, these are kept by male guardians. To successfully register to vote, women thus relied on the cooperation/consent from their male guardians and the wider family, which in many cases proved to be difficult to obtain or not at all forthcoming (Anon 2015b, 2016; Luck 2015; Pearson 2015).[21]

Unlike the low uptake in passive voting rights, the number of female candidacies, meanwhile, was refreshingly robust, with women accounting for a respectable 15 per cent of all contestants in the 2015 poll, and this despite the fact that the MOMRA had disqualified several contestants allegedly due to their involvement in rights activism (Anon 2015b; Gorney 2015).[22] Most of these pioneering female candidates knew, of course, that the odds of winning a council seat were rather slim not only because of their inexperience at the polls, but because they had to navigate several gender-specific barriers affecting their ability to reach out to the country's predominantly male electorate. Some of these barriers were borne out of the country's electoral law, which mandated, amongst others, that all electioneering had to be gender-segregated. For female contestants this meant that any communication with the bulk of their potential voters could only happen indirectly, either through appointed male representatives or from behind a partition, which of course significantly diminished their visibility at campaigning events and in the election campaign more widely (Alswaid 2015). This visibility was further diminished also by the legal proviso introduced in 2015, which forbade candidates from using photographic images on any of their campaigning literature and which, according to the MOMRA, had been introduced to safeguard the modesty of female candidates in accordance with Wahhabi doctrine (Alswaid 2015).

Other barriers to effective voter outreach and mobilisation, meanwhile, carried a more patriarchal undertone and concerned the difficulties many female contestants encountered in securing vital support from tribal/community elders for their election campaigns and in overcoming

Table 15.4 Registered female voters and turnout, 2015

Total number of registered voters	1,480,096
Registered female voters	130,637
Percentage of total registered voters	8.8
Voter turnout	702,539
Female turnout	~100,000
Percentage female turnout	~14

Sources: Information collated from multiple sources, including Anon. 2015b; Pearson 2015; Quamar 2016, p. 438.

wider societal misgivings about the role of women in domestic politics (Alswaid 2015; Batrawy 2015; Gorney 2015).[23] In this, female candidates were decidedly disadvantaged *vis-à-vis* many of their male counterparts, who were little burdened by any of these prejudices and found it overall much easier to secure the necessary electoral support from their families, local communities and tribes. Cognisant of these challenges, many of the female candidates nevertheless remained incredibly optimistic about the electoral experience, asserting that the act of participation itself was significant in challenging cultural barriers to female empowerment and in inspiring other women to follow suit (Alswaid 2015; Gorney 2015).

In the end, 20 of the female contestants in the race were victorious, capturing roughly 1 per cent of all elective council seats (Anon 215e). Of these, several had succeeded in rural municipalities, evidencing that their chances of success are not necessarily confined only to the more liberal metropoles of the Kingdom – where support for female empowerment is strongest and where women have already made some noticeable strides in associational elections – but that they can even win in the more conservative corners of the country, such as for instance in the Al-Qassim region (Batrawy 2015).

This said, the overriding take away from this poll, of course, is that with only a handful of seats captured, the road ahead to anything approximating an equitable representation of Saudi women on the municipal councils is likely to be long and arduous. A glimpse across the fence to other conservative Peninsula countries, where women too have struggled to make any sustained electoral inroads, seems to support this assessment,[24] and so does the MOMRA's reticence thus far to use its powers of appointment to strengthen female representation on the country's municipal councils. Indeed, by picking a mere 17 women out of a total of 1,053 appointed councillors, the MOMRA in 2015 signalled unmistakably to the wider Saudi public – and to its female segment in particular – that it places a little premium on affirmative action as a tool for advancing the empowerment of women in local politics, even though it has the authority to do so (Muhammad 2019).

Conclusion

Saudi Arabia's latest experience with plural elections is less than two decades old, and hence considerably shorter than that of any of the other country cases covered in this edited volume. As of mid-2021, the Kingdom had organised a mere three municipal polls of which only one was held under universal adult suffrage. Caution is therefore warranted when it comes to making any broader claims about the nature and trajectory of Saudi municipal elections, particularly *vis-à-vis* female engagement, and the emergence in the longue durée of a vibrant local participatory culture.

Table 15.5 Female candidacies and winners, 2015

Total number of candidates	6,440
Number of male candidates	5,502
Number of female candidates	978
Percentage female candidates	15.2
Number of male winners	2,086
Number of female winners	20
Percentage of female winners	~ 1

Sources: Quamar 2016: 438.

With this in mind, the chapter offers two concluding thoughts on the municipal polls and their wider impact on the Saudi government and politics. For one, it seems evident that whilst these elections may have helped repair some of the reputational damage inflicted on the Kingdom in the wake of 9/11; they certainly did not provide the impetus for the wider democratic reforms many commentators of Saudi politics had hoped for in the early 2000s. Indeed, if anything, over the past decade Saudi authoritarianism has been further upgraded, rather than downgraded, particularly under the reign of King Salman bin Abdulaziz al-Saud (2015–) and his heir apparent, Mohammed bin Salman al-Saud who, whilst initiating social reforms, have shown no appetite for further political liberalisation (Al-Rasheed 2021). In light of all this, one might hence be tempted to regard the municipal elections as largely cosmetic and irrelevant to the machinations of Saudi politics, which to some extend they are of course. However – and this takes me to the second of my concluding thoughts – this is only one side of the story, the other being the multiple occurrences when municipal elections and affairs managed to spill over into national-level politics, precipitating a politicisation of the public sphere that at times has gone well beyond the more mundane matters of everyday local governance. As highlighted above, this politicisation was evident, for instance, in the Islamist undertones and victories characterising the 2005 and 2011 campaigns as well as the regime's resort to electoral engineering to undercut any such future victories and with it the potential for further ideologisation of the municipal realm. It also shines through the MOMRA's recurring interventions in the electoral process, particularly during the candidate registration phase, during which it disqualified many candidates with an activist background. These interventions were only possible, of course, due to the absence of a truly independent electoral commission and grievance procedure. Lastly, it was apparent in the government's decision to limit suffrage rights in 2005 and the national suffragist campaign and women's rights discourse this engendered between 2004–2005 and 2011.

For the Saudi government, one likely take away from all of this is that, no matter how authoritarian the context and at what level of governance, by their very nature elections are political and prone to inject an element of uncertainty and disruption into an otherwise by and large depoliticised *status quo*. What precisely this means for the government's approach towards municipal elections going forward, and the possibility of introducing elections at regional and/or national levels, remains to be seen, of course, but given the regime's ongoing clampdown on political activism and broader de-liberalisation trends in the region, it seems highly unlikely that Saudi citizens will witness an expansion of these participatory rights any time soon.

Notes

1 The author thanks Marwa Ammar for her assistance in collating data for this research.
2 In Oman too, the authorities have since introduced plural municipal elections, with the first being held under universal adult suffrage in 2012 (Anon 2012).
3 The second municipal elections were originally scheduled for 2009, but postponed for two years due to non-specified 'technical reasons' (Sadek 2011). In 2020, scheduled elections were again postponed, this time due to the COVID-19 pandemic. According to unverified accounts, the term of the municipal councils has since been extended by two years to facilitate a reform of the municipal framework. As of autumn 2021, no new date has been set for the next elections.
4 For an excellent account of local elections in Saudi Arabia pre-2005, see Toby Matthiessen, 2015. 'Centre–periphery relations and the emergence of a public sphere in Saudi Arabia: The municipal elections in the Eastern Province, 1954–1960'. *British Journal of Middle Eastern Studies* 42(3), 320–338.
5 Municipalities in Saudi Arabia are classified into A, B, C and D municipalities, depending on their population size. Overall, they hold responsibility for discharging local services, maintaining local infra-

6. In 2005 municipal councils ranged in size from four seats in the smallest districts to 14 seats in the larger metropolitan areas, including Jeddah, Makkah, Medina and Riyadh. By 2015, the size of municipal councils had been revised upwards, with the largest councils now holding 30 seats (Abdulaal 2006: 10; Royal Decree No. 61, 2013).
7. That same year, the MOMRA also lowered the voting age from 21 to 18 years in a bid to shore up fledging interest in the municipal elections from among the younger citizen population. See Table 15.1.
8. For voters this meant that, depending on the size of their councils, they were asked to select candidates from up to seven separate electoral lists and from areas of their municipality which they were often little familiar with (Kraetzschmar 2010: 520–522).
9. Candidates are entitled to place adverts in the local press, but not on radio and/or TV (Kraetzschmar 2010: 529).
10. For a breakdown of voter registration figures by province and year of election, see Md Muddassir Quamar, 2016. 'Municipal Elections in Saudi Arabia, 2015', *Contemporary Review of the Middle East* 3(4): 439–440.
11. The comparatively high number of candidates per elective seats in 2005 is in all likelihood attributable to the novelty of the electoral experience at the time.
12. As noted earlier, the peculiar division between nomination and voting districts in place for the 2005 and 2011 elections has meant that voters were required to select a candidate not only from the district they reside in, but from across all districts of their municipality. Particularly in the country's larger municipalities voters were thus asked to choose candidates from neighbourhoods far afield, where they often hardly knew any of the contestants and/or anything about the issues facing the local community (Kraetzschmar 2010: 520–522).
13. An Okaz poll conducted prior to the 2005 founding elections revealed widespread scepticism towards the municipal councils and their powers, with no less than 65 per cent of respondents concurring with the view that these held very limited substantive powers (cited in Alghamdy 2011: 135) A study by Amir Al-Alwan referenced in Alaraby also suggests that over 50 per cent of the population remain unaware of the municipal councils and their workings and that less than 10 per cent of those interviewed felt satisfied with the workings of the councils (Anon 2015d).
14. It has also been reported that some candidates appear to have resorted to vote buying as an illicit campaigning device, although it is unclear how widespread this was and what impact it had on the election campaign and its outcome (e.g. Al Hakeem 2005; Kraetzschmar 2010: 522).
15. Some of the wealthier candidates in the bigger cities spend millions of Saudi riyals on their campaigns (Kraetzschmar 2010: 522).
16. For a detailed account of the Saudi electoral law and its impact on the formation of informal pacts, see Hendrik Kretzschmar, 2010. 'Electoral rules, voter mobilization and the Islamist landslide in the Saudi municipal elections of 2005', published in *Contemporary Arab Affairs*, 3(4), 515–533.
17. In the same speech, King Abdullah bin Abdulaziz al-Saud also announced the appointment for the first time of female representatives to the Consultative Assembly.
18. Another such group was the 'Saudi Women Revolution' which, founded in 2011, fought for women's suffrage rights alongside the abolition of the male guardianship system and other discriminatory laws and practices in the Kingdom (Davies 2011).
19. Saudi Arabia is a signatory of the *Convention in the Elimination of all Forms of Discrimination against Women* (CEDAW) as well as the *Arab Charter of Human Rights*, the latter of which stipulates in Art. 24.3 that '[E]very citizen has the right to stand for elections and to choose his representatives in free and impartial elections, in conditions of equality among all citizens that guarantee the free expression of his will' (Anon 2011a; Arab Charter on Human Rights).
20. In the absence of official figures, this author relied on unverified estimates presented by the ADHRB in its analysis of the 2015 elections (Anon 2015b). These figures must be treated with care, of course.
21. Also, informal conversation with four female Saudi citizens resident in York/UK, 28 May and 12 June 2021.
22. For comparison, in the 2015 and 2019 municipal elections in neighbouring Qatar female candidates made up less than 5 per cent of all contestants, and this although women have here held full suffrage rights since 1999 (Al-Khateeb 2015; Anon 2019a).
23. Also, informal conversation with four female Saudi citizens resident in York/UK, 28 May and 12 June 2021.

24 The fellow GCC monarchies of Kuwait and Qatar, for instance, both introduced universal adult suffrage ahead of Saudi Arabia, and yet there are few signs in either of the two countries that female representation on the municipal councils has risen over time. In the most recent 2018 municipal elections in Kuwait female candidates failed to win a single council seat (though one woman was later appointed to the council), whilst in the Qatari municipal elections of 2019 they captured only two seats (Toumi 2018; Anon 2019b).

References

Aazam, Salwa H.F. 2004. *Assessing the Efficiency and Effectiveness of Local Authorities in Saudi Arabia: A Case Study of Jeddah Municipality* (Doctoral thesis, University of Hertfordshire, UK).

Abdulaal, Waleed A. 2006. 'Municipal councils in Saudi Arabia: Context and organization'. *Journal of King Abdulaziz University: Environmental Design Science* 1: 1–25.

Alghamdy, Saeed S.G. 2011. *A Step towards Democracy? 2005 Municipal Elections in Saudi Arabia* (Doctoral thesis, Cardiff University, UK).

Al Hakeem, Mariam. 2005. 'Fear of malpractice surfaces as election fever grips Riyadh'. *Gulf News*, 3 February. Available at: https://gulfnews.com/world/gulf/saudi/fear-of-malpractice-surfaces-as-election-fever-grips-riyadh-1.276005.

Al-Hatlani, Ibrahim. 2015. 'Saudi elections: Serious or just for show?' *Al Monitor*, 20 December. Available at: www.al-monitor.com/originals/2015/12/saudi-arabia-municipal-elections-women.html.

Al-Khateeb, Anwar. 2015. 'Five women to contest Qatar municipal elections'. *The New Arab*, 16 April. Available at: https://english.alaraby.co.uk/analysis/five-women-contest-qatar-municipal-elections.

Al-Rasheed, Madawi. 2009. 'Modernizing authoritarian rule in Saudi Arabia'. *Contemporary Arab Affairs* 2(4): 587–601.

Al-Rasheed, Madawi. 2021. *The Son King: Reform and Repression in Saudi Arabia*. New York: Oxford University Press.

Al-Sulmani, Mishal F. 2008. 'Reform in Saudi Arabia: The case of municipal elections'. *Journal of King Abdulaziz University: Arts and Humanities* 16(2): 113–135.

Alswaid, Dalal. 2015. 'Saudi women poised to make history, but some doubt impact'. *The Arab Gulf Institute in Washington*. Blog Post, 11 December. Available at: https://agsiw.org/saudi-women-poised-to-make-history-but-some-doubt-impact/.

Alswaid, Dalal. 2016. 'The Saudi municipal council elections: Gender, tribalism and religious identity, 2005–2015'. George Washington University, *GSPM Working Paper # 2*.

Anon. 2003. 'Saudi Arabia announces first local council elections, but no date'. *The New York Times*, 14 October. Available at: www.nytimes.com/2003/10/14/world/saudi-arabia-announces-first-local-council-elections-but-no-date.html.

Anon. 2011a. 'Saudi Arabia: Let women vote, run for office. No excuse for exclusion from upcoming municipal elections'. *Human Rights Watch*, 31 March. Available at: www.hrw.org/news/2011/03/31/saudi-arabia-let-women-vote-run-office.

Anon. 2011b. 'Saudi Women respond to exclusion from voting: Baladi campaign [My Country Campaign]'. *Jadaliyya Report*, 16 May. Available at: www.jadaliyya.com/Details/23994.

Anon. 2011c. 'السعودية: المرأة ستشارك في التصويت وستدخل مجلس الشورى' [Saudi Arabia: Women will participate in the vote and enter the Shura Council]. *Human Rights Watch*, 26 September. Available at: https://www.hrw.org/ar/news/2011/09/26/244088.

Anon. 2011d. 'Saudi Arabia – Polls'. *The Middle East Reporter*, 29 September. Retrieved from LexisNexis Academic Database.

Anon. 2012. 'Oman to hold municipal council elections for the first time'. *Gulf News*, 7 May. Available at: https://gulfnews.com/world/gulf/oman/oman-to-hold-municipal-council-elections-for-the-first-time-1.1019363.

Anon. 2014. 'Saudi Arabia: Women take a step closer to municipal elections'. *Asharq Al-Awsat*, 19 February. Available at: https://eng-archive.aawsat.com/bandar-sharida/news-middle-east/saudi-arabia-women-take-step-closer-to-municipal-elections.

Anon. 2015a. 'First Saudi women register to vote'. *Aljazeera*, 20 August. Available at: https://www.aljazeera.com/news/2015/8/20/first-saudi-women-register-to-vote.

Anon. 2015b. '"My country": How Saudi Arabia is undermining women's newfound right to vote'. *Americans for Democracy and Human Rights in Bahrain (ADHRB) Blog Post*, 24 August. Available at: www

.adhrb.org/2015/08/my-country-how-saudi-arabia-is-undermining-womens-newfound-right-to-vote/.

Anon. 2015c. 'Women candidates warned against addressing voters directly'. *Arab News*, 11 October. Available at: www.arabnews.com/saudi-arabia/news/818681.

Anon. 2015d. 'مرشحون مجهولون..وجاهة اجتماعية في الانتخابات البلدية السعودية' [Unknown candidates…social image of Saudi municipal elections] *Alaraby*, 23 October. Available at: https://tinyurl.com/49f98jsn

Anon. 2015e. 'Saudi women are victorious in the first municipal elections they participate in'. *Alsharq Al-Awsat*, 14 December 2015. Available at: https://eng-archive.aawsat.com/theaawsat/news-middle-east/55345824.

Anon. 2016. 'Boxed in: Women and Saudi Arabia's male guardianship system'. *Human Rights Watch*, 16 July. Available at: www.hrw.org/report/2016/07/16/boxed/women-and-saudi-arabias-male-guardianship-system.

Anon. 2019a. 'Five women among 94 candidates in final phase of CMC elections'. *The Peninsula*, 21 March. Available at: www.thepeninsulaqatar.com/article/21/03/2019/Five-women-among-94-candidates-in-final-phase-for-CMC-elections.

Anon. 2019b. 'Central municipal council election winners'. *The Peninsula*, 16 April. Available at: https://thepeninsulaqatar.com/article/16/04/2019/Central-Municipal-Council-election-winners.

Arab Charter on Human Rights. 1997. Available in English at: www.equalrightstrust.org/ertdocumentbank/Arab%20Charter%20on%20Human%20Rights.pdf.

Batrawy, Aya. 2015. 'Saudi women vote, run in elections for first time'. *CTV News*, 12 December. Available at: www.ctvnews.ca/world/women-in-saudi-arabia-vote-and-run-as-candidates-for-first-time-1.2697776.

Bin Abdulaziz al-Saud, Abdullah. 2011. 'Speech by King Abdullah to the Majlis Al-Shura' [Speech transcript]. *Al-Bab.com*. Available at: https://al-bab.com/documents/speech-king-abdullah.

Davies, Catherine. 'Saudi women revolution' makes a stand for equal rights'. *CNN Inside the Middle East*, 4 May. Available at: http://edition.cnn.com/2011/WORLD/meast/05/04/saudi.women.revolution.rights/index.html.

Dickinson, Elizabeth. 2015. 'What is Saudi Arabia threw an election for women and nobody came?' *Foreign Policy*, 9 December. Available at: https://foreignpolicy.com/2015/12/09/what-if-saudi-arabia-threw-an-election-for-women-and-nobody-came/.

Fathallah, Hadi. 2018. 'The failure of regional governance in Saudi Arabia'. *Carnegie Endowment for International Peace*, 26 July. Available at: https://carnegieendowment.org/sada/76928#:~:text=The%20unresolved%20infrastructure%20problem%20of%20Jeddah%20reflects%20the,organizational%20structures%20at%20the%20regional%20and%20local%20levels.

Gorney, Cynthia. 2015. 'In history Saudi elections, these women stepped up as voters and candidates'. *National Geographic*, 12 December. Available at: www.nationalgeographic.com/history/article/151212-saudi-arabia-election-women-vote.

Hamzawy, Amr. 2006. *The Saudi Labyrinth: Evaluating the Current Political Opening*. Washington, DC: Carnegie Endowment for International Peace.

Henderson, Simon. 2005. 'Saudi municipal elections: Royal caution and citizen apathy'. *Policy Watch*, 937(3). The Washington Institute for Near East Policy. Available at: www.washingtoninstitute.org/policy-analysis/saudi-municipal-elections-royal-caution-and-citizen-apathy.

Kapiszewski, A. 2006. 'Elections and parliamentary activity in the GCC states: Broadening political participation in the Gulf Monarchies'. In Abdulhadi Khalaf and Giacomo Luciani (eds.), *Constitutional Reform and Political Participation in the Gulf*. Dubai: Gulf Research Centre, 88–131.

Kraetzschmar, Hendrik. 2010. 'Electoral rules, voter mobilization and the Islamist landslide in the Saudi municipal elections of 2005'. *Contemporary Arab Affairs* 3(4): 515–533.

Kraetzschmar, Hendrik. 2015. 'Associational life under authoritarianism: The Saudi chamber of commerce and industry elections'. *Journal of Arabian Studies* 5(2): 184–205.

Luck, Taylor. 2015. 'Saudi women finally get right to vote, so why aren't more registering?' *Christian Science Monitor*, 28 August. Available at: www.csmonitor.com/World/Middle-East/2015/0828/Saudi-women-finally-get-right-to-vote-so-why-aren-t-more-registering.

Mandeli, Khalid N. 2016. 'New public governance in Saudi cities: An empirical assessment of the quality of the municipal system in Jeddah'. *Habitat International* 51: 114–123.

Matthiesen, Toby. 2015. 'Centre–periphery relations and the emergence of a public sphere in Saudi Arabia: The municipal elections in the Eastern Province, 1954–1960'. *British Journal of Middle Eastern Studies* 42(3): 320–338.

Ménoret, Pascal. 2005. 'The municipal elections in Saudi Arabia 2005: First steps on a democratic path'. *Arab Reform Brief*. Available at: https://s3.eu-central-1.amazonaws.com/storage.arab-reform.net/ari/2005/12/18152528/Arab_Reform_Initiative_2005-12__en_The_Municipal_Elections_in_Saudi_Arabia_2005.pdf.

Muhammad, Fatima. 2019. 'No gender segregation at Saudi municipal council meetings'. *Arab News*, 23 October. Available at: www.arabnews.com/node/1572911/saudi-arabia.

Nelson, Soraya S. 2011. 'In Saudi Arabia only men vote, and not often'. *NPR*, 29 September. Available at: www.npr.org/2011/09/29/140930771/for-saudis-voting-is-still-for-men-only.

Ottaway, David B. 2015. 'Saudi women go to the polls – Finally'. *Viewpoints No. 88*, Wilson Centre Middle East Programme. Available at: www.wilsoncenter.org/sites/default/files/media/documents/publication/saudi_women_go_to_polls_finally.pdf.

Pearson, Michael. 2015. 'First women elected to office in Saudi Arabia'. *CNN*, 14 December. Available at: https://edition.cnn.com/2015/12/13/world/first-women-elected-to-office-in-saudi-arabia/index.html.

Peterson, John E. 2012. *The GCC States: Participation, Opposition, and the Fraying of the Social Contract. Kuwait Programme on Development, Governance and Globalisation in the Gulf States (26)*. London: London School of Economics and Political Science.

Quamar, Md Muddassir. 2016. 'Municipal elections in Saudi Arabia, 2015'. *Contemporary Review of the Middle East* 3(4): 433–444.

Royal Decree No. 61, 2013. Bureau of Experts at the Council of Ministers. Available at: https://laws.boe.gov.sa/BoeLaws/Laws/LawDetails/9da91b16-62ba-41d8-b6f7-a9a700f21d07/1.

Sadek, George. 2011. 'Saudi Arabia: The second municipality elections in the Kingdom's history'. *Library of Congress Blog*, 21 April. Available at: https://blogs.loc.gov/law/2011/04/saudi-arabia-the-second-municipality-election-in-the-kingdoms-history/.

Sadek, George. 2015. 'FALQs: Saudi Arabia municipal elections – Women participate for the first time'. *Library of Congress Blog*, 22 December. Available at: https://blogs.loc.gov/law/2015/12/falqs-saudi-arabia-municipal-elections-women-participate-for-the-first-time/.

Toumi, Habib. 2018. 'Kuwait's municipal council to elect president on Thursday'. *Gulf News*, 23 May. Available at: https://gulfnews.com/world/gulf/kuwait/kuwaits-municipal-council-to-elect-president-on-thursday-1.2225777.

Wagner, Rob L. 2011. 'Saudi Arabia's municipal elections: Lessons learned from Islamic Conservatives'. *Eurasia Review*, 9 September.

World Bank Open Data. *Population Total – Saudi Arabia*. Available at: https://data.worldbank.org/indicator/SP.POP.TOTL?locations=SA.

16
ELECTIONS IN THE ARAB WORLD

International monitoring and assistance

Pietro Marzo

Introduction

Beginning in the late 1980s, and particularly after the fall of the Soviet Union, international organizations (IOs), such as the United Nations (UN), the Organization of American States (OAS), the European Union (EU), and international non-governmental organizations (INGOs), began a series of programs aimed at encouraging liberal economic and pro-democracy reforms in non-Western states. These international actors sought to establish themselves first in the post-Soviet space and the across the globe to further their conceptions of democratic development and 'good governance.' Their democracy promotion programs drew extensively on the minimalist conceptualization of democracy, theorized by Joseph Schumpeter (1942). According to it, the foremost component of a democracy is the ability of citizens to select their political representatives through free, fair, and competitive elections. Schumpeter's conceptualization of democracy gained traction in the late 1980s and 1990s when scholars of democratization widened its theoretical tenets (Diamond 1990; Schmitter and Karl 1991; Huntington 1991). The *Journal of Democracy*, supported by the National Endowment for Democracy (NED),[1] became home to a debate that developed the concepts of procedural democracy. In his seminal article 'Third Wave of Democracy' – later an influential book – Huntington (1991) argues that elections represent the moment where democracy appears. According to Huntington, two rounds of free, fair and competitive elections signal the end of a democratic transition and the beginning of consolidation.

The debate unfolding on the pages of the *Journal of Democracy* had a significant influence on Western policymakers as well as on the agenda of IOs, INGOs, and political foundations engaged in promoting democracy. Support for free and competitive elections became the cornerstone of foreign assistance and diplomatic endeavors to foster democracy in illiberal settings. Western decision makers believed that enhancing citizens' ability to freely and fairly elect their representatives was the most effective tool to curb authoritarianism.

Under international pressure, many authoritarian leaders around the world accepted to introduce elections into their political system, although they did not seem willing to ensure fair competition. Therefore, to improve the integrity of elections, Western IOs, INGOs and state actors sent delegations to observe electoral processes abroad. Although missions of electoral monitoring were not a novelty – the Organization of American States, was the first organization to observe elections in the 1960s – this practice gained momentum during the 1990s, while democracy was expanding around the globe. The 2005 *Declaration of Principles for International Election Observation and its Code of Conduct* (commonly known as the Declaration of Principles or DoP), was the latest of a series of documents setting standards and norms for electoral observation organizations.[2] Over the course of the last three decades, organizations monitoring elections have mushroomed. Prominent IOs and INGOs have trained their personnel to monitor elections around the world, and have designed programs of assistance aimed at preparing for elections.

The emphasis on competitive elections as the panacea to foster democracy worldwide produced mixed results. On the one hand, political processes in Eastern and Central Europe suggested that elections, if genuine, could be drivers of rapid political change and democratization. Bunce and Wolchick (2006) contended that post-communist countries started their journey to democratization through an 'electoral revolution,' where liberal forces defeated the illiberal ones in pluralistic competitions. They also point out the role that international democracy promoters and electoral observers played in deterring manipulation and fraud during elections, allowing for the possibility of opposition forces to replace incumbent elites. In his research on the politics of Sub-Saharan countries, Lindberg (2006) hailed the routinization of elections as central to the improvement of democratic practices and political culture. On the other hand, scholars warned that Western states and organizations were diffusing a sort of 'electoral fetishism' (Carothers 1997; Sadiki 2009), losing sight of the other key components of a qualitative democratic society such as the rule of law, individual freedoms, participation, socioeconomic justice, institutional accountability and responsiveness, among others (Schedler 2002).

Furthermore, the euphoria surrounding the holding of democratic elections forced their introduction into regional settings where democratic procedures were completely unknown and where incumbents had arbitrary control over national institutions and a strong capacity to manipulate elections. In this respect, the idea that elections were the 'hallmark of democracy' (Huntington 1991) had obvious limitations in the Arab World. Rulers across the region accepted to hold elections regularly, yet they recurred to authoritarian undemocratic practices (Brumberg 2002), which included coercive mechanisms and irregularities and produced fraudulent results (Kraetzschmar and Cavatorta 2010). In addition, national institutions, which authoritarian rulers firmly controlled, were instrumental in manipulating electoral procedures (Gandhi and Lust-Okar 2009). More than in other regions of the world, elections in the Arab World were a 'façade' competition under the control of the authoritarian leaders, despite the fact that they involved a number of parties (Sadiki 2009).

The 2011 Arab uprisings led to a renewed enthusiasm for democratization and competitive politics in the region, and the emphasis on holding competitive, free and fair elections to boost transitions to democracy re-gained traction. It followed that Western IOs, INGOs and states have remained overwhelmingly focused on enhancing the procedures of democratic elections. However, they have devoted less attention to programs that improve citizens' understanding of how elections function, what are the specific mechanisms regulating them and what their meaning is in terms of accountability of elected representatives. In addition, international promoters of democracy have neglected almost completely the empowerment of other components of democracy, which not only influence the fairness of electoral contests but affect the quality of the competition. For instance, very little effort is devoted to increasing citizens 'informed' participation in elections – especially among political and religious minorities, youth and women – to ensure citizens' freedom to access competitive information, and to foster participatory governance. As a result, while international monitoring organizations have considered elections taking place in Arab post-authoritarian settings such as Tunisia, Egypt (before the military coup), and Libya, competitive and fair from a procedural point of view, these assessments continue to be based on minimalistic standards that fail to gauge the quality of elections and governance more broadly.

This chapter argues that post-2011 international organizations supporting and monitoring elections are primarily concerned with the respect of procedures rather than the quality of democratic elections. International organizations *de facto* boost the legitimacy of elected representatives, although these are elected through 'defective' elections (very low turnout, widespread patronage and clientelism, lack of clear information) and prove to be unresponsive to their citizens.

The chapter examines international electoral monitoring and electoral assistance in the Arab World. It focuses both on the impact that international electoral observers have when elections are held under authoritarian constraints and during democratization processes. Before delving into the analysis of the interplay between international electoral observers and national groups, the chapter reviews and problematizes the existing knowledge on international electoral assistance.

International monitoring and assistance of elections: the state of the art

For a long time, the literature has focused on the geopolitical factors behind foreign intervention in third state's elections (Miller 1983; Rubin 1999; Brown 2001; Kuzio 2005), as these are decisive moments that give direction to a country's foreign and domestic policy and allow specific groups to control national resources. Corstange and Marinov (2012) identify two main clusters of foreign intervention in national elections. The first – partisan intervention – is the intervention of a foreign actor in support of a specific political group in an electoral competition. Partisan intervention spurs divisions at the national level and may generate polarizing feelings across national groups vis-à-vis the intervening foreign actors. The second type – interventions in the process – consists of the attempt of a foreign power to enhance the quality of the electoral process, without backing any participant in particular. Although this theoretical distinction seems neat, in reality these two categories may overlap. Indeed, foreign states or organizations supporting a country's electoral process may end up inadvertently favoring a specific competitor. A similar conceptual dyad is offered by Godinez (2018), as he distinguishes between globally motivated and self-motivated interventions. The former occurs when a country – or an international organization – intervenes in the elections of another country in the interests of the international or national public. This type of intervention can take place if a candidate/party poses a threat to specific national groups, such as ethnic or religious minorities, or may jeopardize the security of another. The latter occurs instead when a foreign actor intervenes in the elections of another country to promote its geostrategic interests, or to prevent a hostile party from gaining/maintaining power.

In addition to the debate that conceptualizes the types of foreign interventions in electoral processes, scholars have recently focused their attention on the international monitoring of elections. Starting in the 1990s, sending delegations of observers abroad constituted an international norm to ensure the integrity of the electoral process in unconsolidated or slowly liberalizing regimes. The practice of monitoring elections revolves around two main ideas. First, electoral observers could internationally report abuse and fraud occurring during the elections. Second, electoral observers have the ability to put pressure on the incumbent to discourage the arbitrary use of power and institutions to win elections (Kelley 2009). As Merloe argues (2015: 80), 'the sanctioning of international election observation became a common practice of sovereign states. Although it is not yet universal, it is now widely recognized as central to the task of holding genuine elections in the developing world.'

Scholars have debated the impact international electoral observers have on the quality of elections in unconsolidated regimes. Generally speaking, scholars agree that electoral observers have some ability to detect election irregularities (Kelley 2009; Hyde 2011). Some scholars believe that reports issued by credible and authoritative electoral observers may influence national citizens' perception of the fairness of the electoral process (Hyde and Marinov 2014). However, Bush and Prather (2017) demonstrate that the effects electoral observers' statements have on national public opinion are more limited than previously thought. In a later study, Bush and Prather (2018) illustrated how voters tend to instrumentalize electoral observers' assessments of elections. Individuals leaning toward the winning parties tend to emphasize electoral observers' reports of elections if they are positive, as it allows to strengthen the legitimacy of the incumbents, while they tend to diminish the reports' relevance if they are critical. Arguably, individuals who voted for the losing parties behave similarly, instrumentalizing electoral observers' reports.

National voters are not the only actors who instrumentalize international monitoring activities for their benefit. The international monitoring of elections has received criticism because it may produce 'perverse effects,' playing out in favor of the incumbent authoritarian regime. In a seminal study, Beaulieu and Hyde (2009: 393) suggest that 'some international benefits to minimally democratic elections gave electoral autocrats the incentive to invite international observers and manipulate the election in ways that observers were less likely to catch or criticize; in other words, what we call "strategic manipulation."' Hyde (2011: 159) finds three mechanisms that authoritarian incumbents employ to circumvent foreign observers:

> first, pseudo-democrats can attempt to use different forms of election manipulation that are less likely to be caught by observers. Second, they can invite low quality or 'friendly' observers in order to ensure that at least one observer group endorses the elections as democratic. Third, if they are caught manipulating the election (or if they choose to cheat blatantly), they can work to discredit the reports of observers after the election.

It is worth pointing out that electoral monitoring organizations are allowed to observe rounds of elections under the adamant conditions that national authorities invite them. Therefore, wise authoritarian rulers invite delegations or advocate for specific individuals – e.g., members of sibling political parties, affiliates of allied governments and well-known individual supporters of the incumbents – precisely because 'friendly observers' reduce the likelihood of a critical report (Merloe 2015: 88).

In most cases, denying well-respected international organizations or powerful state actors to monitor the integrity of elections may backfire on incumbents. It exposes ruling parties or rulers to international suspicion, casting a shadow on the elections. Needless to say, leaders from aid-dependent states in the Global South have a strong interest in pleasing the international community. As mentioned, denying Western organizations or states the permission to observe elections may lead to the adoption of sanctioning mechanisms or provoke the disruption of economic aid. International organizations such as the World Bank, the International Monetary Fund, the European Union, and the United Nations often condition development aid to the respect of democratic procedures; the holding of competitive elections is one of the main requisites. A second factor that motivates aid-dependent states to open their doors to electoral observers is due to the ability of human rights groups to 'name and shame' ruling parties that do not abide by the rules. Falling under the spotlight of the international community can escalate into closer scrutiny of other components of governance, such as freedom of the press, respect for the rule of law and minority rights. This can have potentially negative consequences for the regime's relations with international actors.

In some authoritarian settings, however, *realpolitik* limits the action of electoral observers. Delegations of observers sent abroad are usually aware, before their mission begins, that electoral reports and assessments should carefully take in consideration the relation between their home country, their donors, and the country where the ballot is taking place. As a result, electoral observers may avoid reporting cases of manipulation and fraud and might therefore fail to directly accuse the incumbent of fraud. Through a systemic examination of three decades of electoral missions, Kelley (2009) demonstrated that when election flaws and irregularities are moderate, international observers tend to consider elections free and fair.

Electoral observers take into consideration the consequences that negative assessments of elections can generate for the country's politics. Daxecker (2014: 504) argues that 'fraudulent elections observed by international observers are more likely to be followed by post-election violence.' Indeed, reports that unveil blatant irregularities may aggravate existing social and political conflicts and may trigger protests and riots against the incumbent (Kuntz and Thompson 2009). Furthermore, electoral observers take into account the consequences that a negative post-election report may entail for specific nationals. Indeed, international electoral observers usually collaborate with national civil society groups or hire nationals that serve as observers during elections. These individuals run the risk of being victims of retaliation from the incumbent, as they report irregularities and frauds. Merloe (2015: 86) explains that 'the intimidation of national monitors may begin with threats to have them fired from their jobs or to take away their children's scholarships, and can even escalate to physical violence.' Criticism has been directed at prominent international organizations, such as the EU, the OSCE, and the UN, for having released positive statements about flawed elections, in addition to not being neutral and failing to apply rigorous standards in their monitoring activities (Nielson et al. 2019). Western countries have received similar criticism as the action of their delegations is not only considered ineffective, but their reports tend to omit fraudulent procedures of the electoral process. Some scholars have called these delegations 'zombie observers' (Merloe 2015: 86–88).

In any case, allowing electoral observers to monitor elections helps the incumbent to use his victory as a source of legitimacy, unless reports of massive fraud are released, and elections' results lose credibility both at the international and national levels. Indeed, international recognition of the election as 'fairly regular' boosts the national legitimacy of the incumbent. Williamson (2021: 2) argue that individuals

> should be more likely to obey a ruler as they perceive them to be more legitimate. Of course, authoritarian regimes also rely heavily on coercion and co-optation to secure compliance, but regimes perceived to be more legitimate by more of their citizens will have less need of these other two mechanism to maintain control.

Thus, in order to minimize the effectiveness of electoral observers, authoritarian regimes have improved their ability to manipulate elections in ways that are hard to detect (Beaulieu and Hyde 2009). These 'competitive authoritarians' (Levitsky and Way 2010) are increasingly relying on subtle mechanisms to weaken political adversaries, eluding the control or mandate of electoral observers.

Manipulation of elections can indeed begin much earlier than the start of the competition, affecting its integrity, and making it difficult for electoral observers to detect flaws. Competitive authoritarian regimes disempower political opponents, who may represent a threat during elections, by introducing administrative hurdles that render electoral registration of candidates more complex. Obstacles may include the lack of transparency about the procedures and the requisites to be eligible as a candidate, or the arbitrary change of deadlines to submit the candidature. In this respect, the incumbent tries to appoint election commissions that include government supporters to administer partisan elections. In some cases, when the incumbent has tight control of the judiciary system, opposition candidates can be the target of timely legal accusations that prevent him or her from joining the electoral competition (Beualieu and Hyde 2009). By integrating harmless opposition in the political competition, ruling autocrats secure their win while displaying multiparty competition (Gandhi and Lust-Okar 2009). The control of national institutions is key to the survival of competitive authoritarianism. Gandhi (2008: 56) argues, 'political institutions are instrumental for allowing dictatorships to deal with two prominent challenges: first, they prevent the formation of opposition that can endanger their hold on power, second they strengthen the top-down legitimacy through maintaining consensus and support.' This tactic prevents charismatic opposition leaders from being at the forefront of the electoral campaign and often forces political parties to opt for second-choice candidates, thereby losing the grip on the electoral base.

All these stratagems are beyond the control of the organizations and delegations observing elections, especially if their monitoring activities start a few weeks before the elections and stop once the elections have taken place. Carothers (1997: 22) points out that due to an 'overemphasis on election day by observers, efforts by entrenched leaders to manipulate electoral processes to their advantage have become more subtle as such leaders have been socialized into the new world of global democracy and internationally observed elections.' Likewise, Hyde (2011: 165) argues that observers often 'engage in electoral tourism, ignore fraud in the pre-election period, issue statements prematurely, distract from more qualified domestic observers, and practice "electoral fetishism" by overemphasizing election day with respect to the broader democratization process.'

Aware of such shortcomings, recently some international organizations have realized that they need to launch more comprehensive missions to counter incumbents' ability to shape electoral outcomes. These more comprehensive missions should not only consider sending delegations well before elections take place, but should complement electoral monitoring with programs engaging large portions of citizens. Based on the author's interviews with officers working at internationally established democracy-promoting organizations, there is a growing consensus about the need to prepare the ground for free and fair competitive elections by enhancing citizens' understanding of the electoral process. Prominent international NGOs that promote democracy and assist elections, such as the Carter Center, Democracy Reporting International, the German Political Foundations, US NGOs Freedom House and the National Democratic Institute, have been realizing gradually that to improve the quality of elections, they have to empower other components of democracy. This includes enhancing the understanding of how elections function and what they mean for the population, fostering participatory governance, encouraging participation and inclusion of minorities, supporting freedom of the press and access to information, supporting civil society advocacy for national institutions' accountability, and improving institution responsiveness, among others.

Electoral Assistance in authoritarian regimes in the Arab World

While the activities of electoral assistance organizations are becoming more comprehensive in many regions of the world, including Latin America, sub-Saharan Africa, and Eastern Asia, the Arab World, remains a complicated environment for the work of democracy-supporting organizations.

Issues regarding international electoral observation and electoral assistance are more relevant when it comes to the Arab World, which has been historically one of the most resistant regions to liberal democracy. Since elections became the 'thermometer' of democracy, the majority of Arab autocrats have arranged elections to please the international community, although these electoral competitions were not genuinely competitive (Sadiki 2009; Schedler 2013). The ability of Arab regimes to routinize multiparty elections, although rigged and unfair, posed a serious limit to the standard of electoral monitoring and democratic assistance. Multiparty elections have often taken the form of 'façade competition,' where authoritarian leaders secure landslides. There is a burgeoning literature questioning the real capacity of international actors to monitor elections and support competitive democracy in the Arab World (Durac and Cavatorta 2009; Bush 2015; Abbott 2018; Van Hüllen 2019). Focusing on Jordan's elections, Lust-Okar (2009) suggested that, in the Arab World, elections assume the form of a confrontation over groups' access to resources rather than a debate over policies.

In the majority of cases, Western organizations, including the European Union and United Nations, have limited their monitoring activities to sending small observation teams during the days when elections were taking place, thus failing to ensure their fairness and/or to promote political pluralism and liberal values. For instance, during Ben Ali's regime (1987–2011), Western countries and organizations sent small delegations to monitor election days, thereby ignoring what happened before and after. In particular, during the 2005 Tunisian presidential elections, Ben Ali won 94% of the vote, and Western democracies like the US, Italy, and France welcomed Ben Ali's re-election, although reports from human rights organizations raised criticism about opposition co-optation election irregularities and arbitrary exclusion of candidates.[3]

Another example comes from Egypt. In 2005, under pressure from the Bush administration, Egyptian president Hosni Mubarak organized the first multi-candidate presidential elections of his tenure. Unsurprisingly, Mubarak was re-elected, gaining 88% of the votes. Among other candidates, Ayman Nour received 7% of the popular vote, and Nunam Gumaa received 3%. Turnout, however, was estimated at only 30% of the adult population, and fear of voting against Mubarak was widespread among Egyptians. Egyptian parliamentary elections in 2005 and 2010 were no exception, with the candidate Ahmed Nazif, from the National Democratic Party – under the control of Mubarak and its family – winning the near-totality of seats in the People's Assembly. Yet, reports from international monitoring organizations were mild and emphasized the positive aspect of the election. In the post-election report on the 2005 Parliamentary Election Assessment in Egypt, the International Republican Institute (IRI) wrote:

> Despite negative aspects of the 2005 parliamentary elections, it is possible to highlight several notable achievements when compared with elections in the past. First, the role played by the domestic monitoring groups and the Judges' Club – as with the presidential election – has been important, as elements of civil society begin to take a more active role in advocating for greater democratic freedom and pluralism. In addition, between monitoring groups and independent media, the government has permitted a new level of scrutiny from the domestic and international community. Several of IRI's delegates had spent time in Egypt in the late 1980s and early 1990s, and noted that the current public debate about political reform and criticism of the ruling party and the government would have been unthinkable 10 or 15 years ago. The relative freedom with which state-run and independent press can debate these issues is an indicator of progress that should not go unmentioned.[4]

Although human rights groups such as Amnesty International and Human Rights Watch were more vocal in denouncing elections regularity, their warning remained unheard. Following both presidential and parliamentary elections, Western states such as Italy, France, the US, and the UK congratulated Mubarak and its party for winning the election. As an example, in 2005, the White House released an official statement congratulating Egyptian President Mubarak on re-election, barely touching upon unfair procedures.

> The United States congratulates the Egyptian people and government for holding Egypt's first multi-candidate presidential elections on September 7. This election represents an important step toward holding fully free and fair competitive multiparty elections, and both supporters and opponents of the government have told us that it has occasioned a vigorous national debate in Egypt on important issues. We expect it will be part of a process of continuing political reforms and that the flaws that were visible in this election will be corrected for November's parliamentary election. The President called President Mubarak this morning to congratulate him on his victory, and say he looks forward to continuing to work with him in the coming years.[5]

Similar to Egyptian and Tunisian cases, elections in Jordan, Iraq, Algeria, and Syria during the 2000s assumed the formation of a 'charade' to demonstrate to the international public that a minimum of competition existed. International electoral observers were quite irrelevant, as the electoral competition relied on networking and patronage and authoritarian leaders had control of national institutions and resources (Lust-Okar 2009; Corstange 2018). In contrast, authoritarian regimes gained some legitimacy kudos from the introduction of elections in their political system and the activities of international electoral observers. Indeed, large and routinized electoral victories helped to solidify their legitimacy both at the national and international levels. This belongs, in part, to the conceptual framework of 'upgrading authoritarianism' (Heydemann 2007), through which Arab autocrats nominally accept Western demands to promote liberal reforms and to open their political system, while ensuring that real decision-making power remains in informal networks they control.

Ruling leaders employed strategies such as ruling out candidates who could threaten their hold on power, co-opting harmless opponents into competition, using subtle coercive means, and controlling sources of information. Many Arab autocrats spread fear of potential chaos and instability deriving from political change. For instance, during the 1990s and 2000s many authoritarian leaders used the 1991 elections in Algeria as a showcase to indicate that political change could lead the country into uncharted territory, jeopardizing security and the economy. Indeed, following widespread protests and riots in 1988, Algeria held its first-time-in-history multiparty and competitive legislative elections in 1991. The Front Islamic du Salut (FIS) won the first round (Algeria had adopted the same electoral system as France) of the competition securing 47% of the popular votes and gaining the majority of seats in the Parliament. Yet, shortly after the first round, a military coup was carried out to prevent the FIS from taking power. Election results were declared invalid, and the transition to democracy was suspended under the 'silence' of the international community (Cavatorta 2013). As a result, Algeria fell into ten years of civil war that devastated the country and further polarized its citizens.

Arab autocrats played the 'Algerian card' to convince their citizens that they remained the only alternative to Islamism and chaos. This narrative resonated among Western policymakers, who believed that friendly despotic leaders were a bulwark against instability. In short, until 2010, while programs of electoral assistance existed and missions of election monitoring continued to be organized in many countries across the Arab World, their impact was irrelevant.

Electoral assistance during democratization in the Arab World

The 2011 Arab revolts blew a wind of hope across the region and spread enthusiasm about its changing political direction. The MENA seemed finally ready to welcome democracy and political pluralism. In transitional settings, international actors immediately intervened to assist national political groups in scheduling a roadmap for the organization of democratic elections. The international focus on elections re-gained momentum, as the ability of international actors to enhance the process heightened. Indeed, as soon as an authoritarian regime collapsed, international organizations providing electoral and democracy assistance increased their activism considerably. As a result, in the Arab region, elections held during transitions away from authoritarianism have shown greater international involvement. Tunisia organized parliamentary and presidential elections in 2011, 2014, and 2019, and they included a multitude of political parties and candidates running for office. International electoral observers have largely agreed on the fact that Tunisian elections were free and fair (Murphy 2013).[6] The 2012 Egyptian parliamentary and presidential elections were, likewise, deemed free and fair by many international observers, and the turnout for the first time surpassed 50% of the adult population.[7]

International actors working on electoral assistance managed to have more direct access to political parties and civil society. In Tunisia, they assisted pre-electoral arrangements, provided extensive training to candidates, supported logistics during elections and empowered local NGOs in their advocacy activities (Marzo 2020). Nascent national institutions became the target of specific training aimed at bolstering their capacity to ensure that each candidate would abide by the rule of law and the constitution. In addition, democracy promoters carried out initiatives that empowered political candidates to convey their messages to voters. They also delivered training to a broad spectrum of political parties to improve the ability of candidates to debate policy and politics (Marzo 2020). As international attention increased, candidates or political parties were less likely to manipulate procedures. From a procedural point of view, all these activities boost the fairness of electoral competitions.

However, as the Tunisian case demonstrates, electoral assistance has devoted overwhelming attention to the procedures of democracy, believing that the holding of competitive elections represents an accomplishment from which democracy would naturally take off. A minimalist conception of democracy still dominates the agency of electoral assistance organizations, which erroneously assume that competitive elections will improve the quality of democracy. The international emphasis on elections as the 'essence of democracy' creates great expectations among citizens, who think that elections will trigger immediate and tangible changes in their lives. As elections are only a moment, however important, of a democratic system, post-election periods generate disillusion and cynicism among citizens.

The contrast between people's expectations about competitive elections and the post-elections assessment finds illustration in survey results. On the one hand, public opinion polling from the region between 2011 and 2015 indicated that most Arab citizens want to be governed by rulers chosen in free and fair elections (Tessler et al. 2012; Robbins 2015). On the other hand, survey evidence suggests that elections are not perceived as having any effect on the quality of democracy and the relationship between citizens and institutions. ArabBarometer and ArabTrans surveys indicate that after ten years since the Tunisian democratic transition began citizens are not cognizant of democratic mechanisms and are not aware of their role and rights within the democratic system (Teti et al. 2019).

In this context, democratic elections remain an 'externally sponsored' mechanism that complies with international standards, but are devoid of meaning and material benefits for those who vote. Instead, international democracy promoters and election observers tend to consider their mission accomplished as soon as a round of free and fair competitive elections has taken place.

Iraq is a clear example of the deep cleavage between the Western ideal that elections are a driver of democratization and the reality on the ground. Unlike the Tunisian and Egyptian cases, where popular uprising and demands for change managed to overthrow incumbent powers, the Iraqi political transition away from authoritarianism originated from a foreign invasion – the US occupation of Iraq in 2003. Following Saddam's demise, international actors attempted to arrange a schedule for the transitional period, emphasizing their preference for establishing democracy through competitive elections, despite citizens having a very limited understanding of their functioning and meaning. Elections in Iraq were held twice in 2005 (in January and December), then again in 2010, in 2015, 2018 and 2021. International organizations have devoted attention to enhancing the competitiveness of elections. Yet, assistance has not been directed toward bolstering citizens' participation, inclusiveness and understanding of electoral processes. In addition, other components of democracy that heavily affect election dynamics and results, such as freedom of the press, minority and youth participation, institutional responsiveness and accountability, seem not to be the priority.

International assistance should spend more time and money on strengthening voters' understanding of – and inclusion in – the electoral process, and promoting other long-term actions to enhance citizens' constructive and active participation in elections, rather than focusing on elections strictly speaking. The success of elections in democratizing setting is not necessarily proportional to their fairness and competitiveness. Indeed, without preparing societies for elections, involving actively as many citizens as possible, and defining a democratic political process that is the *raison d'être* of elections, it will be impossible to conduct 'good' elections and establish a democratic relationship between citizens and their government through them.

Conclusion

For decades, international monitoring of elections has been considered the best way to ensure the integrity of elections in authoritarian settings and unconsolidated regimes. However, as this chapter discussed, electoral observers were not only ineffective but also ended up reinforcing ruling autocrats. Electoral observers allowed incumbents to arrange multiparty 'façade elections,' while they controlled resources, national institutions, information and the opposition. The chapter discussed how, in the Arab World, the practice of international monitoring produced stronger 'perverse effects' than elsewhere in the world and contributed to the resilience of authoritarianism.

Elections were 'externally' encouraged in illiberal settings where the population had very limited preparedness and poor understanding of the mechanisms of democracy, and where rulers arbitrarily controlled national institutions, the press and resources. Thus, they were able to manipulate elections in a way that was hard to detect for electoral observers, who often limited their monitoring activities to the days of elections. When the Arab uprisings led to the demise of authoritarianism and the political space opened up, electoral assistance increased its room for maneuvering, and multiparty free, fair, and competitive elections took place in a number of Arab countries. Yet, the overwhelming focus on the procedural aspects of elections has remained the foremost concern for IOs and INGOs that promote democracy. This chapter argues that the paradigm of electoral fetishism has not changed after the 2011 revolts. In democratizing countries – or in the ones not yet fully back to full authoritarianism – the enormous emphasis on competitive elections created considerable expectations among voters, who believed economic benefits and stability could originate from elections. This did not occur, leading to disillusion.

Holding elections, regardless of how fair and competitive they are, is not as significant in the democratic life of a country if the quality of other components of democracy is low or absent. While this reasoning can be applied to all settings, it holds particularly true in the Arab World, a region where authoritarian rulers have always manipulated elections in their favor. To enhance the capacity of elections as a driver of democracy, international electoral assistance should complement the programs enhancing procedural aspects, with a series of long-term activities that foster participatory governance, promote the understanding of democracy's principles and mechanisms, support inclusion, quality of information, encourage public debate and improve citizens' capacity to demand institutional accountability and responsiveness.

Notes

1 NED was created in 1983 as the US engine for democracy promotion.
2 The UN declaration of Principle for International Election Observation and its Code of Conduct is the latest document that set standard and norm for observation. International Human Rights Law Group's 1984 publication of Guidelines for International Election Observing was perhaps the first to standardize election-monitoring practices across organizations, and it set out some very basic guidelines for election observation. The Inter-Parliamentary Union published Free and Fair Elections: International Law and Practice in 1994, written by a prominent international human rights lawyer Guy Goodwin-Gill and updated in 2006.23 The OSCE /ODIHR's Election Observation Handbook, now in its fifth edition, was first published in 1996. NDI contributed a number of guides and handbooks on election-monitoring techniques (also aimed at domestic observers), including the quick count, monitoring of voter registration, and media monitoring. The Handbook for European Union Election Observation was first published in 2002 and is now in its second edition.2 Initiated by the Carter Center, NDI, and the UN, and commemorated in 2005 at the UN headquarters in New York, 23 organizations signed on to the Declaration of Principles and Code of Conduct for International Election Observation, a document that individual election observers are now expected to sign and to which they must adhere. The full text of the Declaration of Principle for international election observation and code of conduct can be consulted at http://scm.oas.org/pdfs/2008/CP20254-Anexo%20IV%20English.pdf
3 See for instance the Human Right Watch Report: www.hrw.org/world-report/2005/country-chapters/tunisia
4 To read the full text of "IRI Election Assessment in Egypt, November 15–21, 2005"
5 https://georgewbush-whitehouse.archives.gov/news/releases/2005/09/20050910-11.html
6 National democratic Institute (NDI) International foundation for electoral system (IFES), the European Union, The United National, and Carter Centre, among others concluded that the 2014 elections were particularly important in consolidating the country's democratic gains since the 2011 revolution including registration procedure, transparency, and election day.
7 For more information see the Carter Center report: www.cartercenter.org/resources/pdfs/news/peace_publications/election_reports/egypt-2011-2012-final-rpt.pdf

References

Abbott, Lucy. 2018. 'International democracy promotion and democratization in the Middle East and North Africa'. *Democratization* 25(1): 178–184.
Beaulieu, Emily and Susan Hyde. 2009. 'In the shadow of democracy promotion: Strategic manipulation, international observers, and election boycotts'. *Comparative Political Studies* 42(3): 392–415.
Brumberg, Daniel. 2002. 'Democratization in the Arab world? The trap of liberalized autocracy'. *Journal of Democracy* 13(4): 56–68.
Brown, Stephen. 2001. 'Authoritarian leaders and multiparty elections in Africa: How foreign donors help to keep Kenya's Daniel arap Moi in power'. *Third World Quarterly* 22(5): 725–739.
Bunce, Valerie and Sharon Wolchik. 2006. 'International diffusion and post-communist electoral revolutions'. *Communist and Post-Communist Studies* 39(3): 283–304.
Bush, Sarah. 2015. *The Taming of Democracy Assistance*. Cambridge: Cambridge University Press.
Bush, Sarah and Lauren Prather. 2017. 'The promise and limits of election observers in building election credibility'. *The Journal of Politics* 79(3): 921–935.

Bush, Sarah and Lauren Prather. 2018. 'Who's there? Election observer identity and the local credibility of elections'. *International Organization* 72(3): 659–692.

Carothers, Thomas. 1997. 'The rise of election monitoring: The observers observed'. *Journal of Democracy* 8(3): 17–31.

Corstange, Daniel and Nikolay Marinov. 2012. 'Taking sides in other people's elections: The polarizing effect of foreign intervention'. *American Journal of Political Science* 56(3): 655–670.

Corstange, Daniel. 2018. 'Kinship, partisanship, and patronage in Arab elections'. *Electoral Studies* 52: 58–72.

Cavatorta, Francesco. 2013. *The International Dimension of the Failed Algerian Transition: Democracy Betrayed?* Manchester: Manchester University Press.

Daxecker, Ursula. 2014. 'All quiet on Election Day? International election observation and incentives for pre-election violence in African elections'. *Electoral Studies* 34: 232–243.

Diamond, Larry. 1990. 'Three paradoxes of democracy'. *Journal of Democracy* 1(3): 48–60.

Durac, Vincent and Francesco Cavatorta. 2009. 'Strengthening authoritarian rule through democracy promotion? Examining the paradox of the US and EU security strategies: The case of Bin Ali's Tunisia'. *British Journal of Middle Eastern Studies* 36(1): 3–19.

Gandhi, Jennifer. 2008. *Political Institutions under Dictatorship*. New York: Cambridge University Press.

Gandhi, Jennifer and Ellen Lust-Okar. 2009. 'Elections under authoritarianism'. *Annual Review of Political Science* 12(1): 403–422.

Godinez, Jonathan. 2018. 'The vested interest theory: Novel methodology examining US-foreign electoral intervention'. *Journal of Strategic Security* 11(2): 1–31.

Heydemann, Steven. 2007. *Upgrading Authoritarianism in the Arab World*. Washington, DC: Saban Center for Middle East Policy at the Brookings Institution.

Huntington, Samuel. 1991. 'Democracy's third wave'. *Journal of Democracy* 2(2): 12–34.

Hyde, Susan. 2011. *The Pseudo-Democrat's Dilemma: Why Election Observation Became an International Norm*. Ithaca, NY: Cornell University Press.

Hyde, Susan and Nicolay Marinov. 2014. 'Information and self-enforcing democracy: The role of international election observation'. *International Organization* 68(2): 329–359.

Kelley, Judith. 2009. 'D-minus elections: The politics and norms of international election observation'. *International Organization* 63(4): 765–787.

Kraetzschmar, Hendrik and Francesco Cavatorta. 2010. Bullets over ballots: Islamist groups, the state and electoral violence in Egypt and Morocco'. *Democratization* 17(2): 326–349.

Kuntz, Philipp and Mark Thompson. 2009. 'More than just the final straw: Stolen elections as revolutionary triggers'. *Comparative Politics* 41(3): 253–272.

Kuzio, Taras. 2005. 'Russian policy toward Ukraine during elections'. *Demokratizatsiya* 13(4): 491–517.

Levitsky, Steven and Lucan Way. 2010. *Competitive Authoritarianism: Hybrid Regimes after the Cold War*. Cambridge: Cambridge University Press.

Lindberg, Staffan. 2006. *Democracy and Elections in Africa*. Baltimore, MD: John Hopkins University Press.

Lust-Okar, Ellen. 2009. 'Reinforcing informal institutions through authoritarian elections: Insights from Jordan'. *Middle East Law and Governance* 1(3): 3–37.

Marzo, Pietro. 2020. 'International democracy promoters and transitional elites: Favourable conditions for successful partnership. Evidence from Tunisia's democratization'. *Cambridge Review of International Affairs* 33(3): 307–329.

Merloe, Patrick. 2015. 'Authoritarianism goes global: Election monitoring vs. disinformation'. *Journal of Democracy* 26(3): 79–93.

Miller, James. 1983. 'Taking off the gloves: The United States and the Italian elections of 1948'. *Diplomatic History* 7(1): 35–56.

Murphy, Emma. 2013. 'The Tunisian elections of October 2011: A democratic consensus'. *The Journal of North African Studies* 18(2): 231–247.

Nielson, Daniel, Susan Hyde and Judith Kelley. 2019. 'The elusive sources of legitimacy beliefs: Civil society views of international election observers'. *The Review of International Organizations* 14(4): 685–715.

Robbins, Michael. 2015. 'After the Arab spring: People still want democracy'. *Journal of Democracy* 26(4): 80–89.

Rubin, Barry. 1999. 'External factors in Israel's 1999 elections'. *Middle East Review of International Affairs* 3(4): 30–48.

Sadiki, Larbi. 2009. *Rethinking Arab Democratization: Elections without Democracy*. Oxford: Oxford University Press.

Schmitter, Philippe and Terry L. Karl. 1991. 'What democracy is... and is not'. *Journal of Democracy* 2(3): 75–88.

Schedler, Andreas. 2002. 'Elections without democracy: The menu of manipulation'. *Journal of Democracy* 13(2): 36–50.

Schedler, Andreas. 2013. *The Politics of Uncertainty: Sustaining and Subverting Electoral Authoritarianism*. New York: Oxford University Press.

Schumpeter, Joseph. 2010 [1942]. *Capitalism, Socialism and Democracy*. London: Routledge.

Tessler, Mark, Amaney Jamal and Michael Robbins. 2012. 'New findings on Arabs and democracy'. *Journal of Democracy* 23(4): 89–103.

Teti, Andrea, Pamela Abbott and Francesco Cavatorta. 2019. 'Beyond elections: Perceptions of democracy in four Arab countries.' *Democratization* 26(4): 645–665.

Williamson, Scott. 2021. 'Elections, legitimacy, and compliance in authoritarian regimes: Evidence from the Arab world'. *Democratization* 28(8): 1483–1504.

Van Hüllen, Vera. 2019. 'Negotiating democracy with authoritarian regimes: EU democracy promotion in North Africa'. *Democratization* 26(5): 869–888.

17
THE INDEPENDENCE REFERENDUM IN KURDISTAN

Sara Dilzar Mustafa

Introduction

On September 25, 2017, the independence referendum in the Kurdistan region of Iraq (KRI), an autonomous region in Northern Iraq, shook the Iraqi state to its core. The Kurds have been struggling for their independence from repressive Iraqi regimes for almost a century and in 2005 were granted autonomy through a written constitution declaring Iraq a federal state. Yet, this did not stop the Kurdish aspiration for self-determination and independence, even though neither the political elite nor civil society acted genuinely to bring it about up until the 2017 referendum. The referendum itself was not organized by the federal Iraqi or Kurdistan regional government, nor was it a decision initially agreed upon by either parliament. Rather, it was coordinated under the instructions of the at-that-time president of the KRI, Masoud Barzani, who is also the leader of the Kurdistan Democratic Party (KDP), one of the two main parties ruling in the Kurdistan region together with the Patriotic Union of Kurdistan (PUK). The Kurdistan region has a multiparty system with the KDP and the PUK as the two dominant ruling parties alongside smaller parties such as the Goran Party (Change Movement), the Kurdistan Islamic Group (KIG), the Kurdistan Islamic Union (KIU), and even smaller parties representing diverse groups in the region. The two main parties have managed to shape the politics of the region and established their own spheres of influence in different cities with separate military forces and intelligence agencies.

The common explanation for why the Kurds did not push for independence before the 2017 referendum is that, due to the power and influence granted to both parties, they were able to settle for being a part of Iraq within a federal system and cooperate in the Kurdistan region through dividing power and resources. It is then the competition between the KDP and the PUK that was a major catalyst in launching the 2017 referendum, which was more an instrument for intra-Kurdish political struggle rather than a genuine move toward establishing independence (Mustafa 2020).

Accordingly, this chapter shows that party politics and internal Kurdish rivalries led to the campaign process that defined the issue and mobilized public opinion on the referendum question. Generally, the campaign was grounded in nationalist rhetoric, and the arguments and statements the political elite made were aimed at creating a clear-cut path toward independence, although it was known that such a move would not please the central Iraqi state and the international community more broadly. To further substantiate these points, this chapter explores the political party dynamics in the Kurdistan region of Iraq, how they influence public opinion, and to what extent their internal competition impacts the region. The organization and campaign structure of the independence referendum will then be clarified, with a focus on public opinion, nationalist rhetoric, and the timing of events that created a window of opportunity for the referendum to occur.

Iraqi Kurds go to the polls

On March 1, 2015, the Kurdistan Independent High Elections and Referendum Commission (KHEC) was established with the specific role of organizing the referendum (Bogers 2019). Although it has been emphasized that the KHEC should have remained an independent and impartial body immune to party politics, the core of the KHEC membership consisted of members loyal to the major political parties. The KDP retained the Chair position, a PUK member became the Deputy Chair, and the Kurdistan Islamic Union held the Executive Director's post, while the Goran Party took on the role of Head of the Electoral Division. The KHEC documented the entire process and even set up a committee of journalists and media workers to broadcast the Kurdish referendum and keep the world updated on the Kurdish referendum on Kurdish terms. Many other committees were formed within the KHEC, including a committee in charge of negotiations with representatives of disputed areas, a political and economic committee, an international and diplomatic committee that managed all foreign relations, committees to deal with neighboring countries, and a committee to deal with Baghdad.

Regardless of the fact that the KHEC was established in 2015 for the purpose of organizing the referendum, the actual campaign was not held until three weeks before the referendum date. This delay in the campaign process was due to the uncertainty surrounding the referendum, as during that time the Kurdish political elite held various meetings with Iraqi and international representatives whom all warned against holding the referendum (Barzani 2020).

Upon its establishment, the KHEC began making preparations for both in-person voting at polling stations and e-voting procedures. The Commission finally announced the campaign for the referendum on September 5, 2017, and the region saw an escalation of official negotiations coinciding with the timing of the referendum (Palani et al. 2019). The organization of the voting process itself consisted of preparing more than 2000 polling stations, which required hiring around 17,000 employees (Rzepka 2017). Polling stations were organized in the four provinces of Erbil, Sulaymaniyah, Duhok, and Halabja, as well as in the disputed regions of Kirkuk, Diyala, and Nineveh. The ballot paper and question was prepared by the KHEC and was written in Kurdish, Arabic, Turkish, and Syriac to represent the diverse population of the region. The question given to voters was: 'do you want the Kurdistan Region and the Kurdistani areas outside the administration of the Region to become an independent state?'

Visual campaigns in the form of billboards, posters, and banners covered some cities, especially the capital, and rallies attended by Barzani and the political elite were organized in across the region (Bogers 2019). Large banners advocating a 'Yes' vote written in English and Kurdish were hung around the cities, especially in Erbil and Duhok, where the KDP influence had always been most dominant. The referendum was held on September 25, 2017, and the KHEC released the initial results two days later, on September 27. Overall, the number of eligible voters in the region and abroad were 4,581,255 citizens, while the number of actual participants in the referendum vote totaled 3,305,925 voters; 98,945 voters were eligible for e-voting online, with which the results were 76,623 'Yes' votes (99.13%) and 699 'No' Votes (0.87%), while 21,623 votes were discounted. The Commission suspects that these individuals did not complete the voting process online after registering their names (S.H. Karim, Personal Communication, April 20, 2021). The results, released through an official document by the Commission's Council, recorded that the number of invalid votes in total was 40,011 (1.21%), the number of blank ballots, in which neither 'Yes' or 'No', was chosen was 9,368 (0.28%), and the number of votes that did not meet the conditions stipulated was 170,611 (5.16%) (H. Karim, Personal Communication, April 20, 2021). Voter turnout had been 72.16%, and exactly 92.73% of eligible voters voted 'Yes', while 7.27% of voters voted 'No'. The nature of counting the paper ballots was peculiar, as in each city the votes were counted and were not brought back physically to Erbil for the votes to be counted together by one committee. The PUK-affiliated cities blocked their ballots from going to Erbil, and the same occurred in KDP-dominated areas. Thus the two parties counted the votes separately and then communicated them to each other to be added together to form the total number of votes, but no central counting occurred (H. Karim, Personal Communication, April 20, 2021). The KHEC – formed for the referendum – had been given the task of managing other elections as well, but after the referendum the KHEC stopped functioning, as it did during the years before the referendum.

The independence referendum as a result of inter-party competition

Referenda are a way of assessing, rather crudely, the people's stances on specific social or political issues, and they are sometimes employed to make decisions about self-determination or secession. A referendum is a method of measuring peoples' direct votes, and these votes can either bind or prevent a government from enacting a law (Boyer 1982). In the context of self-determination, this definition is simplified as 'an important measure submitted to direct vote of the people' (Boyer 1982: 13). Secession, on the other hand, is the 'formal withdrawal from an established, internationally recognized state by a constituent unit to create a new sovereign state' (Griffiths 2014: 559). One of the reasons for decisions made toward secession is that those groups that lose their autonomy are most prone to seeking self-determination (Hechter 2000; Hale 2004; Siroky and Cuffe 2015). Ethnic groups that suffer the most under central governments are likely to seek self-determination to escape the host state, and when these groups' living standards deteriorate it is more likely that they seek self-determination.

Anderson and Erk (2009) ask whether self-rule accommodates or exacerbates ethnic divisions within a state. This raises the question of what kind of conditions are necessary for a minority group given as much autonomy and self-rule as the KRI to inevitably bring up secession at a certain point. This broad argument is found in the literature on federalism and how some federal arrangements, including the one for the Iraq-Kurdistan region, can actually be detrimental to federalism itself, as it can lead to secessionist movements (Craven 1991; Buchanan 1995; Adeney 2004; Mohammed 2013; Le Billon 2015). A few of these authors note that the way Iraqi federalism was established, rushed, and under American influence, as well as the extent of autonomous powers granted to Kurdistan, paved the way for a resulting secessionist movement (Dawoody 2006; Moore 2006; Stansfield and Anderson 2009; Mohammed 2013; Le Billon 2015). Constitutional errors and the unresolved tension between Kurds and Arabs have allowed the KRI the freedom to turn away from Iraq and any obligation toward the central government, particularly in the context of historical conflicts. In terms of 'constitutional errors', the emphasis on territorial integrity in the absence of the actual ability to control vast swathes of it, as the rise of IS clearly indicated, suggested to Kurds that their future might not be within such a weak state. As Dawoody (2006: 494) illustrates, 'the Constitution obligates the federal government alone with the task of maintaining the integrity of the Iraqi state by stating' (Article 107) that 'the federal authority will maintain the unity of Iraq, its integrity, independence, sovereignty and its democratic federal system'. This did not really stand up to scrutiny in reality and allowed the KRI to turn away from Iraq. Thus, the referendum became an opportunity to grasp at a time when the Iraqi state was significantly weakened by the onslaught of IS.

Opportunities for secession arise for ethnic groups when the host government is vulnerable and weak. A loss of autonomy is a major basis for secessionist movements (Horowitz 1985; McGarry and O'Leary 1993; Hale 2000). Siroky and Cuffe (2015) mention that those ethnic groups that are autonomous and have their own institutional arrangements are more likely to secede. In the Kurdistan region, independence had been considered an option since 2014. The Iraqi state had been under extreme pressure from IS, its own population, and a deteriorating economy, which compared rather unfavorably to the KRI's relative stability and development. When the region lost its access to oil revenues and received a lower budget from the central Iraqi government in 2015, plans for an independence referendum were designed.

The holding of the referendum was therefore justified as necessary at a time when Baghdad had been failing to meet the responsibilities it had to the Kurdistan Regional Government (KRG) and the Constitution (O'Driscoll and Baser 2019). The 2017 referendum was neither declared as a move toward secession nor did the Kurdish political elite acknowledge that secession was the aim of the referendum. In fact, the political elite in the region maintained that the referendum process was a way to garner Kurdish society's opinion and was established and funded through the KDP structures (Strachota and Lang 2017).

The influence political party competition has had on the referendum is tremendous. In fact, without the competition between the two parties, there would not have been an opportunity for one. This competition, alongside PUK's own internal frictions, and the impact of the fight against battle intersected to create the opportunity for the KDP to further their plans for the independence referendum, as the PUK's adamant policy on a united Iraq prevented the KDP from pursuing independence in the past. The PUK has always had some influence in Baghdad, and any movement that might strain this relationship would harm the party's influence, which it uses for the benefit of the cities it rules (PUK Official, Personal Communication, July 25, 2021). The PUK's close relationship with the central government of Iraq (Palani et al. 2021) also prevented the KDP from garnering extra concessions or disputed territories. The KDP's loss of support from the public, shown through demonstrations in Kurdish cities against corruption and for the return of monthly wages, as well as a sharp decline in the economy from the war with the Islamic State, further influenced the KDP to pursue a referendum to revitalize its role and primacy in Kurdistan. The call for a referendum occurred when the PUK's position was weakening in the competition between them. Such weakness was due to both intra-party dynamics and the unpopularity of Iraq's central government, which the PUK supported. More specifically, on the one hand, an internal split that followed the death of its leader Talabani in 2017 debilitated the party. On the other hand, Baghdad's inability to deal effectively with the presence of the IS undermined PUK's political appeal.

In addition to inter-party rivalry and competition, the shock of the IS military gains in Iraq provided a further impetus to the referendum in two distinctive ways. When IS overtook Iraq's oil fields, the revenues that the Iraqi government was supposed to forward to the Kurdistan Regional Government dried up, creating an internal socio-economic and political crisis. As a result of this, in 2014, the Kurdish population had their salaries cut (O'Driscoll and Baser 2019). This provided an incentive for the KDP to try to address the internal economic and political crisis by channeling internal displeasure toward independence. Second, the Kurdish political elite thought that the Kurds' role as frontline fighters in the battle against IS increased its international standing. The president of Kurdistan autonomous region at the time, Masoud Barzani, acted on this belief by promoting Kurdish aspirations for independence. Moreover, as they fought off IS, the Kurdish Peshmerga took control of the disputed oil fields in the oil-rich city of Kirkuk. This was a significant step for the Kurds, as the city and its resources would be crucial to their success if Kurdistan ever acquired its independence. The timing of these events paved the way for the campaign and organization of the referendum to occur with little resistance and in a manner that can only be described as nationalistic in nature.

Campaign and timing

Barzani's presidency should have ended in 2013, but his term was extended for two years by parliament (Mohammedali and Movileanu 2020). As mentioned, by 2015, the region was in a critical situation due to the fight against IS, the financial crisis, and the political inter-party struggle. At this point in time, Barzani's extension had ended, and the KDP pushed for another extension citing two main arguments: the situation the KRI was in required an experienced and strong executive and, at the same time, there was no alternative to Barzani, who enjoyed considerable public support (Hama and Abdullah 2021). The Goran Party rejected this extension and caused a political upheaval by protesting against Barzani and attacking KDP offices. Due to these actions, Goran Party members and the Speaker of Parliament were prevented from entering parliament (O'Driscoll and Baser 2019). As no decision could be achieved amidst the political inter-party rivalry, the Kurdistan Parliament was suspended, and Barzani continued as President of the Region. This allowed Barzani and the KDP to continue in their trajectory toward independence without a parliamentary opposition.

It is crucial to emphasize here that Masoud Barzani himself had called for the referendum, and this was not a decision made by the Kurdistan regional parliament, suggesting that political party competition had a significant impact on the timing of the referendum (Mustafa 2020). In the end, it was the KDP that became the leading instigator of the referendum, which included the campaign and the role of the main party in the region. As it has been made clear, both the PUK and the Goran Party had begun to lose influence in the region throughout the years 2015–2017, and tensions had developed with the KDP. This explains how the PUK and the Goran Party eventually lost authority in decision-making procedures, and the KDP pushed forward as the main driver of the referendum process. The referendum itself furthered KDP's dominance in the region, ousting other parties from power (O'Driscoll and Baser 2019).

The campaign before the referendum is usually a decisive moment in defining the issue at hand and mobilizing public opinion for it and therefore emphasizing that the way the question and issue are framed is important to the outcome of the referendum in general (De Vreese and Semetko 2004). The campaign for the referendum focused on three main elements: Kurdish identity, the historic denial of a nation-state for the Kurds, and the failure of the Iraqi state.

O'Driscoll and Baher (2019) emphasize how throughout the campaign process both 'rally around the flag' rhetoric and ethnic nationalism were used by the political elite. They highlight, specifically, how political parties in the KRI used nationalist rhetoric to gain power from Baghdad, thus suggesting that the KDP used the referendum to gain and maintain power in the region and against Baghdad, allowing the region to be almost completely independent from Baghdad. However, the campaign for the referendum and the rhetoric used was employed in a way to convince the people that they were the ultimate decision-makers in the process and that the referendum was not elite-driven, but elite-accommodated for the people to decide whether they wanted an independent Kurdistan region. This was combined with rhetoric on the historic denial of a nation-state for the Kurds unfolding from the time the Ottoman Empire was fragmented and up until Saddam Hussein's tyrannical regime (Vali 1998; O'Drsicoll and Baser 2019;

Mohammed and Alrebh 2020). This rhetoric was followed by the argument from the political elite that Iraq had failed as a federal state, and the Kurds could no longer continue living in a state that had detrimental implications for the region and its citizens (Barzani 2020). The failures that were highlighted were the incompetence and corruption of the government, economic grievances, and its inability to meet the basic needs of its population, which included electricity, water, education, job opportunity and reconstruction of cities (Cordesman and Molot 2019). In addition to these failures of the Iraqi state, the Kurdish elite also expounded on the constitutional violations committed against the Kurdistan region. The supposed violations of the Iraqi state are related to 55 Articles in the Constitution, with 12 Articles unimplemented or unfulfilled since the making of the Constitution in 2005.

All these violations have been documented and published as a constitutional justification for the referendum (KRG 2017). It is highlighted that Iraq has first and foremost failed to establish itself as a federation and has failed to establish a Supreme Court. Articles referring to the Kurdistan region's ownership and control over its own oil and gas resources have been violated and the region has never been paid its full portion of revenues as stipulated in the Constitution, suffering a significant loss of revenue in 2014–2015 and onwards. Article 140 on disputed territories, including Kirkuk, has been continuously violated, and Iraq has failed to protect its citizens and territories equally (KRG 2017). The Kurdish political elite highlighted the lack of democratic procedures in the state and was determined to show that their immediate concern was democracy and legitimacy.

Throughout the referendum preparations and campaign process, the political elite attempted to make the procedures as democratic as possible. However, parliament had been suspended, and it only reconvened ten days before the referendum to approve the KHEC's activities. Some factions within the PUK, KIU, and the Goran Party boycotted the referendum up until days before it took place, suggesting that they were not willing to risk losing power, territory, resources, or their political positions. These parties had been against the independence referendum from the very start. However, the campaign process, the elite speeches and rallies all created the sense that being against the holding of the referendum was equivalent to being unpatriotic and against the Kurdish cause.

The outcome of the referendum clearly favored an independent Kurdistan, but the referendum was not 'campaigned' on as an official move toward independence. Barzani explicitly stated that he had no plans for immediate declarations of statehood after the referendum, but instead he would begin talks with Baghdad to solve the difficult issues between Baghdad and Kurdistan. Barzani emphasized that the aim of the Kurdish referendum was to grant future generations a better opportunity for self-determination and that the referendum would not serve any political agenda but would simply express the will of the Kurdish nation (Barzani 2020). The Prime Minister at the time, Nechirvan Barzani (Rudaw 2017), also stated that '[t]he outcome does not mean we will immediately embark (on independence), but it will show the international community what the population wants'.

Barzani had signed a regional order to form the KHEC to leave the management of the referendum to an entity that would appeal to the public as an institution with no political ties to reaffirm the notion that the referendum was for the purpose of voicing the nation's will and not the political parties' one. Although the KHEC included members from many different political parties, the KDP was the ruling party and the only party to lead the referendum process. This was made clear after the PUK and Goran Party were significantly weakened and no longer competitors in the historical political party rivalry within the region. Therefore, the role the KHEC played in the referendum and campaign process was possible because of the KDP.

Conclusion

The aftermath of the referendum proved deleterious to the region and its institutions. Barzani (2020) contended that the referendum was a legitimate political, geographical, national, and historical cause, the outcome of a century-long struggle against tyrannical regimes, genocide, mass execution, and displacement. The Iraqi response to the referendum was to exclude all Kurdish members of its parliament from meetings, conduct violent military interventions in disputed areas, block border crossings, and ban all air travel to and from the Kurdistan region. A significant event occurred in October 2017 that rattled the KDP–PUK relations, in which the PUK signed an agreement with the Iraqi force, *Hashd al-Shaabi*, brokered by the late Iranian General Qassem Suleimani (Hama and Jasim 2017). This agreement was for the purpose of surrendering the oil-rich city of Kirkuk, protected at the time by Peshmerga forces. The Peshmerga under PUK leadership withdrew from the disputed area under PUK orders, catching the KDP Peshmerga off-guard as the Iraqi army took over the area.

This event created a deep chasm between the KDP and the PUK, leading to a fragmentation and factionalism that had not occurred in decades. While the PUK was weakened during the referendum process, the KDP was able to allocate resources, and public support, and push the independence agenda forward. The October event weakened both parties though and it allowed Baghdad to gain the upper hand, and, most significantly, destroyed public support for the two political parties, as the event had resonated within the region's citizens, reminding them that the political parties had not altered their drive for power in the region. The rhetoric of the referendum and the campaign was nationalistic, and yet events after the referendum proved that consolidation of power by the political elite would always be at the forefront of political party politics to the detriment of citizens. The PUK's need to regain legitimacy, resources, and power undid the unity the referendum had brought about in the region. This has been a repeating theme in the political party competition in the Kurdistan region, clarifying that when one party is weakened the other will take the opportunity to further its own agenda.

References

Adeney, Katharine. 2004. 'Between federalism and separatism'. In Ulrich Schneckener and Stefan Wolff (eds.), *Managing and Settling Ethnic Conflicts*. London: Palgrave Macmillan, 161–175.

Anderson, Lawrence and Jan Erk. 2009. 'The paradox of federalism: Does self-rule accommodate or exacerbate ethnic divisions?' *Regional and Federal Studies* 19(2): 191–202.

Barzani, Masoud. 2020. *Staking Our Claim*. Erbil: Roksana Printing House.

Bogers, Tim. 2019. *Organising and Contesting the 2017 Kurdish Referendum on Independence: Political Opportunities, Mobilisation Structures and Framing Processes in Iraqi-Kurdistan*. Utrecht University – MA Thesis. Available at: https://studenttheses.uu.nl/bitstream/handle/20.500.12932/33863/Thesis%20Final.pdf?sequence=2&isAllowed=y.

Boyer, J. Patrick. 1982. *Lawmaking by the People: Referendums and Plebiscites in Canada*. Toronto: Butterworths.

Buchanan, Allen. 1995. 'Federalism, secession, and the morality of inclusion'. *Arizona Law Review* 37: 53–63.

Cordesman, Anthony and Max Molot. 2019. *Iraq as a Failed State*. Washington, DC: Center for Strategic and International Studies/Working Paper 12. Available at: https://csis-website-prod.s3.amazonaws.com/s3fs-public/publication/191118_Iraq_Failed_state_report.pdf.

Craven, Greg. 1991. 'Of federalism, secession, Canada and Quebec'. *Dalhousie Law Journal* 14(2): 231.

Dawoody, Alexander. 2006. 'The Kurdish quest for autonomy and Iraq's statehood'. *Journal of Asian and African Studies* 41(5–6): 483–505.

DeVreese, Claes and Holli Semetko. 2004. *Political Campaigning in Referendums: Framing the Referendum Issue*. London: Routledge.

Griffiths, Ryan. 2014. 'Secession and the invisible hand of the international system'. *Review of International Studies* 40(3): 559–581.

Hale, Henry. 2000. 'The parade of sovereignties: Testing theories of secession in the soviet setting'. *British Journal of Political Science* 30: 31–56.

Hale, Henry. 2004. 'Divided we stand: Institutional sources of ethno-federal survival and collapse'. *World Politics* 56(2): 165–193.

Hama, Hawre Hasan and Farhad Hassan Abdullah. 2021. 'Political parties and the political system in Iraqi Kurdistan'. *Journal of Asian and African Studies* 56(4): 754–773.

Hama, Hawre Hasan and Dastan Jasim. 2017. 'The loss of disputed territories: What is next for the Kurdistan region?' *Middle East* 21(2): 58–68.

Hechter, Michael. 2000. 'Nationalism and rationality'. *Studies in Comparative International Development* 35(1): 3–19.

Horowitz, Donald. 1985. *Ethnic Groups in Conflict*. Berkeley, CA: University of California Press.

Kurdistan Regional Government (KRG). 2017. *The Constitutional Case for Kurdistan's Independence & A Record of the Violation of Iraq's Constitution by Successive Iraqi Prime Ministers and Ministers, the Council of Representatives, the Shura Council, the Judiciary and the Army*. Erbil: Author.

Le Billon, Philippe. 2015. 'Oil, secession and the future of Iraqi federalism'. *Middle East Policy* 22(1): 68–76.

McGarry, John and Brendan O'Leary. 1993. 'Introduction: The macro-political regulation of ethnic conflict'. In John McGarry and Brendan O'Leary (eds.), *The Politics of Ethnic Conflict Regulation: Case Studies of Protracted Ethnic Conflict*. London: Routledge, 1–40.

Mohammed, Ala Jabar. 2013. *The Politics of Iraqi Kurdistan: Towards Federalism or Secession?* PhD Thesis. University of Canberra. Available at: https://researchsystem.canberra.edu.au/ws/portalfiles/portal/33685752/file.

Mohammed, Jihan and Abdullah Alrebh. 2020. 'Iraqi Kurds: The dream of nation state'. *Digest of Middle East Studies* 29(2): 215–229.

Mohammedali, Yaseen Taha and Angela Movileanu. 2020. 'Kurdistan parliament: Emergence and development of a non-state parliamentary system'. *PalArch's Journal of Archaeology of Egypt/Egyptology* 17(6): 1117–1125.

Moore, Margaret. 2006. 'The ethics of secession and post-invasion Iraq'. *Ethics and International Affairs* 20(1): 55–78.

Mustafa, Sara Dilzar. 2020. 'Iraqi Kurdistan independence referendum: Political parties, opportunity and timing'. *British Journal of Middle Eastern Studies* 48(5): 890–907.

O'Driscoll, Dylan and Bahar Baser. 2019. 'Independence referendums and nationalist rhetoric: The Kurdistan Region of Iraq'. *Third World Quarterly* 40(11): 2016–2034.

Palani, Kamaran, Jaafar Khidir, Mark Dechesne and Edwin Bakker. 2019. 'The development of Kurdistan's de facto statehood: Kurdistan's September 2017 referendum for independence'. *Third World Quarterly* 40(1): 2270–2288.

Palani, Kamaran, Jaafar Khidir, Mark Dechesne and Edwin Bakker. 2021. 'De facto states engagement with parent states: Kurdistan's engagement with the Iraqi Government'. *British Journal of Middle Eastern Studies* 48(4): 770–788.

Rudaw News. 2017. *Independence Referendum Will Be Held This Year: PM Barzani*. Available at: http://www.rudaw.net/english/kurdistan/250320171.

Rzepka, Marcin. 2017. 'Recalling the past, voting for the future. Reflections and observations after the independence referendum in Kurdistan, September 25 2017'. *Orientalia Christiana Cracoviensia* 9: 143–147.

Siroky, David and John Cuffe. 2015. 'Lost autonomy, nationalism and separatism'. *Comparative Political Studies* 48(1): 3–34.

Stansfield, Gareth and Liam Anderson. 2009. 'Kurds in Iraq: The struggle between Baghdad and Erbil'. *Middle East Policy* 16(1): 134–145.

Strachota, Krzysztof and Jozef Lang. 2017. 'Iraqi Kurdistan–the beginning of a new crisis in the Middle East?' *OSW Commentary* No. 247. Available at: https://www.osw.waw.pl/sites/default/files/commentary_247.pdf.

Vali, Abbas. 1998. 'The Kurds and their others: Fragmented identity and fragmented politics'. *Comparative Studies of South Asia, Africa and the Middle East* 18(2): 82–95.

18
GENDER QUOTAS, CONSTITUENCY SERVICE, AND WOMEN'S EMPOWERMENT

Lessons from Algeria

Meriem Aissa

Introduction

Due to the adoption of gender quotas, women's descriptive representation, measured as the proportion of seats held by women in a national legislature, increased over time in several countries in the Middle East and North Africa (MENA) (IPU 2020).

Since 1995, women's descriptive representation has increased significantly in Algeria, Mauritania, Morocco, Saudi Arabia, and United Arab Emirates (IPU 2020: 11). Reflecting global trends (Krook 2009), gender quotas played a key role in increasing women's representation in decision-making bodies. But what is the impact of gender quotas? What role do they play in women's empowerment in the MENA region? Gender and politics scholars have increasingly sought to examine the role that women legislators play in legislatures in the MENA region (Benstead 2016, 2019; Darhour 2012; Moghadam and Haghighatjoo 2016; Nanes 2015; Sater 2007; Shalaby 2016). Similar to scholars who focus on democratic contexts, these scholars have examined whether there is a link between women's descriptive representation and women's substantive representation.

In the seminal work on representation, Pitkin (1967: 209) defines substantive representation as 'acting in the interest of the represented, in a manner responsive to them.' Gender and politics further theorized the importance of having women present in politics (Phillips 1995). Phillips argued that due to their unique life experiences, women are more likely than men to represent women's interests. Empirical research on democratic contexts tends to find that women legislators are more likely than their male counterparts to represent women's interests (Carroll 2002; Franceschet and Piscopo 2008; Schwindt-Bayer 2006; Thomas 1991). Other scholars are more skeptical. For example, Tremblay and Pelletier (2000) argue that political party affiliation may be more important for substantive representation than gender. They conclude that electing feminists affiliated with leftist political parties, whether women or men, is more likely to lead to women's substantive representation than electing conservative women. Moreover, while women legislators prioritize women's issues, this does not necessarily lead to policy gains (Franceschet and Piscopo 2008).

Concerning authoritarian regimes, the evidence is mixed. For example, Tripp (2001) distinguishes between African countries where there are autonomous women's movements and others where they do not exist. She argues that in contexts where there are autonomous women's movements, women representatives affiliated with the regime may forge alliances with women's movements and advocate on behalf of women. On the other hand, Goetz and Hassim (2003) draw a distinction between democratic South Africa and authoritarian Uganda to argue that while both countries experienced improvements in women's descriptive representation, authoritarianism, patronage, and male party leaders prevent women from substantively representing women in Uganda. Other scholars argue that gender quotas still matter and find evidence that in contexts like Uganda, gender quotas have empowered ordinary women who in the aftermath of quota adoption became more outspoken and involved in their communities (Burnet 2011).

Research on the MENA region has also produced inconsistent findings. While some scholars find that women advocate on behalf of women (Benstead 2016, 2019; Darhour 2012; Moghadam and Haghighatjoo 2016), other scholars are more skeptical (Sater 2007; Shalaby 2016). Relevant to this study is the finding that women's presence in politics increases the likelihood that female citizens will request access to services (Benstead 2016, 2019), and that in the aftermath of quota adoption perceptions of women leaders change (Benstead 2011).

To build on these studies, I focus on the case of Algeria, where women's descriptive representation increased from 8% to 31.6% after the adoption and implementation of a gender quota in 2012. The chapter draws from semi-structured interviews with Algerian women parliamentarians. Moreover, to further theorize the agency of women legislators in the MENA region and the impact of gender quotas on women's empowerment, I draw on existing gender and politics scholarship, which has sought to challenge the notion that women in the region are powerless victims waiting to be saved by the West (Abu-Lughod 2013; Mohanty 1991).

In the aftermath of 9/11, the notion that Muslim women are 'oppressed' and 'need to be saved by the West' dominated Western discourse (Abu-Lughod 2013; Young 2003). The Bush administration argued that Afghan women needed to be saved, as it sought to build support for the US invasion of Afghanistan (Young 2003). Young (2003: 10) argues that 9/11 led to the emergence of a security state that portrayed itself as 'protector of innocent citizens and liberator of women and children to justify consolidating and centralizing executive power at home and dominative war abroad.' The notion that women in Afghanistan needed to be saved was even taken up by Laura Bush, who made a radio address to the nation on November 17, 2001, highlighting the violence that Afghan women experienced under the rule of the Taliban (Young 2003). Ever since, various actors, including some feminists in the West, used the images of Afghan women in burqa to create the category 'Muslim woman.' Similarly, Mahmood (2005) critiques scholars, both feminist and non-feminist, for employing the binary concepts 'resistance' and 'subordination' when studying agency of Muslim women. For example, she finds that men are no longer the only ones who are reading and interpreting the Quran and the Hadith (sayings of the Prophet). One particular woman, Hajja Faiza, who led lessons in an Egyptian mosque, did not give specific instructions or her own opinion when other women asked about what Islam says about female genital mutilation. Instead, she said that the Hadith that has been used to justify female circumcision is weak, meaning that the Prophet did not actually support female circumcision, but she concluded by saying that it is up to individuals to decide and that they should speak to a doctor (Mahmood 2005). Another example that Mahmood gives is the decision by Hajja Faiza to lead prayer, which is usually done by men in mosques. After receiving criticism from both women and men for this act, Hajja Faiza did not justify her action in terms of gender equality or women's rights but instead said that male scholars disagreed about whether women could lead prayer.

These contributions suggest that women in the Arab world have an interest in making their voices heard, but they do not necessarily prioritize women's issues and rights. One of the main findings that emerged from my interviews is that Algerian women parliamentarians rejected the notion that they have an obligation to introduce women's rights laws, emphasizing that they have a responsibility to represent all Algerians. But, they added that they want to change perceptions of women leaders, which I find they work toward achieving via constituency service and helping male citizens solve their everyday problems. Thus, unlike previous research, which focuses on the link between women's descriptive representation and the gendering of the policy-making process, I find that there is a link between women's descriptive representation and *men's* substantive representation.

Consistent with the themes of this volume, the argument here is that the institutional features of elections matter. Gender quotas played a key role in increasing women's presence in Algerian politics and helping women parliamentarians transform public spaces, which used to be dominated by men. Moreover, the context matters. The case of Algeria is complex for several reasons. Algeria is particularly unique in the region because of its political history and the impact of settler colonialism. As Lazreg (1990: 759) points out: 'the French chose Islam as the Algerians' common denominator and as grounds on which to fight them. Likewise, Algerians responded by making Islam the bastion of their resistance to colonialism.'

Algeria's complex political history is important to understanding why women parliamentarians rejected the notion that they have an obligation to introduce and pass women's rights laws. Like their predecessors, women parliamentarians were strategic actors who focused on achieving women's empowerment not via the passage of laws, but on changing perceptions of women leaders and transforming public spaces. This is because women's rights continue to be controversial and perceived as a threat to Algeria's culture (Lazreg 2019). Like women freedom fighters, women parliamentarians expressed agency even though they did not push for women's rights laws. I argue that this period of Algeria's political history was as significant for women's status in Algeria as the participation of women freedom fighters in the Algerian War of Independence. Even though women's descriptive representation has since decreased after the 2019 Hirak and the 2021 parliamentary elections, it is still worth examining the role that these women played.

Background

Algeria has been shaped by two key historical moments. Unlike its counterparts in the region, Algeria experienced a brutal form of settler colonialism and a seven-year war of liberation that continues to shape state-society relations. The main debate and source of conflict has revolved around how to undo the impact of colonialism and reclaim Algerian culture (Lazreg 2019). The civil war of the 1990s further exacerbated conflict as elites disagreed about the participation of Islamists (Roberts 2003; Werenfels 2007). In the aftermath of the civil war, Algeria's culture and women's rights continue to be inextricably tied (Lazreg 2019). Below, I briefly introduce the case of Algeria and explain how its complex history and politics have impacted women's empowerment.

Algerian War of Independence (1954–1962)

During the Algerian War of Independence (1954–1962), a diverse group of male elites, including communists, Islamists, intellectuals, military officers, Arabs, Kabyles (non-Arab Algerians), conservative nationalists, and secular nationalists, came together to form the National Liberation

Front (FLN) and officially declare war against France on November 1, 1954 (Derradji 2016; Quandt 1969). But, as Quandt (1969) argues, after independence, intra-elite power struggles became a key feature of state institutions.

Women's rights were particularly controversial because state actors sought to protect Algeria's Islamic identity (Lazreg 2019). This in turn is because when French colonizers invaded Algeria in 1830, they were obsessed with Islam, which they saw as an obstacle to their missionary activity, and they treated the veil and women as the symbol of Islam (Bradford 1999; Clancy-Smith 1996; Lazreg 1990, 2019). As a result, during the Algerian War of Independence, both men and women were united in their struggle against French colonialism.

Women in particular played an important role in the Algerian War of Independence. As Lazreg (2019) argues, even though the women freedom fighters did not push for women's rights laws, their legacy is undeniable. For example, in the 2019 Hirak, women protesters carried slogans declaring that they were the 'daughters of Hassiba Ben Bouali [woman freedom fighter].' In the post-independence period, although the Constitution prohibited discrimination on the basis of sex and guaranteed women's right to work and equal pay, the state did not pursue specific policies to improve women's status (Amrane-Minne 1999; Lazreg 2019; Moghadam 2001). In the 1980s, Algeria experienced an economic crisis that led ordinary citizens and opposition groups to protest against the state and its policies. The greatest threat that the regime faced was a growing Islamist movement. To placate Islamist groups, the regime adopted a conservative Family Code in 1984 that institutionalized polygamy, repudiation, and inequality in inheritance (Charrad 2001). Moreover, the regime enacted political and economic reforms, including the establishment of a multi-party system (Bouandel 2003). For the first time in Algeria's political history, the FLN, which had led the anti-colonial struggle, had to compete with other parties for seats in parliament and local and regional assemblies. This led to the legalization of Islamist political parties, such as the Islamic Salvation Front (FIS), the Movement of Society for Peace (MSP or Hamas), and the Islamic Renaissance Movement (an-Nahda), and secular political parties such as the Rally for Culture and Democracy (RCD), the Socialist Forces Front (FFS), and the Workers' Party (PT) led by women's rights activist Louisa Hanoune. The RCD and FFS also represent Kabyle Algerians.

The Black Decade

In 1990–1991, the FIS emerged victorious in local and parliamentary elections. To prevent Islamists from controlling parliament and local and regional assemblies, the military canceled the second round of the legislative elections and banned the FIS. This led to a decade-long civil war between armed groups affiliated with the FIS and the regime. About 200,000 people died, and several thousand disappeared.

The civil war further exacerbated the intra-elite conflict. The regime was divided between those who supported the repression of Islamists and their exclusion from formal politics and those who argued that the regime should negotiate with Islamists (Werenfels 2007). Secular opposition parties were also divided on this issue (Roberts 2003).

In 1999, Abdelaziz Bouteflika was elected. He stayed in power until his removal from office after the 2019 Hirak protest movement. He negotiated an agreement with extremist groups, which brought an end to the civil war, but neither civil society actors nor opposition parties participated (MacQueen 2009). Bouteflika also advanced women's rights to sideline extremist groups and to signal to the international community that Algeria was a modern state (Tripp

2019). Important reforms included the criminalization of sexual harassment in 2004, reforms to the family and nationality codes in 2005, the adoption of a gender quota in 2012, and the criminalization of domestic violence in 2015. Scholars argue that these reforms took place due to pressure from the women's movement (Tripp 2019; Youssef 2020). But, despite reforms, women's rights remain weaker in Algeria compared to Morocco and Tunisia (Lazreg 2019; Tripp 2019). This is due to unresolved debates around the role of Islam, women's rights, and Algeria's identity (Lazreg 2019). Moreover, after the civil war, there were divisions among secularists (Roberts 2003). While some secular parties support the inclusion of Islamists, others argue that Islamist parties should be excluded from formal politics (Roberts 2003).

Due to these divisions, some Islamists and secular leaders decided to forge an alliance with the Bouteflika regime. For example, Khalida Toumi, a feminist who was an opponent of the regime in the 1980s and member of the secular Kabyle party, the RCD, became an ally of Bouteflika in the 2000s. Amar Ghoul, member of the Islamist party the MSP, defected to the regime and created the Rally of Algerian Hope (TAJ), which became one of the four main parties in the Bouteflika alliance. Finally, Amara Benyouness, member of the secular opposition, also defected to the Bouteflika coalition. Thus, the regime, which was already divided along ideological, ethnic, and regional lines in the aftermath of independence became even more fractured under the leadership of Bouteflika.

Quota adoption

In 2012, Algeria adopted and implemented a gender quota that led to a significant increase in the proportion of seats held by women from 8% to 31.6%, making Algeria the leader in the Arab world in terms of women's descriptive representation (Ould Ahmed 2012). Gender and politics scholars have argued that women's movements have played a crucial role in pressuring regimes in Africa to increase women's presence in politics (Tripp 2016; Kang and Tripp 2018). In her case study of quota adoption in Algeria, Tripp (2016) challenges the argument made by Ross (2008), who argued that in oil-producing countries like Algeria, women's representation is lower due to economic underdevelopment and low levels of women's labor force participation. Instead, Tripp argues that the presence of a strong women's movement played a key role in pressuring the regime to adopt and implement the gender quota in 2012. First, the women's movement became more active after the civil war ended in the early 2000s. Women's rights activists were particularly concerned with reforming the Family Code, criminalizing sexual harassment and domestic violence, and increasing women's representation in elected assemblies (Tripp 2016). To build on the work of Tripp (2016, 2019), I focus on the impact of one of these reforms, the gender quota. What impact did the gender quota have on women's empowerment? What takes place after elections? How do women parliamentarians represent their constituents?

Gender quotas and women's empowerment

To examine the impact of the gender quota on women's empowerment, I carried out semi-structured interviews with women parliamentarians, male parliamentarians, and women's rights activists. In this chapter, I draw from my interviews with women parliamentarians. I interviewed 30 women parliamentarians from different political parties, including the FLN, the National Rally for Democracy (RND), TAJ, Algerian Popular Movement (MPA), RCD, PT, NAHDA-ADALA-BINA, and MSP.

Building on the work of Benstead (2016, 2019), I focused on constituency service. I asked female parliamentarians: Do women citizens reach out to you when they face a particular problem? Do you receive more requests from men or women? Out of the 30 women I interviewed, 16 reported that they received about an equal number of requests from women and men. Women parliamentarians reported that women approach them because they feel more comfortable talking to another woman, while male citizens approach women parliamentarians because they trust them. I also found that women parliamentarians do more than just help citizens who face personal and community problems. They added that they are 'therapists,' i.e., women and men come to see them to ask for personal advice and talk about their personal problems. Moreover, some of the women parliamentarians reported that male citizens approach them when they face a community problem. Some of the male citizens I spoke to reported that women are more helpful than men.

Requests from women and men

More than half of the women deputies reported that they receive about an equal number of requests from men and women.[1] Interviewees suggested that men approach women because they trust them, while women citizens approach women deputies because of their shared gender. As one of the women parliamentarians said, 'I get both women and men. Women tell me, "You can feel our pain." Men approach me because they trust us. Many men send me messages on Facebook. They say that "women are honest and do not ask for bribes."'[2] An RND deputy added, 'it is not only women. Men trust women more than they trust men. We have proved our competence on the field.'[3]

Women parliamentarians also reported that, unlike their male colleagues, they do not ask for anything in exchange for helping citizens.[4] This might explain why men approach women. Women also approach women due to gender segregation, especially in small towns. As one of the women parliamentarians told me, women who come from small towns are not used to interacting with men who are not their family members.[5] Women parliamentarians added that they are like 'therapists' and that their constituents talk to them about their personal problems when they visit their offices.[6] As one of the women parliamentarians said, 'sometimes I am a therapist. I tell women to spend more time with their husbands, go to dinner.'[7] One of the Islamist women added that a young couple came to see her about public housing and that by the end of the conversation, she found herself giving them advice about marriage. She said, 'even if I do not solve their problems, they leave feeling better because at least I listened to them.'[8] Another woman parliamentarian said, 'I welcome them with a smile. They say, "Even if you cannot get our problem solved, we are satisfied."'[9]

Some women parliamentarians also added that they try to interact with ordinary citizens on a daily basis.[10] As one, 'I use public transportation. I try to show to people that I am just like them.'[11] An RND deputy added that she interacts on a daily basis with her neighbors, helps them clean the building, talks to ordinary Algerians when buying her groceries, and that her daughter uses public transportation. She also added that she once told Ouyahia, secretary general of the RND, 'I do not live in Club des Pins [gated neighborhood where generals, party leaders, and other elites live] like you.'[12]

Another woman parliamentarian with a background in academia reported that after the uprising started in 2019 and even as protests intensified in October 2019, her neighbors told her that they were opposed to the regime but stated 'you are different.'[13] This is because it is common for Algerians to assume that parliamentarians are opportunists and that they just raise their hand to vote for laws that serve the interests of the regime. Corruption also increased in the past few elections. Ordinary citizens refer to parliament as '*parlement ta3 chkara*' (parliament of the bag of the money).

As a result, women parliamentarians, due to their gender and positive interactions with ordinary citizens, seem to be perceived as different from male politicians who engage in corruption. In the 2019 Hirak, one of the main slogans was 'you thieves, you ate the country.'

As one of the women parliamentarians said, 'Algeria won't succeed until women reach leadership positions. We have seen that men love the chair and the power and the money that comes with it. Men are selfish. Women think about others, their families, their society.'[14]

Critical actors and women's substantive representation

I also find that there are 'critical actors,' women who advocate on behalf of women. Childs and Krook (2006) developed the concept of critical actors to describe legislators who advocate on behalf of women and play a key role in shaping the policy-making process. There are some critical female actors who are more active in doing constituency service on behalf of female citizens, particularly on issues related to gender equality.[15] Parliamentarians with a background in law, for example, work with women going through a divorce.[16] One of the women does not have a background in law, so she hired a lawyer who takes on the cases of divorced women.[17]

Women who held leadership positions in local and regional assemblies reported that they are still in contact with women citizens whom they helped in the past.[18] Even the security guards in parliament know who the critical actors are. A woman with a background in academia affiliated with TAJ said that a security guard approached her when a divorced woman with two children went to parliament asking for help. She said,

> The security guards know that I see everyone. They do not even have to make an appointment. A lot of the time, if the husband does not work, he can kick her out. The other problem is that parents tell their daughters, 'You can come but leave your kids with their father.' I investigated and I found out that her husband lived with his family and did not work. The law does not help her. For now, she is in an apartment. I had to go to the governor of Algiers. She also has a job.[19]

This particular woman parliamentarian, and others, noted that constituency service is not sufficient on its own. She noted that Algeria needs more laws to protect marginalized groups, especially divorced women.[20] Due to unemployment and a housing crisis, it is common for women to live with their husband's family. But, as this example illustrates, if a husband divorces his wife and he does not have a stable income, the law does not protect women.[21] An RND deputy with a background in law also said that she proposed the establishment of publicly funded centers for women who get married to someone who lives in another province and then have to complete the divorce proceedings in their husband's province.[22]

Women citizens also contact women parliamentarians when they experience sexual harassment in the workplace.[23] Women parliamentarians reported that they have had to intervene on behalf of women by writing letters to directors if the women complain about their colleagues or report the problem to government officials if the abuser is a director. Further, women deputies reported intervening on behalf of women who needed access to public housing. One of the women deputies told me, 'I have helped a lot of women get housing. I contact authorities and ask that they give special consideration to women who are not employed, single, divorced, and women whose parents died. We give them priority.'[24] Lastly, one of the FLN women reported that she confronted the Minister of Women's Affairs after she marginalized the female staff.[25]

Women's descriptive representation and men's substantive representation

The findings that I have presented above are consistent with previous work (Benstead 2016 and 2019; Chattopadhyay and Duflo 2004; Childs 2004), which finds that female representatives are more responsive to female constituents than their male counterparts. However, based on surveys that she carried out in Tunisia, Benstead (2019) finds that women local councilors are less likely to receive requests from male citizens who need access to community resources such as electricity, roads, transportation, and water. She argues that this might be because 'men are more likely to have professional competencies and networks in the construction and industrial sectors, greater political clout, and denser political networks needed' (Benstead 2019: 108). My research nuances this conclusion. I found that there are women who receive requests from men when they face community problems.[26] Problems that affect local communities include floods, access to electricity and heat, and the poor condition of hospitals, roads, and schools.

According to the women parliamentarians, their presence in the 'field' is important for changing perceptions of women leaders. As one of the women deputies told me, the principal of a school in a remote area was surprised to see her when she showed up wearing boots and pants.[27] She distinguished herself and other women. She said, 'there are deputies of hair salons and there are deputies of the field.' A female mayor told me that she works on weekends and holidays to help with trash pickup and that people are surprised to see a mayor cleaning.[28]

There are also differences among women parliamentarians depending on their backgrounds. For example, a woman deputy who was a party activist before entering parliament told me that she helped men and local party leaders in her province and that by helping them, she restores confidence in the party and changes perceptions of women leaders. She said, 'women who are competent can represent the party and women.'[29]

Women parliamentarians also help men who come from impoverished neighborhoods. One of the RND women explained to me that she works with men from conservative towns, and they contact her anytime there is a problem.[30] She called two of them and told them to tell me about their experience. One man said, 'I first went to her to ask for heat and blankets. She helped 20 families in my neighborhood. In Algeria, one woman is better than 1000 men.'[31] Another male constituent I spoke to on the phone said, 'women do not forget about the people after the elections. The men do not help us after the election is over.'[32] This RND woman emphasized that she works with men from conservative towns.

As we were talking, she showed me the messages that she had received from people who wanted to register to vote and support her party's candidate in the presidential election. I saw not only voter identification cards of individuals but also of entire families. One other woman deputy also told me that citizens she helped in the past contacted her to ask whom they should vote for.[33] One woman affiliated with TAJ mentioned that poor people vote in elections, but she did not specifically say that voters contact her.[34] One of the women deputies reported that even parliamentarians ask for her help.[35] She said, 'they think that because I am the president of an important committee, I can intervene.'[36] But, she added that she would rather spend her time helping the people who elected her.

Moreover, I found that women parliamentarians who do not have political experience interact with constituents from their own professions.[37] One of the female doctors affiliated with the FLN said, a group of doctors experienced a problem and went on strike. They contacted me and we were able to find a solution. With dialogue, we can find solutions. I spoke to them then I spoke to the governor of the province. I organized a meeting between them, and they reached an agreement.[38] Similarly, a female professor affiliated with TAJ reported that she invited university students to parliament.[39] She said that they even got to attend the committee meetings. She said that she introduced them to both hard-working male and female deputies. She even added that the group was so large that the head of security was worried and was checking in on her. And, after they spent the whole day in parliament, they were impressed.

Islamist opposition women also receive requests when there is a community problem.[40] One stated, however, that she cannot help citizens solve their problems because the regime does not want Islamist parties to build a reputation for helping ordinary citizens.[41] She said, 'I receive requests from many citizens. But, because I am affiliated with an Islamist party, ministers and governors refuse to help me. The regime does not want people to receive help from Islamist parties.' But her colleague reported that it depends on the parliamentarian and her strategies.[42] She said that the regime tries to sabotage women parliamentarians affiliated with the opposition, but she resists. She said, 'when the prime minister was in parliament, I was scheduled to address my colleagues. The FLN decided to reschedule me for a very late time slot. My colleague left but I stayed and made my statement. I drove home alone very late and I live far from Algiers.' This particular Islamist woman said that when ordinary citizens contact her about a community problem, she voices their concerns in parliamentary sessions when ministers are in parliament.

Conclusion

One of the main findings of this study is that women's descriptive representation contributes to ordinary men's substantive representation, which might help change attitudes toward women leaders in the long term. My study adds to existing theoretical work on women's representation. Gender and politics scholars argue that since women's interests have been overlooked, women are more likely to represent women (Phillips 1995). This is especially important in contexts where there is a history of mistrust, and in situations where new issues arise that require gendered expertise (Mansbridge 1999). Nonetheless, in Algeria, women deputies emphasize that they are representatives of all citizens and reject the notion that they have an obligation to introduce and pass women's rights laws.

Still, consistent with previous work (Benstead 2016, 2019), I find that women parliamentarians do receive requests from female citizens. But I further nuance previous work on the MENA region by adding that there is a link between women's descriptive representation and *men's* substantive representation. Building on the work of Childs and Krook (2006), I argue that there are certain critical women actors who receive requests from men facing community problems. Additional research is necessary to theorize men's substantive representation, which I argue also deserves attention in gender and politics scholarship in the MENA region.

Notes

1. FLN interview 2 (02/2019); FLN interview 3 (02/2019); FLN interview 4 (02/2019); FLN interview 5 (02/2019); FLN interview 7 (03/2019); FLN interview 8 (03/2019); RND interview 2 (02/2019); RND interview 5 (04/2019); RND interview 6 (04/2019); MSP interview 1 (02/2019); NAHDA-ADALA-BINA interview 1 (03/2019); NAHDA-ADALA-BINA interview 2 (04/2019); TAJ interview 3 (03/2019); RCD interview 1 (03/2019); PT interview 1 (02/2019); RPR (former RND) interview 1 (04/2019)
2. NAHDA-ADALA-BINA interview 2 (04/2019)
3. RND interview 6 (04/2019)
4. FLN interviews 3 (02/2019); 13 (02/2019); RND interview 7 (10/2019); NAHDA-ADALA-BINA interview 2 (04/2019)
5. FLN interview 13 (11/2019)
6. TAJ interview 1 (03/2019); MSP interview 1 (02/2019); TAJ interview 3 (03/2019); FLN interview 10 (04/2019)
7. TAJ interview 1 (03/2019)

8 MSP interview 1 (02/2019)
9 TAJ interview 3 (03/2019)
10 FLN interview 2 (02/2019); RND interview 7 (10/2019); TAJ interview 1 (03/2019)
11 FLN interview 2 (02/2019)
12 RND interview 7 (10/2019)
13 TAJ interview 1 (03/2019)
14 FLN interview 9 (04/2019)
15 RND interviews 1 (02/2019); 3 (02/2019); 4 (04/2019); FLN interviews 3 (02/2019); 4 (02/2019); 6 (03/2019); 7 (03/2019); 9 (04/2019); 10 (04/2019); 12 (05/2019); RCD interview 1 (03/2019); TAJ interview 1 (03/2019)
16 FLN interview 6 (03/2019); RND interview 4 (04/2019); RCD interview 1 (03/2019)
17 RND interview 1 (02/2019)
18 FLN interview 9 (04/2019); RND interview 3 (02/2019)
19 TAJ interview 1 (03/2019)
20 TAJ interview 1 (03/2019)
21 RCD interview 1 (03/2019); Women's rights activist interview (05/2019)
22 RND interview 4 (04/2019)
23 FLN interviews 3 (02/2019); 7 (03/2019); 12 (05/2019); RND interview 3 (02/2019)
24 FLN interview 4 (02/2019)
25 FLN interview 10 (04/2019)
26 FLN interviews 1 (02/2019); 2 (02/2019); 3 (02/2019); 5 (02/2019); 7 (03/2019); RND interviews 1 (02/2019); 7 (10/2019); TAJ interview 1 (03/2019); MSP interview 1 (02/2019); NAHDA-ADALA-BINA interviews 1 (03/2019); 2 (04/2019); TAJ interviews 2 (03/2019); 3 (03/2019)
27 FLN interview 1 (02/2019)
28 Front Moustakbal interview 1 (10/2019)
29 FLN interview 7 (03/2019)
30 RND interview 7 (10/2019)
31 Male constituent phone conversation (10/2019)
32 Male constituent phone conversation (10/2019)
33 FLN interview 13 (11/2019)
34 TAJ interview 3 (03/2019)
35 FLN interview 13 (11/2019)
36 FLN interview 13 (11/2019)
37 FLN interviews 3 (02/2019); TAJ interview 1 (03/2019)
38 FLN interview 3 (02/2019)
39 TAJ interview 1 (2nd interview, 10/2019)
40 MSP interview 1 (02/2019); NAHDA-ADALA-BINA interviews 1 (03/2019); 2 (04/2019)
41 NAHDA-ADALA-BINA interview 1 (03/2019)
42 NAHDA-ADALA-BINA interview 2 (04/2019)

References

Abu-Lughod, Lila. 2013. *Do Muslim Women Need Saving?* Cambridge, MA: Harvard University Press.

Amrane-Minne, Danièle Djamila. 1999. 'Women and Politics in Algeria from the War of Independence to Our Day'. *Research in African Literatures* 30(3): 62–77.

Benstead, Lindsay J. 2011. 'Do Gender Quotas Affect Popular Support for Women as Good Political Leaders? A Cross-National Study of Gender Quotas and Political Attitudes in the Muslim World'. Presented at "Beyond the Numbers: The Effects of Electoral Gender Quotas", St. Louis, MO.

Benstead, Lindsay J. 2016. 'Why Quotas are Needed to Improve Women's Access to Services in Clientelistic Regimes'. *Governance* 29(2): 185–205.

Benstead, Lindsay J. 2019. 'Do Female Local Councilors Improve Women's Representation?' *The Journal of the Middle East and Africa* 10(2): 95–119.

Bouandel, Youcef. 2003. 'Political Parties and the Transition from Authoritarianism: The Case of Algeria'. *Journal of Modern African Studies* 41(1): 1–22.

Bradford, Vivian. 1999. 'The Veil and the Visible'. *Western Journal of Communication* 63(2): 115–139.

Burnet, Jennie E. 2011. 'Women Have Found Respect: Gender Quotas, Symbolic Representation, and Female Empowerment in Rwanda'. *Politics and Gender* 7(3): 303–334.

Carroll, Susan J. 2002. 'Representing Women: Congresswomen's Perceptions of Their Representational Roles'. In Cindy Simon Rosenthal (ed.), *Women Transforming Congress*, 50–68. Norman: University of Oklahoma Press:

Charrad, Mounira. 2001. *States and Women's Rights: The Making of Postcolonial Tunisia, Algeria, and Morocco*. Berkeley, CA: University of California Press.

Chattopadhyay, Raghabendra, and Esther Duflo. 2004. Women as Policy Makers: Evidence from a Randomized Policy Experiment in India'. *Econometrica* 72(5): 1409–1443.

Childs, Sarah. 2004. *New Labour's Women MPs: Women Representing Women*. New York: Routledge.

Childs, Sarah, and Mona Lena Krook. 2006. 'Should Feminists Give Up on Critical Mass? A Contingent Yes'. *Politics and Gender* 2(4): 522–530.

Clancy-Smith, Julia. 1996. 'The Colonial Gaze: Sex and Gender in the Discourses of French North Africa'. In L. Carl Brown, and Mathew S. Gordon (eds.), *Franco-Arab Encounters*, 201–228. Beirut: American University of Beirut.

Darhour, Hanane. 2012. *Implementation of Electoral Gender Quotas: Evidence from the 2002 Moroccan Elections*. Saarbrucken: LAP Lambert Academic Publishing.

Derradji, Abder-Rahmane. 2016. 'Account of the Algerian Urban Guerrilla Network and Its Role in the FLN's Campaign during the Battle of Algiers (1956–1958)'. *Alternatives: Turkish Journal of International Relations* 14(2): 39–59.

Franceschet, Susan, and Jennifer M. Piscopo. 2008. 'Gender Quotas and Women's Substantive Representation: Lessons from Argentina'. *Politics and Gender* 4(3): 393–425.

Goetz, Anne Marie, and Shireen Hassim. 2003. *No Shortcuts to Power: African Women in Politics and Policy Making*. New York: Zed Books.

Inter-Parliamentary Union. 2020. '25 Years after Beijing, IPU Analysis Shows that Gender Parity is Possible'. Available at: https://www.ipu.org/news/press-releases/2020-03/25-years-after-beijing-ipu- analysisshows-gender-parity-possible.

Kang, Alice J., and Aili Mari Tripp. 2018. 'Coalitions Matter: Citizenship, Women, and Quota Adoption in Africa'. *Perspectives on Politics* 16(1): 73–91.

Krook, Mona Lena. 2009. *Quotas for Women in Politics: Gender and Candidate Selection Reform Worldwide*. New York: Oxford University Press.

Lazreg, Marnia. 1990. 'Gender and Politics in Algeria: Unraveling the Religious Paradigm'. *Signs: Journal of Women in Culture and Society* 15(4): 755–780.

Lazreg, Marnia. 2019. *The Eloquence of Silence: Algerian Women in Question*. New York: Routledge.

MacQueen, Benjamin. 2009. *Political Culture and Conflict Resolution in the Arab World: Lebanon and Algeria*. Carlton, VIC: Melbourne University Press.

Mahmood, Saba. 2005. *Politics of Piety: The Islamic Revival and the Feminist Subject*. Princeton, NJ: Princeton University Press.

Mansbridge, Jane. 1999. 'Should Blacks Represent Blacks and Women Represent Women? A Contingent Yes'. *Journal of Politics* 61(3): 628–657.

Moghadam, Valentine M. 2001. 'Organizing Women: The New Women's Movement in Algeria'. *Cultural Dynamics* 13(2): 131–154.

Moghadam, Valentine M., and Fatemeh Haghighatjoo. 2016. 'Women and Political Leadership in an Authoritarian Context: A Case Study of the Sixth Parliament in the Islamic Republic of Iran. *Politics and Gender* 12(1): 168–197.

Mohanty, Chandra Talpade. 1991. 'Under Western Eyes: Feminist Scholarship and Colonial Discourses'. In Chandra Talpade, Ann Russo, and Lourdes Torres (eds.), *Third World Women and the Politics of Feminism*, 51–80. Bloomington, IN: Indiana University Press.

Nanes, Stefanie. 2015. '"The Quota Encouraged Me to Run": Evaluating Jordan's Municipal Quota for Women.' *Journal of Middle East Women's Studies* 11(3): 261–282.

Ould Ahmed, Hamid. 2012. 'Arab World Gets New Trailblazer for Women in Politics'. Reuters. Available at: https://www.reuters.com/article/us-algeria-parliament-women-idUSBRE85C0UH20120613.

Phillips, Anne. 1995. *The Politics of Presence*. New York: Oxford University Press.

Pitkin, Hanna. 1967. *The Concept of Representation*. Berkeley, CA: University of California Press.

Quandt, William. 1969. *Revolution and Political Leadership: Algeria 1954–1968*. Cambridge, MA: MIT Press.

Roberts, Hugh. 2003. 'The Algerian Catastrophe: Lessons for the Left'. *Socialist Register, Fighting Identities: Race, Religion, and Ethno-Nationalism*. Available at: https://socialistregister.com/index.php/srv/article/view/5797.

Ross, Michael L. 2008. 'Oil, Islam, and Women'. *American Political Science Review* 102(1): 107–123.

Sater, James N. 2007. 'Changing Politics from Below? Women Parliamentarians in Morocco'. *Democratization* 14(4): 723–742.

Schwindt-Bayer, Leslie A. 2006. 'Still Supermadres? Gender and the Policy Priorities of Latin American Legislators'. *American Journal of Political Science* 50(3): 570–585.

Shalaby, Marwa. 2016. 'Women's Political Representation and Authoritarianism in the Arab World'. Policy Brief, POMEPS: Project on the Middle East in Political Science, George Washington University.

Thomas, Sue. 1991. 'The Impact of Women on State Legislative Policies'. *The Journal of Politics* 53(4): 958–976.

Tremblay, Manon, and Réjean Pelletier. 2000. 'More Feminists or More Women? Descriptive and Substantive Representations of Women in the 1997 Canadian Federal Elections'. *International Political Science Review* 21(4): 381–405.

Tripp, Aili Mari. 2001. 'The Politics of Autonomy and Cooptation in Africa: The Case of the Ugandan Women's Movement'. *The Journal of Modern African Studies* 39(1): 101–128.

Tripp, Aili Mari. 2016. 'Women's Mobilization for Legislative Political Representation in Africa'. *Review of African Political Economy* 43(149): 382–399.

Tripp, Aili Mari. 2019. *Seeking Legitimacy: Why Arab Autocracies Adopt Women's Rights*. Cambridge: Cambridge University Press.

Werenfels, Isabelle. 2007. *Managing Instability in Algeria: Elites and Political Change Since 1995*. New York: Routledge.

Young, Iris Marion. 2003. 'The Logic of Masculinist Protection: Reflections on the Current Security State'. *Signs: Journal of Women in Culture and Society* 29(1): 1–25.

Youssef, Maro. 2020. 'Algerian Feminists Navigate Authoritarianism'. In Rita Stephan, and Mounira M. Charrad (eds.), *Women Rising: In and Beyond the Arab Spring*, 129–134. New York: New York University Press.

PART 4

Elections and campaigning

19
A MINORITY GOES TO THE POLLS
Arab voters in Israel

Arik Rudnitzky

Introduction

The first elections to the Israeli parliament, the Knesset, were held in January 1949, shortly after the cessation of hostilities between the nascent State of Israel and surrounding Arab countries. In the aftermath of the 1948 war, some 160,000 Arab inhabitants remained within the borders of the new state, comprising about 17% of the total Israeli population. In December 1948, on the eve of the elections to the first Knesset, the leaders of the new state, including Prime Minister David Ben-Gurion, decided to grant Israeli citizenship to those Arab inhabitants. Since then, by virtue of their citizenship in the new state, Israeli Arabs have the right to participate in Knesset elections. At the end of 2022, Israel's Arab population amounted to almost 2 million.

Arab politics in Israel has been conducted on two interconnected levels. One level concerns the organizational patterns of political bodies operating at the national or local level, such as official political parties and popular extra-parliamentary movements. A second level concerns the political behavior of Arab voters as reflected in their participation rate in the elections as well as the distribution of the actual votes to parties according to their political orientation. This chapter deals with the interaction between these two levels.

Political and ideological streams in Arab society in Israel

Arab society in Israel is not a homogenous political or ideological community, but rather a mosaic made up of four main streams: Arab-Israeli (Zionist); Arab-Jewish non-Zionist (Communist); Islamist; and Nationalist. These four approaches have been dominant in the Arab sector since the State of Israel was founded in 1948, although they were not all politically represented at local (municipal) or national (parliamentary) levels (Ghanem 2001).

Supporters of the Arab-Israeli (Zionist) stream accept the minority status of Arab citizens within a Jewish majority state, and they do not aim to undermine the balance of power between the Jewish majority and the Arab minority. They consider the Arab minority a national minority, but in contrast to the supporters of the other streams, voice no unequivocal demand for its recognition as such by the state. Arab representatives of this stream are members of Jewish-Zionist parties, both left and right. They rarely address ideological issues related to the desired nature of the state for Arab citizens, and in any case do not challenge the definition of Israel as a Jewish state. Instead, they focus on civic equality between Jews and Arabs within Israel, expressed in the demand for equal distribution of economic resources, equal opportunities in employment, and so on. Their tone is conciliatory, and their demands for change are articulated in ways designed to appeal to the sensitivities of the Jewish majority. For these reasons, in the past this stream was known as the 'moderate camp.'

The Arab-Jewish Communist stream has been part of the Israeli political scene since the first Knesset elections in 1949. They argue that discrimination against Arab citizens, which is intrinsic to the Zionist nature of the state, is effectively manifested in the privileging of Jewish over Arab citizens. Therefore, they openly call for the elimination of Israel's Zionist character, a step that they consider a precondition for the country's transformation into a democratic state. At the same time, they have demanded recognition of the Arab minority as a national minority. However, they fully accept the prevailing balance of power in Israel between a Jewish majority and an Arab minority. Furthermore, they hold joint Arab-Jewish political and social activism in high regard and reject separate political organizations on a national Arab basis, concerned that such separatism would undermine the promotion of Arab minority interests within Israel.

The ideology of the Islamist stream is grounded in the ideology of the Muslim Brotherhood, which advocates the establishment of an Islamic state operating according to Islamic law (*sharia*). Proponents of the Islamist stream believe that the Islamic religious component is the most important component of the identity of Arabs in Israel and therefore should be cultivated. They do not, however, deny Israel's Muslim citizens additional identities, such as Palestinian, pan-Arab, and civic Israeli. They reject Israel's Zionist nature, yet accept Israel's Jewish majority and dominant Hebrew culture as a *fait accompli*. Based on these understandings, Islamists urge the Arab minority to organize along Islamic religious lines, taking into consideration Israel's existing political reality.

The ideology of the Nationalist stream is based on the principles of the Pan-Arab nationalist movement, led in the 1950s and 1960s by Egyptian President Gamal Abd al-Nasser, and on the principles of the Palestinian national movement that crystallized throughout the 1970s and 1980s. The basic assumption of its proponents is that the Arabs in Israel are Palestinians. Their ultimate goal is to establish a single democratic state on the entire territory of Mandatory Palestine and unite with their Palestinian brethren in a single political entity. This stream holds a definite anti-Israeli and anti-Zionist approach, but given the historical balance of power between Israel and the Palestinian people, its proponents accept Israel as a given, and their desired unification with their Palestinian brethren has been limited to joint national and political aspirations. Proponents of the Nationalist stream demand cultural autonomy for Arabs in Israel as the first step toward a bi-national arrangement within Israel. Although they are organized for political action on a national Arab basis, they are not averse to Jewish-Arab collaboration at the tactical level.

While the Arab-Israeli and the Communist streams have taken part in Israeli parliamentary politics since the first Knesset elections in 1949, the Islamists and the Nationalists entered the parliamentary arena only at a later period, owing to political changes in the Israeli–Arab conflict and social changes in Arab community in Israel. These changes, which will be discussed below, entailed changes in the patterns of political organization of these four ideological streams and were also manifested in the political behavior of Arab voters. Therefore, the discussion of Arab citizens' participation in Israeli Knesset elections from a historical perspective can be divided into three distinct periods. The first period began in 1949 (1st Knesset elections) and ended in 1973 (8th Knesset elections); the second period began in 1977 (9th Knesset elections) and ended in 1999 (15th Knesset elections); the third period began in 2003 (16th Knesset elections) and continues up to this day.

Political recruitment, 1949–1973

Initially, the Arabs had to accommodate their new status as a minority in the state, and Arab politics was adaptive in nature for several reasons. First, the Arabs who remained in the country after the 1948 war were a defeated minority, overwhelmed by feelings of the loss and destruction of their homeland. It was a rural and conservative population, whose political, religious, and social leadership had left the country during the 1948 war (Bishara 1993). Second, the close supervision of the military government apparatus, which was active for 18 years between 1948 and 1966, made political activity in the Arab sector a tool in the hands of the Israeli establishment. On the one hand, the military government imposed strict sanctions on opposition elements in the Arab sector and thwarted any political organization on an Arab national basis. On the other hand, it granted benefits to traditional, notable figures and clan leaders who were not skilled in parliamentary political activity (Cohen 2010). Third, the physical detachment from Arab countries combined with the initiation of the Israeli government's economic development policy in the Arab sector led most of the Arab minority to come to terms with the state as a *fait accompli* and to accept the rules of the political game. This paved the way to the compartmentalization approach, that is, the separation between the Arabs' national identification with their Arab brethren across the border and their acceptance of Israeli civic identity (Rouhana 1997).

During the first period, only three of the four political streams historically structuring the Arab society – Israeli-Arab, Communist, and Nationalist – were active. The main feature of earlier Arab politicization within the State of Israel is the absence of autonomy or political initiative, which would begin to develop only in the early 1960s as a consequence of Nasser's pan-Arabism and especially following the 1967 war.

The Israeli-Arab Zionist stream was mainly constituted by Arab satellite lists of the main Jewish-Zionist parties, namely the Workers' Party of the Land of Israel (*Mapai*, from its Hebrew acronym) led by David Ben-Gurion and the United Workers Party (*Mapam*). The first stood for the status quo, while the second was in opposition to the military government and included Arab representatives in its ranks (Landau 1969). The hallmark of the Israeli-Arab stream was the absence of programmatic party-voters linkage and genuine politicization. For instance, Mapai's Arab satellite lists were *ad-hoc* political organizations established only at election time and not real parties. Local Arab leaders who drew their power from their strong ties with the Israeli political establishment and military government commanders headed these. Arab representatives were part of the coalition and were committed to parliamentary discipline dictated by Mapai, but they were never given ministerial posts. They did not deal with political or national issues, and gained the support of Arab voters based on local frameworks of affiliation, such as the clan, village, or religious community (Mendales 2018).

The second active stream was the Arab-Jewish Communist one, which was represented by the Israeli Communist Party (Maki, from its Hebrew acronym). While most of Maki's members were Jewish, the party won support among the Arab public for three main reasons: its hostility to Zionist ideology and criticism of the military government; its political platform in support of Arab nationalism in the Middle East and Israel's Arab population national distinctiveness; a legitimate political organization representing these Arab Nationalist features and at the same time operating within the framework of Israeli parliamentarism (Rekhess 1988). In 1965, Maki experienced an ideological divide when most of the Arab members, who espoused an Arab Nationalist approach to resolving the Israeli–Arab conflict, withdrew and formed the New Communist List (*Rakah*), a parallel mixed Arab-Jewish party in which most members were Arabs. By the early 1970s, *Rakah* established itself as the dominant party among Arab voters.

In clear rupture with the rest, the Nationalist stream, which began to organize in the late 1950s, was forced largely to operate underground. Influenced by the pan-Arab ideology of Egyptian President Gamal Abdel Nasser, several small nationalist movements emerged in the Arab sector and operated at the extra-parliamentary level. The most prominent movement was *al-Ard* ('the land,' in Arabic), established in 1959. Its members supported pan-Arab political unity and called for self-determination for the Arabs within Israel. In 1964 the Israeli authorities outlawed the movement. A year later, *al-Ard* members sought to run in the Knesset elections through an independent Arab list called the 'Socialist List,' but the Israeli Central Elections Committee disqualified it on the grounds that the list exploited Israeli democracy to undermine the state's foundations. That was the only initiative by the Nationalist stream to organize parliamentary activity during the period under discussion (Dallasheh 2010).

During the first period, the average voter turnout in Knesset elections in Arab localities – 83.8% – was higher than the average nationwide turnout, at 81.4%. Except for the first Knesset elections in 1949, which were held shortly after citizenship and the right to vote were granted to Arab inhabitants in the country, Arab turnout in Knesset elections was higher than the general turnout (see Table 19.1). The high participation rate of the Arabs was mainly due to the massive recruitment of voters under the auspices of the military government, which took advantage of the traditional, patriarchal structure of Arab society. It used clan leaders to influence voters to cast their ballot for the 'right party,' especially the Arab satellite lists affiliated with Mapai, the ruling party (Jiryis, 1976; Bäuml, 2017). For this reason, the period in question can be described as one of 'political recruitment.' Some scholars define Arab politics at that time as characterized by 'politics of coexistence' or 'politics of representation' (Ghanem and Mustafa 2009), explaining that the political behavior of the Arab minority was merely an attempt to live peacefully in coexistence with the Jewish majority. Therefore, according to this critical point of view, Arab representation in the Knesset was not effective. It was an ostensible representation that only served as a tool in the hands of the majority to present to the world how well representatives of the minority were integrated into conventional political institutions, as befits a democratic state.

During the first period, about half of Arab voters on average voted for the Arab satellite lists, which enjoyed dominant status. A considerable portion voted for Jewish-Zionist parties (mainly *Mapai* and *Mapam*) that enjoyed stable support (29% on average). A relatively small portion voted

Table 19.1 Knesset elections turnout (%), 1949–1973

Year	Knesset no.	Nationwide turnout	Arab turnout
1949	1	86.9	69.3
1951	2	75.1	85.5
1955	3	82.8	91.0
1959	4	81.6	88.9
1961	5	81.6	85.5
1965	6	83.0	87.8
1969	7	81.7	82.0
1973	8	78.6	80.0
Average		81.4	83.8

Sources: Reiter and Cohen, 2013; Israel's Central Bureau of Statistics website, www.cbs.gov.il; Israel's Central Elections Committee; The Israel Democracy Institute web site, www.idi.org.il

A minority goes to the polls

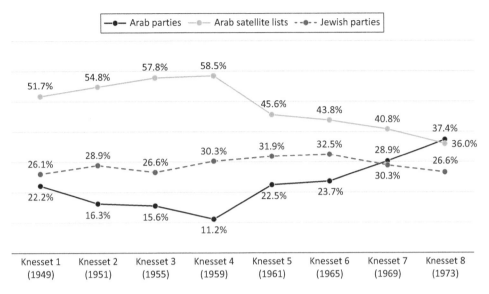

Figure 19.1 Breakdown of the Arab vote in Knesset elections, 1949–1973

for the Arab parties' bloc that included the Communist Party in its various incarnations (*Maki* and *Rakah*). By the late 1960s and early 1970s, the change in the political behavior of Arab voters was already evident. Support for the Arab satellite lists gradually eroded, as support shifted to the Arab parties' bloc. In the 1973 elections, for the first time, the vote for the Arab parties' bloc (mainly for *Rakah*) exceeded the vote for the Arab satellite lists and the Jewish-Zionist parties (see Figure 19.1).

The main reason for this change was the 1967 Six Day War, which almost overnight brought an end to the physical division between the 1948 Arabs and their 1967 Palestinian brethren when Israel captured the West Bank and the Gaza Strip. The Green Line, which was marked on the maps of the 1949 armistice agreements between Israel and its Arab neighbors, and for 18 years served as the country's borders, had virtually disappeared.

Political mobilization, 1977–1999

The second period witnessed the strengthening of Palestinian identity among Israeli-Arab citizens as a result of the renewed connection with their Palestinian brethren in the West Bank and Gaza Strip following the Six Day War (1967), the rise of the Palestinian Liberation Organization (PLO) in the late 1960s, and the development of Palestinian national leadership in the West Bank during the second half of the 1970s. The immediate manifestation of this process were the 'Land Day' events in March 1976, when dozens of demonstrators in Arab localities in the northern Galilee region took to the streets to protest the government's policy of expropriating Arab-owned land. Israeli police killed six young Arab citizens who participated in these demonstrations.

The Nationalist wave that swept the Arab sector during the late 1970s and early 1980s served as fertile ground for the establishment of non-parliamentary Arab organizations. The two most prominent bodies were the National Committee of the Heads of Arab Local Authorities, established in 1975 on the eve of the 1976 Land Day events, and the Supreme Monitoring Committee of the Arab Public in Israel, established in 1982 following Israel's military intervention in Lebanon. Nationalist sentiments in Arab society continued to surge during the late 1980s and early 1990s on the back of the First Intifada (1987–1993), the Gulf War (1991), and the establishment of the Palestinian Authority following the 1993 Oslo Accords (Rekhess 2007). However, the Arab political leadership was careful not to violate the rules of the game. Arab leaders emphasized that the Palestinian people's struggle to establish an independent state in the territories captured by Israel in 1967 was completely different from the struggle of the Arab public for equality and full civil rights within Israel (Rouhana 1991). Paradoxically, even as the results of the 1967 War brought Israel's Arabs citizens closer to their Palestinian brethren across the Green Line, events and conditions on the ground caused these two Palestinian populations to develop in different directions.

During this period, the political map of the Arab sector became more diverse and increasingly decentralized. At first, it seemed that *Rakah* had become the most powerful party among Israeli Arabs. Its platform, emphasizing national affiliation and solidarity with the Palestinian people as well as Israeli citizenship, had become accepted among most of the Arab public in Israel (Kaufman 1997). Popular support for *Rakah* was then translated into political achievements. In the run-up to the 1977 Knesset elections, *Rakah* established the Democratic Front for Peace and Equality (*Hadash*) as a large-scale Arab-Jewish political organization. *Hadash* won the support of more than half of the Arab voters, thus weakening the stand of the Arab satellite lists, leading to their total erosion in the 1981 elections. By the mid-1980s, *Hadash*, the representative of the Arab-Jewish Communist stream, established itself as the dominant party on the Arab streets.

In the second half of the 1980s, however, *Hadash*'s dominant status gradually eroded, as the political power of the Nationalist and Islamist streams increased. The Nationalists, who until the early 1980s had confined their activism to the extra-parliamentary arena, now made several attempts to enter parliament. The first attempt took place during the 1984 Knesset elections with the establishment of the Progressive List for Peace (PLP). The list was established as a new Arab-Jewish party, similar to *Hadash*, but it included former senior members of the *al-Ard* nationalist movement. The PLP's platform resembled to that of *Hadash*, but it considered the Arabs within Israel part of the Palestinian national movement. It also demanded the establishment of self-governing institutions in the fields of education, culture, and religion for Arabs in Israel (Miari 1984; Reiter and Aharoni 1992). *Hadash* opposed such separatist initiatives. By the late 1980s, the PLP lost its popular stand mainly due to disagreements between its Arab and Jewish members. In the 1992 Knesset elections, it failed to overcome the electoral threshold and disappeared from the political map. Ahead of the 1996 Knesset elections, a new nationalist party, the Democratic National Alliance (*Balad*), was formed with Azmi Bishara, a former member of *Rakah*, at its helm. *Balad* was established as a Palestinian nationalist party. It included political activists who had previously boycotted Knesset elections, as well as senior former PLP members. The new party called for abolishing Israel's Zionist character and turning it into 'a state of all its citizens.' It also demanded to recognize the Arab minority as a Palestinian national minority, and to grant it self-government through cultural autonomy. *Balad* was the first party to put the Palestinian national identity of Arab citizens at the top of its agenda (Sultany 2018). The fact that it did so within the framework of Israeli parliamentarism enabled it to establish itself on the political map in the Arab sector. *Balad* had been represented in the Knesset from the second half of the 1990s until the 2022 elections, when the party failed to overcome the electoral threshold.

During the same period, the Islamist stream increased its political power. In the early 1980s, the Islamic Movement was founded by a group of young Muslim clerics, led by Sheikh Abdullah Nimer Darwish, who acquired religious education at Islamic colleges in the West Bank in the 1970s and returned to their communities within Israel. The Islamic Movement drew on the religious sentiment deeply ingrained in the Arab public, and by preaching a return to the foundations of Islam, it gained remarkable achievements at the municipal level (Rekhess 1993). However, until the mid-1990s, the Islamists refrained from participating in the Knesset elections, pondering on how to justify Islamic participation in the Knesset, the symbol of Jewish sovereignty over historic Palestine. The controversy led to a split within the movement's ranks ahead of the 1996 Knesset elections. One faction, led by Sheikh Darwish, opted to run in the Knesset elections on the grounds that such participation would benefit Arab citizens. Another faction, led by Sheikh Ra'ed Sallah, refused to recognize the legitimacy of the Knesset and called for a boycott of the elections (Aburaiya 2004). The attempt of the parliamentary faction led by Sheikh Darwish was crowned with success. Members of the Islamic Movement first ran in the 1996 Knesset elections through a new party, the United Arab List (UAL), thus becoming an important parliamentary force.

Ahead of the 1996 Knesset elections, another Arab party, the Arab Movement for Renewal (*Ta'al*), was formed. At its helm was Ahmad Tibi, an Arab-Israeli citizen who had served as a political adviser to Yasser Arafat in the early 1990s. Tibi withdrew from the 1996 elections, but in the 1999 elections his party established a political alliance with *Balad* and won a seat in the Knesset. The alliance broke up after the election, but Tibi's party had already established its position and has been since represented in the Knesset.

Throughout this period, the Arab-Israeli stream changed its face. In the mid-1970s, the ruling Zionist parties opened their gates to Arab members, and since then Arab members have been represented in these parties. This development led to the disappearance of the Arab satellite lists and enabled the Zionist parties themselves, instead of their Arab proxies, to establish their grip on the Arab streets. However, in the late 1980s and early 1990s, under the influence of the Intifada and the Oslo Accords, the moderate camp changed its orientation.

Ahead of the 1988 Knesset elections, a new Arab party, the Arab Democratic Party (ADP), was formed by 'Abd al-Wahhab Darawsheh, who resigned from the Labor Party in protest at Israeli government policy in the Palestinian Territories after the outbreak of the Intifada. The new party established itself and gained representation in the 1988 and 1992 Knesset elections. In the 1996 elections, ADP joined the UAL and established a political alliance with the Islamic Movement. The emergence of new, authentic Arab parties clearly contributed to the development of political awareness among Arab citizens. However, in the second period, the average turnout of Arabs in elections – 73.4% – was lower than the nationwide average at 78.9%, and also considerably lower than the average Arab turnout in the first period, which stood at 83.8% (see Table 19.2). Indeed, as the political awareness of Arab citizens developed, so did the internal debate among them on the advantages and disadvantages of their participation in Knesset elections.

The decline in voter turnout reflected the maturity of the political discourse regarding Arab citizens' civil and national status in the country. Nevertheless, it would remain relatively high due to two key developments: the entry of new nationalist parties into the parliamentary fray – the PLP and Balad, and the Islamic Movement – and the change in the Israeli domestic and foreign policy during the 1992–1996 Rabin-Peres government. The official Israeli recognition of the PLO and the allocation of budgets for the development of Arab localities strengthened the sense of belonging to the state among Arab citizens (Reiter 2009).

In the 1977 Knesset elections, Hadash had won half the votes of the Arab voters. The rest of the votes were divided between the Jewish parties and the Arab satellite lists. This unprecedented achievement clearly rested on the charged national mood on the Arab streets following the events of the 1976 'Land Day.' It heralded the beginning of a new trend: an increase in voting for Arab parties that included in their ranks authentic representatives from the community and not ones dictated by the Jewish ruling parties, as was the case of the Arab satellite lists. Following

Table 19.2 Knesset elections turnout (%), 1977–1999

Year	Knesset no.	Nationwide turnout	Arab turnout
1977	9	79.2	75.0
1981	10	78.5	69.7
1984	11	79.8	73.7
1988	12	79.7	73.9
1992	13	77.4	69.7
1996	14	79.3	77.0
1999	15	78.7	75.0
Average		78.9	73.4

Sources: Reiter and Cohen, 2013; Israel's Central Bureau of Statistics website, www.cbs.gov.il; Israel's Central Elections Committee; The Israel Democracy Institute web site, www.idi.org.il

the disappearance of the Arab satellite lists in 1981, the struggle for the Arab vote was waged between Arab nationalist parties – *Hadash*, PLP, and ADP – and Jewish-Zionist parties.

During the tense period of the 1980s and early 1990s, the Zionist parties maintained the constant support of about half of the Arab voters on average. It clearly signaled the common understanding within the Arab public that despite national solidarity with the Palestinian cause, its political future rested within the borders of the state – nationalist slogans could not attract voters. However, the second half of the 1990s witnessed an increase in voting for Arab parties due to several developments (see Figure 19.2). First, all political streams were represented in the parliamentary arena when Balad and the Islamic Movement started running in elections and won seats in the Knesset. Second, all Arab parties highlighted their struggle for civil and national rights for Arab citizens of Israel, while the issue of the Palestinian struggle for independence in the 1967 territories became less important. Voting for Arab parties was no longer perceived as a tendency for nationalistic separatism, but rather an expression of growing political awareness within the Israeli context. Third, in the 1996 and 1999 election campaigns, a new voting system was introduced in Israel: one ballot for a candidate for prime minister, and another for a party. Many Arab citizens could now vote for any Arab party close to their worldview, while at the same time voting for their preferred candidate for prime minister. Indeed, the portion of votes cast for Arab parties increased significantly in these two election campaigns compared to past ones, exceeding 60% of the actual vote in the Arab sector. At the same time, an overwhelming majority of the Arab voters elected a Zionist Labor Party candidate for prime minister. In 1996, in fact, 94.7% of Arab voters voted for Shimon Peres, who eventually lost to Likud's leader, Benjamin Netanyahu, while in 1999, 94.3% of Arab voters voted for Ehud Barak, who defeated the same Netanyahu (Frisch 2000). The return to the one-ballot voting system in the 2003 Knesset elections did not bring Arab voters back to the Jewish parties. Since then, the vote for Arab parties has increased steadily.

To conclude, the 1990s can be seen as the heyday of the parliamentary era in the political history of Arab citizens in Israel. At the time, many Arab citizens still believed that parliamentary action could bring about a positive change in their civil and national status. The strong grip of the parties and political movements on the Arab streets, which was expressed in their ability to mobilize the public for occasional collective protests, paid off for them on election day.

A minority goes to the polls

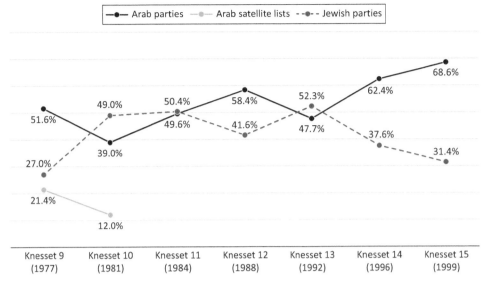

Figure 19.2 Breakdown of the Arab vote in Knesset elections, 1977–1999 Sources: Reiter and Cohen, 2013; Israel's Central Bureau of Statistics website, www.cbs.gov.il; Israel's Central Elections Committee; The Israel Democracy Institute web site, www.idi.org.il

In search of political efficacy, 2003–2022

The third period, extending from the 2003 Knesset elections up to the 2022 elections, began under the shadow of the October 2000 events and the Second Palestinian Intifada in the Palestinian Territories. The October 2000 events, in which 13 Arab civilians were killed in clashes between Arab demonstrators and Israeli police, caused profound alienation and a crisis of trust between the Arab public and state institutions. This resulted in an ongoing decline in the rate of participation of Arab citizens in Knesset elections.

The beginning of the 2000s also witnessed the escalation of the conflict between Israel and the Palestinians following the collapse of the Israeli–Palestinian peace talks and the conflict between Israel and the Hamas regime in the Gaza Strip. However, over the years, the effect of the Israeli–Palestinian conflict on the political worldview of Israeli Arabs began to wane. The death of Palestinian leader Yasser Arafat in 2004 and the political split in 2006 between the Palestinian Authority in the West Bank and the Hamas regime in the Gaza Strip has led to a deep crisis in the Palestinian national movement. At the same time, the 2011 Arab uprisings, and particularly the signing of the 'Abraham Accords' between Israel and several Arab countries in 2020, caused Arab citizens to reshape their perspective vis-à-vis the Israeli–Arab conflict in its broader context (Rudnitzky 2021). The cumulative result of these developments has led many Arab citizens to adopt a new approach that values the benefits of Israeli citizenship, despite its limitations, in a state that defines itself as a Jewish nation-state, according to the Nation State Law passed in the Knesset in July 2018.

Since the beginning of the third period, all four ideological streams in Arab society hold political representation in the Knesset. Members of the Arab-Israeli stream are represented within the Jewish-Zionist parties, but their institutionalized partisan presence in the Arab sector has virtually disappeared. In fact, Arab representation in the Zionist parties in the last decade is largely reminiscent of the Arab satellite lists typical of the first period. In quite a few cases, these are *ad-hoc* appointments at election time, placing candidates on the list slots not by virtue of their membership and seniority in the party but by considering their chances of attracting Arab votes on election day. The other three streams are represented in four main parties: the Arab-Jewish *Hadash*, the Nationalist *Balad*, the Islamist UAL, and Ahmad Tibi's *Ta'al,* whose positions are close to those of UAL and *Balad*. Until 2015, a tripartite structure in Arab politics was maintained: *Hadash* and *Balad* ran each on an independent list, while UAL and *Ta'al* ran on a united list. Following the rise in the election threshold ahead of the 2015 Knesset elections, the four Arab parties were forced to join forces, fearing that if they ran separately, all or some of them would not pass the threshold. Against this backdrop, the Joint Arab List was established.

In the 2015 elections, the Joint List obtained an unprecedented score: 13 out of 120 seats in the Knesset, two more seats than the average combined power of its four components when they used to run separately. However, the political partnership between the four parties did not go smoothly. Chronic political instability in Israel, leading to five election campaigns in less than four years between April 2019 and November 2022, caused instability in the patterns of political organization of the Arab parties. They oscillated between unity and division. In the 21st Knesset elections (April 2019), the Joint List disintegrated, and its constituent parties competed in two small alliances, thus securing only ten seats in the Knesset. In the next two election campaigns (Knesset 22, September 2019 and Knesset 23, March 2020), the four parties reunited in the Joint List and won 13 and 15 parliamentary seats, respectively.

However, political disagreements and personal rivalries led to the withdrawal of the Islamist UAL from the Joint List. In the March 2021 Knesset elections, three parties – *Hadash, Balad*, and *Ta'al* – ran under the Joint List, while UAL ran independently. Despite the historic slump in Arab turnout in these elections (44.6%) the Joint List and UAL managed to pass the threshold, but together they won only ten seats. In the leadup to the November 2022 elections, the Joint List experienced yet another crisis which led to its eventual split into two electoral lists, Hadash-Ta'al and Balad. Thus in the 2022 elections, Arab politics returned to the tripartite structure that characterized it before the Joint List was first established in 2015. In the 2022 elections, Balad failed to pass the electoral threshold, but the other two lists – UAL and Hadah-Ta'al – won together ten seats in the Knesset, thus preserving the Arab representation in the Knesset at the same level as the previous elections.

One salient phenomenon during the period in question is the continuing decline in the Arab public's participation in the Knesset elections. One reason is the loosening of the bond between the parties and citizens. This process is not unique to Arab politics. It characterizes Israeli politics, as well as quite a few democracies in Europe, where civil society organizations began to play a significant role as intermediaries between the citizen and state authorities (Galnoor and Blander 2013: 417–474). Indeed, Arab civil society organizations play an important role in promoting the status of Arab citizens in the field of legal rights or social change, for instance (Jamal 2008). Yet, their popularity at the expense of political parties denotes public disaffection toward traditional representative institutions (first and foremost political parties). Another reason is the emergence of a popular movement to boycott Knesset elections for ideological reasons. This phenomenon emerged following the events of October 2000. The outrage among the Arab public served as fertile ground for the establishment of the 'Popular Committee for the Boycott of the Knesset Elections' ahead of the 2003 elections by several small non-parliamentary nationalist movements that opposed the participation of Arabs in Knesset elections. Since then, the committee has been calling to boycott the elections before each Knesset election campaign. It is an *ad-hoc* body that operates only during election time (Haidar 2007).

The cumulative impact of these processes is reflected in a continuing decline in the rate of participation of Arab citizens in Knesset elections. In the last two decades, the average Arab turnout in Knesset elections dropped to 56.3%, significantly lower than the nationwide average

Table 19.3 Knesset elections turnout (%), 2003–2022

Year	Knesset no.	Nationwide turnout	Arab turnout
2003	16	67.8	62.0
2006	17	63.5	56.3
2009	18	64.7	53.4
2013	19	67.8	56.5
2015	20	72.3	63.5
April 2019	21	68.5	49.2
September 2019	22	69.8	59.2
2020	23	71.5	64.8
2021	24	67.2	44.6
2022	25	70.6	53.2
Average		68.4	56.3

Sources: Reiter and Cohen, 2013; Israel's Central Bureau of Statistics website, www.cbs.gov.il; Israel's Central Elections Committee; The Israel Democracy Institute web site, www.idi.org.il

turnout of 68.4% (see Table 19.3). Only when Arab parties ran as part of the Joint List – first in the 2015 elections, and again in the September 2019 and March 2020 elections – did Arab voter turnout in the elections increase, but these were temporary phenomena that did not herald a renewed interest among Arab citizens in Israeli politics. As mentioned, part of the decline in turnout is indeed explained by an active and organized ideological election boycott campaign. A further explanation is the political indifference and lack of interest in the Knesset elections, which characterize Israeli society as a whole. However, the main explanation for the decline in the turnout is the deliberate abstention from voting both in protest at the political ineffectiveness of the Arab vote in Israeli politics, and as a means of criticism of the poor functioning of Arab parties (Rudnitzky 2020). Indeed, twice following the disintegration of the Joint List – first in April 2019 and then in March 2021 – Arab turnout in the elections reached historic lows: 49.2% and 44.6%, respectively.

Despite the expansion of Arab non-participation in parliamentary elections, all Arab parties have succeeded in maintaining constant political representation in the Knesset. This can be explained by the increase in the voting for Arab parties at the expense of Jewish-Zionist parties. While Jewish parties enjoyed solid support among Arab voters in the elections held in the 1990s, in the last two decades their standing on the Arab streets has almost completely waned. In other words, turnout among Arab voters has been declining, but among actual voters the vote for Arab lists is higher than in the past. For this reason, the steady decline in Arab turnout did not harm the representation of Arab parties in the Knesset. Thus, even before 2015 when the Joint List was first established, all Arab parties passed the threshold and the total number of representatives elected on their behalf to the Knesset steadily increased: 8 in 2003, 10 in 2006, and 11 in 2009 and 2013 (see Figure 19.3 below). In fact, for the past two decades, the real battle for the support of Arab eligible voters has been waged between Arab parties and the 'non-voters party,' that is, those who do not participate in the elections. The Arab parties gained the upper hand only in those elections in which they ran in the Joint List (2015, September 2019, and 2020), and received the support of about half of the eligible voters in Arab society. In all other cases, the percentage of non-voters was higher than the actual support for Arab parties by eligible Arab voters, and in two cases over the last few years exceeded 50%.

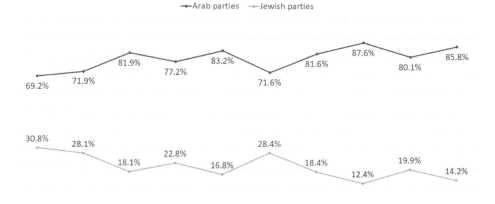

Figure 19.3 Breakdown of the Arab vote in Knesset elections, 2003–2021 Sources: Reiter and Cohen, 2013; Israel's Central Bureau of Statistics website, www.cbs.gov.il; Israel's Central Elections Committee; The Israel Democracy Institute web site, www.idi.org.il

Conclusion

The literature argues that parliamentary election turnout among national and ethnic minorities in democracies is generally lower than the turnout of the majority. A sense of discrimination and lack of political effectiveness, as well as a reality of the national conflict between majority and minority in deeply divided societies, adversely affects the participation of national minorities in general elections (Tavčar Krajnc et al. 2012; Sanders et al. 2014; Kook 2017; Oskooii 2020). The case of the Arab minority in Israel is no exception, but there are unique aspects that at times counter the literature's assumption.

Several Knesset elections were held during times of intense political mobilization on the Arab streets, resulting in a relatively high Arab turnout. In the 1977 Knesset elections, a year after the 1976 'Land Day,' Arab turnout reached 75%, and the Communist Party (*Hadash*) won more than half of the votes in the Arab sector. In the 1996 elections, Arab turnout reached 77% when the nationalist *Balad* party and the Islamic Movement participated for the first time in the parliamentary game, thus expanding the options for political representation of Arab citizens in the Knesset. In the 2015 and 2020 Knesset elections, when the Arab parties competed through the Joint List, the turnout reached almost 65%, thus reversing to some extent the trend of steady decline in Arab turnout in the period following the October 2000 events.

These cases display two shared conditions that highlight 'exceptional moments' when the main trend is bucked. First, Arab citizens are united around a common collective goal, and even if they do not gain Jewish recognition of their collective national status, they nevertheless believe that parliamentary politics may promote their civil status in the country. Second, the parliamentary game has reached a critical point where Arab representation in the Knesset may play an effective role in the balance between the ruling Jewish parties.

The high turnout in the elections held during the first two decades following the establishment of the State of Israel was not a sign of a developed political consciousness among Arab citizens. Rather it was the political behavior of a small and weak minority, whose only desire was to survive and adapt to the new reality of life in a Jewish state. Participation in the elections in those days was the lip service paid by the Arab minority to Israeli democracy to demonstrate its allegiance to the state. The decline in the rate of participation in Knesset elections in the last two decades is not an expression of political indifference or an ideological boycott of the elections, but rather a sign of their growing understanding of their political power. Abstaining from voting is a tactical step aimed at conveying a message: Arab citizens yearn for political influence in the Israeli parliamentary game, but unlike in the past, their participation in elections is not self-evident.

Today the Arab citizen seeks a direct connection to the government and sense of belonging to the state. However, his or her cooperation with the Israeli establishment has changed: instead of voting for Jewish parties as in the past, he or she votes mainly for Arab parties. The Arab public expects these parties to exhaust all possibilities for political cooperation with the Jewish establishment to fulfill the full potential of its political power. The decision is therefore in the hands of the Arab voter: if satisfied with the conduct of the parties, he or she will go to the polls, if not – he or she will abstain.

Against the backdrop of a continuing decline in the Arab participation rate in Knesset elections, the historical precedent set in the 2021 elections with the integration of an Arab party (UAL) into a government coalition led by right-wing Jewish-Zionist parties may become a turning point in patterns of political action. If the political influence of the Arab members of the Knesset is strengthened and they gain real achievements for the Arab public, this political development may give rise to a renewed interest in the Knesset elections among the Arab citizens of Israel.

References

Aburaiya, Issam. 2004. 'The 1996 Split of the Islamic Movement in Israel: Between the Holy Text and Israeli-Palestinian Context'. *International Journal of Politics, Culture, and Society* 17(3): 439–455.

Bäuml, Yair. 2017. 'Israel's Military Rule over Its Palestinian Citizens (1948–1968)'. In Nadim N. Rouhana and Sahar S. Huneidi (eds.), *Israel and Its Palestinian Citizens: Ethnic Privileges in the Jewish State*, 103–136. Cambridge: Cambridge University Press.

Bishara, Azmi. 1993. 'On the Question of the Palestinian Minority in Israel'. *Theory and Criticism* 3(1): 7–20. [In Hebrew].

Cohen, Hillel. 2010. *Good Arabs: The Israeli Security Agencies and the Israeli Arabs, 1948–1967*. Berkeley, CA: University of California Press.

Dallasheh, Leena. 2010. 'Political Mobilization of Palestinians in Israel: The al-Ard Movement'. In Rhoda Ann Kanaaneh and Isis Nusair (eds.), *Displaced at Home: Ethnicity and Gender among Palestinians in Israel*, 21–38. Albany, NY: State University of New York Press.

Frisch, Hillel. 2000. 'The Arab Vote in the Israeli Elections: The Bid for Leadership'. *Israel Affairs* 7(2–3): 153–170.

Galnoor, Itzhak and Dana Blander. 2013. *The Political System of Israel*. Tel Aviv and Jerusalem: Am Oved Publishers and The Israel Democracy Institute. [In Hebrew].

Ghanem, As'ad. 2001. *The Palestinian-Arab Minority in Israel, 1948–2000: A Political Study*. Albany, NY: State University of New York Press.

Ghanem, As'ad and Mohanad Mustafa. 2009. *The Palestinians in Israel: Minority Politics in an Ethnic State*. Ramallah: Madar Center. [In Arabic].

Haidar, Aziz. 2007. 'Election Boycott by the Arab Public: A One Decade Perspective, 1996–2006'. In Elie Rekhess (ed.), *The Arab Minority in Israel and the 17th Knesset Elections*, 89–92. Tel Aviv University: Konrad Adenauer Program for Jewish-Arab Cooperation. [In Hebrew].

Jamal, Amal. 2008. 'The Counter-hegemonic Role of Civil Society: Palestinian–Arab NGOs in Israel'. *Citizenship Studies* 12(3): 238–306.

Jiryis, Sabri. 1976. *The Arabs in Israel*. New York: Monthly Review Press.

Kaufman, Ilana. 1997. *Arab National Communism in the Jewish State*. Gainesville, FL: University Press of Florida.

Kook, Rebecca. 2017. 'Representation, Minorities and Electoral Reform: The Case of the Palestinian Minority in Israel'. *Ethnic and Racial Studies* 40(12): 2039–2057.

Landau, Jacob M. 1969. *The Arabs in Israel: A Political Study*. London: Routledge.
Mendales, Ben. 2018. 'A House of Cards: The Arab Satellite Lists in Israel, 1949–77'. *Israel Affairs* 24(3): 442–459.
Miari, Mohammed. 1984. 'The Making of a Political Movement'. *Journal of Palestine Studies* 14(1): 36–45.
Oskooii, Kassra A.R. 2020. 'Perceived Discrimination and Political Behavior'. *British Journal of Political Science* 50(3): 867–892.
Reiter, Yitzhak. 2009. *National Minority, Regional Majority: Palestinian Arabs Versus Jews in Israel*. Syracuse: Syracuse University Press.
Reiter, Yitzhak and Reuven Aharoni. 1992. *The Political Worldview of the Arabs in Israel*. Beit Berl: The Center for Israeli Arab Society Studies. [In Hebrew].
Reiter, Yitzhak and Orna Cohen. 2013. *Arab Society in Israel: Information Manual*, 2nd edition. Neve Ilan: Abraham Initiatives. [In Hebrew].
Rekhess, Elie. 1988. 'Jews and Arabs in the Israeli Communist Party'. In Milton J. Esman and Itamar Rabinovich (eds.), *Ethnicity, Pluralism, and the State in the Middle East*, 121–139. Ithaca, NY: Cornell University Press.
Rekhess, Elie. 1993. 'Resurgent Islam in Israel'. *Journal of Asian and African Studies* 27(1–2): 189–206.
Rekhess, Elie. 2007. 'The Evolvement of an Arab-Palestinian National Minority in Israel'. *Israel Studies* 12(3): 1–28.
Rouhana, Nadim. 1991. 'Palestinians in Israel: Responses to the Uprising'. In Rex Brynen (ed.), *Echoes of the Intifada: Regional Repercussions of the Palestinian-Israeli Conflict*, 97–117. Boulder, CO: Westview Press.
Rouhana, Nadim. 1997. *Palestinian Citizens in an Ethnic Jewish State: Identities in Conflict*. New Haven, CT: Yale University Press.
Rudnitzky, Arik. 2020. *Arab Voter Turnout in Knesset Elections: The Real, the Ideal, and Hope for Change*. Jerusalem: Israel Democracy Institute. [Hebrew].
Rudnitzky, Arik. 2021. 'The Arab Minority in Israel and the Normalization Agreements with Arab Countries'. In Brandon Friedman (ed.), *The New Normal? Arab States and Normalization with Israel*, 31–34. Jerusalem: Konrad Adenauer Stiftung Israel.
Sanders, David, Stephen D. Fisher, Anthony Heath and Maria Sobolewska. 2014. 'The Democratic Engagement of Britain's Ethnic Minorities'. *Ethnic and Racial Studies* 37(1): 120–139.
Sultany, Nimer. 2018. 'The National Democratic Assembly'. In Nadim N. Rouhana and Areej Sabbagh-Khoury (eds.), *The Palestinians in Israel: Readings in History, Politics and Society*, 215–229. Haifa: Mada al-Carmel.
Tavčar Krajnc, Marina, Sergej Flere and Andrej Kirbiš. 2012. 'Ethnic Minorities and Political Participation: A Comparative Study of Post-Yugoslav Countries'. *Innovative Issues and Approaches in Social Sciences* 5(1): 6–23.

20
ELECTIONS IN OCCUPIED PALESTINE

Control, resistance and contention

Francesco Saverio Leopardi

Introduction

Palestinians living in the Occupied Palestinian Territories (OPTs), namely the West Bank, Gaza Strip and East Jerusalem, have participated, although not regularly, in multiple elections at different levels since the beginning of the Israeli occupation in 1967. Over a 50-year span, the political, social and economic backgrounds against which elections were held changed dramatically. However, the colonial paradigm behind Israeli rule in the OPTs remains the underlying factor defining power relations and informing all political processes. Thus, Palestinian elections in the OPTs can be analysed by looking at how the different actors involved acted to stabilise, challenge or benefit from the political regimes founded upon such colonial relations of power.

Based on this premise, this chapter highlights the function and significance that elections in the OPTs had for Palestinian and Israeli political actors and whether and how their approach changed over time. It also argues that the Israeli authorities consistently looked at Palestinian elections as an instrument to build and strengthen a form of Palestinian self-rule in the OPTs that favoured its own strategic objectives, while granting a 'liberal' cover to their military occupation.

The Palestine Liberation Organisation (PLO), notably its main faction Fatah, evolved significantly in its position and strategy toward elections according to its priority to either challenge or stabilise the existing political system. In the 1970s, the PLO saw elections first as a threat to its representative role of the Palestinian people and, afterwards, as an opportunity to deepen its presence in the OPTs. Conversely, in the context of the ostensible state-building phase stemming from the Oslo Accords, the Fatah-dominated PLO used elections to legitimise and stabilise its rule in the OPTs, both in the 1990s and the mid-2000s. Following Hamas' rise as the main rival to the PLO, the Islamist movement too shifted its approach toward elections according to its overall goal of challenging the leadership of the Palestinian national movement.

Ultimately, this historical review of Palestinian elections disputes their connection to the democratisation of the non-sovereign and militarily occupied Palestinian society. At the same time, it also questions their potential role in reviving popular participation within a fragmented and demobilised official Palestinian national movement.

Municipal elections in the 1970s: control and resistance during the occupation's first decade

After occupying the West Bank and the Gaza Strip in June 1967, and until the early 1980s, Israel pursued a policy of 'normalisation' in its administration of the OPTs. The occupation was supposed to remain 'invisible', meaning that Israel should not establish its own administration in the OPTs, but let the Palestinians continue to rely on the existing administrative infrastructure. Therefore, municipal institutions such as mayors and councils functioned as a connection between the population and the occupation authorities. The occupation authorities also expected the municipal leaders to play a role against the activities of PLO-affiliated armed groups. Israel thus renewed the appointment of mayors and municipal councils in the West Bank, where Jordan, unlike Egypt in the Gaza Strip, had organised local elections in 1963 (Ma'oz 1984).

In 1972, the Israeli authorities decided to upgrade their efforts to normalise the occupation of the OPTs and organised a new round of municipal elections. Renewing the municipal councils through a democratic vote would have provided local administrations with stronger political legitimisation, which would have also facilitated cooperation with the military administration. Moreover, while symbolising a 'return to normal life' following the first years of occupation, the elections also amounted to a challenge to both the PLO and Jordan. Israel upheld the 1955 Jordanian law on elections, which granted the right to cast a ballot to men owning properties, above the age of 21, who had paid their property tax: this meant that only 5% of the West Bank population could participate in the elections (Gazit 2003). Such a limited electorate promoted the traditional power of the *hamulas*, the extended families or clans and of notables, some of whom were willing to collaborate with the occupation authorities (Peretz 1986).

Predictably, both the PLO and Jordan called on the West Bank population to boycott the elections, but their appeals had little influence on the upper-class voters. The elections were held in two rounds in the major municipalities of the West Bank with an 85% turnout and saw a majority of council members belonging to the notable class winning seats. In Israel's eyes, this result was a success, as it not only demonstrated that 'democratic' elections could be organised despite military occupation. It also allowed the occupation to continue the co-optation of local notables in their administration of the OPTs: fostering a power system that rested upon social divisions was much more attractive to Israel, as it provided a chance to discourage radical and nationalist forms of political organisation (Gordon 2008).

In 1976, when the four-year mandate of the municipalities expired, the Israeli authorities hoped to repeat the success of the 1972 elections, further entrenching the normalcy of their occupation, but deep changes in both the social balance of the West Bank and in the political standing of the PLO led to a much different result. By 1976, the PLO had achieved global recognition as the sole, legitimate representative of the Palestinian people. Moreover, following the 1972 elections, the PLO had worked on strengthening its position in the OPTs. That year, the PLO, while praising popular resistance against the 'illegitimate municipal elections', called for greater popular mobilisation, especially within the framework of trade unions (PNC 1972). The PLO's call for trade union mobilisations also reflected its understanding of the social impact that the Israeli occupation had had on the OPTs population. After 1967, Israel's normalisation policies allowed a growing number of Palestinian workers to find employment in the Israeli economy. Due to the higher wages, many Palestinian peasants, who still represented the majority of the OPTs population, left their work in the fields to become commuting labourers. In addition, increasing land appropriation by the military occupation further undermined the social configurations that had dominated rural life in the OPTs and upon which rested the power of the traditional elites. The decline in influence of the traditional elites, the exposure of workers to exploitation and discrimination in Israel and the expansion of settlement activity contributed to the politicisation of Palestinians in the OPTs along nationalist lines, thus pushing them closer to the PLO (Robinson 1997).

The Israeli government was aware of the changed political environment of the West Bank, as the intensity of demonstrations and strikes against the military occupation had been rising. However, Defence Minister Shimon Peretz, while aiming at strengthening the image of a 'liberal' occupation, also hoped that the new round of municipal elections would lay the bases for an actual Palestinian 'self-administration', which could also represent an alternative to the PLO. The Israeli authorities also amended the 1955 Jordanian law extending the right to vote to women and to all residents who had paid the municipal sewage tax. Peretz had been advised against holding the elections in a climate of rising nationalist mobilisation, but he believed that the extended pool of voters would favour the re-election of outgoing conservative mayors. However, unlike in 1972, the PLO actively promoted the participation of nationalist candidates and voters and mobilised its affiliated organisations in an effective electoral campaign. The PLO was joined by the local communist movement, which still enjoyed a significant presence in the West Bank. Conversely, the traditional elite had a much weaker social base and was *de facto* forced to run in the elections by the Israeli authorities. As predicted, nationalist and leftist candidates obtained a remarkable victory: 72.3% of the 88,462 eligible voters elected 14 new mayors, while only 10 achieved re-election. Moreover, 75% of the elected municipal councillors were newcomers who supported nationalist and leftist platforms. For the PLO, this was a major victory, as it was able to strengthen its power base in the West Bank by electing a younger, more radical and better-educated generation of local activists (Ma'oz 1984).

Between 1972 and 1976, the significance of municipal elections in the OPTs changed dramatically for the actors involved. The Israeli authorities went from conceiving the electoral process as instrumental to their control infrastructure in 1972, to realising the political challenge that it posed in 1976. The PLO and the local national movement not only undermined Jordanian claims over the West Bank, but also relied on the municipal elections to build an infrastructure of resistance, turning Israel's strategy upside down. In the following years, Israel would reverse its normalisation policy and pursue a more interventionist strategy that would lead to increased repression against nationalist mobilisation (Gordon 2008). In this context, it would take 20 years before Palestinians in the OPTs would be allowed to vote again under completely revolutionised circumstances.

Elections in the Oslo Era: realising the 'democratic' occupation

In September 1993, the PLO and Israel signed the Declaration of Principles (DoP), also known as the Oslo Accords. The Accords, which envisaged the creation of a Palestinian 'interim self-government authority' in the West Bank and Gaza, represented a lifeline for the PLO leadership that could now rebuild its power on new terms. In this context, elections, and their legitimising cover, would play a central role in the ascent of Yasser Arafat's dominant position as head of the newly established Palestinian National Authority (PNA).

The DoP referred to elections in its first articles, as it mandated the creation of an 'elected council' representing Palestinians in the West Bank and the Gaza Strip for a five-year interim period. According to Article 3, free and direct elections to select the council were to be held within nine months after the DoP came into effect (UN General Assembly Security Council 1993). The Israeli-Palestinian Interim Agreement on the West Bank and the Gaza Strip, or Oslo II, signed in September 1995, provided further details on the rules and the institutions governing the electoral process. The members of the council and the President of the PNA would be elected in two separate but simultaneous ballots. The right to vote was granted to all Palestinians residing in the West Bank and Gaza Strip, as well as in Jerusalem, who were above the age of 18 on election day and whose name was on the electoral register. Oslo II also dictated the creation of a Palestinian Central Election Commission (CEC) that, following appointment by the PNA, would administer the electoral process (The Israeli-Palestinian Interim Agreement 1995).

Arafat and the general elections: entrenching the PNA, asserting personal power

For PNA interim president, Yasser Arafat, general elections were a key step to strengthen the self-governing entity and support the peace process. The elections were an instrument to lend popular legitimisation to the PNA, which had been imposed on the Palestinian national movement and OPTs population within the context of a secretly negotiated political settlement with Israel. Moreover, through the electoral process, Arafat could expand the support base of the Oslo Accords and include local representatives of the national movement. This step was paramount for a leadership that had been based in the diaspora and had suddenly returned to the homeland in 1994. Elected members of the council would also gain membership in the Palestinian National Council (PNC), the PLO highest political body, allowing the PNA president to secure support for peace negotiations. Democratic elections would also enhance Arafat and the PNA's image on the global stage, especially since Oslo II called for international monitoring of the electoral process (Parsons 2005).

To achieve these goals, Arafat did not hesitate to manipulate the electoral process. He charged the CEC, with Mahmud Abbas at its head, to draft an Electoral Law that he eventually issued by decree in December 1995. The law divided the West Bank and the Gaza Strip into 16 districts, which would elect council members according to the size of their population. A majoritarian system envisaged that voters could vote for as many candidates as those assigned to their district, and seats were allocated to those who obtained the most votes (PNA President 1995). The district-based voting system allowed Arafat to promote local networks of power, thus favouring notables and extended families that were able to mobilise support within their reference area. Conversely, militant representatives of the national movement, especially those who had emerged from the First Intifada would have found more support at the national level, namely in a proportional system through which local leverage of power would have had less influence (Robinson 1997).

Arafat tried to convince both his leftist and Islamist opposition to participate in the elections, as this would have meant a wider acceptance of the PNA's state-building project. Internal debates divided the local and exiled branches of opposition factions, such as Hamas and the Popular Front for the Liberation of Palestine (PFLP), on whether to take part in the elections or not. Both movements ultimately decided to boycott the elections, although militants in the OPTs favoured participation to counterbalance Arafat's centralisation of power. Within the PFLP, many feared that the exiled leadership's choice of boycott risked marginalising further the declining Palestinian left, but except for minor defections, the decision to 'withdraw' all national legitimacy to the Oslo process was abided by opposition activists – of either Hamas and the PFLP – in the OPT (Leopardi 2020).

The 1996 elections were *de facto* transformed into a competition within Arafat's party, Fatah. The PNA president wanted to use the composition of Fatah electoral lists to secure the allegiance of future council members and rein in the emerging local leaders whose popularity was based on their militancy during the First Intifada. Arafat conceded on the request coming from Fatah ranks to hold primaries in each district to decide the composition of Fatah lists. Nonetheless, while the primaries predictably designated as candidates those leaders with a strong record of local militancy, Arafat intervened to promote loyal candidates, regardless of their actual political experience. The PNA president enlisted members of notable traditional families that had been weakened over the past two decades due to the emergence of the modern Palestinian national movement. These individuals, deprived of a meaningful popular base, owed their political fortunes entirely to their personal allegiance to Arafat (Robinson 1997). Arafat also favoured the candidacy of Fatah returnees who had spent their political lives in exile. These interferences hindered local leaders who in several cases decided to run on independent lists. Arafat tried to dissuade the formation of alternative Fatah lists, for instance, by promising posts in the PNA's bureaucracy in exchange for candidacy withdrawal, but ultimately several Fatah-affiliated independent lists were presented nonetheless (As'ad Ghanem 1996).

The electoral infrastructure: successes and obstacles in exercising the vote

Both the formulation of the Electoral Law and Arafat's interference showed the limits of Palestinian elections as a democratic process. However, during the 1996 general elections, fair electoral procedures usually associated with the entrenchment of democracy emerged nonetheless. The Palestinian Central Bureau of Statistics (PCBS) was charged with ensuring voter registration and performed its role quite effectively despite significant obstacles that the Israeli occupation authorities placed in its way. For instance, the Israeli authorities tried to discourage and hinder participation in the elections in East Jerusalem to weaken Palestinian claims of sovereignty over it. Rumours alleging that Jerusalemites participating in the ballot would lose the Jerusalem ID card and the benefit that this granted were deliberately spread. This, coupled with movement restrictions and Israeli soldiers pushing away voters on election day, depressed turnout in the Jerusalem area. Nonetheless, the PCBS was able to register more than a million voters thanks to the contribution of thousands of volunteers, who in Jerusalem collected names house by house (As'ad Ghanem 1996).

The PNA authorities undermined the fairness of elections as well to pursue their goal of favouring Fatah candidates and ensuring the best score possible for Arafat in the presidential ballots. The electoral campaign was reduced from 22 to 14 days, and notwithstanding the provision of the Oslo Accords, the CEC was appointed later in the process, leaving the administration of the elections to the Ministry of the Interior. Moreover, while much of the media was biased in favour of *Fatah*, pressure was also exerted on independent outlets, leading as far as the arrest of the *Al-Quds* newspapers' editor, who did not dedicate sufficient prominence to Arafat's image. Finally, some independent candidates were bribed in exchange for their withdrawal, while others were simply threatened or arrested (Parsons 2005).

Results and significance of the 1996 vote

On 20 January 1996, 71.6% of registered voters participated in the ballot, delivering Yasser Arafat his first important result: the vast majority of the OPTs population decided to participate in the first elections of the PNA, thus rejecting the calls for boycott coming from the opposition. The high turnout ensured the popular legitimacy of the policies that the PNA president had been pursuing towards Israel. In the presidential ballot, predictably, Arafat won a resounding victory, receiving 88.2% of the votes, while 11.8% went to his opponent, Samiha Khalil. Khalil, loosely associated with the Democratic Front for the Liberation of Palestine (DFLP), had a strong militant record, and ran on a campaign based on the rejection of the Oslo Accords. In the first elections for the Palestinian Legislative Council (PCL), 62 out of 88 seats were won by Fatah affiliates, ensuring Arafat's party total domination over the legislative body. The district-based system delivered the expected results, as candidates of Fatah official lists won 55 seats, although they received only 30% of the total votes (Central Elections Commission – Palestine 1996; As'ad Ghanem 1996).

Through the elections, the PNA seemed to have achieved a significant success: Arafat and the new Palestinian polity not only proved capable of organising democratic elections but could also show widespread approval for the peace process to the international community. The leftist and Islamist opposition seemed in disarray, as their attempts to delegitimise and derail the peace process through either political or military means had appeared to have little impact on the PNA orientations or those of public opinion (Milton-Edwards and Farrel 2010; Leopardi 2020). However, after this peak in its state-building process, the PNA would quickly be forced to reckon with its own limits and those imposed by the ongoing Israeli occupation and colonial approach towards the Palestinian self-government. As Arafat centralised powers in his hands, corruption spread across the PNA bureaucracy while its security forces duly abided by the provisions of 'security coordination' with Israel by ensuring the repression of political dissent within the territory under its control. This, coupled with the inability to achieve further progress towards Palestinian statehood, crippled the PNA's popular legitimacy and credibility (Khalidi 2007).

The 1996 Palestinian general elections were a success for Israel too, notwithstanding the outright opposition of the Likud government to Palestinian statehood. As it would become clear with the failure of the final status negotiations in 2000, the Oslo Accords represented a framework that did not allow for the emergence of a viable Palestinian state but, conversely, a reorganisation of power relations enabling continued Israeli dominance and overall sovereignty over Israel/Palestine. None of the core issues of the Palestinian question, such as the end of military occupation and settlements expansion, Israeli control over borders and natural resources, the return of Palestinian refugees or the status of Jerusalem was resolved. The Oslo process further favoured the territorial fragmentation of Palestinian land; it prevented the emergence of a viable Palestinian economy and led to the social and political demobilisation of the OPTs population (Roy 2007). The Oslo Accords represented an effective mechanism to outsource the Israeli occupation, as they created a Palestinian entity that relieved Israel from its obligation as occupying force and started to police the population of the West Bank and Gaza Strip on its behalf. The electoral legitimisation of the PNA provided a liberal cover to the ongoing occupation and gave the impression that the preliminary steps towards Palestinian statehood were in fact being taken (Gordon 2008).

In December 2000, the second Palestinian mass uprising in the OPTs broke out due to the contradictions of a peace process preventing Palestinian independence while allowing further entrenchment of Israeli settler colonial endeavour. The *Al-Aqsa Intifada* brought five years of asymmetric warfare throughout Israel/Palestine, the total Israeli re-occupation of the West Bank and Gaza Strip and an increasingly polarised Palestinian political camp. Following Yasser Arafat's death in November 2004, his prospective successor Mahmud Abbas needed popular legitimisation, while relations of power within the Palestinian national movement had to be reconfigured. Such process went through both presidential and legislative elections that, contrary to their initial goals, would lead to unbridgeable divisions in Palestinian politics and growing delegitimisation of its main actors.

Elections in the post-Arafat era: ultimate impasse

After the Oslo Accords, Arafat became the sole decision-maker in both the PNA and the PLO by centralising power through corruption, neo-patrimonial policies and repression. He also relied extensively on internal divisions within Fatah to avoid the emergence of alternative leaders by positing itself as the ultimate point of balance. Thus, his death risked opening a phase of harsh political competition within the PNA ruling party. In this context, a reconfiguration of power and of the rules and institutions governing the Palestinian polity was an urgent need, especially as Palestinian politics emerged from a destructive uprising. The whole Palestinian political spectrum needed reform and elections appeared to be a fundamental instrument to achieve it (As'ad Ghanem 2010).

Municipal and presidential elections: announcing Hamas' rise

The PNA announced in late 2004 the decision to hold municipal elections throughout the West Bank and Gaza Strip in four stages. This was the first time that municipalities and mayorships were elected after the establishment of the PNA, and it saw the participation of Fatah, the leftist organisations, Hamas and many independent candidates. The 1996 Law on Local Councils was amended several times in between the four electoral rounds, mainly with the aim of bolstering Fatah's position against the backdrop of Hamas' growing popularity. The direct election of mayors was abolished, leaving this task to the newly elected municipal councils. Later, a proportional system of representation replaced the previous majoritarian one, favouring local and familial groupings over political identities. Although political affiliations at a local level were not necessarily clear, candidates close to Hamas obtained significant results and won several municipalities: in the Gaza Strip, Hamas took over seven out of ten densely populated municipalities, thus receiving tens of thousands of votes (Central Elections Commission – Palestine 2005b; As'ad Ghanem 2010). In some cases, the Islamist movement formed tactical alliances with leftist factions and succeeded in beating the local Fatah candidate: in Ramallah, the PFLP-affiliated candidate Janet Mikha'il was elected mayor thanks to Hamas support (Jamal 2013).

Between the first and second rounds of municipal elections, Palestinians were also summoned to elect a new PNA president in January 2005. The new PLO Chairman, Mahmud Abbas, sought popular legitimisation for its bid to succeed Arafat to the PNA presidency and a strong mandate to resume negotiations with Israel. Unlike in 1996, the leftist opposition joined the presidential race, although the different factions did not agree on a single candidate. Hamas, alongside Islamic Jihad, maintained its boycott of the presidential elections, claiming its unwillingness to recognise the institutions created by the Oslo Accords. However, the movement was experiencing an intense internal debate on the issue of running in elections for PNA bodies, as the remarkable performance achieved in the municipal elections had emboldened those in favour of greater political engagement. Their different choice concerning the 2006 legislative elections would show where internal balances had shifted (Baconi 2018).

The presidential ballot recorded a 66.5% turnout and delivered the expected result, as Mahmud Abbas was elected with 62% of the votes. While achieving his goals, Abbas did not really receive an undisputed national seal of approval, considering the lower turnout to which Hamas' boycott contributed. The absence of a Hamas candidate possibly also helped Mustafa Barghouthi, founder of the Palestinian National Initiative (PNI) and supported by the PFLP, in obtaining 19.5% of the votes (Central Elections Commission – Palestine 2005a; Jamal 2013).

The new PNA president negotiated a ceasefire with Israeli Prime Minister Ariel Sharon and engaged in a dialogue with other Palestinian factions to maintain calm in the OPTs. Intra-Palestinian talks led to the so-called 'Cairo Declaration' signed by the major Palestinian factions, including Hamas, which reaffirmed abidance to the ceasefire and called for overall reform and democratisation of the Palestinian polity. Palestinian factions agreed on holding legislative elections and recommended to amend the Electoral Law, abandoning the majoritarian system in favour of a mixed one (I'lan al-Qahira 2005). The elections for the second PLC appeared as the crucial ballot to determine the future of Palestinian politics and to lay the basis for the renewal of Palestinian institutions.

The 2006 legislative elections and beyond: the impossibility of Palestinian elections

In hindsight, the stage appeared set for a major crisis in the run-up to the 2006 legislative elections. After Arafat's death, Fatah lost its unifying figure, letting the deep divisions that affected the movement emerge, while its status as the PNA ruling party made it the main target of ordinary Palestinians' grievances for its corruption and authoritarianism. Hamas entered the electoral competition as the party of armed resistance, rejection of a failed peace process and change within the national movement. As these two poles were on a colliding trajectory, leftist factions appeared increasingly unable to coalesce to provide a third option. Moreover, in the aftermath of the Second Intifada, Palestinians were forced to live under a tighter Israeli military grip, symbolised by the construction of the Separation Wall in the West Bank. The Sharon government decided to withdraw the army and settlers from the Gaza Strip but enforced a sealing of its borders. While the withdrawal was largely seen as a success of armed resistance, the unabated Israeli policies of fragmentation of the West Bank and the continued harshness of its occupation further pushed Palestinian voters closer to Hamas (Usher 2006).

After the Cairo Declaration of March 2005, a majority within Hamas favoured entering electoral politics. The document calling for the reform of the PLO and the implementation of pluralism within Palestinian institutions provided the guarantees that the Islamist movement had been seeking. Hamas looked at the PLC elections as a way to gain a foothold within Palestinian institutions to break Fatah's monopoly and turn the PNA into a site of resistance to the Israeli occupation rather than just a self-administering entity that facilitated it (Baconi 2018).

Once the decision to enter the electoral fray was taken, Hamas showed remarkable organisational unity. Conversely, Fatah appeared increasingly unable to end the divisions between its own factions. Chaos dominated Fatah's selection of electoral lists: after the first round of primaries held in the West Bank delivered victory to the younger generation of Fatah leaders led by Marwan Barghouthi, the old guard worked to rig the Gaza second round. Due to mass fraud, Abbas cancelled the primaries, but this led to the emergence of two different Fatah lists embodying the rifts between the old and the new guard. The chaotic situation was best symbolised by the fact that Barghouthi headed both the official and independent Fatah lists. The botched formulation of electoral lists and the insistence of some independent candidates contributed to dispersing the Fatah vote, compromising its score in the new mixed electoral system (Usher 2006; Giacaman 2006).

Leftist factions experienced similar problems, as their chronic fragmentation re-emerged during discussions to form a united list. The main problem was the disagreement over its composition and how it should reflect the weight of different factions. The order of candidates' appearances on the list led to a dispute between the DFLP and the PFLP, while the latter also clashed with the PNI. Both factions thought that they deserved credit for Mustafa Barghouthi's score of 20% in the presidential election, hence their right to provide 20% of candidates to the unified list. Ultimately, the Palestinian left presented three distinct lists, irremediably dispersing the vote of their supporters (Jamal 2013; Leopardi 2020).

Fatah and leftist problems reflected their superficial understanding of the new Electoral Law and of the mutated political climate. As the Cairo Declaration envisioned, the PLC seats were expanded from 88 to 132: 66 were to be elected through a district-based system while the other half would be allocated following a nationwide, proportional principle (Central Elections Commission – Palestine 2005c). Fatah campaigned poorly, fielding more candidates than seats available and disregarding the popularity of candidates who sought seats at the district level. On the contrary, Hamas demonstrated a great understanding of the electoral system and devised a strategy that would ensure an unexpected success. Its strongest candidates ran at the district level, while less popular members were placed at the national one, where the party's name was more important than the public profile of individual candidates. The 'Change and Reform' list appealed to a disillusioned Palestinian population who looked at the elections as an opportunity for a fresh start. Furthermore, Hamas led a targeted campaign that featured public gatherings, media interviews and posters, effectively conveying its message centred on domestic issues such as the reform of the PNA and the end of corruption (Milton-Edwards and Farrel 2010).

On 25 January 2006, electoral operations unfolded without major disruptions and both local and international observers certified their conformity to international democratic standards. Turnout was high, as 77% of registered voters cast their ballot. Their democratic choice, however, shocked all actors with a stake in the elections: Hamas won an overwhelming victory, gaining 74 seats and thus securing an absolute majority in the PLC. Its performance at the district level, wherein 45 of its candidate were elected, was key to delivering such a resounding result. As the election of only 17 of its district candidates shows, Fatah had clearly underestimated the impact of a district-based system, thus allowing Hamas to enjoy total control of the PLC with only 3% of vote share advantage. The three leftist lists managed to have only seven candidates elected, all from the national level, as they stood no chance of winning seats in the districts (Central Elections Commission – Palestine 2006a, 2006b).

The international community recognised the 2006 legislative elections as free and fair but would quickly join Israel in isolating the new Hamas-led government. International donors, notably the US and the European Union, conditioned financial support to Hamas' acceptance of previous PLO–Israel agreements and its recognition of Israel's 'right to exist', although this, in the spirit of Oslo, was not tied to a mutual Israeli recognition of the Palestinian right to statehood. Following Hamas' refusal, international donors froze most funds to the PNA and redirected some money only to departments and offices under presidential control. Israel stopped forwarding taxes that, under the provisions of the Oslo Accords, it collected on behalf of the PNA. The ensuing economic crisis fuelled social and political tension in the OPTs while a group of Fatah hard-liners in the security forces, such as Muhammad Dahlan, began working with US and Israeli security officials to prepare a military takeover. Despite an official agreement between Fatah and Hamas to form a national unity government, tensions continued to rise as rumours of an impending coup against the Islamist movement appeared corroborated by Fatah's efforts to recruit new military personnel loyal to the PNA president. In this context, Hamas too had reinforced its military apparatus and in June 2007 decided to launch a pre-emptive coup in the Gaza Strip, ousting all PNA and Fatah military personnel from the enclave. Afterwards, two separate governments were formed in Gaza and the West Bank, sanctioning an unprecedented polarisation in Palestinian politics (Dabed 2010).

The events that unfolded after the 2006 PLC elections demonstrated the contradictions and dangers of holding elections under occupation. The alignment of international actors to Israel's position strengthened the colonial asymmetry existing in Israel/Palestine, while highlighting the inconsistency of their promotion of democracy through the electoral process. As Jamil Hilal (2010) argued, international support for parliamentary elections in the PNA, ignored that the conditions for 'effective democracy' are denied in the context of colonial domination. At the same time, the 2006 PLC elections also showed that lacking an effective debate on the goals of holding the elections under occupation in terms of their role toward self-determination, Palestinian politics were bound to polarise between alternative power groups (Hilal 2010: 35–37).

Over the last 15 years, the Hamas–Fatah division appeared unresolvable despite the ostensible efforts of local and regional political actors to mediate between the two. Furthermore, both the rule of the Hamas government in Gaza and that of Fatah-dominated PNA in the West Bank have long passed the expiry date of their electoral mandates. In this context, Palestinian political forces hinted at presidential and legislative elections as a way to return popular legitimisation to Palestinian institutions, revive the national movement and end divisions. However, the continuation of the Palestinian impasse has underscored the deepening of the fundamental issues preventing the success of electoral politics. Accordingly, while presidential and legislative elections had been scheduled for July 2021, only to be cancelled in April (Aljazeera 2021), even local votes were subjected to delay and cancellations. Israel's repression of political activity has intensified and has specifically targeted electoral activities to influence the overall process on several occasions, as testified by the threats and the arrests to which candidates, frequently from Hamas, have been subjected during the 2016–2017 local elections. Notwithstanding numerous rounds of negotiations, Fatah and Hamas never implemented the signed reconciliation agreements, underscoring their unwillingness to achieve real power sharing. Fatah continues to suffer from deep-rooted internal conflicts which emerged during the run-up to the 2021 general elections as more than three lists affiliated to the party were registered (Al-Omari 2021). Furthermore, the authoritarian practices of both the PNA and Hamas have alienated the Palestinian public and contributed to social and political demobilisation, depriving civil society of the means to contest power in an election (Shahin 2016).

Palestinian analysts have long called for the resolution of such long-standing problems before holding new elections and for the reactivation of PLO institutions as better-suited instruments to renew the membership and the initiative of the Palestinian national movement. Without consensus on a political programme for national liberation and self-determination, and against the backdrop of dysfunctional institutions, elections proved unfit to provide new legitimacy to Palestinian politics. In the context of unchallenged colonial relations of power and deep international interferences, voting also appeared unable to promote democratisation (Fatafta and Tartir 2020; El-Kurd 2021).

Conclusion

Over the last 50 years, the different ruling actors in Occupied Palestine resorted to elections to stabilise a political regime that served their short and long-term goals. This was the case despite the changing scenarios and the different levels at which elections were held. In the asymmetric context of colonial relations of powers, elections also represented opportunities to mobilise popular support for a political project aiming at challenging such a system. Even in the heydays of the US-sponsored settlement of conflicts across the Middle East, voting in Palestine had little to do with the expansion of Western liberal democracy and much more with the reconfiguration of power relations, notwithstanding the Palestinians' eagerness for democratic participation.

After 1967, Israel's strategy to normalise political and administrative relations with Palestinians was articulated from a colonial perspective. Municipal elections in the 1970s were meant to select an abiding ruling class, whose power rested on the traditional, clan-based distribution of power. The Israeli authorities aimed to rely on such a local ruling class to prevent the crystallisation of nationalist and modern political organisation, while projecting the image of liberal government. While such operation was successful in 1972, the evolution and modernisation of the Palestinian national movement, allowed the PLO to exploit the 1976 local elections to mount an effective challenge to the Israeli power system and turn the municipalities into sites of resistance.

Paradoxically, in 1996, within the framework of the Oslo Accords, presidential and legislative elections for the newly formed PNA contributed to turning the representatives of the modern Palestinian national movement into a local elite to which Israel outsourced the administration and policing of the occupied population. Arafat also needed the electoral process to legitimise the new Palestinian political regime and therefore he resorted to significant electoral manipulation to achieve a result validating his statehood project. Elections strengthened colonial relations of powers between Israel and Palestinians, while legitimising an increasingly authoritarian polity that prevented democratisation and achieved the political demobilisation of its population in coordination with the colonial ruler.

After the end of the *Al-Aqsa Intifada*, elections became again an instrument to stabilise the political situation in the OPTs and legitimise Abbas' succession to Arafat. However, Hamas' organisational and political rise meant that elections were also the site of renewed contention over the status quo. In seeking to expand and institutionalise its power while turning the PNA into a new base for resistance, Hamas capitalised on popular grievances toward the PNA. Despite the transparency of the 2006 legislative elections, the events that followed Hamas' victory demonstrated that a democratic vote could only be tolerated as long as it served the international and Israeli vision of political settlement.

The rejection of the legislative elections demonstrated the unviability of democratic voting in the context of military occupation and colonial power relations. In such a context, Palestinian elections cannot favour the democratisation of local politics nor contribute to the goal of lasting political stabilisation. Elections also appear unfit to renew Palestinian political mobilisation in the context of a fossilised Hamas–Fatah polarisation and in the absence of a debate on a long-term programme for national liberation.

References

Aljazeera. 2021. 'Abbas Delays Palestinian Parliamentary Polls, Blaming Israel', 30 April. Available at: https://www.aljazeera.com/news/2021/4/30/palestinians-polls-hamas-plo.

'Al-Nass al-Harfi li-I'lan al-Qahira al-Sadir 'an al-Fasa'il al-Filastiniyya 17-03-2005 (The Text of the "Cairo Declaration" Issued from the Palestinian Factions)'. 2005. Wafa Info. Available at: http://info.wafa.ps/atemplate.aspx?id=4894.

Baconi, Tareq. 2018. *Hamas Contained: The Rise and Pacification of Palestinian Resistance*. Stanford, CA: Stanford University Press.

Central Elections Commission – Palestine. 1996. 'The 1996 Presidential and Legislative Elections'. Available at: https://www.elections.ps/Portals/0/pdf/Resultselection1996.pdf.

Central Elections Commission – Palestine. 2005a. 'Elections Final Results-(Voters' List)- by District'. Available at: https://www.elections.ps/Portals/0/pdf/Voters'.ListDistrict2005.pdf.

Central Elections Commission – Palestine. 2005b. 'Qanun Intikhab Majalis al-Hay'at al-Mahalliyya Raqm 10 li-Sanat 2005 wa Ta'dilatihi (Local Councils Electoral Law No. 10. Year 2005 and Amendments)'. Available at: https://www.elections.ps/Portals/30/pdf/LocalElections_Law_Nr10_2005_Updates_AR.pdf.

Central Elections Commission – Palestine. 2005c. 'Qanun Raqm 9 Li-Sanat 2005 bi-Sha'n al-Intikhabat (The 2005 Law No. 9 on the Elections)'. Available at: https://www.elections.ps/Portals/30/pdf/GeneralElections_Law_Nr9_2005_AR.pdf.

Central Elections Commission – Palestine. 2006a. 'The Second 2006 PLC Elections Lists Voters per Districts'. Available at: https://www.elections.ps/Portals/0/pdf/Votes%20for%20lists%20per%20districts.pdf.

Central Elections Commission – Palestine. 2006b. 'The Second 2006 PLC Elections. The Final Distribution of PLC Seats.' Available at: https://www.elections.ps/Portals/0/pdf/The%20final%20distribution%20of%20PLC%20seats.pdf.

Dabed, Emilio. 2010. 'Decrypting the Palestinian Political Crisis: Old Strategies Against New Enemies: Chile 1970–73, Palestine 2006–09'. *Arab Studies Quarterly* 32(2): 73–91.

El-Kurd, Dana. 2021. 'Elections Can't Fix the Palestinian Authority'. *+972 Magazine*, 24 February. Available at: https://www.972mag.com/palestinian-authority-elections-democracy/.

Fatafta, Marwa, and Alaa Tartir. 2020. 'Why Palestinians Need to Reclaim the PLO'. *Foreign Policy*, 20 August 2020. https://foreignpolicy.com/2020/08/20/palestinians-reclaim-plo-palestinian-authority-democracy/.
Gazit, Shlomo. 2003. *Trapped Fools: Thirty Years of Israeli Policy in the Territories*. London – Portland: Frank Cass.
Ghanem, As'ad. 1996. 'Founding Elections in a Transitional Period: The First Palestinian General Elections'. *Middle East Journal* 50(4): 513–528.
Ghanem, As'ad. 2010. *Palestinian Politics after Arafat. A Failed National Movement*. Bloomington, IN: Indiana University Press.
Giacaman, George. 2006. 'Al-Intikhabat al-Tashri'iyya al-Filastiniyya wa al-Tahawwul al-Siyasi (The Palestinian Legislative Elections and Political Change)'. *Majallat Al-Dirasat al-Filastiniyya* 17(65): 60–69.
Gordon, Neve. 2008. *Israel's Occupation*. Berkeley, Los Angeles, CA: University of California Press.
Hilal, Jamil. 2010. 'The Polarization of the Palestinian Political Field'. *Journal of Palestine Studies* 39(3): 24–39.
Jamal, Manal. 2013. 'Beyond Fateh Corruption and Mass Discontent: Hamas, the Palestinian Left and the 2006 Legislative Elections'. *British Journal of Middle Eastern Studies* 40(3): 273–294.
Khalidi, Rashid. 2007. *The Iron Cage: The Story of the Palestinian Struggle for Statehood*. Oxford: Oneworld Publication.
Leopardi, Francesco Saverio. 2020. *The Palestinian Left and Its Decline Loyal Opposition*. Singapore: Palgrave Macmillan.
Ma'oz, Moshe. 1984. *Palestinian Leadership on the West Bank the Changing Role of the Arab Mayors under Jordan and Israel*. London: Routledge.
Milton-Edwards, Beverley, and Stephen Farrel. 2010. *Hamas: The Islamic Resistance Movement*. Cambridge: Polity Press.
Omari, Ghaith al. 2021. 'Palestinian Politics are More Divided Than Ever'. *The Washington Institute for Near East Policy*, 27 May. Available at: https://www.washingtoninstitute.org/policy-analysis/palestinian-politics-are-more-divided-ever.
Parsons, Nigel. 2005. *The Politics of the Palestinian Authority: From Oslo to Al-Aqsa*. London: Routledge.
Peretz, Don. 1986. *The West Bank: History, Politics, Society, and Economy*. Boulder, CO: Westview Press.
PNA President. 1995. 'Qanun Raqm 13 li-Sanat 1995 bi-Sha'n al-Intikhabat (Law n. 13, 1995 on the Elections)'. Available at: http://muqtafi.birzeit.edu/pg/getleg.asp?id=9671.
PNC. 1972. 'Al-Dawra al-'Ashira al-Istithna'iyya, Al-Qahira (The 10th Extraordinary Session, Cairo)'. Wafa Info. Available at: http://www.wafainfo.ps/atemplate.aspx?id=3247.
Robinson, Glenn E. 1997. *Building a Palestinian State: The Incomplete Revolution*. Bloomington, IN: Indiana University Press.
Roy, Sara. 2007. *Failing Peace: Gaza and the Palestinian-Israeli Conflict*. London and Ann Arbor, MI: Pluto Press.
Shahin, Khalil. 2016. 'Indama Tatahawwal al-Furas ila Tahdidat. Al-Intikhabat wa al-Wahda al-Wataniyya Numudhajan. (When Opportunities Turn into Challenges: Elections and National Unity as a Example)' *Majallat Al-Dirasat al-Filastiniyya* 108: 206–211.
'The Israeli-Palestinian Interim Agreement'. 1995. Available at: https://mfa.gov.il/MFA/ForeignPolicy/Peace/Guide/Pages/THE%20ISRAELI-PALESTINIAN%20INTERIM%20AGREEMENT.aspx.
UN General Assembly Security Council. 1993. 'Declaration of Principles on Interim Self-Government Arrangements'. Available at: https://peacemaker.un.org/sites/peacemaker.un.org/files/IL%20PS_930913_DeclarationPrinciplesnterimSelf-Government%28Oslo%20Accords%29.pdf.
Usher, Graham. 2006. 'The Democratic Resistance: Hamas, Fatah, and the Palestinian Elections'. *Journal of Palestine Studies* 35(3): 20–36.

21
ELECTORAL CAMPAIGNS IN POST-BEN ALI'S TUNISIA

Electoral expertise and renewed clientelism[1]

Déborah Perez-Galan

Introduction

If anything, the Tunisian electoral campaign for the 2014 legislative elections proved Paul Lazarsfeld's assertion in *The People's Choice* (2021) right: electoral campaigning does not make an election. It strengthens political preferences, which are already formed, but does not convert voters and fails to make them vote for someone else. For instance, despite organising a series of meetings, opening a multitude of local offices, delivering a very neat canvassing operation, and distributing electoral goods, the *Ennahda* party failed to gain a majority in parliament in October 2014. The Islamist movement, whose members led the government between 2011 and 2014 as part of a coalition called the Troïka composed of the leftist Congress for the Republic and the socialist *Ettakatol*, only came in second. The majority of votes and seats went to its main opponent, *Nidaa Tounes* (Tunisia's Call), a broad motley coalition of leftists, unionists, highly ranked civil servants and members of the former regime, that was built around the personality of Beji Caïd Essebsi, an 88-year-old former minister under Habib Bourguiba, to counter Islamism. On October 26, 2014, Rached Ghannouchi, the founder and president of *Ennahda*, called Beji Caïd Essebsi and acknowledged his party's defeat, triggering the first peaceful transition of power in the region (McCarthy 2015). Studying this long-awaited electoral campaign in revolutionary Tunisia is interesting to understand not only how new ways of campaigning arise, but also how old ways persist. What is at stake during an electoral campaign and, more specifically, during an electoral campaign that takes place right in the middle of regime change?

The Tunisian revolution promptly led to organising constituent elections in October 2011 in a context of liberalisation, and to creating numerous political parties (Geisser and Perez 2016). However, it was only after the approval of the road map drafted by the Quartet[2] in autumn 2013 that elections became 'the only game in town' (Guilhot and Schmitter 2000). International observers of the Arab uprisings insisted on the importance of holding elections as key to the democratisation process. The Constitution adopted in January 2014 paved the way for parliamentary and presidential elections which were held for the first time in October and December 2014, and then again in September and October 2019. Local elections were also held in May 2018. For the first time, political actors could campaign freely, introducing a whole new range of political goods such as posters, leaflets, and music representing the candidates. Campaigning thus became a way to display political legitimacy and to show one's expertise in the political field. However, it was also a moment when people's needs – and especially their need for jobs – were expressed at several levels. Studying campaigning shows how the importance of these socio-economic issues overshadowed the bipolarity of the political field between Islamist and anti-Islamist organisations.

My fieldwork, conducted before, during, and after the 2014 elections, and the observations made during the 2019 elections, show that a contradictory dynamic structures Tunisian electoral campaigns. They can be analysed, at the same time, as a moment when new political actors display their strength and build up their legitimacy, and as a crisis of patronage relations. Electoral mobilisation paradoxically led to the demobilisation of voters. Through an ethnographic approach to electoral campaigning in post–Ben Ali Tunisia, this chapter argues that studying electoral campaigns is key to understanding politics in the making. Electoral campaigns during the Tunisian regime change act as a catalyst for new political actors, as a revealing moment for building up local anchoring, and as a moment when new political norms are shaped and spread. Hence, studying electoral campaigns casts a new light on the issues of rupture and continuity during regime change: elections since 2011 may have been the first free elections in Tunisia, but they belong to a history of elections that started in the 19th century.

Getting the party started: electoral campaigns and specialisation of political wannabes?

Campaigns during the Tunisian regime change can be understood as a moment for new political forces to build themselves up and display power to strengthen their legitimacy to rule over the country. Regime change and the liberalisation of political life triggered the creation of new political organisations, as well as the revitalisation of old ones. In a context of pluralist effervescence (Allal and Vannetzel 2017), more than 150 parties were created and legalised (Storm 2013; Geisser and Perez 2016) in 2011. Many electoral initiatives turned into political alliances. Studying these political organisations foregrounds how campaigning can act as a catalyst for political organisations that are new to the official political sphere – triggering electoral mobilisation and activating political cleavages. These actors are in great need not only of members but also of skills on how to run a campaign and win an election, which leads them to expand by enrolling new members and people who have expertise in electoral matters.

Enrolling new members

Political parties formed alliances in an attempt to access positions of power through elections, whereas before the revolution, they were opposition movements with very little experience in the field of elections, as most had been banned from competing. Campaigning led these organisations to define or redefine their political identity in post–Ben Ali Tunisia. The case of *Ennahda* is particularly interesting here since it was (re)created in advance of the 2011 election. The movement had almost been eradicated from Tunisian soil and only survived in exile, mostly in France and United Kingdom (Ayari 2016; Wolf 2017; Zederman 2019). In 2011, list-making and campaigning were a rush job: even a movement as structured as *Ennahda* was not organised homogeneously across the whole territory. For instance, in order to comply with the electoral rule providing for full parity[3] of electoral lists, the party lacked women members to invest in as candidates in some constituencies. One female Member of Parliament (MP) stated:

I was supposed to be a candidate in France, I had been internally elected. But they lacked women to run in Bizerte, my hometown. And in Paris, they had other good candidates. So I did my campaign there and Meherzia Labidi was nominated in Northern France.[4]

Political organisations remained fragmented. Their means differed, even from one constituency to the next. Many political organisations opened their doors – willingly or not – to newcomers to organise candidate lists according to the electoral laws and especially to the requirement of gender parity. However, during the campaign, a hierarchy between old activists and newcomers persisted and triggered a specific division of political work.

Professionalising in communication

Candidates and party members became more professionalised and learned to tailor their communication during campaigns. They were able to talk to the mass media both nationally and internationally, to develop and present a programme, and to organise meetings. Most of them learned by doing, since free access to media was new. Novel formats, including debates, were introduced on national television. The Superior Instance for the Independence of the Elections (ISIE) and electoral laws regulated access to the media, but some private channels were closely linked to the interests of a given political party. This was the case of *Al-Mustakillah* in 2011, a private television channel owned by a London-based businessman, Hechmi Hamdi, with a turbulent past as a member of *Ennahda* and of Ben Ali's party, the Democratic Constitutional Rally (RCD). During the 2011 campaign, Hamdi created a party, *Al-Aridha Chaabeya*,[5] whose candidates were particularly successful in rural areas where *Al-Mustakillah* was popular. Every day, they were on air to present the movement's 'populist' programme, which included free health care, basic income for the unemployed, and respect for Islam.

However, some candidates had prior experience in communicating with international media, a skill they had developed under Ben Ali, when, as members of the political opposition, they were unable to access national media outlets (Zederman 2019). In revolutionary Tunisia, the international presence was quite noteworthy (Marks 2013; Marzo 2020), as Western 'democracy makers' (Guilhot 2005) participated in developmentalist configurations (Olivier de Sardan 1995) along with foreign observers from countries that joined forces with new domestic political forces. International observers, embassies representatives project managers from international organisations, and journalists contributed to the professionalisation of political actors in both obvious and discreet ways. Members of international non-governmental organisations (NGOs) and foundations organised training for new political actors, as well as conferences and workshops. Participants learned new skills and how to behave as legitimate actors in the political field. They incorporated new norms in terms of dress code, presentation, and public speaking (Perez 2021) to conform to global political norms.

Campaigning was used to display the ability of these actors to play by those rules and to be seen as legitimate in the political sphere after spending years in exile or operating illegally. The international presence served both as a resource for and as a constraint on these political actors. During the 2014 campaign for instance, *Ennahda*'s women candidates were put forward by the party but were given strict guidelines on how to behave: heels and makeup were compulsory,[6] as a candidate told me. *Ennahda*'s leaders also tried to control their image: they hired journalists to cover some of their meetings and campaign activities[7] when former ministers of the Troïka were involved.

Setting partisan identities

Campaigns crystallised partisan identities not only on the political spectrum but also as a set of tools as part of the communication strategies of the candidates. They had to decide on a logo that would be printed on the ballot with the colour, name, and motto contributing to the identification of the party. Most of these visual signifiers were aimed at showing that the party represented the whole of Tunisia. The purple colour favoured by deposed President Ben Ali was ruled out. So was green, a colour usually associated with Islamist movements, especially the Egyptian Muslim Brotherhood (MB), and *Ennahda*'s leaders were particularly keen to differentiate themselves from the MB. *Ennahda*'s logo is a blue dove flying towards a red star. It echoes the colours of the Moroccan Party for Justice and Development (PJD)[8] and the Turkish Justice and Development Party (AKP),[9] which served as major inspirations for *Ennahda*'s leadership. Most party leaders chose red – the colour of the Tunisian flag – such as with *Joumhouri*'s[10] red tree, *Union Patriotique Libre*'s (UPL[11]) red lion, and *Parti Communiste des Ouvriers de Tunisie*'s (PCOT)[12] red sickle and hammer. *Nidaa Tounes* leaders opted for a red palm tree. These visual identities would go on to be seen on the T-shirts that *Nidaa Tounes* provided its activists, on caps distributed by members of *Ennahda*, and on little cards showcasing the logo of a given party. The latter were handed out by most of the major parties when campaign directors realised that ballots were confusing voters. The ballots did not include the name of the candidates or the party, only logos and their number on the list, which could reach as high as 70. To counter this confusion, parties printed cards with the logo and the number of the candidate list as well as the name of the head of the list.

Identifying one's position on the political spectrum

Moreover, for candidates, campaigning provided the opportunity to explain the party's electoral programmes and to clarify where they stood on the political spectrum. In the case of *Nidaa Tounes*, several internal committees composed of academics led by a former leftist opponent of Ben Ali and human rights advocate, wrote the programme for the 2014 elections. Its binary rhetoric juxtaposed a 'Tunisian way of life' and 'modernist' model in keeping with Bourguibism to what was presented as an Islamist project aimed at dissolving Tunisian identity into Islam. However, programmes are also political objects in 'a good campaign kit' that conform to Westerners' expectations. For *Nidaa Tounes*, drafting a programme allowed the party leadership to showcase how many academics supported them and to appear as technocrats and members of the intelligentsia.

This 'Tunisian way of life' was not only defended in the *Nidaa Tounes* programme, but was also performed during meetings. '*Nidaa* is not just a political party, it's Tunisia itself!'[13] was a sentiment hammered into the political consciousness by the movement's founding fathers and reflected in the electoral motto they adopted: '*Tahya Tounes*' (Long Live Tunisia). Its members opposed political Islam and foregrounded a more Mediterranean- and European-oriented Tunisian lifestyle and identity. Meetings in the rural governorates were designed to promote Tunisia's national history. In Haïdra, a small district famous for its Roman ruins, a meeting took place in front of the archaeological site and the colonial-era train station had been transformed into a stage.[14] A band played traditional music, and two horse riders were dressed in the traditional clothes of the region, well known for its *zarda*.[15] After the meeting, members of the list paraded in the street along with the band and the horsemen. In Thala, in the northern part of Kasserine's electoral district, party leaders inaugurated *Nidaa Tounes*' new office with a freshly painted fresco of Habib Bourguiba.[16]

The international pressure to professionalise and run a 'good' campaign was accompanied by catch-all strategies that parties developed, calling into question the apparent bipolarity of political life. Indeed, bipolarisation was only apparent and aimed at mobilising voters during the elections (Netterstrom 2015). However, even during the electoral campaigns, the cleavage opposing secular to religious positions was instrumentalised and lost its salience at specific moments. For instance, *Nidaa Tounes* leaders quoted the Quran, including *suras* on posters,[17] and mobilised imams during the campaign (Grasso 2021). For its part, *Ennahda*'s meetings during the 2014 campaign displayed the party's wish to become a 'normal' actor after decades of operating in secrecy. Here, normalisation was enacted through displays of patriotism. Members of the campaign paid attention to having as many Tunisian flags as flags with *Ennahda*'s logo. Meetings opened and closed by singing the national anthem. They foregrounded young people and women and outlined their attachment to Tunisian history. Even *Ennahda*'s slogan for the 2014 campaign placed Tunisia at its heart: 'My love for Tunisia isn't just hot air'.[18] The party's candidates chanted it while canvassing. Yet, they also insisted on the importance of the revolution by reading poems about it and paying respect to the martyrs.[19] Patriotism and attachment to the revolution were thus two of the resources used to reinforce the new political actor's claims to respect and legitimacy.

Meetings displayed the ability of each list of candidates to be present on the ground, to distribute goods, and to enlist supporters. They relied on electoral machines whose functioning calls into question the very possibility of studying post-revolutionary elections without taking into account previous electoral experiences in Tunisia.

Electoral machines in transition

One cannot have wandered around Tunis in October 2014 without noticing groups of people distributing political tracts for one party or another. These people usually looked similar: they were young, they wore T-shirts or caps with the logo of their party, and they shared a hope to get 'the help' the party leaders or candidates had promised them. Some of them had a more formal role in campaigning, but they were all tasked with securing votes in a specific neighbourhood, monitoring voting on election day, and collecting voters' demands. In sum, they acted as brokers between the party leadership and voters. They all played a part in the electoral machine of the largest political organisations. This section focuses on those machines and how parties relied on a repertoire of electoral contention shaped by international norms and inherited from the authoritarian period. It calls into question the bipolarity of political life between Islamists and modernists, as the focus was largely socio-economic in nature. It also foregrounds the way political leaders and candidates display their personal wealth as a political resource, allowing them to address people's needs. Such a presentation of political actors blurs the borders between public and private goods and eventually strengthens neo-patrimonial conceptions of the state.

From the study of local anchorage to that of political machine

The strength of the democratisation paradigm looms large in the literature dealing with elections in the Middle East and North Africa (MENA) region. In authoritarian regimes, election results are known beforehand, so why study them? And even more so, why should we study electoral campaigns if everyone knows the outcome? Within a critical approach to democratisation processes focused on regime hybridisation, Tunisian elections have been studied as ways for the regime to reinforce control over the population (Camau et al. 1981). Moreover, studies on the Moroccan electoral scene (Bennani-Chraïbi et al. 2004; Zaki 2009) and on Egyptian elections (Arafat and Ben Nefissa 2005) foreground how, in a constrained context, electoral competition invests other spaces. When elections take place under authoritarian rule or are based on patronage dynamics, their competitiveness does not vanish and competition is displaced to other spaces (i.e. who is nominated as a candidate, who gets administrative support to organise their campaign, who builds up a strong local anchorage, and so on). These studies invite us to take seriously the historicity of the electoral process and its effect on campaigning, even during regime change. Vannetzel (2016) especially insists on the small degree of specialisation of political candidates and MPs, and on the intertwinement of political organisations and local charitable associations.

In pre-2011 Tunisia, political parties' local anchoring was very limited. MPs were expected to be in Tunis and serve as representatives of the whole nation (Camau et al. 1981). The local district was not considered to be a relevant place for political debate: campaigning before 2011 thus consisted of organising formal encounters between the candidate and the population, with the candidate running through a speech dealing mostly with national issues. Local issues were dealt with at the scale of the governorate, by nominated *walis*, who were part of the RCD (Camau et al. 1981; Hibou 2006). In post–Ben Ali Tunisia until 2018, MPs were the only elected political actors, which is why they crystallised people's expectations and were expected to answer to them. Political organisations and campaigning candidates therefore went to the people and tried to answer their demands: from the 2014 elections onwards, they openly tried to do so by building up electoral machines.

This concept was first studied in the United States and outlines the clientelist functioning of the representative regime (Bonnet 2010). Focusing on electoral machines allows for a critical approach to voting in democratic regimes. Campaigns therefore read like a show of strength. In Tunisia, the 2014 campaign configuration was quite different from that of 2011, when political organisations, with the exception of *Ennahda* and *Al-Aridha Chaabeya*, mostly campaigned in very limited areas through small gatherings and meetings. A socio-geographical analysis of the electoral results at the scale of the polling station outlines a sharp discrepancy between *Al-Aridha Chaabeya*, whose candidates achieved strong results in rural neighbourhoods, *Ennahda*, which took first place in urban deprived areas, and secularist leftists whose lists performed best in affluent neighbourhoods (Gana and Van Hamme 2016).

In 2014, many political actors, and especially those who lost the 2011 election (i.e. the left), explained that it was time to 'do what it takes' to win the elections, and condemned the naïveté of those who still did not want to 'get their hands dirty'.[20] This strategy implied a greater commitment in districts designated as the interior regions, which are at a socio-economic disadvantage compared to the coast and big cities (Beheldi 2012). Candidates then tried to build up their local anchoring in those regions whose representation had been increased by the electoral laws after the revolution (Gobe 2017).[21] Political leaders hence built up electoral machines composed of not only volunteers, but also a number of workers specifically hired for the campaign. On the one hand, electoral engineering allowed for some important locally grounded feedback on the citizens' needs. On the other hand, it paved the way for redistributing collective resources.

Displaying electoral expertise

These electoral machines are inherited from RCD structures, with former RCD members labelling their participation in elections prior to 2011 as 'expertise'. They enter the electoral competition by occupying elective or non-elective positions such as head of the regional campaign or head of a local office. Brokers can be found at several levels: inside the constituency to access socio-economically disadvantaged families and direct charitable actions towards them; inside the local well-known families and institutions of the electoral district; and at the head of the party in the capital.

Particularly striking in the Tunisian case is how some of the candidates and their political entourage tend to display their knowledge of how to campaign to appear more professional or legitimate. Indeed, a number of them do not hesitate to legitimise their presence by explaining their role during electoral campaigns in the RCD at several levels (as local brokers, as responsible for the campaign in one region, as member of the national committee). Surprisingly enough, they use the same rhetoric, whether or not they occupied prominent positions at the head of political parties.

They define this expertise as their ability to organise smoothly run meetings and to respect the new framework for transparent elections set by the ISIE. It also includes being able to hire workers for the campaign (who will distribute flyers, canvass, attend meetings) and to collect vote promises. Brokers display their expertise both to national actors and to international organisations observing the elections. During interviews, they emphasised their electoral experiences prior to 2011 and repurposed their participation in elections under authoritarian rule as 'skills'. MPs and members of political organisations had tense relationships with voters in particular regions. The relation to political organisations echoed the sharp territorial contrast not only between the coast and the hinterland, but also within each district, between the centre of cities and their peripheries be they rural or urban (Gana et al. 2012). The difficulty in accessing certain neighbourhoods showcased the limitations of state penetration and identity formation. In this context, political organisations relied on electoral brokers to secure access to some districts. Electoral brokers then insisted that their local knowledge of power networks and important families allowed them to negotiate access to poor neighbourhoods that were typically unwelcoming to candidates and political parties.[22] Some also identified their previous work experience with social services as political resources, since it provided contacts and access to state authorities, and to potential voter pools in the poorest neighbourhoods.

Electoral brokers and party employees also demonstrate their skills through canvassing. In doing so, they insist on two types of expertise: on the one hand, international experience in how elections should be run – with a recurrent reference to 'American methods' – and on the other hand, local experience of influential networks built before 2011. This calls into question the ambivalent interactions between international norms imported from Western international organisations and the heritage of authoritarianism in the new context of pluralism. These two references are intertwined in what the machines do: they not only canvass constituencies and organise meetings, but they also develop charitable actions before the official campaign starts.

Canvassing and meetings: what the machines do

For each candidate, meetings were primarily a way to display local strength and solid connections to the local community. They accounted for the strength of the candidates and political parties. In this regard, it is considered important for the head of the list to be invited to lunch by one of his relatives after the meeting. This also allowed for more informal exchanges between the candidate, his supporters, and local notables. Where the meeting took place was also of symbolic importance. For instance, both *Nidaa Tounes* and the electoral held one of their largest meetings in the very modest neighbourhood of Mellassine in the capital. For *Nidaa Tounes*, it was a way to show that the party not only catered to rich people living in the northern suburbs like La Marsa or Carthage but it also demonstrated that they were welcome in this neighbourhood where demonstrations can be explosive and that they could 'control' the young *hittists*[23] living there. Moreover, the composition of attendees is important. During most meetings I attended, women were often in the minority but were sitting in the front row. Young people wearing the colour of the party would often welcome the candidate and his entourage. Even though meetings differed from place to place and depended on the candidate's resources, they read like scripted moments: special occasions for the candidate to display local strength and his ability to come and talk to the population.

While the meetings were described as 'party time, music, flags',[24] canvassing was presented as a more serious campaign activity, which took place more discreetly. It was presented by both candidates and electoral brokers as the most important part of the campaign and the best way to 'go to the people'. Canvassing brought together not only candidates and voters but also brokers, who sold their local knowledge and anchoring. With canvassing, candidates could display their professionalism and expertise when it came to campaigning: the largest meeting room of the *Ennahda* office in Kasserine town during the 2014 campaign was replete with maps of the governorate, showing where to go and with whom. This technique was taken up by most political organisations whose leaders and candidates canvassed their electoral districts. This activity was conducted rationally. For instance, during the 2014 campaign, many UPL offices had a secretary in charge of coordinating canvassing using phones and large notebooks where they wrote down who went where every afternoon.[25] In some offices, the brokers employed by the party used notebooks to record various data on the people they met: name and ID number, number of inhabitants in the house, phone numbers, demands and needs such as help in financing a small project or finding a job in the civil service.[26] Phone numbers were used for a mass SMS campaign on the day of the election: people received a text message exhorting them to go and vote and reminding them of the number on the list they had agreed to support. Each broker was hoping to be paid one Tunisian dinar for each vote promised. Here, the difference between brokers and clients – two types that the literature usually distinguishes – was blurred since the local brokers were usually also clients of the party. They were paid to work for the party and benefitted from the candidates' displays of generosity and munificence (i.e. a feast in a restaurant for the campaign teams).

From state patrimonialism to party-based patrimonialism

Political leaders positioned themselves as capable of funding and addressing people's needs thanks to their own personal wealth. It is their own wealth they displayed when campaigning, as multiple interactions with candidates and party leaders show. For instance, the head of the *Nidaa Tounes* campaign insisted that he was the one directly paying all the brokers, all the offices of the party, and such from his own personal resources.[27] These attitudes outline the remaining importance of state neo-patrimonialism (Eisenstadt 1973), which has been thoroughly analysed in independent Tunisia as the blur between personal and public resources at the head of the state, and as a key aspect of authoritarianism(Moore 1970). The campaigning organisation revealed a transition from state neo-patrimonialism to a party-based one. It outlined the inheritance of patrimonialism practices among party leaders who took up Ben Ali's former practices. Personal wealth became a campaign issue for some candidates. Candidates displayed their ability to use their personal wealth to solve the country's problems in order to present themselves as suitable and capable candidates for the presidency. They managed to reverse the stigma: the blur between state and private resources is shown not as a problem and the result of a plunder of public resources, but as a solution.

Major political organisations started organising meetings with local authorities to negotiate support long before the official campaign. Others distributed goods to the population such as schoolbags to families with school-age children, financial help to buy a sheep for *Eid*, or new clothes for children on *Eid-Essrir*. These distributions took place before the official campaign period, but they were also part of the campaigning process. They could be done directly in the name of the party or through a charitable association. These practices were also inherited from the authoritarian period when the strength of the Ben Ali system relied on its ability to keep the security pact (Hibou 2006) mostly by distributing goods to the poorest parts of the population.

However, one can distinguish between different ways of 'doing good'. Some political parties, especially *Ennahda*, emphasised their charitable activities by associating them with a discourse on Islam and the necessity to behave in a 'good' way. Thus, not only were their charitable organisations active before the electoral campaign, but they also functioned throughout the year (Sigillò 2020). While they specialised in assisting the poorest parts of the population, they also developed specialised resources on topics linked to democratisation; for instance, how to claim one's right in the transitional justice process (Kebaïli 2022). Conversely, when other parties resorted to charitable actions, either they did them only at the time of the campaign or these actions were done by only one personality within the party who, for instance, funded young people's studies or provided them with jobs in his firm (Perez 2021).

Despite the differences between meetings and canvassing sessions, one cannot but note how political practices and an electoral repertoire of electoral contention (Desrumaux and Lefebvre 2016) circulated during the campaign from one list to the other. The transposition of the concept of a repertoire of contention, coined by Charles Tilly (1978), proves heuristic in exploring the continuity of pre-2011 practices after Ben Ali's departure, as well as the circulation of a mode of action imported from abroad (such as canvassing). The candidates, who often had contrasting individual resources, imitated each other even while defending different programmes and occupying opposing positions on the political spectrum. They adjusted former electoral practices to the new context. However, this actualisation of practices inherited from authoritarianism failed to retain the voters' loyalty and paved the way for a crisis of clientelist relations.

'Politics of the belly' and crisis of patronage

Even though political actors resort to practices that have been established for a long time in Tunisia, they do so in a context of crisis. The revolutionary configuration in Tunisia has been analysed as the result of a crisis of patronage (Hibou 2011), a crisis reinforced by the electoral period. Clientelism no longer hinges on Ben Ali's hegemonic party but irrigates multiparty politics. It takes specific forms in political organisations where some party leaders represented themselves as rich benefactors able to solve the personal needs of their staff and the country's problems with their personal resources. However, clientelism is no longer tolerated as it was before 2011; nor is neo-patrimonialism. The revolution has transformed the perception of what was tolerable or unacceptable, and the spreading of clientelism during electoral campaigns only increases voters' dissatisfaction.

Such a configuration enriches our grasp on what has been analysed as the 'politics of the belly' in sub-Saharan Africa (Bayart 1989). In Banégas' study on the democratisation process in Benin, he describes how clientelism is reinforced and transforms from state- to party-centric. He shows that 'the building up of a pluralist public space, and the possible emergence of new regimes of democratic subjectivity paradoxically operate through clientelist logics' (Banégas 2003: 424). Electoral campaigns provide evidence of the level of expectations towards the state and elected candidates. We argue that the Tunisian case works differently: distributing material or immaterial goods leads to anti-parliamentarianism and voter abstention.

We have seen how electoral machines employed young *hittists* to buy the 'right' to campaign: these odd jobs sometimes last for the whole campaign or sometimes only for one day and are not sufficient to retain voters. *Hittists* are often responsible for security during the meetings of different parties; they are not party activists, but youngsters considered to be potential threats to the meeting and who need to be neutralised. Such a configuration echoes what Banégas describes as the revenge of those 'from the bottom of the bottom' upon those 'in the upper part of the upper part': 'the majority of citizens perceive the electoral campaign as a time when it is possible to take back from politicians the money they made since they came to power, and even more so since independence' (Banégas 2003: 433). During meetings, not only do political parties boast of their power and capacity to hold a meeting in a sensitive area, but youngsters also demonstrate their ability to monetise access to the neighbourhood. For a short time, they embody a symbolic inversion of this balance of power. Such an inversion is quite fragile, as the number of incidents during meetings and campaigns shows.[28]

'Why do you think we're here? It's because of misery, and if we had a job, we wouldn't be here'.[29] This statement outlines the disenchanted link to politics developed by people working for the campaign. What is more, it foregrounds the main demand: employment. Observations during the 2014 campaign showed that leaders or candidates often did not pay their brokers and workers what was expected. A number of misunderstandings between 'staff' expecting to be paid for their work and partisan leaders who considered them unpaid volunteers triggered suspicion towards partisan politics and limited partisan loyalty. The contrast between the wealth of some partisan leaders and the non-payment of small salaries to people in precarious situations strengthened the collective feeling of betrayal among the staff who could then decide to rebel and turn against the party.

The Tunisian electoral campaign therefore reads like a case study to understand how the limits of the acceptable and the intolerable may change during a political crisis. It foregrounds how different registers of moral economy are conjured up by clients to denounce partisan clientelism. The label of clientelism designates different practices, local or national, considered as morally reprehensible or not. One can only observe a hiatus between the concept that is morally condemned (vote buying) and its practical requalification ('he gave new clothes to my son'), which is accepted. However, accepting new clothes or money is no indication of a vote in Tunisia as elsewhere (Garrigou 1992). Patrons fail to pay in due time the people who had worked for them and their clients. They do not even reward them symbolically. These electoral brokers, whether they were active at the local or the national level, no longer feel obliged to vote for the party for which they worked. If presents for children or food and medicine for those in need are accepted and play a part in the promotion of candidates, inaction when it comes to jobs in the public service is considered unacceptable and can generate tensions – as does the non-payment for odd jobs completed during the campaign. Electoral campaigning is a moment when money is 'eaten': it provides a number of odd jobs and individual goods for families. Yet, in this electoral job market, jobs remain transitory and rarely lead to permanent positions. Partisan actors fail to promote loyalty between voters and their organisation. The irregularity of the distribution of goods prevents the forming of any strong bond between most clients and parties. The revolution transformed the border between the unacceptable and the acceptable when it comes to clientelism and it is even more blatant during the electoral campaigning process: even though voters are recruited by political organisations and electoral machines are built, many campaign workers do not vote, and do not hesitate to affirm their disgust towards partisan politics. Such a fracture between political candidates and voters contributed to the denunciation of the party system that the Constitution provides for and paved the way for populist initiatives.

Conclusion

What does the first peaceful alternation of power in Tunisia mean? Electoral campaigning in revolutionary Tunisia is characterised by a tension between new forms of campaigning produced by an electoral pluralist competition organised under international pressure and the legacy of former electoral practices. Campaigns are privileged moments when new political organisations form, define their identity, enrol new members, and develop their local anchoring. However, most political actors are confronted with their need for competence on how to run an election. These actors who accessed the institutions and political sphere in 2011 are new to them and lack electoral skills. Such a configuration brings them to rely on former RCD members and to observe and imitate one another when it comes to communicating, organising meetings or going to the people. They set up electoral machines, personalise political bonds, and canvass the poorest neighbourhoods. In order to gain access to areas where state representatives are not particularly welcome, they employ a number of brokers and often resort to former members of Ben Ali's party. Yet, these electoral machines are caught in the same crisis of clientelism as the one that led to the collapse of the RCD system: the demand for dignity and the 2011 mobilisation shape new conceptions of what is tolerable and what is unacceptable when it comes to clientelism. While campaigns are generally analysed as a moment of electoral mobilisation that deepens political cleavages, post–Ben Ali campaigns have had the reverse effect. Parties instrumentalised the cleavage opposing religious and secular actors. They enhanced this cleavage to position themselves on the political spectrum and made it the major point of their programme. Yet, during their meetings, they tried to appeal to a broader set of voters by asserting their attachment to Islam and Islamic values in society, as well as their modernism and patriotism. Political practices circulated between parties, even when it came to quoting the Quran, and Bourguiba. The result is a strong movement of de-mobilisation on the voters' side. Citizens tend to demonstrate their will to abstain from voting and express their disgust towards partisan politics, paving the way for counterrevolutionary and radical behaviour.

Notes

1 The fieldwork this chapter is based on was funded by the ERC WAFAW. I would also like to thank Zoe Petkanas and Hugo Bouvard for their efficient proofreading, as well as the coordinators of the book for their insightful suggestions.
2 The Quartet refers to the four organisations (the Tunisian General Labour Union and Tunisian Confederation of Industry, Trade, and Handicrafts, Tunisian League of Human Rights, and Tunisia's National Bar Association) that facilitated a national dialogue between the majority and the opposition during the constitutional process.
3 The electoral law disposes that every list of candidates should be paritarian. This parity is vertical, which is to say that every list is composed of the same number of men and women but that it's not compulsory to have the same number of men and women as head of the list. Hence the number of elected men was far superior to that of women.
4 Author's interview with MP, Tunis, September 2014.
5 The full name of the party is the Popular Petition for Freedom, Justice and Development.
6 Author's interview with a candidate from the diaspora, Paris, September 2014.
7 Author's observations, Ben Arous, October 2014.
8 The Party for Justice and Development (PJD) is the predominant Moroccan Islamist party. It was part of the opposition until 2011 when its leaders won the elections held after the 2011 reform of the Constitution.

9 AKP is the Turkish Islamist movement and is also translated as Party for Justice and Development. Its leader Erdogan has been in power since 2003 and it is considered a model for other Islamist formations moving from opposition to being in power.
10 *Joumhouri* (Republican Party) is the new name of the Popular Democratic Party, a political organisation founded in 1983 by one of the most famous historical opponents to Bourguiba and Ben Ali: Ahmed Nejib Chebbi.
11 Free Patriotic Union (UPL) is a neoliberal movement created by a businessman in advance of the 2011 elections.
12 Tunisian Workers' Communist Party is Tunisia's main communist party and was founded in 1986.
13 Author's interview with one of *Nidaa Tounes*' vice-presidents, Tunis, November 2015.
14 Author's fieldwork, Haïdra, October 2014.
15 A *zarda* is a party organised on the annual pilgrimage to a saint's tomb and is generally accompanied by horse shows (Ltifi 2006).
16 Author's fieldwork, Thala, October 2014.
17 Author's fieldwork, Tunis, October 2014.
18 Author's fieldwork, Ben Arous, October 2014.
19 Author's fieldwork, Majen Bel Abbes, October 2014.
20 Author's fieldwork, Tunis–Sfax–Kef, June–October 2014.
21 The electoral law drafted in 2011 increases the number of MPs for the hinterland constituencies: in addition to the quota of one MP seat for 60,000 citizens, each 'hinterland' constituency received an extra seat.
22 Author's interviews, Tunis, Kasserine, September 2014–November 2015.
23 *Hittist* is the term used to refer to a young unemployed man who literally 'holds the wall' (Allal 2011).
24 Author's interview with *Nidaa Tounes* candidate in El Kef, October 2014.
25 Author's fieldwork, Kasserine, October 2014.
26 Author's fieldwork, Tunis, October 2014.
27 Author's interview with the vice-president of *Nidaa Tounes*, Mellassine, November 2015.
28 Fieldwork, Kasserine, October 2014.
29 Fieldwork, Tunis, October 2014.

References

Allal, Amin. 2011. 'Avant on tenait le mur, maintenant on tient le quartier !. Germes d'un passage au politique de jeunes hommes de quartiers populaires lors du moment révolutionnaire à Tunis'. *Politique Africaine* 121(1): 53–67.
Allal, Amin and Marie Vannetzel. 2017. 'Des lendemains qui déchantent? Pour une sociologie des moments de restauration'. *Politique Africaine* 146(2): 5–28.
Allal, Amin and Geisser Vincent. 2018. *Tunisie, une démocratisation au-dessus de tout soupçon*. Paris: CNRS Éditions.
Arafat, Alaa ed-Din and Sarah Ben Nefissa. 2005. *Vote et Démocratie dans l'Egypte contemporaine*. Paris: IRD-Karthala.
Ayari Michael, Béchir. 2016. *Le Prix de l'engagement politique dans la Tunisie autoritaire, gauchistes et islamistes sous Bourguiba et Ben Ali (1957–2011)*. Tunis: IRMC-Karthala.
Banégas, Richard. 2003. *La démocratie à pas de caméléon, transition et imaginaires politiques au Bénin*. Paris: Karthala.
Bayart, Jean-François. 1989. *L'État en Afrique, la politique du ventre*. Paris: Fayard.
Beheldi, Amor. 2012. 'La question spatiale'. ACMACO & CEMAREF. *Tunisie Perspective 2040*. Tunis: Sud Éditions.
Bennani-Chraïbi, Mounia, Maryam Catusse and Jean-Claude Santucci. 2004. *Scènes et coulisses de l'élection au Maroc. Législatives 2002*. Paris: Karthala.
Bonnet, François. 2010. 'Les machines politiques aux États-Unis. Clientélisme et immigration entre 1870 et 1950'. *Politix* 92(4): 7–29.
Bono, Irene, Béatrice Hibou, Hamza Meddeb and Mohamed Tozy. 2015. *L'État d'injustice au Maghreb, Maroc et Tunisie*. Paris: Karthala.
Camau, Michel, Fadila Amrani and Rafaa Ben Achour. 1981. *Contrôle politique et régulations électorales en Tunisie*. Aix-en-Provence: Édisud.

Cavatorta, Francesco and Lise Storm. 2018. *Political Parties in the Arab World Continuity and Change*. Edinburgh: Edinburgh University Press.
Desrumaux, Clément and Rémi Lefebvre. 2016. 'Pour une sociologie des répertoires d'actions électorales'. *Politix* 113(1): 5–16.
Eisenstadt, Schmuel. 1973. *Traditional Patrimonialism and Modern Neopatrimonialism*. Beverly Hills, CA: Sage Publications.
Ferjani, Mohamed Chérif. 2012. 'Révolution, élections et évolution du champ politique tunisien'. *Confluences Méditerranée* 82(3): 107–116.
Gana, Alia and Gilles Van Hamme. 2016. *Élections et territoires en Tunisie. Enseignements des scrutins post-révolution (2011–2014)*. Tunis: IRMC-Karthala.
Gana, Alia, Gilles Van Hamme, and Maher Ben Rebah. 2012. « La Territorialité du vote pour l'Assemblée Nationale Constituante Tunisienne de 2011 ». *Confluences Méditerranée* 82(3): 51–69.
Garrigou, Alain. 1992. *Le Vote et la Vertu. Comment les français sont devenus électeurs*. Paris: Presse de la FNSP.
Geisser, Vincent and Déborah Perez. 2016. 'De la difficulté à "faire parti" dans la Tunisie post-Ben Ali'. *Confluences Méditerranée* 98(3): 21–44.
Gobe, Éric. 2017. 'De la dialectique du «local» et du «national» dans les lois électorales tunisiennes ou comment représenter le «peuple» dans la Tunisie post-Ben Ali'. *L'Année du Maghreb* 16(16): 153–170.
Gobe, Éric and Larbi Chouikha. 2014. 'La Tunisie politique en 2013: de la bipolarisation idéologique au «consensus constitutionnel» ?' *L'Année du Maghreb* 11(11): 301–322.
Grasso, Anna. 2021. 'L'utilisation de la ressource religieuse par un parti «laïque» dans: la Tunisie de l'après-révolution'. *Revue Internationale de Politique Comparée* 28(1–2): 111–134.
Guilhot, Nicolas. 2005. *The Democracy Makers: Human Rights and the Politics of Global Order*. New York: Columbia University Press.
Guilhot, Nicolas and Philippe C. Schmitter. 2000. 'De la transition à la consolidation. Une lecture rétrospective des *democratization studies*'. *Revue Française de Science Politique* 50(4–5): 615-632.
Hibou, Béatrice. 2006. *La Force de l'obéissance: Économie politique de la répression en Tunisie*. Paris: La Découverte.
Hibou, Béatrice. 2011. 'Tunisie. Économie politique et morale d'un mouvement social'. *Politique africaine* 121(1): 5–22.
Kebaïli, Sélima. 2022. 'Repenser le rôle des victimes dans la justice transitionnelle en Tunisie: le cas de la «Journée de la loyauté»'. *L'Année du Maghreb* 26(26): 157–174.
Lazarsfeld, Paul F., Bernald Berelson and Hazel Gaudet. 2021 [1948]. *The People's Choice: How the Voter Makes up His Mind in a Presidential Campaign*. New York: Columbia University Press.
Ltifi, Adel. 2006. 'La Famille maraboutique de Sidi Ahmad Tlili: Un exemple d'alliances matrimoniales de notables'. In Abdelhamid Henia (ed.), *Être no table au Maghreb*. Tunis: IRMC-Maisonneuve et Larose, 167–182.
Marks, Monica. 2013. *Inside the Transition Bubble: International Expert Assistance in Tunisia*. Barcelona: Institute for Integrated Transition.
Marzo, Pietro. 2020. *The International Dimension of Tunisia's Transition to Democracy. From Consensus over Democracy to Competitiveness within Democracy*. PhD Thesis, Department of Political Science, Université Laval.
McCarthy, Rory. 2015. 'What happens when Islamists lose an election?' *Monkey Cage, Washington Post*, June 11.
Moore, Clement Henry. 1970. *Politics in North Africa: Algeria, Morocco, Tunisia*. London: Little, Brown & Company.
Netterstrøm, Kasper Ly. 2015. 'After the Arab Spring: The Islamists' compromise in Tunisia.' *Journal of Democracy* 26(4): 110–124.
Olivier de Sardan, Jean-Pierre. 1995. *Anthropologie et Développement: Essai en socio-anthropologie du changement social*. Marseille: Karthala.
Perez, Déborah. 2021. *Devenir député en situation révolutionnaire. Expérimentations démocratiques et restaurations autoritaires en Tunisie (2011–2015)*. PhD in Political Science, IEP d'Aix-En-Provence.
Salamé, Ghassan. 1991. 'Sur la causalité d'un manque: pourquoi le monde arabe n'est-il donc pas démocratique?' *Revue Française de Science Politique* 41(3): 307–341.
Sawicki, Frédéric. 1994. 'Configuration sociale et genèse d'un milieu partisan. Le cas du parti socialiste en Ille-et-Vilaine'. *Sociétés Contemporaines* 2(1): 83–11.
Sigillò, Ester. 2020. 'Islamism and the rise of Islamic charities in post-revolutionary Tunisia: Claiming political Islam through other means?' *British Journal of Middle Eastern Studies*. https://doi.org/10.1080/13530194.2020.1861926.

Stepan, Alfred. 2018. 'Toward a "democracy with democrats" in Tunisia: Mutual accommodation between Islamic and secular activists'. In Jean-Pierre Filiu and Stephane Lacroix (eds.), *Revisiting the Arab Uprisings: The Politics of a Revolutionary Moment*, 9–28. London: Hurst & Company.

Storm, Lise. 2013. *Prospects for Democracy in North Africa: Parties and Party System Institutionalization in the Maghreb*. Boulder, CO: Lynne Rienner.

Tilly, Charles. 1978. *From Mobilization to Revolution*. Reading, MA: Addison-Weasley Publishing Co.

Vannetzel, Marie. 2016. 'Grandeur et déclin des Frères musulmans égyptiens: les mutations de l'élite parlementaire frériste de Moubarak à Morsi, 2005–2012'. *Actes de la Recherche en Sciences Sociales* 211–212(1–2): 36–53.

Wolf, Anne. 2017. *Political Islam in Tunisia: The history of Ennahda*. London: Hurst & Company.

Zaki Lamia. 2009. *Terrains de campagne au Maroc: les élections législatives de 2007*. Paris and Tunis: Karthala et Institut de Recherche sur le Maghreb Contemporain.

Zederman, Mathilde. 2019. '«Faire parti» à distance. Partis politiques tunisiens pro- et anti-régime Ben Ali en France.' *Revue Internationale de Politique Comparée* 26(2–3): 33–56.

22
DIGITAL STRATEGIES OF TUNISIAN POLITICAL PARTIES

The case of the 2018 municipal elections

Bader Ben Mansour

Introduction

Since the 2011 revolution, social media platforms have been the backbone of electoral campaigns in Tunisia. Indeed, in a country where 7 million of the 11 million inhabitants are connected to Facebook (M'rad 2020; Hammami 2020) and where political advertising is forbidden in traditional media, it is not surprising to see electoral campaigns taking place on social media. While a darker side of digital political communication has been observed in recent years, including the rise of fake news and trolling (Hammami 2020), the web is still valued in Tunisia and remains the primary tool for political information for citizens (Bougamra 2015; Hammami 2020). Recently, Elswah Mona and Philip Howard (2020: 2) noted that

> after ousting Ben Ali, Tunisian activists continued to engage in online civic actions with Facebook being the most popular social media platform…. About 66% of Tunisians have subscribed to Facebook, making Tunisia the top country in the Maghreb to use Facebook.
>
> *(Elswah and Howard, 2020:2)*

Despite the importance of the web, the strategies and practices of the digital electoral campaigns of political parties are still largely unknown. There is a gap between the rapid development of digital campaigns across the world and the lack of studies on this subject in Tunisia, where the field of research remains largely unexplored in theoretical and empirical terms, as most of the work on digital campaigns is devoted to the study of Western democracies.

Research into emerging democracies is scarce, but to fully understand the role of social media in politics, it is essential to analyze different contexts. As several researchers point out, the impact of social media on election campaigns varies from one country to another, depending on the cultural, social and political context (Enli and Moe 2013; Vaccari 2013; Gibson 2020; Lilleker et al. 2015; Giasson and Small 2017; Gibson et al. 2014). Thus, there is a need to study 'less obvious' cases today (Giasson et al. 2018; Giasson and Small 2017; Larsson and Svensson 2014). While social media is important in Western democracies, it is equally important in countries that do not have a free and independent press, according to Shelley Boulianne (2017, 2020).

In countries where politicians have limited access to traditional media or in countries where political advertising is banned, such as Tunisia, the role of social media could be more decisive. Each context has specificities that may have an impact on how partisan organizations establish and conduct their digital election campaigns.

This chapter looks at political parties' motivations behind their use of social media. This involves analyzing – through the discourse of strategists – the objectives that anchor the digital campaigns of the political parties in our sample for the 2018 municipal elections.

We first determine the extent to which political parties have integrated social media into their campaign strategies. We then analyze the strategic objectives assigned to social media by political parties for these municipal elections.

Interviews with communications strategists were conducted prior to the municipal elections during the period from 04/07/2017 to 06/12/2017. Made in person, they lasted on average 113 minutes. The objective was to identify the strategic intentions that anchored the digital campaigns. A content analysis of the responses to questions about the use of social media was conducted using QDA Miner 5 software to identify the objectives of digital campaigns.

Social media and politics

In recent years, scientific production on the political web has been greatly enriched by the rapid development of digital technology and its links with various events that have marked the international political scene. From Barack Obama's 2008 presidential campaign to the Arab Spring uprisings in 2011, these events prompted the scientific community to consider the potential of social media to transform citizens' political participation (Bimber 2012; Boulianne 2015 and 2020; Enli and Moe 2013). Social media opened the question of whether it would have the power to create a new space for participation and interaction between political elites and citizens (Graham et al. 2013; Vergeer and Hermans 2013; Ben Mansour 2017).

This question has attracted the interest of several researchers in communication and political science, who have so far mainly studied the web aspects of national election campaigns in established Western democracies. In the practices observed, social media has not really made it possible to strengthen citizens' participation and political commitment; rather, it has replicated traditional forms of communication that limit political participation by citizens and favor the dissemination of partisan information (Giasson et al. 2013; Koc-Michalska et al. 2014; Ben Mansour 2017).

Although social media has created an egalitarian campaign environment for small political parties (Gibson and McAllister 2015; Koc-Michalska et al. 2014), the 'politics as usual' thesis continues to win support from the research community in the era of the participatory web. Most of the empirical research reached strong conclusions about the normalization of the role of social media in political communication strategies. The communication that political parties proposed would thus take a one-way, controlled and professionalized vertical form (Giasson et al. 2013; Graham et al. 2013; Koc-Michalska et al. 2014; Larsson and Moe, 2014; Small 2008; Williams and Gulati 2013; Magin et al. 2017), which is, of course, the opposite of the philosophy of the participatory web and the logic of the social network (Ben Mansour 2017). In addition, the extensive use of micro-targeting practices in recent years through the exploitation of large volumes of personal voter data from the web (Römmele and Gibson 2020; Theviot 2019) has led to the emergence of an even more unbalanced new field of communication – an environment described as 'hyper normality' (Gibson 2020: 2).

Starting in 2016, a darker side to digital campaigns has emerged, resulting in the rise of disinformation, demobilization, bots and trolls (Chadwick 2017; Theviot 2019). According to

Römmele and Gibson (2020), this is a more manipulative approach that goes beyond the application of simple principles of political marketing (Bradshaw and Howard 2017). These aspects, which probably represent the new characteristics of the fourth age in which political communication evolves, justify the cyber-pessimism a large part of the scientific community displays toward social media in politics.

Hybrid election campaigns

With the emergence of social media and its increasing use by citizens, political parties have had no choice but to change the way they design campaign strategies. Digital technology now plays an increasingly important role in the preparation and implementation of political parties' election campaigns (Giasson 2017).

In reality, it is not a question of replacing traditional means of communication with new technologies, but rather of developing communication strategies where the logic of the 'new media' and the traditional means of communication co-exist, complement and reinforce each other within the campaign (Chadwick 2013; Giasson et al. 2018; Chadwick et al. 2016).

Beyond the integration of online and offline communication channels, a cohabitation between the action of the militant base and the control exercised by the elites in the design of electoral strategies is observed (Giasson et al. 2018). These hybrid campaigns emphasize the online participation of activists and sympathizers, while keeping control of the campaign (Vaccari 2010; Giasson et al. 2018; Chadwick 2013). This is a hybridity between a bottom-up and a top-down logic that is being proposed, qualified as controlled interactivity by Jennifer Stomer-Galley (2014). The hypothesis of hybridity has been investigated empirically and confirmed in several established democracies (Chadwick 2013; Vaccari 2010; Gibson 2015; Giasson et al. 2018, 2019). However, no study has attempted to verify the level of hybridity of election campaigns in a context other than that of established Western democracies.

The internal component of digital election campaigns

Digital campaigns have undergone a remarkable evolution over time, marked by a distinct configuration of tools, objectives, human and organizational resources and proximity to one of the two ends of the innovation–standardization spectrum (Gibson 2020). Paradoxically, with the evolution of digital campaigns, research has focused primarily on the analysis of the technical object, namely the digital platforms mobilized by political parties during election campaigns (Gibson 2020; Theviot 2015). Gibson notes though that what is observed on the web is only one component of the digital campaign. While the public external 'showcasing' (websites, email, Facebook pages, Twitter accounts) is important to understand and analyze, it is only part of the underlying binary ecosystem. Jungherr (2016) suggests that to understand the impact of digital tools on campaigns today, researchers should go beyond the content analysis of digital platforms and focus more on integrating digital tools into organizational structures. In addition to the front end, which clearly represents the visible part of the iceberg, there is a back end (Kreiss 2015) that is not observable and consists of important elements that characterize a digital campaign, such as personnel, infrastructure (hardware and software), modes of communication, organizational structures and a set of activities (Gibson 2020; Kreiss 2015). Strategic choices that may concern various aspects of campaigning ranging from targeting practices, to community development, to informal relationships with non-campaign structures are not immediately available in the study of partisan content posted online (Penney 2017; Dommett and Temple 2018).

Thus, behind the use of platforms such as Facebook and Twitter by political parties, digital strategies are designed, developed and implemented based on several considerations, some of which are related to the perceptions of strategists, and the context, timing and affordances of digital platforms (Kreiss et al. 2018). It is this latter aspect of digital campaigning that needs to be explored further.

Strategic objectives assigned to digital campaigns

Given the development of digital tools and their increasing use by citizens, political parties have had no choice but to adapt and comply with these developments, bringing about changes in the development of their digital strategies (Tenscher et al. 2016; Gibson 2020: 17; Lobera and Portos 2020). In some cases, these policy changes have resulted in an openness to engage activists and volunteers by providing opportunities for dialogue or facilitating their involvement in the election campaign (Klinger and Russman 2017; Kalsnes 2016).

This strategic objective adopted by some political parties has led to the emergence of the notion of citizens-initiated campaigning (Gibson 2020; Koc-Michalska et al. 2016) based on community building, resources generation and mobilizing activists/members. The commitment here moves from a mode of consumption of campaign content to a mode of redistribution, where supporters become vectors of digital party content distribution via their online networks, thereby reaching a wider audience (Gibson 2020; Koc-Michalska et al. 2020).

This logic, which is essentially based on the role of party activists and supporters, is based on the two-step model of flow of communication that Katz and Lazarsfeld developed in 1955 (Stromer-Galley 2014; Penney 2017). However, online autonomy is often guided and directed toward certain actions by political organizations, which are constantly wary of losing control of their campaigns. They therefore require coordination with online activists and generally maintain centralized control over the agenda of electoral issues on which to act (Giasson et al. 2018; Chadwick 2013). While some political parties agree to give more freedom to volunteers under certain conditions (Giasson and Small 2017), others categorically refuse to venture in this direction and prefer to remain in known territory (Giasson et al. 2013; Vaccari 2013), adopting numerical strategies dominated by a top-down hierarchical logic (Gibson and Ward 2012; Koc-Michalska et al. 2020). This is a more cautious, targeted and personalized form of communication that generally results in the increased personal visibility of candidates (Giasson 2017; Jackson and Lilleker 2011; Gibson 2020: 41; Koc-Michalska et al. 2020; Enli and Skogerbø 2013).

This choice is not due to complications related to the management of activists and the digital component for political organizations, but rather to tactical reasons. Political parties are allergic to negative controversies and communication slippages that can become viral on digital platforms (Theviot 2018; Giasson et al. 2013). Depending on the context, the timing and the type of campaign, the strategic objectives are set long before the launch of the campaign and constitute the guidelines of the usages that political parties will make of the digital platforms in the campaign (Kalsnes 2016; Bor 2013; Klinger and Russmann 2017; Kreiss et al. 2018).

Based on recent work on the analysis of digital campaigns of political parties (Bor 2013; Chadwick 2013; Kreiss 2012; Vaccari 2010), Giasson and colleagues (2018, 2019) have come up with three types of objectives that strategists generally aim to achieve in the development of digital strategies. First are *communicative objectives* such as disseminating a partisan message, disseminating information about the activities of the party and the leader, reframing/control messages and attacking the adversary. Second are *political objectives* associated with winning the election, generating resources, promoting a political project or ideology, gaining visibility, online and offline mobilizing and getting the vote out. Finally, *marketing objectives* are activities such as

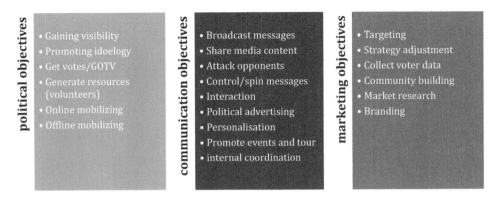

Figure 22.1 Strategic objectives assigned to digital campaigns (inspired by Giasson et al., 2018, 2019)

collecting voter information data, managing a community of internet users, studying the electoral market, targeting voters, obtaining feedback to adjust the strategy, managing databases and protecting the brand and image of the party.

Figure 22.1 presents the classification we adopted for the Tunisian case study to analyze the objectives pursued by political parties in their use of social media for the 2018 municipal elections.

Using the content analysis software QDA Miner 5, the analysis allows to determine more specifically in the discourse of strategists for what purposes the political parties use social media.

Results

Objectives common to all political parties

The analysis of the interviews indicates that communication objectives dominate the orientation of the social media uses of the six political parties in our sample. Political objectives come second and marketing objectives third (Figure 22.2).

Giasson and colleagues (2018, 2019) explain this phenomenon suggesting that that in an election campaign the emphasis is more on the communication aspect. In preparation for the 2018 municipal elections, the responses of the strategists analyzed also show the importance of communication objectives. The strong interest expressed in 'broadcasting the partisan message' seems to be the priority for all political parties in their use of social media at the municipal level (Table 22.1 in Appendix). We also note the interest of all strategists in interacting with citizens via Facebook (Table 22.1). Indeed, they report that exchanges, discussions and dialogue with citizens remain essential and crucial in local elections. This was highlighted by Klinger and Russmann (2017) and confirmed by Larsson and Skogerbø (2018) who argued that the self-promotional use of candidates is less present at the local level. According to them, local politicians use social media in an interactive way by adopting essentially two-way communication. However, in the case of Tunisian municipalities, political advertising is of great importance for Tunisian strategists in their use of digital technology (Table 22.1). This is probably due to the ban on political advertising in the audiovisual media by the electoral law. Personalization is also a priority for some political parties and, in this case, the *Mouvement Tunisie Volonté* (MTV) that said it wanted to put forward its leader Moncef Marzouki, the former opponent of Ben Ali.

Our data indicate that party strategists seek to achieve political objectives, including to raise the awareness and visibility of candidates at the municipal level (Table 22.2). This objective is one of the reasons to explain the creation by all political parties of new Facebook pages specific

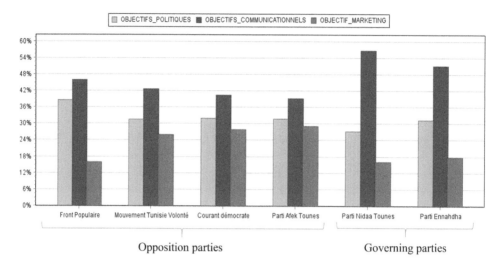

Figure 22.2 Distribution of strategic objectives by political parties. Source: Author

to each municipality, to mark their presence and cover their local activities. In terms of marketing objectives, the data in Table 22.3 show that targeting across the Facebook platform is a priority for all the political party strategists in our sample.

By creating official pages specific to each municipality, geographic targeting seems to be privileged to specifically reach the residents of these municipalities. In addition to geography, the characteristics of targeting revolve around gender and age, according to respondents, one of whom states:

> [o]n targeting by region and locality. The focus is on urban residents. When there is an event in a given region such as a meeting in Sfax for example, all publications for the purpose of mobilization, advertising, and information are directed towards the residents of the city of Sfax… Targeting is also done by age and gender.… (Respondent 22)

Thus, although all political parties use Facebook targeting in these municipal elections, they have not shown a major interest in collecting personal digital data about voters (Table 22.3). Only the *Afek Tounes* party is interested in information systems and has expressed its intention to use companies that collect and manage personal data about citizens to refine their targeting practices. Two of the strategists confirmed that they were in negotiations with several companies specialized in personal data management such as Nation Builder and the French start-up Liegey Muller Pons (LMP) to acquire an information system. They explained that they found difficulties due to certain legal constraints provided for in Tunisian legislation. According to them, companies with a proven track record in managing personal data for electoral purposes are internationally based. Tunisia's Personal Data Protection Act prohibits the storage of Tunisian citizens' data abroad. At the time of the interviews, the *Afek Tounes* party had advanced discussions with Nation Builder to further refine its targeting practices according to criteria including citizen connection habits. As a result, Tunisian political parties do not yet seem to integrate segmentation, micro-targeting and big data analysis into their digital strategies. They seem to be limited only to the technical function of targeting that Facebook pages allow based on information voluntarily disclosed by internet users to the social network such as their place of residence, age or gender. The following sections illustrate some of the ways in which different Tunisian parties approached the municipal elections.

Ennahda and Nidaa Tounes: digital campaigns under control

The analysis of the discourse of the strategists of the two major parties in power at the time (Ennahda and Nidaa Tounes) indicates the existence of several common points regarding the importance given to the different functions of social media. Strategists emphasize the importance of reaching out to citizens through social media by delivering a cohesive, structured, partisan message that reaches its target audience. Ennahda's strategists claim to use Facebook primarily to control their campaign message and thus maintain its coherence.

> There is a lot of denigration of our party, of our views, of our policies and of our orientation on the part of some columnists as well as political opponents. Social media is used to respond and explain our views, decisions, and to deal with disinformation attempts and attacks against us. (Respondent 4)

Similarly for the strategists of Nidaa Tounes, the campaign message must be controlled as stated by this strategist:

> Our use of Facebook is very thoughtful. We must not be too open on social networks [sic]. Any 'mistake' could create a scandal. Political opponents play a lot on these small mistakes to exploit them politically later… Our political opponents sometimes distort our messages and try to discredit the party. We are present on Facebook to remedy this and justify our positions. (Respondent 7)

This characteristic of the ruling parties has been observed in several studies which have shown that these parties are obsessed with controlling their campaign message from which the requirement is to remain 'on message' (Bor 2013; Giasson et al. 2013; Chadwick and Stromer-Galley 2016).

Regarding the political objectives these political parties pursued, we note the interest accorded to the category 'gaining visibility'. The Facebook platform was thus deployed primarily to publicize the voters' lists and candidates running in the municipalities by trying to improve the image of their parties.

Beyond message targeting, the marketing objectives for Ennahda and Nidaa Tounes did not appear to be a priority. In this sense, on Facebook, Ennahda would seek to target women first according to three of its strategists, one of whom stated that

> One million women voted for President Béji Caid Essebssi in 2014. They are the foundation of Tunisian society and the most important electoral base. Tunisian women are very active in society, and it is fundamental to reach them as much as possible via Facebook. In Tunisia, you cannot win elections without their support. (Respondent 1)

The strategists for the Islamist Ennahda stated that they sought to reach out to and 'seduce' women to get rid of the negative image of a party opposed to women's rights that its political opponents attach to them. In this sense, the party was the only one to respect horizontal and vertical gender parity in all the electoral lists presented in the 350 municipalities (Nafti 2019). In the municipality of Tunis, a woman was presented as the head of the list and was elected mayor, a first in the history of Tunisia. Ennahda's strategy was clearly expressed by its strategists and was transposed into the digital component of its municipal campaign. Moreover, the analysis of the strategists' discourse indicates that neither those of Ennahda nor those of Nidaa Tounes were concerned about the adjustment of their strategies following feedback on Facebook or indeed the dissemination of content co-produced by users (Table 22.3). Both parties did not seem to attach any importance to the development of an online community and were not in favor of giving freedom to their activists/supporters. The lack of openness to citizen participation in respondents' responses reveals the prudence and control that anchored the digital communication of Ennahda and Nidaa Tounes at the municipal level.

These findings confirm those of several researchers who believe that political parties in power remain reluctant to be overly open to social media (Giasson 2017; Chadwick 2013; Giasson et al. 2013). Moreover, as Bor (2013) points out, digital media is integrated into the campaign strategies of all political parties, but it mainly allows the parties in power to control their campaign message.

Front Populaire

The Front Populaire does not have great financial resources, but it has the advantage of being a party of militants given its ideological anchorage of the extreme left (Hmed 2019). The party strategists interviewed for this study recognize the weaknesses of their formation in terms of communication in general and digital communication in particular. Despite these weaknesses and considering social media as an alternative to their marginalization in the traditional media, they recognize that Facebook allows them to speak directly to citizens:

> [w]e are so prejudiced by traditional media and [sic] today social media represent our only alternative. They allow us to speak directly to citizens and to spread our messages. This is what is most important to us at this time. (Respondent 24)

According to respondents, the use of social media is essentially based on the dissemination of political releases, views and some media interventions. The 'broadcast message' category is at the top of the communication objectives (Table 22.1) of the Front Populaire.

Respondents give two reasons for this 'trivialized' use of digital tools: the lack of financial resources on the one hand and the low importance given to the digital component by party leaders on the other. Despite communication and intra-organizational difficulties, the Front Populaire campaign teams claim to have developed a digital strategy for local elections. Facebook was mobilized not only to speak directly to citizens but also to interact with them on topics that specifically concern their municipalities (Table 22.1). Mobilization on Facebook seems to be a priority for the Front Populaire (Table 22.2). However, offline mobilization is preferred to online mobilization and this can be explained by the fact that the Front Populaire is a coalition of traditional left parties with a relatively large militant base. Thus, the Front Populaire relies more on fieldwork, a point that strategists highlighted on a number of occasions.

The analysis reveals the existence of other commonalities with Ennahda in particular, for example publicizing events and activities such as partisan rallies and promoting party ideology (Table 22.2). This is explained by the fact that these two formations are programmatic parties with marked ideological roots: the first is an Islamist party and the second is Marxist-Leninist.

Afek Tounes, MTV and Courant Démocrate: 'citizen' digital strategies

There are several similarities in the discourse of the strategists of these three center political parties. These similarities are reflected in the order of priorities given to the different categories.

In anticipation of the municipal elections, respondents indicated that the Facebook platform would be used to communicate a message built around local issues. Facebook pages created for each municipality would be used to spread the message and raise awareness of their parties at the municipal level (Table 22.1). From this perspective, *Courant Démocrate* and MTV strategists explained that social media is an alternative to their absence in traditional media.

> Today in Tunisia, the private media dominates the media landscape … We find ourselves with TV channels, radios and newspapers controlled by financial and advertising lobbies that have a direct influence on the editorial line of these media. These lobbies are linked to the parties in power, Nida Tounes and to a lesser degree the party Ennahda. As an opposition party we are excluded from private media. Our alternative is social networks [sic] which are the only communication tool that allows us to address citizens directly. We have developed a whole strategy in this sense. (Respondent 23)

To compensate for their weak presence in traditional media, they turn to what they call alternative media (mainly Facebook) to address citizens directly. The mobilization of such practices by oppositional third parties has been confirmed by several researchers in different contexts (Gibson and McAllister 2015; Koc-Michalska et al. 2016; Larsson 2016; Klinger and Russmann 2017). Political objectives account for 31.7% of mentions for *Afek Tounes*, 31.9% for the *Courant Démocrate* and 31.5% for MTV of the total strategic goals pursued by these political parties (Figure 22.2). We note that the strategists of these same formations sometimes mobilize social media to attract the attention of traditional media. The objective is to gain more visibility. One of the MTV strategists said: 'when used intelligently, social media can give access to traditional media. Sometimes we provoke an invitation via Facebook with a provocative status, sometimes with a virulent attack on the ruling parties' (Respondent 16). In the same context, one of the *Courant Démocrate* strategists stated:

> [T]oday, we provoke traditional media via social media … We are forced to operate in this way to make our voice heard. Nowadays, if a political party is not present in traditional media, it risks disappearing from the spotlight … We try to always be present in the media landscape despite attempts to exclude us. (Respondent 23)

Indeed, by trying to attract the attention of traditional media via Facebook, the platform becomes a means for these political formations to access the public space and voters who consume the major national traditional media. While mobilization in general is widely exploited by all political parties, online mobilization seems to be a priority for the strategists of *Afek Tounes*, the Democratic Movement and MTV as stated by this strategist: 'one of our goals on social media is to open up to the public. It is essential to have an audience that campaigns itself and relays political messages on Facebook' (Respondent 15). Particularly for *Courant Démocrate* strategists, activists must be constantly mobilized to campaign themselves on Facebook by sharing videos and photos, and relaying news, political messages and hashtags:

> We rely heavily on the viral phenomenon and the logic of sharing on Facebook. The content must be shared massively by the activists. These thousands of activists play a crucial role in digital communication [sic] by disseminating information on a large scale and promoting the party … They must be constantly mobilized on Facebook. (Respondent 22)

Strategists believe that effective digital campaigning is about adopting forms of citizen mobilization that rely on the central role of activists/sympathizers/volunteers (Table 22.2). This approach, which relies on relative freedom for activists and supporters, is deployed in other national contexts through mobilization platforms that allow for some elite control over activism (Chadwick 2013; Gibson 2020; Vaccari 2010; Giasson et al. 2019). Contrary to what is observed in Western democracies, Tunisian political parties do not have the kind of platform that allows them to control militant action. In this context, the organization of activists would only be on Facebook via private groups. Therefore, although the strategists seem to care about the direction of the campaign by giving instructions upstream, it remains difficult to control the actions of activists on Facebook especially when official campaigns overlap with unofficial ones.

Regarding marketing objectives, we note the interest in online community development on the part of *Afek Tounes*, *Courant Démocrate* and MTV strategists (Table 22.3). According to them, it is important to create groups of activists to organize and coordinate actions and to campaign:

> [w]e uses social media and mainly Facebook to exchange with the activist community through closed groups. Important information is relayed within these groups ... Activists discuss, debate among themselves and organize. This is the case of the Facebook group named [...] composed of 450 people who coordinate and organize their next actions related to the municipal campaign in Tunis.... (Respondent 20)

Through private Facebook groups, political parties can keep their teams and activists mobilized to relay messages and campaign. One strategist stated:

> Members are active in internal Facebook groups created by section presidents. Each local office president creates his or her group and leads his or her community in a Facebook group where activists constantly interact to organize and coordinate actions online and, on the ground, (80, 100, 200 members depending on the locality/delegation, 10,000 at the national level). (Respondent 10)

On the other hand, while all political party strategists consider exchanges with citizens on local issues to be essential, those from the *Courant Démocrate* are more open to adjusting their strategy based on interactions with citizens on Facebook (Table 22.3). One states:

> [w]e are very present and open on Facebook to the point where we have even taken political positions and sometimes changed course as a result of citizen feedback ... Several points have allowed us to adapt our communication without changing our position but rather adapting our strategy. I think the strong point of Facebook is the feedback it generates and that we take seriously. (Respondent 19)

We also note the interest given to market research and surveys by the *Afek Tounes* party. Indeed, the party collaborates with national and international firms and conducts studies with the help of focus groups for planning and determining themes to address at the level of regions and localities. Thus, the question arises: why is this the only party whose strategists are open about their targeting, data collection and market research practices? We believe this can be explained by the sources of inspiration of some of its campaign staff, for whom foreign models, particularly French ones, are the reference in terms of political marketing and digital campaigns. Inspired by marketing practices common in other national contexts, they seem to import them into their own training. For example, it appears that all three of these alternative center opposition parties are interested in developing online communities, recruiting volunteers and new cyber activists to coordinate and organize online and offline actions. Similarly, online mobilization appears to be a priority for these political parties to engage activists on Facebook.

Discussion and conclusion

Conducted to better understand how political parties would deploy their digital campaigns in the 2018 municipal elections, the interviews with strategists reveal that political parties are giving social media an important place in their electoral strategies. They have been forced to integrate it into their strategies for two reasons: first, because of its influence on the Tunisian political scene since the 2011 revolution and, second, in reaction to the ban on political advertising on audiovisual media during elections. As Bruce Bimber (2014) has pointed out, the communication environment is changing with technological transformations. This environment, described as a hybrid by Andrew Chadwick (2013), is increasingly incorporating the digital platform in the development and implementation of election campaigns (Giasson 2017; Lilleker et al. 2015, 2017).

Our interviews reveal that electoral strategies for municipal elections were developed by combining digital tools with more traditional offline practices. This hybridity allows the major governing parties to benefit from wider media coverage of their campaign activities. It allows alternative opposition parties to counteract their weak presence in the traditional media and, in some cases, to attract the attention of the traditional media, which they need in order to reach voters who still overwhelmingly use it for political information. The logic of hybridity is also revealed by the dissemination on digital platforms of passages taken from traditional media and, conversely, when strategists hope that Facebook publications will be relayed through traditional media to reach a wider audience. Hybridity is also expressed through the deployment of private and public Facebook groups for the organization of mobilization actions that are intended to materialize in the field, such as partisan rallies in municipalities or door-to-door campaigns.

Integrated into the official campaign strategy of the political parties, the social media is mobilized for external functions (disseminate the message, become known, control the message) and internal functions (development of communities, internal coordination, recruitment of volunteers, adjustment of the strategy). At the intra-organizational level, the logic of hybridity is observed more in the strategies of *Afek Tounes*, MTV and *Courant Démocrate*, whose strategists seemed to be more in favor of what Gibson describes as citizen-initiated campaigning (Gibson 2015, 2020; Koc-Michalska et al. 2016), digital actions based on community building, online mobilization and the dissemination of user-generated or co-generated content (Giasson et al. 2018; Lilleker et al. 2017).

However, opening up participation to activists and supporters requires maintaining some control over their actions, a phenomenon described by Daniel Kreiss (2012) as managed interactivity. The scope of this control remains uncertain in the Tunisian context since political organizations do not have platforms for managing and marketing militant action. By resorting to these more engaging and innovative practices in developing digital strategies, alternative opposition formations adopt a new approach to digital campaigning at the municipal level that draws on the deliberative conception of political communication (Theviot 2018). In contrast, the ruling parties (Ennahda and Nidaa Tounes) rely more on hierarchical and controlled digital campaigns.

These findings are consistent with David Karpf's (2012) hypothesis that opposition parties are generally more likely than traditional formations to adopt technological innovations and take risks in their digital electoral communication. Some researchers (Small 2008; Koc-Michalska et al. 2016; Vergeer and Hermans 2013) have offered explanations for this phenomenon. Small formations with little chance of forming a government can afford to adopt these kinds of bottom-up, open and more participatory digital strategies. Moreover, the indifference of the traditional media in its election coverage would also explain their active presence on the web, which aims to attract media attention and allow them to gain more visibility (Giasson et al. 2013; Theviot 2018; Klinger and Russmann 2017; Gibson and McAllister 2015).

Conversely, the digital campaigns of governing parties are constantly monitored and scrutinized by the press, the media and their opponents. Digital mishaps could create negative repercussions for the campaign and potentially for the party's re-election (Giasson et al. 2018). This would lead ruling party strategists to consider more conservative, more controlled and less participatory digital campaigns.

Appendix

Table 22.1 Number of mentions of communication objectives

Communication objectives	Front Populaire	MTV	Courant Démocrate	Afek Tounes	Nidaa Tounes	Ennahda
Broadcast message	39	29	59	38	32	32
Share media content	8	6	14	16	3	2
Attack opponent	9	9	14	1	1	1
Control/spin message	3	5	2	3	29	27
Interaction	27	20	49	23	25	28
Political advertising	10	14	19	18	28	24
Personalization	10	16	4	12	8	1
Promote events and tours	15	3	6	5	16	9
Internal coordination	4	13	14	20	2	–

Table 22.2 Number of mentions of political objectives

Political objectives	Front Populaire	MTV	Courant Démocrate	Afek Tounes	Nidaa Tounes	Ennahda
Getting known/visibility	22	21	39	20	18	24
Promote ideology/values	22	1	3	2	–	17
Get votes/GOTV	13	10	15	28	10	14
Generate resources (volunteers)	8	9	10	16	6	–
Online mobilizing	6	28	52	30	7	6
Offline mobilizing	34	16	24	14	28	15

Table 22.3 Number of mentions of marketing objectives

Marketing objectives	Front Populaire	MTV	Courant Démocrate	Afek Tounes	Nidaa Tounes	Ennahda
Targeting	25	26	50	41	21	25
Strategy adjustment	10	9	18	6	2	1
Collect voter data	1	3	7	8	8	3
Community building	7	25	33	26	3	3
Market research	–	3	5	16	6	10
Branding	–	4	11	4	1	1

References

Ben Mansour, Bader. 2017. 'Le rôle des médias sociaux en politique: Une revue de la littérature'. *Regards Politiques* 1(1): 3–17.

Bimber, Bruce. 2012. 'Digital media and citizenship'. In Holli Semetko and Margaret Scammell (eds.), *The SAGE Handbook of Political Communication*. London: Sage Publications, 115–127.

Bimber, Bruce. 2014. 'Digital media in the Obama campaigns of 2008 and 2012: Adaptation to the personalized political communication environment'. *Journal of Information Technology & Politics* 11(2): 130–150.

Bougamra, Mayssa. 2015. 'Internet et démocratie: Les usages sociopolitiques de Facebook dans l'après-révolution en Tunisie', MA thesis in commnuication. Université du Québec à Montréal, Montréal.

Boulianne, Shelley. 2015. 'Social media use and participation: A meta-analysis of current research'. *Information, Communication & Society* 18(5): 524–538.

Boulianne, Shelley. 2017. 'Revolution in the making? Social media effects across the globe'. *Information, Communication & Society* 22(1): 39–54.

Boulianne, Shelley. 2020. 'Twenty years of digital media effects on civic and political participation'. *Communication Research* 47(7): 947–966.

Bor, Stephanie. 2013. 'Using social network sites to improve communication between political campaigns and citizens in the 2012 election'. *American Behavioral Scientist* 58(9): 1195–1213.

Bradshaw, Samantha and Philp N. Howard. 2017. 'Troops, trolls and troublemakers: A global inventory of organized social media manipulation'. *Oxford Internet Institute* 12: 1–37.

Chadwick, Andrew. 2013. *The Hybrid Media System: Politics and Power*. 1st edition. Oxford: Oxford University Press.

Chadwick, Andrew. 2017. *The Hybrid Media System: Politics and Power*. 2nd edition. Oxford: Oxford University Press.

Chadwick, Andrew, James Dennis and Amy Smith. 2016. 'Politics in the age of hybrid media: Power, systems, and media logics'. In Axel Bruns, Gunn Sara Enli, Eli Skogerbø, Anders Olof Larsson and Christian Christensen (eds.), *The Routledge Companion to Social Media and Politics*. London: Routledge, 7–22.

Chadwick, Andrew and Jennifer Stromer-Galley. 2016. 'Digital media, power, and democracy in parties and election campaigns party decline or party renewal?' *The International Journal of Press/Politics* 21(3): 283–293.

Dommett, Katharine and Luke Temple. 2018. 'Digital campaigning: The rise of Facebook and satellite campaigns'. *Parliamentary Affairs* 71(1): 189–202.

Elswah, Mona and Philip N. Howard. 2020. 'The challenges of monitoring social media in the Arab world: The case of the 2019 Tunisian elections'. *The Computational Propaganda Project*. COMPROP DATA MEMO 1/23. Available at: https://demtech.oii.ox.ac.uk/research/posts/the-challenges-of-monitoring-social-media-in-the-arab-world-the-case-of-the-2019-tunisian-elections/.

Enli, Gunn and Hallvard Moe. 2013. 'Introduction to special issue: Social media and election campaigns–key tendencies and ways forward'. *Information, Communication & Society* 16(5): 637–645.

Enli, Gunn Sara and Eli Skogerbø. 2013. 'Personalized campaigns in party-centred politics: Twitter and Facebook as arenas for political communication'. *Information, Communication & Society* 16(5): 757–774.

Giasson, Thierry. 2017. 'Du marketing politique à la science électorale'. In Réjean Pelletier and Manon Tremblay (eds.), *Le parlementarisme canadien*. Québec: Presses de l'Université Laval, 153–168.

Giasson, Thierry, Gildas Le Bars and Philippe Dubois. 2019. 'Is social media transforming Canadian electioneering? Hybridity and online partisan strategies in the 2012 Quebec election'. *Canadian Journal of Political Science* 52(2): 323–341.

Giasson, Thierry, Fabienne Fabienne Greffet and Geneviève Chacon. 2018. 'Relever le défi de l'hybridité: Les objectifs des stratégies de campagnes numériques lors des élections française et québécoise de 2012'. *Politique et Sociétés* 37(2): 19–46.

Giasson, Thierry, Gildas Le Bars, Frédérick Bastien and Mélanie Verville. 2013. '#Qc2012. L'utilisation de Twitter par les partis politiques'. In Frédérick Bastien, Éric Bélanger et François Gélineau (eds.), *Les Québécois aux urnes: les partis, les médias et les citoyens en campagne*. Montréal: PUM, 135–148.

Giasson, Thierry and Tamara A. Small. 2017. 'Objectives of Canadian opposition parties'. In Alex Marland, Thierry Giasson and Anna Lennox Esselment (eds.), *Permanent Campaigning in Canada*. Vancouver: UBC Press, 109–126.

Gibson, Rachel. 2015. 'Party change, social media and the rise of « citizen-initiated » campaigning'. *Party Politics* 21(2): 183–197.

Gibson, Rachel. 2020. *When the Nerds Go Marching in: How Digital Technology Moved from the Margins to the Mainstream of Political Campaigns*. Oxford: Oxford University Press.

Gibson, Rachel, Andrea Römmele and Andy Williamson. 2014. « Chasing the digital wave: International perspectives on the growth of online campaigning ». *Journal of Information Technology & Politics* 11(2): 123–129.

Gibson, Rachel and Ian McAllister. 2015. 'Normalising or equalising party competition? Assessing the impact of the web on election campaigning'. *Political Studies* 63(3): 529–547.

Gibson, Rachel and Stephen Ward. 2012. 'Political organizations and campaigning online'. In Holli Semetko and Margaret Scamell (eds.), *Sage Handbook of Political Communication*. London: Sage, 62–74.

Graham, Todd, Marcel Broersma and Karin Hazelhoff. 2013. 'Closing the gap? Twitter as an instrument for connected representation'. In Richard Scullion, Roman Gerodimos, Daniel Jackson and Darren Lilleker (eds.), *The Media, Political Participation and Empowerment*. New York: Routledge, 71–88.

Hammami, Sadok. 2020. 'Élections 2019 ou les apories de la nouvelle communication politique'. *Revue Tunisienne de Science Politique* 1(3): 137–164.

Hmed, Choukri. 2019. 'Les décu-e-s de l'autoritarisme partisan. Engagement et désengagement dans les organisations de la gauche radicale après 2011'. In Amin Allal and Vincent Geisser (eds.), *Tunisie. Une démocratisation au-dessus de tout soupçon?* Tunis: Nirvana Éditions, 123–137.

Jackson, Nigel and Darren Lilleker. 2011. 'Microblogging, constituency service and impression management: UK MPs and the use of Twitter'. *The Journal of Legislative Studies* 17(1): 86–105.

Jungherr, Andreas. 2016. 'Four functions of digital tools in election campaigns: The German case'. *International Journal of Press/Politics* 21(3): 358–377.

Kalsnes, Bente. 2016. 'The social media paradox explained: Comparing political parties' Facebook strategy versus practice'. *Social Media + Society* 2(2): 1–11.

Karpf, David. 2012. *The MoveOn Effect: The Unexpected Transformation of American Political Advocacy*. Oxford: Oxford University Press.

Klinger, Ulrike and Uta Russmann. 2017. 'Beer is more efficient than social media Political parties and strategic communication in Austrian and Swiss national elections'. *Journal of Information Technology & Politics* 14(4): 299–313.

Koc-Michalska, Karolina, Rachel Gibson and Thierry Vedel. 2014. 'Online campaigning in France, 2007–2012: Political actors and citizens in the aftermath of the Web. 2.0 Evolution'. *Journal of Information Technology & Politics* 11(2): 220–244.

Koc-Michalska, Karolina, Darren Lilleker and Thierry Vedel. 2016. 'Civic political engagement and social change in the new digital age'. *New Media & Society* 18(9): 1807–1816.

Koc-Michalska, Karolina, Darren G. Lilleker, T. Michalski, Rachel Gibson and J. M. Zajac. 2020. 'Facebook affordances and citizen engagement during elections: European political parties and their benefit from online strategies?' *Journal of Information Technology & Politics*, 2: 1–14.

Kreiss, Daniel. 2012. *Taking Our Country Back: The Crafting of Networked Politics from Howard Dean to Barack Obama*. Oxford: Oxford University Press.

Kreiss, Daniel. 2015. 'Digital campaigning'. In Stephen Coleman and Dean Freelon (eds.), *Handbook of Digital Politics*. London: Edward Elgar Publishing, 118–135.

Kreiss, Daniel, Regina G. Lawrence and Shannon C. McGregor. 2018. 'In their own words: Political practitioner accounts of candidates, audiences, affordances, genres, and timing in strategic social media use'. *Political Communication* 35(1): 8–31.

Larsson, Anders Olof. 2016. 'Online, all the time? A quantitative assessment of the permanent campaign on Facebook'. *New Media & Society* 18(2): 274–292.

Larsson, Anders Olof and Hallvard Moe. 2014. 'Triumph of the underdogs? Comparing Twitter use by political actors during two Norwegian election campaigns'. *Sage Open* 4(4): 1–13.

Larsson, Anders Olof and Jakob Svensson. 2014. 'Politicians online–Identifying current research opportunities'. *First Monday* 19(4). Available at: https://journals.uic.edu/ojs/index.php/fm/article/download/4897/3874.

Larsson, Anders Olof and Eli Skogerbø. 2018. 'Out with the old, in with the new? Perceptions of social (and other) media by local and regional Norwegian politicians'. *New Media & Society* 20(1): 219–236.

Lilleker, Darren G., Karolina Koc-Michalska, Ralph Negrine, Rachel Gibson, Thierry Vedel and Sylvie Strudel. 2017. 'Social media campaigning in Europe: Mapping the terrain'. *Journal of Information Technology & Politics* 14(4): 293–298.

Lilleker, Darren G., Jens Tenscher and Václav Štětka. 2015. 'Towards hypermedia campaigning? Perceptions of new media's importance for campaigning by party strategists in comparative perspective'. *Information, Communication & Society* 18(7): 747–765.

Lobera, Josep and Martín Portos. 2020. 'New-old parties, grassroots and digital activism'. *Information, Communication & Society*, 24: 1–22.

Magin, Mélanie, Nicole Podschuweit, Jörg Haßler and Uta Russmann. 2017. 'Campaigning in the fourth age of political communication: A multi-method study on the use of Facebook by German and Austrian parties in the 2013 national election campaigns'. *Information, Communication & Society* 20(11): 1698–1719.

M'rad, Hatem. 2020. 'Présidentielles: D'une élection atypique à un élu néophyte'. *Revue Tunisienne de Science Politique* 1(3): 31–64.

Nafti, Hatem. 2019. *De la révolution à la restauration, où va la Tunisie?* Paris: Riveneuve éditions.

Penney, Joel. 2017. 'Social media and citizen participation in "official" and "unofficial" electoral promotion: A structural analysis of the 2016 Bernie Sanders digital campaign'. *Journal of Communication* 67(3): 402–423.

Römmele, Andrea and Rachel Gibson. 2020. 'Scientific and subversive: The two faces of the fourth era of political campaigning'. *New Media & Society* 22(4): 595–610.

Small, Tamara. 2014. 'The not-so social network: The use of Twitter by Canada's party leaders'. In Alex Marland, Thierry Giasson and Tamara A. Small (eds.), *Political Communication in Canada: Meet the Press and Tweet the Rest*. Vancouver: UBC Press, 92–110.

Small, Tamara. 2008. 'Equal access, unequal success – Major and minor Canadian parties on the net'. *Party Politics* 14(1): 51–70.

Stromer-Galley, Jennifer. 2014. *Presidential Campaigning in the Internet Age*. Oxford: Oxford University Press.

Tenscher, Jens, Karolina Koc-Michalska, Darren G. Lilleker et al. 2016. 'The professionals speak: Practitioners' perspectives on professional election campaigning'. *European Journal of Communication* 31(2): 95–119.

Theviot, Anaïs. 2015. 'Historiciser et sociologiser les études sur le numérique. Porter le regard sur les processus historiques et les acteurs pour étudier les dispositifs web'. *Interfaces Numériques* 4(3): 473–490.

Theviot, Anaïs. 2018. *Faire campagne sur Internet*. Villeneuve d'Ascq: Presses universitaires du Septentrion.

Theviot, Anaïs. 2019. *Big data électoral. Dis-moi qui tu es, je te dirai pour qui voter*. Lormont: Le Bord de l'eau.

Vaccari, Cristian. 2010. 'Technology is a commodity: The Internet in the 2008 United States presidential election'. *Journal of Information Technology & Politics* 7(4): 318–339.

Vaccari, Cristian. 2013. *Digital Politics in Western Democracies: A Comparative Study*. Baltimore, MD: Johns Hopkins University Press.

Vaccari, Cristian. 2017. 'Online mobilization in comparative perspective: Digital appeals and political engagement in Germany, Italy, and the United Kingdom'. *Political Communication* 34(1): 69–88.

Vergeer, Maurice and Liesbeth Hermans. 2013. 'Campaigning on Twitter: Microblogging and online social networking as campaign tools in the 2010 general elections in the Netherlands'. *Journal of Computer-Mediated Communication* 18(4): 399–419.

Williams, Christine and Jeff Gulati. 2013. 'Social networks in political campaigns: Facebook and the congressional elections of 2006 and 2008'. *New Media & Society* 15(1): 52–71.

23
THE ROLE OF MEDIA IN ELECTORAL CAMPAIGNS IN THE PANDEMIC ERA: THE CASE OF KUWAIT

Geoffrey Martin

Introduction

Kuwait is the scene of some of the Gulf region's only elections, free press, and displays of free speech. A long tradition of democratic dialogue and discussion often places the small Gulf state at the center of public discussions about the role of media in a region known for its authoritarian governments. Equally important conversations emphasize the region's only electoral process, and the myriad of political, economic, and social issues that come with it. How do the politics of campaigning and the underlying use of mass media impact electoral outcomes? What is the role of mass media and social media? How is the public invested in it and how does it influence voters?

There is a gap in the literature concerning these questions. Much of the emphasis in the literature is on the fragmented relationship between regime type, electoral systems, or other structural factors upholding durable authoritarianism (Herb 2014). None of the above strands of literature looks at campaigns themselves, and what important role, if any, media plays in elections. Work on the role of media in general is minimal, with a few exceptions (Alfadhli 2013; Miller and Ko 2015).

This chapter looks at the role of media in the election campaign of December 2020. The 2020 election can be used as an important gauge for the role of media in election campaigning, as the COVID-19 pandemic led to restrictions at *diwaniyaat* and campaign headquarters and on personal visits, creating a "barrier between candidates and voters" (Al Mulla 2020a).[1] At the start of the election, many media outlets and analysts predicated that restrictions "'leveled the playing field between women and men' as well as independent candidates by allowing social media to play a larger role and reducing the role of vote buying and identity politics by blocking their organizing venues" (Al Mulla 2020b). This chapter is a contribution to the literature on elections and media by looking at the dynamics and micro-processes of campaigning and media.

Literature review

The literature on Kuwaiti elections is dominated by discussions of regime type and election systems and how they could lead to democratization/liberalization or reinforce authoritarianism tendencies (Brumberg 2003; Schedler 2002; Szmolka 2011). Seminal pieces on Kuwaiti electoral politics focus on how political, social, cultural, and geopolitical structures impact the "meaningfulness" of elections. The motive is often to study how and why certain groups are marginalized from electoral processes (Tétreault and Al-Ghanim 2009; Tétreault 2000: 40–42). Another focus is how elections are a by-product of "managed reform" by monarchs without endangering their own power by coopting potential opposition, prohibiting political parties, manipulating electoral districts or voting systems, encouraging Islamist candidates, setting up informal tribal primary elections (*far'iyyat*), naturalizing pro-government Bedouin tribes,[2] or diluting potential opposition (Crystal 1989; Al Ghanim 2010; Brumberg 2003; Tétreault 2000; Azoulay 2020; Salih 2011; Aiko 2011; Kraetzschmar 2018). Members of Parliament (MPs) generally function as de facto personal intermediaries between their voters and the government, and the (KNA) is largely used as a forum for patronage to avoid the creation of cross-cutting parliamentary opposition (Azoulay 2020). Azouley argues that one can consider this system of informal rule as "both pyramidal and circular": a hierarchy and an ever-growing circle of elites, groups, or clans of new and old elites.

Unfortunately, this literature makes little mention of the role of mass media and social media as it pertains to elections, election campaigns, or electoral outcomes. There are a few outliers though on media in elections that are worth mentioning. Wheeler (2003) argues that the emergence of social media is supplementing the traditional role of the *diwaniyas*, as the introduction of the internet has negatively affected *diwaniya* attendance. However, the use of social media has also become an extension of the *diwaniyas*, where people can interact with politicians online, discuss politics, and share their opinions (Wheeler and Mintz 2010). More recently, Kononova and Akbar (2015) also investigated how Kuwaiti citizens used traditional and new media during the December 2012 parliamentary election. Those surveyed spent more time in personal discussions or on social media than using traditional media to obtain political information. Martin (2019) conducted a study looking at the use of Twitter during the Arab Spring in Kuwait. He argued that protests transformed public discussion, with public criticism of important political issues and corruption becoming more commonplace on social media. Since the protests, the Kuwaiti government has attempted to remedy a perceived lack of openness and availability in the public sphere by expanding its presence on Instagram, in order to respond to a rising crescendo of criticism and engage with citizens' concerns (Martin 2019).

Alfadhli (2013) conducted a study of 317 Kuwaiti Twitter users to look at whether voters felt that Twitter had an important impact on their opinions during elections. In the study, 55% of the respondents used Twitter to follow the news, 54% of the participants agreed or strongly agreed that they received statements from candidates on Twitter, although only 21% of the participants thought that what was published on Twitter was credible. Overall, Alfadhli (2013) argues that there is a significant relationship between social media and vote choice and that Twitter can be an effective means of shaping voters' decisions. Miller and Ko (2015) investigated the role of social media in Kuwait's February 2012 parliamentary election by conducting an empirical analysis of Twitter use by the 50 winning candidates. In a content analysis of 329 tweets, they found that 239 tweets were direct personal communication with voters (Miller and Ko 2015). Thus, Twitter might act as a natural extension of offline engagements and is a cost-effective platform with high levels of public exposure (Miller and Ko 2015).

Finally, Selvik et al. (2015) looked at the political effect of print media liberalization in Kuwait based on a content analysis of Arabic language newspapers in the 2009 parliamentary election. The analysis found no systematic favoring of pro-government candidates in electoral coverage, but did find a statistically significant bias for candidates from the ruling *hadar* (urban) class, at the expense of the Bedouin tribal population. Selvik et al. (2015) explains that the pro-*hadar* bias in Kuwaiti newspapers relates to the historical dominance of Sunni *hadar* families in

Kuwaiti politics.[3] Selvik et al. (2015) also found that the level of newspaper coverage strongly correlates with election success.

Methodology

Studying the role of media has many challenges in Kuwait. Assigning causality to online campaigning for elections to offline events, such as electoral outcomes, is difficult, if next to impossible due to the lack of transparent election financing, access to candidates and their staff, or a social environment conducive to surveys and focus groups. Researchers studying online media can get "stuck at one level of analysis or get bogged down by simple anecdotal arguments or methodological purism" (Martin 2018: 229).

To study the role of media in electoral campaigns, this chapter observed the December 2020 election. The author implemented a content analysis of the various news posts and articles leading up to election day, looking at 15 media platforms (Table 23.1). Each post was coded by topic. In total, the author analyzed and coded 850 posts and articles.

The author was present in Kuwait before, during, and after the election and observed the events first hand. He conducted semi-structured interviews with 38 Kuwaiti citizens, and he also conducted interviews with the campaign teams of three different candidates in the second, third, and fourth voting districts. One of these candidates won the election campaign while the others lost. Finally, in-person snowball surveys were implemented in each of the five voting districts in Kuwait capturing the views of 241 participants between January and April 2021 (Table 23.2). Each survey was conducted at a *diwaniyaat* in groups of approximately 10–17 people. A total of 19 *diwaniyaat* were visited. The survey was conducted informally with a show of hands to answer various questions followed by informal discussions.

Context of the 2020 elections

Upon independence in 1961, Kuwait adopted a parliamentary form of government (Salameh and Al Sharah 2011). The Kuwaiti Constitution was ratified on November 11, 1962, and enshrined the legislative Kuwait National Assembly (KNA) to authorize laws. The KNA is a unicameral legisla-

Table 23.1 Media analysis

Publication	Media type
Al-Qabas	Newspaper
Al-Rai	Newspaper
Al-Anbaa	Newspaper
Al-Annhar	Newspaper
KUNA	Government agency
Al-Majlis TV	Government agency
KuwaitCM	Government Twitter account
Kuwait MOH	Government Twitter account
Hadith Al Balad	Twitter account
Al Majlis	Twitter account
Arab Times	Newspaper
Kuwait Times	Newspaper
Times Kuwait	Newspaper
Kuwait News	Twitter account
MajlesAlOmmah	Government Twitter account

Table 23.2 Survey

Voting district	No. of respondents
First circle	36
Second circle	27
Third circle	43
Four circle	63
Fifth circle	72

ture composed of 50 elected seats with members serving a four-year term. The 50 members are directly elected through five constituencies. Up to 16 additional voting members are appointed by the prime minister as part of the ministerial cabinet. The legislature relies heavily upon the discretionary powers of the Emir to evaluate the exercise of power and the duration of the assembly (Das 2017). The first election to the Kuwaiti parliament was held on January 23, 1963 (Olimat 2009) and, to date, 19 elections have been called. The voting age is 21, with bans on police and military personnel from taking part in elections. Women have been allowed to vote since 2005.

Kuwait enjoys a more outspoken and critical media environment than several other Arab countries. It is ranked as having a "partly free" press system (Freedom House 2020). The internet is considered to be a relatively free medium and is protected by freedom of expression in the Constitution. This being said, government restrictions and electronic criminal laws – the Cyber Crimes Law 63/2016 and the National Unity Law 19/2012 – mean that users have to practice self-censorship when engaging in political debate and criticism (Alsalem 2021; Al Mulla 2020b). These laws allow the government to police online activities due to the internet's vague and unclear terms. The four newspapers considered the most influential are *Al-Rai, Al-Seyasah, Al-Qabas*, and *Al-Anbaa*. Al-Rai TV and Al Qabas provide the vast majority of televised candidate coverage. More recently, social media has become an essential political tool in Kuwait and ranks first in terms of internet penetration in the Middle East with 100% of the population having access to the internet (Al-Qassemi 2011; Wheeler and Mintz 2010). Twitter and Instagram are heavily used; Twitter for news and discussion, and Instagram for shopping and advertising products (Greenfield 2013).

The 2020 elections were called after the cabinet resigned on October 6, 2020 (Egypt Independent 2020), and differed from previous electoral campaigns, as they were the first under the country's new Emir, Nawaf Al-Ahmad Al-Jaber Al-Sabah, who took over following the death of Sheikh Sabah Al-Ahmed Al-Jaber Al-Sabah on September 28. Symbolically, the first election under a new Emir is supposed to be a time of unity. Newspapers and social media accounts of both pro-government and opposition figures praised the Emir and proclaimed a new era (Gulf States Newsletter, 2020e; Gulf News 2020c). In an interview, a former MP stated that

> you have to understand that a new Emir is a reset button. Old grievances can be dismissed, as the system uses the personalized nature of politics to circumvent the paralysis. This is momentary you see, but leads to moments of reformist attitudes or more often, performances.
>
> *Former Parliament Member of : Interview February 2020*

Yet, the transition left more questions than answers. Sheikh Nawaf is an unknown quantity, keeping an apolitical and low-key role, and is the founder of the National Guard (Martin, 2020).

Crown Prince Meshaal Al Ahmed Al Jaber Al Sabah was thrust into the position based on lineage rather than ambition. Sheikh Meshaal has been one of the strong men of the Sabah for over 50 years. It was he who was behind various repressive measures during the Arab Spring protests in Kuwait (Gulf States Newsletter, 2020e).

The other major factor was the global pandemic, which tested the capacity of the Kuwaiti government. Kuwait's initial response to the pandemic was one of the strictest in the world, proactively closing non-essential services, stopping all travel, and quarantining highly infected districts (Hashem and Martin 2020a). In spite of this, from early August, the Ministry of the Interior and the Ministry of Health had begun discussing the need to prepare for elections (Gulf News 2020d).

Inadvertently, COVID-19 ushered in a new era for electoral campaigning due to strict health requirements. Campaign headquarters, banquets, tribal gatherings, and other events for candidates were banned under Ministerial Resolution 156 of 2020 (Euro News 2020). Additional recommendations for the elections included preventing entry to polls for those not wearing a mask, physical distancing, and banning any gathering outside polling stations (Al Qabas 2020a). In October, the government imposed a six-month prison sentence and a fine of 10,000 dinars (US$33,000) on violators at electoral rallies. Concerns about whether citizens infected by COVID-19 could vote were at the heart of government discussions during the lead up to elections (Al Qabas 2020b). In the end, clinics were set up in each polling station with over 600 medical staff to prepare for any medical emergency. Additionally, the Elections Committee announced that only government media would be allowed to enter the polling stations. Private news channels would have to remain outside (Al Khaleej 2020).

A campaign headquarters is an important factor for candidates as it is a place for the campaign staff to congregate, voters to speak directly with the candidates, and candidates to hold lectures in front of a large audience. The *diwaniyaat* play the most significant role in elections and act as the primary place for candidates to listen to what their constituents have to say in private, as well as a way to get their campaign messages out. Unofficially, this is where deals are made to "service" constituents with patronage, or to enact vote-buying strategies, which are rife (Gulf States Newsletter, 2020b).[4] The limited possibilities for those involved in elections to do all this had a significant impact on the perception of how social media was going to be used during the election period.

The role of the media in the 2020 elections

By election time there were 567,694 registered voters (273,940 males and 293,754 females). Voter registration had increased by 18% after 2016, with 84,694 new registered voters. The number of candidates registered to run in the National Assembly 2020 elections was 297 males and 29 females, including 43 deputies from the 2016 Assembly running again for re-election (Gulf States Newsletter, 2020b).

In general, the government media's role in elections is passive. Their main focus is issuing statements about regulations, such as how to register as a candidate for elections and the eligibility requirements (Al Anbaa 2020). They also provide lists of approved candidates and press releases to private newspapers (KUNA 2020a, 2020b). A commentator told Gulf News that government media is "neither active nor interacting, but rather passively silent" (Gulf News 2020a). One campaign manager noted that "citizens and bystanders are forced to get their news from the local media outlets, through social media accounts, or the rumour mill, which are not independent or credible news agencies" (Interview 2020).

Yet, more than any other time in its history, the government was very active on social media and media accounts. They set up special daily health briefings and weekly meetings of the Council of Ministers were published online and on state television (KuwaitCM). Due to the restrictions, Al Majlis TV, the parliamentary channel, prepared more comprehensive coverage. The channel showed more than 60 reports every Saturday with academic, media, and political personalities (Al Majlis 2020). A prominent program on the channel was "Kuwait Votes" hosted by government officials, activists, and civil society institutions to talk about the official preparations for the elections (Parliamentary Constitution Network 2020). But as one informant noted, "none of this was critical content, it was all vanilla" (Interview February 2020). Another campaign manager noted

> this coverage has no analysis, guests and hosts simply read off prompters like auctioneers. Often the bar is set so low that government employees managing to put together a program is considered a success, the content is a secondary concern. It's only about performance, there is no substance to it.
>
> *Kuwaiti Political Activist*

The media sample illustrated the quantity of government reports in the media. Of the 850 posts and articles, 40% were government announcements (Figure 23.1).

Those surveyed noted the general feeling about the government media's role in the election (Figure 23.2). The government does not really have much of a role. Yet, the participants also believed that it was important to follow the news, even if it wasn't very useful.

Much of the focus in the media sample leading up to the elections was how campaigns would be cheaper because of the pandemic-related restrictions. Mass media in Kuwait is often focused on the mechanics of elections, including spending, versus the actual election itself. In previous elections, candidates spent between 100,000 and 500,000 KD on a campaign headquarters, salaries, banquets, and advertising (Al Qabas 2020c; Gulf News 2020b; Euro News 2020). During the election period, Al Rai and Al Qabas charged 2,000–30,000 KD per televised candidate interview. Fees varied depending on the date of the interview (the closer to the election date the more expensive) and whether it was on TV or the internet.

As candidates shifted their messaging online due to the COVID-19 restrictions, media and advertising companies increased their prices by 20%–50% (SMS Box 2020). Packages are divided into three levels, the lowest ranging between 5,000 and 30,000 KD, the average ranging between 50,000 and 70,000 KD, and the higher level starting from 100,000 KD (Al Jazeera 2020). One marketing site described social networking sites as a "stock exchange for advertising" during the election period (SMS Box 2020). Candidates paid up to 10,000 KD to hire "tweeps" to promote political campaigns on Twitter, Instagram, and other platforms. The cost of publishing a single tweet ranged between 100 and 300 KD, depending on the popularity and spread of the online account, the large number of followers, and the quality of the published tweet (SMS Box 2020). The survey participants thought that social media accounts were the most important medium for campaigns (Figure 23.3). They talked informally after the *diwaniya* about how they were the best source for analysis and criticism, because the traditional media was too uncritical.

Concerns about voter turnout or political dynamics in the pandemic environment were at the heart of many early media discussions. As one article noted, the pandemic "may push numbers of voters to refrain from participating and voting, to avoid infection, or weary of the participation procedures" (Al Qabas 2020d). The same article argued that the pandemic had helped tribes, and Sunni or Shia religious candidates who have more loyal followers (Al Qabas 2020d).

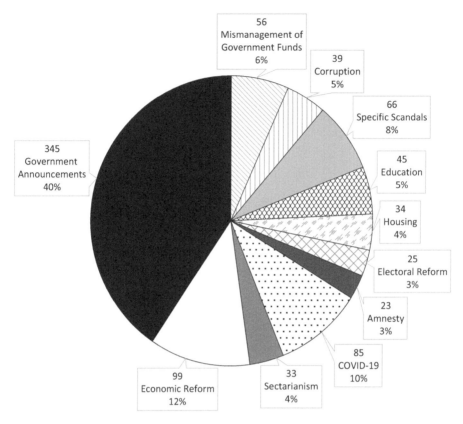

Figure 23.1 Media sample topics.

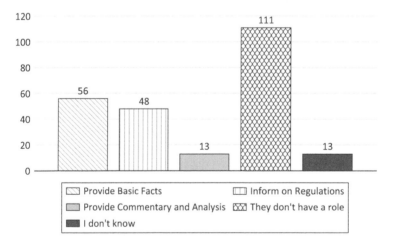

Figure 23.2 What is the role of government media in elections?

The role of media in electoral campaigns in the pandemic era

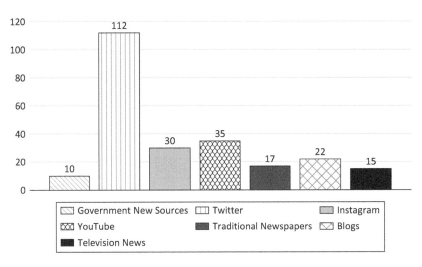

Figure 23.3 What is the most important medium for campaigning?

Hadar candidates might suffer more "due to the absence of the tribal bond, and the inability of family ties to keep pace with the tribe's role in mobilization" (Al Qabas 2020d).

Another theme widely spread in media exhorted the in-person ban as a way for independent candidates, especially women, to win against more traditional political opponents. Since 2006, only six women have won seats in parliament. *Diwaniyaat* are often pointed out as the main reason women cannot meet and discuss with constituents during election campaigning. Kuwaiti women do not have a social equivalent to male *diwaniyas*. This narrative of a new chance was encouraged by *hadar* elite women, embassies eager to tap into elite networks, and foreign think-tanks, which often promote less than accurate commentary on the political and social dynamics of Kuwait. Alanoud Sharekh, head of Ibtkar Consulting, founded the Mudhawi's List in September 2020 (Middle East Eye 2020), purporting to help women reach elected positions, whether in the assembly, municipal councils, student unions, boards of sports clubs, or non-governmental organizations (NGOs), through seminars, social media assistance, and public presentations/debates (Mudhawi's List; Al Qabas 2020f; AGSIW 2020). The Arab Gulf States Institute in Washington noted that "the move to online campaigning, which could actually work to the advantage of women candidates… Their reliance on bottom-up campaigns could prove to be an antidote to traditional political practices" (AGSIW 2020).

Perhaps the most seminal belief in the pre-election environment was that social media would transform the potential of candidates now that *diwaniyaat* were closed. In an article titled "Vote for Programs, not People", Dr Bader Khaled Al-Khalifa wrote that

> "all candidates must submit clear-cut programs and work schedules to implement these programs away from personal relationships, and communicate directly with voters through interactive programs in social communication with personal visits as the prevailing health conditions allow" (Al Qabas 2020e).

Candidates themselves played up the importance of the cyber-optimist narrative. Candidates Alia Al-Khaled, Ahmed Al-Hamad, Sheikha Al-Jassem, and Ali Al-Ali discussed how social media platforms played a more important role in their campaigns (AlKhaleej 2020; Anadolu Agency

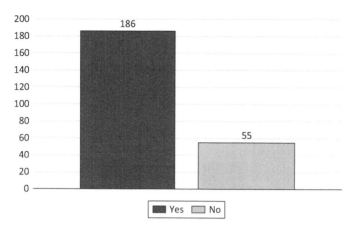

Figure 23.4 Was the quality of media content by candidates better than in previous elections?

2020). Al-Jassem said that "the arena for legislative elections this time is social media". According to Al-Jassem, even if she did traditional media interviews she must put them on social media, "otherwise, no one can see or follow them" (Euro News 2020).

It is true that Twitter has become more influential and effective than traditional media in the country. The circulation of daily Kuwaiti newspapers does not exceed 50,000, while the most popular Twitter accounts have over 500,000 followers (Selvik et al. 2015: 272). Working with traditional media is difficult in Kuwait with fake interviews, bribes, and gatekeeping *hadar* owners controlling the narrative. It is common to see the label "the corrupt media" (*al-i'lam al-fasid*) in social media posts.

In general, the marketing content for campaigns was more sophisticated than previous elections, according to 186 out of 241 survey participants (Figure 23.4). Catchy videos, slogans, and graphics were the norm.[5]

Yet, the impact of these marketing messages may not have been that great. There was an information overload and most people surveyed were not very impressed (Figure 23.5). As one pundit pointed out, "The disadvantage that candidates and voters face is the fact that there is a large number of political messages, many of which are repeated, so the public loses the chance of being influenced" (Interview March 2020). Another pundit discussed "the suffering of most candidates in formulating a distinctive media message, as most messages are similar and devoid of the distinctive proposition and personality" (Al Jazeera 2020).

One journalist commented that citizens' social media

> Accounts will be swept by a tsunami of speeches, leaving no room for thought. Most candidates will be keen on the propaganda sent and with professional video productions, the candidate will appear as if he were Martin Luther King… In this propaganda atmosphere that will not include direct meetings between candidates and voters, any opportunity to test the candidates' abilities to address people directly will vanish, so it will not be possible to judge their political abilities.
>
> *(Al Qabas 2020g)*

Those surveyed tended to agree, with 171 participants stating that candidates were generally of poor quality (Figure 23.6).

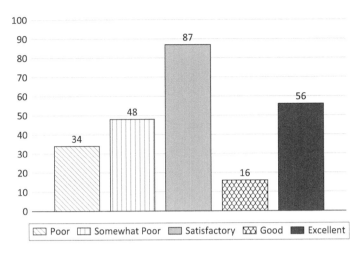

Figure 23.5 Overall, how would you rate the quality of media content in 2020?

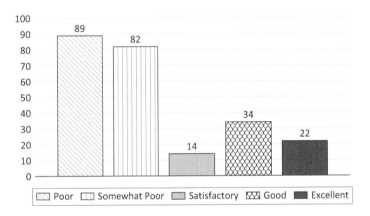

Figure 23.6 How would you rate the quality of candidates?

Those surveyed highlighted what they thought were the most important issues in the election (Figure 23.7). Of the voters surveyed, 27% thought the most important issue was economic reform.

The most trending topic focused on how COVID-19, low oil prices, and the shutdown impacted the Kuwaiti economy, which was floundering even before the pandemic. Kuwait relies on oil for 90% of its public revenues, and price fluctuations in early 2020, which saw oil prices plunge to US$25 per barrel, meant the country was struggling with historic deficits (Gulf States Newsletter, 2020d).

Several initiatives were taken to highlight the mounting economic challenges, including a report titled "Before It's too Late" written by 29 Kuwait University scholars and issued on the eve of the elections (Kuwait impakt 2020). However, these types of initiatives were only noticed by "a select group of elite citizens or foreign embassies. Most of the electorate didn't even know they existed" (Interview January 2020). As a Bloomberg article aptly described, the economy was a sideshow in the election campaign even though reforms were the most pressing issue (Bloomberg 2020a). Paradoxically, most of the candidates used populist rhetoric in

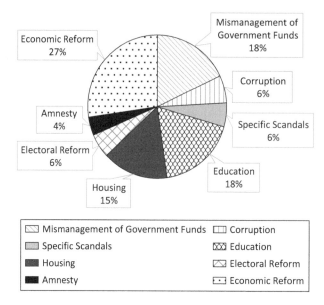

Figure 23.7 What were the most important topics in the election?

their campaigns, arguing to improve or protect subsidies, salaries, and public services. The topic that evoked the most passion amid the pandemic was related to the demographic situation and "Kuwaitisation" plans that seek to redress the expats-to-nationals ratio. The main proposal, which passed its initial reading in the KNA in July 2020, was to introduce a quota system for specific nationalities, as well as to label anyone over age 60 without a secondary education as ineligible for a work permit (Gulf Business 2020, Al Arabiya 2020a). Such a demographic plan is logistically improbable due to the structure of the labor market, "but is widely popular publicly" (Interview January 2020). The issue was popular in the sample and with media sources, candidates, and citizens more broadly (Gulf News, 2020b). A campaign manager expressed dismay at the way populism impacted campaigns. "There was no way to insert serious analysis about cutting spending or salaries for citizens. For a candidate to say this publicly is a death sentence, even though the economic realities are stark" (Interview January 2020). Most candidates attempted to capture voters by announcing populist platforms that often made unrealistic economic promises and xenophobic statements. Another campaign manager noted that "much of the issue is that people are living in denial about the future of the country and they lash out, with rhetoric and hate; and the expats are the easiest ones to push around" (Interview 2020).

Education was another hot topic. Kuwait was the only country in the world to halt public education entirely for eight months. More than 450,000 students were forced to stay at home as of March 2020. The indecision of the Ministry of Education left students without proper formal education for over eight months, and the shift to online learning fell short of educational requirements (Hashem and Martin 2020b).

Political reform and corruption also remained at the top of the agenda. There are a variety of issues here. Citizens are unhappy with the one-vote law, passed in 2012 to replace the four-vote list system. The new system is deeply unpopular with many people, who claim that it strengthens the government and it does not allow opposition groups to build coalitional blocs (Al Rai 2020; Martin 2021). Various scandals were also points of discussion (Figure 23.8). The Malaysian 1MDB scandal which implicated former Prime Minister Jaber Mubarak Al Sabah, visa trading

The role of media in electoral campaigns in the pandemic era

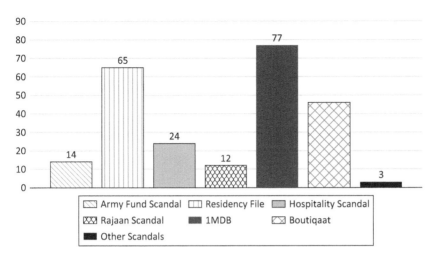

Figure 23.8 What are the most important topics concerning corruption?

scandals, the embezzlement of billions of dollars in the Ministry of Defense, and a scheme to defraud the Ministry of the Interior of hotel booking budgets were all hot topics of conversation (Gulf States Newsletter, 2020a;; Daily Star 2020; Gulf States Newsletter, 2020c). During the election, a scandal arose that brought into public view ten well-known social media influencers, whose assets were frozen for alleged money laundering after their accounts dramatically inflated by between US$32.5 and US$35 million without reason. Four perfume companies, including Boutiqaat, a leading Kuwaiti beauty e-commerce platform, are implicated in the scam, believed to be used as a cover for the sale of drugs and alcohol and other illicit activities. Abdulwahab Al Essa, the founder and CEO of Boutiqaat, was registered to run for parliamentary elections but was removed from the docket pending further investigation (Gulf States Newsletter, 2020c).

Election campaigns felt more like an escape from this reality, rather than a frank assessment of it. One writer wrote, "these days, with the election date approaching, we have seen the seasons of deception, lying and selling illusions from some to the helpless masse". In fact, those who review the *Al-Qabas* archive find that Kuwait's problems have been the same for more than 45 years (Al Qabas 2020h). Yet, according to the survey, voters argued that they were not influenced by media (Figure 23.9). Instead, their main voting preferences were family, ideology, and tribe (Figure 23.10).

In the end, the results were no different from previous elections. On the evening of December 5, the 18th legislative electoral process ended. Voter turnout was surprisingly quite high in the context of a pandemic, with unofficial polling numbers between 68% and 69% out of 567,694 eligible voters, a 1%–2% increase from the last parliamentary election in 2016. For the most part, this election did "not break from the past" (Washington Post 2020). Of 326 candidates, 44 of the previous 50 MPs in the 2016 parliament ran for re-election, and only 19 of them won, which is something to be expected in the one-vote system as it is designed to encourage low rates of incumbent re-election. The big winners of the election were the tribes, with the Al Mutairi, Awazem, and Ajmi tribes winning 29 seats. Tribal primaries continued to be an important factor in electoral politics. Of the 29 tribal MPs, 14 won in primaries held before the election.

Of the 29 women who ran for office, not one gained a seat. Safa Al Hashem, the sole female parliamentarian, lost her seat in a landslide, securing less than 400 votes and placing thirtieth in the third constituency. For female promoters and candidates there was a gnashing of teeth.

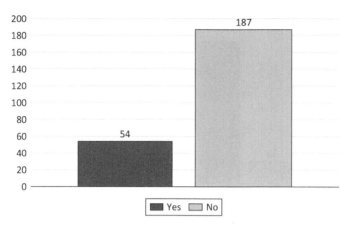

Figure 23.9 Does media influence your voting preferences?

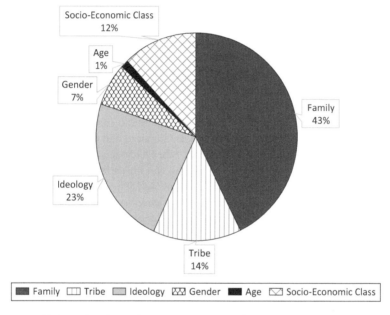

Figure 23.10 What does influence your voting preferences?

"People in Kuwait are still not convinced of women's political leadership", Alanoud Al-Sharekh said. Often, these conversations of elite women are decontextualized in media and are more for foreign audiences than local ones. Women turned out to vote in large numbers. One article stated that "the fall of women is caused by the woman herself" (Al Qabas 2020i). There was praise for the strong participation of fully veiled women; a reporter described them as "the black army". Different female candidates and organizers rarely work together, a collective action issue that hampers women's ability to win in Kuwaiti elections. Female candidates have historically split their vote in critical districts. If one of them withdrew or coordinated with the other, women would win at least one seat. The biggest divide is along class lines between middle-class and merchant-class women (Olimat 2009; Krause 2013; alMughni 2001). Those surveyed

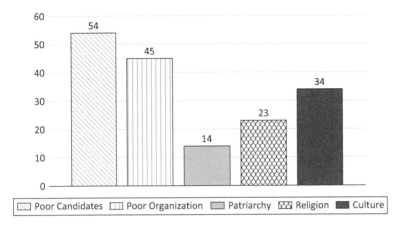

Figure 23.11 What were the main challenges for women candidates winning in the 2020 elections?

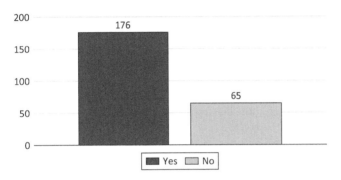

Figure 23.12 Were you surprised by the election results?

thought that poor candidates and poor campaign organization were the root cause of the failure of women to win (Figure 23.11). The majority of those surveyed were not surprised by the election outcome (Figure 23.12).

Discussion

It was clear from the results that very little had changed during the election even with restrictions. "While social media has become the main driver of this year's media campaign", as one commentator mentioned, this has little do to with the outcome (Bloomberg 2020b). Elections and campaigning are often mired in confusion simply because there are no details in the media about how they work in practice. Government media does not help because there is no clear idea of its role. The government plays almost no role in managing the media scene, meaning there is little tangential influence on campaigns other than to confuse voters. Elections are a perplexing process in the Kuwaiti media, more about insiders and outsiders understanding what the differences are from surface-level events. Overall, the role of media in elections in Kuwait is contradictory: a cacophony of voices, fake news, contradictory statements, and irresponsible proposals.

The role of media is an echo chamber, full of populist statements, rather than a serious explanation of a candidate's policy platform. The reality outside the media façade is that parliamentarians continue to act largely as service MPs for their constituents with few exceptions. Much of the performative actions on Twitter, for example, are delinked from the potential of the candidate, and voters know this. Looking past the role of media, the failure of female candidates is due to the poor planning and execution of their media campaigns. In general, social media does not influence voters; in fact, many of the most successful candidates did not use social media. Unfortunately, due to increased social media use, the echo chamber will only become louder and drown out more thoughtful analysis in the future. "All in all, politics in Kuwait represent more of a social safety valve than a vehicle for major policy changes, whether of the progressive or regressive sort" (Polluck 2017: 4).

Conclusion

The December 2020 election illustrated that the politics of campaigning and the use of mass media are paradoxical in Kuwait. Mass media does not really have an impact on the elections per se, and it does not improve the ability of candidates to win elections, especially those outside the political establishment. In fact, because it acts as more of a release valve or echo chamber, reactive and toxic, it is more of a sideshow to the real politics of patronage, vote-buying, and identity politics.

In the end, it breeds apathy and patronage voting because it encourages populism, which is a shallow veneer for identity interests. The literature on elections in Kuwait and the wider region has never really focused on the mass media in elections, focusing instead on cooptation or on authoritarianism. More studies and investigations of the micro dynamics of elections would be a much-needed contribution to fill this gap in the literature.

Notes

1 *Diwaniya* (plural *diwaniyaat*) are male-only tribal gatherings that are a focal point of politics and society in Kuwait.
2 Good examples of naturalized tribes are the Ajman, the Dawasir, the Uteibi, and the Mutran tribal confederations.
3 While Kuwait is de facto a "city state", distinctions are often made between the "urban" population (the "hadhar") and those who live in the outlying city districts (the "badu"). The former are long-established groups in the town of Kuwait and the latter are of Bedoiun tribes who settled in Kuwait during the 20th century.
4 Vote buying is a common and recurring problem in Kuwait with 1,000–2,000 KD the price of one vote, or gifts such as mobile phones or Ipads.
5 For an example, see this thread on some of the most popular videos: https://twitter.com/ALYOUSEF94/status/1333382806597152770?s=20.

References

AGSIW. 2020. 'Mudhawi's list: Advocating for Kuwaiti women in politics'. Available at: https://agsiw.org/mudhawis-list-advocating-for-kuwaiti-women-in-politics/.
Aiko, Hiramatsu. 2011. 'The changing nature of the parliamentary system in Kuwait: Islamists, tribes, and women in recent elections'. *Kyoto Bulletin of Islamic Area Studies* 4(1–2): 62–73.
Al Anbaa. 2020. 'The ministry of the interior: Candidacy for membership'. Available at: https://www.alanba.com.kw/ar/kuwait-news/parliament/1000922/.
Al Arabiya. 2020a. 'Expats over age 60 with no degree have until year's end to leave Kuwait'. Available at: https://english.alarabiya.net/en/News/gulf/2020/08/27/Expats-over-age-60-with-no-degree-have-until-year-s-end-to-leave-Kuwait.html.
Al'Ghanim, Mohammed. 2010. 'Do elections lead to reform? Assessing the institutional limits of representative bodies in Bahrain, Kuwait and Saudi Arabia'. *Contemporary Arab Affairs* 3(2): 138–147.

Alfadhli, Salah. 2013. 'The impact of Twitter on the voters of parliamentary elections in Kuwait'. *Journal of the Social Sciences* 41(2): 9–19.

Al Hashem, Shaikha and Geoffrey Martin. 2020a. *COVID-19's Implications for Foreign Labour Outflow in Kuwait*. LSE Middle East Blog. Available at: https://blogs.lse.ac.uk/mec/2020/05/19/covid-19s-implications-for-foreign-labour-outflow-in-kuwait/.

Al Hashem, Shaikha and Geoffrey Martin. 2020b. *The Elephant in the Room: Kuwait's Labour Crisis*. Gulf International Forum. Available at: https://gulfif.org/the-elephant-in-the-room-kuwaits-labor-crisis/.

Al Jazeera. 2020. 'Because of corona's measures, social networking sites are the most prominent propaganda field in the Kuwaiti parliamentary election.' Available at: https://www.aljazeera.net/news/politics/2020/11/26.

Al Khaleej Online. 2020. 'Fearing corona… Precautionary mechanisms to cover the Kuwaiti national assembly's vote'. Available at: https://alkhaleejonline.net.

Al-Majlis. 2020. Twitter account. Available at: https://twitter.com/AlmajlisChannel/status/1334908766240780292?s=20.

Al-Mughni, H. 2001. *Women in Kuwait: The Politics of Gender*. London: Saqi Books.

Al Mulla, Yasmena. 2020a. 'Kuwait elections: Citizens head to the polls'. Available at: https://gulfnews.com/world/gulf/kuwait/kuwait-elections-citizens-head-to-the-polls-1.1607142485106.

Al Mulla, Yasmena. 2020b. 'How election campaigning works in Kuwait - And how it is being impacted by COVID-19. Available at: https://gulfnews.com/world/gulf/kuwait/how-election-campaigning-works-in-kuwait---and-how-it-is-being-impacted-by-covid-19-1.1605103024526.

Al Rai. 2020. 'A field survey by the Center for Gulf and Arabian Peninsula Studies at Kuwait University monitors increasing calls for its amendment 'One Voice'… the controversy continue'. Available at: https://www.alraimedia.com/article/1510275/.

Al Qabas. 2020a. 'Cabinet: No celebrations after the announcement of the election result'. Available at: https://www.alqabas.com/article/5820009.

Al Qabas. 2020b. 'Preventing 'corona' patients from voting…opens the door to challenge the election'. Available at: https://alqabas.com/article/5816007.

Al Qabas. 2020c. '100,000 Dinars is the lowest cost of an election campaign'. Available at: https://alqabas.com/article/304203.

Al Qabas. 2020d. 'Political analysis. Reluctance to participate strengthens the positions of tribes and Islamists'. Available at: https://www.alqabas.com/article/5821163.

Al Qabas. 2020e 'The upcoming elections.. Vote for programs, not people'. Available at: https://www.alqabas.com/article/5809741.

Al Qabas. 2020f. 'British Ambassador: It's time to empower women to make decisions'. Available at: https://alqabas.com/article/5808177.

Al Qabas. 2020g. 'Free speech, the worst elections in the history of Kuwait'. Available at: https://alqabas.com/article/5800830.

Al Qabas. 2020h. 'The season of lies and hypocrisy..!' Available at: https://alqabas.com/article/5814244.

Al Qabas. 2020i. 'At the core, Kuwait is on its way to Lebanonization'. Available at: https://alqabas.com/article/5829220.

Al-Qassemi, Sultan. 2011. 'Gulf governments take to social media'. *Huffpost*. Available at: https://www.huffpost.com/entry/gulf-governments-take-to-_b_868815.

Alsalem, Fatima. 2021. 'Kuwait: From 'Hollywood of the Gulf' to social media diwaniyas'. *Arab Media Systems 3*. Available at: https://books.openbookpublishers.com/10.11647/obp.0238/ch10.xhtml.

Anadolu Agency. 2020. 'Twitter, Instagram and Snapchat are electoral campaigning tools in Kuwait'. Available at: https://www.aa.com.tr/ar/.

Azoulay, R. 2020. *Kuwait and Al-Sabah: Tribal Politics and Power in an Oil State*. Bloomsbury Publishing.

Bloomberg. 2020a. 'Kuwaiti economy in crisis a sideshow as nation goes to polls'. Available at: https://www.bloomberg.com/news/articles/2020-12-05/kuwait-s-economy-in-crisis-a-sideshow-as-nation-goes-to-polls.

Bloomberg. 2020b. 'Kuwait's voter "uprising" ousts more than half of parliament'. Available at: https://www.bloomberg.com/news/articles/2020-12-06/kuwaiti-voters-replace-more-than-half-of-sitting-parliament.

Brumberg, D. 2003. 'Liberalization versus democracy: Understanding Arab political reform'. Available at: https://policycommons.net/artifacts/977386/liberalization-versus-democracy/1706512/.

Crystal, J. 1989. 'Coalitions in oil monarchies: Kuwait and Qatar'. *Comparative Politics* 21(4): 427–443.

Daily Star. 2020. 'Human trafficking case: Kuwait court denies bail to MP Shahid'. Available at: https://www.thedailystar.net/frontpage/news/human-trafficking-case-kuwait-court-denies-bail-mp-shahid-1963597.

Das, Hirak. 2017. 'National assembly elections in Kuwait, 2016'. *Contemporary Review of the Middle East* 4(2): 193–210.

Egypt Independent. 2020. 'Kuwait's emir asks government to stay on, prepare for elections'. Available at: https://www.egyptindependent.com/kuwaits-emir-asks-government-to-stay-on-prepare-for-elections/.

Euro News. 2020. 'Legislative elections in Kuwait in the shadow of corona: Electronic campaigns and the absence of gathering'. Available at: https://arabic.euronews.com/2020/12/01/legislative-elections-in-kuwait-in-the-time-of-corona.

Freedom House. 'Kuwait: Freedom in the world 2020 country report'. Available at: https://freedomhouse.org/country/kuwait/freedom-world/2020.

Greenfield, Rebecca. 2013. 'In Kuwait, Instagram accounts are big business'. *The Atlantic Wire*, July 12. Available at: https://www.theatlantic.com/technology/archive/2013/07/kuwait-instagram-accounts-are-big-business/313382/.

Gulf Business. 2020. 'Kuwait's national assembly approves expat quota bill'. Available at: https://gulfbusiness.com/kuwaits-national-assembly-approves-expat-quota-bill-report/.

Gulf News. 2020a. 'How election campaigning works in Kuwait - And how it is being impacted by COVID-19'. Available at: https://gulfnews.com/world/gulf/kuwait/how-election-campaigning-works-in-kuwait---and-how-it-is-being-impacted-by-covid-19-1.1605103024526.

Gulf News. 2020b. 'Kuwait: Parliament and government discuss demographic imbalance bill'. Available at: https://gulfnews.com/world/gulf/kuwait/kuwait-parliament-and-government-discuss-demographic-imbalance-bill-1.74588982.

Gulf News. 2020c. 'Kuwait election youth issues absent from political discourse'. Available at: https://gulfnews.com/world/gulf/kuwait/kuwait-election-youth-issues-absent-from-political-discourse-1.75355684.

Gulf States Newsletter. 2020a. *Crisis Pushes Illegal Residents Up the Political Agenda*. Volume 44, Issue 1,101, April.

Gulf States Newsletter. 2020b. *First Elections of the Nawaf Era Take Place Under a Covid Cloud*. Volume 44, Issue 1,114, November.

Gulf States Newsletter. 2020c. *Kuwait Struggles to Adjust to Impact of Covid-19 and Low Oil*. Volume 44, Issue 1,103, May.

Gulf States Newsletter. 2020d. *Kuwait Struggles to Find Viable Response to Covid-19 Crisis*. Volume 44, Issue 1,106, June.

Gulf States Newsletter. 2020e. *With New Crown Prince in Place, Kuwaiti Leaders Turn Focus to Domestic Challenges*. Volume 44, Issue 1,112, October.

Herb, Michael. 2014. *The Wages of Oil: Parliaments and Economic Development in Kuwait and the UAE*. Ithaca: Cornell University Press.

Kononova, Anastasia and Mohammad Akbar. 2015. 'Interpersonal communication, media exposure, opinion leadership, and perceived credibility of news and advertising during December 2012 parliamentary election in Kuwait'. *International Journal of Communication* 9: 1206–1228.

Kraetzschmar, Hendrik. 2018. 'In the shadow of legality: Proto-parties and participatory politics in the emirate of Kuwait'. In Francesco Cavatorta and Lise Storm (eds.), *Political Parties in the Arab World: Continuity and Change*. Edinburgh: Edinburgh University Press, 230–251.

Krause, Wanda. 2013. 'Gender and participation in the Arab Gulf'. In David Held and Kristian Ulrichsen (eds.), *The transformation of the Gulf*. London: Routledge, 105–124.

KUNA. 2020a. 'A total of 395 male and female candidates with the closing of nominations for elections'. Available at: https://www.kuna.net.kw/ArticleDetails.aspx?id=2937118&language=ar.

KUNA. 2020b. 'Social media plays role in Kuwaiti parliament's by-elections'. Available at: https://www.kuna.net.kw/ArticleDetails.aspx?id=2782194&language=en.

Kuwait impakt. 2020. 'Before it's too late'. Available at: https://kuwaitimpakt.com/.

Martin, Geoffrey. 2018. 'Researching Twitter'. In Janine Clark and Francesco Cavatorta (eds.), *Political Science Research in the Middle East and North Africa: Methodological and Ethical Challenges*. Oxford: Oxford University Press: 218–230.

Martin, Geoffrey. 2019. 'The consequences of some angry re-tweets: Another medium is the message'. *Review of Middle East Studies* 53(2): 259–293.

Martin, Geoffrey. 2020, October. *Kuwait at a Crossroads*. ZENITH Magazine. Available at: https://magazine.zenith.me/en/politics/succession-kuwait.

Martin, Geoffrey. 2021. 'The failure of Karamat watan: State legitimacy and protest failure in Kuwait'. *Partecipazione e Conflitto* 14(2): 702–726.

Middle East Eye. 2020. 'Ahead of Kuwait elections, women push for further representation'. Available at: https://www.middleeasteye.net/news/kuwait-election-women-representation-candidates-vote.

Miller, Noah and Rosa Ko. 2015. 'Studying political microblogging: Parliamentary candidates on Twitter during the February 2012 election in Kuwait'. *International Journal of Communication* 9: 2933–2993.

Mudhawis List. 2020. Available at: https://mudhawislist.com/mudhawis-milestones.

Olimat, Muhamad. 2009. 'Women and politics in Kuwait'. *Journal of International Women's Studies* 11(2): 199–212.

Parliamentary Constitution Network. Available at: http://www.kna.kw/clt-html5/news-details.asp?id=33955.

Polluck, David. 2017. 'Kuwait: Democracy trumps reform'. In *Beyond Islamist & Autocrats: Prospects for Political Reform Post Arab Spring*. The Washington Institute for Near East Policy. Available at: https://www.washingtoninstitute.org/policy-analysis/beyond-islamists-and-autocrats-prospects-political-reform-post-arab-spring.

Salameh, Mohammad and Mohammad al-Sharah. 2011. 'Kuwait's democratic experiment: Roots, reality, characteristics, challenges, and the prospects for the future'. *Journal of Middle Eastern and Islamic Studies (in Asia)* 5(3): 57–81.

Salih, Kamal Eldin Osman. 2011. 'Kuwait primary (tribal) elections 1975–2008: An evaluative study'. *British Journal of Middle Eastern Studies* 38(2): 141–167.

Schedler, Andreas. 2002. 'Elections without democracy: The menu of manipulation'. *Journal of Democracy* 13(2): 36–50.

Selvik, Kjetil, Jon Nordenson and Tewodros Aragie Kebede. 2015. 'Print media liberalization and electoral coverage bias in Kuwait'. *Middle East Journal* 69(2): 255–276.

SMS Box. 2020. 'How to conduct a successful advertising campaign for the national assembly elections'. Available at: https://www.smsbox.com/en/.

Szmolka, Inmaculada. 2011. 'Democracias y autoritarismos con adjetivos: La clasificación de los países árabes dentro de una tipología general de regímenes políticos'. *Revista Española de Ciencia Política* 26: 11–62.

Tétreault, M. A. 2000. *Stories of democracy: Politics and society in contemporary Kuwait*. New York: Columbia University Press.

Tétreault, M. A. and Al-Ghanim, M. 2009. 'The day after "victory": Kuwait's 2009 election and the contentious present'. *Middle East Report Online* 8. https://merip.org/2009/07/the-day-after-victory-kuwaits-2009-election-and-the-contentious-present/

Wheeler, Deborah. 2003. 'The Internet and youth subcultures in Kuwait'. *Journal of Computer-Mediated Communication* 8(2): 1–26.

Wheeler, D. and Mintz, L. 2010. The Internet and political change in Kuwait. *Foreign Policy*. https://foreignpolicy.com/2010/04/15/the-internet-and-political-change-in-kuwait/

24
OPPOSITION COORDINATION UNDER A COMPETITIVE AUTHORITARIAN REGIME: THE CASE OF THE 2019 LOCAL ELECTIONS IN TURKEY

Berk Esen[1] and Hakan Yavuzyılmaz

Introduction

On 31 March 2019, Turkish voters headed to the polls to elect their mayors and municipal council members in 30 metropolitan areas, 51 provinces, 922 districts and 386 sub-districts. This was the first municipal contest under Turkey's presidential system, which further eroded institutional checks and balances and tilted the playing field in favour of the incumbent. After a highly divisive campaign, the opposition parties achieved an impressive victory against candidates supported by the ruling Justice and Development Party (*Adalet ve Kalkınma Partisi*, AKP) and the National Action Party (*Milliyetçi Hareket Partisi*, MHP) in major metropolitan areas and provinces across the country, including Istanbul and Ankara. This was the biggest electoral upset the ruling party had faced since it first came to power in 2002. This electoral outcome was all the more surprising for two particular reasons. First, aside from its incumbency advantage in a competitive authoritarian regime (Esen and Gumuscu 2016), the AKP had built a pre-electoral alliance with the MHP, which had been in the opposition camp during the previous local elections. Second, the AKP's control of major metropolitan areas like Istanbul and Ankara dated back to 1994 (Esen and Gumuscu 2019).

The results reinforced the downward trend of AKP votes in major metropolitan districts that had first become apparent in the June 2015 parliamentary elections (Kemahlıoğlu 2015) and confirmed in the 2017 constitutional referendum (Esen and Gumuscu 2017b). Although the ruling party obtained a plurality of votes, its electoral base was eroded in Turkey's major metropolitan areas and among young voters, shifting instead towards sparsely populated Anatolian provinces. Interestingly, the AKP and its electoral ally, the MHP, lost votes and mayoral seats to all major opposition parties. In particular, the main opposition Republican People's Party (*Cumhuriyet Halk Partisi*,

---

[1] Dr. Esen acknowledges the financial support of the Young Scientist Award (BAGEP) of the Science Academy, Turkey.

CHP) benefited the most from the AKP's decline, as it gained control of municipal governments in four of the top five most populated provinces in the country. The pro-Kurdish People's Democratic Party (*Halklann Demokratik Partisi*, HDP) regained control of municipal governments in its strongholds in the south-eastern provinces, whereas the recently established Good Party (*İYİ Parti*, IYIP) won its first district mayoral seats but fell short of scoring victories at the provincial level.

In this chapter, we argue that three important factors account for the opposition's ability to outperform the AKP and the MHP. First, the ruling party experienced a significant decline in its performance legitimacy due to the ongoing economic downturn and migration crisis. In the past, the AKP had expanded its electoral base because of its good economic performance (Çarkoğlu 2008). In recent years, however, the Turkish economy took a severe hit that resulted in sharp rises in inflation and unemployment figures after 2018. For the urban poor, these economic woes were exacerbated by the fact that hundreds of thousands of Syrian migrants had taken refuge in Turkey over the previous decade, thus requiring the allocation of public resources. Second, opposition parties managed to coordinate their campaigns to nominate joint candidates in many provinces. Thus, the opposition's strong performance in the 2019 local elections affirmed those studies that suggest opposition coordination increases electoral competitiveness under an electoral authoritarian regime (Jimenez 2021; Donno 2013). Third, the opposition campaign was largely centred on an 'active depolarizing strategy' (Somer et al. 2021) that sought to defuse the identity conflicts the incumbent had created and emphasize cross-cutting ties among the electorate. Instead of engaging in polemics with the incumbent, opposition candidates adopted an inclusionary discourse, addressed local problems and promised redistribution to disadvantaged groups (Esen and Gumuscu 2019; Yavuzyılmaz 2021). This 'inverted populist' strategy (Demiralp and Balta 2021) allowed opposition candidates to overcome the incumbent's polarizing discourse and appeal to AKP voters in major metropolitan areas.

The 2019 local elections affirmed that the political regime in Turkey exhibited competitive authoritarian features (Esen and Gumuscu 2016, 2019) and had not yet drifted to a closed autocracy as some analysts feared (Çalışkan 2018). As we had already seen in previous elections (Kemahlıoğlu 2015; Sayarı 2016; Esen and Gumuscu 2017a), the playing field was tilted against the opposition both prior to and during the campaign. However, the opposition's strong performance did not result in a democratizing outcome. As the AKP's electoral hegemony waned, the incumbent turned to various post-election mechanisms to reverse the electoral outcomes and retain the authoritarian features of the regime (Tepe and Alemdaroğlu 2021). Yet, winning municipal governments in major metropolitan areas has provided the opposition parties with resources that are vital for challenging the incumbent under a competitive authoritarian regime. But unless these local victories are followed by success in the upcoming presidential elections, democratization is not possible.

Political background of the local elections

After its victory in the 2002 general election, the AKP relied on its popular support to entrench its rule at the national and local levels (Gumuscu 2013). The ruling party retained the plurality of the votes in five successive parliamentary elections and captured the majority of municipal governments, including major metropolitan areas like Istanbul and Ankara, in the 2004, 2009 and 2014 local elections. Its control over municipal governments endowed the AKP with an array of resources for providing social assistance and public services and distributing patronage (Eligür 2010; Kemahlıoğlu and Özdemir 2018). Thanks to its electoral hegemony, the ruling party tilted the playing field against the opposition, captured state institutions and eroded institutional checks and balances to establish a competitive authoritarian regime (Esen and Gumuscu 2016;

Esen 2021). Accordingly, elections are neither free nor fair in Turkey under the rule of the AKP, which enjoys disproportionate access to public and private resources and systematically targets its opponents in media and civil society.

In recent years, however, the AKP has faced increasing electoral competition from opposition parties. In the June 2015 elections, for instance, the ruling party lost its parliamentary majority for the first time since 2002 (Kemahlıoğlu 2015) and remained in power largely due to the opposition parties' failure to form an alternative government. When coalition talks failed, President Erdoğan called for a snap election in November that his party won decisively (Sayarı 2016). Later, faced with a coup attempt in 2016 (Esen and Gumuscu, 2017b), Erdoğan declared emergency rule, which allowed him to purge his critics from the bureaucracy and to govern the country by decree. He sidelined several prominent figures within the AKP (Yardımcı-Geyikçi and Yavuzyılmaz 2020) and tightened his grip over state institutions, especially following the transition to an executive-presidential system (Esen and Gumuscu 2018).

Prior to this systemic transition, the electoral system had changed to allow political parties to build pre-electoral coalitions. In the lead up to the 2018 twin elections, Erdoğan pushed for an electoral alliance between his party and the MHP, a conservative-national bloc called the People's Alliance (*Cumhur İttifakı*). During the last decade, Turkish politics experienced 'pernicious polarization' (Somer et al. 2021) into two mutually distrustful camps. Having come to power by mobilizing previously marginalized sectors in society, Erdoğan has since adopted a polarizing discourse to consolidate his electoral base and to fend off both democratic and extra-judicial challenges against his rule (Somer 2019).

During the 2017 referendum campaign, the opposition actors engaged in what Jimenez (2021) refers to as 'informal coordination', which included private agreements to oppose proposed constitutional amendments and a cross-ideological platform to lead the 'no camp'. Although such efforts were not sufficient to defeat the government, the 'no camp' received support from almost half of the electorate and carried several major metropolitan areas (Esen and Gumuscu 2017a). Since the presidency was invested with more substantial powers, the stakes of the 2018 presidential elections increased for opposition parties. On the eve of the 2018 twin elections, the CHP took the lead in forming an electoral alliance, Nation Alliance (*Millet İttifakı*), with the IYIP and two other minor right-wing parties (Esen and Yardımcı-Geyikçi 2020; Sozen 2019). Not surprisingly, the autocratization process in Turkey compelled ideologically distant parties to engage in formal opposition coordination to increase their chances of victory under the new system.

2019 local campaign
The ruling bloc

Prior to the 2019 elections, the AKP and the MHP revitalized the People's Alliance and agreed to nominate joint candidates in 51 provinces (27 metropolitan areas and 17 provinces for AKP candidates), while each party would run their own nominees in the remaining 30 provinces (DW 2019). At the time, the AKP was already in charge of the municipal government in many of these provinces and thus enjoyed incumbency advantage.

As a party that, for years, had capitalized on its successful provision of public services and social assistance, the AKP campaign promoted service-oriented local governance (*hizmet belediyeciliği*) with an emphasis on the importance of community outreach. Its campaign slogan – local governance from the heart (*gönül belediyeciliği*) – highlighted the party's emotional bonds with the electorate (AK Parti 2018). The ruling party promised a new urban development model and a political vision in its electoral agenda that sharply differed from its past practices (Esen and Gumuscu 2019). Its platform pledged more transparency, sustainable development fitting local needs, urban planning, increased infrastructural investments and social assistance, greater openness and civic engagement, and strong commitment to environmental protection (AK Parti 2019). Obviously, there was a clear mismatch between this platform and the AKP's local policies to date and its polarizing rhetoric.

The AKP campaign was largely centred on President Erdoğan. Due to the process of de-institutionalization observed in the ruling party, the AKP's party–voter linkage had weakened, and many voters began to identify more closely with Erdoğan, who was given almost free rein over his party (Yardımcı-Geyikçi and Yavuzyılmaz 2020). Accordingly, Erdoğan picked his party's mayoral candidates and replaced some sitting mayors with little consideration of local dynamics. The replacement of long-time mayors with political outsiders disrupted AKP rank-and-file members and weakened the party's efforts to mobilize voters. Furthermore, Erdoğan's dominant presence distracted from the campaign focusing on local issues and kept the candidates out of the spotlight. He campaigned across the country, holding rallies in 57 provinces and several districts and gave special emphasis to Istanbul and Ankara towards the end of the campaign (Sabah 2019).

As the minor partner in the People's Alliance, the MHP adopted a far more consistent message during the 2019 campaign. Given its ultra-nationalist origins, the MHP leaders highlighted the security threats Turkey faced in an attempt to justify their continued partnership with the AKP and promote the party's own importance within that alliance (Cumhuriyet 2019a). The MHP platform, which made only scant references to local issues and lacked concrete policy proposals, emphasized the party's ideology at the expense of individual candidates (Esen and Gumuscu 2019).

In addition to buttressing the regime electorally, the MHP's presence in the People's Alliance allowed Erdogan to portray his government as native and national (*yerli ve milli*), while accusing his opponents of endangering national security. The MHP leadership made a concerted effort to link the CHP and the IYIP with the Kurdish separatist organization the Kurdistan Workers' Party (PKK; via the HDP) to discredit their appeal.

The opposition

Their defeat in the 2018 twin elections compelled the CHP and IYIP leadership to deepen their alliance to survive against government pressure and fend off intra-party challenges. While mutual concessions were unacceptable to some ideologically committed voters in each party, both party leaders benefited from the preservation of the Nation Alliance, as it increased the costs of repression for the incumbent and boosted their competitiveness under the presidential system. Accordingly, the CHP and the IYIP agreed to preserve the Nation Alliance on the eve of the 2019 local elections, while the Felicity Party (*Saadet Partisi*, SP) and the Democrat Party (*Demokrat Parti*, DP) refused to join the coalition and instead ran their own candidates. After long negotiations, the CHP and the IYIP nominated joint candidates in 23 metropolitan areas (13 CHP and 10 IYIP candidates) and 27 provinces (15 CHP and 12 IYIP candidates) and, as mentioned, ran separate candidates in the remaining 30 provinces. The agreement allowed both parties to concentrate their resources on their own strongholds; the CHP local organizations were entrenched in economically advanced metropolitan areas, whereas the IYIP could better appeal to moderate Turkish nationalists and conservatives in the Anatolian heartland.

The CHP's campaign relied heavily on an 'active depolarizing strategy' (Somer et al. 2021) that refused to engage the incumbent's divisive discourse and emphasized cross-cutting ties within the electorate. In particular, the party leadership focused on local issues and offered concrete policy proposals to appeal directly to voters. The party's communication strategy changed dramatically to serve this purpose. Its campaign slogan revolved around a message of hope. CHP candidates were asked to avoid confronting pro-government voters with anger, ridicule or sarcasm and challenging Erdoğan directly (Wuthrich and Ingleby 2020). Instead of focusing on its own electoral base, the main opposition party adopted an inclusionary discourse to reach out to marginalized groups within the electorate.

In major metropolitan areas, the CHP nominated candidates who fit this campaign strategy. The CHP's leader, Kılıçdaroğlu, was able to obtain the support of the IYIP to pick figures who had wide popular appeal and moderate ideological views. His preference for centrist candidates generated strong intra-party opposition but, in the end, was accepted. In many metropolitan areas, CHP candidates were successful district mayors with a strong public record and genuine local support (Esen and Gumuscu 2019). CHP candidates criticized the incompetence of incumbent mayors, highlighted economic challenges voters faced and promised redistribution through social assistance programmes. Their non-polemic and positive campaign highlighted ongoing economic difficulties and engaged with AKP voters through concrete policy proposals that addressed pressing local problems (Esen and Gumuscu 2019; Yavuzyılmaz 2021). For instance, İmamoğlu highlighted the need to put an end to partisanship through transparent and inclusive governance and refrained from directly attacking Erdoğan who was still popular with AKP voters. A clear manifestation of this strategy was his decision during the campaign to consult with all former İstanbul mayors, including President Erdoğan, about the city's problems (Cumhuriyet 2019b).

As a newly established party in a competitive authoritarian regime, the IYIP had difficulty in reaching out to voters and propagating its views and ideology. Its candidates got limited media coverage, while business and civil society actors linked with the IYIP faced pressure from the regime. Furthermore, the IYIP experienced intra-party rifts on its political direction and ideological platform that the ruling party exploited. During the campaign, IYIP's leader, Meral Aksener, tried to position the party as a moderate nationalist organization that would simultaneously appeal to middle-class voters and conservatives disillusioned with the government's poor management of the economy. However, the party lacked resources and strong cadres to follow this course; many party members came from an ultra-nationalist background and veered away from the official line.

The IYIP's primary goal was to win some municipalities to gain access to resources crucial for building strong local organizations, recruiting better candidates and achieving visibility and credibility among voters (Esen and Gumuscu 2019). Having splintered from the ultra-nationalist MHP, the IYIP campaign borrowed many centre-right themes that had dominated Turkish politics for decades, such as effective economic management, the resolution of local problems and the provision of public goods and social assistance to the needy. Accordingly, the IYIP was careful to strike a balance between right-wing values and support for the republican regime so as to overcome the secular–Islamist divide. Its party manifesto promised voters people-centred local governance, in sharp contrast to the nepotistic measures of mayors from the People's Alliance. The IYIP leadership heavily criticized the government for its poor management of the economy and the migration crisis.

Due to her popularity, the IYIP's campaign centred on Meral Akşener who could appeal to both conservative and nationalist Turkish voters and, as a female politician, court women voters more effectively. Akşener held rallies in 20 provinces and 55 districts in less than two months and participated in campaign events with the CHP leader Kılıçdaroğlu and CHP candidates (Sabah 2019). Her speeches promoted the IYIP as a right-wing alternative to the ruling bloc, dismissed Bahçeli as a junior partner of the government and took on Erdoğan directly. In so far as it elicited a response from Erdoğan, Akşener's criticism kept the IYIP under the media spotlight and elevated the party's political standing among right-wing voters.

Due to its nationalist ideology, the IYIP was vulnerable to criticism that it was openly cooperating with the HDP. In response, the IYIP leadership made painstaking efforts to sever any ties with the HDP, openly criticizing its leadership and even standing down its candidate in favour of the pro-government candidate in Iğdır and Ahlat so as not to divide the anti-HDP vote in both areas. The IYIP's response demonstrates the dilemmas faced by opposition parties under a competitive authoritarian regime against the incumbent's efforts to divide the opposition on identity lines. Ultimately, the IYIP's uncompromising stance against the HDP did not break the Nation Alliance nor did it end the AKP's and MHP's criticism of Akşener and her party.

The pro-Kurdish HDP ran an independent campaign. After surpassing the 10% electoral threshold to gain parliamentary representation in the June 2015 elections, the pro-Kurdish party came under severe government pressure that resulted in the arrest of scores of Kurdish politicians, including its charismatic former co-chairman Selahattin Demirtaş. After 2016, the government appointed trustees (*kayyum*) to replace mayors from the HDP and its sister party, the Democratic Regions Party (*Demokratik Bölgeler Partisi*, DBP), allegedly due to their support for terror activities. The use of trustees was an instrument to further tilt the playing field against the opposition and expand the ruling party's patronage networks for retaining electoral dominance in the region (Tepe and Alemdaroğlu 2021). Trustees enabled the AKP to reward its supporters through patronage and clientelism, to intimidate and divide the opposition camp and to take away the HDP's incumbency advantage in the lead up to the 2019 campaign.

The HDP saw the local elections as a way to regain these municipal governments and consolidate its power base in the heavily Kurdish-populated south-eastern and eastern provinces. HDP candidates were confronted with government-sponsored attacks, police intimidation and biased or limited media coverage throughout the campaign (Esen and Gumuscu 2019). The party also decided not to field candidates in seven metropolitan municipalities where CHP candidates were on the ballot, urging its supporters to vote against candidates from the ruling coalition. In the words of party co-chair Sezai Temelli, the HDP's goal in this election was 'winning in Kurdistan, making AKP and MHP lose in the West' (SonDakika 2019).

Election results

As shown in Figures 24.1 and 24.2, the 2019 local elections ended the AKP's electoral hegemony and produced a more balanced political map. While the AKP still controls municipal governments across the Anatolian heartland, its areas of strength are generally confined to the sparsely populated and economically underdeveloped provinces – with some exceptions like Samsun, Konya, Bursa, Gaziantep and Denizli. Even in these areas, the ruling party experienced a sharp decline in its vote share and lost mayoral seats to the MHP in central and eastern Anatolia regions. The MHP too experienced a major electoral upset. Although the Turkish ultra-nationalist party increased its mayoral seats to 11 (up from 8 in the 2014 local elections), it lost two major metropolitan municipalities – Adana and Mersin – to the CHP and saw a sizable portion of its voters switch support to the IYIP, especially in economically advanced parts of the country. However, the MHP experienced an upward shift in provincial parts of central and Eastern Anatolia, the Black Sea and Aegean regions. It captured seven provincial mayoralties – Amasya, Çankırı, Bayburt, Karaman, Kastamonu, Kütahya and Erzincan – from the AKP and only lost one provincial mayoralty – Isparta – to the ruling party.

Despite trailing the AKP in overall vote share, the CHP emerged as the real winner of this election. It seized control of municipal governments in five major metropolitan areas – taking Mersin

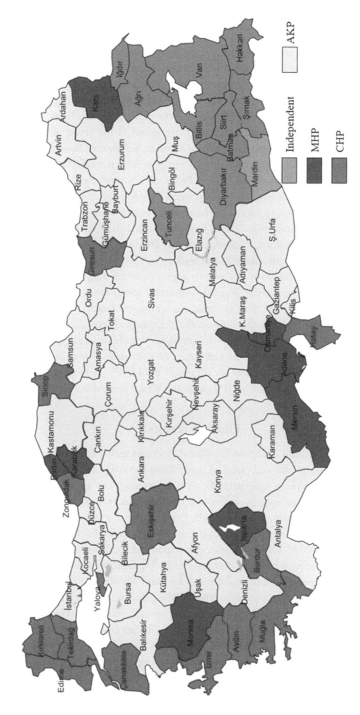

Figure 24.1 The 2014 local election results in Turkey by province. Source: Esen and Gumuscu (2019).

Opposition coordination under a competitive authoritarian regime

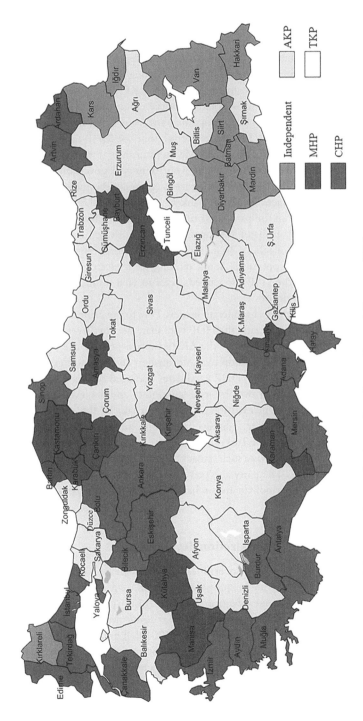

Figure 24.2 The 2019 local election results in Turkey by province. Source: Esen and Gumuscu (2019).

and Adana from the MHP and Istanbul, Ankara and Antalya from the AKP – and in five provinces – Artvin, Bilecik, Bolu, Ardahan and Kırşehir – from the People's Alliance. In total, the CHP won mayoral races in 21 provinces (up from 14 in the 2014 local elections) and widened its geographical reach across the country (Esen and Gumuscu 2019). By contrast, the main opposition party lost only two of its mayoral seats (Giresun and Zonguldak) to the AKP in closely contested races and one to an independent candidate (Kırklareli), who resigned from the main opposition party on the eve of the election when he was not picked as the CHP nominee; however, he has recently rejoined the party. In total, the CHP currently controls municipal governments that govern more than half of the electorate. This is a major success for a party that has long experienced electoral ghettoization (Ciddi and Esen 2014) and faced difficulty in appealing to AKP voters over the last two decades.

The election results produced a mixed picture for the nationalist IYIP, which took credit for the Nation Alliance's victory in major metropolitan areas but failed to win a single municipal government at the provincial level. Having splintered from the MHP in 2017, the IYIP gained strength in the coastal areas of the Aegean and Mediterranean regions with a heavy concentration of moderate right-wing Turkish voters. It won municipal governments in 19 provincial districts in former strongholds of centre-right parties (Esen and Gumuscu 2019), while losing closely contested provincial races in Afyon, Balıkesir, Denizli and Uşak. The IYIP leadership consolidated its support within the party after the 2019 elections. Two reasons account for this outcome. First, AKP's defeat in major metropolitan areas motivated opposition parties with a view to the next presidential elections. In light of the MHP's declining electoral trend in metropolitan areas, the IYIP felt optimistic about its long-term electoral prospects. Second, as a partner of Nation Alliance, the IYIP also gained access to vital municipal resources and cadres in areas where the CHP candidates won.

The pro-Kurdish HDP achieved moderate success. Due to government crackdowns, organizational challenges and intra-party rifts, the HDP vote share declined even in some of its strongholds (Esen and Gumuscu 2019). Due to the AKP's *kayyum* politics, the HDP did not enjoy any incumbency advantage in the lead up to this campaign and was no longer in a position to expand its electoral base. In the end, HDP candidates managed to win back many municipal governments that had been taken over by state appointees and achieved a surprising victory in Kars but lost three key provinces (Bitlis, Ağrı and Şırnak) to the ruling party (Tepe and Alemdaroğlu 2021). Moreover, after a divisive campaign, the HDP lost the mayoral race in Tunceli against a candidate from the Turkish Communist Party, which won in a provincial race for the first time in its history. Despite such setbacks, the HDP remains the strongest party in the predominantly Kurdish cities. The party also played a strong role in influencing the outcome of elections in several major metropolitan areas where its decision not to field candidates contributed to CHP's victory.

Post-election developments

After the 2019 local elections, the government engaged in post-election mechanisms to reverse some election results while keeping the facade of democratic institutions (Tepe and Alemdaroğlu 2021). The Supreme Election Council (SEC) played a crucial role in facilitating the incumbent's efforts to retain control over some municipal governments despite unfavourable electoral results (Esen and Gumuscu 2019). The SEC exhibited a systematic bias in deliberating the post-election objections against vote counts filed by candidates from the People's Alliance and the opposition parties. For example, on 11 April, the SEC ruled to confirm the district election board's decision to deny mandates for 6 elected mayors as well as 62 municipal and provincial councillors from the HDP with the justification that these candidates were dismissed from public office in 2016 on terrorism charges (CoE 2019). In the case of these six mayors, the candidate with the second highest number of votes – conveniently from the AKP – was declared the winner. In what was a clear violation of political rights, the SEC decision ignored the fact that these HDP candidates were reviewed and approved by SEC district boards prior to the election.

The SEC's most controversial ruling was its decision to annul the result of the metropolitan mayoral election in Istanbul and ask for a re-run in response to complaints filed by the AKP. On election night, the AKP declared victory with a very close margin based on early results released by the pro-government Anatolian Agency. Although İmamoğlu immediately challenged these results in a series of press conferences, the ruling party refused to concede and declared victory again the next day (Esen and Gumuscu 2019). When, several days later, the SEC announced İmamoğlu as the winner with 48.8%, the AKP leadership started an organized campaign to cast doubt on and reverse the result. Backed up by a coordinated media campaign, they even accused the opposition of committing election fraud (Hürriyet 2019). The ruling party managed to get a recount in its strongholds, albeit with no decisive change to the outcome. The AKP subsequently mobilized police forces to gather evidence on alleged voter irregularities and petitioned to have the mayoral election annulled (BBC News Türkçe 2019).

Faced with intense pressure from the ruling party, the SEC ultimately reached the 'inconsistent and politicized' decision (CoE 2019: 21) to annul the election on the grounds that electoral board committees included individuals who were not civil servants and that incorrect entries were detected in electoral rolls. The fact that the SEC only annulled the metropolitan mayoral election, while confirming the results of mayoral elections at the district level was further testament to the decision's biased nature. If the AKP leaders hoped to reverse the electoral outcome with this decision, they miscalculated severely. Even AKP voters saw the decision to be unfair and switched their support to the CHP candidate İmamoğlu who won the re-run with 54.2% in what was clearly the biggest upset of the 2019 local election.

What was different this time?

These results beg the question of 'what was different?' in this election. Understanding the causal factors behind this electoral outcome can also contribute to the literature on opposition success under a competitive authoritarian regime (Jimenez 2021; Donno 2013; Bunce and Wolchik 2010). Specifically, compared to other electoral contests – including the 2014 local elections – three important factors stand out in contributing to the opposition's electoral success despite the uneven playing field: (1) the decreasing performance legitimacy of the incumbent party; (2) a successful opposition campaign centred on a discourse of de-polarization; and (3) effective coordination among opposition parties.

Decreasing performance legitimacy of the regime

One of the most important structural factors that hampered the performance of incumbent candidates was the economic deterioration in the country (Esen and Gumuscu 2019; Yavuzyılmaz 2021). Several studies have shown that the most important factor behind the AKP's electoral dominance has been the party's successful combination of a sustained macroeconomic balance and clientelistic distributive politics (Gidengil and Karakoç 2016; Esen and Gumuscu 2020). Nevertheless, on the eve of the local elections, the macroeconomic situation had deteriorated. The most visible symptoms were the sharp rise in inflation and unemployment levels since

2018. Overall, unemployment had reached 25.2% and the inflation rate had risen to 19.7% in March 2019, with an even larger increase in the price of foodstuffs. In response, AKP metropolitan municipalities began selling subsidized fresh food products in poor neighbourhoods, but this policy further confirmed the sharp rise in poverty levels and hurt the government's public image (Esen and Gümüşcü 2019; Yavuzyılmaz 2021). Considering the socio-economic profile of the core AKP electorate, rising food prices and other living expenses significantly hurt the performance legitimacy of the AKP.

In tandem with the economic crisis, the AKP's resource allocation to Syrian refugees further derailed the party's performance. Although some studies suggest that refugees have a negative yet insignificant impact on the AKP's vote share in districts with concentrated refugee populations (Fisunoğlu and Sert 2019), Esen and Gumuscu (2019) suggest that macroeconomic deterioration, especially rising unemployment, intensified the reaction against Syrian refugees during the pre-election period and contributed to the party's electoral decline in major metropolitan areas. The main impetus behind this reaction was the increasing preference for recruiting Syrian refugees in the service sector instead of Turkish ones. Together with the AKP government's dismal economic performance, widespread corruption rumours and nepotism also hurt pro-government candidates at the local level.

Successful opposition campaign that centred on de-polarization

Compared to previous electoral contests in which both the governing AKP and opposition parties engaged in polarizing discourse (Somer 2019), the opposition campaign centred on de-polarization in the 2019 local elections. In sharp contrast to the People's Alliance, opposition candidates generally refrained from commenting on macro-political developments to highlight instead the failures of incumbent mayors and their own solutions to these problems. At the leadership level, the opposition parties highlighted the importance of and the need for political change through the electoral process. This campaign strategy, alongside the decreasing performance legitimacy of the regime, enabled opposition candidates to disrupt the strong bond between the People's Alliance and its voters (Yavuzyılmaz 2021).

Effective coordination among the opposition parties

After the transition to an executive-presidential system, opposition parties increased their efforts to coordinate formally. Although these parties lacked a coherent ideology, their shared commitment to parliamentary democracy solidified opposition coordination and facilitated their efforts to bring together different segments of the electorate, especially in major metropolitan areas. Although the CHP and the IYIP faced intra-party rifts in the aftermath of the 2018 twin elections, the durability of the Nation Alliance was a major factor behind the opposition's electoral performance. Apart from increasing electoral competitiveness, successful opposition coordination also helped candidates prevent electoral manipulation and fraud in closely contested races.

Implications of local elections on the durability of competitive authoritarian regime in Turkey

In competitive authoritarian regimes, an election that signals the electoral weakness of the incumbent parties has important repercussions for the regime, such as increasing the likelihood of elite defections and counter mobilization against the incumbent and strengthening the pre-electoral coordination among opposition parties (e.g., Lindberg 2009; Bunce and Wolchik 2010; Donno 2013). Accordingly, the outcome of the 2019 local elections disrupted the ruling party's capacity to undertake popular mobilization and sustain intra-elite cohesion both directly and indirectly. The loss of municipal governments in the country's largest metropolitan areas deprived the incumbent of vital public resources to keep its popular base intact and reward elite supporters through clientelism and patronage. Certain organizational and mobilizational characteristics of the AKP have amplified these possible implications for the sustainability of the Turkish competitive authoritarian regime.

Organizational and mobilizational characteristics of AKP

In the extant literature on the sustainability of competitive authoritarian regimes, organizationally strong ruling parties are considered a major factor behind regime durability (e.g., Levitsky and Way 2010; Svolik 2012; Handlin 2016). Not only are they effective in terms of maintaining elite-level coherence and prevent elite defections, but they also prove useful when it comes to social control and electoral mobilization (Svolik 2012).

The AKP was established as a splinter party of the Nationalist View Movement in 2001 (Hale and Özbudun 2011), and over time it has developed the organizational features of mass and personalistic parties (Baykan 2018). First, the party has a complex, hierarchically routinized and territorially comprehensive party organization (Kumbaracıbaşı 2009; Baykan 2018; Yardımcı-Geyikçi and Yavuzyılmaz 2020). The V-Party dataset shows that the AKP scores high on the indicators that are used to measure the level of local organizational strength (Figure 24.3).

Party membership figures and membership density figures also show the AKP's high capacity to penetrate to its core electorate (Table 24.1).

While maintaining the above-mentioned organizational features, the ruling party became increasingly personalized under Erdoğan after 2007 (Lancaster 2014). Several studies have already suggested that this personalization and the increasing incidence of ad-hoc decision-making inside the party are signs of de-institutionalization (Yardımcı-Geyikçi and Yavuzyılmaz 2020).

Within this complex, territorially comprehensive, hierarchical and personalized organization, local party organizations both at the provincial and the sub-provincial levels have functioned as the 'nerve ends' of the party (Hale and Özbudun 2011). Together with AKP-controlled metropolitan municipalities, these local party organizations have been critical in

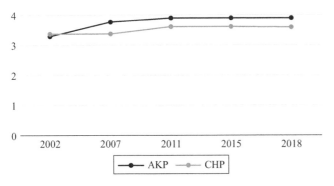

Figure 24.3 The local organizational strength (AKP and CHP). Four indicates that the party has local offices in all municipalities, zero indicates that the party has negligible presence locally. Source: V-Party dataset (Lührmann et al. 2020).

Table 24.1 Membership density and membership strength figures of AKP 2006–2018

Year	No. of members	Party votes[a]	Membership density (m/party voters) (%)	Membership strength (m/total electorate) (%)
2006	1,834,520	16,327,291 (07)	11.2	5.2
2011	7,844,15	21,399,082 (11)	36.7	18.3
2018	9,949,451	21,338,690 (18)	46.6	19.8

Source: Yavuzyılmaz (2021).
[a] Numbers in parentheses indicate the year of the general election.

routinizing and strengthening the relationship between the party and its voters at the base level (Ark-Yıldırım 2017).

Alongside the organizational characteristics of the AKP, the level of value infusion stands out as a critical factor to understand the implications of the 2019 local elections for sustaining competitive authoritarianism. Value infusion is a concept that constitutes the attitudinal component of a political party's institutionalization (Levitsky 1998). It indicates a process by which a party becomes an end in itself for its members and personnel rather than being an instrument to attain other rewards and benefits. Thus, internal value infusion occurs when party actors demonstrate allegiance to the party itself separately from any momentary leader or special ambitions of the moment (Harmel et al. 2018). External value infusion refers to a similar solidified relationship between the party and its electorate.

The electoral mobilization strategy of the party stands as an important measure to understand the AKP's level of external value infusion, because the party's mobilizational strategy becomes critical in determining the voting rationale of its core electorate. V-Party data shows that the AKP's electoral mobilization strategy largely centres on clientelism (Figure 24.4). The prominence of clientelism as an electoral mobilization strategy shows the intensity of the instrumental linkage between the party and its electoral base.

Turning to the internal value infusion both at the central and the base levels of the party organization, a similar picture emerges due to the high level of instrumental linkage between the party and its cadres. Apart from the level of personalization, which is indicative of low value infusion (Harmel et al. 2018), the AKP's patronage politics significantly instrumentalizes the relationship between the party organization and its cadres. Rather than perceiving the party as an end in itself, the majority of the party personnel – especially at the local level – perceives the AKP as an instrument to gain economic benefits (Gürakar 2016). Low levels of value infusion

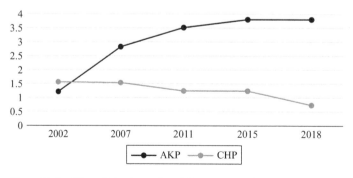

Figure 24.4 Clientelistic electoral mobilization in Turkey (AKP and CHP). Four indicates that the party uses clientelist voter mobilization as its main mobilizational strategy. Source: V-Party dataset (Lührmann et al. 2020).

can also be traced in the relationship that the party establishes with its members. Despite the high membership density levels of the party (Table 24.1), the relationship between the party members and the party remains highly instrumental. First and foremost, most of the members are not due-paying party members and their relationship with the party rests on receiving benefits either in the form of patronage or clientelism (Hale and Özbudun 2011).

These features of party organization amplify the negative implications of recent local elections for the sustainability of competitive authoritarianism in Turkey. To better delineate the political implications of recent local elections for competitive authoritarianism in Turkey, the following section analyzes the role of local governments in the AKP's politics of patronage and clientelism.

The role of local governments in AKP's politics of clientelism and patronage

Scholars have suggested that the sustainability of competitive authoritarian regimes depends on the capacity of incumbents to distribute rewards, both to their elite supporters and to their voter base (e.g., Greene 2007; Svolik 2012). As already mentioned in the previous section, the smooth functioning of resource distribution requires a political party with high organizational strengths. In addition to the party's local organizations, municipal governments serve as key institutional hubs for partisan delivery of benefits, not only in the form of in-kind and cash transfers to voters, but also in the distribution of public jobs and contracts (Eligür 2010; Sayarı 2014; Kemahlıoğlu and Özdemir 2018).

The politics of clientelism and patronage has been a prevalent feature of Turkish politics and predates the AKP era (Sayarı 2014). Nevertheless, under AKP rule, the politics of patronage and clientelism has become more systematic through a combination of old vertical networks of patron–client relations with horizontal social networks of mutual help (Aytaç 2014). Several studies have shown that the epicentre of AKP's politics of clientelism has centred on the sustained provision of social goods to lower-income households in major metropolitan areas (Esen and Gumuscu 2020). Municipal governments, which were uninterruptedly governed by the party and its Islamist predecessors following the 1994 local elections, have served as critical units both in terms of classical/vertical patron–client relationships and horizontal forms of clientelism and patronage (Ark-Yıldırım 2017). Such a combination constitutes the composite form of the new politics of clientelism and patronage in Turkey under the AKP through which the ruling party has managed to build routinized and strong connections among its different clients through a network of local municipalities and religious charities (Buğra and Candaş 2011; Kemahlıoğlu and Özdemir 2018).

The municipal-level procurement of services to private firms stands out as an important channel for non-programmatic distributive politics to regime allies. Through several amendments to the public procurement law, the AKP government replaced the default open tender method with restricted and negotiated ones to distribute public resources in a more partisan manner (Gürakar 2016). Under AKP rule, municipal enterprises emerged as a major distributor of public contracts. Since municipal governments appoint the board members of these enterprises, AKP cadres control the list of winning bids in public tenders. Municipal-level procurement contracts are also used in creating employment opportunities for potential voters and ordinary party members (Gürakar 2016).

Together with local organizations, municipal governments served as a strong auxiliary body for the party's clientelistic electoral mobilization strategy (Ark-Yıldırım 2017; Kemahlıoğlu and Özdemir 2018). The ruling party systematized several social welfare programmes, which are selectively distributed to its voters in exchange for support among low-income voters. The AKP-controlled metropolitan government systematically engaged in several in-kind and cash transfers, especially in areas where its vote share remained high (Aytaç 2014).

What does the future hold?

Both the specific organizational and mobilizational characteristics of the ruling party and the primacy of municipal governments in its clientelist policies turned the 2019 electoral defeat into a major blow for AKP rule. The election's repercussions can be grouped under three headings: (1) increased oppositional coordination; (2) significant blow to the non-programmatic distributive politics of the AKP; and (3) increased prospects of the AKP's institutional decay.

Oppositional coordination

The extant literature on the conditions of democratization in competitive authoritarian regimes suggests that the outcome of oppositional victory is more likely when opposition parties forge electorally viable coalitions (Howard and Roessler 2006; Donno 2013). As a culmination of the emerging democracy–authoritarianism cleavage in response to the breakdown of Turkish democracy, opposition parties have recently increased their coordination efforts (Selçuk and Hekimci 2020). The 2019 local elections stand out as an important learning process for the opposition in terms of increasing their coordination efforts for better electoral mobilization and effective prevention of electoral manipulation and fraud under a competitive authoritarian regime. Its defeat in major metropolitan areas severely hampered the AKP's perception of electoral invincibility in the eyes of the electorate and increased the prospects of an opposition victory in the upcoming presidential elections. Considering the importance of opposition coordination for subverting competitive authoritarianism (Gandhi and Reuter 2013; Jimenez 2021), the 2019 local elections constitute an important blueprint for opposition parties in Turkey.

Politics of clientelism and patronage

Since the 2019 local elections, the AKP's distributive networks have taken a severe hit due to the opposition's control over the country's largest municipalities. These metropolitan municipalities were critical hubs for the partisan delivery of rewards to AKP voters. Since their electoral victory, opposition-controlled municipal governments have engaged in successful redistributive policies which are more transparent and programmatic. Among these are several social assistance programmes based on mutual help such as the 'hanging bill' (*Askıda Fatura*) programme and the Package for Educational and Family Support (*Eğitime Destek Paketi, Aile Destek Paketi*). Coupled with the loss of the AKP's ongoing performance legitimacy, these policies are further highlighted in the eyes of voters.

Repercussions for the AKP

Although the sudden institutional decay of the AKP continues to be improbable, its poor electoral performance significantly increased the prospects of factional rivalry inside the party. First and foremost, in competitive authoritarian regimes election victories by themselves matter as they create an aura of invincibility for the incumbent parties. This aura significantly derails coordination efforts among opposition parties and decreases the prospects of elite defections and vote shifts to the benefit of opposition parties (Simpser 2013). In that regard, the 2019 local election results have decreased the ruling party's aura of invincibility and increased the likelihood of vote shifts and elite defections on the eve of the next election. Secondly, the failure to distribute rewards increased the risk of defections among party cadres. In the immediate aftermath of the 2019 local elections, two splinter parties – the Democracy and Progress (DEVA) Party and the Gelecek Party – were established by former AKP elites. The decline in AKP's membership figures and the resignations of party cadres to join the DEVA Party and the Gelecek Party reflect this trend (Cumhuriyet 2020). The establishment of these parties which have the potential to reach AKP cadres and voters could amplify the institutional decay process of the AKP. This process will significantly derail the elite co-optation and societal control/electoral mobilization functions of the ruling party which have hitherto been critical in the breakdown of Turkish democracy.

Conclusion

The 2019 local elections in Turkey were a typical case of an electoral contest under competitive authoritarianism. The incumbent AKP and its junior ally the MHP had the advantage of campaigning under a heavily skewed electoral playing field to their benefit. Moreover, the post-election developments also revealed that Turkey's political regime still shows characteristics of competitive authoritarianism. Nevertheless, the results of recent local elections have also been atypical. Thanks to opposition coordination, for the first time the opposition parties managed to win several metropolitan municipalities including Istanbul and Ankara which had been controlled by the incumbent AKP for decades.

The results of recent local elections will also have important repercussions for the sustainability of competitive authoritarianism in Turkey. Thus far, several indications such as the formation of new parties by former cadres of the AKP and the decrease in party membership levels have demonstrated an increase in the fragility of the competitive authoritarian regime in Turkey. At the same time, opposition parties have successfully turned the potentiality of local governments to their advantage through successful social policies which have weakened the ruling block's hold on its voters in metropolitan municipalities.

Notwithstanding these repercussions of the recent local elections for the ruling block, the prospect of democratization still depends on the opposition parties' success in effective pre-electoral coalition making and coordination and in maintaining a discourse that centres on de-polarization in the upcoming presidential and parliamentary elections. Opposition parties are currently in the process of preparing a joint electoral platform and nominating a single candidate. This is not only important for electoral gains, but is also crucial for maintaining effective control over the ballot box and securing the election results for the upcoming general election against likely attempts of electoral fraud and manipulation. The opposition's electoral success has increased the prospects of subverting the competitive authoritarian regime in Turkey.

References

AK Parti. 2018. 'Gönül Belediyeciliği Vatandaşa Dokunabilmektir'. Available at: https://www.akparti.org.tr/haberler/gonul-belediyeciligi-vatandasa-dokunabilmektir/.
AK Parti. 2019. 'Manifesto'. [Electoral Platform]. Available at: https://akadaylar.com/Manifesto_28Ocak2019.pdf.
Ark-Yıldırım, C. 2017. 'Political Parties and Grasroots Clientelist Strategies in Urban Turkey'. *South European Society and Politics* 22(4): 473–490.

Aytaç, S. Erdem. 2014. 'Distributive Politics in a Multiparty System: The Conditional Cash Transfer Program in Turkey'. *Comparative Political Studies* 47(9): 1211–1237.

Baykan, Toygar Sinan. 2018. *The Justice and Development Party in Turkey: Populism, Personalism, Organization*. New York: Cambridge University Press.

BBC News Türkçe. 2019. 'Olağanüstü itiraz: İstanbul'da yeni seçim isteyen AKP'nin YSK'ya sunduğu dilekçede neler var?'. Available at: https://www.bbc.com/turkce/haberler-turkiye-47956420.

Buğra, Ayşe and Ayşen Candaş. 2011. 'Change and Continuity under an Eclectic Social Security Regime: The Case of Turkey'. *Middle Eastern Studies* 47(3): 515–528.

Bunce, Valerie and Sharon Wolchik. 2010. Defeating Dictators: Electoral Change and Stability in Competitive Authoritarian Regimes. *World Politics* 62(1): 43–86.

Çalışkan, Koray. 2018. 'Toward a New Political Regime in Turkey: From Competitive to Full Authoritarianism'. *New Perspectives on Turkey* 58: 5–33.

Çarkoğlu, Ali. 2008. 'Ideology or Economic Pragmatism: Profiling Turkish Voters in 2007'. *Turkish Studies* 9(2): 317–344.

Ciddi, Sinan and Berk Esen. 2014. 'Turkey's Republican People's Party: Politics of Opposition under a Dominant Party System'. *Turkish Studies* 15(3): 419–441.

Council of Europe. 2019. 'Local Elections in Turkey and Mayoral Re-run in Istanbul: 31 March 2019 and 23 June 2019'. *Council of Europe Monitoring Report*. Available at: https://rm.coe.int/local-elections-in-turkey-and-mayoral-re-run-in-istanbul-committee-on-/1680981fcf.

Cumhuriyet. 2019a. 'MHP'nin seçim sloganı belli oldu'. Available at: https://www.cumhuriyet.com.tr/haber/mhpnin-secim-slogani-belli-oldu-1211487.

Cumhuriyet. 2019b. 'Erdoğan-İmamoğlu görüşmesi başladı'. Available at: https://www.cumhuriyet.com.tr/haber/erdogan-imamoglu-gorusmesi-basladi-1197064.

Cumhuriyet. 2020. 'Cumhur İttifakı partilerinin üye sayısında büyük düşüş!'. Available at: https://www.cumhuriyet.com.tr/turkiye/cumhur-ittifaki-partilerinin-uye-sayisinda-buyuk-dusus-1897081.

Demiralp, Seda and Evren Balta. 2021. 'Defeating Populists: The Case of 2019 Istanbul Elections'. *South European Society and Politics* 26(1): 1–26.

Donno, Daniel. 2013. 'Elections and Democratization in Authoritarian Regimes'. *American Journal of Political Science* 57(3): 703–716.

DW. 2019. '31 Mart seçimleri için aday listeleri teslim edildi'. Available at: https://www.dw.com/tr/31-mart-se%C3%A7imleri-i%C3%A7in-aday-listeleri-teslim-edildi/a-47591193.

Esen, Berk and Şebnem Gumuscu. 2016. 'Rising Competitive Authoritarianism in Turkey'. *Third World Quarterly* 37(9): 1–26.

Esen, Berk and Şebnem Gumuscu. 2017a. 'A Small Yes for Presidentialism: The Turkish Constitutional Referendum of April 2017'. *South European Society and Politics* 22(3): 303–326.

Esen, Berk and Şebnem Gumuscu. 2017b. 'Turkey: How the Coup Failed'. *Journal of Democracy* 28(1): 59–73.

Esen, Berk and Şebnem Gumuscu. 2018. 'The Perils of "Turkish Presidentialism"'. *Review of Middle East Studies* 52(1): 43–53.

Esen, Berk and Şebnem Gumuscu. 2019. 'Killing Competitive Authoritarianism Softly: The 2019 Local Elections in Turkey'. *South European Society and Politics* 24(3): 317–342.

Esen, Berk and Şebnem Gumuscu. 2020. 'Why Did Turkish Democracy Collapse? A Political Economy Account of AKP's Authoritarianism'. *Party Politics* 27(6): 1075–1091.

Esen, Berk and Şebnem Yardımcı-Geyikçi. 2020. 'The Turkish Presidential Elections of 24 June 2018'. *Mediterranean Politics* 25(5): 682–689.

Esen, Berk. 2021. 'Competitive Authoritarianism under the AKP Rule'. In Joost Jongerden (ed.), *The Routledge Handbook on Contemporary Turkey*, 153–167. London: Routledge.

Eligür, Banu. 2010. 'Turkey's March 2009 Elections'. *Turkish Studies* 10(3): 469–496.

Fisunoğlu, Sert and Deniz Ş. Sert. 2019. 'Refugees and Elections: The Effects of Syrian on Voting Behavior in Turkey'. *International Migration* 57(2): 298–312.

Gandhi, Jennifer and O.J. Reuter. 2013. 'The Incentives for Pre-electoral Coalitions in Nondemocratic Elections'. *Democratization* 20(1): 137–159.

Gidengil, Elisabeth and Ekrem Karakoç. 2016. 'Which Matters More in the Electoral Success of Islamist (Successor) Parties – Religion or Performance? The Turkish Case.' *Party Politics* 22(3): 325–338.

Greene, K.F. 2007. *Why Dominant Parties Lose: Mexico's Democratization in Comparative Perspective*. Cambridge: Cambridge University Press.

Gumuscu, Şebnem. 2013. 'The Emerging Predominant Party System in Turkey'. *Government and Opposition* 48(2): 223–244.

Gürakar, Esra Çeviker. 2016. *Politics of Favoritism in Public Procurement in Turkey: Reconfigration of Dependency Networks in the AKP Era*. New York: Palgrave Macmillan.

Hale, William and Ergun Özbudun. 2011. *Islamism, Democracy and Liberalism in Turkey: The Case of AKP*. London: Routledge.

Handlin, Samuel. 2016. 'Mass Organization and the Durability of Competitive Authoritarian Regimes: Evidence from Venezuela'. *Comparative Political Studies* 49(9): 1238–1269.

Harmel, Robert, Lars Svasand, and Hilmar Mjelde. 2018. *Institutionalization (and De-Institutionailzation) of Right-Wing Protest Parties: The Progress Parties in Denmark and Norway*. London: Rowman & Littlefield International in Partnership with ECPR.

Howard, Marc Morje and Philip G. Roessler. 2006. 'Liberalizing Outcomes in Competitive Authoritarian Regimes'. *American Journal of Political Science* 50(2): 365–381.

Hürriyet. 2019. 'Yıldırım'dan "seçim neden iptal oldu?" sorusuna cevap: Çok basit, çünkü çaldılar'. Available at: https://www.hurriyet.com.tr/gundem/yildirimdan-secim-neden-iptal-oldu-sorusuna-cevap-cok-basit-cunku-caldilar-41211059.

Jimenez, Maryhen. 2021. 'Contesting Autocracy: Repression and Opposition Coalition in Venezuela'. *Political Studies*. Online First. https://doi.org/10.1177/0032321721999975.

Kemahlıoğlu, Özge. 2015. 'Winds of Change? The June 2015 Parliamentary Election in Turkey'. *South European Society and Politics* 20(4): 445–464.

Kemahlıoğlu, Özge and Elif Özdemir. 2018. 'Municipal Control as Incumbency Advantage: An Analysis of AKP Era'. In Sabri Sayarı, Pelin Ayan Müsil, and Özhan Demirkol (eds.), *Party Politics in Turkey: A Comparative Perspective*, 116–136. New York: Routledge.

Kumbaracıbaşı, Arda Can. 2009. *Turkish Politics and the Rise of the AKP: Dilemmas of Institutionalization and Leadership Strategy*. London: Routledge.

Lancaster, Caroline. 2014. 'The Iron Law of Erdogan: The Decay from Intra-party Democracy to Personalistic Rule'. *Third World Quarterly* 35(9): 1672–1690.

Levitsky, Steven. 1998. 'Institutionalization and Peronism: The Concept, the Case and the Case for Unpacking the Concept'. *Party Politics* 4(1): 77–92.

Levitsky, Steven and Lucan Way. 2010. *Competitive Authoritarianism: Hybrid Regimes After the Cold War*. New York: Cambridge University Press.

Lindberg, I. Staffan. 2009. *Democratization by Elections: A New Mode of Transition*. Baltimore, MD: Johns Hopkins University Press.

Lührmann, Anna, Nils Düpont, Masaaki Higashijima, Yaman Berker Kavasoglu, Kyle L. Marquardt, Michael Bernhard, Holger Döring, Allen Hicken, Melis Laebens, Staffan I. Lindberg, Juraj Medzihorsky, Anja Neundorf, Ora John Reuter, Saskia Ruth-Lovell, Keith R. Weghorst, Nina Wiesehomeier, Joseph Wright, Nazifa Alizada, Paul Bederke, Lisa Gastaldi, Sandra Grahn, Garry Hindle, Nina Ilchenko, Johannes von Römer, Daniel Pemstein, and Brigitte Seim. 2020. 'Varieties of Party Identity and Organization (V–Party) Dataset V1'. *Varieties of Democracy (V-Dem) Project*.

Sabah. 2019. 'Liderler yerel seçim için yoğun mesai harcadı'. Available at: https://www.sabah.com.tr/gundem/2019/03/29/liderler-yerel-secim-icin-yogun-mesai-harcadi.

Sayarı, S. 2014. 'Interdisciplinary Approaches to Political Clientelism and Patronage in Turkey'. *Turkish Studies* 15(4): 655–670.

Sayarı, Sabri. 2016. 'Back to a Predominant Party System: The November 2015 Snap Election in Turkey'. *South European Society and Politics* 21(2): 263–280.

Selçuk, Orçun and Dilara Hekimci. 2020. 'The Rise of the Democracy-Authoritarianism Cleavage and Opposition Coordination in Turkey (2014–2019)'. *Democratization* 27(8): 1496–1514.

Simpser, Alberto. 2013. *Why Governments and Parties Manipulate Elections: Theory, Practice and Implications*. New York: Cambridge University Press.

Somer, Murat. 2019. 'Turkey: The Slippery Slope from Reformist to Revolutionary Polarization and Democratic Breakdown'. *The Annals of the American Academy of Political and Social Science* 681(1): 42–61.

Somer, Murat, Jennifer McCoy and Russell Evan Luke IV. 2021. 'Pernicious Polarization, Autocratization and Opposition'. *Democratization* 28(5): 929–948.

SonDakika. 2019. 'Sezai Temelli'nin "Batıda Kaybettireceğiz" Açıklaması' Available at: https://www.sondakika.com/politika/haber-sezai-temelli-nin-batida-kaybettirecegiz-11745443/.

Sözen, Yunus. 2019. 'Competition in a Populist Authoritarian Regime: The June 2018 Dual Elections in Turkey'. *South European Society and Politics* 24(3): 287–315.

Svolik, Milan W. 2012. *The Politics of Authoritarian Rule*. New York: Cambridge University Press.

Tepe, Sultan and Ayça Alemdaroğlu. 2021. 'How Authoritarians Win When They Loose'. *Journal of Democracy* 32(4): 87–101.

Wuthrich, F.M. and Melvyn Ingleby. 2020. 'The Pushback against Populism: Running on 'Radical Love' in Turkey'. *Journal of Democracy* 31(2): 24–40.

Yardımcı-Geyikçi, Şebnem and Hakan Yavuzyılmaz. 2020. 'Party (de)institutionalization in Times of Political Uncertainty: The Case of the Justice and Development Party in Turkey'. *Party Politics* 28(1): 71–84.

Yavuzyılmaz, Hakan. 2021. 'When Local becomes General: Turkey's 31 March 2019 Elections and its Implications for Dynamics of Polarization and Sustainability of Competitive Authoritarianism'. *Journal of Balkan and Near Eastern Studies* 23(4): 622–642.

25
POLARISATION AND ELECTIONS UNDER COMPETITIVE AUTHORITARIANISM

The case of Turkey after 2013

Şebnem Yardımcı Geyikçi

Introduction

There is widespread agreement in the literature on contemporary Turkey that severe polarisation characterises its politics and society (Aydın-Düzgit and Balta 2019; Somer 2019). This phenomenon has also been documented in the latest research (Erdoğan 2016, 2018). Most recently, a survey conducted by Erdoğan and Uyan-Semerci (2020) demonstrated that the country suffers from extreme polarisation to the extent that 66.6% of people report they would not want their kids to be friends with the kids of those who support the most distant political party, and 74.9% would not want their daughter or son to marry a supporter of the most distant party. In an effort to unpack the why and how of polarisation, several works have explored different aspects of it. Some have looked at how polarisation damaged democracy in Turkey, ultimately leading to the breakdown of democracy (Esmer 2019; Somer 2019), while others have been concerned with the Justice and Development Party's (*Adalet ve Kalkınma Partisi*, AKP) role in the processes of polarisation (Tepe 2013), as well as how the party benefited from polarisation in its rise to become the dominant party (Keyman 2014). Still others have focused on how the Turkish elite perceive the extent of polarisation (Aydın-Düzgit and Balta 2019).

One common theme that unites these works has been their emphasis on the role that polarisation has played in Turkey's democratic backsliding and, ultimately, democratic breakdown. This chapter moves beyond these works and focuses on the relationship between polarisation and elections after the Gezi Park protests of 2013, which was a watershed moment for the AKP. In its struggle to hold on to power during this period, the party leadership sought to reconfigure the country's traditional religious–secular divide as one of saviours versus traitors, new versus old Turkey, and ultimately a choice between the AKP and insecurity, between Erdoğan's regime and democracy. The period after the Gezi Park protests also represents the moment when democratic breakdown became irrevocable. In light of these developments, this chapter focuses on two presidential elections (2014 and 2018) and three general elections (June–November 2015 and 2018), covering a four-year period, to uncover the function of polarisation in relation to elections in competitive authoritarian settings. Although the strength of competitive authoritarianism has varied, in all these elections voters went to the ballot box with parties competing on an uneven playing field and favouring the incumbent at the expense of all other political forces. However, in line with the introduction of this volume, this chapter also argues that 'elections do matter and are worth investigating as autonomous processes', even when they are not free and fair.

Rather than defining polarisation as an ideological distance between political parties, following Mccoy et al. (2018) polarisation here is conceptualised as relational and instrumental, used by incumbents as an electoral strategy in competitive authoritarian settings. As such, this chapter is concerned with the supply side of political polarisation rather than the societal bases of the phenomenon and looks at the period after the Gezi protests. Based on a detailed analysis of election campaigns, the contention here is that by adopting and redefining the terms of polarisation in each election, the AKP has deployed it as a campaign tool which performs two tasks simultaneously. First, polarisation keeps the opposition divided, which is a must for the longevity of authoritarian regimes (Bunce and Wolchik 2010; Gandhi and Reuter 2008; Levitsky and Way 2010). Secondly, it works to consolidate the incumbent's voter base by demarcating the line between AKP supporters and others. Although polarisation should be conceived as a mutually constructed process led by both government and opposition, the opposition's ability to determine the political agenda declined significantly with the consolidation of the competitive authoritarian regime after 2013. Only with the introduction of a presidential system in 2018, have the terms of politics changed, creating incentives for the opposition to unite and respond to the polarisation the AKP fostered. As such, this chapter mostly focuses on the ways in which the AKP employed polarisation as a campaign tool. However, it goes on to argue that as the capacity of opposition coordination and cooperation increases, the AKP's power to adopt and employ polarisation as a political strategy declines and this is when the opposition's role can counteract it. The most vivid manifestation of this decline occurred during the 2019 local elections, wherein the incumbent lost control of major cities (see Chapter 24). Furthermore, unable to respond to the economic and governance crisis the country has been experiencing since 2018, the AKP's ability to design politics from above has continued to diminish sharply, making it extremely challenging to employ polarisation as a campaign strategy.

Polarisation: bottom-up or top-down?

In the literature on party politics, polarisation is the primary metric by which the character of party systems is measured. Referring to the ideological distance among political parties and among the electorate (Sartori 1976), polarisation tells us whether political competition in a particular country is centrifugal or centripetal. As such, political polarisation 'points at large differences in policy positions between opposed "camps" or "coalitions" of political parties, and high similarities in policy positions within these coalitions' (Oosterwaal and Torenvlied 2010: 261). Political polarisation also rests on the number and strength of anti-system parties (Tepe 2013) in that, as the relative power of anti-system parties increases, polarisation and the radicalisation of politics surge (Casal Bertoa and Rama 2021).

While the literature on cleavages tends to see the emergence of political divisions as a bottom-up process (Lipset and Rokkan 1967), following Schattschneider (1975), who underlined the role played by elites in framing political issues to shape the dynamics of political conflict, recent scholarship suggests that they can also be a product of top-down processes (LeBas 2018; Torcal and Mainwaring 2003; Tworzecki 2019). As such, political entrepreneurs would successfully create and deepen divisions within the political sphere, which would then be replicated in social life (Enyedi 2008). Although the presence of deep-seated socio-cultural divides would contribute to the process, they are neither necessary nor sufficient for political crafting (McCoy and Rahman 2016).

LeBas (2006: 435), for instance, argues that political parties can act as major agents of polarisation, as it fulfils several functions, such as 'mobilizing constituencies and maintaining party cohesion', as well as making 'boundary crossing – or defection – from the party difficult'. Likewise, McCoy and Rahman (2016: 13) underpin the possibility that 'politicians may polarize as an electoral strategy, seeking a wedge issue and thus magnifying an existing cleavage'. Furthermore, contemporary examples of extreme or 'pernicious' polarisation observed in countries as varied as Venezuela, Hungary, Israel, the United States and Turkey have been characterised as elite driven and a by-product of political entrepreneurs' search for electoral gain (McCoy et al. 2018).

In a similar vein, many scholars researching Turkey assert that social and political polarisation in the country is employed instrumentally by President Erdoğan and has been orchestrated by the incumbent AKP for electoral gains in the last 15 years (Aydın-Düzgit and Balta 2019; McCoy and Somer 2019). To that extent, the instrumental use of polarisation has been defined as one of the major factors behind the incremental erosion of democracy in the country (Somer and McCoy 2018; McCoy and Somer 2019). Although since the beginning of multiparty politics polarisation has been a defining characteristic of the party system in Turkey (Özbudun 1981, 2013), it never before reached its current levels (see Figure 25.1) and never became inherent to the political regime. As argued elsewhere, both the deep-seated socio-cultural divides and the majoritarian nature of institutions have offered fertile ground upon which polarisation could flourish (McCoy and Rahman 2016), but polarisation was not inevitable and intrinsic to the political system. What has changed is that the AKP increased its vote share up

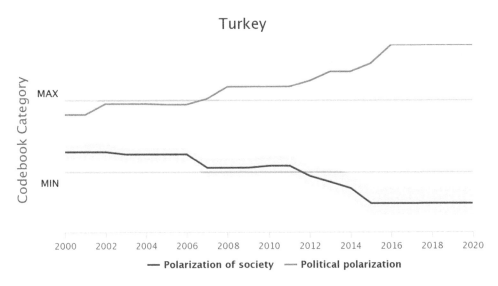

Figure 25.1 Social and political polarisation in Turkey. Source: V-Dem Varieties of Democracy Version 11.1. Polarisation of society (0: serious polarisation, 4: no polarisation), political polarisation (0: not at all. Supporters of opposing political camps generally interact in a friendly manner. 4: yes, to a large extent. Supporters of opposing political camps generally interact in a hostile manner).

to around 50% from its second term onwards. This meant the incumbent put all its energy into keeping this vote concentration and the privileges that come with it by eliminating horizontal accountability and relying on vertical accountability. The ultimate consequence of this process of democratic breakdown was the introduction of a presidential government system in 2018, which made polarisation part and parcel of the institutional system with a winner-takes-all modality. This chapter discusses how polarisation is instrumentalised in elections as a campaign tool to demonstrate the relationship between elections and polarisation in a competitive authoritarian setting.

The 2014 presidential elections

In 2007, a constitutional amendment stipulating that the president be elected by popular vote was approved in a referendum. The first popular election for a five-year presidential term was scheduled for 2014 and Recep Tayyip Erdoğan emerged as the natural candidate of the incumbent party. The main opposition party, the Republican People's Party (*Cumhuriyet Halk Partisi*, CHP), coordinated with the Nationalist Action Party (*Milliyetçi Hareket Partisi*, MHP), and together nominated a joint candidate, Ekmeleddin İhsanoğlu, an academic with a diplomatic background and conservative centre-right leanings. Selahattin Demirtaş was the candidate of the People's Democratic Party (*Halkların Demokrasi Partisi*, HDP), the party of the Kurdish political movement. Erdoğan's electoral campaign mostly targeted İhsanoğlu rather than Demirtaş, calculating that in the event of a run-off, the candidate who could mobilise the Kurdish electorate would have a better chance of defeating him.

Two major developments occurred before the elections that shaped the campaign agenda. The first one was the Gezi Park protests in 2013 – the largest mass civil movement in the republic's history. Fed up with the government's increasingly authoritarian tendencies, people around the country took to the streets to call for change. What makes the Gezi protests unique is the multi-identity composition of the protestors. For the first time, groups as diverse as Islamists, seculars, Turkish nationalists and Kurdish nationalists – who historically had an uncompromising attitude towards one another – came together against increasing AKP authoritarianism. Therefore, Gezi signified an existential threat to the AKP, a party owing its success to the persistence of societal divisions. Erdoğan and the AKP attempted to retake control over the discourse on the protests by claiming they had been orchestrated by international actors and their domestic allies to slow Turkey's economic growth and undermine its international credibility.

The second development was a corruption scandal, known as the 17–25 December Operations, which emerged due to the conflict between the government and the Gülen movement, one of the strongest religious communities in the country. The scandal occurred when allegations were disclosed in December 2013 involving important AKP cabinet members. Erdoğan, once again, related these allegations to the same 'axis of evil' that had initiated the Gezi protests and was composed of internal and external enemies. This time though one culprit was clearly identified, namely the Gülen movement, which had collaborated with the AKP government since 2002, but with whom relations had started to deteriorate from 2012 onwards (Özbudun 2014). Erdoğan claimed that the parallel state's moves were an extension of the Gezi protests, in that they both had the same goal of preventing Turkey from becoming an important world power (Nefes 2017).

With the Gezi protests, the incumbent realised that the social divisions upon which the party constructed its political discourse might crumble. The clash with the Gülen movement, on the other hand, demonstrated that elite unity might have eroded. Faced with two potential challenges (Yardımcı-Geyikçi and Yavuzyılmaz 2022), the AKP realised that the only way out was to centralise power in the hands of Erdoğan and to reframe its political discourse from one that highlights long-standing cleavages between the centre and periphery, elite versus popular or secular versus religious divides into one of Turkey's saviours versus traitors, and later one of the new versus old Turkey. Both cleavages carry the overtones of previous ones, but with a new twist. This change in tone can be observed in all elections after the Gezi protests.

Accordingly, the gist of the 2014 presidential election campaign rested on these divisions. On the one hand, Erdoğan portrayed the CHP and the MHP's joint candidate, İhsanoğlu, as the candidate supported by the Gülen movement and a covert agent of international actors and their domestic allies. Erdoğan often called calling İhsanoğlu the candidate of the Gülen movement and a representative of old elites:

> You are going to lose anyway. You could have stood yourself and lost with dignity. Pennsylvania [*referring to the Gülen movement*] pointed and monsieur [*referring to the elite identity of İhsanoğlu*] entered the game. Shame on you and also on the ones who nominated you.
>
> *(Türkiye 2014)*

During his electoral campaign, he also directly referred to the Gezi movement and related it to the graft allegations of 17–25 December as a plot against the government organised by traitors and supported by international actors:

> They first said Gezi, then 17–25 December. They tried to oust the government chosen by the people by plotting games. You made them account for it in the local elections. With the power that you delegate to us, we now fight against them.
>
> *(Milat 2014)*

On the other hand, Erdoğan presented himself as an executive president, and his election as the dawn of a new era within a presidential system, explicitly stating his intentions to change the system of government into a presidential one (Aksam 2014). The opposition's joint candidate İhsanoğlu, conversely, stated that he was in favour of the parliamentary system and would be impartial if he were elected (Türkiye 2014). This was emblematic of the division between the two candidates, and Erdoğan exploited this division, framing İhsanoğlu as a representative of old Turkey who was nominated by a conglomerate of the Gezi protesters, the Gülen movement and their domestic and international allies. As a result, the theme of new Turkey versus old Turkey emerged in his campaign speeches several times:

> 'Old Turkey was a dark Turkey for everyone except for elites and gangs which were clustered in the state institutions' (Akşam 2014).

The emphasis on a new Turkey against an old Turkey also included several references to the dominant centre and periphery socio-cultural cleavage, reminding the people that the old Turkey was represented by the secular elites and their party, the CHP. He referred to the single-party era led by the CHP in the 1920s and 1930s to relate the old cleavage to the new one:

Now we are opening the doors of a new Turkey. Our goal is 2023. Under the CHP rule they closed our mosques, forbade our book. They did not allow our veiled daughters to enter the universities. How can the CHP ask for votes today from the people?

(Milat 2014)

Furthermore, threatened by the potential for opposition cooperation, he also expressed surprise that the MHP was standing with the CHP, accusing the party leadership of siding with the traitorous representatives of old Turkey (Yeni Şafak 2014). Erdoğan's approach to the MHP was informed by his understanding of the party's voter base. A careful analysis of election results demonstrates why he took this approach; for example, a significant number of people who voted for the MHP in the March 2014 local elections voted for Erdoğan in the presidential race (see Kalaycıoğlu 2015; Özbudun 2015). More importantly, his discourse was fine-tuned to avoid cooperation among the opposition by stigmatising part of the opposition as terrorists or traitors while blaming others for cooperating with terrorists. With the same polarising discourse, he could also consolidate his voter base, motivating them to stand behind the saviour Erdoğan.

Ultimately, Erdoğan received 51.79% of the vote (Table 25.1) and was elected to the office of the presidency. His presidential campaign had aimed to redraw the lines of polarisation as being between saviours and traitors, between new and old Turkey. Erdoğan positioned himself as the embodiment of the saviour and the founder of new Turkey, while all others were agents of old Turkey, plotting against the government through protests and allegations of corruption.

The twin general elections of 2015

Relieved by his easy victory in the presidential elections, Erdoğan and the AKP, with Davutoğlu now at the helm, established the foundation of its June 2015 election campaign on the notion of a new Turkey, which, according to the party, required a new constitution and a new presidential regime. In the election manifesto, discussions on the presidential system to be adopted dominated the debate. The claim was that the current parliamentary system was the product of military interventions, and therefore it had reserved domains of power such as the presidency created to oversee the parliament (AKP 2015a). In the AKP's view, this tutelary position had been responsible for weak and unstable coalition governments in the 1990s, and precluded Turkey's democratically elected governments from reaching a number of desired development goals. An effective presidential system would be the most appropriate regime for a country looking to establish a new Turkey.

Thus, the AKP's electoral campaign employed once more the rhetoric of new versus old Turkey. However, as the process was coordinated along with Davutoglu, Erdoğan could not dominate the whole election campaign. Despite receiving 40% of the total vote, the AKP lost the June 2015 elections insofar as, for the first time in its history, it did not win an outright

Table 25.1 Results of 2014 presidential elections in Turkey

Candidate	Supporting parties	Vote (%)
Recep Tayyip Erdoğan	AKP	51.8
Ekmeleddin İhsanoğlu	CHP–MHP	38.4
Selahattin Demirtaş	HDP	9.8
Total	–	100

majority and was forced to form a coalition with other political parties. While the CHP held its position with almost no change from the previous ballot, the MHP and the HDP were both winners, significantly increasing their numbers of seats. As the upwards trend of MHP votes in the local elections suggested, the party gained the support of a portion of conservative-nationalist voters fed up with AKP rule and suffering from economic decline, political instability and leadership confusion following Erdoğan's presidency. The major success of the HDP, conversely, was first to appeal to almost all Kurdish voters, including conservative ones who had previously opted for the AKP, and second, to convince at least a segment of left-leaning voters that it had become a party of Turkey and could therefore be a 'national' player rather than simply the representative of the Kurds. Thanks to both factors, the party managed to receive 13.1% of the vote – well above the 10% election threshold which had previously been the major hurdle to Kurdish representation.

The outcome of the June 2015 elections obviously surprised Erdoğan, who was looking for a clear parliamentary majority for the AKP to draft the new constitution without the need for an agreement with the other parties. As president of the country, he was rather quick to assert that if the parties were unable to form a coalition, there would be a second election (T24 2015a). Many observers argued that this statement indeed signified his unwillingness to support any coalition government (Cemal 2015). According to the Constitution, after the swearing-in ceremony in parliament, parties have 45 days to form a government, and if they fail the president has the right to call early elections. Ultimately, and with the parties unable to form a coalition government, President Erdoğan used his constitutional mandate to call for snap elections – the first in Turkish history – on 1 November 2015.

The June 2015 election marked the moment when Erdoğan realised that he needed to recalibrate his strategy to maintain control of the 50% plus 1 vote support upon which he had built his political legitimacy. He observed that he had lost his ability to reach Kurdish voters, who now preferred HDP representation, and in the absence of Kurdish support he had to turn to Turkish nationalists. However, this recalibration required a wholesale change in the political discourse. He had been the one who initiated peace talks with the Kurdish political movement in the hope that his party could continue to rely on Kurdish support; however, he now changed his tone, reframing the Kurdish issue as one of terrorism.

Interestingly enough, between the June and November 2015 elections, the country experienced violence and polarisation on a scale unseen in Turkish politics since the tumultuous 1990s, which shaped the November election campaign. In July 2015, for instance, scores of Kurdish and socialist activists were killed and many others injured because of a suicide attack carried out by ISIL militants in Suruç (T24 2015b). In retaliation, two days after the deadly attack, the Kurdish Workers' Party (PKK) executed two police officers in Şanlıurfa (Akşam 2015), thus reigniting

Table 25.2 Results of June and November 2015 general elections in Turkey

Party	June 15 Vote (%)	Seats	November 15 Vote (%)	Seats	Change Vote (%)	Seats
AKP	40.8	258	49.5	317	+8.7	+59
MHP	16.2	80	11.9	40	−4.3	−40
CHP	24.9	132	25.3	134	−0.4	+2
SP	2	0	0.68	0	−1.3	0
HDP	13.1	80	10.76	59	−2.3	−21

the bloody conflict between the PKK and Turkish security forces. On 10 October, at a peace rally, two explosions occurred, leaving 109 dead and many injured.

The campaign was affected by increasing fear and terror in the country. This time, Erdoğan took a greater role in the election process and changed the content of his polarising discourse from new Turkey versus old Turkey to new Turkey or insecurity. Somer (2019) defines this turn as a move from a positive polarising frame to a negative polarising frame. It is not a coincidence that during the campaign, Erdoğan attended the funerals of soldiers and used it to his political advantage (Cumhuriyet 2015). Winning the November 2015 general elections with an outright majority, Erdoğan has continued this negative polarising discourse, which has only worsened since the 2016 coup attempt and the 2017 constitutional referendum over the presidential system. This was part of the political strategy of keeping the opposition divided and consolidating the voter base; however, this time the line of polarisation was drawn along anti-Kurdish politics, while voter consolidation was defined through Turkish nationalism.

The 2018 presidential and general elections

The 2018 presidential and general elections were conducted under the newly established presidential system. As was the case for all the elections after 2013, the 2018 election was neither fair nor free in so far as government control over the media and state resources created an uneven playing field favouring the incumbent (Çarkoğlu and Yıldırım 2018; Esen and Yardımcı-Geyikçi 2022; Çalışkan 2018; Sözen 2019).

Two major developments before the elections determined the 2018 electoral agenda. The first was the coup attempt of 2016. Since the failed military intervention allegedly organised by the Gülen movement, Erdoğan's securitisation of politics has only increased. The government framed the coup attempt as an attack against the state, and called on all political forces to unite behind the government. After the coup attempt, the AKP government was also quick to declare a state of emergency and began ruling by decree (Esen and Gümüşçü 2017). As such, the government's struggle with the Gülen movement quickly turned into a purge against all oppositional forces. Furthermore, with increasing statist and nationalist discourse, Erdoğan and the AKP managed to form a political alliance with the MHP by framing itself as the saviour of the state. This rapprochement with the MHP served several purposes. First, it eliminated the only remaining right-wing alternative to the AKP as a rival, thereby allowing Erdoğan to consolidate right-wing voters, who constitute the bulk of the electorate. Secondly, after losing Kurdish support, retaining 50% plus 1 of the votes could only be achieved through an alliance with Turkish nationalists. Leaving aside the costs of this strategy, such as being trapped in Turkish nationalist discourse and strengthening a junior partner like the MHP at the expense of the AKP, the cooperation between the two parties framed within a right-wing Turkish nationalist conservative identity allowed Erdoğan to maintain his political control.

The second development was the 2017 referendum over the establishment of a presidential system. Due to the collaboration between the AKP and the MHP, the presidential system first passed the three-fifths parliamentary majority necessary to call for a referendum (Sözen 2019). The referendum took place in a tense, securitised context with the 'Yes' camp, composed of the AKP and the MHP, employing a polarising discourse of new Turkey versus old Turkey, and more prominently as the saviour of the state against the traitors and/or terrorists (Dikici-Bilgin and Erdoğan 2018).

The 'Yes' camp was the winner, with 51.4% of the vote. Keeping in mind all the irregularities in the election process, the small margin between the two camps demonstrated the fragility of the support for the presidential system, and for Erdoğan. The referendum process

Table 25.3 Results of November 2015 and June 2018 parliamentary elections in Turkey

Party	November 15 Vote (%)	Seats	Alliance	June 18 Vote (%)	Seats	Change Vote (%)	Seats
			People's Alliance	**53.7**	344	–	–
AKP	49.5	317	AKP	42.6	295	–6.9	–22
MHP	11.9	40	MHP	11.1	49	–0.8	+9
			Nation Alliance	**34**	189	–	–
CHP	25.3	134	CHP	22.7	146	–2.6	+12
SP	0.68	0	SP	1.3	0	+0.6	0
	–	–	IYI Party	10	43	+10	+43
HDP	10.76	59	HDP	11.7	67	+1	+8

They are the total vote share of parties which form the alliance so for people's alliance (AKP+MHP) and for nation alliance (CHP+SP+IYI)

once again significantly polarised the country, and according to Aytaç et al. (2017), voters mostly acted according to partisan preferences, without really knowing the content of the constitutional amendments. Leaving aside the establishment of a presidential system *à la Turca* without any checks and balances, the referendum process ultimately enhanced the division between the AKP and the anti-AKP, as well as the Erdoğan and anti-Erdoğan blocks. This division was the continuation of new versus old Turkey, new Turkey being embodied by Erdoğan himself.

The 2018 elections took place against the backdrop of these developments, and the discourse employed in the referendum was mostly maintained. However, due to the constitutional changes brought about by the referendum, which created a very strong presidency, the campaign, as well as the political discourse of Erdoğan and the party, became increasingly personified in Erdoğan himself (Yardımcı-Geyikçi and Yavuzyılmaz 2022); the party became the state and Erdoğan started to portray himself as its embodiment. This extreme personalisation made it easier for Erdoğan to label his opponents' traitors, but, conversely, it consolidated the opposition through an anti-Erdoğan and pro-democracy discourse, creating a new division on the political scene.

The incumbent President Erdoğan was nominated as the presidential candidate of the AKP–MHP Alliance (*Cumhur Ittifaki*, People's Alliance), while the opposition forces this time decided to compete with their own candidates in the first round, assuming that this move would clear a path to a second round. In the second round, the strategy was to rally behind the surviving opposition candidate. As for the parliamentary elections, thanks to amendments to the electoral law which allows parties to run as a coalition, the CHP, the İYİ Party and the Felicity Party (SP, *Saadet Partisi*) formed the Nation Alliance (*Millet Ittifaki*) against the People's Alliance, leaving only the pro-Kurdish HDP out of the opposition front. The new electoral alliance system made it possible for all parties within the coalition to enter parliament if they could together garner more than 10% of the vote, eliminating the threshold for the smaller parties. The central goal of the opposition was to stop Erdoğan from using the secular versus religious or nationalist versus traitor divides by including the pro-Islamist SP and the nationalist İYİ Party, which was a newly founded nationalist centre-right party, whose leaders had defected from the MHP. Thus, the opposition coordination was more effective in the 2018 elections.

In the meantime, Erdoğan followed a dual strategy to overcome opposition coordination. In the presidential race, relying on the old secular–religious divide, he chose to compete against the CHP's candidate Muharrem İnce – a party man who emerged from the rank and file – and did not refer to either Meral Akşener – chair of the nationalist right-wing İYİ Party – or to Temel Karamollaoğlu – chair of the Islamist SP. Meanwhile, the Kurdish political movement HDP's candidate Selahattin Demirtaş was incarcerated, curtailing his ability to lead an assertive campaign and making it easier for Erdoğan to ignore his candidacy. Erdoğan's goal was to keep the race between himself and İnce so that he could maintain his polarising discourse built around the secular–religious, as well as new Turkey and old Turkey, divide. The unfair nature of elections was felt particularly in 2018. Media coverage of the opposition candidates was limited, and they had almost no access to the national media, while sitting President Erdoğan enjoyed not only abundant private and public resources but also extensive coverage in the public and private media (OSCE 2018). İnce was the only candidate allowed to appear on some media outlets, while there was a deliberate attempt to prevent the visibility of Akşener, a prominent critic of Erdoğan rising from the ranks of the nationalist centre-right. It should be noted that under emergency rule, throughout the campaign process opposition parties' activists were also harassed by vigilantes, as well as public officials (Esen and Yardımcı-Geyikçi 2020). Due to the unfair nature of the elections, Erdoğan could continue to shape the election agenda and build his campaign against the CHP candidate, positioning himself again as the face of new Turkey. He did not refrain from making several references to the headscarf issue to portray himself as the sole representative of right-wing religious voters, while accusing İnce of being a staunch secularist who was part and parcel of the so-called state suppression apparatus against religious people in the previous era.

In the parliamentary elections, conversely, Erdoğan and the AKP aimed to sustain the polarising discourse based on a division between the saviour of Turkey and the traitors, and defended the idea that the People's Alliance protected the state against domestic and international terrorists. Siding with the MHP, the AKP maintained a strong anti-Kurdish discourse, while at the same time accusing the İYİ Party – the only centre-right alternative left within the opposition front – of collaborating with the Gülen movement. His goal was to suggest that the opposition were traitors and terrorists (Sözen 2019). As a corollary of this strategy, any attempt by the Nation Alliance to coordinate with the HDP was directly labelled as collaboration with terrorists. As the Organisation for Security and Co-operation in Europe (OSCE 2018: 14) observed, Erdoğan 'repeatedly referred to other candidates and parties as supporters of terrorism', openly calling the HDP candidate a 'terrorist' and 'the CHP presidential candidate as a supporter of terrorism'. Overall, Erdoğan maintained the intense polarising and securitising discourse in the 2018 parliamentary elections with the goal of keeping the opposition divided and consolidating the nationalist right-wing support base. However, this time the opposition forces were well prepared and tried to keep the election discourse within the context of Erdoğan's regime versus democracy. All opposition forces shared the common vision of returning to the parliamentary system, which they considered the only way out of the single-man regime ushered in with the new presidential system.

Erdoğan won the presidency with 52.6% of the votes in the first round, increasing his vote share by only 0.8% from the 2014 presidential elections despite forming an alliance with the third largest party, the MHP (Table 25.4). In the parliamentary elections, the AKP's vote share decreased to 42.6% from 49.5%, so for a second time the party could not secure a majority. Although the AKP was the first party once again, it lost votes in all regions apart from southeastern Turkey – an HDP stronghold (Çarkoğlu and Yıldırım 2018). The total vote share of the People's Alliance was 53.7%, while the Nation Alliance received 34% of the votes and the HDP garnered 11.7%. Despite the unfair nature of the elections, as well as their securitisation by Erdoğan, the AKP–MHP alliance's total vote share decreased significantly, from 61.9% down

Table 25.4 Results of 2018 presidential elections in Turkey

Candidate	Supporting parties	Vote (%)
Recep Tayyip Erdoğan	AKP–MHP	52.6
Muharrem İnce	CHP	30.6
Selahattin Demirtaş	HDP	8.4
Meral Akşener	IYI Party	7.3
Temel Karamollaoğlu	SP	0.9
Other	–	0.2
Total	–	100

to 53.7%. The opposition, composed of the Nation Alliance and the HDP, were united in their anti-authoritarian and pro-democracy stance regardless of their different identities.

The relative decline of the AKP in the parliamentary elections indicated that Erdoğan's capacity to polarise the electorate over the religious–secular or saviour–traitor divide has also begun to diminish. There are two main reasons for the decreasing effectiveness of Erdoğan's use of polarisation as an electoral strategy. First, the opposition forces have become diversified, including not only secular centre-left but also centre-right, religious-right and Kurdish political actors. Significantly, with the establishment of the İYİ Party, the AKP could not absorb an alternative centre-right force, as it had several times before (Gümüşçü 2013). Secondly, the move from parliamentarism to presidentialism in 2017 created a single-man regime which strengthened the authoritarian character of the political system. Increasing authoritarianism and decreasing competitiveness, conversely, banded the opposition together within a pro-democracy camp.

Conclusion

Looking at the period after 2013, this chapter has analysed the relationship between polarisation and elections under competitive authoritarian rule in Turkey. The contention is that polarisation in Turkey is an elite-driven process that has been used by the incumbent party as an electoral strategy, serving two purposes: dividing the opposition while consolidating the right-wing voter base. However, this strategy has required constant recalibration in that the terms of polarisation have to be constantly redefined depending on the changing electoral calculus. While before 2013, the major dividing line was drawn between centre and periphery, as well as secularity and religion, as the opposition began to include more diverse social groups, the AKP had to create new divisions, such as the saviours versus traitors and later on new Turkey versus old Turkey, in order to maintain electoral dominance. It must be noted that these divisions have carried overtones of the previous divides. However, its power to determine politics from above by polarising voters has begun to diminish.

The results of the 2019 local elections, in which opposition forces succeeded in gaining control of the country's largest cities including Istanbul and Ankara, validated the contention that Erdoğan and the AKP's capacity to shape politics from above has diminished significantly. Additionally, with burgeoning economic problems and further depreciation of the Turkish lira, social demands have begun to dominate the political agenda, which further diminishes the incumbent's attempts at political engineering. Overall, as the incumbent's capacity to instrumentalise polarisation has waned, so has the likelihood of competitive authoritarianism surviving in Turkey.

References

AKP. 2015a. *Yeni Türkiye Yolunda Daima Adalet Daima Kalkınma: 7 Haziran 2015 Genel Seçimleri Seçim Beyannamesi* [On the Road to New Turkey Forever Justice Forever Development: Manifesto for the June 7, 2015 General Elections]. Available at: file:///C:/Users/sebnem/Downloads/2015-secim-beyan namesi-20nisan%20(1).pdf.

Akşam. 2014. 'Başbakan Erdoğan vizyon belgesini açıkladı!'. July 12. Available at: Başbakan Erdoğan vizyon belgesini açıkladı! (aksam.com.tr).

Akşam. 2015. 'Şanlıurfa'da 2 polisin şehit edilmesini PKK üstlendi'. July 22. Available at: Şanlıurfa'da 2 polisin şehit edilmesini PKK üstlendi - Son Dakika Haberleri (haberturk.com).

Aydın-Düzgit, Senem and Evren Balta. 2019. 'When elites polarize over polarization: Framing the polarization debate in Turkey–Retracted'. *New Perspectives on Turkey* 60: 153–176.

Aytaç, Erdem, Ali Çarkoğlu and Kerem Yıldırım. 2017. 'Taking sides: Determinants of support for a presidential system in Turkey'. *South European Society and Politics* 22(1): 1–20.

Bilgin, Hasret and Emre Erdoğan. 2018. 'Obscurities of a referendum foretold: The 2017 constitutional amendments in Turkey'. *Review of Middle East Studies* 52(1): 29–42.

Bunce, Valerie and Sharon Wolchik. 2010. 'Defeating dictators: Electoral change and stability in competitive authoritarian regimes'. *World Politics* 62(1): m43–m86.

Casal Bertoa, Fernando and Jose Rama. 2021. 'Polarization: What do we know and what can we do about it?' *Frontiers in Political Science* 3. Available at: https://www.frontiersin.org/articles/10.3389/fpos.2021 .687695/full.

Cemal, Hasan. 2015, August 14. 'Koalisyon yolunu Erdoğan kesti, nokta!' [Erdoğan Prevented Coalition], T24. August 14. Available at: http://t24.com.tr/yazarlar/hasan-cemal/koalisyon-yolunu-erdogan-kesti -nokta,12508.

Cumhuriyet. 2015, August 17. 'Şehit cenazesinde AKP mitingi'. August 17. Available at: 'Şehit cenazesinde AKP mitingi' (cumhuriyet.com.tr).

Çarkoğlu, Ali. and Kerem Yıldırım. 2018. 'Change and continuity in Turkey's June 2018 elections'. *Insight Turkey* 20(4): 153–183.

Çalışkan, Koray. 2018. 'Toward a new political regime in Turkey: From competitive toward full authoritarianism'. *New Perspectives on Turkey* 58: 33.

Enyedi, Zsolt. 2008. 'The social and attitudinal basis of political parties: Cleavage politics revisited'. *European Review* 16(3): 287–304.

Erdogan, Emre. 2016. 'Turkey: Divided we stand'. *On Turkey* 118: 1–4.

Erdoğan, Emre. 2018. 'Dimensions of polarization in Turkey: Social distance, perceived moral superiority, and political intolerance'. *The German Marshall Fund of the United States*. Available at: https:// www.gmfus.org/sites/default/files/Dimensions%2520of%2520Polarization%2520in%2520Turkey %2520edited.pdf.

Erdoğan, Emre and Pinar Semerci. 2020. *Dimensions of Polarization in Turkey 2020*. Turkuazlab Report. Available at: https://www.turkuazlab.org/en/dimensions-of-polarization-in-turkey-2020/.

Esen, Berk and Sebnem Yardimci-Geyikçi. 2020. 'The Turkish presidential elections of 24 June 2018'. *Mediterranean Politics* 25(5): 682–689.

Esen, Berk and Sebnem Gumuscu. 2017. 'Turkey: How the coup failed'. *Journal of Democracy* 28(1): 59–73.

Esmer, Yilmaz. 2019. 'Identity politics: Extreme polarization and the loss of capacity to compromise in Turkey'. In Ursula van Beek (ed.), *Democracy under Threat*. London: Palgrave, 121–146.

Gandhi, Jennifer and Ora John Reuter. 2008. 'Opposition coordination in legislative elections under authoritarianism'. *Prepared for presentation at the Annual Meeting of the American Political Science Association, Boston, MA*. Available at: http://ojreuter.com/wp-content/uploads/2015/06/Gandhi_Reuter_ Coordination_Legislative_Elections_APSA08.pdf.

Gumuscu, Sebnem. 2013. 'The emerging predominant party system in Turkey'. *Government and Opposition* 48(2): 223–244.

Kalaycıoğlu, Ersin. 2015. 'Turkish popular presidential elections: Deepening legitimacy issues and looming regime change'. *South European Society and Politics* 20(2): 157–179.

Keyman, Fuat. 2014. 'The AK party: Dominant party, new Turkey and polarization'. *Insight Turkey* 16(2): 19–31.

LeBas, Adrienne. 2006. 'Polarization as craft: Party formation and state violence in Zimbabwe'. *Comparative Politics* 38(4): 419–438.

LeBas, Adrienne. 2018. 'Can polarization be positive? Conflict and institutional development in Africa'. *American Behavioral Scientist* 62(1): 59–74.

Levitsky, Steven and Lucan Way. 2010. *Competitive Authoritarianism: Hybrid Regimes after the Cold War*. Cambridge: Cambridge University Press.

Lipset, Seymour Martin and Stein Rokkan. 1967. *Cleavage Structures, Party Systems, and Voter Alignments: An Introduction*. New York: Free Press.

McCoy, Jennifer and Tahmina Rahman. 2016. 'Polarized democracies in comparative perspective: Toward a conceptual framework'. *International Political Science Association Conference, Poznan, Poland*. Available at: https://www.researchgate.net/publication/336830321_Polarized_Democracies_in_Comparative_Perspective_Toward_a_Conceptual_Framework.

McCoy, Jennifer, Tahmina Rahman and Murat Somer. 2018. 'Polarization and the global crisis of democracy: Common patterns, dynamics, and pernicious consequences for democratic polities'. *American Behavioral Scientist* 62(1): 16–42.

McCoy, Jennuifer and Murat Somer. 2019. 'Toward a theory of pernicious polarization and how it harms democracies: Comparative evidence and possible remedies'. *The Annals of the American Academy of Political and Social Science* 681(1): 234–271.

Milat. 2014. 'Tamam İnşallah!' August 4. Available at: 4 Ağustos 2014 tarihli Milat Gazetesi – Gazeteler.

Nefes, Turkay Salim. 2017. 'The impacts of the Turkish government's conspiratorial framing of the Gezi Park protests'. *Social Movement Studies* 16(5): 610–622.

Oosterwaal, Annemarije and Rene Torenvlied. 2010. 'Politics divided from society? Three explanations for trends in societal and political polarisation in the Netherlands'. *West European Politics* 33(2): 258–279.

OSCE. 2018. 'ODIHR election observation mission final report'. Available at: https://www.osce.org/odihr/elections/turkey/397046?download=true.

Özbudun, Ergun. 1981. 'The Turkish party system: Institutionalization, polarization, and fragmentation'. *Middle Eastern Studies* 17(2): 228–240.

Özbudun, Ergun. 2013. *Party Politics & Social Cleavages in Turkey*. Boulder, CO: Lynne Rienner.

Özbudun, Ergun. 2014. 'AKP at the crossroads: Erdoğan's majoritarian drift'. *South European Society and Politics* 19(2): 155–167.

Özbudun, Ergun. 2015. The 2014 presidential elections in Turkey: A post-election analysis. *Global Turkey in Europe III: Democracy, Trade, and the Kurdish Question in Turkey-EU Relations*. Available at: https://www.iai.it/sites/default/files/gte_pb_18.pdf.

Sartori, Giovanni. 1976. *Parties and Party Systems*. Cambridge: Cambridge University Press.

Schattschneider, Elmer. 1975. *The Semisovereign People: A Realist's View of Democracy in America*. Belmont: Wadsworth Publishing Company.

Somer, Murat. 2019. 'Turkey: The slippery slope from reformist to revolutionary polarization and democratic breakdown'. *The Annals of the American Academy of Political and Social Science* 681(1): 42–61.

Somer, Murat and Jennifer McCoy. 2018. 'Déjà vu? Polarization and endangered democracies in the 21st century'. *American Behavioral Scientist* 62(1): 3–15.

Sözen, Yunus. 2019. 'Competition in a populist authoritarian regime: The June 2018 dual elections in Turkey'. *South European Society and Politics* 24(3): 287–315.

T24. 2015a. 'Erdoğan: Önce birinci, sonra ikinci partiyi görevlendiririm, hükümet kurulamazsa tekrar seçime gidilir' [Erdoğan: I will give mandate to the first party and then the second one, if the government cannot be formed then there would be a re-election]. June 14. Available at: http://t24.com.tr/haber/erdogan-once-birinci-sonra-ikinci-partiyi-gorevlendiririm-hukumet-kurulamazsa-tekrar-secime-gidilir,299598.

T24. 2015b. 'Suruç'ta bombalı katliam!'. Available at: Suruç'ta bombalı katliam! (t24.com.tr).

Tepe, Sultan. 2013. 'The perils of polarization and religious parties: The democratic challenges of political fragmentation in Israel and Turkey'. *Democratization* 20(5): 831–856.

Torcal, Mariano and Scott Mainwaring. 2003. 'The political recrafting of social bases of party competition: Chile, 1973–95'. *British Journal of Political Science* 33(1): 55–84.

Türkiye Gazetesi. 2014. 'Milyonların verdiği mesaj'. August 4. Available at: Milyonların verdiği mesaj: Değişim zamanı (turkiyegazetesi.com.tr).

Tworzecki, Hubert. 2019. 'Poland: A case of top-down polarization'. *The Annals of the American Academy of Political and Social Science* 681(1): 97–119.

Yardımcı-Geyikçi, Şebenm and Hakan Yavuzyilmaz. 2022. 'Party (de) institutionalization in times of political uncertainty: The case of the justice and development party in Turke'. *Party Politics* 28(1): 71–84.

Yeni Şafak. 2014, August 4. 'Erdoğan: Operasyon yapan demir yumruğumuzu yer'. Available at: Erdoğan: Operasyon yapan demir yumruğumuzu yer - Yeni Şafak (yenisafak.com).

26
FROM BALLOTS TO BULLETS

Libyan 2012 elections as the origin
of the unachieved transition

Chiara Loschi

Introduction

Libya held its first post-Al-Qadhdhāfī parliamentary elections on July 7, 2012, resulting in the country's first elected parliament, the General National Congress (GNC). However, shortly thereafter, a legitimacy battle began and tensions between elected representatives grew. Such tensions between former revolutionary groups and members of the armed forces and security apparatus escalated, eventually leading to civil conflict. Since then, hopes for a peaceful democratic transition have disappeared. This chapter is concerned with the following questions: What problems affected the planning and implementation processes? What factors impacted the elections on democratization and reconciliation processes?

This chapter contends that Libyan instability has its roots in the rules of the game and the processes established for the 2012 parliamentary elections. In particular, the argument put forth here is that the election preparations and results paved the way for the emergence of long-lasting cleavages that not only exacerbated pre-existing frictions but also created new deep cleavages/ divisions outside the ballot boxes. Thus, the 2012 Libyan elections did not erase or substitute older societal-deep rifts, but, on the contrary, they amplified their reach. Against this background, new transitional institutions did not emerge as mediators between competing parties and could not agree on a unifying national interest or the necessity for a monopoly on the use of force.

Post-conflict elections have many more challenges than routine elections. Indeed, they aim at building legitimized institutions and governments; setting up democratic procedures and opening political participation; and establishing and consolidating peace and demilitarization. In short, voters and candidates should be able to participate and compete without fearing for their lives.

During times of transition, transitional institutions establish new rules and allow freedom of the press and speech, but against a context of highly polarized societies seeking to revive conflicts. Libya was no exception to these risks. The Libyan 2012 elections provide a useful case study in the frame of post-2011 political processes in Arab countries. The process set in motion for the preparation of the elections and the following dynamics confirm that elections matter, but not only to explain institutional developments in newly democratizing states (Lust-Okar and Jamal 2002). In particular, in the Libyan case the electoral process called into question the understanding of post-conflict state building. The election preparations caused fragmentation along both new and old cleavages that influenced the process in the short term and paved the way toward subsequent political crises and security instability. The parliament elected with the July 2012 elections became an additional arena in which members could strive for a privileged position vis-à-vis local constituencies and privileged access to the process of nation building, instead of building strong national transitional institutions.

The chapter focuses on pivotal events concerning the preparation for elections and the following phase to analyze their consequences. The argument is that several critical processes launched with the planning of the elections had long-lasting negative effects on the outcomes and on the political processes initiated after the results. Specific gaps and exclusionary politics that emerged with the post-2011 phase did not disappear with the elections, but were amplified, creating the conditions for the subsequent deepening of conflict and the intervention of foreign actors. This is of utmost importance to better capture the impact of the electoral process, as well as international sponsorship of electoral mechanisms, on subsequent political developments and the reconstruction process in post-conflict countries. This is particularly salient in Libya, where international actors and the UN continue to call for national elections, but they are consistently sabotaged by domestic and the very same international institutions and actors. It is in this context that experts question the idea of promoting elections as a process for political stabilization (Wehrey and Badi 2022).

Setting the scene: Libya's ten years of impossible transition

Beginning on February 15, 2011, the Arab revolts that broke out in Tunisia and Egypt reached Libya. The regime established on September 1, 1969, by Colonel Mu'ammar Al-Qadhdhāfī was targeted by protests, and on February 27, 2011, the National Transitional Council (NTC) was established as the transitional political authority, ready to take over in case of regime collapse. In response, the colonel embarked on a campaign of repression against the protests. This marked the beginning of a conflict that continued until Al-Qadhdhāfī was captured and killed on October 20, and Sirte – the leader's hometown and the loyalists' last stronghold – fell to the opposition forces.

On October 23, the NTC proclaimed the end of the revolution and the liberation of the country. At the request of the Libyan authorities and to support the new transitional authorities of the country in their post-conflict efforts, the United Nations Security Council created a special integrated political mission, the United Nations Support Mission in Libya (UNSMIL), on September 16, 2011.

The creation of the National Transitional Council in 2011 appeared to be one of the most promising steps for a peaceful transition. In July 2012, elections were held for a 200-member unicameral parliament called the General National Congress to replace the NTC. However, this was the start of a prolonged crisis. In 2014, the weakness of the GNC and escalating internal conflicts led to the creation of two rival parliaments and their associated governments: one in western Libya and one in the east. However, already in 2013, insecurity and conflict had been spreading, and the ability of Libya's national authorities to provide basic services was collapsing, contributing to calls for the dissolution of the GNC. The political transition definitively collapsed in 2014. In March 2014, parliament expelled Prime Minister Ali Zeidan in a vote of no confidence and appointed Defense Minister Abdallah al-Thani as interim prime minister. Amid renewed militarization of the civil conflict, in June 2014 a House of Representatives (HoR) was elected to replace the GNC. However, the Islamist political coalition in the GNC rejected the legitimacy of the HoR elections and the shift in power. At this point, the political and military conflict truly erupted. National and local forces organized around two main warring alliances against each other: Libya Dawn (*Fajr Libia*) and Operation Dignity (*Karama*). In July 2014, Tripoli-based militias allied with the GNC leadership and launched 'Operation Dawn' to control key areas of the capital. Following these clashes, the HoR moved to Tobruk in the east of the country without a formal transfer of power from the GNC. In Tobruk, the HoR voted to establish an interim government chaired by Abdullah al-Thinni. In the west, the GNC was reinstated in September by a coalition of armed militias united under the name of Fajr Libya, which had extended its control over central Tripoli.

These events were crucial for the establishment of two distinct centers of powers. Although UNSMIL sponsored negotiations in Skhirat between parliaments and governments and appointed the Government of National Unity (GNU), in the longer term, this resulted in a reconfiguration of the conflicting parties and security actors rather than marking a political change. In the east, the HoR failed to vote to formally recognize it, instead recognizing the role of the Libyan Arab Armed Forces (LAAF), under the command of General Khalifa Haftar. At the same time, external interference led to an escalation of militarization, exacerbating the internal conflict. The LAAF, supported by Russia, the United Arab Emirates (UAE) and Egypt, also relied on foreign fighters from Syria, Sudan and Chad, as well as Russian mercenaries. Armed groups in western Libya, an area nominally under their control, supported the UN-recognized GNU. Turkey and Qatar supported the GNU with weapons, ammunition, training and foreign fighters. Adding to this conflict scenario, in 2014 the Islamic State claimed its presence in the country as the Islamic State Organization in Libya, further polarizing the internal conflict by occupying cities such as Derna and Sirte, and organizing attacks on oil terminals in early 2016, before being virtually eliminated in late 2016.

Paradoxically, since 2011, any military support for the parties in the conflict, including from European Union member states, has been in violation of UN Security Council resolutions, which imposed an arms embargo on Libya. This, however, has been totally ineffective so far. At the same time, the lack of demilitarization of political actors and militias in the west of the country and especially in the capital Tripoli, led to a proliferation of armed groups and militias and further fragmentation of power. This went hand in hand with the progressive efforts of European institutions to establish a Libyan institutional interlocutor within the framework of political cooperation, which was increasingly based on the need for European institutions to establish control over migratory flows through Libya.

The overlapping of several and often contradictory international policies strongly conditioned and constrained the evolution of the phenomena that emerged in Libya after 2011. In this context, claims of particularism and demands for political pluralism, opportunities for cultural mobilization, freedom of protest, the participation of women and the role of young men and women in the cultural life of the country experienced increasingly greater obstructions. After further Libyan conflict broke out in 2019, which ended with the ceasefire of October 2020 and the launch of a Libyan Political Dialogue Forum (LPDF), the national debate has reopened on a sustainable democratic transition for the country and a political solution leading to institutional reunification may have been set in motion. In February 2021, after two rounds of voting, the LPDF selected a new executive council, creating an interim Government of National Unity, which is still in power. The GNU was tasked with overseeing the presidential and parliamentary elections that had been set for December 2021. However, due to prolonged debates over the legal and constitutional basis of the elections and disputes over candidate eligibility, the High National Election Commission (HNEC) announced the postponement of the elections. At the time of writing, elections seem to be off the Libyan political agenda. How have the 2012 elections spread the seeds of such long-lasting instability in Libya?

Preparations for elections

The transitional period should have led to the establishment of state institutions and nationwide support for a new political leadership. In preparation for the elections and discussions around the electoral law, transitional institutions, embodied by the National Transitional Council (NTC), faced the most complicated challenges of the process. Elections became the cornerstone of the transition and the NTC persisted with them from the start and during the following months. The first issue to emerge was the legalization of new political parties such as the Muslim Brotherhood and the Salafi movements. Their arrival on the scene opened the debate over the political system that the new institutions had to acquire. Second, instrumental reactivation of older political agendas such as those that the federalist movements from east Libya put forward, also influenced both pre- and post-election phases.

In any case, in 2011, the death of Al-Qadhdhāfi and the declaration by the NTC of Libya's liberation on October 23 set in motion the process toward parliamentary elections to designate the 200 members of the General National Congress (*Al-mutamar al-wataniyu al-aamu*). Elections took place on July 7, 2012, and the NTC, headed by Abdul Rahim El-Kleib, handed over power to the GNC. The GNC was consequently charged with appointing and overseeing the constituent assembly and the election of a new government. The NTC's temporary constitutional declaration (TCD) of August 3, 2011, had charged the NTC with the promulgation of an electoral law and the establishment of an electoral commission within 90 days of the declaration of liberation in preparation for elections that would take place within 240 days of this same date. Based on the legal framework sketched in the TCD, the NTC promulgated election, political party and constituency laws, and appointed the High National Election Commission to implement the ensuing registration, preparation and electoral process.

It first promulgated Law No. 2-2012 to formally legalize political parties, which had been outlawed during the Al-Qadhdhāfi regime. The NTC established the High National Election Commission with Law No. 3-2012 on January 19 to oversee the GNC elections. The law provided a mandate for an independent commission composed of 17 members, amended twice with Laws No. 31- and 44-2012 to a final membership of 11. The drafting of the electoral legal framework led to the emergence of the first divisive issues. Drafts of the electoral law were released in January 2012 on social media to give Libyan civil society groups and individuals the opportunity to submit feedback online. The drafts raised opposition against the electoral system (AFP 2012; Pack and Cook 2015) and a revised version of the law, Law No. 4-2012, was issued in late January. The final law set that 80 of the 200 seats would go to party lists while the majority, elected by proportional representation, 120 seats, would go to independents, elected by majority vote. This system aimed at avoiding a strong party-ruled majority in Congress, which reflected liberal technocrats' concerns over a possible Islamist takeover. It also aimed at ensuring a broad-based national unity government, which would be necessary for the GNC to reach the two-thirds majority demanded by the TCD to pass major legislation, such as a new constitution. Some argued that an individual-based system would exacerbate regional divisions by empowering local elites and notables rather than national figures, but others argued that a party-based system would provide too much power to established groups such as the Muslim Brotherhood. To counter this latter argument, the NTC proposed to ban political parties formed on the basis of religious, ethnic or tribal affiliations with the aim of reducing the influence of social cleavages on the electoral process. However, due to the opposition of Islamist groups, the NTC dropped this proposal in the final version of Law No. 29-2012. Ultimately, to secure seats, those candidates running in single-member districts had to engage with and find support among local concerns and issues; however, in so doing, the system crystalized and acknowledged the political relevance of pre-existing local configurations of power (Pack and Cook 2015).

Another significant fracture emerged with the federalism issue, which recalled older political demands. Libyan independence sanctioned in January 1952 from Italian colonial occupation led to a federal arrangement of three regions ruled by King al Idris al Senusi as a result of UN-led mediation that started in 1949. Claims of Cyrenaica's status as a largely autonomous and influential province from 1951 re-emerged after 2011 due to strong political marginalization during the Al-Qadhdhāfī regime and political groups in the east began appealing to the sentiments of Cyrenaican political power. The majority of Libya's water and oil reserves are in Cyrenaica, but only around one-fourth of the country's population lives in the region, so that federalist demands for preferential resource allocation represented a salient source of conflict. Indeed, in March 2012, a number of political leaders in the east declared the establishment of the Cyrenaica Regional Transitional Council, an independent body with no affiliation to the NTC that echoed the independence aspirations that had emerged in the early post-colonial years (Baldinetti 2010).

According to NTC law, 100 seats went to western Libya, and only 60 to the east and 40 to the south. The ratio was based on population districts, but federalists demanded that the NTC allocate 100 seats for the future GNC to each of Libya's three historic regions. With the aim of controlling federalist influence, the NTC issued a first constitutional amendment on March 13, 2012. This amendment modified several points of Article 30 of the TCD and required that the members of the GNC select (outside of its members) a body composed of 60 people to draft a new constitution. The solution replicated the model of the original 1951 constitutional committee with 20 representatives from each region, that is Cyrenaica, Tripolitania and Fezzan (Sawani and Pack 2013). With a similar rationale, the NTC issued a second constitutional amendment on June 10, 2012, to delineate the proposed membership of the constitutional council, namely specifying the appointment of 20 representatives from each of Libya's three historic regions for a total of 60 members (Pack and Cook 2015).

Only 48 hours before election day, on the morning of July 5, boxes and other election tools in Ajdabiya were destroyed by allegedly federalist groups. Later that day, a group of protesters not officially affiliated with the Cyrenaica Regional Transitional Council shut down the five oil installations of Sidra, Haruj, Zuwaytina, Brega and Hariqa. During the night, the NTC issued a third amendment to the constitutional declaration that mandated the creation of a constitutional assembly elected through free and direct suffrage rather than one appointed by members of the GNC. This amendment aimed at reducing the tensions mounting in the east over the GNC seats distribution.

However, the NTC's last-minute decision did not accommodate all federalists; hundreds of people demonstrated in Benghazi the day before the election calling for a boycott because the GNC seats were still not divided equally by region. Nevertheless, many citizens in the east participated in the elections, presumably as they would have had the amendment not been promulgated. This chain of events made it clear that emerging institutions were prone to consider amendments, suggesting that they could be blackmailed into sitting at the table and accommodate spoilers' threats. In other words, calls for a boycott and a disruption of the system emerged as a winning strategy for the extraction of concessions outside electoral participation. This called into question the strength of central institutions and their capacity to establish nationwide systems and electoral mechanisms, and even to establish a monopoly on the use of force, while local and particular political agendas increased their political relevance in the fissures of society.

Electoral outcomes and the end of the democratic process

The HNEC declared preliminary results on July 17, 2012, and confirmed them on August 1. The elections were conducted with minimal violence and led to a full transfer of power from the outgoing NTC to the incoming General National Congress. It thus appeared that despite the initial difficulties and the rising tensions due to the emergence of religious parties and federalist demands, the Libyan transition could proceed and succeed.

With a final turnout of 61.58%, the GNC was finally elected. Mahmoud Jibril's National Forces Alliance (NFA) won 39 seats, followed by the Justice and Construction Party (JCP), which received 17 seats. In third, the National Front Party with three seats organized old 1980s anti-Al-Qadhdhāfī alliances and strong pro-parliamentary advocates. The National Centrist Party, a faction of the NFA, won two seats in a separate list. The Union for the Homeland (al-Ittihad min ajl al-Watan), the Bloc of Wadi El Haya gathering and the National Centrist Party elected two candidates each. A total of 15 political entities lists, organized at both national and local level, gained one seat each. The 120 independents seats created a heterogeneous assemblage of personalities, out of which only one woman won a seat (Table 26.1).

On October 14, 2012, with the support of the National Forces Alliance and a number of independents, the General National Congress appointed Ali Zeidan, an independent, as prime minister. After prolonged negotiations over the composition of the new government, Congress approved his cabinet nominees and Zeidan took office on November 14.

The electoral system prevented the organization of clear ideological and larger blocks, rendering the GNC fragmented and based mostly on local and individual interests, with strong ties to micro-level constituencies. In addition, it led to several shifting alliances, undermining the coherence of the government's actions. Negotiations between the national and local levels persisted on an *ad hoc* basis, making the government more vulnerable and suggesting that despite the election of a government, there was no moving away from this plurality of power centers (Lacher 2013). One of the direct consequences was that the new GNC failed, crucially, in securing a monopoly over the use of legitimate force. On November 23, 2011, the NTC established a transitional administration, headed by Prime Minister Abdul Rahim al-Keeb, with the highest priority to assert national authority over the assortment of armed groups and impose security on uncontrolled areas. One case in point is Decision No. 7 taken in October 2012, which authorized the use of force in Bani Walid. On October 2, 2012, clashes erupted in Bani Walid, an ex-Al-Qadhdhāfī stronghold, between the pro-government militias from Misrata and

Table 26.1 Composition of General National Congress' seats (party lists and independents). Personal elaboration based on Lacher 2013 and Smith 2012

Political parties	
National Forces Alliance (Tahaluf al-Quwah al-Wataniya)	39
Justice and Construction Party (Hizb al-Adala wa al-Bina) (Muslim Brotherhood)	17
National Front Party (Hizb al-Jabha al-Wataniya)	3
Wadi al Hayah	2
Union for the Homeland	2
National Centrist Party	2
Local interest groups	15
Independents (including personalities associated with National Forces Alliance; associated with Justice and Construction; Salafis, independent or associated with party lists)	120
Total	200

local militiamen. The stronghold was shelled a few days later, and government and government-aligned military forces led the military offensive and entered Bani Walid on October 24, 2012. This decision uncovered the existence of competing camps within the GNC, and opened the way for a military offensive. The military operation caused the destruction of local institutions, businesses and homes in Bani Walid by militias from Misrata and other local strongholds.

The vote to show force in Bani Walid was disrupted and many deputies left the chamber to avoid having to vote. Eventually, only about two-thirds of GNC members were present. According to Lacher, the resolution was accepted with 65 votes in favor, just 7 against and about 55 abstentions (Lacher 2013). Despite weak formal support, the alliance between the revolutionary forces within the GNC was sufficient to launch the attack. The same fissure emerged with the debate on the political isolation law, which would exclude from office those who had served under the Al-Qadhdhāfī regime. The Muslim Brotherhood, Salafis and representatives of the revolutionary strongholds supported the exclusion of those who had served under Al-Qadhdhāfī, and, on the other side, the Alliance and many independents from the south and center opposed the proposal. The vote over the issue stalled between December 2012 and early May 2013, also forestalling progress on other major policy issues. When a vote was finally put on the agenda in March 2013, armed protesters affiliated with the Islamist current surrounded the GNC offices. The law was finally adopted on May 5, 2013, while armed groups organized barricades in front of several ministries to push their demands for political exclusion.

The episodes and escalation since late 2012 confirm that central institutions were subject to the blackmailing strategies of armed groups that considered the GNC a tool to legitimize their use of force. In other words, those transitional institutions based on democratic rule were easily highjacked. Although the elected GNC and government continued to issue laws and decrees, their ability to enforce decisions was extremely limited.

As mentioned, another long-lasting divisive element is the instrumental re-emergence of the regionalist/federalist movement, which established a new arena of political bargain outside ballot boxes. After the election, Libya's Oil Ministry appointed 32-year-old militia leader Ibrahim Jadhran from Ajdabiya, in eastern Libya, as a regional commander of its Petroleum Facilities Guard (PFC) to ensure the protection of eastern oil fields. Jadhran had federalist sympathies and used his position to advance that agenda (DeVore 2014; Mezran and Eljarh 2014). Indeed, Jadhran's guards launched an oil blockade in July 2013 and seized three petroleum-exporting ports. Libyan oil exports shrunk from 1.7 million to 110,000 barrels per day. Zeidan opted for negotiation rather than confrontation due to Jadhran's military strength and the unreliability of pro-government forces. In the longer run though, the federalists found themselves cut off from oil revenues and funds because governmental threats deterred companies from doing business with them. However, Jadhran's blockade denied Libya's government its main source of revenue and despite being short-lived, it exposed the inner fragility of the Libyan transitional authorities and provoked a governmental crisis. In particular, governmental military personnel eventually blamed the government for inadequately supporting them when trying to negotiate with Jadhran's PFC (DeVore 2014).

Islamist and Salafi movements: electoral results, instability, and international concerns

The Islamist forces within and outside the GNC represent a heterogeneous field. After the regime's downfall and in preparation for elections, some forces played a pivotal role in establishing long-lasting fractures, both intentionally and unintentionally. During the electoral process and the post-election phase, a wide spectrum of Islamist parties, jihadists and Salafi movements appeared on the political scene and played a pivotal role in determining the subsequent political set-up. In particular, the emergence of multiple religious-oriented movements and parties after 42 years of regime repression captured the attention of not only Libyan political actors but also Western and European governments and experts.

Islamist parties and movements not only directly participated in the political rivalries within and outside institutions, and in the fragmentation of the security apparatus, but they were also the target of Western and neighboring countries' concerns, or support, legitimizing the ideological cleavage opposing Islamist against liberals. This process allowed Libyan personalities, whose aim was to gain international support, to define their role in subsequent domestic conflicts based on this ideological divide, thus paving the way for an escalation of foreign intervention in the country.

In preparation for the elections, the electoral legal framework hampered the creation of major ideological blocks in the GNC, but it permitted the Muslim Brotherhood party and the Salafis groups to enter the political scene. However, the idea of a deep divide between Islamists and seculars was based on a non-existent ideological cleavage. Western media outlets referred to this divide in their titles when interpreting the elections' results: 'Libya's First Post-Gaddafi Vote to Test Islamists', said Reuters on July 5, 2012; 'Liberals Claim Lead in Libyan Election', according to France 24 on July 8, 2012[1]; 'Election Results in Libya Break an Islamist Wave' for the *New York Times*;[2] and 'Libya Election Success for Secularist Jibril's Bloc', titled the BBC news website.[3] Thus, it seemed that the Islamists of the Justice and Construction Party and the liberals, represented by Mahmoud Jibril's National Forces Alliance party, were clearly ideologically opposed.

This was a misleading interpretation of the results, but it had an impact on Western and European constituencies. While the NFA led by Jibril, who was considered a liberal, did win 39 out of the 80 seats, the larger picture including the 120 independent personalities' profiles reveals that Muslim and Salafi together won a greater number of seats than individual so-called liberals (Lacher 2013). In fact, 'liberal' and 'secular' labels are extremely problematic in this case: 'liberal' cannot account for the diverse personalities in the GNC, and 'secular' does not describe any Libyan candidate running in the election. In any case, such nuance mattered little for external actors who responded to the Libyan crisis using the trite, but simple framework of Islamists versus liberals.

Among jihadist movements, older generations of Libyan jihadist had created a number of groups during the Al-Qadhdhāfī regime, among them the largest was the Libyan Islamic Fighting Group (LIFG; *al-Jama'a al-Islamiya al-Muqatila bi-Libiya*). It operated in secret until they declared their existence in 1995. Following several attempts to assassinate Al-Qadhdhāfī during that decade, the regime ruthlessly repressed it (Fitzgerald 2016). Several former LIFG figures subsequently played key roles in the revolution and opted for participating in the Libyan democratic transition, forming political parties and running in elections.

The Zeidan cabinet had some LIFG members among its ministers: Sami al Saadi as Minister of Martyrs and Missing Persons, who resigned his post at the end of 2012,[4] and Khaled al-Sharif, a relevant figure in the organization (Lacher 2013). After the fall of Al-Qadhdhāfī, a second generation of jihadist established *Ansar al-Sharia* Libya. The movement's largest support came from Benghazi, and later from the neighborhoods of Derna and Ajdabiya. *Ansar al-Sharia* was highly heterogeneous, and some members persuaded the leaders not to physically disrupt them (Fitzgerald 2016). The movement had transnational aspirations, and it is reported that fighters from Derna and some members of *Ansar al-Sharia* from Benghazi joined the struggle of Qaeda-linked groups in northern Mali against French forces (Lacher 2013). *Ansar al-Sharia* Libya decided to focus on charitable work and social services to create a society based on its definition of Islamic principles, eventually leading to an Islamic state overseen by its interpretation of sharia (Fitzgerald 2016), in line with *Ansar al-Sharia* Tunisia's strategy (Merone 2017). In 2012, a series of attacks against Western institutions revealed the existence of organized extremist groups in Libya. Among these attacks, the assault against the US diplomatic mission in Benghazi on September 11, 2012, which resulted in the death of Ambassador Christopher Stevens and three staff members, had considerable international repercussions. Subsequently, mass protests took place in Benghazi against *Ansar al-Sharia*, although the organization had not claimed the attack and argued that it stood against violent extremism. In any case, public opinion both inside and outside Libya was heavily influenced by the idea that radical groups were an actual threat to security and stability and this was impossible to ignore.

These feelings increased when in November 2014 militants from different groups and former combatants in the Syrian civil war pledged allegiance to IS leader Abu Bakr al-Baghdadi. The belief of an Islamist plot to gain control of the government began to circulate in Libya and neighboring countries. In Tunisia, there was a growing sense of insecurity which politicized the management of the Tunisian security sector and the borders with Libya (International Crisis Group 2014). The establishment of the Islamic State organization in the region of Sirte and in the city of Sabrata, close to the Tunisian border, raised concerns among Tunisian authorities because of security spillover from the border. Indeed, the jihadi group set up a camp in Sabrata to attract Tunisian jihadists seeking to flee the country, especially after the Ennahda-led government in August 2013 declared *Ansar al-Sharia* a terrorist organization (Meddeb 2016). In 2013, military officers in Egypt removed the country's first democratically elected president, Mohamed Morsi, representative of the Muslim Brotherhood, and eventually established a new authoritarian regime led by Abdel Fattah el-Sisi. Inevitably, this built a rationale for anti-Islamism support in Libya (Anderson 2017). It also opened the door to external actors and contributed to the legitimization of a strong anti-Islamist political and military stance among Libyan leaders who wished to acquire international and regional credit.

Against this background, General Khalifa Haftar increased his public support in Benghazi for his unilateral offensive against Islamist armed groups, including *Ansar al-Sharia*. Haftar launched operation *Karama* (Dignity) on May 16, 2014, with the aim of cleansing Libya of 'terrorism and extremism'.[5] Haftar's rhetoric replicated the rhetoric that el-Sisi had employed in Egypt against the Muslim Brotherhood. As early as May 2014, Egypt indeed supported Haftar, having as a priority to secure its long and porous border with Libya that stretches for 1115 km, against infiltration by Islamist militants, including members and affiliates of al-Qaeda and the Islamic State and against the influence of the Muslim Brotherhood (Mourad 2021). As international observers, including the UN Panel of Experts, have been continuously recording, Haftar also gained support from France in the form of weapons (United Nations Security Council 2019) and intelligence support for Haftar's military staff (United Nations Security Council 2017). Indeed, one guiding principle of French foreign policy in North Africa is 'stabilization at any costs', which goes hand in hand with the regional approach against Islamist insurgency in the Sahara–Sahel belt and terrorism at home (Bensaâd 2019).

Conclusion

This chapter has argued that a number of events and factors established in preparation for the 2012 Libyan parliamentary elections created the context for the emergence of long-lasting political divisions and hampered a peaceful transition. In particular, the chapter contends that the election preparations and results paved the way for the emergence of long-lasting cleavages that not only exacerbated pre-existing frictions but prevented the suppression of new inevitable post-revolutionary divisions appearing outside the ballot boxes. The elections were held in a difficult context, but it was hoped that a democratic institutional framework would contribute to appeasing tensions. This did not occur and the resulting political dynamics did not erase social cleavages. On the contrary, the issues that emerged after the elections and the political choices made by transitional institutions amplified pre-existing exclusionary politics and reinforced local-based power centers. Furthermore, the emergence of the Muslim Brotherhood party, Salafi movements and organized extremist groups reinforced an ideological cleavage that aroused the concerns of several external actors, who eventually directly participated in the disruption of the transition and the civil conflicts resulting from its collapse.

In preparation for the elections, two pivotal factors stand out. First, the electoral law prevented the establishment of strong parties that could make a positive contribution to the constitutional process. In particular, the law was designed to avoid an Islamist takeover. In doing so though, it favored candidates with strong localized ties and this exacerbated the political relevance of local configurations of power to the detriment of national interests. To secure a seat, one had to have very deep connections to a specific locality, and this favored local notables and kin ties over ideological or policy-related ones. Secondly, the regional/federalist issue re-emerged during the electoral campaign, and the days before the elections confirmed the weakness of transitional institutions and their openness to *ad hoc* solutions when threatened with force by local militias and armed groups. While this could have disappeared in the post-election phase, the weakness of the central institutions amplified the blackmailing power of militias and their political offshoots. The GNC could not gain control of the security apparatus and appointed a supporter of the federalist agenda as head of security for the eastern oil fields; however, the loss of control over the monopoly on the legitimate use of force could not be halted. After the election, it became evident that the security sector was subject to multiple influences and actors' strategies, thus leading to a heavily fragmented security apparatus. In addition to these two elements, the emergence of Islamist political representatives, both inside and outside parliament, created the conditions for external actors to interfere in Libyan domestic politics. The scenario that emerged after 2012, combined with the establishment of an IS presence in Libya in late 2014, paved the way for the legitimization of clear anti-Islamist political and military stances among Libyan leaders who wished to acquire international and regional credit. This marked the beginning of the strong positioning of external actors in Libyan policies.

Notes

1 'Liberals Claim Lead in Libyan Election'. *France24*, July 8, 2012, https://www.france24.com/en/20120708-liberals-claim-lead-libya-election-muslim-brotherhood-benghazi-tripoli.
2 'Election Results in Libya Break an Islamist Wave'. *The New York Times*, July 9, 2012, https://www.nytimes.com/2012/07/09/world/africa/libya-election-latest-results.html.
3 'Libya Election Success for Secularist Jibril's Bloc'. BBC, July 18, 2012, https://www.bbc.com/news/world-africa-18880908.
4 'Three New Ministers Named'. *Libya Herald*, December 31, 2012, https://www.libyaherald.com/2012/12/new-ministers-named-report/.
5 معركة "كرامة ليبيا".. الصراع وأطرافه, *al-Arabiya*, May 19, 2014, https://bit.ly/3H0vD75

References

AFP. 2012. 'Libya's NTC Adopts Election Law, Drops Women Quota'. *Al Arabyia News*. January 28, 2012. Available at: https://english.alarabiya.net/articles/2012%2F01%2F28%2F191161.
Anderson, Lisa. 2017. '"They Defeated us all": International Interests, Local Politics, and Contested Sovereignty in Libya'. *The Middle East Journal* 71(2): 229–247.
Baldinetti, Anna. 2010. *The Origins of the Libyan Nation: Colonial Legacy, Exile and the Emergence of a New Nation-State*. Abingdon: Routledge.

Bensaâd, Ali. 2019. 'Luttes de Pouvoir, Réseaux Transnationaux entre Configurations Territoriales dans le Fezzan, Libye'. *Maghreb, – Machrek* 240(2): 121–138.

DeVore, Marc R. 2014. 'Exploiting Anarchy: Violent Entrepreneurs and the Collapse of Libya's Post-Qadhafi Settlement'. *Mediterranean Politics* 19(3): 463–470.

Fitzgerald, Mary. 2016. 'Jihadism and its Relationship with Youth Culture and Ideology: The Case of Ansar Al-Sharia in Libya'. In Narbone, Luigi, Favier, Agnès and Collombier, Virginie (eds.), *Inside Wars: Local Dynamics of Conflicts in Syria and Libya, Middle East Directions*. Florence: European University Institute-Robert Schumann Centre for Advanced Studies, 44–48.

International Crisis Group. 2014. 'Tunisia's Borders (II): Terrorism and Regional Polarisation'. *Middle East and North Africa Briefing 41*. Tunis and Brussels.

Lacher, Wolfram. 2013. 'Fault Lines of the Revolution Political Actors, Camps and Conflicts in the New Libya'. *SWP Research Paper* 4/2013, Berlin.

Lust, Ellen and Amaney Ahmad Jamal. 2002. 'Rulers and Rules: Reassessing the Influence of Regime Type on Electoral Processes'. *Comparative Political Studies* 35(3): 337–366.

Mezran, Karim and Mohamed Eljarh. 2014. 'The Case for a New Federalism in Libya'. *Atlantic Council*, Issue Brief, December 23, 2014. Available at: https://www.atlanticcouncil.org/in-depth-research-reports/issue-brief/the-case-for-a-new-federalism-in-libya/.

Mourad, Hicham. 2021. 'Égypte: Affaiblir les islamistes en Libye'. *Confluences Méditerranée* 118(3): 65–76.

Meddeb, Hamza. 2016. 'Tribes and Militias. The Rise of Local Forces in the Tunisia-Libyan Border Region. In Narbone, Luigi, Favier, Agnès and Collombier, Virginie (eds.), *Inside Wars: Local Dynamics of Conflicts in Syria and Libya, Middle East Directions*. Florence: European University Institute-Robert Schumann Centre for Advanced Studies, 38–43.

Merone, Fabio. 2017. 'Between Social Contention and Takfirism: The Evolution of the Salafi-Jihadi Movement in Tunisia'. *Mediterranean Politics* 22(1): 71–90.

Pack, Jason and Haley Cook. 2015. 'The July 2012 Libyan Election and the Origin of Post-Qadhafi Appeasement'. *Middle East Journal* 69(2): 171–198.

Sawani, Youssef and Jason Pack. 2013. 'Libyan Constitutionality and Sovereignty Post-Qadhafi: The Islamist, Regionalist, and Amazigh Challenges. *The Journal of North African Studies* 18(4): 523–543.

Smith, Ben. 2012. 'Libya's General Assembly election 2012, SNIA/6389'. London: House of Commons Library.

United Nations Security Council. 2017. 'Letter dated 1 June 2017 from the Panel of Experts on Libya Established Pursuant to Resolution 1973 (2011) Addressed to the President of the Security Council'. S/2017/466. 1 June 2017.

United Nations Security Council. 2019. 'Letter dated 29 November 2019 from the Panel of Experts on Libya Established Pursuant to Resolution 1973 (2011) Addressed to the President of the Security Council'. S/2019/914. 9 December 2019.

Wehrey, Frederic and Emaddedin Badi. 2022. 'Flames on the Horizon?' *Carnegie Middle East Center*. January 7, 2022. Available at: https://carnegie-mec.org/diwan/86145?s=09.

PART 5

Voting behaviour

27
THE RATIONALITY OF ARAB VOTERS: WHY AND HOW PEOPLE VOTE IN NON-DEMOCRATIC REGIMES ACROSS THE MENA REGION

Valeria Resta

Introduction

Since the introduction of nominally democratic institutions as part of the process of authoritarian upgrading in the late 1990s, a rich literature has explained how elections were far from democratizing the Middle East and North Africa (MENA) region. Rather, they were aimed at consolidating unaccountable authoritarian power across the region. Much has been written trying to explain why and how nominally democratic institutions can serve to consolidate authoritarianism. For instance, we now know that elections in the MENA region have largely served to convey internal and international legitimacy, the latter fundamental – at least in the past – to obtain loans to refund internal debts and carry out economic modernization projects. Elections helped in dividing and co-opting opposition, solving conflicts within the ruling coalition, and ensuring dictators' seemingly credible commitment to power-sharing agreements with it (Gandhi and Lust-Okar 2009; Heydemann 2007; Khiari and Lamloum 1999; Sadiki 2009; Schedler 2006). Yet, little is known about the perspective of citizens in the MENA region. A first set of questions has to do with the very act of voting on the part of citizens living under competitive authoritarianism. Why should they go to the polls and cast their vote if elections are aimed at consolidating incumbents' power? Why should MENA citizens lend themselves to this farce? A second set of question has to do with how individuals in the MENA region cast their vote. What is the rationale guiding their choice? Why do people continue to cast their votes for the ruling party or its affiliates? What is the link between individuals and political parties?

These questions are of paramount importance to fully grasp individual-related micro-level mechanisms of authoritarian resilience and breakdown. After all, elections can be called, but can nonetheless be ignored by the people, if they are convinced that they are only aimed at sustaining a despotic status quo. From this perspective, in fact, the widespread understanding according to which voters cast their vote out of duty to do so (that is when voting is compulsory) or for fear of retaliation in case of defection falls short in explaining how the threat of violence managed to be so effective in presenting to the world a spectacle of elections for so long. Similarly, the overwhelming role of patronage and vote-buying used to account for voters' choice at the ballot box no longer chime with the complexity of party politics in the region.

This chapter aims to account for the increasing complexity of party politics in the MENA region, which cannot but be sustained by voters. Building on a rational choice reading and on the emerging literature on electoral behavior in the MENA region, this chapter discusses the main determinants of voting behavior in the MENA. Building on a rational choice model, the chapter investigates why MENA citizens show up to the polls when called to do so and how they cast their vote in different types of electoral contests. In so doing, it will emerge that Arab voters are as rational as their Western counterparts when it comes to turning out and that they are also rational when it comes to picking a preference, because they use their vote to maximize their expected payoff.

The paradox of voting: a rational choice perspective

For rational choice theory, voters are deemed to be rational inasmuch as they use their vote instrumentally to maximize their expected payoff (Aldrich 1993; Blais 2000; Fisher 2004). From this, given individuals' preferences, not all vote choices are equally rewarding. Also, the very act of heading to the polls on election day, even though it is a low-cost/low-benefit choice, might not always be worthwhile. According to the basic model (Downs 1957):

$$R = PB - C > 0$$

individuals are better off turning out if the expected utility of voting outweighs the costs of so doing.

The expected utility (R) is the result of the expected benefits deriving from voting for one's preferred candidate (B) multiplied by the probability that that outcome will eventually happen (P) – or, put differently, by the probability that one's vote will actually make a difference – minus the costs of voting (C). These costs are related to getting prepared for voting, for example registering to vote and gathering information about the candidates (Converse 2000; Highton 2004), and to the very act of voting on the election day, like wasting time going to the polling station (Niemi 1976). Even though these costs are rather small, the main implication of this formulation is that for individuals abstention would be the most rational choice because the probability that one's vote would make a difference to the expected outcome is *close to* zero in most cases. This is true in established democracies, whence this literature has been produced, and it is even truer for competitive authoritarianism elections, which are rigged in order to rule out the possibility of significant political change. Yet, people do vote in both settings and this constitutes, at least from a purely rational choice perspective, the 'paradox of voting', which is even more paradoxical in electoral autocracies where P is, by definition, *equal to* 0.

In trying to account for this apparent paradox, several contributions have been put forward by either changing the perspective from which turnout is approached or by adding some elements to the basic equation. New approaches to turnout have relied on the minimal regret model and game theoretic accounts. Building on the assumption that voting occurs amidst uncertainty, the minimax regret model conceives turnout decision as ruled by individuals' pursuit of minimal regret in the worst-case scenario (Ferejohn and Fiorina 1974). While this model predicts higher levels of turnout if compared to the basic formulation, it has been set aside in light of theoretical and empirical flows. Theoretically, the calculus of probability of the different case scenarios it leaves to individuals seems untenable, as it is the belief that elections will be decided by exactly one vote. Empirically, the model is not able to explain the strategic vote or the different levels of turnout depending on the closeness of the election. Game theoretic models, for their part, depart from the non-strategic assumption of the basic model, for which the level of turnout is just the aggregated decision of individuals regardless of others' decisions, and conceive individuals' turnout decision as one influenced by what others do (Ledyard 1984; Palfrey and Rosenthal 1985). In other words, P, i.e. the probability of affecting the outcome of the election through one's own vote, is now endogenous to the model and is given by others' turnout decisions. If everybody votes, then one's vote will only have a small impact on the final outcome (P close to zero, as it emerges from the basic formulation) and abstention will be the rational choice, but if only a few people vote, then turning out is a rewarding choice. The assumption behind such reasoning is that one's decision occurs in situations of perfect information, that is that each individual knows exactly the preferences (and hence the final decision) of the other potential voters, which is – again – unrealistic, especially when large audiences are considered. Because of this, the model might work well with very small electorates but when shifting to larger ones the assumption of perfect information is not tenable and the probability of affecting the final outcome (P) approaches zero, again making abstention the most rational choice (Aldrich 1993; Mueller 2003).

Returning to the basic formulation, another set of contributions aims at integrating it with the 'missing element' able to account for why people turn out. If people do not vote in light of their belief in affecting the electoral outcome, what can explain it? Some students have pointed to how the role of information might increase the value of the B term. This is because the better informed an individual is, the greater the awareness that their choice will be a good one (Matsusaka 1995).Yet, while this line of reasoning is apt at explaining different levels of turnout across voters, the question of why people vote remains unanswered since the P value (which is always close to 0) nullifies B (Geys 2006).

A more fruitful avenue of research had already been traced by Down's introduction of a D term to the equation, whereby D represents the value of seeing democracy continue (Downs 1957), for which the basic model of turning out becomes

$$R = PB + D - C$$

With the passing of time, the D term expanded its meaning and ended up denoting the 'expressive' components of the vote. This stands for the value of voting itself, regardless of its outcome. It can stand for citizens' willingness to legitimize the elections, and thus consolidating and reinforcing democracy, as per Downs' formulation, but it can also be a means of voicing one's own evaluation about the political status quo, or to just act in accordance with one's own ethics and moral persuasions. The problem of such 'consumption voting' (Fiorina 1976) by which citizens consume voting for its own sake, is the risk of making rational choice models tautological inasmuch as D adds nothing to their explanatory power. The theoretical challenge is then that of making D endogenous to the model, or as Aldrich (1993: 258) states: 'if the answer to the question "Why did you vote?" is that "I voted because I wanted to", then it moves the theoretically important question back to one step to "Why did you want to vote?"'

For a more recent body of scholarship, D is determined by the role of learning from one election to another (Fowler 2015). Drawing on the concept of bounded rationality, for which learning proceeds along a win-stay/lose-shift strategy, learning models link the decision to turn out for an upcoming election not to the expected outcome of the election but to the actions and the outcomes of past elections (Kanazawa 2000). In this sense, one's willingness to vote is given by individuals' rewards and punishments from past elections. In a slightly different acceptation, the D term can also be conceived as a result of group involvement (Grossman and Helpman 2001). For individuals embedded in a group, turning out is rational in order 'to build a reputation of trustworthiness towards other group members' (Geys 2006: 24) or because of the benefits expected, which are larger for groups than individuals, as the impact that groups have on the election outcome is larger when compared to that of one individual. As Geys observes (2006), group models are theoretically sound in that they are apt at explaining high-level voter turnout against the odds of the basic formulation. In addition, they can also cover a broad range of empirics, like the positive impact of group identity on turnout; stylized facts like individual-level predisposition to turn out based on their socio-economic characteristics; and also different levels of turnout depending on the order of the election and strategic vote. An asset of group models–like formulations is that they have something to say about strategic politicians and turnout, a point Aldrich had already raised when he stated that 'strategic politicians will invest more heavily in the closest contests, and this investment will be reflected in increasing levels of turnout, even if voters do not consider the closeness of the contests' (Aldrich 1993: 268). The active involvement of politicians in altering the P value (the probability of the outcome to happen) along with the B parameter (the desirability of one electoral outcome over the other) has found broad support in empirical studies. Strategic politicians can thus play on the construction of strong group identity and/or use pork barrel politics to reward their voters, which will be a strong incentive to turn out (Boubekeur 2016; Catalinac et al. 2020; Gao 2016).

Turning out in the Arab world

As for the Arab region, it is hard to believe that learning models can be applied to explain turnout, given that the vast majority of elections regularly produce victories for the incumbent party and its ruling coalition. In fact, from a purely theoretical point of view, the main conundrum in accounting for the turnout in the Arab world lies in the fact not only that P is equal to zero (as is virtually the case for all consolidated democracies), but also that B approaches zero, in that elections are aimed at producing victories for the incumbents and therefore have a predetermined outcome.

In acknowledging this, the act of voting across the region is often explained with reference to vote-buying and patronage politics. However, this kind of explanation falls short in accounting for lively and complex party systems and does not take into account the point that only a tiny minority of Arab voters can accede to such benefits. In a recent study on seven Arab countries between 2006 and 2009, de Miguel et al. (2015) noted that patronage is strong among high-income individuals, especially when government *wasta* is involved, 'presumably because these individuals are better connected to the state and thus stand to gain substantially from trading their electoral support' (de Miguel et al. 2015: 1377). From such a perspective, the B term is not understood as a policy outcome, as in the basic model, but for the personal benefits deriving from patronage.

A more policy-based understanding of the B term is offered in those accounts linking the decision to vote to expected policy outcomes. From this perspective, Masoud (2014) has, for instance, shown that Egyptians turned out and voted for the party because of their policy preferences over the economic programming in the founding elections of 2011/2012. Yet, Masoud's take is that such a perception was not driven by actual congruence between voters' preference and parties' policy positions, but by individuals' exposure to parties' propaganda. In sum, the more a given party was able to get to the voters, the more likely those voters were to vote for the party, regardless of the party's closeness to their policy preferences. The great merit of this account is that of highlighting the effects of the unevenness of the opportunity structure available to parties in the elections as a result of previous electoral authoritarianism (Masoud 2014;

Resta 2018) and of speaking to the widespread incongruence between voters' policy preferences and their final vote choice across the region due to low levels of party system institutionalization (Çarkoğlu, Krouwel, and Yıldırım 2018). Moreover, it also has the merit of linking the B term to the role of strategic politicians, as Aldrich (1993) suggested. By exploiting an extremely volatile electorate, they can thus mobilize potential voters by playing on different levels, depending on the circumstances. Strategic politicians can, for instance, invest different amounts of resources depending on the closeness of the electoral race (or by altering the perception of closeness), so they can mobilize their voters not only by promising personal benefits and policy outcomes but also by acting on the 'expressive vote' embodied by the D term.

In fact, an important body of literature emphasizes the importance of the networks of kinship, the role of strategic politicians and the expressive valence of the vote even in the MENA region. Confirming the theory of group models, in a study of voting behavior within the Arab community in Israel, Ben-Bassat and Dahan (2010) find an inverted U-shaped relationship between group size and voter turnout, meaning that voters belonging to a group find it rational to vote if they are expected to make a difference – and are therefore unlikely to vote if their group is too small to impact the final outcome or if their group is so big that they do not see their vote as decisive. However, another reading has stressed how, in such contexts, turnout can be read under individuals' belief that the other groups constitute a threat to their own or when the survival of their group is at stake (Zeedan 2018). In these contexts, the role of strategic politicians is that of fomenting group identity discourse to mobilize their following. This might occur when group identities are instrumentalized for the sake of power maintenance (Brumberg 2013), as was, for instance, the case when secularly legitimated incumbent dictators called on their constituencies to vote to counterbalance the Islamist threat, but it has also been observed within recent populist trends (Ben Salem 2021). Another, yet different conceptualization of the D term that nonetheless remains within the boundaries of group identity is that of horizontal voting, usually associated with preferences for Islamist parties. In fact, quite in contradiction with the modernization theory (Inglehart and Welzel 2005; Norris and Inglehart 2011), it has been observed that the middle class is more likely to vote for an Islamist party out of identity and cultural concerns (Pellicer and Wegner 2014). The salience of such issues is further corroborated by subsequent studies aimed at explaining the voting behavior of the Arab electorate (Resta 2022; Wegner and Cavatorta 2018).go

The D term has also been understood in terms of retrospective evaluation, meaning that, beyond their desire to vote to express their group membership, Arab voters turn out because of their willingness to voice their views over regimes' performances. This means that Arab voters turn out to voice not only their dissatisfaction with the regime's conduct but also to endorse it. As for this latter acceptation, de Miguel et al. (2015) found that turnout is correlated with individuals' positive evaluation of the regime's economic policies. Rephrasing Downs, it might then be the case that Arab voters vote when they want a positive economic trend to continue. At the same time, higher levels of turnout are also associated with increasing support for opposition parties, first and foremost the Islamist ones. In this sense, in addition to identity and cultural concerns, the act of voting is also seen as a means to express discontent with a regime's conduct (Frantz 2018). Understanding the D term as voters' retrospective evaluation is in line with one of the many instrumental uses ruling parties across the region make of the elections. Even though competitive authoritarian elections are not deemed to provoke radical political change – even if, in some cases, this might occur as the 2011 Justice and Development Party (PJD)-led government in Morocco testifies – they nonetheless provide information to the incumbents in order to calibrate policy concessions (Miller 2014), thus somewhat resembling what elections are deemed to do in their pure and original acceptation.

From this perspective, the turnout in the Tunisian elections from 2011 onward seems to assume a punitive valence. In the 2011 founding elections, turnout was around 49% and marked by difficulties for citizens to register. Turnout went up to 67.7% for the 2014 legislative elections only to go down to 41.7% in 2019. The unprecedented rate of Tunisians willing to cast their vote in 2014 was accompanied by a net loss for the incumbent parties, first and foremost the Islamist *Ennahda*, and the overwhelming victory of the *Nida Tounes* party, which was created after the 2011 elections with the declared aim to rally all the secular forces to curb the power of the Islamists. In contrast with this narrative, the overwhelming 2011 and 2016 victories of the Justice and Development Party, the main opposition party in Morocco, do not correlate with higher levels of turnout. In the same way, the 2005 Egyptian election, which saw victory for the Muslim Brotherhood, is also among those with the lowest level of turnout (28.1%), notwithstanding the provision of compulsory voting.[1] In this sense, a first rough differentiation can be made between electoral authoritarianism and consolidating democracies in the region. While the former turnout is accompanied by citizens' belief of having a real alternative to the status quo (as it was *Nida* in 2014), in electoral authoritarianism the data confirm the hypothesis of expressive voting with retrospective positive evaluations about regimes' conduct, meaning that Arab voters in non-free contexts are more likely to vote to support the regime when they have reasons to do so than to vote to express dissatisfaction with the status quo.

Patterns of voting behavior across the Arab region
Voting in first-order elections

Even though conceptually different, practically speaking the decision to turn out is necessarily entangled with the decision for whom to vote. Far from the conventional wisdom, which portrays elections in the MENA region as a gigantic sham for showing off consensus around the leader, even in electoral autocracies voting assumes an instrumental valence for the maximization of voters' payoff.

In this regard, a great number of studies have dealt with the determinants of the vote choice for either the ruling party or its main opposition, namely Islamist parties. The former is usually associated with patronage voting and, only partially, with identity-driven concerns. As for the latter reading, individuals vote for the incumbent party if they perceive it as the guarantor of their group's survival (Brumberg 2002; Lust 2011). This is the case, for instance, when individuals living under 'secular' regimes vote for the incumbent parties to prevent an Islamist takeover. However, for the majority of the literature, it is clear that voters cast their choice for the ruling party because of material benefits. This is pretty much in line with de Miguel et al.'s findings that turnout in a number of MENA countries is correlated with the voters benefiting from *wasta*, which implies access to such benefits and is therefore more likely to involve the upper classes. Another strand of the literature though argues that voting for the ruling party is associated with the poorer strata of society. In this sense, the strongholds of the ruling party are deprived areas where low-income and illiterate voters live (Blaydes 2006). This is because vote-buying is deemed to be cheaper and notables associated with the ruling party and the regime have the means to pay for such votes.

Intriguingly, the poor strata of MENA societies are often also portrayed as the main constituencies for the competitor of the ruling parties, the Islamists. Scholars have provided several explanations for why this would be the case. For those adhering to the modernization theory, low-income and poorly educated voters are more likely to be seduced by religious rhetoric and appeals, insofar as they are not yet 'disenchanted' with religion. The same classes are deemed to be a key constituency for Islamist parties because, out of their state of necessity, they are the first beneficiaries of the services that charitable religious associations linked to Islamist parties provide (Masoud 2014). In this regard, Islamist parties are deemed to build their popularity from their reputation for providing a sort of welfare their voters would like to see the state deliver (Clark 2004; White 2012). Another reading argues that the poor support Islamist parties due to 'grievance voting' (Pellicer et al. 2020). Far from voting because of their pious convictions or for the services received, poor voters left at the margins of state-led programs of economic modernization, and in some case exploited by it, support Islamists' economic proposals and their rhetoric of emancipation from the crony capitalism sustaining the ruling elite across the region (Van Hamme et al. 2014; Merone 2015). Grievance voting also entails that Islamists find supporters among well-educated individuals who did not manage to find an appropriate place in society in terms of work opportunities because of the dysfunctional economic paradigm adopted in many post-populist regimes (Pellicer and Wegner 2015). In addition to the socio-economic determinants of the Islamist vote, its identity-driven component has been acknowledged. This is what has been called the horizontal vote, meaning that many individuals from the middle and upper classes, and hence well integrated within the economic structure, also choose to vote for Islamist parties because they want to distance themselves from the regime and, in particular, from its imposed secular identity (Pellicer and Wegner 2015).

With the exclusion of the 'modernization' hypothesis, which indeed has found little support in empirical evidence, it is then quite evident that the support for Islamist parties comes from their oppositional stances to the regime and cross-cuts across voters' socio-economic conditions for a variety of reasons. This is because, Islamists, and in particular the moderate political wing of the Muslim Brotherhood, have managed to monopolize the protest vote. Evidence of the socio/economic miscellaneous composition of the electorate for Islamist parties has recently appeared. Studies aimed at detecting the individual determinants of the religious divide that emerged after the 2011 uprisings have found that these are confined to denominational elements that have to do with the role of religion in the public sphere and the role of women in society, often mediated by individuals' embeddedness in religious networks (Masoud 2014; Wegner and Cavatorta 2018; Resta 2022).

Last but not least, departing from the contrapositions between ruling vs. Islamist parties, numerous contributions have demonstrated how religious and tribal affiliations are good predictors of voting in a great number of countries. The role of denominational elements in the decision to vote is greater in the context of societies divided along identity lines – religious, tribal or ethnic (Ben-Bassat and Dahan 2010; Corstange 2018; Freer 2019; Zeedan 2018). Yet, this is again the result of the divide-and-rule strategies employed by the ruling elites to maintain their grip on power (Brumberg 2002; Resta 2021; Salloukh et al. 2015).

Voting in second-order elections

What has been said thus far about the behavior of Arab voters when casting their electoral choice derives from the observation of first-order elections, namely legislative and, to a limited extent, presidential elections. In fact, much of what concerns these kinds of electoral contests does not apply to second-order elections. Differently from the first-order elections which have an impact on who governs the country, second-order elections determine the outcome for lesser offices, such as regional, municipal and local councils, and are therefore considered of less importance (Norris and Reif 1997; Reif and Schmitt 1980). According to the literature developed in consolidated democracies, the turnout for second-order elections is usually lower and the role of national parties might be somewhat scaled down, with different – and sometimes non-partisan – actors having the lion share instead. Moreover, when local elections occur at a different time from the parliamentary or presidential elections, they are also used to signal approval of or disappointment with the governing party or parties (Norris and Reif 1997).

Even though the literature on voting in second-order elections in the MENA region is scarce, the available data confirm these trends. To begin with, turnout for local elections is lower than the turnout registered in parliamentary and presidential elections. Further, the role of national political parties is reduced. This is because different determinants come into play for local elections. For instance, individuals might prefer a candidate who is recognized as capable of enacting a series of initiatives for the local population, even if they do not hold the same ideological outlook or political views. This attitude can even lead voters to prefer women candidates as they are perceived to be less corruptible (Benstead and Lust 2018). In a similar vein, individuals might prefer to vote for somebody they personally know in order to have access to information and social services (Benstead 2019). Pushing this argument further, the choice may fall on the candidate who can guarantee material benefits in exchange for one's vote (Blaydes 2010). Moreover, as per group theories hypotheses, at a local level one is more likely to vote for kinship-led considerations. Yet, the Lebanese case shows that the opposite is also true, in that local elections can be seen as a unique opportunity to forge a new civic culture breaking away from sectarianism and other denominational identities (Deets 2018).

Yet, besides these individual considerations, the reasons why national parties give way to other actors in second-order elections have also to do with differences at the system level that have recently emerged. In local elections in predominant party(ies) electoral authoritarianisms, ruling parties are overshadowed by the role of individual candidates, who are generally notables affiliated with the regime and who use elections to build or consolidate – depending on the case – a patronage network to increase their influence which, in turn, augments their power position within the ruling elite (Lust 2009; Vollmann et al. 2020). However, the consolidating democracy of Tunisia sees a different trend. From the data received thus far, the 2018 local elections saw the rollback of the parties that had a prominent role in the process of democratic transition from authoritarianism and the concomitant blossoming of a myriad of independent and non-partisan lists. For instance, the party *Nida Tounes* that won the 2014 parliamentary elections with more than 37% of the vote and managed to have its leader elected in the presidential elections, gained only 20% of the vote in the 2018 local elections, thereby controlling only 76 of 350 local councils. In this way, local elections in the Arab region are beginning to resemble second-order elections in consolidated democracies when it comes to their power to punish or reward the national government and the national party system. Looking back, it emerges how local elections not only in Tunisia but also in the MENA region – one can think, for instance, of the 1990 Algerian local elections – should no longer be disregarded for the predictive insights they can provide about national politics.

Conclusion

From the perspective of rational choice theory, voting in Arab electoral competitive authoritarian systems is as (ir)rational as voting in Western consolidated democracies. This is because in both cases, the probability that one's vote will actually make a difference to the final outcome is close to zero, regardless of the fact that in consolidated democracies this is a consequence of the size of the electorate while in electoral authoritarianism this is due to a system deliberately designed to prevent any change in the status quo. Yet, of course, the vast majority of Arab voters do not have the same incentives to turn out as their counterparts living in democratic settings. In fact, Arab voters living in autocracies are more likely to turn out when they want to express their support for the regime. This is because they have learned to use elections as a signaling game toward the regime. And they do so in the best possible way for their safety – avoid voicing their discontent, but mark their satisfaction with economic conditions. Only in the newly democratic Tunisia is the trend reversed with higher levels of turnout associated with the victory of the challenging party.

Equally rational is the vote choice. The possibility of provoking regime change through elections is ruled out from the start, but Arab voters have nonetheless learnt to use their vote instrumentally to maximize their payoffs. This is because Arab voters, as anyone else around the world, cast their vote to make their life better. Depending on their socioeconomic conditions, their embeddedness in social networks or simply their political orientation (even though the latter might be driven by the former), their vote choice is aimed at either materially improving their living conditions or satisfying immaterial needs, as the horizontal vote testifies.

Far from being a long-deemed apathetic public, Arab citizens have constantly demonstrated that they are willing to participate in public life and to have a say in the future of their country. However, the problem lies in the structures of opportunity available to them that are purposely aimed at preventing competition and inclusion, which are the two basic dimensions of a democratic polity. Against this backdrop, political learning has induced voters living under electoral authoritarianism to take advantage of the electoral moment. However, 'voting by the rules' reinforces these kinds of regimes inasmuch as elections are deemed to sustain them, which is why in the last decades the democratization-through-elections hypothesis has been discarded. Yet, it remains to be seen what the repercussions are of such political learning on the new democracies of the region, when and where they might emerge.

Note

1 Source: IDEA dataset.

References

Aldrich, John H. 1993. 'Rational Choice and Turnout'. *American Journal of Political Science* 37(1): 246–278.

Ben-Bassat, Avi, and Momi Dahan. 2010. 'Social Identity and Voting Behavior'. *Public Choice* 151(1): 193–214.

Ben Salem, Maryam. 2021. 'The Delegitimation of Political Parties in Democratic Tunisia'. In Francesco Cavatorta, Lise Storm, and Valeria Resta (eds.), *Routledge Handbook on Political Parties in the Middle East and North Africa*. London: Routledge, 165–178.

Benstead, Lindsay J. 2019. 'Do Female Local Councilors Improve Women's Representation?' *The Journal of the Middle East and Africa* 10(2): 95–119.

Benstead, Lindsay J., and Ellen Lust. 2018. 'Why Do Some Voters Prefer Female Candidates? The Role of Perceived Incorruptibility in Arab Elections'. In Helena Stensöta, and Lena Wängnerud (eds.), *Gender and Corruption: Historical Roots and New Avenues for Research*. London: Palgrave Macmillan, 83–104.

Blaydes, Lisa. 2006. "*Who votes in authoritarian elections and why? Determinants of voter turnout in contemporary Egypt*" Annual Meeting of the American Political Science Association. Philadelphia, PA, August.

Blaydes, Lisa. 2010. *Elections and Distributive Politics in Mubarak's Egypt*. Cambridge: Cambridge University Press.

Boubekeur, Amel. 2016. 'Islamists, Secularists and Old Regime Elites in Tunisia: Bargained Competition'. *Mediterranean Politics* 21(1): 1–21.

Blais, André. 2000. *To Vote or Not to Vote?: The Merits and Limits of Rational Choice Theory*. Pittsburgh: University of Pittsburgh Press.

Brumberg, Daniel. 2002. 'The Trap of Liberalized Autocracy'. *Journal of Democracy* 13(4): 56–68.

Brumberg, Daniel. 2013. 'Transforming the Arab World's Protection-Racket Politics'. *Journal of Democracy* 24(3): 88–103.

Çarkoğlu, Ali, André Krouwel, and Kerem Yıldırım. 2018. 'Party Competition in the Middle East: Spatial Competition in the Post-Arab Spring Era'. *British Journal of Middle Eastern Studies* 46(3): 440–463. https://doi.org/10.1080/13530194.2018.1424620.

Catalinac, Amy, Bruce Bueno de Mesquita, and Alastair Smith. 2020. 'A Tournament Theory of Pork Barrel Politics: The Case of Japan'. *Comparative Polityical Studies* 53(10–11): 1619–1655.

Clark, Janine. 2004. *Islam, Charity, and Activism: Middle-Class Networks and Social Welfare in Egypt, Jordan, and Yemen*. Bloomington, IN: Indiana University Press.

Converse, Philip E. 2000. 'Assessing the Capacity of Mass Electorates'. *Annual Review of Political Science* 3(1): 331–353. www.annualreviews.org.

Corstange, Daniel. 2018. 'Kinship, Partisanship, and Patronage in Arab Elections'. *Electoral Studies* 52: 58–72.

de Miguel, Carolina, Amaney A. Jamal, and Mark Tessler. 2015. 'Elections in the Arab World'. *Comparative Political Studies* 48(11): 1355–1388.

Deets, Stephen. 2018. 'Consociationalism, Clientelism, and Local Politics in Beirut: Between Civic and Sectarian Identities'. *Nationalism and Ethnic Politics* 24(2): 133–157.

Downs, Anthony. 1957. *An Economic Theory of Democracy*. New York: Harper and Brothers.

Ferejohn, John A., and Morris P. Fiorina. 1974. 'The Paradox of Not Voting: A Decision Theoretic Analysis*'. *American Political Science Review* 68(2): 525–536. https://www.cambridge.org/core/journals/american-political-science-review/article/abs/paradox-of-not-voting-a-decision-theoretic-analysis/0F89DD7019DEC0A1D8B0F4F33CB69CBE.

Fiorina, Morris P. 1976. 'The Voting Decision: Instrumental and Expressive Aspects'. *The Journal of Politics* 38(2): 390–413. https://www.journals.uchicago.edu/doi/10.2307/2129541.

Fisher, Stephen D. 2004. 'Definition and Measurement of Tactical Voting: The Role of Rational Choice'. *British Journal of Political Science* 34(1): 152–166. https://www.cambridge.org/core/journals/british-journal-of-political-science/article/abs/definition-and-measurement-of-tactical-voting-the-role-of-rational-choice/A961F83E7E2FDCB97A670817EEF0A733.

Fowler, James H. 2015. 'Habitual Voting and Behavioral Turnout'. *The Journal of Politics* 68(2): 335–44. https://doi.org/10.1111/j.1468-2508.2006.00410.x.

Frantz, Erica. 2018. 'Voter Turnout and Opposition Performance in Competitive Authoritarian Elections'. *Electoral Studies* 54: 218–225.

Freer, Courtney. 2019. 'Clients or Challengers?: Tribal Constituents in Kuwait, Qatar, and the UAE'. *British Journal of Middle Eastern Studies* 48(2): 271–290.

Gandhi, Jennifer, and Ellen Lust-Okar. 2009. 'Elections Under Authoritarianism'. *Annual Review of Political Science* 12(1): 403–422.

Gao, Eleanor. 2016. 'Tribal Mobilization, Fragmented Groups, and Public Goods Provision in Jordan'. *Comparative Political Studies* 49(10): 1372–1403.

Geys, Benny. 2006. 'Rational Theories of Voter Turnout: A Review'. *Political Studies Review* 4(1): 16–35.

Grossman, Gene M., and Elhanan Helpman. 2001. *Special Interest Politics*. Cambridge, MA: MIT Press.

Heydemann, Steven. 2007. *Upgrading Authoritarianism in the Arab World*. Washington, DC: The Saban Center for Middle East Policy at the Brooking Institution.

Highton, Benjamin. 2004. 'Voter Registration and Turnout in the United States'. *Perspectives on Politics* 2(3): 507–515. https://www.cambridge.org/core/journals/perspectives-on-politics/article/abs/voter-registration-and-turnout-in-the-united-states/B923E70DBA76C8A0B23C1E6A243AD674.

Inglehart, Ronald, and Christian Welzel. 2005. *Modernization, Cultural Change, and Democracy: The Human Development Sequence*. Cambridge: Cambridge University Press.

Kanazawa, S. 2000. 'A New Solution to the Collective Action Problem: The Paradox of Voter Turnout'. *American Sociological Review* 65(3): 433–442.

Khiari, Sadri, and Olfa Lamloum. 1999. 'Tunsie: Des élections en trompe-l'œil'. *Politique africaine* 76(4): 106–115.

Ledyard, John O. 1984. 'The Pure Theory of Large Two-Candidate Elections'. *Public Choice* 44(1): 7–41. https://link.springer.com/article/10.1007/BF00124816.

Lust, Ellen. 2009. 'Competitive Clientelism in the Middle East'. *Journal of Democracy* 20(3): 122–135.

Lust, Ellen. 2011. 'Missing the Third Wave: Islam, Institutions, and Democracy in the Middle East'. *Studies in Comparative International Development* 46(2): 163–190.

Masoud, Tarek. 2014. *Counting Islam: Religion, Class and Elections in Egypt*. New York: Cambridge University Press.

Matsusaka, John G. 1995. 'Explaining Voter Turnout Patterns: An Information Theory'. *Public Choice* 84(1): 91–117. https://link.springer.com/article/10.1007/BF01047803.

Merone, Fabio. 2015. 'Enduring Class Struggle in Tunisia: The Fight for Identity beyond Political Islam'. *British Journal of Middle Eastern Studies* 42(1): 74–87.

Miller, Michael K. 2014. 'Elections, Information, and Policy Responsiveness in Autocratic Regimes'. *Comparative Political Studies* 48(6): 691–727.

Mueller, D. C. 2003. *Public Choice III*. Cambridge, MA: Cambridge University Press.

Niemi, Richard G. 1976. 'Costs of Voting and Nonvoting'. *Public Choice* 27: 115–119. https://www.jstor.org/stable/30022903#metadata_info_tab_contents.

Norris, Pippa, and Ronald Inglehart. 2011. *Sacred and Secular: Religion and Politics Worldwide*. Cambridge: Cambridge University Press.

Norris, Pippa, and Karlheinz Reif. 1997. 'Second-Order Elections'. *European Journal of Political Research* 31(1): 109–124.

Palfrey, Thomas R., and Howard Rosenthal. 1985. 'Voter Participation and Strategic Uncertainty'. *American Political Science Review* 79(1): 62–78. https://www.cambridge.org/core/journals/american-political-science-review/article/abs/voter-participation-and-strategic-uncertainty/BDB260823206A1247AA66E73E67B84EA.

Pellicer, Miquel, Ragui Assaad, Caroline Krafft, and Colette Salemi. 2020. 'Grievances or Skills? The Effect of Education on Youth Political Participation in Egypt and Tunisia'. *International Political Science Review* 43(2): 191–208.

Pellicer, Miquel, and Eva Wegner. 2014. 'Socio-economic Voter Profile and Motives for Islamist Support in Morocco'. *Party Politics* 20(1): 116–133.

Pellicer, Miquel, and Eva Wegner. 2015. *Who Votes for Islamist Parties – And Why?* GIGA Focus. Available at: https://www.files.ethz.ch/isn/189975/gf_international_1501.pdf.

Reif, Karlheinz, and Hermann Schmitt. 1980. 'Nine Second-Order National Elections - A Conceptual Framework for the Analysis of European Election Results'. *European Journal of Political Research* 8(1): 3–44.

Resta, Valeria. 2018. 'Leftist Parties in the Arab Region before and after the Arab Uprisings: Unrequited Love?' In Francesco Cavatorta, and Lise Storm (eds.), *Political Parties in the Arab World: Continuity and Change*. Edinburgh: Edinburgh University Press, 23–48.

Resta, Valeria. 2021. 'The Terminal: Political Parties and Identity Issues in the Arab World'. In Francesco Cavatorta, Lise Storm, and Valeria Resta (eds.), *Routledge Handbook on Political Parties in the Middle East and North Africa*. London: Routledge, 331–343.

Resta, Valeria. 2022. 'The "Myth of Moderation" Following the Arab Uprisings: Polarization in Tunisia and Egypt's Founding Elections'. https://doi.org/10.1080/13530194.2021.2023353.

Sadiki, Larbi. 2009. *Rethinking Arab Democratization: Elections without Democracy*. Oxford: Oxford University Press.

Salloukh, Bassel, Rabie Barakat, Jinan Al Habbal, Lara Khattab, and Shoghig MIkaelian. 2015. *The Politics of Sectarianism in Postwar Lebanon*. London: Pluto Press.

Schedler, Andreas. 2006. *Electoral Authoritarianism: The Dynamics of Unfree Competition*. Boulder, CO: Lynne Rienner Publishers.

Van Hamme, Gilles, Alia Gana, and Ben Rebbah Maher. 2014. 'Social and Socio-territorial Electoral Base of Political Parties in Post-revolutionary Tunisia'. *The Journal of North African Studies* 19(5): 751–769.

Vollmann, Erik, Miriam Bohn, Roland Sturm, and Thomas Demmelhuber. 2020. 'Decentralisation as Authoritarian Upgrading? Evidence from Jordan and Morocco'. *The Journal of North African Studies* 27(2): 1–32.

Wegner, Eva, and Francesco Cavatorta. 2018. "Revisiting the Islamist–Secular Divide: Parties and Voters in the Arab World." *International Political Science Review* 40(5): 558–575.

White, Jenny B. 2012. *Islamist Politics in the Middle East: Movements and Change*. London: Routledge.

Zeedan, Rami. 2018. 'Predicting the Vote in Kinship-Based Municipal Elections: The Case of Arab Cities in Israel'. *Journal of Muslim Minority Affairs* 38(1): 87–102.

28
CLIENTELISM IN MENA ELECTIONS

Miquel Pellicer and Eva Wegner

Introduction

Middle East and North Africa (MENA) elections are often described as clientelistic affairs and void of programmatic appeals. Because elections in many countries are either uncompetitive (e.g. Egypt under Mubarak and again under al-Sisi or Tunisia pre-transition) or have no bearing on core policymaking (e.g. Morocco or Jordan), parties are organizationally weak and few invest in party manifestoes or concrete policy proposals (Gandhi and Lust-Okar 2009; Lust-Okar 2006). As Lust-Okar (2006: 459) argues 'in authoritarian elections, the distribution of state resources trumps by far any role of elections as arenas for contests over the executive or critical policies'. In this context, it makes sense for voters to demand clientelistic benefits – both individual and collective – in return for their vote.

Indeed, there is a general sense that politics in the Middle East and North Africa is essentially clientelistic. Beyond the autocratic setting, two factors contribute to this perception. First, the so-called Arab social contract (El-Haddad 2020), in which MENA post-independence regimes exchanged public sector jobs, education, and healthcare for political acquiescence and loyalty from their citizens, is a clientelist bargain in nature. Second, many studies document the pervasive role of mediation/connections (*wasta*) to access jobs and services (Benstead et al. 2019; Harris et al. 2017).

As a result, much work on the region mentions clientelism and patronage. It is then surprising that actual research on clientelism in MENA *elections* is much rarer than in other world regions such as Latin America and South-East Asia.[1] Instead, most MENA work mentioning clientelism either studies phenomena that are not in line with the generally accepted definition of political clientelism as the exchange of particularistic benefits for *political* support (Stokes 2007b; Kincaid et al. forthcoming; Pellicer et al. 2020) or focuses on clientelism at the elite level, emphasizing the role of 'patronage networks' (Ruiz de Elvira et al. 2018; Heydemann 2004).[2] As a result, these types of study cannot shed much light on how much clientelism matters for voter mobilization and support in electoral contests.

Research that explicitly addresses political clientelism in the context of MENA *elections* mostly focuses on Turkey (Güneş-Ayata 1994; Yıldırım 2020). Outside Turkey, it is limited to a few contributions such as the work by Lust (2009) Lust-Okar (2006) on competitive clientelism in Jordan; Blaydes (2006) and Corstange on vote-buying (2016 and 2012) in Egypt, Lebanon, and Yemen; or Pellicer and Wegner (2013) on electoral rules and clientelism in Morocco. In addition, several findings on clientelism in elections emerge from studies where it is not the core focus. For example, some studies describe how clientelistic goods are exchanged or at least requested during electoral campaigns (Shehata 2008), or discuss clientelism in the context of charity organizations run by Islamist movements (Clark 2004) or of voting behaviour more generally (Pellicer and Wegner 2014; Wegner and Cavatorta 2019).

So how much of a role does clientelism really play in MENA elections? What forms does it take and what do citizens think about it? This chapter seeks to address these questions by drawing on existing expert and opinion surveys as well as on our own project on the 'Demand Side of Clientelism' in Tunisia.

How much clientelism is there in MENA electoral politics?

The extent and types of clientelism

Recent research on clientelism has settled on a set of core types of clientelism that differ in the kinds of goods that are exchanged, the relationship between patrons and clients, as well as in the trade-offs they imply for citizens (Pellicer et al. 2020). In *vote-buying*, votes are exchanged for money and small gifts during electoral campaigns or on election day. In *relational clientelism*, citizens exchange different forms of political support (voting, campaigning, attending rallies) with politicians for access to social policy benefits (e.g. public work programmes) and general assistance in more iterative exchanges during and outside electoral campaigns. In *collective clientelism*, citizens exchange a block of votes for local public goods, in exchanges that are typically brokered by a community leader.

Four recent datasets shed some light on the prevalence of these types of clientelism in the MENA. Table 28.1 lists the datasets, the types of clientelism, and the countries included in the survey. What all the datasets have in common is that they target the *supply side* of clientelism, that is, they ask about party investment in clientelism and clientelistic offers to citizens. The Varieties of Democracy (V-DEM) dataset is the most extensive survey and includes 15 MENA countries (Coppedge et al. 2021). It is also the only survey that includes two variables on clientelism, one about vote-buying and one about the type of party linkages, differentiating programmatic linkages from collective clientelism and particularistic clientelism (akin to relational forms). The other three surveys include smaller – and only partially overlapping – sets of countries and focus on one type of clientelism only: vote-buying in the Afrobarometer (Afrobarometer Round 6)

Table 28.1 Data on clientelism in the MENA

Dataset	Country name	Variables	Type of survey
V-Dem	Algeria, Bahrain, Egypt, Iran, Iraq, Israel, Jordan, Kuwait, Lebanon, Libya, Morocco, Oman, Syria, Turkey, Yemen	Vote-buying and type of party linkages (programmatic, collective clientelism, relational clientelism)	Expert
DALP 2008	Morocco, Egypt, Israel, Lebanon	Clientelistic effort of parties	Expert
Afrobarometer R6	Morocco, Algeria, Tunisia, Egypt	Offers of vote-buying	Public opinion
Electoral integrity	Morocco, Iran, Kuwait, Syria, Jordan, Algeria	Extent of bribes in latest elections	Expert

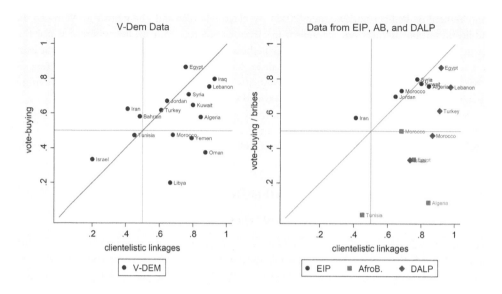

Figure 28.1 Clientelistic linkages and vote-buying in the MENA. Source: Author

and the Electoral Integrity Project (EIP) (Norris and Grömping 2019), and party linkages in the Democratic Accountability and Linkages Project (DALP). Importantly, three of these surveys are expert surveys, which implies that they might reflect not only local knowledge about clientelism but also established perceptions of politics in the MENA as clientelist.

Figure 28.1 plots the prevalence of vote-buying with the extent of clientelistic party–voter linkages from these different surveys. The left panel shows the V-Dem data only, whereas the right panel plots the data from the other surveys.[3] The left panel reveals several interesting insights about the level and nature of clientelism in the MENA. First, most of the countries are in the top right quadrant, which suggests that electoral politics in the MENA is indeed highly clientelistic. Second, parties tend to be below the 45-degree line, which indicates that the nature of clientelism in the MENA is more tilted in the direction of collective and relational strategies rather than vote-buying. Third, there is no obvious pattern in the data: countries with particularly high levels of clientelism include more and less competitive systems as well as monarchies and republics. We will return to this issue below.

The right panel generally confirms these basic insights. However, it also suggests some important limitations. First, a few countries change their position in the plot. For example, the EIP data considers vote-buying in Morocco to be far more pervasive, whereas the DALP data considers that linkages in Israel and Turkey are substantially more clientelistic than V-Dem. Second, according to Afrobarometer, the only one of these datasets that is not based on experts, there is considerably less vote-buying than according to the expert surveys.[4] These differences are, of course, partly the result of different types of measurements in the surveys, but they also highlight that measuring the extent of clientelism is generally difficult. This implies that we should not give too much weight to specific differences between countries but focus on the overall picture. This overall picture shows that first, there is quite a lot of clientelism in MENA elections and second, it is less geared toward vote-buying and more toward collective or relational forms.

Figure 28.2 further investigates if there is a relationship between the degree of polyarchy and the prevalence of vote-buying and clientelistic linkages in MENA countries. The left panel plots

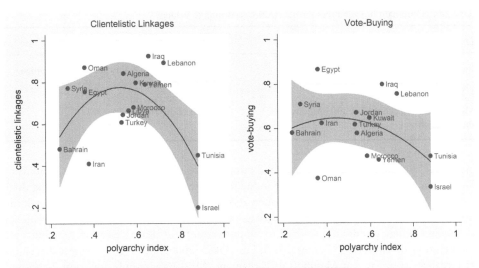

Figure 28.2 Polyarchy and clientelism in the MENA. Source: Author

polyarchy and clientelistic linkages and polyarchy and vote-buying. For clientelistic linkages, the data shows an inverted U-pattern, suggesting that at low and high levels of polyarchy, we tend to see less clientelism whereas the most clientelistic activity from parties exists at intermediate levels of polyarchy (by MENA standards) in countries such as Algeria, Kuwait, Jordan, and Morocco.[5] For vote-buying, there does not seem to be much of a relationship, with the possible exception that the most democratic countries in the region, Israel and Tunisia, tend to experience less vote-buying than others.

In both panels, the confidence interval is large as there are few observations and the findings should be treated with caution. Nevertheless, it is interesting to note that the findings for clientelistic linkages are in line with the general literature on corruption, which shows that an inverted U-shaped relationship exists between democracy and corruption (McMann et al. 2017). Similarly, one can argue that clientelism makes little sense when elections are rigged to an extent that investing in clientelism has few returns; it becomes more appealing as elections become more transparent, and again less when elections are free and fair.[6]

The nature of party linkages in the MENA

V-Dem and DALP allow a closer look at the nature of party linkages in the MENA. V-Dem provides an ordinal ranking of strategies, differentiating between programmatic linkages, collective clientelism, and individual clientelistic strategies, whereas DALP provides more information about the type of voters targeted by clientelistic offers.

Table 28.2 shows the V-DEM ordinal ranking of strategies. This information suggests that the most common way in which parties link with voters in the MENA is by promising local public goods (such as schools, clinics, and paved roads and footpaths) to areas where supporters live (collective clientelism) or by helping individual voters in exchange for support (individual clientelism).

Shehata's (2008) and Lust-Okar's (2006) work illustrates how collective and individual clientelism function in the MENA. Shehata describes a parliamentary campaign in Egypt focus-

Table 28.2 Dominant linkage types in the MENA according to V-Dem

Linkage type	Countries
Individual and collective clientelism	Algeria, Egypt, Iraq, Kuwait, Lebanon, Oman, Syria, Yemen
Collective clientelism	Jordan, Morocco, Libya
Mixed collective clientelism and programmatic	Bahrain, Iran, Tunisia, Turkey
Programmatic	Israel

ing on the appeals made in neighbourhood campaign meetings. In these meetings, candidates focused on the number of jobs they had found for people from the constituency during their last term in office as well as the local public goods brought to the districts, including education centers and trash removal. Individual goods provision had clear features of relational clientelism, where goods are provided to supporters not just during election time but over the duration of the term (Nichter 2018). Lust-Okar (2006) shows that a core expectation of Jordanian voters is that Members of Parliament (MPs) provide jobs for constituents and generally help them access state resources. To be able to help with this, voters expect MPs to have good relations with the government, rather than criticising it or attempting to hold it accountable for programmatic goods. Lust-Okar and Shehata's work also shows that rather than politicians targeting voters with clientelistic goods, it is the voters themselves who demand such services and threaten not to vote for MPs who do not deliver on particularistic goods, pushing MPs into what Nichter and Peress (2017) describe in Latin America as 'request fulfilling'.

Table 28.3 shows who, according to DALP experts, is targeted by clientelism in the MENA. One of the core findings of the literature on clientelism is that it is mostly targeted at poor voters (Stokes et al. 2013). These patterns broadly appear in the MENA data. The rich are the least likely to be targeted by clientelistic offers compared to the middle class, which, in turn, is less likely to be targeted compared to the poor.

What is particularly interesting about the nature of clientelism is the specific pattern it takes in the MENA. In the MENA, the big drop in targeting is not between the poor and the middle class, as observed in Latin America (Brusco et al. 2004; Stokes 2005) and Sub-Saharan Africa (Jensen and Justesen 2014), but between the middle class and the rich, insofar as the poor and the middle class are almost equally targeted with offers of clientelism. This suggests that the nature of electoral clientelism in the MENA is distinctive, as it appears to involve better-off socio-economic groups than in other world regions.[7]

Clientelism and elections in Tunisia

In the context of our research project on the 'Demand Side of Clientelism', we conducted several surveys in Tunisia. Different from the data presented so far that focuses on the supply side of clientelism in MENA elections, our project looks at citizens' perspectives on clientelism. We present some insights from two surveys, one that taps into the demand for clientelism alongside other attitudinal aspects, and a second that looks at moral evaluations of clientelism. Both surveys were conducted in 2019 (the first in February, the second in November and December).[8] Both targeted mostly poor rural and urban communities in Tunisia. We draw on findings from this project to explore the following three questions: (1) How much demand is there for different forms of clientelism in Tunisia? (2) What are the social norms around different forms of clientelism? (3) How does clientelism relate to support for democracy and trust?

Table 28.3 Targeting of different types of voters according to DALP

Country	Poor	Middle	Rich
Egypt	0.7	0.5	0.2
Israel	0.6	0.6	0.3
Lebanon	0.8	0.7	0.5
Morocco	0.7	0.6	0.4
Turkey	0.5	0.4	0.2

Demand for clientelism and the role of social norms

We begin by presenting the demand for three forms of clientelism from the 2019 survey, as described above: vote-buying, relational clientelism, and collective clientelism. The questions were asked as hypothetical questions. For each type, the respondents were presented with a scenario where the terms of the exchange were spelt out: 70 TD in exchange for your vote (vote-buying), help when you need it in exchange for campaigning for the candidate (relational clientelism), and local public goods in exchange for a block of votes (collective clientelism). After each scenario, the respondent was asked how likely they were to vote for the candidate proposing the respective deal on a scale from 1 to 10. Table 28.4 shows the share of respondents who indicated a likelihood above 5 of voting for the candidate.[9] In addition, we asked respondents if they have experienced such a form of clientelism.

The results show a clear ranking in demand, with about a quarter of respondents expressing demand for collective clientelism, 12% for relational clientelism, and only 5% for vote-buying. These differences are mirrored by the forms of clientelism that respondents indicated having experienced in the past and by a behavioural measure of clientelism included in the survey. The numbers for demand and experience shown in Table 28.4 are probably lower than in reality given that respondents might be reluctant to indicate demand or admit to experiences of clientelism. However, they do indicate that preferences for clientelism have a clear hierarchy, where there is more demand for exchanges with more valuable goods whereas outright vote selling is less appealing or indeed offered. They also suggest that demand for clientelism might be higher than actual offers by politicians and parties.

Our survey also included an open text question asking about the exact nature of the goods that were offered when respondents indicated that they had experienced a particular form of clientelism. For vote-buying, the typical offer was between 20 and 70 TD; for relational clientelism, politicians tended to offer jobs or help with housing improvements; and for collective clientelism, the most common goods were streetlights and roads, housing, and jobs for the community.

Overall, these findings echo the findings of Lust and Shehata for Egypt and Jordan, where jobs and community infrastructure were also the most sought-after goods. At the same time, the results also suggest that clientelism is less dominant in Tunisia than in other countries, a finding that matches those of the Afrobarometer and V-Dem. The needs of people are likely to be important drivers of these preferences. Clearly, in a middle-income country with little extreme poverty such as Tunisia, small handouts at election time are not considered valuable by most people. In contrast, promises of individual or community-level jobs and improvements are much more attractive.

Additionally, research suggests that moral evaluations of clientelism matter for its attractiveness (Gonzalez Ocantos et al. 2014; Mares and Young 2019; Pellicer and Wegner 2021). When citizens find clientelism morally acceptable, no stigma is attached to engaging in a form of clientelism and vice-versa. In our work, we find that the different types of clien-

Table 28.4 Demand for different types of clientelism in Tunisia

	Hypothetical demand (%)	Experienced (%)	Behavioral (%)
Vote-buying	5.0	3.6	9.3
Relational clientelism	12.7	8.1	–
Collective clientelism	26.5	22.7	26.7

Source: Data from the 'Demand Side of Clientelism' Project.

telism do indeed carry different forms of social stigma in Tunisia. Tunisians evaluate vote-buying most unfavourably by far and collective clientelism most positively (Pellicer and Wegner 2021). Vote-buying is clearly perceived to be unacceptable (a value of 3 on a scale from 1 to 10, where 10 is 'totally acceptable' and 1 is 'totally unacceptable'), whereas collective clientelism is borderline acceptable. In an open text follow-up on why an exchange was evaluated as unacceptable, almost 50% of the time the depicted exchange was said to be an abuse of citizens, 20% that it was corruption, and around 15% that it showed opportunistic behaviour by politicians. This suggests that citizens who are critical of clientelism partly feel that it violates the dignity of voters and partly that it was operating in a grey zone, suggesting illegal practices and self-interested politicians.

Overall, these findings suggest that there is a high stigma and little admitted demand for individual forms of clientelism (vote-buying and relational) relative to collective forms.

Demand for clientelism and demand for democracy

Clientelism is generally perceived to be undemocratic. As Stokes (2007a) shows, clientelism violates several important principles of democracy, such as equality of the vote. Clientelism erodes political accountability and the influence of poorer voters, as they give up political rights in exchange for access to benefits. These features might have consequences for attitudes toward democracy. Kitschelt and Wilkinson (2007) note that, at the country level, absence of programmatic party competition is associated with cynical and disenchanted attitudes toward democratic institutions. Such a mechanism is problematic as clientelism erodes demand for democracy, which in turn, allows clientelism and, in the case of the MENA, authoritarianism to persist.

Our survey contains standard indicators from the Barometer series about trust in politicians and support for democracy.[10] Investigating how they relate to demand for different types of clientelism yields some interesting results.

Table 28.5 shows ordinary least square (OLS) regressions of demand for different forms of clientelism on the two different measures of support for democracy (one measures willingness to give up democracy for service delivery and the second measures that the type of regime does not matter to the respondent) and trust in politicians. In line with the findings reported by Kitschelt and Wilkinson (2007) at the country level, individual demand for clientelism is associated with less support for democracy. Respondents who are more willing to give up democracy for service delivery or believe that the kind of government does not matter tend to have a higher demand for clientelism. This is strongest for relational clientelism, a type of clientelism that involves repeated interactions between patrons and clients that extend beyond electoral campaigns.

At the same time, trust in politicians appears to be positively related to demand for clientelism, especially demand for relational clientelism and potentially collective clientelism.[11] This

Table 28.5 Support for democracy, trust, and demand for clientelism

	(1) Demand relational CL	(2) Demand relational CL	(3) Demand collective CL	(4) Demand collective CL	(5) Demand VB CL	(6) Demand VB CL
Give up democracy for service delivery	0.791***		0.690***		0.317**	
	(0.164)		(0.203)		(0.116)	
Kind of regime does not matter to me		0.562**		0.231		0.249*
		(0.175)		(0.220)		(0.123)
Trust in politicians	0.486**	0.510**	0.361	0.369	0.142	0.135
	(0.188)	(0.190)	(0.232)	(0.238)	(0.133)	(0.134)
Observations	1155	1121	1155	1121	1155	1121

Standard errors are in parentheses. Controls: education and gender.
*$p < 0.05$; ** $p < 0.01$; ***$p < 0.001$.
VB=Vote-buying ; CL=Clientelism.

implies that those with higher demand for particularistic goods feel that politicians are more reliable than those who are not willing to engage in clientelistic exchanges.

These findings suggest that, in the MENA, demanding clientelism is potentially incompatible with demand for democracy – instead, citizens make the system work for them through clientelism. Citizens who feel positive about clientelism also feel positive about the politicians who deliver it to them. This suggests a circle where autocratic politicians deliver goods in exchange for support and are appreciated by citizens for this service. Demand for democracy and demand for clientelism seem to be antagonistic in the MENA.

Future research: how does clientelism work in the MENA?

The data presented in this chapter confirms the generally held view that politics in the MENA is mostly clientelistic. Electoral appeals appear to be made with either collective or individual clientelistic offers in most countries, especially in those at intermediate levels of electoral competition.

What remains an open question are the mechanisms of clientelism in elections. Whereas much focus is on elite-level patronage networks or the role of *wasta*, we know much less about how clientelism works at the citizen and party level. The expert surveys presented in this chapter might be partly driven by commonly held views that clientelism is ubiquitous in the MENA, without offering specific empirical details that would allow us to know who does what, how, and why. This impression is, for example, suggested by answers to a question in the DALP that asks the experts which goods MENA parties use when targeting voters. The possible goods are consumer goods, jobs, access to social policies, preferential access to government contracts, or lax 'interpretation' of regulations. DALP MENA experts answer that parties use all these goods *in equal measure* for generating political support. This is highly unlikely. The first three types of goods are goods that are valuable to ordinary citizens, whereas the other types are relevant to companies or entrepreneurs. Likewise, the latter type of goods is only accessible to parties in government. This suggests that experts might communicate a general impression that all these goods are used 'a great deal' without making (or being able to make) a distinction and report on nuances.

This does not mean that the experts are necessarily wrong. However, it does suggest that how clientelism in elections works in practice in the MENA remains, to some extent, an open question that has not been satisfactorily answered. We believe that there are two potential ways of addressing this issue. The first is to use better methods for estimating the prevalence of and preferences for clientelism in the MENA in surveys. One option is list experiments that allow truthful answers to sensitive questions to be measured. This method has been successfully used by Corstange (2010) to measure the prevalence of vote-buying in Lebanon. One problem with this method is that it is difficult to use to measure more complex forms of clientelism such as relational (with repeated interactions) or collective (involving a community-level exchange) clientelism. Another option that we pursued in our project is to develop a behavioural measure of preferences for different types of clientelism. We offered respondents money at the end of the survey and asked them to make a choice between selling us their vote in the survey or putting the money toward a charity in the community (collective clientelism) or a charity at the province level (programmatic voting). While this method does not capture the prevalence of clientelism, it allows us to measure demand more accurately, irrespective of supply. In addition, conjoint experiments can help address how demand and evaluations depend on varying features of clientelism.

The second approach to learn more about the nature and mechanisms of clientelism would be ethnographic research. Although there is a lot of good qualitative work on MENA politics, much of it engages with elites; for example, the work on Islamist parties by Schwedler (2006), Wegner (2011), and Wickham (2002). In contrast, for our meta-analysis of ethnographic work on clientelism from the client's perspective, we were unable to find suitable work on the MENA whereas there was an oversupply for countries in other world regions, such as Argentina and Indonesia (Pellicer et al. 2020). Work such as Auyero's (1999, 2000) on Argentina, Gay's (1999) on Brazil, or Arghiros's (2001) on Thailand would be extremely useful to move away from the standard wisdom on clientelism in the MENA to a more sound empirical base.

Notes

1 For Latin America, see Nichter and Peress (2017), Nichter and Nunnari (2019), or Stokes et al. (2013); for South-East Asia, see Berenschot (2018), Berenschot and Aspinall (2020), or Aspinall and Sukmajati (2016), among many others.
2 For example, *wasta* does not imply that there is an exchange of jobs and services for *political* support as in clientelism in the same way as clientelism is distinct from gaining access to jobs and services through bribe-paying.
3 Because the other surveys only have either vote-buying (Afrobarometer, Electoral Integrity Project) or linkages (DALP), the right panel uses the DALP variables to add the respective missing information in order to plot the data in the two-dimensional space (e.g. the Afrobarometer has only a vote-buying variable, so the graph uses the V-Dem linkage information for the country to supply an x-coordinate).
4 The numbers in the graph show the share of respondents who indicated offers divided by the turnout in the election preceding the survey. We use this measure to account for the fact that brokers typically target likely voters with offers (Szwarcberg 2015; Brusco et al. 2004). These lower levels of clientelism according to the Afrobarometer might at least partly result from social desirability bias which might be rather high in the MENA. In a list experiment in Lebanon, Corstange (2010) finds that twice as many people admit to vote-selling when asked with a list experiment, compared to asked directly.

5 The polyarchy index ranges from 0 (full absence of polyarchy) to 1 (full presence of polyarchy). Empirically, MENA countries' degree of polyarchy ranges mostly between 0.3. and 0.7. Intermediate levels of polyarchy in the MENA are thus around 0.5 of the index.
6 The finding that Israel has the lowest extent of clientelism also fits with Keefer (2007) and Keefer and Vlaicu (2008) who argue that longer experience with democratic elections increases the credibility of policy promises and thereby decreases the appeal of clientelism for politicians and voters.
7 This matches with Corstange's (2012) findings on Lebanon. He also observes that better-off groups are targeted with offers of vote-buying.
8 Both surveys use face-to-face interviews and data entry on tablets. We designed the surveys to be representative of the respective locality. We assigned enumerators a starting point in an enumeration area who then selected households with a random walk. The enumerators selected individual respondents in the household with a Kish grid. For the first survey, the sample size is only 300 respondents in each country, but as each respondent evaluated six exchanges, our data contains around 1900 evaluations of clientelism by country. The sample size of the second survey was 1200 respondents in Tunisia.
9 The answers to these questions are very polarized with most respondents indicating either a 1 (not at all likely) or 10 (extremely likely) so that looking at the shares of 10 (relative to 1) does not change the picture significantly (4.4 for vote-buying, 9.7 for collective, and 21% for relational).
10 For democracy we use two questions: First, 'If a non-elected government or leader could impose law and order, and deliver houses and jobs, how willing or unwilling would you be to give up regular elections and live under such a government?'. Second, we ask which of three statements is closest to the respondents' own opinion: (A) Democracy is preferable to any other kind of government. (B) In some circumstances, a non-democratic government can be preferable. (C) For someone like me, it doesn't matter what kind of government we have. The first question measures the trade-off between democracy and the delivery of goods whereas the third statement in the second question measures disinterest in the political system. For trust, we use agreement with the statement 'Generally speaking, most politicians can be trusted'.
11 We find a similar result in the survey on moral evaluations of clientelism where trust in politicians is strongly associated with finding clientelistic exchanges more acceptable (Pellicer and Wegner 2021).

References

Afrobarometer. 'Round 6. "Morocco, Algeria, Tunisia, Egypt"'. Available at: http://www.afrobarometer.org.
Arghiros, Daniel. 2001. *Democracy, Development and Decentralization in Provincial Thailand*. Richmond: Curzon.
Aspinall, Edward, and Mada Sukmajati, eds. 2016. *Electoral Dynamics in Indonesia: Money Politics, Patronage and Clientelism at the Grassroots*. Singapore: NUS Press.
Auyero, Javier. 1999. 'From the client's point (s) of view: How poor people perceive and evaluate political clientelism'. *Theory and Society* 28(2): 297–334.
Auyero, Javier. 2000. 'The logic of clientelism in Argentina: An ethnographic account'. *Latin American Research Review* 35(3): 55–81.
Benstead, Lindsay J., Lonna Rae Atkeson, and Muhammad Adnan Shahid. 2019. 'Does wasta undermine support for democracy?' In Ina Kubbe and Aiysha Varraich (eds.), *Corruption and Informal Practices in the Middle East and North Africa*. New York: Routledge, pp. 77–99.
Berenschot, Ward. 2018. 'The political economy of clientelism: A comparative study of Indonesia's patronage democracy'. *Comparative Political Studies* 51(12): 1563–93.
Berenschot, Ward, and Edward Aspinall. 2020. 'How clientelism varies: Comparing patronage democracies'. *Democratization* 27(1): 1–19.
Blaydes, Lisa. 2006. Who votes in authoritarian elections and why? Determinants of voter turnout in contemporary Egypt. Presented at the Annual Meeting of the American Political Science Association. Philadelphia, PA, August.
Brusco, Valeria, Marcelo Nazareno, and Susan Stokes. 2004. 'Vote buying in Argentina'. *Latin American Research Review* 39(2): 66–88.
Clark, Janine. 2004. 'Social movement theory and patron-clientelism: Islamic social institutions and the middle class in Egypt, Jordan, and Yemen'. *Comparative Political Studies* 37(8): 941–68.
Coppedge, Michael, John Gerring, Carl Henrik Knutsen, Staffan I. Lindberg, Jan Teorell, Nazifa Alizada, David Altman, Michael Bernhard, Agnes Cornell, M. Steven Fish, Lisa Gastaldi, Haakon Gjerløw,

Adam Glynn, Allen Hicken, Garry Hindle, Nina Ilchenko, Joshua Krusell, Anna Luhrmann, Seraphine F. Maerz, Kyle L. Marquardt, Kelly McMann, Valeriya Mechkova, Juraj Medzihorsky, Pamela Paxton, Daniel Pemstein, Josefine Pernes, Johannes von Römer, Brigitte Seim, Rachel Sigman, Svend-Erik Skaaning, Jeffrey Staton, Aksel Sundström, Ei-tan Tzelgov, Yi-ting Wang, Tore Wig, Steven Wilson, and Daniel Ziblatt. 2021. "V-Dem [Country–Year/Country–Date] dataset v11.1". ed.V. o. D. Project.

Corstange, Daniel. 2010. 'Vote buying under competition and monopsony: Evidence from a list experiment in Lebanon'. Paper presented at APSA. Available at: https://citeseerx.ist.psu.edu/viewdoc/download?doi=10.1.1.175.2531&rep=rep1&type=pdf.

Corstange, Daniel. 2012. 'Vote trafficking in Lebanon'. *International Journal of Middle East Studies* 44(3): 483–505.

Corstange, Daniel. 2016. *The Price of a Vote in the Middle East: Clientelism and Communal Politics in Lebanon and Yemen*. Cambridge: Cambridge University Press.

El-Haddad, Amirah. 2020. 'Redefining the social contract in the wake of the Arab Spring: The experiences of Egypt, Morocco and Tunisia'. *World Development* 127: 104774. Available at: https://www.sciencedirect.com/science/article/pii/S0305750X19304231.

Gandhi, Jennifer, and Ellen Lust-Okar. 2009. 'Elections under authoritarianism'. *Annual Review of Political Science* 12(1): 403–22.

Gay, Robert. 1999. 'The broker and the thief: A parable (reflections on popular politics in Brazil)'. *Luso-Brazilian Review* 36(1): 49–70.

Gonzalez Ocantos, Ezequiel, Chad Kiewiet de Jonge, and David W. Nickerson. 2014. 'The conditionality of vote-buying norms: Experimental evidence from Latin America'. *American Journal of Political Science* 58(1): 197–211.

Güneş-Ayata, Ayşe 1994. 'Roots and trends of clientelism in Turkey'. In Luis Roniger and Ayşe Güneş-Ayata (eds.), *Democracy, Clientelism, and Civil Society*. London: Lynne Rienner Publishers, pp. 49–64.

Harris, Adam, Kristen Kao, Ellen Lust, Jens Ewald, and Petter Holmgren. 2017. 'Governance and service delivery in the Middle East and North Africa'. *Program on Governance and Local Development Working Paper* (10). Available at: https://openknowledge.worldbank.org/bitstream/handle/10986/26201/112976-WP-PUBLIC-WDR17BPGovernanceinServiceDelivery.pdf?sequence=1&isAllowed=y.

Heydemann, Steven. 2004. *Networks of Privilege in the Middle East: The Politics of Economic Reform Revisited*. London: Palgrave.

Jensen, Peter Sandholt, and Mogens K. Justesen. 2014. 'Poverty and vote buying: Survey-based evidence from Africa'. *Electoral Studies* 33: 220–32.

Keefer, Philip. 2007. 'Clientelism, credibility, and the policy choices of young democracies'. *American Journal of Political Science* 51(4): 804–21.

Keefer, Philip, and Razvan Vlaicu. 2008. 'Democracy, credibility, and clientelism'. *Journal of Law, Economics, and Organization* 24(2): 371–406.

Kincaid, Harold, Miquel Pellicer, and Eva Wegner. forthcoming. 'Philosophy of science issues in clientelism research'. In Harold Kincaid and Jeroen Van Bouwel (eds.), *Oxford Handbook of the Philosophy of Political Science*. Oxford: Oxford University Press. Available at: https://global.oup.com/academic/product/the-oxford-handbook-of-philosophy-of-political-science-9780197519806?cc=us&lang=en#.

Kitschelt, Herbert, and Steven Wilkinson. 2007. 'A research agenda for the study of citizen-politician linkages and democratic accountability'. In Herbert Kitschelt and Steven Wilkinson (eds.), *Patrons, Clients, and Policies: Patterns of Democratic Accountability and Political Competition*. Cambridge: Cambridge University Press, pp. 1–49.

Lust, Ellen. 2009. 'Competitive clientelism in the Middle East'. *Journal of Democracy* 20(3): 122–35.

Lust-Okar, Ellen. 2006. 'Elections under authoritarianism: Preliminary lessons from Jordan'. *Democratization* 13(3): 456–71.

Mares, Isabela, and Lauren Young. 2019. *Conditionality and Coercion: Electoral Clientelism in Eastern Europe*. Oxford: Oxford University Press.

McMann, Kelly M., Brigitte Seim, Jan Teorell, and Staffan I. Lindberg. 2017. 'Democracy and corruption: A global time-series analysis with V-Dem data'. *V-Dem Working Paper* 43.

Nichter, Simeon. 2018. *Votes for Survival: Relational Clientelism in Latin America*. New York: Cambridge University Press.

Nichter, Simeon, and Salvatore Nunnari. 2019. 'Declared support and clientelism'. *CEPR Discussion Paper* January (DP13460). Available at: https://papers.ssrn.com/sol3/papers.cfm?abstract_id=3319779.

Nichter, Simeon, and Michael Peress. 2017. 'Request fulfilling: When citizens demand clientelist benefits'. *Comparative Political Studies* 50(8): 1086–117.

Norris, Pippa, and Max Grömping. 2019. 'Perceptions of electoral integrity, (PEI-7.0)'. Harvard Dataverse.

Pellicer, Miquel, and Eva Wegner. 2013. 'Electoral rules and clientelistic parties: A regression discontinuity approach'. *Quarterly Journal of Political Science* 8(4): 339–71.

Pellicer, Miquel, and Eva Wegner. 2014. 'Socio-economic voter profile and motives for Islamist support in Morocco'. *Party Politics* 20(1): 116–33.

Pellicer, Miquel, and Eva Wegner. 2021. 'What is bad about clientelism? Citizen evaluations in poor communities in South Africa and Tunisia'. *Unpublished Manuscript*.

Pellicer, Miquel, Eva Wegner, Markus Bayer, and Christian Tischmeyer. 2020. 'Clientelism from the client's perspective: A meta-analysis of ethnographic literature'. *Perspectives on Politics*: 1–17. https://doi.org/10.1017/S153759272000420X.

Ruiz de Elvira, Laura, Christoph H. Schwarz, and Irene Weipert-Fenner, eds. 2018. *Clientelism and Patronage in the Middle East and North Africa: Networks of Dependency*. London and New York: Routledge.

Schwedler, Jillian. 2006. *Faith in Moderation: Islamist Parties in Jordan and Yemen*. Cambridge: Cambridge University Press.

Shehata, Samer. 2008. 'Inside Egyptian parliamentary campaigns'. In Ellen Lust-Okar and Saloua Zerhouni (eds.), *Political Participation in the Middle East*. Boulder, CO: Lynne Rienner Publishers, pp. 95–120.

Stokes, Susan. 2005. 'Perverse accountability: A formal model of machine politics with evidence from Argentina'. *American Political Science Review* 99(3): 315–25.

Stokes, Susan. 2007a. 'Is vote buying undemocratic?' In Frederic Schaffer (ed.), *Elections for Sale: The Causes and Consequences of Vote Buying*. Boulder, CO: Lynne Rienner Publishers, pp. 81–100.

Stokes, Susan. 2007b. 'Political clientelism'. In Carles Boix and Susan Stokes (eds.), *The Oxford Handbook of Comparative Politics*. Oxford: Oxford University Press, pp. 604–627.

Stokes, Susan, Thad Dunning, Marcelo Nazareno, and Valeria Brusco. 2013. *Brokers, Voters, and Clientelism: The Puzzle of Distributive Politics*. Cambridge: Cambridge University Press.

Szwarcberg, Mariela. 2015. *Mobilizing Poor Voters*. Cambridge: Cambridge University Press.

Wegner, Eva. 2011. *Islamist Opposition in Authoritarian Regimes: The Party of Justice and Development in Morocco*. Syracuse: Syracuse University Press.

Wegner, Eva, and Francesco Cavatorta. 2019. 'Revisiting the Islamist–Secular divide: Parties and voters in the Arab world'. *International Political Science Review* 40(4): 558–75.

Wickham, Carrie Rosefsky. 2002. *Mobilizing Islam: Religion, Activism, and Political Change in Egypt*. New York: Columbia University Press.

Yıldırım, Kerem. 2020. 'Clientelism and dominant incumbent parties: Party competition in an urban Turkish neighbourhood'. *Democratization* 27(1): 81–99.

29
THE CONSEQUENCES OF ARAB PARTIES' DIVIDE AND QUEST FOR POWER IN ISRAELI POLITICS ON ARAB VOTERS

Sawsan Khalife

Introduction

Israel's Arab citizens are faced with a hard task in their attempt to influence politics in Israel's parliament, the Knesset. Arab citizens of Israel have been pushing for improved citizenship status alongside advancing the Palestinian national struggle for justice for quite some time. They compose over 20% of the population in Israel and lead separate social, cultural and political lives from those of the Israeli Jewish population. They have endured systematic inequality and second-class status in Israel since its foundation in 1948 and lived under military rule until 1967. However, their citizenship allows them a voice in Israeli politics, although the Arab parties in Israel often find themselves on the margins of political decision-making processes even when they were the third largest block in the Knesset, as was the case in 2019 and 2020. This is especially true when it comes to decisions on Israeli national security issues.

This chapter examines the politics of the Arab parties in Israel in recent elections, seeking to understand how an Islamist party managed to become the first Arab party in Israel to be part of a coalition government in May 2021. Crucially, the chapter also examines the implications of this for the Palestinians and their citizenship status in Israel, as the consequences of this shift in Israeli politics might be momentous. The historic event of forming a government coalition with an Islamist party is indeed driving scholars to investigate the ways in which Arab legislators are integrated in the decision-making processes in Israel, their behavior, and the impact they can make on the political status and perceptions of Palestinian identity. The chapter begins with a background on Arab Palestinian politics in Israel. It then looks at the campaigns that Arab parties led in recent elections with a brief introduction to the establishment of the Muslim party of Ra'am, and concludes with looking at the implications of taking part in an Israeli Zionist coalition government.

Arab Palestinian party politics in Israel

Arab party politics in Israel exists within a complicated political and historical context. After Israel's victory over the land of mandatory Palestine in the 1948 war, the Palestinian population in the newly founded Israel found themselves a minority within a growing Jewish majority, and the Arab parties aimed to adjust their approach to Arab voters according to the unique, constantly changing political dynamics.

Following the 1948 war, Palestinians who remained in Israel became a national minority and were subject to repressive military rule and *de facto*, the civilian citizenship rights of the Palestinians in Israel were halted until 1967 (Shafir and Peled, 2005: 141). Shafir and Peled also argue that military rule primarily allowed the state of Israel to transfer ownership of the land from the Palestinians to the Jews, and to control Palestinian access to the job market. Aryeh Dayan (2021) also found that military rule between 1948 and 1966 aimed to prevent the return of Palestinian refugees, to limit the Palestinians from seeking employment in Jewish towns to preserve employment for newly arrived Jews (*Olem Hadashim*), and to prevent any Arab collaboration and mobilization for political, economic, or cultural aims. In essence, the Arab citizens of Israel were placed under severe conditions that limited their political and economic prospects in the country; it also prevented them from communicating with their neighboring towns in the West Bank and the Gaza Strip, where many had relatives, creating a social and political vacuum between the two sides. In addition, it aimed at isolating the Israel's Arab citizens from the regional dynamics, societies, and politics, where anti-Israeli sentiment had grown considerably. The Israel archive that was recently made public reveals that the reason military rule ended in 1966 after almost 19 years was after the state of Israel made sure that Palestinian refugees could return to their homes and towns (Burger 2019). Rouhana and Khoury (2016) mapped major points in the history of the Palestinian citizens of Israel that impacted the political demands and ambitions of the Arab population in the country. Following military rule, between the 1970s and the 1990s, the Arabs in Israel worked to achieve genuine equality with Jewish citizens without challenging Israel's Jewish Zionist identity. The aftermath of the 1993 Oslo Accords witnessed the rise of political claims to transform Israel into a democratic state for all its citizens. It was only after the Second Intifada's tragic killing of 13 Arabs in in Israel's Galilee and Triangle regions in October 2000 in October 2000 that the Arab political elite began to gradually shift the relationship between Palestinians and the state, demanding greater recognition and collective rights.

Today, Arab parties in Israel exist within a unique political and social reality. They represent a population that is unique in its own right: a national minority within a larger Jewish population, which lives in social and political separation from other Palestinians in the West Bank, and is inaccessible to the Palestinians in the Gaza Strip. They are also an estranged Arab community within the Middle East, as they have no access to most Arab and Muslim neighboring countries because they hold an Israeli passport, a document that restricts travel and is mostly unwelcome in all Arab countries except Jordan, Egypt, and more recently the United Arab Emirates.

Within Israel, Arabs compose 21.1% of the overall population, totaling 1.956 million people (Central Bureau of Statistics 2020). Arab citizens of Israel are systematically discriminated against, and continue to live in underdeveloped towns and villages, separate and unequal from the Israeli Jewish population due to a series of legal measures, from property rights to public services, that render them virtually second-class citizens. Within Israel, only eight cities are considered mixed (Hag-Yehya and Ron 2018) and even within these cities, the Arab and Jewish populations are largely segregated, separate and unequal, including their residential areas and neighborhoods, education systems, job market, and within local political representation in the municipalities (Hag-Yehya and Ron 2018).

The Arab citizens in Israel are increasingly aware of their status as non-Jewish citizens, and the implications that follow. In 2015, 38% of Arabs in Israel said they felt discriminated against by the Israeli authorities, and only 9% believed equality was fully achievable (Radai et al. 2015). The survey also found that Arab citizens showed interest in integrating into Israeli society

(Radai et al. 2015) having by now accepted their reality. Reasons for this interest in further integration can be related to the expansion of the Arab middle class in recent years and is demonstrated in increasingly loud calls to improve the status and share of resources within the existing system (Fakhouri 2021: 191).

Arab party politics

The political behavior of the Arab parties in Israel cannot be understood without accounting for local, national, and regional levels of analysis. First and foremost, party politics among Palestinians in Israel is influenced by the continuous and fluid Israeli–Palestinian conflict. The political and cultural continuity between Palestinians in Israel and Palestinians in the Territories never ceased to exist despite the territorial divide following the 1948 war and the measures in place to restrict contact, particularly with Gaza. This continuity intensifies during times when the conflict takes a violent turn, resulting in Arab citizens of Israel taking to the streets to protest against attacks on Palestinians in the Palestinian territories. Fear of increased proximity between Palestinians on both sides of the geographical divide, in turn, leads Israel at times to announce and enforce national emergency measures, as was the case in the Second Intifada 2000, and more recently during the violent events in May 2021. In fact, the actual state of emergency declared in 1948 for a mere few days was never canceled, and the Knesset renews it every year, leading to continuous debates over its ability to legitimize security actions that violate citizens' rights, in contradiction with basic laws (Sheked and Margalit 2021).

In addition to the 'domestic' Israeli–Palestinian conflict, the politics of Arab parties is influenced by the broader regional context and the relations Israel has – or does not have – with its Arab neighbors. The peace accords with Jordan and Egypt, the 1967 war and the decline of Pan-Arabism, and more recently, the split between Hamas and Fatah, all influenced the political behavior of Arab parties in Israel (Fakhouri 2021). The Arab Spring and its regional insecurity, and the sense of abandonment by powerful Arab countries following the Abraham Accords in 2021, also drove Arab parties to consider pragmatic approaches to politics, preferring citizenship rights and citizen services over national Palestinian rights and prioritizing the conflict (Fakhouri 2021). This is a particularly important aspect, as it clearly demonstrates that Arab parties in Israel – and Arab citizens too – react to regional events. Recent developments have further pushed the Arab parties in Israel to seek further integration into Israeli institutions to secure equality. As the current situation illustrates, members of the Arab parties take seats in finance, social issues, education committees, and on international delegations, but the security and intelligence committees have always seen the exclusion of Arab parliamentarians (Barrenada 2021).

It follows that the impact of Arab parties on the conflict with the Palestinians in the Territories and with Israel's regional rivals through the Knesset remains very limited in comparison with Jewish parties. Arab parties find themselves 'alien' and distant from the Jewish consensus over state identity, and therefore from the state's approach to Palestinian demands for justice and from Israeli regional diplomacy. In short, Arab parties find themselves *de facto* incapable of influencing the conflict and are kept outside the peace processes. As mentioned though, their participation in the elections is aimed at influencing Israeli politics and improving the citizenship status of its Arab voters. However, participation in the elections does not mean that the Arab parties get their fair share of the democratic process. Rather, it takes place in a broad exclusionary structure (Barrenada 2021).

Despite the limitations, Arab voters in Israel find elections a legitimate tool for political change, and Arab parties as a result benefit from a higher turnout when political tensions are on the rise. Rudnitzky (2020) argues that turnout increases when 'intense' events in the history of Palestinians in Israel occur, such as the Land Day in 1976, and after the Oslo Accords. In both these cases, turnout was significantly high. Turnout reached 75% during the ninth Knesset elections in 1976, and 77% during the fourteenth Knesset elections in 1996. Rudnitzky argues that when Arab voters are united under one cause, they make use of elections to try to influence the balance of power between the right and left Israeli parties. Historically, Arab parties also served as a bloc for Rabin's minority coalition, and Balad (التجمع Tagamoe') founder Azmy Bishara repeatedly mentioned that Arabs should play an active role in Israeli democracy (2021 פאח'ורי). Koren also studied Palestinian-Arab political behavior following the 2008–2009 attack on Gaza and found evidence indicating that Arab voters were using Israeli elections to influence and benefit their social and political lives (Koren 2010).

Campaigns and dynamics in Israeli elections during the political crisis between 2019 and 2021

Elections in Israel are held every four years for 120 electoral seats in the Knesset under a proportional representation system. When the electoral threshold was increased and set at 3.25%, Arab parties collectively decided to form the Joint List in 2015 to ensure that the threshold would be overcome. The objective of unity was to at least ensure survival and eventually increase their influence in the Knesset. The alliance consisted of the most prominent parties that had held seats in the Knesset for years, namely Hadash (الجبهة Al Jabha), Balad (التجمع Al Tagamo'), Ta'al (العربية للتغيير Arab Movement For Renewal), and Ra'am (العربية الموحدة United Arab List).

Sweid (2017) investigated the influence and significance of the Joint List on the Arab leadership in Israel, especially given that Arab representation in the Knesset was disproportionate to the population in Israel, a mere 5%–10% of the overall seats in the parliament since the 1980s, whereas the population stood at around 20%. The results of the elections were unprecedented. The Joint List won 13 seats, obtaining 88% of the votes cast by Arab voters, and allowing them to make history and become the third largest party in the country. Sweid (2017) also mapped turnout in accordance with the different types of Arab voters and the impact of this union on their votes. The small number of Arab voters who traditionally aligned with Zionism and supported Israeli-Jewish parties dropped drastically, from 52.3% in 1992 to 16.8% in the 2015 elections. In addition, leftist Arab voters, who cast their votes for Hadash, became the most prominent party within the List in 2015, winning five seats. More nationalist voters who most likely found a home in Balad allowed the party to win three seats. Finally, the Islamists voter increased its presence to three seats as a result of the Joint List.

Despite running and winning together, the ideological differences between the Arab parties in the Joint List were significant and this applied to voters and leaders. As a result of such differences – as well as personality clashes – Arab unity within the Joint List did not survive for the April 2019 elections for the 21st Knesset. Ra'am and Balad ran separately from Hadash and Ta'al, winning ten seats combined, a three-seat drop from the 2015 elections. The turnout was relatively low, reflecting the disappointment of the Arab electorate with the political system and, crucially, with the internal divisions in the Joint List (Levi et al. 2019). Since 2019, Israel has been going through a political crisis with elected representatives unable to form a government due to unresolved internal disputes between Israeli-Jewish parties. This resulted in four elections in a two-year span: in April and September 2019, in March 2020, and more recently in March 2021.

The crisis in Israel's political system was also an opportunity to test the effectiveness of a higher turnout for Arab parties under the Joint List. For a limited time, Arab parties gained momentum and ground from the political crisis affecting the Jewish side of Israel's politics.

Following the drop in seats when the Joint List ran in two separate parties in April 2019, Arab voters pressured their Arab parties to bring back the Joint List for the September 2019 elections for the 22nd Knesset. The elections saw the Joint List winning 13 seats and an even greater accomplishment occurred in the March 2020 elections when the Joint List obtained 15 seats, the highest representation of Arab party parliamentarians parliamentarians in the history of Israel.

Barrenada (2021) examined the 2015 and 2019–2020 elections and found that when Arab parties run in a Joint List, turnout increases, and when party fragmentation occurs, many Arab voters either migrate, preferring to vote for Jewish Zionist lists, or decide to stay home, depressing the turnout. Furthermore, the ability of the Joint List to raise the Arab voter turnout, from 349,000 in 2013 to 444,000 in 2015 – an increase of 27.3 percentage points – proves that there is growing trust among Arab voters in the ability of Israeli politics to generate change (Navot et al. 2017).

This turbulent political climate though had an impact on the Joint List as well, leading to its break-up before the March 2021 elections. Unable to form a coalition due to internal ideological, religious, and economic disputes, some of the Jewish parties began to consider including Arab parties in cabinet in order to save the country millions of tax money, avoid international embarrassment, and deal with growing security risks in a hostile region. The Israeli-Jewish parties' dispute increased the tensions with the Joint List, as the different parties had opposing views on how to react to a potential offer to join a government coalition. This weakened and eventually split the Joint List. The Islamist party left the Joint List and became an 'available' potential government partner for Israeli-Jewish parties.

The Joint List thereafter came to an end. While Arab turnout was higher, and in the March 2020 elections for the 23rd Knesset it was the highest, following the departure of Ra'am from the Joint List, the turnout for the 24th Knesset in March 2021 was the lowest in two decades, at 44.6% (Rudnitzki 2021).

The divide in Arab party politics and the Islamist party of Ra'am making history

The political divide between the Arab parties was never as blunt and noticeable as during the 24th Knesset elections in March 2021. During the election campaign, the liberal and conservative streams of the Arab parties, and their respective voters, clashed and offered significantly diverging choices on social issues to undecided Arab voters. In essence, the campaign Ra'am ran and the justification for removing the party from the Joint List can be interpreted as the inevitable outcome of social and ideological diverging worldviews between the Islamist party and the rest of the non-Islamist Arab parties (Hadash, Balad, and Ta'al). Following a Palestinian businesswoman's publicized donation to the lesbian, gay, bisexual, transgender, queer, or questioning (LGBTQ) community in Israel, and the 'yes' vote of three members of parliament of the leftist party Hadash to the banning of 'gay conversion therapy', LGBTQ rights became a central topic of dispute between conservative and liberal Arab voters. Opposing stances on individual rights and freedoms partly explain the split of Ra'am from the Joint List (Fakhouri, 2021) and facilitated Ra'am's distancing from fellow Arab parties.

While the Joint List parties took more liberal approaches to social issues and aligned with the Israeli 'left bloc' in forming an opposition to Netanyahu, Ra'am instead focused on Arab citizenship status as its top concern (Navot et al. 2021) while signaling its social conservatism. Ra'am's campaign stood out for its declared intention to collaborate with Israeli right-wing parties if the opportunity arose. When the Joint List's leader, Ayman Odeh, rallied to the election cry 'anyone but Bibi' (Odeh, 2020), coined by all those who no longer wanted Netanyahu re-elected as prime minister, Mansour Abbas, Ra'am's leader, was signaled to his voters and to the other parties 'on second thought, why not Bibi?'.

Focusing on the history and policy preferences of Ra'am is important in understanding Arab parties' politics going forward. Ra'am is not only the first and only party to enter an Israeli coalition of parties that hold Zionist ideology, but its choice also reflects a fundamental divide in Arab parties' politics and can shed light on the repercussions on Arab parties' politics in Israel. Ra'am can be considered a politically courageous party willing to sacrifice the Palestinian cause for the sake of improving the status of Israel's Arab citizens. In fact, it avoided using the word 'Palestinian' during the campaign and has distanced its politics from broader Palestinian politics. The Ra'am party slogan – *realist, influential, conservative* (Bein-Levovich and Zakan 2021) – relies on the assumption that an effective approach to get political gains for Arabs in Israel should be accomplished through participation in government coalitions (Fakhouri 2021)

The campaign results were staggering for Ra'am, which won four seats, while the combined three Arab parties in the Joint List won only six. This was a drastic fall from the 15 seats won during the March 2020 elections, and a 20 percentage points drop in turnout (Navot et al. 2021). These numbers show that the Islamic party Ra'am gained electoral power at the expense of the drastic fall of the Joint List. Ra'am made the right choice in running separately from the Joint List, as it established itself as an independent party not only capable of overcoming the electoral threshold, but also relevant for Israeli national politics more broadly. In May 2021, Ra'am reached an agreement with Jewish parties and joined the Bennet–Lapid government coalition, which required a few more seats to be able to form a majority government to avoid another round of elections.

Ra'am was established as a result of several local and regional developments: the modernization and urbanization of the Muslim communities in Israel, which saw a decline in conservative traditions that the party wanted to revive; West Bank activism – *waedoun* – aiming to attract Palestinians back to Islam; (in)accessibility to holy Muslim sites; the collapse of Arab ideologies during the 1960s; the Arab defeat in 1967; the 1973 Arab victory; and the awakening of Islam. This is very much in line with developments elsewhere that saw the emergence of Islamist parties. Ase'ed (2019) argues that there are four main phases in the evolution of the Islamist party. The first is the foundational phase between 1972 and 1982, the second is the establishment phase between 1980 and 1996, and the third is the split into Northern and Southern factions in the period 1996–2015. Finally, there is the renewal phase from 2015 onwards, the same year the Northern faction was outlawed following its involvement in mobilizing demonstrations in 2015 that began outside the Al-Aqsa Mosque, and the subsequent violent events that occurred. The renewal phase is most significant in contributing to a more modern image of the party. Through volunteer work, the provision of services for the community, the establishment of advisory organizations for political branches across the country, with 25% of administrative positions going to women, and a solid representation in national elections (2019 אסעיד), the party gained credibility and support.

Ali (2018) investigated the ideology and establishment of the Ra'am party. As a fundamentalist movement that aims to create an autonomous Muslim society in Israel, it relies on the universal Islamist ideology of similar parties in the region. Its mission is to create the 'new Muslim' man who would serve the vision of the movement, and regards this as essential for the whole process – to create a new man, who would create a new community that would ultimately result in a new society (Al Anani 2016).

Even though Ra'am first ran in Israeli elections in 1996, it managed to win 100,000 more votes between the 2003 and the 2021 elections (Israeli Institute of Democracy). Ali (2018) argues that Ra'am is a success story because it faced significant challenges in establishing its new

Muslim vision, such as the low socioeconomic status of the majority of Arab towns, underdeveloped infrastructure deterring the evolution of an independent community, and the geographic divide of the Muslim population that prevents local Muslim governance. The main tools that Ra'am uses to accomplish its vision are education and community building. Palestinian identity is also used by Ra'am to attract new voters and supporters (Ali 2018: 226). As a nonviolent movement, the party makes use of democratic tools to achieve its objectives, such as educational and religious community projects (Ali 2018).

While both Balad and Hadash aimed to influence Israeli politics, Ra'am differed in that it was willing to collaborate with right-wing parties to gain such influence (Fakhouri 2021). This collaboration gained momentum when Netanyahu began flirting with Arab voters, and advancing talks with the Ra'am party (Hendrix and Rubin 2021). This is the same prime minister who made national headlines when he incited against Arab citizens by warning Jewish voters in the 2015 elections that Arabs were voting 'in droves', to motivate them to go to the polls and vote (Throor 2015). However, Netanyahu soon retreated from the possibility of collaborating with Ra'am and a short time before the elections, he announced that the Likud party would not rely on Ra'am support to form a coalition (Lys, 2021). As history would soon reveal, the Bennet–Lapid government had no qualms about going where Netanyahu did not go. They reached a coalition deal with Abbas in May 2021.

Implications for Palestinian politics in Israel

The political influence of Ra'am on the politics of Arab parties remains unclear. Zriek, (in Margalit, 2021) a political philosophy scholar, argues that Ra'am is trying to move the conversation around the conflict between Israelis and Palestinians from a dispute over history and territory to a dispute over the cultural differences between Muslims and Jews, a classic religious prism of Islamist movements. This would suggest that what matters are not the questions of national self-determination that the Palestinians in Israel have been working toward, but cultural misunderstandings (Margalit 2021), which can be solved more easily insofar as the principal enemy of many Arabs and Jews is secular liberalism. Other approaches label Ra'am leadership attempts as a stepping-stone in establishing a 'non-Zionist Israeli identity' and argue that during its campaign a broader conception of Israeli identity seemed to emerge (Navot et al. 2021). However, Ra'am's leader, Mansour Abbas, is leading a Zionist discourse. Soon after he took office, Abbas repeated the Zionist statement of a God-given birthright for the Jewish people over state power, stating that 'the State of Israel was born as a Jewish state, and the question is how we integrate Arab society into it' (Pfeffer 2021). This is a blunt departure from the political discourse of non-Zionist Arab parties.

The political impact of Ra'am entering the coalition government is not necessarily found in the Israeli political system as a whole, but in Arab parties' politics and Arab voting behavior. The exclusion of Arab parties from government coalitions over the past seven decades was a reflection of a fundamental contradiction between embracing the state of Israel as foremost a Jewish state that Jewish parties adopted, and striving for a state of equal rights and self determination of its non-Jewish citizens that the Arab parties adopted. Arab parties held on to their self-proclaimed national identity as Palestinians, and their attempts to balance power relations between Arab and Jewish populations in Israel. Ra'am's novelty is that it did not challenge the Israeli exclusionary political system. Quite the contrary, it reinforced it by disengaging from the Palestinian national struggle, and limiting the conversation to cultural disputes, and religious differences to overcome in the context of a Zionist framework. Ra'am was given a seat at the big table that lacked any political prospects for equal rights for the non-Jewish population in Israel.

Thus, it is not surprising that Ra'am succeeded in negotiating its way into a coalition government. What is surprising is that its constituencies were receptive to a campaign strategy built on disengaging from national identity issues. Historically, Arab parties have been reluctant to sacrifice the Palestinian cause because it would be unprecedented, and could lead to a collapse of Arab parties' foundations and support base. Yet, Ra'am found support among voters for its disengagement from the Palestinian cause. That the first party to be part of an Israeli coalition is an Islamist and conservative party is, however, not entirely surprising either. Israel is an increasingly theocratic state and within this framework of rejection of secular individualism and liberalism, Ra'am is at 'home'.

At the same time, Ra'am politics is setting a new and more challenging standard for the Arab parties, as its presence in government reinforces the exclusionary structure of Israeli politics. An outcome of this historic move is that Arab parties might now feel under increasing pressure to distance their political behavior from the national Palestinian struggle in order to get a seat in government. Not only do Arab parties face hostility toward their history and Palestinian national identity from the Israeli parties, but now they also need to face an Arab party's alternative political stance that marginalizes the significance of the Palestinian conflict.

The Islamist party of Ra'am is pragmatic not only in its institutional tactics, but also in its strategy toward Arab voters. It attracted voters who hold a Palestinian national identity, but who are also socially conservative and concerned with other issues, gradually testing its appeal among voters when highlighting grievances of violence and unemployment in society at the expense of the national Palestinian struggle. Ra'am is foremost an Islamist party and its political behavior in the 24th Knesset is likely to strengthen its own ambition of creating a stronger conservative Muslim society, rather than attending to the grievances of the whole of the Arab community. Ra'am is more likely to push for Islamizing the education system, for example, than providing resources for the underfunded school systems in Arab towns. Given where Israeli politics is at the moment, this strategy could pay off, although, as mentioned, it remains unclear how pragmatic or strategic Ra'am is in influencing Israeli politics as well.

At a regional level, the Islamist party of Ra'am will have bigger challenges to deal with if it adopts a strategy of disengaging from the Palestinian cause altogether and establishing a new Muslim society. Reasons for that are that, by default, it will align itself with Muslim Brotherhood parties and initiatives in the region. This can pose further challenges to its integration within Israeli political institutions. In fact, Ra'am regards itself as a 'temporary minority' Muslim community in Israel, looking to the regional Muslim majority as proof of this temporary status (Ali 2018: 202). This can place it at odds with Jewish parties in so far as removing the Palestinian national aspect might work in the short term to ensure a presence in a government coalition, but it might backfire in the long term given its attachment to an emerging Islamist identity. Eventually, Ra'am will be forced to balance its regional ideological similarities with its current pragmatic approaches in Israeli politics.

References

al-Anani, K. 2016. *Inside the Muslim Brotherhood: Religion, Identity, and Politics*. Oxford University Press. Retrieved April 10, 2022, from https://oxford-universitypressscholarship-com.ezproxy.haifa.ac.il/view/10.1093/acprof:oso/9780190279738.001.0001/acprof-9780190279738.

Ali, N. 2018. 'The Islamic party in Israel: The image of the new believer'. In Aziz Haider (ed.), *Political Aspects in the Arab Citizens of Israel*. Ra'ananah: Van Leer Institute in Jerusalem, 196–228 (In Hebrew).

Ase'ed, R. 2019. 'The Islamist Party in Israel as a supplier of social services: Socio-Historic Evolution and the Main characteristics'. *Society and Welfare*, L'T': 609–632. (In Hebrew).

Barrenada, I. 2021. '"Conventio Ad Excludendum" Palestinian Parties in Israel'. In Francesco Cavatorta, Lise Storm and Valeria Resta (eds.), *Routledge Handbook on Political Parties in the Middle East and North Africa*. Chapter 16. Oxfordshire: Routledge, pp. 205–216. ISBN: 978-0-367-21986-4.

Bein-Levovich, A., and Zakan, D. 2021. 'The campaigner of Mansour Abbas reveals the secrets: "We knew we are passing easily"'. Globes. https://www.globes.co.il/news/article.aspx?did=1001366040.

Burger, Y. 2019. 'Israel canceled its military rule only after it assured no possible return to the villages'. Available at: https://www.haaretz.co.il/news/politics/.premium-1.7257522 (In Hebrew).

Central Bureau of Statistics, State of Israel. 2020. Available at: https://www.cbs.gov.il/he/mediarelease/DocLib/2020/438/11_20_438b.pdf.

Dayan, Aryeh. 2021. *The Military Rule (1948–1966): Its Aim and the Political Opposition to Its Existence*. Haifa: University of Haifa. (In Hebrew).

Fakhouri, A. 2021. 'Arab Palestinian politics in Netanyahu era: Comparison and conflict between the politics of Odeh and the politics of Abbas'. *Theory and Critique* 54: 187–202.

Hag-Yehya, N., and O. Ron. 2018. 'Integrated but unequal: Arab residents representation in mixed cities' municipalities'. Jerusalem: Israel Democracy Institute. (in Hebrew)

Hendrix, Steve and Shira Rubin. 2021. 'In turnabout, Netanyahu courts Arab voters he once called a threat'. *The Washington Post*, 18 March. Available at: https://www.washingtonpost.com/world/middle_east/israel-election-netanyahu-arab-voters/2021/03/18/72bfe4de-85c4-11eb-be4a-24b89f616f2c_story.html.

Koren, David. 2010. 'Arab Israeli citizens in the 2009 elections: Between Israeli citizenship and Palestinian Arab identity'. *Israel Affairs* 16(1): 124–141.

Levi, A., Abu M. Mukh and M. Elran. 2019. 'The Arab society and the 21st and 22nd elections to the Knesset'. *Strategic Update* 22(2): 17–24 (In Hebrew).

Lys, E. 2021. 'The Likud: We will not form a coalition with Ra'am's support'. Haartez. https://www.haaretz.co.il/news/elections/.premium-1.9451678.

Margalit, Ruth. 2021. 'A seat at the table: Is Masour Abbas changing the system or selling out?' *The New Yorker*, 25 October. Available at: https://www.newyorker.com/magazine/2021/11/01/the-arab-israeli-power-broker-in-the-knesset.

Navot, D., R. Aviad, and A. Ghanem. 2017. 'The 2015 Israeli general election: The triumph of Jewish skepticism, the emergence of Arab faith'. *The Middle East Journal* 71(2): 248–268.

Navot, D., S. Swaid, and M. Khalaily. 2021. 'The Arabs in Israel, 2019–2021: Towards a Non-Zionist Israeli Identity?' in Shamir, M., & Rahat, G. (Eds.). (2022). The Elections in Israel, 2019–2021 (1st ed.). Routledge. https://doi.org/10.4324/9781003267911

Odeh, A. 2020. 'Twitter'. Available at: https://twitter.com/AyOdeh/status/1289622786814513152 (In Hebrew).

Pfeffer, Anshel. 2021. 'Why Israel's top political Islamist is so comfortable talking about a Jewish State'. *Haaretz*. Available online: https://www.haaretz.com/israel-news/.premium.HIGHLIGHT-why-israel-s-top-political-islamist-is-so-relaxed-talking-about-a-jewish-state-1.10490325.

Radai, A. T. M. and Y. Alerman Makledah and M. Kornberg. 2015. 'The Arab citizens in Israel: Recent trends and surveys'. *Strategic Update* 18(2): 93–108.

Rouhana, Nadim and Areej Sabbagh-Khoury. 2016. 'Palestinian citizenship in Israel: A settler colonial perspective'. In Frederick Greenspan (ed.), *Contemporary Israel: New Insights and Scholarship*. New York: New York University Press, 32–62.

Rudnitzky, Arik. 2020. *Arab Voter Turnout in Knesset Elections: The Real, the Ideal, and Hope for Change*. Jerusalem: Israel Democracy Institute.

Rudnitzki, Arik. 2021. *Arab Citizens' Voting in the 24th Knesset*, March 2021. Jerusalem: Israel Democracy Institute (In Hebrew).

Shafir, G. and Peled, Y., 2005. *Being Israeli: The dynamics of multiple citizenship*. Tel Aviv: The Tel Aviv University Press (in Hebrew). https://kotar.cet.ac.il/KotarApp/Viewer.aspx?nBookID=62321720#6.530.6.default.

Sheked, T. and L. Margalit. 2021. *On the Importance of Declaring Emergency State: The Permanent Order of Emergency in Basic Law: The Government in Light of the Covid Crisis*. Jerusalem: Israel Democracy Institute (In Hebrew).

Sweid, S. 2017. 'The influence of the Joint List on the Arab-Palestinian leadership in Israel'.

Throor, I. 2015. 'On Israeli election day, Netanyahu warns of Arabs voting "in droves"'. https://www.washingtonpost.com/news/worldviews/wp/2015/03/17/on-israeli-election-day-netanyahu-warns-of-arabs-voting-in-droves/.

30
CLASS AND RELIGIOUS CLEAVAGES: THE CASE OF LEBANON

Joseph Daher

Introduction

Sectarian parties have dominated the Lebanese parliament since the independence of the country in 1943 and after the end of the civil war in 1989, throughout the various legislative elections in 1992, 1996, 2000, 2005, 2009 and 2018.[1] Similarly, sectarian parties have controlled governments. Apart from the independent Lebanese MP Paula Yacoubian, who resigned in 2020,[2] the only self-proclaimed 'non-sectarian' parties represented in parliament and government are the Ba'th party and the Syrian Social National Party (SSNP), both allied to the Syrian regime or Hezbollah. These parties remain relatively small and have not challenged the sectarian system or promoted any class perspective, which would threaten the neoliberal economic system in the country. The implementation of neoliberal policies occurred following the end of the civil war in 1989.

The domination of sectarian parties on all levels of political representation (municipal, legislative and governmental) has pushed sections of the Lebanese population to reject electoral participation. The Lebanese parliamentary elections of 2018, nine years after the last elections in 2009, witnessed a significant diminution of voter turnout, with 49.7 per cent of registered voters casting a ballot in comparison to 54 per cent in 2009 (Sanchez 2021).[3]

Yet, over the last decade, discontent toward the rule of sectarian parties has triggered several protest movements: in early 2011, during the regional revolutionary processes, a movement called 'the people want the fall of the sectarian regime' emerged; in 2012 and 2014, poor labor conditions led to another wave of protests; and in the summer of 2015, the movement 'you stink' arose to protest against sanitation conditions, which then spilled over into a more overt critique of the political system. The latest and most significant challenge to the sectarian party system occurred in October 2019 with the outbreak of a vast protest movement which differed from previous mobilizations because it directly challenged the whole neoliberal sectarian system and explicitly denounced all parties combined as responsible for the deterioration of the country's socioeconomic conditions (Bou Khater and Majed 2020). As one of the main slogans of the protest movement puts it, 'everyone means everyone'.

The resilience of the main sectarian parties is nevertheless still very strong. This chapter seeks to understand the roots and dynamics of sectarianism in Lebanon, and its connections to neoliberalism, while analyzing the reason for the domination of these parties on the electoral scene and how they prevent the emergence of class[4] affiliation–based politics from below. At the same time, this study seeks to demonstrate that the domination of these sectarian parties is not due to the absence of class dynamics on the political scene, but rather their conflation with a particular social class.

The two pillars of the hegemony of ruling Lebanese parties: sectarianism and neoliberalism

The Lebanese sectarian ruling parties have maintained their hegemony on the political scene for decades thanks to two main factors: sectarianism and neoliberalism.

Major world leaders, public intellectuals and analysts have long portrayed all political tensions and mobilizations in the Middle East/North Africa (MENA) region as conflicts between religious sects fighting each other for centuries, if not longer. For instance, US President Barack Obama has spoken on several occasions of 'ancient sectarian differences' as a means of explaining the conflict in Syria. These 'ancient divisions', he argues, propel the inability in the Arab world, which is 'rooted in conflicts that date back millennia' (cited in Hashemi and Postel 2017: 2). Before the uprisings in the Middle East and North Africa in 2011, academic Vali Nasr (2006: 82) explained that the nature of politics in the Middle East was rooted 'in the old feud between Shi'as and Sunnis that forge attitudes, defines prejudices, draws political boundary lines, and even decides whether and to what extent those other trends have relevance'.

Sectarianism in this perspective is the result of an essential and primordial component of the Arab/Muslim mind and on these premises no solution can be found outside the realm of a so-called 'consociational' sectarian political solution (Lijphart 1977).[5] Contrary to this understanding, in this chapter, sectarianism is considered as a product of modern times and not a tradition from time immemorial. As Palestinian Lebanese scholar Ussama Makdissi (2000: 2) has noted, 'sectarianism is a modern story, and for those intimately involved in its unfolding, it is the modern story – a story that has and that continues to define and dominate their lives'. Since 2003, Lebanon and Iraq have, for instance, a political system in which power is officially divided between the various religious communities and ethnicities, while in reality serving the political and economic elites of these groups.

For its part, neoliberalism must be considered as a particular organization of capitalism to ensure the conditions for capitalist reproduction on a global scale and as part of a ruling class offensive, which ran through the recessions of the 1970s and 1980s and resulted in the restructuring and generation of new and expanded forms of capitalist accumulation (Cimorelli 2009). The basic goal of neoliberalism, as David Harvey has emphasized, is the development of a new

> regime of capital accumulation characterized by a minimal direct intervention of the state in the economy, limited to setting up the legal, political and military functions required to guarantee the proper functioning of markets and their creation in those sectors where markets do not exist.
>
> *(cited in Roccu 2012: 72)*

In the framework of neoliberalism, the state has the explicit role of guaranteeing capital accumulation.

Roots and dynamics of sectarianism in Lebanon

Sectarianism in Lebanon is a modern product that has its origins in the mid-19th century and was constructed in the context of European domination and Ottoman reforms. Since its independence in 1943, the Lebanese state defines itself as a consociational confessional democracy inasmuch as political power is shared among the various religious communities.

Such constitutional engineering is based on the 1943 National Pact, an unwritten understanding between Maronite and Sunni notables, and the Constitution of 1926. Both documents maintained political representation along sectarian lines and entrenched the domination of the Maronite community within the top echelons of the state. The president, according to the Constitution, was required to be Maronite, and had extensive powers, while Christian deputies also had a majority in parliament with a 6 : 5 ratio to Muslim deputies (Salibi 1971; Faour 1991).[6]

Emerging from the end of the civil war, the political arrangements codified in the 1989 Ta'if Agreement[7] entrenched sectarian arrangements albeit strengthening the position of the Sunni and Shi'a in the Lebanese political system. These changes reflected the demographic shift toward a Muslim majority in Lebanon and, moreover, the growing power of the Sunni and Shi'a factions of the bourgeoisie in Lebanon vis-à-vis the Maronite faction. The post–civil war era saw, in particular, the increasing influence of the Sunni business community over various sectors of the Lebanese economy. The Christian faction of the bourgeoisie lost much of its power to a Muslim-Sunni capitalist section, which benefited from foreign ties and lucrative connections to diaspora communities, particularly in the Gulf. Hence, the powers of the president (required to be a Maronite Christian) were weakened while those of the prime minister (a Sunni Muslim) increased. Moreover, the ratio of Muslims to Christians in the new Lebanese parliament rose to 6 : 6, as well as their numbers in state institutions. The term of speaker of the parliament, held by a Shi'a, was also increased to four years and constitutionally protected from being voted out during the first two years (Traboulsi 2014).

Lebanese state institutions have also played an important role in promoting sectarianism and primordial identities in society. This system of laws and the political framework – regulated along religious and patriarchal lines – are critical to the maintenance of divisions within society and therefore the domination of sectarian elites. Institutions maintain the divides in society, while different rights and duties exist according to one's religious identity and ethnicity. Lebanese citizens, for instance, are subject to the laws and courts affiliated with their official religious community (Mikdashi 2014). Moreover, Melani Cammett (2014) has demonstrated that charities connected to sectarian parties are mostly located in areas of the same religious communities. Welfare services in this perspective are another channel 'through which sectarianism is consolidated and helps to sustain and solidify communal boundaries' (Cammett 2019).

As Amel (1986: 29) observed, 'communities are not communities unless through and by the state… and the Lebanese state guarantees the sustainability of the dynamics that reproduce communities as political structure, which only by the state becomes institutions'.

For this reason, laws such as the electoral and personal status laws – which are regulated along religious and sectarian lines – are critical to the maintenance of sectarian identity. As Makdisi (1996) has pointed out, 'to be Lebanese meant to be defined according to religious affiliation'. This is why any process of secularization of the state or a path toward it has been rejected by sectarian parties, including the introduction of personal status civil legislation alongside religious laws, and even the promulgation of civil marriage.

At the same time, sectarianism has to be understood as a powerful mechanism of control over the course of the class struggle through its creation of ties of dependence between the popular classes and their bourgeois leadership. In this manner, the popular classes are deprived of an independent political existence and instead are defined (and act politically) through their confessional status. This analysis draws upon Mehdi Amel's observation that sectarian patterns of political mobilization reflect the manner in which sections of the bourgeoisie act to impose themselves as representatives of the popular classes (Amel 1986).[8] Furthermore, in Amel's view, sectarianism needed to be seen as constitutive and reinforcing of current forms of state and class power. The different factions of the Lebanese bourgeoisie sought to give a confessional aspect to the class struggle in order to strengthen their own position (Amel 1986).

In this sense, Lebanon's sectarian system arose alongside the development of Lebanese capitalism and in interaction with colonial rule. Since Lebanon's independence in 1943, the sectarian nature of the state in Lebanon has served the political and economic elites of the ruling sectarian groups, which have relied on the liberal economic orientation of the country to consolidate their power. Following the end of the civil war, such power has only being reinforced.

Neoliberalism in Lebanon and socioeconomic inequalities

Due to its intermediary position between the West and the Arab world, the Lebanese economy in the first two decades after independence was largely dominated by the service sector, which in 1976 constituted 72 per cent of the Lebanese economy (Dubar and Nasr 1976; Owen 1988). Within this sector, banking was dominant. At the same time, following Lebanon's independence in 1943, control of the state and the country's economy continued to be concentrated in the hands of a narrow oligarchy. State policies reflected the interests of these political and economic elites, who aimed to maintain and strengthen Lebanon's position as a key financial intermediary between the Arab world and Europe (Gates 1989).

In the aftermath of the civil war, successive Lebanese governments adopted neoliberal policies, which led to the deepening of the historically constituted characteristics of the Lebanese economy: a finance and service-oriented development model in which social inequalities and regional disparities are very pronounced. The Ta'if agreement was not only the basis of a new political consensus between the Lebanese elite, but also put the country on the path of economic measures that had been pursued elsewhere in the Middle East since the 1980s, with an emphasis on increased integration into the global economy, privatization and the growth of the private sector (Baroudi 2001). Beginning in 1996, government wages were frozen and automatic wage increases were ended; real wages thus tended to decline significantly due to rising inflation, as prices increased by about 120 per cent from 1996 to 2011 (Zaraket 2014).

Lebanese neoliberalism is most notably distinguished by its focus on urban-led restructuring and the financialization of the economy linked to foreign capital inflows. Investments in the construction and real estate sectors reflect the nature of a speculative and commercial capitalism that dominates the region, which is characterized by short-term profit seeking (Achcar 2013). The construction and real estate sectors, a successful economic enterprise in the region, are at the crossroads of land speculation, driven by (1) the search for shelter investments in real estate and (2) an economy of commercial and touristic services funded to a large extent with regional oil revenues, both by capital and consumers alike from rentier states. The importance of real estate's investment by the Lebanese elite was reflected in a study that the Gherbal platform published in 2021, which released a non-exhaustive list of properties held by 66 Lebanese politicians (Lebanese party leaders, ministers and deputies), who owned a total of 1792 properties, an average of 27 properties per capita. The data presented in the report placed the leader of the Progressive Socialist Party (PSP), Walid Joumblatt, at the top of the list, with 505 properties to his name, mostly in the Chouf region. He was followed by the Tripoli member of parliament (MP), Mohamad Kabbara, affiliated with the Future Movement, with 221 properties, mainly in North Lebanon (Hijazi and Tamo 2021).

At the same time, to fund a state rife with corruption and patronage, successive governments offered very high interest rates on public debt securities, purchased by Lebanese banks directly or through the *Banque du Liban* (BdL). In turn, these offered attractive rates to depositors, while achieving very comfortable margins. The mechanism was perfected at the end of the 1990s with the establishment of the parity of the Lebanese pound and the state's debt in dollars, which fueled the inflow of capital and kept afloat the ruling political elite. The banking sector in particular benefited from these policies. Between 1993 and 2019, the Lebanese state paid USD 87 billion in interest to the banks. Over this period, public debt rose from USD 4.2 to USD 92 billion, an increase of more than 2000 per cent, while bank assets increased by more than 1300 per cent (totaling USD 248.88 billion) and gross domestic product (GDP) by only 370 per cent (Maucourant Atallah and Tamo 2020).

In the midst of these economic policies, successive governments failed to tackle problems affecting the majority of Lebanese, such as unemployment, low wages, structural poverty (particularly in the regions of Akkar and the Bekaa Valley), increasing corruption and the poor quality of social services (Baroudi 2002). The political economy of Lebanon was therefore marked by the highly polarized outcomes of neoliberal reform. Between 2010 and 2016, the income of the poorest households stagnated or dropped, and unemployment remained stubbornly high: only one-third of the working-age population had a job, and joblessness among those under 35 ran as high as 37 per cent. Between 40 and 50 per cent of Lebanese residents lacked access to social assistance. Temporary foreign workers, whose numbers are estimated to reach more than 1 million, had no social protection to speak of. According to a study conducted by the Central Statistical Office, half of workers and more than one-third of the country's farmers lived below the poverty line in 2018. Furthermore, according to the latest figures from the International Labor Organization and the Central Statistics Administration in 2018, informal workers, who do not benefit from any protection from their employers, represent 55 per cent of the workforce.

The October 2019 economic crisis and the effects of the pandemic only worsened the lives of Lebanon's popular classes. About 1.7 million individuals, or 45 per cent of the Lebanese population, were already below the upper poverty line (the number of people living on less than USD 14 a day) in April 2019. The pandemic drove the poverty rate above 55 per cent and increased the unemployment rate to over 35 per cent.

The neoliberal economy of Lebanon constitutes an essential component of the sectarian nature of the Lebanese state and strengthens the control of the Lebanese sectarian parties over society, while continuously impoverishing large segments of the population.

Tools to prevent the emergence of class dynamics from below on the electoral scene

The sectarian parties have been able, at different levels, to maintain forms of hegemony on their religious communities through various mechanisms, whether using consent and/or violence, in order to bind the interests of subaltern classes to their party structures and their interests. In so doing, despite their rivalries, they continuously work to prevent the emergence and consolidation of any social and/or political alternative, particularly labor movements and other proletarian/working-class forces, both during and outside electoral campaigns. In addition, the ruling political elite can count on the electoral institutional structure which still serves the interests of sectarianism.

The institutional structure and the hegemony of sectarian parties

The Lebanese electoral system remains an obstacle for the emergence of class politics from below and therefore challenges the sectarian and neoliberal political system and its elites. In this framework, the parliamentary electoral system is still an instrument to institutionalize sectarianism and reproduce and reinforce the sense of sectarian identity and solidarity.

After years of lobbying and pressure from civil society activists, a new parliamentary electoral law was ratified in 2017. This law was able to achieve some improvements, including the adoption of proportional representation and preferential voting, and the possibility for Lebanese in the diaspora to vote from their countries of residence instead of having to travel to Lebanon (El-Ghossain 2017). One of the main objectives through these changes was to favor a more representative parliament, with more space for independent and civil society actors. The 'reforms' of the electoral system for the 2018 elections have, however, not favored the dynamics outside sectarianism; quite the opposite. The requirement of an electoral threshold and preferential voting largely neutralize the effects of the proportional representation provided for in the law and mainly benefit the dominant sectarian parties. The preferential vote actually encourages candidates to seek preferential votes from their co-confessionalists, in a dynamic similar to the 'Orthodox law', rejected a few years earlier and whose main purpose was to force Lebanese citizens to vote exclusively for candidates from their confession. Additionally, the new electoral law also prevents improved representation for women, impoverished strata of society,[9] smaller and independent political parties and personalities.

The 'reforms' of the Lebanese electoral law sustain some major aspects of clientelism through the preferential vote. At the same time, electoral spending limits have not been removed. The new law also allows for an increase in the number of registered election delegates, whose presence on site at polling stations represents forms of favoritism or pressure on voters. Charitable organizations connected to sectarian political groups are still permitted to provide services during elections (Atallah and El-Helou 2018). Furthermore, citizens still have to vote in their place of origin and not of residence, which ensures better control of sectarian parties because of their greater capacity to monitor and assist people to go and vote by transporting them on polling day.

The failure of the electoral reform in meeting its objectives is evident in the 2018 voting behavior, which saw voters once again cast their ballot along sectarian lines. In fact, throughout the different districts, voters whose sect was in the minority or not represented by a seat (and thus had no sectarian political representation) were less likely to cast their vote than voters having a political candidate from their same sect (Sanchez 2021). Moreover, according to a study by the Lebanese Center for Policy Research, the electoral results demonstrated that

> turnout rates were particularly high in districts where voters had a co-confessional candidate that came from a traditional political family or that was wealthy, suggesting that the sectarian system is particularly designed and suited for key influential political families to mobilize the sectarian vote.
>
> *(Sanchez 2021)*

In this context, the emergence of opposition parties is made very difficult, particularly with the very high eligibility threshold as a result of the ratio of voters to seats in the majority of regions, while the main factors promoting sectarian and clientelism patterns are still in operation. In addition to this, sectarian parties have used various tools to build their own popular base.

Maintaining hegemony through consent and violence

The elites of Lebanese sectarian parties have developed several mechanisms to maintain their domination. First, they exploit privatization schemes and their domination of ministries to strengthen networks of patronage, nepotism and corruption. Control over a ministry has been a key instrument for ruling sectarian parties to distribute resources (financial assistance, public investment in particular regions or provision of a job) to its own popular base. These trends affect the entire public sector, from schools to hospitals to the justice system (Abboud et al. 2020). Symbolic of this loyalty to sectarian parties by large segments of public employees was their low participation in the 2019 Lebanese *intifada*. Public sector employees – estimated at around 300,000 or 14 per cent of the total labor force – were largely underrepresented among protesters (1 per cent) at the beginning of the protest movement, although they also suffered from the economic crisis and the loss of purchasing power (Bou Khater and Majed 2020). This was a consequence not only of sectarian clientelism among the public, but also of the cooptation of the Union Coordination Committee (UCC) in 2015, as explained further below. In the election of the Engineer Professional Association in June 2021, representatives of public sector engineers were the only ones to remain within the realm of the ruling sectarian parties, while the coalition of opposition to the sectarian parties, called the 'the union revolts', won all the seats of the civil engineers, architects and agricultural engineers' sections (Meghaphone 2021). Similarly, control of other state institutions such as the Council for Development and Reconstruction (CDR), created to manage reconstruction projects after the country's civil war (1975–1990), allowed sectarian parties to secure numerous significant contracts with companies connected to them, which augmented in electoral years (Atallah, Mahmalat and Maktabi 2021).

The patronage and clientelist networks are also useful to mobilize their own popular bases. If these networks are not sufficient, the buying of votes at election time is also an important tradition of sectarian parties. Vote buying takes different forms, including cash distribution, paying school fees, distributing medicines and even organizing free health campaigns. Sectarian parties have used the provision of particular welfare services to their popular base to bind them to their interests (Corstange 2012).

In this context, the deepening of the financial crisis and the subsequent COVID-19 pandemic provided new opportunities for the sectarian parties to provide services, such as campaigns to sanitize public spaces and distribute food to the needy in an attempt to rehabilitate their image. For example, the Lebanese Forces distributed bread and petrol vouchers to its members and supporters, alongside a health support system in various regions, such as Zahle and Bcharre, where they provided medicines for free and/or guaranteed other drugs at a reduced price, while the PSP also delivered food boxes, fuel and aid in the Chouf region (Tleiss 2021). The allocation of anti-COVID vaccines was also employed as an instrument for political clientelism. The Qubayyat town council, in the northern region of Akkar, advertised at the end of March 2021 that it would vaccinate some of its residents with Chinese vaccines secured 'thanks to a donation' from Saad Hariri's family (Trombetta 2021).

Unsurprisingly, Hezbollah was one of the main actors benefiting from the financial crisis because of its massive networks of institutions and resources, which go back to the end of the 1980s and have continuously expanded. In April 2021, Hezbollah began distributing to its base a card called *al-Sajjad* to assist people in need. This magnetic card is used in the *al-Nour* cooperatives owned by the party, which are otherwise off-limits. The *al-Sajjad* cardholder benefits from a discount of up to 70 per cent on food products available in the cooperative, up to a sum of 300,000 Lebanese pounds, equivalent to USD 21.4 for a value of LP 14,000 for USD 1 at the beginning of June 2021 (Mohammad 2021). In April 2021, Hezbollah MP Hassan Fadlallah asserted that Hezbollah had delivered direct assistance to 50,000 impoverished families (*Orient le Jour* 2021). All these actions contribute to the continual policy of the party to entrench and act as a separate state within Lebanon.

The dual use of coercion and consent has allowed ruling sectarian neoliberal parties to maintain their hegemony on wide segments of the popular classes, particularly in the absence of the emergence of a political alternative since the end of the civil war.

At the same time, elections have generally been, for ruling sectarian parties, an opportunity to mobilize their popular base to show their strength in particular regions. In this perspective, their members and supporters have also often acted as agents of repression to maintain the hegemony of their parties and leaders. Hezbollah has been particularly effective in using forms of intimidation and violence against individuals critical of the party, including activists and journalists during and outside of elections. Intimidation ranges from harassment of family members to limiting access to basic services to concerns about losing one's job – particularly in localities where the party is dominant (Corstange 2012). Moreover, Hezbollah members did not hesitate to attack protesters from the former Lebanese Option Gathering (LOP),[10] and killed the head of the student party's wing Hachem Salman (19 years old) during a protest against Hezbollah's involvement in Syria (Naharnet 2013).

This type of behavior is not restricted to Hezbollah. Amal's members acted in a similar manner in Shi'a majority areas, while individuals affiliated with the Progressive Socialist Party and the Free Patriotic Movement (FPM), in the Chouf and the Metn areas, respectively, also intimidated and even attacked individuals critical of their parties or rivals at election time. Forms of intimidation and violence against activists and journalists critical of ruling sectarian parties have increased considerably since the outbreak of the Lebanese uprising in October 2019. Members and supporters of political parties have used social networks and threats to attack critical journalists and activists, to intimidate and silence them. Furthermore, the refusal of any form of dissent turned to physical assaults against activists and intellectuals opposed to sectarian parties. Hezbollah was the most significant party to use forms of intimidation and violence. Ali Jammoul, an activist from Nabatiya, for instance, received a multitude of threats and a flood of insults from Hezbollah supporters for having criticized the party on Facebook. They also threatened him not to go back to his village. In another case, Mirra Berry, a young activist from Nabatiya, decided to leave Lebanon to live in Turkey after having suffered several campaigns of harassment, after she criticized Hezbollah and Amal on social networks. Her mother also received direct threats from relatives who belong to Hezbollah and Amal because of her daughter's outspoken criticism of these parties (Yassine 2021).

The main objective through these shows of strength and intimidation is to quell the demonstrations and, in some cases, re-occupy public places in the regions where the ruling sectarian parties dominate. Assassinations of protesters and activists have also occurred with total impunity. For example, in February 2021, writer and activist Lokman Slim,[11] a well-known critic of Hezbollah, was murdered. Slim had been the subject of multiple threats because of his political activism, including during the protest movement.[12] While the identity of the killers remains unknown, this murder was viewed as a message to all forms of political dissidence against Hezbollah and Amal. Likewise, individuals associated with the investigation of the August 4 explosion in the port of Beirut have also been murdered. A photographer, called Joseph Bejjani, who visited the port with a number of foreign investigators after the blast, was shot outside his house in December 2020. His assassination was in all likelihood linked to similar killings and mysterious deaths connected to the port of Beirut explosion, including the deaths of Colonel Mounir Abou Rjeily and Colonel Joseph Skaf, both of whom worked at customs (The New Arab 2020).

Violence and repressive tactics, which have increased considerably since the beginning of the uprising in October 2019, were not the sole tool in the hands of sectarian parties to maintain their domination on large sectors of society.

Preventing a class and secular alternative

During the civil war, labor movements and trade unions were important social actors in organizing and coordinating protests and civil resistance against the war, sectarian divisions, the power of militias, Israeli occupation, and in favor of the specific concerns of workers. Following the end of the civil war, the country's elites actively strived to weaken the independent trade union movement and then coopted the main federation of trade unions, firstly the General Confederation of Lebanese Workers (GCLW) in 2000 and then the Union Coordination Committee in 2015.

As a wave of strikes unfolded throughout the 1990s, a clear strategy to undercut the power of the GCLW and associated federations and unions became evident. This strategy was jointly elaborated by the main political elites at the time – the Hariri government, Hezbollah, Amal and other Syrian regime–aligned forces such as the Ba'th party and SSNP – despite their different interests and rivalries. Both the Ba'th and the SSNP parties played a critical role in this process as the Lebanese Ministry of Labor was controlled by political forces close to the Syrian regime between 1993 and 2005. In the main, this strategy rested upon two essential pillars: (1) establishing a rival federation and union bodies organized along sectarian lines and/or submitted to political forces drawing their power from the Syrian regime, and (2) intervention in the internal affairs of the GCLW itself. Through these means, the Lebanese political elite attempted to subordinate the labor movement to the priorities of the government's economic reform measures and to weaken the ability of the GCLW to mobilize across sectarian lines. The objective was to eliminate the main obstacle to the implementation of neoliberal policies and a possible political rival to the sectarian and bourgeois political elite.

This kind of strategy was also used on the Union Coordination Committee, which was at the head of many labor struggles throughout the country between 2012 and 2014. The UCC, however, became less active against the Lebanese government after its victory in the January 2015 internal elections of a list supported by all the sectarian political parties, including Hezbollah. This list defeated the one headed by Hanna Gharib, who had been the main trade union personality in the various labor struggles of the previous few years. The same winning list won 16 of the administrative committee's 18 seats with the support of both March 8 and March 14 forces. The coalition between March 8 and March 14 forces, whose common list was called the Union's Consensus, also prevailed in the February 2015 elections for the regional branches of Beirut, Mount Lebanon, the South and North, and all but two seats in the Bekaa branch (Salloukh 2015). The results of these elections and the collaboration between all sectarian political parties were reminiscent of the actions they had undertaken to subordinate the role of the GCLW a few years earlier to avoid cross-sectarian labor mobilization. In July 2017, the trade unionist Nehme Mahfoud, a former president of the Private Teachers Union, who had struggled alongside the UCC for the implementation of a salary scale, and his list *Niqâbatî* (My Union) were defeated by a list including a coalition of the principal political movements of the country. Nevertheless, Mahfoud won 43 per cent of the votes despite not being backed by any major political actor (Zoghbi 2017). The possibility of cross-sectarian mobilization and the development of class-based movements present a potential threat to all the sectarian political movements in Lebanon. In this context, the GCLW and the UCC have been completely absent from the Lebanese *intifada* of October 2019 to 2021. The absence of autonomous and mass trade unions weakens the protest movement's ability to cohere itself into a social and political challenge to the sectarian parties and their system.

More generally, ruling sectarian parties have also adopted a rather oppositional and/or suspicious position toward any form of popular mobilization from outside parliament challenging the Lebanese political system. In early 2011, for instance, in the wake of the uprisings in the region, protests also erupted in Lebanon, calling for an end to the sectarian regime, and at the end of summer 2015 around the 'you stink' campaign, which was originally triggered after a waste management crisis, but quickly turned into a challenge to the Lebanese political system. In the 2016 municipal elections in Beirut, the sectarian parties of both March 8 and March 14 gathered forces against the independent and non-sectarian electoral coalition of *Beirut Madinati* (Arabic for 'Beirut is my city'), which nevertheless secured around 40 per cent of the votes.

These suspicions toward popular mobilization surfaced again during the 2019 uprising. Attempts by some sectarian movements, such as the *Kataeb*, and to a lesser extent the Lebanese Forces, to portray themselves as part of the protest movement, while seeking forms of collaboration with some liberal sectors are a way to weaken the appeal of the protest movement for radical change (Jalk 2021). At the same time, through these actions, these parties aspire to strengthen their positions in the state's power structure and not to change the system.

The protest movement has lost momentum since October 2019, but has never completely stopped despite the repression, the financial crisis and the COVID-19 pandemic. The protest movement definitely recorded some initial victories in challenging the power of sectarian neoliberal parties after the withdrawal of taxes that had triggered the uprising and the resignation of Prime Minister Saad Hariri on October 29, 2019.[13] Moreover, at the end of 2020, university student elections witnessed significant victories of independent democratic and secular lists opposed to all the ruling sectarian parties, which often decide not to run in major private universities in the full knowledge that they will not do well (Chehayeb 2020). In addition to this, as mentioned above, the coalition 'the union revolts' opposed to the sectarian parties won 15 seats out of 20 for the four sections of civil engineers, architects, agricultural engineers and public sector engineers, and took 220 delegate places of the 283 to be filled (Assaf 2021).

However, the protest movement still lacks a broad united political front capable of gathering parties on a class and secular basis. A number of political parties participated in the movement, notably leftist and democratic forces such as the Lebanese Communist Party, the *Mouwatinoun wa mouwatinat fi dawla* (Citizens in a State) led by former minister Charbel Nahas and civil society movements such as *Beirut Madinati*. Their representativeness at the street level nevertheless remains modest and their programs are sometimes criticized by the most radical elements of the movement. At the same time, smaller sectors of the left are very fragmented within the protest movement and, thus far, have not been able to build a united front capable of channeling demands and organizing demonstrators across the country.

On their side, the more liberal and right-wing sectors of the movement, which do not have a class perspective, have made many attempts to organize themselves, such as the agreement signed in June 2021 between the Bloc National and the *Minteshreen* group advocating a liberal discourse close to the center-right, which is likely to seduce a bourgeoisie eager for change but not at any price (Khoury 2021). In this political context, amid the absence of any significant political alternative and a deep economic crisis, sectarian bourgeois parties will be able to mobilize their confessional bases and maintain their hegemony in any future election.

The results of the 2022's legislative election confirmed this situation. Except former Prime Minister Saad Hariri's Future Movement Party that decided to boycott the elections – in spite of which some of its MPs ran as independent and were elected, the traditional ruling political parties largely maintained their domination on the political scene. The duo Hezbollah and Amal remained in control of the totality of the 27 Shi'a seats in parliament, while the Lebanese Forces and the FPM dominated the Christian political scene. The election of 13 "opposition" MPs, (out of 128 in total), who were considered to be affiliated with the the Lebanese uprising of October 2019, was presented by some medias as a major "breakthrough", but without shedding a light on the major shortcomings of this new opposition. The main weaknesses of the opposition were not its limited number of MPs, however, but rather in its lack of unified and clear political program, and above all in its strategy which remains solely based on change within parliament. In reality, there was no shared, common political vision or platform. The abolition of the sectarian system and an alternative to the neoliberal system were two main issues in which no consensus existed, while no measures were put forward to deal with the economic and social crisis.

Conclusion

In 2010, former Lebanese Maronite Patriarch Nasrallah Sfeir stated that 'if we remove the confessionalism (sectarianism) from the texts before removing it from the minds, nothing will change' (*Orient le Jour* 2010). This statement has become a mantra for the Lebanese ruling class as well as larger segments of society. However, this is the best justification not to challenge the core of the production and reproduction of sectarian identities and divisions within society, which is the political system and its way of ruling by sectarian parties. In this framework, elections are only tools to provide new legitimacy to sectarian parties to continue to rule.

The nature of political institutions is indeed a historically determined reflection of the class structure that has emerged in relation to capital accumulation. In other words, the state is not disassociated from the sphere of politics, which, in turn, is not separated from the economic sphere (Hanieh 2013). This is why the defense of the current nature of the Lebanese state by all the sectarian parties is also a way of guaranteeing not only their domination over society but their forms of capital accumulation.

In this perspective, the struggle against sectarianism is not about a more inclusive society, but is, at its core, a class struggle challenging the dominant ideas reproduced by the political system and its ruling elites. The sectarian nature of the state, along with the promotion of neoliberal policies, is an obstacle to the rise of class dynamics from below, challenging the ruling bourgeois sectarian parties. Alongside these factors, the various mechanisms of control on society that sectarian parties have put in place, including both consent and violence, allow them to maintain their hegemony. A veritable challenge to sectarianism and therefore the political parties ruling through it can only occur with a real break from the ruling system and its ideas. As Lebanese Palestinian academic Ussama Makdissi (2000: 174) wrote 'to overcome sectarianism, if it is at all possible, requires yet another rupture, a break as radical for the body politic as the advent of sectarianism was for the old regime, it requires another vision of modernity'.

In conclusion, social movements protesting against the Lebanese sectarian and neoliberal system are a key element in creating the conditions for an alternative, which still needs to materialize politically through mass non-sectarian organizations and parties rooted in the country's popular classes. In this perspective, the creation of forms of dual power is a political necessity in order to challenge the state and the sectarian neoliberal political parties.

Notes

1 The parliament term is supposed to be four years but it extended its own term several times. The extension was prompted by the failure of the politicians to agree on a new electoral law until June 2017.
2 Yacoubian grabbed an Armenian Orthodox seat in the 2018 parliamentary election, running on the list known as Kulluna Watani, representing a coalition of civil society groups.
3 This turnout was, however, still more important than in other previous elections (46.5 per cent in 2005, 45 per cent in 2000, 43.1 per cent in 1996 and 30.4 per cent in 1992.
4 Class is understood as a social relation, and factors such as gender, age, national and ethnic origin and citizenship status are part of what constitutes class as a concrete social relation (Hanieh 2015).

5 Consociationalism is characterized in this context by four political tenets: (1) a grand coalition; (2) mutual veto power; (3) segmental autonomy; and (4) proportional representation (Lijphart 1977).
6 Similarly, other government positions, including civil service and ministerial staffing positions, were distributed according to a fixed quota of six to five in favor of Christians based on the 1932 census.
7 The Ta'if Agreement of October 22, 1989, the fruits of a Saudi, US and Syrian agreement imposed on Lebanese deputies, confirmed Syria's dominant position in Lebanon.
8 Mehdi Amel, whose real name was Hassan Abdallah Hamdan. Amel was an important figure on the Lebanese left who provided an innovative approach to understanding the character of sectarianism in the Arab world. Assassinated in 1987 by Islamic fundamentalist militants widely believed to be close to Hezbollah, his insights remain highly salient in setting out a theoretical framework for understanding the party.
9 Candidates must, for instance, pay a registration fee of 8 million Lebanese Pounds (equivalent at this period to USD 5,300) – quadruple the 2009 fee – which represents an obstacle for impoverished individuals, small parties and independents. At the same time, the law enhances the financial advantages for ruling and dominant sectarian leaders and political parties. During campaigns, a candidate is allowed to legally disburse up to USD 100,000 plus USD 3.33 per registered voter in a relevant district, a 20 per cent augmentation that permits ruling and dominant sectarian parties and wealthier individuals to disburse millions more in each district than what they spent in 2009 (El-Ghossian 2017).
10 Established in 2007 and headed by Ahmad Al-As'ad, the son of the well-known As'ad feudal family in the south, the LOP is an independent Shi'a political party opposed to March 8, and more particularly to Hezbollah and Amal.
11 Slim was the founder of UMAM Documentation and Research and Dar al-Jadid institutions. He transformed part of his home in Beirut's southern suburb of Haret Hreik into an exhibition and cultural center, and repeatedly expressed his criticism of Hezbollah policies.
12 After Slim was killed, Hezbollah leader Hassan Nasrallah's son Jawad shared a tweet saying 'Loss of some is in reality an unexpected gain and kindness for others' with the hashtag 'no regret'. He then deleted the tweet which he said was personal and was not intended in the way that some understood it as a subtweet on the death of the activist.
13 Melhem Khalaf, an independent candidate from the civil movement, was elected head of the bar association, while the Bekaa League candidate Ali Yaghi, an independent supported by the protest movement, won the elections of the council of the order of dentists.

References

Abboud, Magali, Joseph Farchakh, Kenza Ouazzani, and Anthony Samrani. 2020. 'In Lebanon, the clientelist octopus is in need of food'. *L'Orient Today*. Available at: https://bit.ly/3geO3oE.
Achcar, Gilbert. 2013. *Le peuple veut, une exploration radicale du soulèvement arabe*. Paris: Sindbad-Actes Sud.
Amel, Mehdi. 1986. *In the Sectarian State*. Beirut: Dâr al-Farabi. In Arabic.
Assaf, Claude. 2021. 'Raz-de-marée de la thaoura à l'ordre des ingénieurs'. *Orient le Jour*. Available at: https://bit.ly/3w9bWCt.
Atallah, Sami, and Zeina El-Helou. 2018. 'Lebanese elections: Clientelism as a strategy to garner votes'. *The Lebanese Center for Policy Studies*. Available at: https://bit.ly/3h1GMc0.
Atallah, Sami, Mounir Mahmalat, and Wassim Maktabi. 2021. 'Les marchés publics, symboles du système de partage du gâteau à la libanaise'. *Orient le Jour*. Available at: https://bit.ly/3qFGHhp.
Baroudi, Salim. 2001. 'Conflict and co-operation within Lebanon's business community: Relations between Merchants' and industrialists' associations'. *Middle Eastern Studies* 37(4): 71–100.
Baroudi, Sami. 2002. 'Continuity in economic policy in post war Lebanon: The record of the Hariri and Hoss governments examined, 1992–2000'. *Arab Studies Quarterly* 24(1): 63–90.
Bou Khater, Lea, and Rima Rima Majed. 2020. 'Lebanon's 2019 October revolution: Who mobilized and why?' *Asfari Institute for Civil Society and Citizenship*. Available at: https://bit.ly/3aeEwuR.
Cammett, Melanie. 2014. *Compassionate Communalism, Welfare and Sectarianism in Lebanon*. Ithaca, NY: Cornell University Press.
Cammett, Melani. 2019. 'Lebanon, the sectarian identity test lab'. *The Century Foundation*. Available at: https://bit.ly/2UMnkHs.
Chehayeb, Kareem. 2020. 'Lebanon: Sectarian parties trounced in unprecedented student elections'. *Middle East Eye*. Available at: https://bit.ly/3zjR4eL.

Cimorelli, Eddie. 2009. 'Take neoliberalism seriously'. *International Socialism*. Available at: https://bit.ly/3wBv8ZX.
Corstange, Daniel. 2012. 'Vote trafficking in Lebanon'. *International Journal of Middle East Studies* 44(3): 483–505.
Dubar, Claude, and Salim Nasr. 1976. *Les classes sociales*. Paris: Presses de la Fondation Nationale des Sciences Politiques.
El-Ghossian, Anthony. 2017. 'One step forward for Lebanon's elections'. *Carnegie*. Available at: https://bit.ly/3ei8W0H.
Faour, Muhammad. 1991. 'The demography of Lebanon: A reappraisal'. *Middle Eastern Studies* 27(4): 631–641.
Gates, Carolyn. 1989. *The Historical Role of Political Economy in the Development of Modern Lebanon*. Oxford and London: Center for Lebanese Studies and I. B. Tauris
Hanieh, Adam. 2013. *Lineages of Revolt, Issues of Contemporary Capitalism in the Middle East*. Chicago, IL: Haymarket Books.
Hanieh, Adam. 2015. 'Theorising inequality and difference through a regional lens'. *Arab Council for Social Sciences*, Occasional Paper Series, Beirut, ACSS.
Hashemi, Nader, and David Postel. 2017. *Sectarianization, Mapping the New Politics of the Middle East*. London: Hurst and Company.
Hijazi, Salah, and Omar Tamo. 2021. 'Le patrimoine immobilier des hommes politiques au Liban, des données révélatrices'. *Commerce du Levant*. Available at: https://bit.ly/3uIQCn1.
Jalk, Jeanine. 2021. 'Comment les forces libanaises tentent de surfer sur la révolution'. *Orient le Jour*. Available at: https://bit.ly/35irHMz.
Khoury, Alexandra. 2021. 'Au sein de l'opposition, l'émergence d'un front social-libéral'. *Orient le Jour*. Available at: https://bit.ly/3qAVREQ.
Lijphart, Arend. 1977. *Democracy in Plural Societies: A Comparative Exploration*. New Haven, CT: Yale University Press.
Makdissi, Ussama. 1996. 'Reconstructing the nation-state: The modernity of secularism in Lebanon'. *MERIP*. Available at: https://bit.ly/3wTb71T.
Makdissi, Ussama. 2000. *The Culture of Sectarianism, Community, History and Violence in Nineteeth-Century Ottoman Lebanon*. Berkeley and Los Angeles, CA: University of California Press.
Maucourant Atallah, Nada, and Omar Tamo. 2020. 'Banquiers et politiques, une grande famille'. *Commerce du Levant*. Available at: http://bit.ly/3sDUtln.
Meghaphone. 2021. 'The day October 17 was revived, through the order of architects and engineers'. Available at: https://bit.ly/3x4VSDj.
Mikdashi, Maya. 2014. 'Sex and sectarianism: The legal architecture of Lebanese citizenship'. *Comparative Studies of South Asia, Africa and the Middle East* 34(2): 279–293.
Naharnet. 2013. 'Al-Asaad claims receiving death threat, holds Nasrallah and state responsible for Salman's murder'. Available at: https://bit.ly/3quuNXB.
Nasr, Vali. 2006. *The Shia Revival: How Conflicts within Islam Will Shape the Future*. New York: Norton and Company.
Orient Le Jour. 2010. 'Sfeir désavoue Berry sur la déconfessionnalisation'. Available at: https://bit.ly/3qpcRh5.
Orient Le Jour. 2021. 'Le Hezbollah fournit une aide à 50.000 familles, selon le député Fadlallah'. Available at: https://bit.ly/3gbl05f.
Owen, Roger. 1988. 'The economic history of Lebanon, 1943–1974: Its salient features'. In Halim Barakat (ed.), *Toward a Viable Lebanon*. London: Croom Helm, 27–41.
Roccu, Roberto. 2012. *Gramsci in Cairo: Neoliberal Authoritarianism, Passive Revolution and Failed Hegemony in Egypt under Mubarak, 1991–2010* (PhD thesis). University of London, London School of Economics.
Salibi, Kamal. 1971. 'The Lebanese identity'. *Journal of Contemporary History* 6(1): 76–81+83–86.
Salloukh, Bassel. 2015. 'Sectarianism and struggles for socio-economic rights'. In Jinan Al-Habbal, Rabie Barakat, Lara Khattab, Shogie Mikaelian, and Bassel Salloukh (eds.), *The Politics of Sectarianism in Postwar Lebanon*. London: Pluto Press, 70–87.
Sanchez, Daniel Garrote. 2021. 'Understanding turnout in the Lebanese elections'. Available at: bit.ly/3GqcfSz
The New Arab. 2020. 'Lebanese ex-army photographer shot dead outside his home'. Available at: https://bit.ly/3xaKPrR.

Tleiss, Hussein. 2021. 'Lebanon returns to the era of "rations"… and the parties display their "primitive achievements" with high technologies'. *Al-Hurra*. In Arabic. Available at: https://arbne.ws/3cFjUfN.

Traboulsi, Fawaz. 2014. 'Social classes in Lebanon Lubnân: Proof of existence'. *Heinrich Boll Stiftung*. In Arabic. Available at: https://bit.ly/2T362p1.

Trombetta, Lorenzo. 2021. 'COVID vaccines used for political clientelism in Lebanon'. *Ansa Med*. Available at: https://bit.ly/3vfZxMA.

Zaraket, Maha. 2014. 'A – B ranks of wages and salaries'. *Al-Akhbar*. Available at: https://bit.ly/36ysE42.

Yassine, Mohammad. 2021. 'Ces militants chiites menacés pour avoir critiqué le Hezbollah'. *Orient le Jour*, 19 April. Available at: https://bit.ly/3vHuudv.

Zoghbi, Imad. 2017. 'Scenario Hana Gharib repeats itself in the teachers' union: Remove mahfudh'. *Al-Modon*. Available at: http://bit.ly/3awv7h9.

31

IDEOLOGY AND ELECTORAL CHOICES IN ARAB ELECTIONS

Enea Fiore[1]

Introduction

The understanding of an ideology's impact on casting ballots has always been rather puzzling. When it comes to politics, ideologies enable individuals to appraise their conditions and prospects and act accordingly through mobilization (Mullins 1972). Historically, groups and parties rallied around ideological tenets and forged their own agendas relying on a set worldview. Despite the difficulties that social scientists faced over decades in grasping the nuances of a phenomenon as subtle as ideology and its effects on individuals, we can confidently affirm that ideologies are highly fluid – they quickly adapt to agents' shift in rationales and programmes due to changing circumstances (Goldstone 1991). Ideologies do not exist in a vacuum; they are not static and monolithic phenomena. Instead, they evolve (or not) over time, and more importantly, they are the by-products of a particular historical moment's perceived necessities. In short, ideologies, and their (in)evolutions, are historically contextualized phenomena.

Over recent decades, scholars have observed the rise and fall of several ideologies across the Middle East and North Africa (MENA): post-independence nationalism, pan-Arabism, communism and its Arab socialist variants, revolutionary Islam, and the vision of a sober and pious theocracy. Broadly speaking, ideologies have principles and views on almost every aspect of life, and their 'agents' – such as political parties or social movements – constantly engage in framing issues to mobilize support for contentious or electoral politics (Benford and Snow 2000; Slothuus and de Vreese 2010). In this regard, in the MENA we can observe the presence of all those preconditions that could ensure the flourishing of ideologies in electoral choices: political parties are in place and elections are held in almost every country – albeit with remarkable differences in voters' freedom and potential political impact. However, the MENA region is split into several countries with diverse political regimes – all with their own characteristics that shape different local ideological variations.

The generalization of regimes' composition in the MENA around the broad categories of 'authoritarianism' and 'democracy' has been made for analytical convenience (e.g., Democracy Index 2020). However, looking in greater detail, several sub-types of political regimes are detectable in both categories: democracies (Tunisia and Israel), quasi-democracies (Iraq), consociational democracies (Lebanon), autocratic rentier monarchies (Gulf countries except Yemen), monarchies (Jordan and Morocco), theocracies (Iran), personalistic party regimes (Syria and, to a certain degree, Turkey), and military regimes (Egypt, Mauritania, Algeria). Political regimes have different characteristics depending on when they are born and, furthermore, they change over time. In this constantly changing environment, ideologies also change, and subsequently voters' preferences.

In short, the MENA region could not be strictly analysed as a *unicum*, nor could the ideologies that historically emerged in the region. Therefore, tracing the role of ideology in electoral choices in the MENA region is difficult, and every generalization should be taken with a grain of salt.

The methodological implications of this complexity in understanding ideology and voting behaviour in MENA countries affect both quantitative and qualitative studies. In social science, quantitative studies usually infer causal relation(s), patterns, or predictions relying on a reasonably large case population and numerical data (Franklin 2008). These data are usually collected through questionnaires administered to a representative sample of the population. This methodology is rapidly becoming mainstream in investigating voting behaviour in the region due to its strong potential for generalization. However, despite scholars' efforts to construct reliable databases, biased answers in surveys, context-dependent data reliability due to the authoritarian nature of most regimes and collinearity among independent variables are substantial risks (Bogner and Landrock 2016; Johnston et al. 2018). For their part, qualitative studies generally offer an in-depth analysis of case studies interpreting non-numerical data, providing details and insights to better interpret a given phenomenon. However, basing their causal inference on a limited set of cases, qualitative approaches do not possess much potential for generalization. Moreover, in studying voting behaviour, qualitative analyses are at risk of case selection biases that could ultimately lead to a 'truncation' problem, nullifying potential inference (Collier and Mahoney 1996). However, the good news is that scholars have developed and deployed several effective countermeasures and mixed methods to cope with these problems (Cavatorta 2020). Thus, today there is sufficiently varied material to discuss how ideology impacts voting behaviour in the MENA region.

This chapter contributes to the debate by identifying and analysing meaningful trends in authoritarian and democratic environments through the comparative method. An in-depth analysis of the primary and secondary literature reveals that the two main analytical lenses – namely, the patronage and the religious–secular divide hypotheses – are both valid and present in almost every case study. However, they are eventually insufficient when it comes to identifying which determinants are dominant in voting behaviour. In this regard, the present analysis argues that introducing contextual variables – namely voter turnout, regime types, and democratic desirability – could help to enrich the understanding of MENA elections and voting behaviour.

Do parties, elections, and electoral behaviour(s) matter?

When we try to understand ideologies and electoral choices in a modern state, we cannot exclude party politics and, of course, elections from our analysis. Indeed, they represent the preconditions that enable competitive institutional politics firstly, and to turn ideological stances into political agendas secondly. Historically, analyses on MENA's political parties often discarded them as empty vessels either marginalized or subordinate to dictators, monarchs, or the military: those considered to truly hold decision-making power (Willis 2002). However, parties exist in two-thirds of MENA countries and experience various degrees of governance (Hinnebusch 2017). Thus, their role cannot be quickly discarded. In the region, political parties are seen as costly machines within which social climbers and rent-seekers dominate, have weak social roots, and can be personalistic in nature and highly fractured. In this respect, data reveal that a decline in trust towards political parties affects different countries regardless of their regime type (WVS Wave 6; WVS Wave 7). Nevertheless, parties are still essential to the existence of democratic polity and to channel voters' individual and aggregate interests: this is as true in the West (Ignazi 2014) as it is in MENA countries (Hinnebusch et al. 2021).

Elections are also an essential part of a pluralistic and democratic political environment. In a democracy, elections provide a powerful mechanism to choose representatives based on programmatic voting. However, despite the clear numerical majority of authoritarian regimes in the MENA, elections have become increasingly important here too. Even closed autocracies understand that their prospects for survival increase if elections are held regularly (Ghandi and Przeworski 2007). The consequence is visible in the flourishing of 'competitive authoritarianism' in the area, where parties and elections have become even more central (Cavatorta and Storm 2018).

For quite some time, the combination of the mainstream cognitive bias that parties in MENA are weak, with no deep roots in society, and that elections do not effectively allocate power, relegated the understanding of voting behaviour to an instrumental vote – aimed only to extract material benefits – or automatic ideological-identity affiliation without considering party agendas or performance (Cavatorta 2020). However, the literature on electoral behaviour in the MENA is evolving, with a growing number of studies looking at regime party voters' electoral dynamics (Gao 2016), voter profiles (Pellicer and Wegner 2014; Mohamed 2018), and voters' ideological commitment or lack thereof (Corstange 2013; Wegner and Cavatorta 2019). Voting in the MENA region is an important affair; selecting political elites at the local or national level reveals much about citizens' preferences and satisfaction with the current political and economic situation. Moreover, to understand who turns out, it is essential to individuate the determinants that shape political configurations.

The results of these studies are not always in harmony with each other, but there are different trends that we can identify in the literature on ideology and voting behaviour.

Is it patronage, or is it ideology?

Two analytical lenses have dominated the academic debate on MENA's elections. On the one hand, scholars argue that elections and electoral choices are highly ideologized along a religious–secular divide. These analyses look at Islamist parties and their secular counterparts' responses regarding the divisive role that religion has in politics (e.g., Schwedler 2011). On the other hand, other scholars argue that elections are deprived of their political and ideological content, patronage, clientelism, and crony relations that characterize electoral contests in authoritarian regimes (Ghandi and Lust-Okar 2009; Lust 2009) as well as in democracies (Cammett and Issar 2010; Corstange 2018). For the latter group of scholars, ideology is almost an irrelevant dimension in the face of clientelist transactions. To what extent the absence of ideology during electoral contests is accurate across different countries and political regimes has been a question that several analyses have considered, given that patronage and clientelism are believed to be the backbone of MENA electoral politics.

The patronage hypothesis assumes that incumbents – in both MENA authoritarian and pluralistic regimes – have multiple instruments to manage elections, and direct repression to maintain the status quo is rarely needed. Gerrymandering, malapportionment, and the exploitative use of the public sector are some examples of the tools used to ensure the continuation of clientelistic transactions to the detriment of programmatic voting. Ruling elites engage in malapportionment and gerrymandering in an authoritarian context to shape the legislature, ensuring that it is composed of the regime's supportive candidates (Gandhi and

Lust-Okar 2009). These practices are also at work in democratic settings: for instance, Israeli authorities have employed gerrymandering of the Palestinian population to accommodate nationalist demands (Lovatt 2020). In Lebanon, gerrymandering and malapportionment have been deployed by sectarian elites to reproduce sectarian modes of subjectification and mobilization (Salloukh et al. 2015). Furthermore, the public sector in the MENA is vast and in constant growth: seven of the MENA's countries have an average of 26 per cent of the total workforce employed in the public sector compared to 15 per cent of 108 non-MENA countries (Monroe 2020). In Lebanon, for instance, the size of the public sector grew from 75,000 employees in 1974, to 175,000 in 2000, to almost 300,000 in 2017 (Salloukh 2019). Incumbents utilize the public sector to feed their crony network through access to state resources, thus making elections a moment to (re)define the patron–client relation between voters and the regime. In some cases, patronage is so widespread that it becomes a nation-building strategy, such as in Qatar (Shockley and Gengler 2020). Here, candidates are perceived as intermediaries in 'competitive clientelism'. Accordingly, voters choose candidates instrumentally, selecting them not on their policy positions but to obtain state resources. Usually, those elected tend to be closer and better connected with the incumbents, such as in Jordan (Lust-Okar 2006), or credibly committed to providing services, such as in Palestine (Tuastad 2008). To summarize, in an environment of competitive clientelism – present in both democratic and authoritarian regimes – voters are expected to look at elections as a distributive mechanism where candidates are intermediaries (*wasta*) or power brokers (*zu'ama*) providing jobs and financial and political favours. In short, voters choose those candidates close to the incumbents to obtain state resources. Democratization scholars usually perceive these elections as destined to become a distributive mechanism that gradually reduces the call for political change (Lust 2009).

Clientelism is thus the most utilized paradigm to analyse and describe electoral politics and voting behaviour in the MENA. However, other scholars – dissatisfied with the realist rationale of the clientelist hypothesis – looked at other ascriptive and moral determinants that could equally shape voting behaviour. The analysis of electoral behaviour in Arab countries often arises from the need to explain mass support for Islamists, especially after their post-Arab uprising *exploits* in Egypt and Tunisia. The religious–secular divide hypothesis emerged from the assumption that these two main ideological fields dominate the electoral competition in the whole area (Blaydes and Linzer 2012). On the one hand, the political use of religious discourses to enhance candidates' moral credentials and boost their appeal in the face of autocratic regimes or dysfunctional democracies has become a powerful factor in Islamists' mobilization strategy. The latter usually appeal to a conservative audience focusing on the 'moral superiority' of a religion-based political system, economic justice, and preserving clear gender roles (Wickham 2004). On the other hand, secular parties generally promote a state's secularism, with religion confined to a private dimension, commitment to modernity and economic development, and improvement in individual liberal rights – such as on gender issues (Wolf 2018). However, when it comes to practice, Wegner and Cavatorta (2019) found that the religious–secular divide does indeed exist at the voter level but is limited to religion's role in politics and gender roles. Not surprisingly, being female had a strong positive effect on voting for secular *Nidaa Tounes* in Tunisia's 2014 election (Dennison and Draege 2020).

Given the complexity of Arab electoral dynamics, a growing number of scholars have left behind the antithetical opposition between these two analytical lenses, introducing several other variables which shape voting behaviour – thus making the previous analytical boundaries among vote determinants more complex. In Tunisia, for instance, the relevance of the religious–secular divide seems to strongly affect electoral choices on the surface, but this is true only to the extent that other multiple variables are involved. In the 2014 election, a retrospective vote seems not to be relevant among electors, instead distrust against Islamists fomented by the secular opponent (i.e., *Nidaa Tounes*), the nostalgia of the 'golden days' of Bourguiba's regime, and living in big cities instead of rural areas, are found to be better predictors of casting ballots for secular parties (Ozen 2020). Also, in Tunisia, gender and religiosity are identified as major sociodemographic vote predictors. The degree of religiosity strongly affects the choice between Islamists and seculars and being male significantly affects voting for Ennahda (Dennison and Draege 2020), supporting Wegner and Cavatorta's (2019) understanding of the Islamist–secular divide. However, in line with Kurzman and Naqvi (2010), Dennison and Draege (2020) also noted that in Tunisia, over time, voters have started to bring economic matters and security to the foreground at the expense of identity issues, which have proved more important in the first electoral contests. In Morocco, the Islamist Justice and Development Party's (PJD) shifts in its political agenda brought a change in the party's electoral roots, from the periphery towards the centre, and from a grievance-based electoral audience to a more educated, reformist, and middle-higher class professionals voters (Pellicer and Wegner 2014). In Lebanon, Hezbollah's management of its municipalities is found to be guided by the neoliberal logic of development. Despite its populist rhetoric, references to Islamic values and practices exist only in legitimizing discourses; conversely, when it comes to governance, Hezbollah has become adept at 'good governance' of international and regional financial institutions and funds support (Harb 2009). As we can see, the religious–secular divide is not a mere binary conflict on a few issues; rather, it is a multidimensional phenomenon involving different variables depending on the context. However, a closer look at patronage dynamics also reveals the presence of other determinants. In Lebanon, for instance, patronage plays a role in voting, but this is strictly intertwined with sectarian considerations (Salloukh et al. 2015). In Yemen, Libya, and Kuwait, tribalism is a key factor in shaping electoral politics (Cavatorta and Storm 2018). In the United Arab Emirates (UAE), personal ties and kinship with candidates have been found to be third in importance after candidates' characteristics and electoral promises (Yaghi and Antwi-Boateng 2015). In Turkey, the Justice and Development Party (AKP) utilized a mass housing programme as its main tool to maintain and enlarge its electoral support (Marschall et al. 2016). However, the same AKP strongly reverted to Manichean pro-Islamic discourses to marginalize left-wing Kurdish parties in an attempt to secure the vote of religious Kurds (Grigoriadis and Dilek 2018).

On the one hand, the ideological dimension of the secular–religious divide does play a role in electoral choices, but it is not the whole story. On the other hand, patronage also exists and plays a role in MENA elections, but it is not the whole story either. The two phenomena are present; indeed, they often coexist and overlap, but to understand which of these dimensions – or what determinants' combination – are dominant, contextual variables must be taken into account. The political regimes' typology, voter turnout, and democratic desirability are here considered of primary importance to understand the extent to which these variables are involved in voters' electoral choices. The deployment of a combination of these three variables reinforces the potential inference on vote behaviour. For instance, an authoritarian regime with high turnout and low democratic desirability might reveal a high degree of citizens' satisfaction with the political and economic environment; conversely, the same regime with low turnout and high democratic desirability may see its legitimacy questioned.

Many signals suggest that including these three variables can further improve our understanding of vote behaviour in the MENA. For instance, before and after the Arab uprisings, Islamist parties performed worse in countries that have the most free elections (i.e., more democratic regimes). Moreover, Islamist parties saw their electoral zenith in those moments of transition from an authoritarian regime to a more pluralistic one (Kurzman and Naqvi 2010; Kurzman and Türkoglu 2015). This is visible in multiple countries: in the 1991 election in Algeria, Islamists gained around 47 per cent of the vote, but in all other elections, they never performed better than 9 per cent of the share of votes, including in the 2021 elections; in 1989, the Jordanian Muslim Brotherhood obtained 17 seats in parliament, but then experienced a downward trend, which brought them to win just 10 parliamentary seats out of 130 in 2020; in Tunisia, Ennahda gained around 37 per cent of the votes in the 2011 elections, then dropped to around 28 per cent in 2014 and below 20 per cent in 2019. This pattern suggests the importance of the regimes' typology: voting for Islamists in a liberalizing regime represents a powerful anti-system stance, but once democracy comes, Islamists are then judged on their performance and no longer on their potential. In addition, a closer analysis of voter turnout in MENA elections reveals that participation is lower in authoritarian regimes compared to more democratic environments.[2] In this regard, de Miguel et al. (2015) found that the choice to abstain from voting in the MENA region could be an ideological stance aimed at expressing favour or disfavour towards the regime. Moreover, Aydogan (2020) pointed out that despite the ideological religious–secular stances that are indeed important – referring to identity values – political reforms and government's role in regulating the economy are also significant. Therefore, instead of a straight secular–religious divide based on gender issues and religion's role in society, or the purely clientelist nature of electoral competition, what shapes electoral behaviour in MENA countries seems to have more to do with the nature of political regimes and the evaluation of their economic performance, particularly over time. In this regard, a closer look at the functioning of voter turnout and democratic desirability in both democracies and authoritarian regimes helps us to better isolate the independent variables' relative weight on the electoral behaviour in the MENA region.

On ideology, competitive authoritarianism, and quasi-democracy

To deepen our understanding of how material or ideological considerations shape electoral behaviour, contextual variables – namely regimes' typology, voter turnout, and democratic desirability – are taken into account. As already partially pointed out above, MENA regimes are very different from each other. However, they tend towards the centre of the political regime spectrum: autocracies gradually refashioned their institutional structure in the face of rapid social changes, thus appropriating certain democratic characteristics (Heydemann 2007). These regimes engaged in self-restructuring, both real and façade, becoming 'competitive authoritarian'. Conversely, those states with a greater democratic environment had weak bureaucratic efficacy and high institutional ineffectiveness in guaranteeing an equal and impartial legal order. MENA 'quasi-democracies' are poorly consolidated; the inability of the state and politics to guarantee equality to all individuals led to the persistence of some authoritarian features. Local spheres of private power (i.e., *Zu'ama*), crony capitalism, state capture by private interests, and use of public resources to buy social peace are characteristics of MENA's quasi-democracies (Fabiani 2018; Baumann 2019).

In both types of regimes, the ideological commitment towards democracy as a political system has been found to be solid since the early 2000s (Norris and Inglehart 2002). Gorman et al. (2019) refreshed and updated those data confirming that Muslims still show a positive attitude towards democracy, which could be compared to those of Protestant and English-speaking countries. The Arab Barometer (AB) (Wave III 2014; Wave IV 2017) registered a growing trend over time in the perception of democracy as a better system of government.[3] However, in the most recent World Value Survey (WVS) – to the question on 'having a democratic system' – a decreasing trend was identifiable in 2018. Iraq had a cumulative positive attitude towards having a democratic system of 83.4 per cent in 2013, and 57.7 per cent in 2018; Jordan went from 86 per cent in 2010, to 63.5 per cent in 2018; Egypt went from 98.7 per cent in 2012, to 82.3 per cent in 2018; and Tunisia went from 85.7 per cent in 2013, to 71.4 per cent in 2019 (WVS Wave VI 2018; WVS Wave VII 2020). The exception is represented by Lebanon, both in AB and WVS, where the perception of democracy and the desirability of a democratic system have remained almost unaltered over time. In short, the democratic appeal among MENA citizens is not in doubt, so they would be expected to turn out and vote in both types of regimes. Furthermore, if the patronage mechanism allocates material benefits effectively, also in this case citizens would be expected to be prone to casting ballots to access resources. So, how can these expectations be squared with the low electoral turnout and growing citizens' depoliticization visible in several cases in the area?

In countries where competitive authoritarianism is solid and controls the provision of resources, turnout rates are lowest, but democratic desirability remains high. Conversely, in quasi-democracies – such as Lebanon, Tunisia, and Iraq – the turnout is much higher, although democratic desirability suffered the most worrying drop. In investigating the democratic desirability in the area, Teti et al. (2019) found evidence that Arab citizens are less keen on liberal democracy when it comes to identity issues, namely gender and the role that religion should have in politics. Instead, they support democratic forms of social security, redistribution, and fighting corruption. In short, voters seem to prioritize socio-economic rights – aimed at reducing inequalities – over civil-political rights. On the basis of these findings, we can argue that a drop in democratic desirability coincides with disappointment with the economic performance of democracies and satisfaction with those of authoritarianisms. Conversely, if democratic desirability is high, it reveals a high degree of satisfaction with democratic regimes' economic performance and a poor degree of satisfaction in the case of authoritarian regimes, thus increasing the appeal for regime change.

If we take a look at recent public opinion surveys (2018–2019) in MENA countries, we find confirmation of Teti et al.'s findings (2019): when asked what were the most important challenges facing Palestinians, the two main answers were the economy (37 per cent) and corruption (21 per cent); in Algeria, they were, respectively, 40 per cent and 22 per cent; in Jordan 71 per cent and 17 per cent; in Iraq 18 per cent and 32 per cent; in Lebanon 45 per cent and 13 per cent; and in Tunisia 48 per cent and 12 per cent (AB Wave V 2019). The few exceptions are Egypt, where the second biggest concern after the economy (36 per cent) was fighting terrorism (18 per cent), and Morocco, where multiple problems, such as drugs and marginalization, represented the biggest concern. Moreover, the COVID-19 pandemic exacerbated economic concerns in 2021: in Lebanon, Algeria, Jordan, Tunisia, Iraq, Libya, and Morocco, an average of 41 per cent of respondents reported the economy as the biggest challenge that their states face in 2021.[4] On a scale from 0 to 10 whether democracy should entail taxing the rich and subsidizing the poor, all Arab countries combined resulted in a mean score above 7, far more than the United States at 5.71 (WVS Wave VII 2020). Considering that democracy is associated with enhancing socio-economic conditions in the MENA region, if mid-term effective redistributive policies do not follow a democratic opening, the outcome leads to democratic disillusionment, social unrest, and turnout collapse. In this regard, Spierings (2020), for instance, found that those regimes that experienced initial political liberalization, but no substantial (economic) democratization after the Arab uprisings (i.e., Bahrain, Egypt, and Morocco) saw a consistent decline in democracy's desirability. Conversely, those that did not experience such conditions (i.e., Algeria, Jordan, Palestine, Sudan, and Yemen) did not face a decline in trust towards democracy.

For competitive authoritarian regimes – whose elections are considered based on patronage and clientelism – it follows that patronage is indeed an important factor in their elections. However, the low turnout and the endurance of democratic desirability also reveal another side of the coin. On the one hand, patronage and clientelism dominate the share of the electorate that votes for independent candidates or for parties close to incumbents (e.g., Gao 2016), and on the other hand, abstention seems to be more related to signal (dis)approval towards the regime (de Miguel et al. 2015). Moreover, the persistence of redistributive-related democratic desirability in an authoritarian context – where the undisputed winner of elections is abstention – is in line with the findings of de Miguel et al. (2015): Arab citizens who decide to use turnout – and abstention – as a way to evaluate the regime, do so by judging harshly the latter largely on its economic performance. To summarize, in competitive authoritarianism, vote behaviour privileges abstention as a rational assessment of the regime's economic performance. Thus, low turnout and high democratic desirability reveal low acceptance of authoritarianism and the management of its resources despite patronage. For those active voters choosing to support opposition parties, the choice is ideological insofar as it reflects dissatisfaction towards the incumbents. Conversely, voting for regime-related parties and independent candidates – usually represented by businessmen or *Zu'ama* – is primarily driven by patronage. Exceptions to this pattern are those Gulf countries where citizens enjoy extensive welfare and low taxation – such as Saudi Arabia, the UAE, and Qatar – where primary candidate selection determinants are more related to religion, candidates' characteristics, and ascriptive identity (Kraetzschmar 2010; Yaghi and Antwi-Boateng 2015; Shockley and Gengler 2020).

For quasi-democracies, democratic disillusionment is strong but in a very specific manner. Given its consociational system, Lebanon's general drop is almost entirely concentrated in the poorest Sunni community. The Lebanese disappointment with their political and economic structure has led citizens to sectarian claims in public discourse, although private preferences seem to be directed more by material interests (Corstange 2013). In Tunisia, while political democratization indeed took place, this is not true for economic growth and redistribution. The result is that the drop in democratic desirability is concentrated among the poorest sectors of the population (Spierings 2020). As already pointed out, in Tunisia, the religious–secular arguments rapidly gave way to economic considerations in voting behaviour: at the end of 2020, the first five problems considered prominent in the country, and those that the government should prioritize, concerned one or other aspect of the economy (IRI 2020). Similarly, in Iraq – a country traditionally characterized by sectarian cleavages – the politicization of ethnic and sectarian identities has lost relevance among citizens in the face of socio-economic issues that transcend religion or ethnicity (Jabar 2018). To summarize, in quasi-democracies, voting behaviour seems to privilege material and retrospective considerations – mainly on socio-economic issues – rather than ideology *a priori*. However, the disappointment of socio-economic expectations seems to be the perfect ingredient for democratic disillusionment, depoliticization, and the subsequent drop in turnout. Therefore, it is no surprise that kinship considerations in candidate's selection have also been found in these countries (Corstange 2018) in so far as they might be helpful in securing resources, suggesting that people use all available means to cope in times of crisis.

Conclusion

Significant shifts in voter turnout according to different contexts indicate that MENA's voters are not passive. On the contrary, they constantly debate, evaluate, and change opinions towards the regime, the incumbents, and their political and economic choices. Elections, as we saw, represent a powerful 'litmus test' on the determinants that shape electoral choices and how this translates into voting behaviour. The two dominant analytical lenses, namely the patronage and religious–secular divide hypotheses, prove to be consistently present. However, they are insufficient to grasp the complexity of the variables involved in shaping how MENA citizens vote.

The inclusion of three contextual variables – namely, regime type, turnout rates, and changes in democratic desirability – helps to better define the dominant voting determinants and to what extent they are related to material or ideological considerations. In authoritarian regimes, the high abstention rates represent a political choice: citizens use turnout to signal their (dis)approval towards the regime based on economic considerations. For their part, active voters supporting opposition parties directly signal their discontent with the regime; for those who support regime-related candidates their choice is mainly patronage driven. In quasi-democracies, the early high turnout after liberalization and the subsequent drop as well as changes in democratic desirability are related to the failure to meet democratic redistributive-related expectations, especially among the poorer sections of the population.

As the findings suggest, the electorate in the MENA region is not composed of entrenched and highly ideologized partisans. Instead, a large part of the electorate are swing voters and cast their ballots based on their evaluation of the regime in place – both democratic and authoritarian – on incumbents' performance, and on economic performance. This is also true for voters of Islamist parties, whose support remains fluid and context dependent (Pellicer and Wegner 2014).

Finally, the persistence of phenomena such as patronage, clientelism, kinship, and sectarianism is not attributable to social or political exceptionalism. The functioning of MENA competitive authoritarian regimes and quasi-democracies disciplines citizens into an environment where detachment from clientelist dynamics is a privilege of the few. Elites' hegemony is often secured with identity affiliation – such as sectarian, kin, or tribal – and control over resources and their mechanisms of redistribution. Moreover, where a democratic government has replaced an authoritarian regime, hopes of economic redistribution and political equity boost citizens' political participation. However, when democracy does not fulfil these expectations, faith in democracy – and consequently turnout – collapses. This trend is in line with the worldwide deterioration of liberal democratic desirability due to its growing difficulties in guaranteeing socio-economic rights for citizens.

Notes

1 Work for this article was supported by a grant (number 435-2020-0539) from the Social Sciences and Humanities Research Council of Canada (SSHRC).
2 In Jordan, the voter turnout was 56.5% in 2013, and 29.9% in 2020; in Egypt it was 28.3% in 2015, and 29.1% in 2020; in Morocco it was 45.4% in 2011, and 43% in 2016. In Palestine, the voter turnout was 77.7% in 2006; in Iraq it was 79.6% in 2005, 62.4% in 2010, 60.5% in 2014, and 44.9% in 2018; in Turkey it was 74.1% in 2014, 85.5% in 2015, and 86.2% in 2018. Source: IDEA – International Institute for Democracy and Electoral Assistance Database.
3 In Algeria, Palestine, Morocco, Lebanon, Tunisia, and Jordan, confidence in the democratic system of governance goes from a minimum of 74% (Algeria) to 86% (Jordan). Source: Arab Barometer IV, 'Democracy in the Middle East and North Africa: Five years after the Arab Uprisings'.
4 Source: AB Wave VI, 'Fact sheet: MENA Region Economy'.

References

Aydogan, Abdullah. 2020. 'Party System and Ideological Cleavages in the Middle East and North Africa'. *Party Politics* 20(10): 1–13.
Arab Barometer (AB). 'Wave III, 2014; Wave IV, 2017; Wave V, 2019'. Available at: https://www.arabbarometer.org/survey-data/data-downloads/.
Baumann, Hannes. 2019. 'The Causes, Nature, and Effect of the Current Crisis of Lebanese Capitalism'. *Nationalism and Ethnic Politics* 25(1): 61–77.
Benford, D. Robert and David Snow. 2000. 'Framing Process and Social Movements: An Overview and Assessment'. *Annual Review of Sociology* 20: 611–639.

Blaydes, Lisa and Drew Linzer. 2012. 'Elite Competition, Religiosity, and Anti-Americanism in the Islamic World'. *American Political Science Review* 106(2): 225–243.

Bogner, Kathrin and Uta Landrock. 2016. 'Response Biases in Standardized Surveys'. *GESIS Survey Guideline*. GESIS – Leibniz Institute for the Social Science. Available at: https://www.gesis.org/fileadmin/upload/SDMwiki/BognerLandrock_Response_Biases_in_Standardised_Surveys.pdf.

Cammett, Melani and Sukritiu Issari. 2010. 'Bricks and Mortar Clientelism: Sectarianism and the Logics of Welfare Allocation in Lebanon'. *World Politics* 62(3): 381–421.

Cavatorta, Francesco. 2020. 'Overcoming Exceptionalism: Party Politics and Voting Behaviour in the Middle East and North Africa'. In Larbi Sadiki (ed.), *Routledge Handbook of Middle East Politics*. London and New York: Routledge, 216–227.

Cavatorta, Francesco and Lise Storm. 2018. *Political Parties in the Arab World*. Edinburgh: Edinburgh University Press.

Collier, David and James Mahoney. 1996. 'Insight and Pitfalls: Selection Bias in Qualitative Research'. *World Politics* 49(1): 56–91.

Corstange, Daniel. 2013. 'Ethnicity on the Sleeve and Class in the Heart: When Do People Respond to Identity and Material Interests?' *British Journal of Political Science* 43(4): 889–914.

Corstange, Daniel. 2018. 'Kinship, Partisanship, and Patronage in Arab Elections'. *Electoral Studies* 52: 58–72.

Dennison, James and Jonas Draege. 2020. 'The Dynamics of Electoral Politics after the Arab Spring: Evidence from Tunisia'. *Journal of North African Studies* 26(4): 756–780.

De Miguel, Carolina, Amaney A. Jamal and Mark Tessler. 2015. 'Elections in the Arab World: Why Do Citizens Turn Out?' *Comparative Political Studies* 48(11): 1355–1388.

Fabiani, Riccardo. 2018. 'Tunisia and the International Community Since 2011: Rentierism, Patronage and Moral Hazard'. *Jadaliyya*. Available at: https://www.jadaliyya.com/Details/35142.

Franklin, Mark. 2008. 'Quantitative Analysis'. In Donatella della Porta and Michael Keating (eds.), *Approaches and Methodologies in the Social Science*. Cambridge: Cambridge University Press, 240–262.

Gao, Eleanor. 2016. 'Tribal Mobilization, Fragmented Groups, and Public Goods Provision in Jordan'. *Comparative Political Studies* 49(10): 1372–1403.

Ghandi, Jennifer and Ellen Lust-Okar. 'Elections Under Authoritarianism'. *Annual Review of Political Science* 12(1): 403–422.

Ghandi, Jennifer and Adam Przeworski. 2007. 'Authoritarian Institutions and the Survival of Autocrats'. *Comparative Political Studies* 40(11): 1279–1301.

Goldstone, Jack. 1991. 'Ideology, Cultural Frameworks, and the Process of Revolution'. *Theory and Society* 20(4): 405–453.

Gorman, Brandon, Ijlal Naqvi and Charles Kurzman. 2019. 'Who Doesn't Want Democracy? A Multilevel Analysis of Elite and Mass Attitudes'. *Sociological Perspectives* 62(3): 261–281.

Grigoriadis, N. Ioannis and Esra Dilek. 2018. 'Struggling for the Kurdish Vote: Religion, Ethnicity and Victimhood in AKP and BDP/HDP Rally Speeches'. *Middle Eastern Studies* 54(2): 289–303.

Harb, Mona. 2009. 'La gestion du Local par les Maires du Hezbollah au Liban'. *Critique Internationale* 42(1): 57–72.

Heydemann, Steven. 2007. 'Upgrading Authoritarianism in the Arab World'. Analysis Paper 13. *Saban Center for Middle East Policy*. Brookings Institution. Available at: https://www.brookings.edu/research/upgrading-authoritarianism-in-the-arab-world/.

Hinnebusch, Raymond. 2017. 'Political Parties in MENA: Their Functions and Development'. *British Journal of Middle Eastern Studies* 44(2): 159–175.

Hinnebusch, Raymond, Francesco Cavatorta and Lise Storm. 2021. 'Political Parties in MENA: An Introduction'. In Francesco Cavatorta, Lise Storm and Valeria Resta (eds.), *Routledge Handbook on Political Parties in the Middle East and North Africa*. Oxon and New York: Routledge, 1–13.

Ignazi, Pietro. 2014. 'Power and the (Il)Legitimacy of Political Parties: An Unavoidable Paradox of Contemporary Democracy?' *Party Politics* 20(2): 160–169.

IRI - International Republican Institute. 2020. 'Public Opinion Survey: Residents of Tunisia'. Available at: https://www.iri.org/sites/default/files/2020-10_iri_tunisia_report_-_final.pdf.

Jabar, A. Faleh. 2018. 'The Iraqi protest movement: From identity politics to issue politics'. *LSE Middle East Centre Paper Series* 25. Available at: http://eprints.lse.ac.uk/88294/.

Johnston, Ron, Kelvyn Jones and David Manley. 2018. 'Confounding and Collinearity in Regression Analysis: A Cautionary Tale and an Alternative Procedure, Illustrated by Studies of British Voting Behaviour'. *Quality and Quantity* 52(4): 1957–1976.

Kraetzschmar, Jan Hendrik. 2010. 'Electoral Rules, Voter Mobilization and the Islamist Landslide in Saudi Municipal Elections of 2005'. *Contemporary Arab Affairs* 3(4): 515–533.

Kurzman, Charles and Ijlal Naqvi. 2010. 'Do Muslim Vote Islamic?' *Journal of Democracy* 21(2): 50–63.

Kurzman, Charles and Didem Türkoglu. 2015. 'After the Arab Spring: Do Muslim Vote Islamic Now?' *Journal of Democracy* 26(4): 100–109.

Lovatt, Hugh. 2020. 'The End of Oslo: A New European Strategy on Israel-Palestine'. *European Council on Foreign Relation*. Available at: https://ecfr.eu/publication/the-end-of-oslo-a-new-european-strategy-on-israel-palestine/.

Lust, Ellen. 2009. 'Democratization by Elections? Competitive Clientelism in the Middle East'. *Journal of Democracy* 20(3): 122–135.

Lust-Okar, Ellen. 2006. 'Elections under Authoritarianism: Preliminary Lessons from Jordan'. *Democratization* 13(3): 456–471.

Marschall, Melissa, Abdullah Aydogan and Alper Bulut. 2016. 'Does Housing Create Votes? Explaining the Electoral Success of the AKP'. *Electoral Studies* 42: 201–212.

Mohamed, Ezzeldin Ahmed. 2018. 'Turnout in Transitional Elections: Who Votes in Iraq?' *The Journal of the Middle East and Africa* 9(2): 153–171.

Monroe, Steve. 2020. 'Public Sector Employment in MENA: A Comparison with World Indicators'. *The Economic Research Forum*. Available at: https://theforum.erf.org.eg/2020/08/31/public-sector-employment-mena-comparison-world-indicators/.

Mullins, A. Willard. 1972. 'On the Concept of Ideology in Political Science'. *American Political Science Review* 66(2): 498–510.

Norris, Pippa and Ronald Inglehart. 2002. 'Islamic Culture and Democracy: Testing the "Clash of Civilizations" Theory'. *Comparative Sociology* 1(3–4): 235–263.

Ozen, H. Ege. 2020. 'Voting for Secular Parties in the Middle East: Evidence from the 2014 General Elections in Post-revolutionary Tunisia'. *The Journal of North African Studies* 25(2): 251–279.

Pellicer, Miquel and Eva Wegner. 2014. 'Socio-economic Voter Profile and Motives for Islamist Support in Morocco'. *Party Politics* 20(1): 116–133.

Salloukh, Bassel. 2019. 'Taif and the Lebanese State: The Political Economy of a Very Sectarian Public Sector'. *Nationalism and Ethnic Politics* 25(1): 43–69.

Salloukh, Bassel, Rabie Barakat, Jinan al-Habbal, Lara Khattab and Shoghig Mikaelian. 2015. *The Politics of Sectarianism in Post-war Lebanon*. London: Pluto Press.

Shockley, Bethany and Justin Gengler. 2020. 'Social Identity and Coethnic Voting in the Middle East: Experimental Evidence from Qatar'. *Electoral Studies* 67: 1–13.

Schwedler, Jillian. 2011. 'Can Islamist Become Moderates?: Rethinking the Inclusion-Moderation Hypothesis'. *World Politics* 63(2): 347–376.

Slothuus, Rune and Claes de Vreese. 2010. 'Political Parties, Motivated Reasoning, and Issue Framing Effects'. *The Journal of Politics* 72(3): 630–645.

Spierings, Niels. 2020. 'Democratic Disillusionment? Desire for Democracy after the Arab Uprisings'. *International Political Science Review* 41(4): 522–537.

Teti, Andrea, Pamela Abbott and Francesco Cavatorta. 2019. 'Beyond Elections: Perceptions of Democracy in Four Arab Countries'. *Democratization* 26(4): 645–665.

Tuastad, Dag. 2008. 'Local Elections in Gaza'. In Ellen Lust-Okar and Saloua Zerhouni (eds.), *Political Participation in the Middle East*. Boulder, CO and London: Lynne Rienner Publishers, 121–139.

Wegner, Eva and Francesco Cavatorta. 2019. 'Revisiting the Islamist-Secular Divide: Parties and Voters in the Arab World'. *International Political Science Review* 40(4): 558–575.

Wickham, Rosefsky Carrie. 2004. 'The Path to Moderation: Strategy and Learning in the Formation of Egypt's Wasat Party'. *Comparative Politics* 36(2): 205–228.

Willis, J. Michael. 2002. 'Political Parties in Maghrib: The Illusion of Significance?' *The Journal of North African Studies* 7(2): 1–22.

Wolf, Anne. 2018. 'What are "secular" parties in the Arab World? Insights from Tunisia's *Nidaa Tounes* and Morocco's PAM'. In Francesco Cavatorta and Lise Storm (eds.), *Political Parties in the Arab World*. Edinburgh: Edinburgh University Press, 49–71.

World Value Survey (WVS). 'Wave V, 2018; Wave VI, 2020'. Available at: https://www.worldvaluessurvey.org/WVSContents.jsp.

Yaghi, Abdulfattah and Osman Antwi-Boateng. 2015. 'Determinants of UAE Voters' Preferences for Federal National Council Candidates'. *Digest of Middle East Studies* 24(2): 213–235.

32

THE ARAB GENERATION Z

From Disillusionment to Pragmatism

Dina Shehata and Abdalmajeed Abualela

Introduction

Generational analysis is a commonly used approach to explaining social and political change. The German sociologist Manheim was among the first to argue that the concept of generation is an important analytical tool that provides possibilities for analyzing the formation of social and intellectual movements and for understanding the rapid transformation of a given society. Mannheim defined a generation as a group of individuals of similar ages whose members have been shaped by important historical events within a given period (Mannheim 1952).

Generational analysis has been used to describe contemporary global social and political phenomena such as the crisis of representative democracy, the emergence of new social movements, the rise of populism and extremism, and the rise of post materialism and identity politics (Foa and Mounk 2019; Giroux 2010; Inglehart 1971, 1977, 2008). In the Arab world, generational analysis has frequently been used to explain phenomena such as the rise of Islamism and violent extremism, and the political uprisings known as the Arab Spring)Tinnes 2020; Cole 2014; Wright 2011; Anderson 2013; Abbott et al. 2017; Sayre and Yousef 2016; Lange 2011; Herrera 2009; Austin 2011).

More recent generational analysis in the Arab world has focused on the rise of a new generation of Arabs, known as the Arab Generation Z. Born between 1997 and 2012, the political consciousness of this generation has been shaped by the turbulent events of the Arab uprisings and their aftermath (Abualela 2020a). Multiple surveys have indicated that this generational cohort, much like its global counterpart, is distrustful of established elites and values, and of dominant political, social, and religious institutions. The Arab Generation Z is much more inclined to reject the dominant ideological and cultural narratives that have defined Arab politics and tends to be more interested in more immediate social and economic issues such as education and employment, climate change, gender equality, and equality of opportunity. They are also more accepting of the values of freedom, equality, and diversity compared to older generations of Arabs (Raz 2019; Population Council 2010; Arab Barometer 2016, 2019; Arab Youth Surveys 2008-2021).

Recent surveys indicate that the Arab Generation Z has low levels of trust in government, little interest in politics, and low levels of participation in elections and in formal political institutions. Moreover, unlike Arab millennials, the generation that actively participated in the 2011 Arab uprisings and that was driven by ambitious visions of political and social change, the Arab Generation Z appears much more pragmatic and issue focused.

Generation Z seems to have renounced plans for radical change and their activism focuses primarily on advancing more immediate social and economic goals (Arab Barometer 2019; Arab Youth Survey 2020). Globally and regionally, this generation has developed new forms of political engagement and mobilization centered primarily on new social media campaigns and issue-specific social change (Abuela 2020b).

The purpose of this chapter is to examine the emergence of the Arab Generation Z as a new political actor in the Arab world, to situate this generation within the broader context of the global Generation Z, to highlight the values and preferences of this generation, to describe how they engage with politics and political participation, and finally to reflect on the implications of this generational change on the future of Arab politics.

Generation Z as a new global political actor

Generation Z is the latest generation to enter the public sphere across the globe. They are beginning to replace millennials as the generation driving new global social and political trends. As shown in figure 32.1 below the Pew Research Center which has been studying the Millennial generation for decades has set a cut-off point between millennials and the next generation: anyone born between 1981 and 1996 is considered a millennial, and anyone born from 1997 to 2012 is part of a new generation which is labeled Generation Z (Dimock 2019; Parker and Igielnik 2020).

Much has been written about Generation Y, or millennials born between 1981 and 1996, and their role in driving social and political phenomena during the past two decades. Millennials are the generation shaped by the 9/11 attacks, the war on terror and the invasions of Iraq and Afghanistan, and the 2008 financial crisis and its social and economic aftermath. Millennials are also considered the first generation of 'digital natives' who have used social media and new technology as a means of acquiring information, communicating with peers, expressing their views, and organizing and mobilizing. Millennials were also the first generation to combine virtual activism with real-life activism to push for social and political change. A large segment of the Millennial generation embraces diversity and upholds

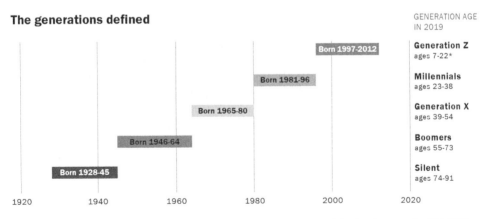

Figure 32.1 The generations defined. Source: www.pewresearch.org/social-trends/2020/05/14/on-the-cusp-of-adulthood-and-facing-an-uncertain-future-what-we-know-about-gen-z-so-far-2/

more progressive values regarding women and lesbian, gay, bisexual, and transexual (LGBT) rights. They are also less religious than older generations, and during the last decade they were active in creating new social movements and in mobilizing grassroots activism in support of progressive goals (Dimock 2019).

In contrast, Generation Z has come of age during the rising tide of right-wing populism. They have grown up in an environment characterized by political polarization and cultural wars between the left and the right, heightened racial tensions, a deepening climate crisis, and a global pandemic (Parker and Igielnik 2020). From a young age, they have been at the forefront of movements such as School Strike for Change and Black Lives Matter. The young climate activist Greta Thunberg has become the face of this young, politically, and socially mobilized generation. A survey of 2,832 students in the United States in August 2020 indicates that recent events, such as the coronavirus pandemic, the climate crisis, and issues of racial and economic justice, have inspired Generation Z students to become more politically active (Anderson 2020).

Like millennials, large segments of Generation Z hold progressive views on issues such as freedom, diversity, women's rights, and LGBT rights and they believe that governments should play a more activist role in addressing issues of inequality and climate change (Williams 2020). Generation Z overwhelmingly believes that climate change is a man-made issue and should be urgently addressed (Annie E. Casey Foundation 2021). Across the world, Generation Z is the most diverse and most educated generation yet. They are also the first generation to be completely regarded as digital natives in the sense that they have not known the world before technology (Dimock 2019), which is reflected in their political activism (Ananthavel and Wheatley 2020). The development of new social media has made it easier for Generation Z to interact, mobilize, and engage in politics (Sivert 2020). Generation Z get their news mainly from social media as opposed to television channels and newspapers and uses social media as the primary means to express their views on political issues (Dugyala and Rahman 2020; Yeretnov 2021).

In their book, Generation Z: A Century in the Making, Seemiller and Grace argue that Generation Z's levels of trust in elites and governments are low. Broad segments of Generation Z believe that political systems do not respond to their concerns, and they want to take issues into their own hands, and to work through protest and social movements. This may explain their lower turnout rate for elections compared to other generations. The authors point to this generation's declining participation in formal institutions compared to digital platforms to protest social issues and to affect social transformation (Seemiller and Grace 2019).

According to Seemiller and Grace, surveys show that Generation Z's disillusionment with politics makes them less convinced of the effectiveness of voting than others. In contrast, these same surveys suggest that Generation Z believes that protest is a very effective means of influencing politics and public affairs. Seemiller and Grace (2019) link the lower rate of Generation Z's voter turnout compared to other generations, and their involvement in social movements, with a decline in trust and expectations in governments, institutions, and political systems (Wike and Castillo 2018).

As indicated in figure 32.2 below, As indicated in figure 32.2 below a Pew Research Center survey conducted in 2018 in 40 countries showed that young people vote less often, thereby supporting these insights. In ten of the nations polled, people aged 50 and older are more likely than 18- to 29-year-olds to say they have voted in at least one election. Those aged 18–29 are also more likely than older adults to post comments online about social or political issues in 12 of the 14 countries surveyed (Wike and Castillo 2018).

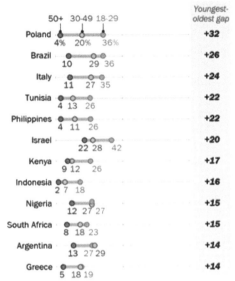

Figure 32.2 Generational difference. Source: www.pewresearch.org/global/2018/10/17/international-political-engagement/

The Arab Generation Z

The Arab Generation Z shares many common traits with its global counterpart, but it also has characteristics peculiar to the Arab context. The events of the Arab Spring raised the political and economic aspirations of Arab youth, especially regarding the prospects for political reform and democratic transformation. Surveys conducted in 2008, 2009, and 2010 showed Arab youth's desire to live in democratic societies (Morell and John 2021; Arab Youth Surveys 2008, 2009, 2010). This desire gained momentum during the protests of the Arab Spring. However, as the Arab Spring gave way to civil strife, political polarization, and renewed authoritarianism, economic and social conditions worsened with youth bearing the brunt of this decline. This led many Arab youth to renounce their enthusiasm and desire for democracy and to focus on more achievable and immediate goals such as education and employment. This becomes apparent when comparing surveys from 2008 to surveys conducted in 2020. In 2008, 90 percent of respondents said democracy was very important, while in 2020, 51 percent said democracy – as defined in the Western world – would never work in the Middle East (Arab Youth Survey 2020). In the wake of the Arab uprisings, Arab youth became more pragmatic and more focused on issues of education, and employment (Morell and John 2021). For many Arab youth, now what they value most is stability (Arab Youth Center 2020; Sky News Arabia 2020).

Declining trust in politics and in electoral participation rates

In line with global trends, the Arab Generation Z also has low political and electoral participation rates. This decline in political participation is associated with low interest in political issues and in joining formal political organizations as well as low rates of political trust. According to a 2019 Arab Barometer report on youth in the Middle East and North Africa (MENA) region, Arab youth appear uninterested in politics, both overall and when compared to older generations. The report states that

> only three-in ten youth in Lebanon (31 percent), Yemen (29 percent), Palestine (29 percent), Sudan (28 percent), and Egypt (27 percent) say they are interested or very interested in politics, while no more than a quarter say the same in Jordan (25 percent), Morocco (23 percent), Iraq (21 percent), and Libya (21 percent). Tunisian and Algerian youth are least politically interested with fewer than two in ten citing interest in politics (17 percent and 15 percent, respectively)
>
> *(Raz 2019).*

The report also maintains that Arab youth are more likely than older age cohorts to evaluate the last parliamentary elections held in their respective country as being neither free nor fair (Raz 2019). Similarly, the results of the Arab Barometer survey conducted in 2020 in 15 countries show a consistent decline in trust in governments among youth in the MENA region over the past decade. As indicated by figure 32.3 below, whereas the regional average for trust in government among youth in the MENA region was 73 percent in 2010–2011, this dropped to 42 percent in 2018–2019 (Jamal et al. 2020).

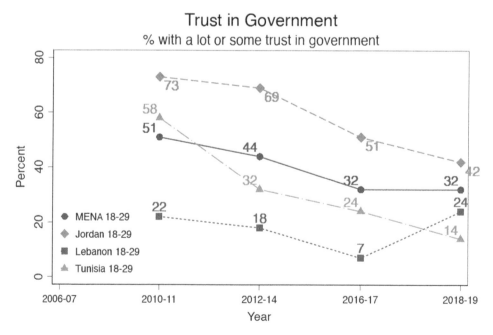

Figure 32.3 Trust in government. Source: www.arabbarometer.org/wp-content/uploads/Youth-in-MENA-2020.pdf

This lack of interest in politics, accompanied by negative evaluations of elections and declining trust in governments, is reflected in low levels of youth engagement in politics and in elections across the Arab world. The findings of the Arab Barometer for the period 2006–2016 reveal a continuous decline in the political participation of Arab youth aged 18–34. The percentage of people who vote in elections in this age group decreased from 43 percent in 2006 to 30 percent in 2016. As indicated in figure 32.4 below the decline in participation rates affected both formal and informal political participation. The percentage of young people who participated in political rallies and demonstrations during the same period decreased from 22 percent to 16 percent and while 81 percent reported using the internet, only 20 percent use it to express political views. In addition, only 33 percent use it to obtain information about political developments in their country (Arab Barometer 2016).

From the political to the social

Like its global counterpart, the Arab Generation Z is interested in new issues and concerns, which distinguishes it from previous generations. These issues include youth empowerment and entrepreneurship, corruption, education, combating sexual harassment, and promoting women's rights (Abulela 2020a; Arab Youth Survey 2020). As in the rest of the world, these issues have become important for Generation Z in the Arab world and are related to growing connectivity, cosmopolitanism, and secularism among members of this generation.

As argued above, the Arab Generation Z is mistrustful of formal institutional frameworks and has turned its back on formal political institutions such as political parties and elections (Arab Barometer 2016). As with Generation Y, social movements and horizontal organizations are more appealing to Generation Z than political parties and vertical hierarchical organizations. However, Generation Z seems to differ from Generation Y in that it is more interested in issue specific social campaigns rather than the structural social movements that were the primary focus of its predecessor. This intersects with the shift in their areas of interest, and with the general decline of ideologies and grand narratives. It is yet another way of by-passing the institutional and organizational structures eschewed by Generation Z. In recent years, many campaigns and social movements have been created in Arab countries by members of Generation Z. These campaigns have focused on social issues such as women's rights, the environment, education, youth, and health. In most cases, they have relied on social media activism, in addition to some actual protests on the ground (Abulela 2020a).

Use of social media

Globalization and modern technology have contributed to connecting Arab youth to the rest of the world. The Arab Generation Z interacts primarily through social media, which they prefer over traditional media. An opinion poll conducted by the Arab Barometer showed that young people in Arab countries trust the information they receive through social media more than the traditional media controlled by governments. More than half of internet users in the 18–30 age group in the countries surveyed see social media sites as a more reliable sources of news than television and newspapers – which they described as biased in their reporting – and prefer social networking sites as a source of information and news (Arab Barometer 2019).

Social media has given youth an alternative space for political engagement. Youth resort to social networking sites to communicate their voice, which is denied in the state-controlled traditional media. As a result, social media has often become a pressure tool. Campaigns created on

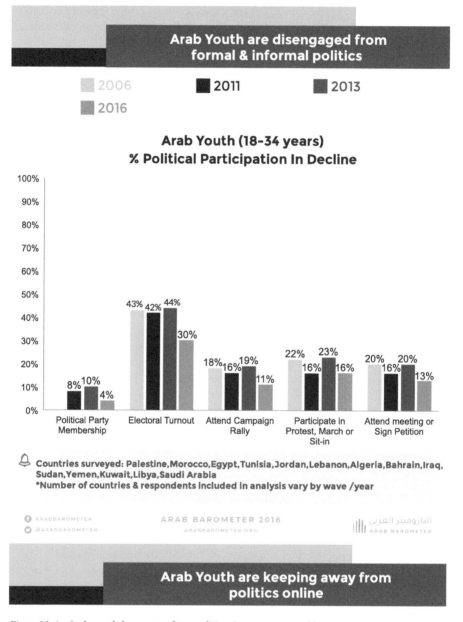

Figure 32.4 Arab youth keep away from politics. Source: www.arabbarometer.org/wp-content/uploads/Arab-Youth-Disengaged-from-Politics.pdf

social media can be a source of pressure on governments and sometimes governments are forced to pay attention to their content (Al Saadi 2018).

Changing values

The Arab Generation Z is embracing different values from previous generations of Arabs. This is reflected in their views on women and religion. According to the results of the Arab Youth Survey 2020, 70 percent of male youth from the Arab Generation Z believe that 'working women benefit the family' (Arab Youth Survey 2020; Alterman and John 2020). The place of religion and other determinants of identity is also witnessing a change for this generation. Religion is the main driver of identity for only 40 percent of those surveyed, compared to 19 percent who consider family and 17 percent who consider nationality the main determinant of identity. Even among those who consider religious identity the main driver, this feeling does not translate into support for governments that define themselves religiously (Arab Youth Survey 2020, 2021).

Similarly, the results of the Arab Barometer survey point to a decline in the phenomenon of religiosity in several Arab states, especially among Arab youth under the age of 30 (Raz 2019). The percentage of young people under the age of 30 who classified themselves as non-religious during the survey period increased from 11 percent to 18 percent, with 46 percent of Tunisian youth under the age of 30 describing themselves in 2018 as not religious, compared to 26 percent among those over 30. This is correlated with declining trust in religious leaders in most of the societies covered by the study, and a corresponding decline in trust in Islamic movements in the wake of the Arab Spring (Arab Barometer 2019). The Arab Barometer survey also documented a decline in trust in clerics by 11 points from 51 percent in 2013 to 40 percent in 2019. Similarly, the percentage of people expressing confidence in Islamist political parties decreased by more than a third from 2011 and reached just 15 percent in 2019. Furthermore, 80 percent of respondents believed that religious institutions needed reform (Raz 2019).

Declining interest in politics and in political participation, growing emphasis on social and economic issues, widespread use of new social media as a vehicle for expression and mobilization, and finally changing social values toward greater secularism and gender equality indicate that while the Arab Generation Z may not transform Arab politics in the short term, it is likely to transform Arab societies in the medium and long term. What this change is going to look like and how it is going to affect Arab politics in the future are subjects worth further exploration..

Case studies

Lebanon

Over the past decade, economic and political crises, and deepening political conflict and polarization along sectarian lines, have alienated a large segment of Lebanese youth. Surveys show that Lebanese youth are disillusioned with the sectarian political system and that most do not participate in the formal political process either by joining political parties or voting in elections, despite the relatively competitive nature of Lebanese elections, albeit along sectarian lines.

According to the SAHWA Youth Survey conducted in 2016, 96 percent of young Lebanese respondents are disillusioned with the corruption and nepotism in their country. Between 80 percent and 90 percent say they have never participated in any associative activities, including demonstrations and strikes (SAHWA Survey – Lebanon 2016). Another survey conducted by the Konrad-Adenauer-Stiftung in 2018 in Lebanon on young people between 21 and 29 years old found that 76 percent of respondents did not plan to participate in the 2018 parliamentary elections. Their reasons for non-participation included lack of trust, the futility of the elections, and that results are determined in advance. According to the same survey, 91 percent of the respondents did not belong to any political party, and 89 percent reported that they did not look forward to participating in public affairs. When asked about the public figure or the Lebanese political figure or the political party that best reflects their opinion, 'no one' was the first answer to the three questions (Konrad-Adenauer-Stiftung 2018).

Another survey conducted by the Rashad Center for Cultural Governance in 2019, found that while 46 percent of Lebanese youth expressed support for a particular political party or group, only 8.4 percent officially belong to a particular party, movement, or political group. Only a third of the respondents knew about the Lebanese Constitution, while only 7.6 percent would consider running for office one day. Furthermore, 42 percent of respondents had participated in one way or another in protests, and their most important demands were the recovery of looted funds, early parliamentary elections, the formation of a government of technocrats, the removal of the dominant sectarian political elite, and the establishment of a secular state. The survey also found that for Lebanese youth social media was the primary source of information about politics, followed by television, and then trusted people (Adyan Foundation 2020).

The Rashad Center survey found that half of Lebanese youth consider themselves religious, but for most of the respondents, religion is a personal matter between them and God. It does not affect their attitudes and relationships with others, nor does it affect the way they act in their daily lives or their own convictions. About half of the respondents stated that their sectarian affiliation does not affect their political orientation. The survey indicated that young people strongly adhere to intellectual, social, and religious pluralism and diversity, as nearly 90 percent of them have participated in religious events by other religious groups, and about 80 percent have attended an education program about different religions (Adyan Foundation 2020). Nearly 90 percent of Lebanese youth believed that the sectarian political system is the basis of the current crises because it generates divisions between sects and causes corruption and quotas, and that it has proven its failure to govern the Lebanese. Approximately 70 percent believed that the sectarian system guarantees the rights of sects, but that it marginalizes individuals and minorities (Adyan Foundation 2020).

This widespread youth disillusionment with the sectarian political system was reflected in the 'You Stink' campaign in 2015. The campaign with its emphasis on the common grievance of failed garbage collection and waste management garnered the support of youth from across the political spectrum. It laid the foundation for the 2019 protests, which raised the slogan 'All means All' in reference to a rejection of elites from all political sects and parties. And while these two movements ultimately proved ineffective against entrenched sectarian interests, they nonetheless reflected a new consensus among youth about the need to transcend the sectarian political system and to address long-standing social and economic problems.

From the 'You Stink' campaign to 'All means All' protests

In 2015, and as a result of the Lebanese government's failure to collect waste and garbage, the 'You Stink' campaign was initiated by young civil society activists. The movement capitalized on feelings of discontent among the public toward politicians, and the growing garbage crisis in Lebanon. It aimed at finding long-term solutions to the problem of waste management, raising awareness about the environment and the importance of waste recycling, and linking this to public health issues. Demonstrations in support of the campaign's demands took place and grew as the waste management crisis intensified. The protest movement, which was initially organized by young people, began to gain support among the older generations and the number of participants in the campaign doubled in just one month (Petré 2015).

The movement used the internet and social media to raise funds and to announce its demonstrations. Its demands focused on finding environmentally friendly solutions for solid waste management, reviving the role of municipalities in waste management by allocating public funds to them instead of private companies, and holding those responsible for the crisis accountable. Other youth movements, such as 'we want accountability' and 'youth against the system' joined the campaign. The protest movement positioned itself against the incompetence of political leaders, and the slogan 'All means All' appeared on social networks in condemnation of all political leaders and parties)Tadamun 2016(.

In 2015, there were disagreements over the slogan 'All means All', as several groups objected to the inclusion of their leaders within the slogan. However, during the 2019 protests, which broke out in response to a deepening economic crisis, Lebanese youth agreed that elites from all the different sects represent one corrupt bloc. As a result, the slogan 'All means All' became the general slogan of the 2019 protests (Fayyad 2019).

An important difference between the 2019 protests and those that preceded it is the generalization of 'All means All'. Equally important is the widespread adoption of demands to overthrow the entire political formula based on sectarianism, clientelism, and corruption along with the leaders upholding it (Halabi 2019). The protests highlighted the widespread conviction among young people that elections no longer offered real options for change or reform (Salloum 2019).

The October 2019 protests saw the emergence of a group of new young leaders, mostly university students, who played an important role in spreading the demand for moving beyond the sectarian system and establishing a secular state that prioritizes individual rights over the rights of the sect. While the average age of the activists leading the 2019 movement was approximately 30, youth in the age group 18–25 constituted most of the demonstrators. This age group is distinguished by the fact that it did not live through the violent civil war that the previous generation had experienced, and their memory is not linked to the war. At the same time, this generation experienced a period of unprecedented corruption in the Lebanese state, and the failure of all party leaders to address it. In sum, it is a generation who does not relate to the current political system and to the civil war that produced it (Halabi 2019).

During the 2019 protests, the *Montashereen* or the spread-out movement also appeared, highlighting that young people wanted to spread their ideas throughout Lebanon. It aimed to establish itself as an independent political party in Lebanon and to introduce political change. *Montashereen* and other Lebanese non-governmental organizations (NGOs) participated in efforts to repair the damage caused by the explosion of the Port of Beirut and they highlight the role of Lebanese youth in volunteering, serving their communities, and carrying out tasks that should be the responsibility of the Lebanese state. After the port explosion, the movement's activists decided to form a political party. The movement aimed to attract Lebanese youth tired of sectarian politicians, some even seeing them as war criminals who left their mark in the civil war. The movement presented itself as inclusive of young people from all religious sects, and as seeking to strengthen the state vis-à-vis the sects. To achieve this goal, *Montashereen* focused on political education. The party is working to appear as an alternative in upcoming elections (DW 2021).

Egypt

The Egyptian Generation Z grew up in an environment characterized by rapid change and volatility. As children, they witnessed rising demands for change, and the ascendance of new social movements leading to the January 2011 uprising, which created a sense of optimism about the possibilities for economic and political change. This was followed by a series of crises, which led to the counter-revolution on June 30, 2013, followed by a return to authoritarianism and repression, and by the Covid-19 pandemic. As a result, the political awareness and maturity of this generation developed significantly at an early age (Abu Sakeen 2020).

While the 2011 uprising had created a momentary surge in political participation among Egyptian youth, the rise of the Muslim Brotherhood, their ouster by the military in 2013, and the consequent reconstitution of authoritarianism, led to widespread demobilization and to a rapid decline in political and electoral participation especially among youth. Moreover, in light of the domestic and regional instability precipitated by the events of the Arab Spring, large segments of the Egyptian Generation Z now see stability and economic security as more important than democracy (Arab Barometer 2019; Roushdy and Sieverding 2014). Moreover, many among them have grown distrustful of religious political groups. According to the Arab Barometer, one-fifth of Egyptian youth described themselves as 'not religious', and trust in the Muslim Brotherhood decreased from 44 percent in 2011 to 17 percent in 2019 (Arab Barometer 2019). These developments have led to a noticeable shift away from political mobilization toward mobilization around social issues such as gender issues.

The rise and fall in youth electoral participation

Electoral participation among Egyptians and Egyptian youth has traditionally been low given the lack of genuine electoral competition and the long-standing hegemony of the ruling National Democratic Party (NDP) which dominated Egyptian politics from its inception in 1976. However, the ouster of Mubarak during the 2011 uprising and the dissolution of the NDP led to a temporary rise in political participation among Egyptians, including youth.

A Baseera Center survey conducted in December 2014, on a national representative sample of 2,027 citizens aged 18 years and above, shows that whereas only 36 percent of Egyptians had participated once or twice in different elections or referendums before 2011 and 59 percent had never voted, in 2014, 83 percent of Egyptians reported that they had voted at least once or twice since January 2011, while the percentage of those who stated they had never voted dropped to 15 percent. Similarly, whereas before January 2011 only 23 percent of youth aged 18–29 had ever voted, in 2014 over 75 percent reported that they had exercised their right to vote in elections or referendum processes (Refaei 2014; Osman 2015).

Two Panel Surveys of Young People in Egypt (SYPEs) conducted by the Population Council in 2009 and 2014 also show a significant rise in electoral participation in the wake of the 2011 uprising. The first round of the SYPE in 2009 found youth to be politically apathetic and disengaged. Only 16 percent of all youth aged 18–29 had voted in a previous election, less than 1 percent belonged to a political party, less than 5 percent were members of a group or organization, and fewer than 3 percent reported having participated in volunteer activities, mainly providing assistance to the poor (Population Council 2010).

The 2011 uprising created a temporary opening in the political process. As a result, millions of Egyptians were eager to vote, and the media reported much higher turnout rates for the elections and referendums that occurred from 2011 through 2012 As indicated by figure 32.5 below (Roushdy and Sieverdin 20114). The SYPE 2014 survey shows that youth participation in national elections increased substantially after 2011, with turnout ranging from 52 percent to 65 percent. Youth turnout was highest for the 2012 presidential elections, with 65.1 percent voting in the first round and 61.5 percent in the second round. Youth participation was higher than the reported overall voter turnout rates of 46 percent and 52 percent, respectively, for these two

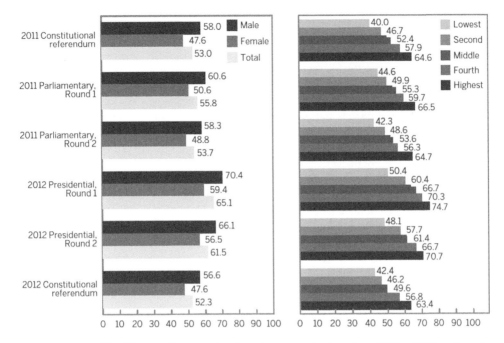

Figure 32.5 Youth's self-reported turnout in referendums and elections from 2011 to 2012, and gender and wealth quintile, 2014 (%). Source: www.unicef.org/egypt/media/4976/file/2014Survey_on_Young_People_in_Egypt.pdf

elections (Carter Center 2012). Youth turnout was lowest in the two constitutional referendums, both around 53 percent. For the 2011 and 2012 referendums, this mirrored the low overall turnout of 41 percent and 32 percent, respectively; however, as demonstrated by these figures, it was still higher than turnout rates for the general population (Sabry 2012).

The rise in electoral participation among youth after 2011 began to ebb in the wake of the 2013 counter-revolution, which led to the reconstitution of authoritarian rule in Egypt. Data from the 2014 and 2018 elections indicate a significant drop in electoral participation especially among youth. Data from the 2014 presidential elections exit polls indicate that the share of young people aged 18–30 who voted constituted only 27 percent of total interviewed voters, although this age group makes up around 37 percent of eligible voters. Similarly, low youth participation was documented during the more recent parliamentary elections in Egypt, with figures not exceeding 20 percent. Furthermore, according to the two polls that Baseera conducted before the 2015 parliamentary elections, only 4 percent of young people knew the correct dates of the elections in their governorates during the first phase of voting, and only 29 percent knew the dates during the second phase. Moreover, the 2014 Survey of Young People in Egypt shows that one in every six young people believes that it is useless to participate in politics. The survey also asked young people to rate their interest in politics, with only 17 percent of respondents describing themselves as interested or very interested in politics, and only 28 percent saying they followed political news (Osman and Girgis 2016).

This drop in youth participation could be clearly seen during the 2018 presidential elections. At the time, the head of the national media accused young people of being too lazy to participate in the electoral process and urged them to cast their votes to show the world the efficiency of the democratic electoral process in Egypt. The pro-state journalist Amr Adib also pointed out that Egyptian youth are in a state of political rebellion. He justified the low levels of young people's participation in elections as part of a global pattern whereby the young participate less than the elderly (El-Behary 2018).

Low youth turnout in the 2018 presidential elections was attributed to discontent with the political process, skepticism about the integrity of the electoral process, lack of conviction about the seriousness of the elections or the importance of their vote, as well as a general loss of confidence in the political process and in the electoral process. Youth cited lack of competition, a declining conviction in the possibility of change, and the lack of individual influence in society, as reasons for abstaining from participating in the 2018 elections (Adam 2014).

Similarly, levels of youth participation in student union elections and of general student mobilization have significantly declined since 2013. Student union elections since 2013 show very low rates of student participation. This stands in sharp contrast to the high level of engagement among university student in the elections that took place in the wake of the January 2011 uprising. Since 2013, student unions have mostly been formed by appointment (Research Unit in the Association for Freedom of Thought & Expression 2021). As an alternative, youth began to shift their focus away from political issues toward social issues such as fighting sexual harassment (Hamdy and Gameel 2018).

From the political to the social: the case of the anti-sexual harassment movement

In the context of the general shift away from political issues toward social issues, Egyptian youth activism also began to shift focus toward social issues such as sexual violence and harassment and gender rights (ACPSS 2021; Abualela 2020b). Over the past decade, many campaigns have been created in Egypt to confront sexual harassment, mainly by providing psychological and legal support to victims, reporting and documenting incidents of harassment, and providing field protection to victims. The 'I saw harassment' initiative worked on monitoring cases of harassment through its volunteers in the streets. The 'Harassment Map' initiative documented cases of harassment and supported victims by referring them to the competent civil society organizations. The 'Force Against Harassment' initiative established a presence in places where harassment is endemic, and its volunteers were ready to engage the aggressors and rescue the victims (Abualela 2020b).

From 2019, the movement to combat sexual harassment gained increased momentum and visibility. This was driven in part by the emergence of the global Me Too movement, which encouraged victims of rape and harassment to expose sexual predators, and by the emergence of local campaigns led by bloggers and social media groups (Abualela 2020b). The most influential of these social media groups is the 'Assault Police' Instagram account, which was created in 2020 and which exposed several important sexual harassment cases. 'Assault Police' sought to expose cases of sexual assault, to name and shame sexual predators, to raise awareness about the legal means available to victims of harassment, and to encourage more women to come forward to expose their aggressors. The account published thousands of testimonies about incidents of harassment against girls and women which highlighted the wide prevalence of this phenomenon in Egyptian society and the failure of cultural, legal, and religious institutions to address it (ACPSS 2021).

The creation of this and similar groups and the widespread societal debate about the incidents of harassment that were disclosed, created growing social pressure on the government to address this issue. This prompted the official media and state agencies such as the National Council for Women and the public prosecutor to investigate the validity of some of the accusations made on

'Assault Police' (ACPSS 2021). Moreover, because of these social media campaigns, the Egyptian parliament has increased the legal punishment for rape and sexual harassment and has adopted legislative amendments that protect victims of harassment by concealing their identities so that they are more willing to file complaints. These steps, in addition to the fear of being exposed on social media, represent important mechanisms that may lead in the future to reducing the phenomenon of harassment. These may also, over time, change the value system that allowed for harassment to occur on a broad scale (ACPSS 2021).

These successful social media campaigns demonstrate the increasing relevance of the internet and social media. They differ from earlier anti-harassment initiatives, which had an actual organizational structure and field role, in that the activity of these pages and blogs is limited to social media campaigns. And while previous initiatives worked to protect women in the streets through the physical presence of their volunteers, the activity of these new social media groups was limited to electronic activities such as social media campaigns, exposing cases of sexual violence, and receiving testimonies from survivors, in addition to publications related to raising awareness levels (Abualela 2020b).

Conclusions and reflections

The Arab Generation Z, like its global counterpart, is the most educated, most connected, most liberal, and least religious (in relative terms) generation of Arabs. It is also the generation that has the lowest levels of trust in politics and in elections and which tends to participate the least in the formal political process. The experiences of the previous generation of Arab youth, the Arab Generation Y, with the uprisings of the Arab Spring seem to have created widespread disillusionment among younger Arabs about the ability of democracy and political reform to solve the problems of the Arab world. The negative outcomes associated with the Arab uprisings in countries such as Libya, Syria, Yemen, Egypt, and even Tunisia seem to have convinced many young Arabs that stability is more important than democracy. Multiple youth surveys indicate that large majorities of young Arabs now prioritize issues such as employment, education, corruption, and security over issues of political reform.

One can thus make the argument that the Arab Generation Z has tended to be more realistic and pragmatic, renouncing grand visions for political change, such as Islamism, Arabism, and democratization, and focusing its energies primarily on social and economic issues and on social activism. In the case of Lebanon this was reflected in the 'You Stink' movement and in Egypt in social media campaigns such as the anti-sexual harassment campaign spearheaded by 'Assault Police'.

This doesn't mean that political activism has completely disappeared from the agenda of the Arab Generation Z. However, where political activism has occurred, it has tended to have an anti-institutional and anti-establishment character. The political protests in Sudan, Algeria, Lebanon, and Iraq in 2020 and 2021 tended to occur outside all established parties and movements and to denounce elites and ideologies in both the regime and the opposition. In Lebanon and Iraq, young protestors denounced the sectarian political systems and elites, and demanded that issues of corruption and employment be given priority. In Algeria, protestors rejected both secularists in the regime and Islamists in the opposition, and in the Sudan a broad alliance of civil society forces rejected the traditional political elites.

Moreover, for the first time in decades, many protestors across the Arab world don't seem to have identifiable political affiliations. Most are neither Islamist, leftist, or liberal nor act on behalf of a particular sect or minority. Most are demanding social and political changes that transcend these traditional divisions and which address issues of unemployment, education, and corruption. However, like the previous protests associated with the Arab Spring, these most recent protests have also failed to affect real political change.

How this general disillusionment with established elites and ideologies, and with the efficacy of political participation, is likely to change Arab politics in the coming years requires further investigation. However, one can make the argument that for large segments of the Arab Generation Z, regime change and democratization are no longer seen as the sole answer to their country's problems, and many now believe that stability, employment, education, and corruption are more pressing issues and hence their activism is more focused on such issues.

References

Abbott, Pamela, Andrea Teti and Roger Sapsford. 2017. *Youth and the Arab Uprisings: The Story of the Rising Tide*. Arab Transformations Project.

Abu Sakeen, H. 2020, October. 'Generation of Trauma and Trust in Institutions'. *Ahwal Masrya* 78: 100.

Abualela, Abdalmajeed. 2020a, October. 'Generation Z between Accepting and Rejecting the Constants'. *Ahwal Masrya* 78: 123–131.

Abualela, Abdalmajeed. 2020b, October. 'The Role of blogs and Social Media Pages in the Movement Against Sexual Violence'. *Democracy Magazine* 80: 32–37.

Adam, Mohamed. 2014. 'The Missing Vote: Where Were the Youth in Egypt's Elections?' The Tahrir Institute for Middle East Policy', 29 May. Available at: https://timep.org/presidential-elections-monitoring/the-missing-vote-where-were-the-youth-in-egypts-elections/.

Adyan Foundation. 2020. *Survey of Lebanese Youth on Politics and Sectarianism*. Beirut: Adyan Foundation.

Al Ahram Center for Political and Strategic Studies (ACPSS). 2021. *The Public Sphere and the "Covid-19" Challenge*. Arab Strategic Report 32.

Al Saadi, Farah. 2018. 'On International Youth Day: Arab Youth Stay out of Politics'. *Raseef 22*, 13 August. Available at: http://bitly.ws/zmhk

Alterman, Jon and Sunil John. 2020. *Surveying Arab Youth*. Center for Strategic and International Studies. Available at: https://www.csis.org/analysis/surveying-arab-youth.

Ananthavel, Sindhu and Regan Wheatley. 2020. 'The Gen Z Vote: Digital Outreach in the 2020 election'. *The Daily Nexus*, 15 November. Available at: https://dailynexus.com/2020-11-15/the-gen-z-vote-digital-outreach-in-the-2020-election/.

Anderson, Charles. 2013. 'Youth, the Arab Spring, and Social Movements'. *Review of Middle East Studies* 47(2): 150–156.

Anderson, Greta. 2020. 'Gen Z Students Plan to Vote in 2020'. *Inside Higher Education*, 24 September. Available at: https://www.insidehighered.com/quicktakes/2020/09/24/report-gen-z-students-plan-vote-2020

Annie Casey Foundation. 2021. *What are the Core Characteristics of Generation Z*. Available at: https://www.aecf.org/blog/what-are-the-core-characteristics-of-generation-z

Arab Barometer. 2016. 'Arab Youth Keep Away from Politics'. Available at: https://www.arabbarometer.org/wp-content/uploads/Arab-Youth-Disengaged-from-Politics.pdf.

Arab Barometer. 2019. 'New Poll: Arab Youth Change Their Beliefs and Impressions'. *Arab Barometer*. Available at: http://bitly.ws/zmhp

Arab Youth Center. 2020. 'Arab Youth Priorities Survey'. Available at: https://arabyouthcenter.org/en/article/our-research/arab-youth-priority-survey.

Arab Youth Surveys. 2008–2021. 'AASD-BCW'. Available at: http://arabyouthsurvey.com/en/.

Austin, Leila. 2011. 'The Politics of Youth Bulge: From Islamic Activism to Democratic Reform in the Middle East and North Africa'. *SAIS Review of International Affairs* 31(2): 81–96.

Carter Center. 2012. *Presidential Election in Egypt: Final Report*. Atlanta: The Carter Center. Available at: www.cartercenter.Org/resources/pdfs/news/peace_publications/election_reports/egypt-final-presidential-elections-2012.Pdf.

Cole, Juan. 2014. *The New Arabs: How the Millennial Generation is Changing the Middle East*. New York: Simon & Schuster.

Dimock, Michael. 2019. 'Defining Generations: Where Millennials End and Generation Z Begins'. *Pew Research Center*, 17 June. Available at: https://www.pewresearch.org/fact-tank/2019/01/17/where-millennials-end-and-generation-z-begins/.

Dugyala, Rishika and Kamran Rahman. 2020. '6 Things to Know about Gen Z, Politics and 2020'. *Politico*. Available at: https://www.politico.com/news/2020/10/11/gen-z-politics-2020-poll-takeaways-426767.

DW. 2021. 'Young Activists Fight for a New Lebanon'. *DW*, 5 June. Available at: https://www.dw.com/en/young-activists-fight-for-a-new-lebanon/a-57788237.

El-Behary, H. 2018, March 28. 'Why Is There Low Youth Turnout in the 2018 Presidential Elections?' *Egypt Independent*. Retrieved February 1, 2022, from https://egyptindependent.com/low-youth-turnout-2018-presidential-elections/.

Fayyad, Mona. 2019. 'The Younger Generation and Getting Lebanon out of the Sectarian Bottle'. *Alhurra*, 17 November. Available at: http://bitly.ws/zmht

Foa, Roberto and Yascha Mounk. 2019. 'Youth and the Populist Wave'. *Philosophy & Social Criticism* 45(9–10): 1013–1024.

Giroux, Henry. 2010. *Politics after Hope: Obama and the Crisis of Youth, Race, and Democracy*. London: Routledge.

Halabi, F. 2019. *From 'Overthrowing the Regime' to 'All Means All': An Analysis of the Lebanonisation of Arab Spring Rhetoric*. Paris: Arab Reform Initiative. Available at: https://www.arab-reform.net/pdf/?pid=8289&plang=en.

Hamdy, Naila and Mohamed Gameel. 2018. 'Egyptian Youth: Networked Citizens but Not Fully Engaged Politically'. *Arab Media & Society 26*. Available at: https://www.arabmediasociety.com/egyptian-youth-networked-citizens-but-not-fully-engaged-politically/.

Herrera, Linda. 2009. 'Pensée 1: Youth and Generational Renewal in the Middle East'. *International Journal of Middle East Studies* 41(3): 368–371.

Inglehart, Ronald. 1971. 'The Silent Revolution in Europe: Intergenerational Change in Post-industrial Societies'. *American Political Science Review* 65(4): 991–1017.

Inglehart, Ronald. 1977. *The Silent Revolution: Changing Values and Political Styles Among Western Publics*. Princeton, NJ: Princeton University Press.

Inglehart, Ronald. 2008. 'Changing Values Among Western Publics from 1970 to 2006'. *West European Politics* 31(1–2): 130–146.

Jamal, Amaney, Salma Al-Shami and Michael Robbins. 2020. *Youth in MENA: Findings from the Fifth Wave of the Arab Barometer*. The Arab Barometer. Available at: https://www.arabbarometer.org/wp-content/uploads/Youth-in-MENA-2020.pdf.

Konrad-Adenauer-Stiftung. 2018. *Election Polling Survey Lebanese Youth Segment*. Konrad-Adenauer-Stiftung. Available at: https://www.kas.de/c/document_library/get_file?uuid=56544a6f-3b7d-b892-a4e9-fa6156f4f325&groupId=284382.

Lange, Michael. 2011. *The Arab Youth and the Dawn of Democracy*. Konrad Adenauer Stiftung International Reports: 1–10.

Mannheim, Karl. 1952. 'The Problem of Generations'. In Paul Kecskemeti (ed.), *Essays on the Sociology of Knowledge: Collected Works. Volume 5*. New York: Routledge, 276–322.

Morell, Michael and Sunil John. 2021. 'What a Seminal Survey Tells Us about the Views of Arab Youth'. *CBS News*. Available at: https://www.cbsnews.com/news/arab-youth-views-opinion-poll/.

Osman, Maged. 2015. 'Political Conditions in Egypt: Press Release'. *Baseera*. Available at: www.baseera.com.eg/pdf_poll_file_en/participation%20in%20parliamentary%20elections-%20En.pdf.

Osman, Magued and Hanan Girgis. 2016. 'Towards Effective Youth Participation'. Policy Brief. Cairo: Population Council. Available at: https://www.popcouncil.org/uploads/pdfs/2016PGY_SYPE-civic-brief.pdf.

Parker, Kim and Ruth Igielnik. 2020. 'On the Cusp of Adulthood and Facing an Uncertain Future: What We Know about Gen Z so Far'. Pew Research Center's Social & Demographic Trends Project. Available at: https://www.pewresearch.org/social-trends/2020/05/14/on-the-cusp-of-adulthood-and-facing-an-uncertain-future-what-we-know-about-gen-z-so-far-2/.

Petré, Christine. 2015. '#youstink: The Environmental Youth Movement in Lebanon'. *World Bank Blogs*. Available at: https://blogs.worldbank.org/arabvoices/youstink-environmental-youth-movement-lebanon.

Population Council. 2010. 'Survey of Young People in Egypt: Final Report'. Available at: https://www.popcouncil.org/uploads/pdfs/2010PGY_sypefinalreport.pdf.

Raz, Daniella. 2019. *Youth in Middle East and North Africa*. Arab Barometer. Available at: https://www.arabbarometer.org/wp-content/uploads/ABV_Youth_Report_Public-Opinion_Middle-East-North-Africa_2019-1.pdf.

Refaei, Mostafa Magdy. 2014. *Political Participation in Egypt: Perceptions and Practice. AECID*. Available at: https://www.aecid.es/centro-documentacion/documentos/documentos%20adjuntos/informe%20final.%20participaci%c3%b3n%20pol%c3%adtica%20en%20egipto_eng.pdf.

Research Unit in the Association for Freedom of Thought & Expression. 2021. *Out of Coverage…The Student Unions' Election in Egyptian Universities during a Decade 2011–2020*. Cairo: Association of Freedom of Thought and Expression. Available at: https://afteegypt.org/wp-content/uploads/2021/04/Out-of-Coverage-Student-Unions.pdf.

Roushdy, Rania and Maia Sieverding. 2014. *Panel Survey of Young People in Egypt (SYPE) 2014: Generating Evidence for Policy, Programs, and Research*. Unicef. Available at: https://www.unicef.org/egypt/media/4976/file/2014Survey_on_Young_People_in_Egypt.pdf.

Sabry, Bassem. 2012. 'The Meaning of Egypt's Referendum'. *Al Monitor*, 23 December. Available at: www.al-monitor.com/pulse/originals/2014/01/egypt-referendum-constitution-evaluation.html.

Salloum, Saad. 2019. 'Key Points about the Protest Movement in Lebanon and Iraq'. *Taadudiya*, 21 November. Available at; http://bitly.ws/zmhu

Sayre, Edward and Tarik Yousef. 2016. *Young Generation Awakening: Economics, Society, and Policy on the Eve of the Arab Spring*. Oxford: Oxford University Press.

Seemiller, Corey and Meghan Grace. 2019. *Generation Z: A Century in the Making*. London: Routledge.

Sivert, Samantha. 2020. 'Generation Z Comes out to the Polls in Record Numbers'. *The Hofstra Chronicle*, 17 November. Available at: https://www.thehofstrachronicle.com/category/news/2020/11/15/recent-election-data-shows-generation-z-is-more-likely-to-be-progressive-and-politically-active-than-older-generations.

Sky News Arabia. 2020. 'Arab Youth Unanimously Agree on 3 Priorities that Form the Basis of Development'. *Sky News Arabia*, 11 August. Available at: http://bitly.ws/zmhv

Tadamun. 2016. 'The Garbage Crisis in Lebanon: From Protest to Movement to Municipal Elections'. *Tadamun*, 19 March. Available at: http://www.tadamun.co/garbage-crisis-lebanon-protest-movement-municipal-elections/?Lang=en#.ytpl3_n7ti.

Tinnes, Judith. 2020. 'Bibliography: Children, Youth, and Terrorism'. *Perspectives on Terrorism* 14(3): 125–167.

Wike, Richard and Alexandra Castillo. 2018. Many Around the World are Disengaged from Politics. *Pew Research Center*. Available at; https://www.pewresearch.org/global/2018/10/17/international-political-engagement/.

Williams, Dalton. 2020. 'How Could Gen Z Impact the 2020 Election'. *KVII*. Available at: https://abc7amarillo.com/news/local/how-could-gen-z-impact-the-2020-election.

Wright, Robin. 2011. *Rock the Casbah: Rage and Rebellion across the Islamic World*. New York: Simon & Schuster.

Yeretnov, Eddy. 2021. 'Generation Z Enters the Political Scene'. *Scot Scoop News*, 23 January. Available at: https://scotscoop.com/generation-z-enters-the-political-scene/.

INDEX

9/11 223
17-25 December Operations, Turkey 332–333
1967 Six Day War 241
1979 Islamic Revolution, Iran 160–161
2008 election law, Lebanon 152–154
2010 referendum, Turkey 138–139
2011 Arab uprisings 2, 18, 32, 202–203
2011 elections, Tunisia 111
2014 parliamentary elections, Tunisia **113**
2014 presidential elections, Turkey 332–334
2015 general elections, Turkey 334–336
2017 election law, Lebanon 154–156
2018 elections, Iraq 128–130
2018 general election, Turkey 336–339
2018 Organic Law, Tunisia 183
2018 presidential election: Egypt 83–86; Turkey 139, 336–339
2019 elections: Tunisia **116**; Turkey 311–318
2020 elections, Kuwait 294–305
2020 parliamentary elections, Egypt (2020) 86–89
2021 elections, Iraq 128–130

Abbas, Mansour 383–384
Abdallahi, Ould 68, 74
Aboul-Fotouh, Abdel-Moneim 80
abstention, voting behavior 408
Adalet ve Kalkinma Partisi (Justice and Development Party, AKP) 134–136, 266, 310–312, 405; 2014 presidential elections 332–333; 2015 general elections 334–336; 2019 elections 312–318; characteristics of 321–323; clientelism 323–324; electoral manipulation 140–141; opposition coordination 324; polarisation 331–332; political hegemony 136–139; popular legitimacy 141–144; repercussions for 324–325
Afek Tounes 282, 285–286
Afghanistan, women 223

Afrobarometer 367, 371
Afro-Mauritanian communities 73
Ahmadinejad, Mahmoud 168
Aksener, Meral 314, 338
Al Hashem, Safa 303
Al Sabah, Jaber Mubarak 302
Al Sabah, Meshaal Al Ahmed Al Jaber 296
al-Adlwa al-Ihsan 45
Al-Anbaa 295
Al-Aridha Chaabeya 265
al-Assad, Bashar 15–16
Al-Badawy, Al-Sayyid 85
al-Baghdadi, Abu Bakr 350
Algeria 26–27; Algerian War of Independence (1954-1962) 224–225; Black Decade 225–226; bureaucratic management of plurality 33–35; clientelism 23; elections as technology of power 30–33; gender quotas 5, 223–224, 226; Hirak 35; popular consultations 27–30; voting behavior 406; women's descriptive representation 222–223; women's rights 225–226
Algerian War of Independence (1954-1962) 224–225
al-Hamid, Sa'ib' Abd 127
Ali, Ben 110–111
Ali, Khaled 85
Alignment party 103
Al-Keeb, Abdul Rahim 347
Al-Mustakillah 265
Al-Nasser, Gamal Abd 238
Al-Nour 82–83
Al-Qabas 295
Al-Qadhdhāfī, Mu'ammar 343, 345, 349
Al-Rai 295
Al-Sabah, Nawaf Al-Ahmad Al-Jaber 295
Al-Sadat, Mohamed Anwar 85

429

Index

Al-Sadr, Muqtada 127
al-Sajjad 393
Al-Saud, Abdulaziz bin Abdul Rahman 187–188
Al-Seyasah 295
Al-Sisi, Abdel-Fattah 78–79; 2014 presidential election 79–81; 2015 parliamentary election 81–83; 2018 presidential election 83–86; 2020 parliamentary elections 86–89
Al-Thinni, Abduallah 344
Al-Wafd 85, 87
Amal 394, 396
Amel, Mehdi 398n8
amir 188
Anan, Sami 80, 84
Annahj Democrati (Democratic Way) 44–45
Ansar al-Sharia 349–350
anti-authoritarian alliances 122
anti-Islamist bloc, Tunisia 112–115
Arab Democratic Party (ADP) 243
Arab Generation Z 412–415, 425–426; changing values 419; declining trust in politics 416–417; Egypt 421–425; electoral participation 416–417; Lebanon 419–421; social media 417, 418
Arab monarchies, legislative elections 19
Arab Movement for Renewal (*Ta'al*) 243
Arab Palestinian party politics, in Israel 378–380
Arab party politics, Israel 380–384
Arab society, in Israel 237–238
Arab World: democracy 202; electoral assistance 206–210; international monitoring 203–206; political role of military 67–68; voter turnout 358–360
Arab-Israeli (Zionist) 237–238, 245
Arab-Jewish Hadash 246
Arab-Jewish non-Zionist (Communist) 237–239
Arabs: citizens of Israel 378–380; democracy 7; participation in Knesset elections 246–247; political mobilization (1977-1999), Israel 241–245; political recruitment of Arabs (1949–1973), Israel 239–241; voter turnout Knesset elections (2003-2021) *248*
Arafat, Yasser 245, 254–255
Assault Police Instagram account 424
authoritarian elections 1
authoritarian regimes 13, 206; election results 267–268; gender quotas 223
autocratic legalism 138
autocratization, Turkey 136–139
autocrats 13
Aziz, Ould Abdel 66, 68, 70, 72

Ba'ath Party 18–19, 395
Balad 242–243, 246, 381, 384
Bani Walid, Libya 347–348
Barak, Ehud 104, 244
Barzani, Masoud 218–219
Begin, Menachem 102

Beirut Is My City List 155; *see also Beirut Madinati*
Beirut Madinati 396
Bejjani, Joseph 394
Benghazi, Libya 349–350
Ben-Gurion, David 100–102
Benyouness, Amara 226
Berry, Mirra 394
Black Decade, Algeria 225–226
Bloc National 396
blood bonds, Lebanon 149
Blue-White party 105
Bouteflika, Abdelaziz 225
boycotts: Algeria 34–35; Lebanon 396; Morocco 44–45; Palestine 252
Bread and Freedom parties 87
brokerage, Iraq 126–128
brokers 269
bureaucratic management of plurality, Algeria 33–35
Bush, Laura 223

Cairo Declaration 257–258
campaigns 263; COVID-19 pandemic 296; hybrid election campaigns 279; independence referendum in Kurdistan 218–219; Israel 381–382; opposition campaigns 320; Saudi Arabia 192–193; social media 7; Tunisia 264–267, 272; *see also* digital electoral campaigns; electoral machines
candidate registration, Saudi Arabia 191–192
candidates, Kuwait *301*
canvassing 269–270
cashirism, Algeria 34
Christians, Lebanon 153–154, 389
circumventing foreign observers 204
cities, local elections 20–23
citizens-initiated campaigning 280
Civic Campaign for Electoral Reform, Lebanon 154
Civil Democratic Movement, Egypt 83
civil society movements, Lebanon 396
class dynamics, preventing in Lebanon 391–393
clientelism 366–367, 373–374; *Adalet ve Kalkınma Partisi* (Justice and Development Party, AKP) 323–324; collective clientelism 367, 371–372; competitive clientelism 404; demand for democracy 372–373; executive elections 17; Lebanon 148, 392; legislative elections 20; local elections 22–23; party linkages 369–370; social norms 371–372; Tunisia 271, 370–373; types of 367–368; vote-buying 367–368, 371–372
Coalition for a Peaceful Alternative 70
collective clientelism 367, 371–372
communication, candidates in Tunisia 265
communicative objectives 280, **288**
Communist Party in Iraq 123–128
competitive authoritarianism 26, 406–408

competitive clientelism 404
competitiveness, Morocco 48–49
consociationalism 5, 398n5
consociativism, Lebanon 148–150
constitutional bodies, Tunisia 179–180
Constitutional Union (UC) 46
consumption voting 357
cooperation, cross-ideological cooperation 122
coordination: informal coordination 312; with opposition parties 320
Coordination of the Democratic Opposition (COD) 70
corruption, Turkey 332
Council for Development and Reconstruction (CDR) 393
Council of Guardians 163–164
coups/coup d'etat 67; Algeria 28–29; Egypt 78; Mauritania 66, 74; Turkey 135
Courant Démocrate 285–286
COVID-19 pandemic 407; Kuwait 296–298; Lebanon 393
critical actors 228
cross-ideological cooperation, Iraq 121–123
cross-ideological social brokerage, Iraq 126–128
Cumhur İttifaki (People's Alliance) 312
Cumhuriyet Halk Partisi (Republic People's Party, CHP) 135–136, 140, 310–313, 332, 337
cyber-pessimism 279

Darawsheh, 'Abd al-Wahhab 243
Dark Decade, Algeria 29, 32
Darwish, Abdullah Nimer 242
Dash party 102
Da'wa 125
debt, Lebanon 390–391
Declaration of Principles for International Election Observation and its Code of Conduct (Declaration of Principles, DOP) 202, 211n2, 253
declining trust in politics, Arab Generation Z 416–417
degree of extremism, electoral districts 57
demand for clientelism and democracy 372–373
Demirtas, Selahattin 338
democracy 201, 403; clientelism 372–373
democracy promotion programs 201
Democratic Accountability and Linkages Project (DALP) 368–371, 373
democratic backsliding 4–5; Turkey 139
Democratic Constitutional Rally (RCD) 109–110
Democratic Front for Peace and Equality (*Hadash*) 242
Democratic National Alliance (*Balad*) 242
Democratic Party for Democracy and Renewal (PRDR) 68
Democratic Socialist Party (PSD) 45, 110
democratic socializing 67

de-polarization 320
deviation ratio, electoral districts 57
digital electoral campaigns 277, 279–280, 287–288; *Afek Tounes* 285–286; objectives of 280–281; *see also* social media
divided structures of contestation 19
diwaniyaat 294, 299
diwaniyas 293, 299
Doha Agreement 153–154
domestic violence, Algeria 226

East Jerusalem 251, 255
Effective Number of Parties in Parliament (ENPP) 97, 99–100
Egypt 2; 2014 presidential election 79–81; 2015 parliamentary election 81–83; 2018 presidential election 83–86; 2020 parliamentary elections 86–89; Al-Sisi, Abdel-Fattah 78–79; electoral assistance 207; executive elections 15–17; Generation Z 421–425; legislative elections 18; local elections 21; National Security Agency (NSA) 87; voter turnout 407
Egyptian Patriotic Movement Party 83
Egyptian Social Democratic Party (ESDP) 82
El Amal Ettounsi 111
election laws: division of electoral districts, Jordan 58–61; Lebanon 152–156
election monitoring, Saudi Arabia 190
electoral architecture 5
electoral assistance: in authoritarian regimes 206–208; during democratization in Arab World 209–210
electoral authoritarian regimes 14
electoral authoritarianism 27
electoral autocracies, Morocco 39
electoral behaviour 403–404; Morocco 48–50; *see also* voter turnout
electoral campaigns, Saudi Arabia 191–193
electoral disorders, Algeria 27–28
electoral districts, Jordan 55; effect on outcomes of electoral process 63; election laws 58–61; geographical division of 56–58; patterns of division 55–56; rationale for geographic division 61–63
electoral engineering 54
electoral fairness, Turkey **142**
electoral fetishism 202
electoral fraud, Algeria 33
electoral infrastructure, Palestine 255
electoral integrity: Morocco 40, 43; Turkey 140–141
electoral machines, Tunisia 267–271
Electoral Management Body (EMB) 175, 180
electoral manipulation, Turkey 140–141
electoral observers, international monitoring 203–206
electoral outcomes, Libya 347–350

Index

electoral participation: Arab Generation Z 416–417; Egypt Generation Z 422–424; Morocco 45–46; women, Saudi Arabia 193–195; *see also* voter turnout
electoral processes, Tunisia 183–184
electoral reform, Lebanon 392
electoral regulations, Saudi Arabia 189–191
electoral revolution 202
electoral system: Israel 100; Lebanon 150–152; Morocco 40–42; Turkey 135–136
El-Kleib, Abdul Rahim 345
emergency rule, Turkey 138
Ennahda 110–111, 113, 115–117, 263–264, 266–267, 283–284
equality of voting 57
Erdoğan, Tayyip 21, 136, 139, 142–144, 312–313, 334–338
Ergenekon 137
Eshkol, Levi 100, 102
Essebsi, Beji Caïd 112, 115, 263
Essebsi, Hafedh Caïd 114
Essid, Habib 113–114
ethnic diversity, Mauritania 70–71
evolution of political parties (2002-2021), Morocco 46–48
executive aggrandizement, Turkey 138–139
executive elections 15–17

Facebook 277, 282–283, 285–286; *see also* social media
Fadlallah, Hassan 393
Faiza, Hajja 223
Fajr Libia (Libya Dawn) 344
Family Code, Algeria 225–226
family ties, Lebanon 149
Fatah 251, 254–255, 257–259
Fateh coalition 125, 128–130
Felicity Party (Saadet Partisi, SP) 313
female circumcision 223
female parliamentarians 227–230
female suffrage, Saudi Arabia 193–195
first-order elections 360–361
foreign intervention in elections 203
foreign observers, circumventing 204
fragmentation, Israel 99
fragmented parliament strategy, Egypt (2015) 81–83
fraudulent elections 205
Free Patriotic Movement (FPM) 394
Front Populaire 284
Future Movement Party 396

Gaza Strip 245, 251, 254
gender parity 264–265
gender quotas 5, 23, 222; Algeria 223–224, 226; women's empowerment 226–230
General Confederation of Lebanese Workers (GCLW) 395

General National Congress (GNC), Libya 342–343, 347–348
Generation Z 413–415; *see also* Arab Generation Z
generational analysis 412
generations, defined 413
geographical division of electoral districts, Jordan 56–58
gerrymandering 403–404
Gezi movement 333
Gezi Park protests, Turkey 329–330, 332
Ghannouchi, Rached 112, 114, 263
Ghariani, Mohamed 111
Gharib, Hanna 395
Ghazouani, Mohamed Ould 66
global deviation rates 57
Good Party (IYI Parti, IYIP) 311
Goran Party (Change Movement) 214, 218
Government of National Unity (GNU) 344
gray regimes 14–15
The Green Line 241
grievance voting 361
Gülen movement 333, 336

Hadar 293, 299
Hadash 242–243, 381, 384
Haftar, Khalifa 344, 350
Halklann Demokratik Partisi (HDP) 311, 315, 318
Hamas 23, 225, 245, 251, 257–259, 380
Hamdi, Hechmi 265
harassment, Lebanon 394
Harassment Map initiative 424
Hare quota, Morocco 42
Hariri, Saad 396
hegemony, Lebanon 392–394
Hezbollah 153, 393–394, 396, 405
High National Election Commission (HNEC), Libya 344, 347
Higher Committee for the Coordination of National Opposition Parties (HCCNOP) 121–123
Hirak, Algeria 35
hittists, Tunisia 272
Hizb al-Rahma 117
Hokumat-e Eslami 165
House of Representatives: Jordan 60; Morocco **41**
hybrid election campaigns 279
hybrid regimes, Islamic Republic 167–169
hybridity 287
hyper normality 278

identifying one's position on political spectrum 266–267
identity issues 7
ideologies 401–403
İhsanoğlu, Ekmeleddin 332–333
İmamoğlu, Ekrem 319
Imtidad party 130

432

Ince, Muharrem 338
independence referendum in Kurdistan 214–220
Independent High Authority for the Elections (ISIE) 110, 175–176, 265; legal guarantees 176–180; transitional context of ISIE independence 181–184
informal coordination 312
International Covenant on Civil and Political Rights 56
international monitoring 203–206; *see also* monitoring
international non-governmental organizations (INGOs) 201–202
international organizations (IOs) 201, 203
inter-sectarian tensions, Iraq 123
interventions in elections 203
intifada 393
IRA-Mauritania alliance 70–71
Iran 160–161; Council of Guardians 163–164; Islamic Republic 167–169; president of the Republic 164; requirements for a passive electorate 164–165; *Vali-ye faqih* 162–163; *Velayat-e faqih (Rahbari)* 161–162
Iraq 1, 121; 2018 elections 128–130; 2021 elections 128–130; consociationalism 5; cross-ideological cooperation 121–123; electoral assistance 210; independence referendum in Kurdistan 214–220; Sadrists and Communists 123–128
Iraqi Communist Party 125
Iraqi Kurdistan 2
Islah 122
Islamic government 161–162; Ayatollah Khomeini 165–166
Islamic institutions: Council of Guardians 163–164; *Vali-ye faqih* 162–163; *Velayat-e faqih (Rahbari)* 161–162
Islamic principles, Iran 160–161
Islamic Renaissance Movement (an-Nahda) 225
Islamic Republic 163; hybrid regimes 167–169; Iran 161; requirements for a passive electorate 164–165
Islamic Salvation Front (FIS) 21, 26, 28, 225
Islamic State, Libya 350
Islamic Supreme Council of Iraq (ISCI) 125
Islamist Justice and Development Party (PJD) 22, 42, 46–50, 52n9, 266, 359, 405
Islamist movement: Libya 348–349; Tunisia 263
Islamist opposition women 230
Islamist party, Israel 382–384
Islamists: *al-Adlwa al-Ihsan* 45; clientelism 21; Israel 237–238; socialists and 22
Islamist-secular divide 405
Israel 1, 97–98, 153; Arab citizens 378–380; Arab Palestinian party politics 378–380; Arab party politics 380–384; Arab society 237–238; campaigns 381–382; electoral system 100; Knesset 237; Palestinian politics 384–385; parliamentary regimes 98–100; policy of normalisation 252; political efficacy (2003-2022) 245–248; political mobilization (1977-1999) 241–245; political recruitment of Arabs (1949-1973) 239–241; prime ministers 100–105; Ra'am 382–384; voting behavior 359
Israeli Arabs 237
Israeli-Arab Zionist 239
Israeli-Jewish parties 382
Israeli-Palestinian conflict 380
Israeli-Palestinian Interim Agreement 253
Israeli-Palestinian peace talks 245
Itilaf al-Karama 117
IYI Parti (IYIP) 311, 313–315, 337

Jabhat al-Islah 117
Jaish al-Mahdi 127
Jammoul, Ali 394
Jibril, Mahmoud 349
Joint List, Israel 381–383
Jordan: election laws 58–61; electoral districts *see* electoral districts (Jordan); executive elections 17; legislative elections 19–20; party linkages 370; rationale for geographic division of electoral districts 61–63; voting behavior 406
Joumblatt, Walid 390
justice, electoral districts (Jordan) **62**
Justice and Development Party *see Adalet ve Kalkinma Partisi* (Justice and Development Party, AKP)

Kabbara, Mohamad 390
Kabyle Algerians 225
Kadima 105
Karama (Operation Dignity) 344
Karoui, Nabil 115
Khalaf, Melhem 398n13
Khomeini, Ruhollah 160–162, 165–166
Knesset (Israel) 237; election turnout (1949-1973) **240**; election turnout (1977-1999) **244**; voter turnout (2003-2022) **247**
Konsowa, Ahmed 84–85
Kurdish New Generation Movement 130
Kurdish People's Democratic Party (Halklann Demokratik Partisi, HDP) 311
Kurdish Peshmerga 218
Kurdistan, independence referendum 214–220
Kurdistan Democratic Party (KDP) 214, 217, 220
Kurdistan Independent High Elections and Referendum Commission (KHEC) 215
Kurdistan Islamic Group (KIG) 214
Kurdistan Islamic Union (KIU) 214
Kuwait 292–293; context of 2020 elections 294–296; media 294–305; scandals 302–303; social media 300, 305–306; women in political leadership 303–305
Kuwait National Assembly (KNA) 293
Kuwait Votes 297

Index

La'ihat al-Biyarta (The Beirutis' List) 155
La'ihat Bayrut Madinati (Beirut Is My City List) 155
Land Day (1976) 243
largest remainder method, Morocco 42
Law on Local Councils (1996), Palestine 257
leadership patterns: prime ministers **105**; prime ministers in parliamentary democracies **101**
Lebanese Communist Party 396
Lebanese Option Gathering (LOP) 394
Lebanon 1–2, 147–148; 2008 election law 152–154; 2017 election law 154–156; Arab Generation Z 419–421; clientelism 148, 392; consociativism 148–150; COVID-19 pandemic 393; electoral reform 392; electoral system 150–152; General Confederation of Lebanese Workers (GCLW) 395; hegemony 392–394; *Montashereen* 421; neoliberal sectarianism 148–150; neoliberalism 388, 390–391; preventing emergence of class dynamics 391–393; protests 396, 421; public sector 404; sectarian parties 387, 391–392; sectarianism 388–390; socioeconomic inequalities 390–391; strikes 395; 'you stink' campaign 396, 420–421
legal guarantees, Independent High Authority for the Elections (ISIE) 176–180
legislative elections 17–20; Mauritania 72–73; Palestine 258
legislatures 17–20
liberalized autocracies 14
Libya 2, 342–343; *Ansar al-Sharia* 349–350; electoral outcomes 347–350; end of democratic process 347–350; General National Congress (GNC) 342; Islamist movement 348–349; military 73; National Transitional Council (NTC) 343, 345–346; preparations for elections 345–346; Salafi movement 348–349
Libya Dawn (Fajr Libia) 344
Libyan Arab Armed Forces (LAAF) 344
Libyan Political Dialogue Forum (LPDF) 344
Likud Party 102, 103, 384
local elections 20–23; Turkey 311–312, 316–317, 320–324
loyal opposition 39

Madaniyoun coalition 125
Mahfoud, Nehme 395
malapportionment 403–404
Mapai 100, 102, 239, 240
marketing objectives **288**; digital electoral campaigns 280–281
Maronite faction, Lebanon 389
Marzouk, Mohsen 111, 114
Mauritania 66–67; coups 66; ethnic diversity 70–71; executive elections 17; legislative elections 72–73; party system 68–71; political actors 70–71; political role of military 73–75;

presidential elections 72; review and control of institutions 71–72
Me Too movement 424
Mechichi, Hichem 118
media, role in Kuwait 2020 elections **294**, 296–305
media bullying, Egypt 79–81
meetings: political machines 269–270; Tunisia 272
Meir, Golda 102
MENA elections 2–4, 6–7; executive elections 15–17; legislative elections 17–20; local elections 20–23
men's substantive representation 229–230
military: Mauritania 66–67, 73–75; political role in the Arab world 67–68
Military Council for Justice and Democracy (CMJD), Mauritania 74
military takeover, Algeria 28–29
millennials 413–414
Millet Ittifaki (Nation Alliance) 312
Milli Selamet Partisi (MSP) 135
Milliyetçi Haraket Partisi (MHP) 310, 334, 336–337
Minteshreen 396
misdistribution, electoral districts (Jordan) **62**
Mohammed VI 14, 20, 40, 47
MOMRA, Saudi Arabia 188–191
monitoring elections: electoral assistance 206–208; international monitoring 203–206
Montashereen 421
Morocco 14–15, 39; electoral behaviour 48–50; electoral integrity 43; electoral participation 45–46; electoral system 40–42; evolution of political parties (2002-2021) 46–48; executive elections 17; Islamists 22–23; Justice and Development Party 405; legislative elections 19–20; local elections 21–23; parliamentary elections **49**; party competition 43–45; party system fragmentation 50; pluralism 39; vote-buying 368
Mousavi, Mir Hossein 168
Moussa, Moussa Mostafa 85–86
Moussi, Abir 116–117
Mouvement Tunisie Volonté (MTV) 281, 284–288
Mouwatinoun wa mouwatinat fi dawla (Citizens in a State) 396
Movement of Islamic Tendency (MTI) 110
Movement Society for Peace (MSP or Hamas) *see* Hamas
Mubarak, Hosni 207–208
muhafaza, Lebanon 150, 153
muhasasa ta'ifyya 123
municipal councils, Saudi Arabia 188, **192**
municipal elections: digital tools 287; Palestine 257–258
municipal elections (1970s), Palestine 252–253
Muslim Brotherhood 78–81, 111, 349, 350, 361, 406

434

Muslim Brothers 18
Muslim women 223–224
Muslims: democracy 406; Lebanon 153–154
Mustamerroun coalition 125

Nahas, Charbel 396
Nation Alliance (Millet Ittifaki) 312–313, 337
Nation's Future Party (NFP) 81, 86, 89
National Action Party (Milliyetçi Hareket Partisi, MHP) 310
National Centrist Party, Libya 347
National Coalition, Tunisia 114
National Commission, Lebanon 154
National Constituent Assembly (ANC), Tunisia 109–111
National Council of Human Rights, Morocco 43
National Democratic Rally, Algeria 33–34
National Endowment for Democracy (NED) 201
National Forces Alliance (NFA), Libya 347
National Independent Electoral Commission (CENI), Mauritania 69, 71
National Liberation Front (FLN) 26, 225
National List, Egypt 88
National Pact for Development and Democracy (PNDD) 68
National People's Army (ANP), Algeria 28
National Progressive Front 18–19
National Rally of Independents (RNI) 46–48
National Security Agency (NSA), Egypt 87
National Security Council (MGK), Turkey 137
National Transitional Council (NTC), Libya 343, 345–346
National Wisdom Movement 125, 129
Nationalists, Israel 237–238, 240, 242
neoliberal sectarianism, Lebanon 148–150
neoliberalism, Lebanon 388, 390–391
neo-patrimonialism 271
Netanyahu, Benjamin 104, 105, 244, 384
Nidaa Tounes 111, 113–116, 266–267, 283–284, 362
no-confidence rule, Israel 105

Obama, Barack 388
objectives of political parties 281–282
occupation authorities, Palestine 252
Occupied Palestinian Territories (OPTs) 251
Odeh, Ayman 382
Olmert, Ehud 105
Operation Dignity (Karama) 344
opposition campaigns, Turkey 320
opposition parties: coordination with 320; Egypt 87; Mauritania 70
Organic Law No. 23-2012, Tunisia 180
Organic Law No. 2012-2023, Tunisia 182
Organic Law of 2012, Tunisia 183
Organization of American States 202
Orthodox Gathering Law, Lebanon 154

Oslo Accords 253–256
Oslo Era elections, Palestine 253–256
Oslo II 254

Palestine 2, 251; 1996 vote 255–256; Arab Palestinian party politics in Israel 378–380; legislative elections 258; municipal elections (1970s) 252–253; Oslo Era elections 253–256; post-Arafat era 256–260
Palestine Liberation Organisation (PLO) 251–253, 380
Palestinian Legislative Council (PCL) 256
Palestinian National Authority (PNA) 254–257
Palestinian politics, in Israel 384–385
Palestinians 238, 244, 245
PAM 48–50, 52n10
Pan-Arab nationalist movement 238
paradox of voting 356–358
parliamentary democracies 98
parliamentary elections: Egypt (2015) 81–83; Egypt (2020) 86–89; Morocco 40–42, **49**
parliaments, legislative elections 17–20
participation: Iraq 130; Morocco 45–46; symbolic voter participation 16; *see also* electoral participation; voter turnout
partisan identities, Tunisia 266
partisan intervention 203
party cohesion 98
party competition, Morocco 43–45
party discipline 98
party linkages 369–370
Party of Independence (PI) 46
Party of Progress and Socialism (PPS) 46
Party of Socialist Workers (PST) 30
party system, Mauritania 68–71
party system fragmentation, Morocco 50
party-based patrimonialism 270–271
party-centred strategy, 2020 parliamentary elections (Egypt) 86–89
patrimonialism 270–271
Patriotic Union of Kurdistan (PUK) 214, 217, 220
patronage 366, 403–404, 408
patterns of electoral district division, Jordan 55–56
People's Alliance (Cumhur Ittifaki) 312
People's National Assembly (APN) 32
People's Progressive Alliance (APP) 70
Perceptions of Electoral Integrity Index (PEI) 43, *44*, 52n5
Peres, Shimon 103
Peretz, Shimon 253
performance legitimacy of the regime, Turkey 319–320
personal data, managing for electoral purposes 282
personalistic politics, Tunisia 113
personalization of electoral politics 99
pluralism 18; Morocco 39; Tunisia 181
polarization: Tunisia 110–112; Turkey 329–332

political actors, Mauritania 70–71
political efficacy (2003-2022), Israel 245–248
political fragmentation 181
political hegemony, Turkey 136–139
political intimidation, Egypt 79–81
political mobilization (1977-1999), Israel 241–245
political objectives **288**; digital electoral campaigns 280
political parties 402–403; objectives of 281–282; strategic objectives *282*
political recruitment of Arabs (1949-1973), Israel 239–241
political regimes 402
political stability, Israel 100–105
politics of consensus, Tunisia 112–115
polycentric regimes, Islamic Republic 167–169
Popular Committee for the Boycott of the Knesset Elections 246
popular consultations, Algeria 27–30
Popular Front for the Liberation of Palestine (PFLP) 254
popular legitimacy, Turkey 141–144
Popular Movement (MP) 46
popular sovereignty, Algeria 30
populism 142–143
praetorian regimes 168
president of the Republic, Iran 164
presidential elections: Egypt (2014) 79–81; Egypt (2018) 83–86; Islamic Republic 167; Mauritania 72; Palestine 257–258
presidentialization of executive politics 99, 104
presidents, executive elections 15–17
preventing emergence of class dynamics, Lebanon 391–393
prime ministerialization 99
prime ministers: executive elections 15–17; Israel 98–105
print media liberalization 293
Progressive List for Peace (PLP) 242
Progressive Socialist Party (PSP) 154, 390, 394
proportional quota 153
protests: Egypt 79; Iraq 124; Lebanon 147, 396, 421; Libya 343; Palestine 256; Turkey 144, 329–330, 332
pseudo-democratic institutions, Morocco 14–15
public sector 404

qada', Lebanon 150, 153
Qalb Tounès 116
Qatar 2
quality of candidates, Kuwait *301*
quality of media content, Kuwait *301*
quantitative pluralism 181
Quartet 273n2
quasi-democracies 406–408
quasi-opposition parties 19

Ra'am 381–384
Rabin, Yitzhak 102–103
Rally for Culture and Democracy (RCD) 225
Rally of Algerian Hope (TAJ) 226
Rally of Democratic Forces (RFD) 70
Rassemblement Constitutionnel Democratique (RCD) 109–110
rate of variance, electoral districts (Jordan) **62**
redistributive-related democratic desirability 408
referenda, independence referendum in Kurdistan 214–220
regional politics, elections 2
regulating political fields, Algeria 30–31
religiosity, Arab Generation Z 417, 419
religious-secular divide 403–405
representation, women's descriptive representation 222–223
Republican People's Party (*Cumhuriyet Halk Partisi*, CHP) 310–311, 332
requirements for a passive electorate, Iran 164–165
Revolutionary Guards, Iran 168
revolutions 67
right to campaign, Tunisia 272

Saadet Partisi (SP) 313
Sadrist-Communist alliance, Iraq 123–128
Sadrists, Iraq 123–128, 130
Saïed, Kaïs 115, 118, 177, 180–181
Sa'irun 123, 125, 128–130
Salafi movement, Libya 348–349
Salafism 110
Saudi Arabia 2, 187–188; campaigns 192–193; candidate registration 191–192; electoral regulations and management 189–191; female suffrage 193–195; voter turnout 191–193
scandals, Kuwait 302–303
secession 216
second-order elections, voting behavior 361–362
sectarian parties, Lebanon 387, 391–392
sectarianism, Lebanon 388–390
secular parties 404
secularism 404
secular-religious divide 405
security dilemma, Iraq 123
self-determination 216
sexual harassment: Algeria 226, 228; Egypt Generation Z 424–426
Shafik, Ahmed 80, 82, 84
Shamir, Itzhak 102–103
shaping subjectivities, Algeria 31–32
Sharon, Ariel 104–105, 257
Shi'a: Iraq 123–125, 129; Lebanon 389
shkara (selling eligible positions to the highest bidder) 31
single non-transferable vote (SNTV) 59
Six Day War (1967) 241
Sledgehammer 137

Index

Slim, Lokman 394, 398n11
social brokerage, Iraq 126–128
Social Democratic Vanguard Party (PADS) 45
social media 7, 277–279, 287, 293, 295; Arab Generation Z 417; Egypt 424–425; Kuwait 305–306; Twitter 293, 300
social norms, clientelism 371–372
Socialist Destourian Party (PSD) 110
Socialist Forces Front (FFS) 30, 225
Socialist Popular Alliance (SPA) 82
Socialist Union of Popular Forces (USFP) 22, 46
socio-economic conditions, voting behavior 361
socioeconomic inequalities, Lebanon 390–391
stacked, electoral districts (Jordan) 56
State of Law coalition 125
state patrimonialism 270–271
Stevens, Christopher 350
strategic manipulation 204
strikes, Lebanon 395
Strong Egypt 87
Structural Adjustments Programmes (SAPs) 2
substantive representation 222; men 229–230; women 228
suffrage, Saudi Arabia 189–190
suffrage rights, Saudi Arabia 193
Sunni, Lebanon 389
Supervisory Commission for Elections, Lebanon 156
Supreme Election Council (SEC), Turkey 318–319
symbolic voter participation 16–17
symbolism, local elections 21
Syria 149; executive elections 15–16; legislative elections 18–19
Syrian Social National Party (SSNP) 387, 395
system Lebanon 147–148
systemic religious constraint, Islamic government, Iran 165–166

Ta'al 243, 381
Ta'if Agreement (1989) 389–390
targeting of voters **371**
Tawassoul 70
Taya, Ould 71
technology of powers, elections, Algeria 30–33
temporary constitutional declaration (TCD) 345
Tishreen movement 130
Touche Pas Ma Nationalité 71
Toumi, Khalida 226
towns, local elections 20–23
trade unions, Lebanon 395
Troïka 263
trust 6; in government, Arab Generation Z 416–417
Tunisia 2, 5, 109–110, 175–176, 263–264; 2011 elections 110–112; 2014 parliamentary elections **113**; 2019 elections **116**; *Afek Tounes* 285–286; anti-Islamist block 112–115; campaigns 264–267; clientelism 271, 370–373; *Courant Democrate* 285–286; digital electoral campaigns 283–284; electoral assistance 207; electoral machines 267–271; Front Populaire 284, **288**; gender parity 264–265; identifying one's position on political spectrum 266–267; Independent High Authority for the Elections (ISIE) 175–176; Islamists versus secularists 115–117; legal guarantees of ISIE 176–180; legislative elections 18; meetings 272; objectives of political parties 281–282; polarization 110–112; politics of consensus 112–115; religious-secular divide 404–405; right to campaign 272; social media 277; transitional context of ISIE independence 181–184; voting behavior 406; *see also Ennahda; Nidaa Tounes*
Tunisian pluralism 181
Turkey 1, 134–135, 310, 329–330; 17–25 December Operations 332; 2010 referendum 138–139; 2014 presidential elections 332–334; 2015 general elections 334–336; 2018 general election 336–339; 2018 presidential election 139, 336–339; 2019 elections 311–318; AKP *see Adalet ve Kalkinma Partisi*; autocratization 136–139; corruption 332; coups 135; democratic backsliding 5, 139; elections as source of popular legitimacy 141–144; electoral manipulation 140–141; emergency rule 138; Gezi Park protests 329, 332; historical background 135–136; impact of local elections 320–324; Justice and Development Party (AKP) 405; local elections 21, 311–312; opposition campaigns 320; performance legitimacy of the regime 319–320; polarisation 331–332; political hegemony 136–139; Supreme Election Council 318–319
Turkish Justice and Development Party (AKP) 266
Twitter 293; Kuwait 300

unescapable necessities, Algeria 29–30
unfree competition 27
Unified Socialist Party (PSU) 45
Union Coordination Committee (UCC) 393, 395
Union for the Republic (UPR) 68, 71
Union of the Democratic Centre (UCD) 68
Union of the Forces of Progress 70
United Arab Emirates 2; voting behavior 405
United Arab List (UAL) 243
United Nations: Declaration of Principles for International Election Observation and its Code of Conduct (Declaration of Principles, DOP) 211n2; Support Mission in Libya (UNSMIL) 343
United Nations Support Mission in Libya (UNSMIL) 343

Vali-ye faqih 161–163, 166
values, Arab Generation Z 419
Varieties of Democracy Project (V-Dem) 139, 367; party linkages 369–370
V-DEM Electoral Component Index (2021) *3*
Velayat-e faqih (Rahbari) 161–162, 166
Victory Alliance 125
villages, local elections 20–23
virtual constituencies 61
virtual electorate law 58
vote-buying 367–368, 371–372
voter shuttling, Mauritania 71
voter turnout 6; in Arab World 358–360; Israel 380–381; Knesset elections (1949-1973) 240–241; Knesset elections (1977-1999) **244**, *245*; Knesset elections (2003-2022) **247**; Kuwait 297–298; Lebanon 392; Morocco 45–46; Saudi Arabia 191–193
voters, targeting **371**
voting 356–358, 403; first-order elections 360–361; second-order elections 361–362; *see also* voter turnout

voting behavior 6, 404, 408; across Arab region 360–362

waedoun 383
West Bank 251–254, 383
will of the people, Turkey 142–143
women: electoral participation, Saudi Arabia 193–195; Islamist opposition women 229; Muslim women 223–224; political leadership, Kuwait 303–305
women freedom fighters, Algeria 225
women parliamentarians 227
women's descriptive representation, Algeria 222–223, 226, 229–230
women's empowerment, gender quotas 226–230
women's quotas 32; *see also* gender quotas
women's rights 224; Algeria 225–226; Morocco 20
women's substantive representation 228
Workers Communist Party of Iraq (WCPI) 125
Workers' Party (PT) 225

Yemen 2; executive elections 16
Yemenite Socialist Party 122
'you stink' campaign, Lebanon 396, 420–421
Youth Coordination Committee, Egypt 88